THE TRIBES AND CASTES

OF THE

CENTRAL PROVINCES OF INDIA

MACMILLAN AND CO., Limited
LONDON · BOMBAY · CALCUTTA
MADRAS · MELBOURNE

THE MACMILLAN COMPANY
NEW YORK · BOSTON · CHICAGO
DALLAS · SAN FRANCISCO

THE MACMILLAN CO. OF CANADA, Ltd.
TORONTO

THE

TRIBES AND CASTES

OF THE

CENTRAL PROVINCES
OF INDIA

BY

R. V. RUSSELL

OF THE INDIAN CIVIL SERVICE
SUPERINTENDENT OF ETHNOGRAPHY, CENTRAL PROVINCES

ASSISTED BY

RAI BAHADUR HĪRA LĀL

EXTRA ASSISTANT COMMISSIONER

*PUBLISHED UNDER THE ORDERS OF THE CENTRAL
PROVINCES ADMINISTRATION*

IN FOUR VOLUMES

VOL. II

MACMILLAN AND CO., LIMITED
ST. MARTIN'S STREET, LONDON

1916

COPYRIGHT

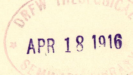

CONTENTS OF VOLUME II

ARTICLES ON CASTES AND TRIBES OF THE CENTRAL PROVINCES IN ALPHABETICAL ORDER

The articles which are considered to be of most general interest are shown in capitals

SUBCASTES OF BANIA

Agarwāla.	Gahoi.	Maheshri.
Agrahari.	Golapūrab.	Nema.
Ajudhiabāsi.	Kasarwāni.	Oswāl.
Asāthi.	Kasaundhan.	Parwār.
Charnāgri.	Khandelwāl.	Srimāli.
Dhūsar.	Lād.	Umre.
Dosar.	Lingāyat.	

v

SUBCASTES OF BRĀHMAN

Ahivāsi.	Mahārāshtra.	Nāramdeo.
Jijhotia.	Maithil.	Sanādhya.
Kanaujia, Kanyakubja.	Mālwi.	Sarwaria.
Khedāwāl.	Nāgar.	Utkal.

CONTENTS

ILLUSTRATIONS IN VOLUME II

PRONUNCIATION

a has the sound of **u** in *but* or *murmur*.

ā   ,,   ,,   **a** in *bath* or *tar*.

e   ,,   ,,   **é** in *écarté* or **ai** in *maid*.

i   ,,   ,,   **i** in *bit*, or (as a final letter) of **y** in *sulky*.

ī   ,,   ,,   **ee** in *beet*.

o   ,,   ,,   **o** in *bore* or *bowl*.

u   ,,   ,,   **u** in *put* or *bull*.

ū   ,,   ,,   **oo** in *poor* or *boot*.

The plural of caste names and a few common Hindustāni words is formed by adding *s* in the English manner according to ordinary usage, though this is not, of course, the Hindustāni plural.

NOTE.—The rupee contains 16 annas, and an anna is of the same value as a penny. A pice is a quarter of an anna, or a farthing. Rs. 1-8 signifies one rupee and eight annas. A lakh is a hundred thousand, and a krore ten million.

PART II

ARTICLES ON CASTES AND TRIBES

AGARIA—FAKĪR

AGARIA

Agaria.[1]—A small Dravidian caste, who are an offshoot of the Gond tribe. The Agarias have adopted the profession of iron-smelting and form a separate caste. They numbered 9500 persons in 1911 and live on the Maikal range in the Mandla, Raipur and Bilāspur Districts. The name probably signifies a worker with *āg* or fire. An Agaria subcaste of Lohārs also exists, many of whom are quite probably Gonds, but they are not included in the regular caste. Similar Dravidian castes of Agarias are to be found in Mīrzāpur and Bengal. The Agarias are quite distinct from the Agharia cultivating caste of the Uriya country. The Raipur Agarias still intermarry with the Rāwanbansi Gonds of the District. The Agarias think that their caste has existed from the beginning of the world, and that the first Agaria made the ploughshare with which the first bullocks furrowed the primeval soil. The caste has two endogamous divisions, the Patharia and the Khuntia Agarias. The Patharias place a stone on the mouth of the bellows to fix them in the ground for smelting, while the Khuntias use a peg. The two subcastes do not even take water from one another.

Their exogamous sections have generally the same names as those of the Gonds, as Sonwāni, Dhurua, Tekām, Markām, Uika, Purtai, Marai, and others. A few names of Hindi origin are also found, as Ahindwār, Ranchirai and Rāthoria, which show that some Hindus have probably been amalgamated with the caste. Ahindwār or Aindwār and Ranchirai mean a fish and a bird respectively in Hindi, while Rāthoria is a *gotra* both of Rājpūts and Telis. The Gond names are probably also those of animals, plants or other objects, but their meaning has now generally been

[1] This article is compiled from papers by Mr. Mīr Pādshāh, Tahsīldār of Bilāspur, and Kanhya Lāl, clerk in the Gazetteer office.

3

forgotten. Tekām or *teka* is a teak tree. Sonwāni is a
sept found among several of the Dravidian tribes, and the
lower Hindu castes. A person of the Sonwāni sept is always
chosen to perform the ceremony of purification and readmission into caste of persons temporarily excommunicated.
His duty often consists in pouring on such a person a little
water in which gold has been placed to make it holy, and
hence the name is considered to mean Sonāpāni or gold-
water. The Agarias do not know the meanings of their
section names and therefore have no totemistic observances.
But they consider that all persons belonging to one *gotra*
are descended from a common ancestor, and marriage within
the *gotra* is therefore prohibited.   As among the Gonds, first
cousins are allowed to marry.

2. Mar-
riage.

Marriage is usually adult. When the father of a boy
wishes to arrange a marriage he sends emissaries to the
father of the girl. They open the proceedings by saying,
'So-and-so has come to partake of your stale food.'[1] If
the father of the girl approves he gives his consent by saying,
'He has come on foot, I receive him on my head.' The
boy's father then repairs to the girl's house, where he is
respectfully received and his feet are washed. He is then
asked to take a drink of plain water, which is a humble
method of offering him a meal. After this, presents for the
girl are sent by a party accompanied by tomtom players,
and a date is fixed for the marriage, which, contrary to the
usual Hindu rule, may take place in the rains. The reason
is perhaps because iron-smelting is not carried on during the
rains and the Agarias therefore have no work to do. A few
days before the wedding the bride-price is paid, which consists
of 5 seers each of *urad* and til and a sum of Rs. 4 to Rs. 12.
The marriage is held on any Monday, Tuesday or Friday,
no further trouble being taken to select an auspicious day.
In order that they may not forget the date fixed, the fathers
of the parties each take a piece of thread in which they tie
a knot for every day intervening between the date when the
marriage day is settled and the day itself, and they then
untie one knot for every day. Previous to the marriage all
the village gods are propitiated by being anointed with oil

---

[1] *Bāsi* or rice boiled in water the previous day.

by the Baiga or village priest. The first clod of earth for
the ovens is also dug by the Baiga, and received in her cloth
by the bride's mother as a mark of respect. The usual
procedure is adopted in the marriage. After the bridegroom's arrival his teeth are cleaned with tooth-sticks, and
the bride's sister tries to push *sāj* leaves into his mouth, a
proceeding which he prevents by holding his fan in front of
his face. For doing this the girl is given a small present.
A *paili*[1] measure of rice is filled alternately by the bride
and bridegroom twelve times, the other upsetting it each
time after it is filled. At the marriage feast, in addition to
rice and pulse, mutton curry and cakes of *urad* pulse fried
in oil are provided. *Urad* is held in great respect, and is
always given as a food at ceremonial feasts and to honoured
guests. The greater part of the marriage ceremony is
performed a second time at the bridegroom's house.
Finally, the decorations of the marriage-shed and the palm-
leaf crowns of the bride and bridegroom are thrown into
a tank. The bride and bridegroom go into the water, and
each in turn hides a jar under water, which the other must
find. They then bathe, change their clothes, and go back
to the bridegroom's house, the bride carrying the jar filled
with water on her head. The boy is furnished with a bow
and arrows and has to shoot at a stuffed deer over the girl's
shoulder. After each shot she gives him a little sugar, and
if he does not hit the deer in three shots he must pay
4 annas to the *sawāsa* or page. After the marriage the
bridegroom does not visit his wife for a month in order to
ascertain whether she is already pregnant. They then live
together. The marriage expenses usually amount to Rs. 15
for the bridegroom's father and Rs. 40 for the bride's father.
Sometimes the bridegroom serves his father-in-law for his
wife, and he is then not required to pay anything for the
marriage, the period of service being three years. If the
couple anticipate the ceremony, however, they must leave
the house, and then are recalled by the bride's parents, and
readmitted into caste on giving a feast, which is in lieu of
the marriage ceremony. If they do not comply with the
first summons of the parents, the latter finally sever connec-

---

[1] A measure containing about 2½ lbs. of grain.

tion with them. Widow marriage is freely permitted, and the widow is expected to marry her late husband's younger brother, especially if he is a bachelor. If she marries another man with his consent, the new husband gives him a turban and shoulder-cloth. The children by the first husband are made over to his relatives if there are any. Divorce is permitted for adultery or extravagance or ill-treatment by either party. A divorced wife can marry again, but if she absconds with another man without being divorced the latter has to pay Rs. 12 to the husband.

3. Birth and death ceremonies.

When a woman becomes pregnant for the first time, her mother goes to her taking a new cloth and cakes and a preparation of milk, which is looked on as a luxurious food, and which, it is supposed, will strengthen the child in the womb. After birth the mother is impure for five days. The dead are usually burnt, but children under six whose ears have not been pierced, and persons dying a violent death or from cholera or smallpox are buried. When the principal man of the family dies, the caste-fellows at the mourning feast tie a cloth round the head of his successor to show that they acknowledge his new position. They offer water to the dead in the month of Kunwār (September-October).

4. Religion and social customs.

They have a vague belief in a supreme God but do not pay much attention to him. Their family god is Dulha Deo, to whom they offer goats, fowls, cocoanuts and cakes. In the forest tracts they also worship Bura Deo, the chief god of the Gonds. The deity who presides over their profession is Lohā-Sur, the Iron demon, who is supposed to live in the smelting-kilns, and to whom they offer a black hen. Formerly, it is said, they were accustomed to offer a black cow. They worship their smelting implements on the day of Dasahra and during Phāgun, and offer fowls to them. They have little faith in medicine, and in cases of sickness requisition the aid of the village sorcerer, who ascertains what deity is displeased with them by moving grain to and fro in a winnowing-fan and naming the village gods in turn. He goes on repeating the names until his hand slackens or stops at some name, and the offended god is thus indicated. He is then summoned and enters into the body of one of the persons present, and explains his reason for being offended with the sick person, as that he has passed by the god's shrine without taking off his shoes, or omitted to make the triennial offering of a fowl or the like. Atonement is then promised and the offering made, while the sick person on recovery notes the deity in question as one of a vindictive temper, whose worship must on no account be neglected. The Agarias say that they do not admit outsiders into the caste, but Gonds, Kawars and Ahīrs are occasionally allowed to enter it. They refuse to eat monkeys, jackals, crocodiles, lizards, beef and the leavings of others. They eat pork and fowls and drink liquor copiously. They take food from the higher castes and from Gonds and Baigas. Only Bahelias and other impure castes will take food from them. Temporary excommunication from caste is imposed for conviction of a criminal offence, getting maggots in a wound, and killing a cow, a dog or a cat. Permanent excommunication is imposed for adultery or eating with a very low caste. Readmission to caste after temporary exclusion entails a feast, but if the offender is very poor he simply gives a little liquor or even water. The Agarias are usually sunk in poverty, and their personal belongings are of the scantiest description, consisting of a waist-cloth, and perhaps another wisp of cloth for the head, a brass *lota* or cup and a few earthen vessels. Their women dress like Gond women, and have a few pewter ornaments. They are profusely tattooed with representations of flowers, scorpions and other objects. This is done merely for ornament.

The caste still follow their traditional occupation of iron-smelting and also make a few agricultural implements. They get their ore from the Maikal range, selecting stones of a dark reddish colour. They mix 16 lbs. of ore with 15 lbs. of charcoal in the furnace, the blast being produced by a pair of bellows worked by the feet and conveyed to the furnace through bamboo tubes ; it is kept up steadily for four hours. The clay coating of the kiln is then broken down and the ball of molten slag and charcoal is taken out and hammered, and about 3 lbs. of good iron are obtained. With this they make ploughshares, mattocks, axes and sickles. They also move about from village to village with an anvil, a hammer

5. Occupation.

and tongs, and building a small furnace under a tree, make and repair iron implements for the villagers.

1. Origin.   **Agharia** [1] (a corruption of Agaria, meaning one who came from Agra).—A cultivating caste belonging to the Sambalpur District [2] and adjoining States. They number 27,000 persons in the Raigarh and Sārangarh States and Bilāspur District of the Central Provinces, and are found also in some of the Chota Nāgpur States transferred from Bengal. According to the traditions of the Agharias their forefathers were Rājpūts who lived near Agra. They were accustomed to salute the king of Delhi with one hand only and without bending the head. The king after suffering this for a long time determined to punish them for their contumacy, and summoned all the Agharias to appear before him. At the door through which they were to pass to his presence he fixed a sword at the height of a man's neck. The haughty Agharias came to the door, holding their heads high and not seeing the sword, and as a natural consequence they were all decapitated as they passed through. But there was one Agharia who had heard about the fixing of the sword and who thought it better to stay at home, saying that he had some ceremony to perform. When the king heard that there was one Agharia who had not passed through the door, he sent again, commanding him to come. The Agharia did not wish to go but felt it impossible to decline. He therefore sent for a Chamār of his village and besought him to go instead, saying that he would become a Rājpūt in his death and that he would ever be held in remembrance by the Agharia's descendants. The Chamār consented to sacrifice himself for his master, and going before the king was beheaded at the door. But the Agharia fled south, taking his whole village with him, and came to Chhattīsgarh, where each of the families in the village founded a clan of the Agharia caste. And in memory of this, whenever an Agharia makes a libation to his ancestors, he first pours a little water on the ground in honour of the dead Chamār. According to

[1] This article is mainly compiled from papers by the late Mr. Baikunth Nāth Pujāri, Extra Assistant Commissioner, Sambalpur ; Sitāram, Head Master of the Raigarh English School, and Kanhyā Lāl, clerk in the Gazetteer office.

[2] Now transferred to Bengal.

another version of the story three brothers of different families
escaped and first went to Orissa, where they asked the Gajpati
king to employ them as soldiers.   The king caused two
sheaths of swords to be placed before them, and telling them
that one contained a sword and the other a bullock-goad,
asked them to select one and by their choice to determine
whether they would be soldiers or husbandmen.   From one
sheath a haft of gold projected and from the other one of
silver.   The Agharias pulled out the golden haft and found
that they had chosen the goad.   The point of the golden and
silver handles is obvious, and the story is of some interest for
the distant resemblance which it bears to the choice of the
caskets in *The Merchant of Venice*.   Condemned, as they
considered, to drive the plough, the Agharias took off their
sacred threads, which they could no longer wear, and gave
them to the youngest member of the caste, saying that he
should keep them and be their Bhāt, and they would support
him with contributions of a tenth of the produce of their
fields.   He assented, and his descendants are the genealogists
of the Agharias and are termed Dashānshi.   The Agharias
claim to be Somvansi Rājpūts, a claim which Colonel Dalton
says their appearance favours.   " Tall, well-made, with high
Aryan features and tawny complexions, they look like
Rājpūts, though they are more industrious and intelligent
than the generality of the fighting tribe." [1]

Owing to the fact that with the transfer of the Sambalpur
District, a considerable portion of the Agharias have ceased
to be residents of the Central Provinces, it is unnecessary to
give the details of their caste organisation at length.   They
have two subdivisions, the Bad or superior Agharias and
the Chhote, Sarolia or Sarwaria, the inferior or mixed
Agharias.   The latter are a cross between an Agharia and
a Gaur (Ahīr) woman.   The Bad Agharias will not eat with
or even take water from the others.   Further local subdivisions are now in course of formation, as the Ratanpuria,
Phuljharia and Raigarhia or those living round Ratanpur,
Phuljhar and Raigarh.   The caste is said to have 84 *gotras*
or exogamous sections, of which 60 bear the title of Patel,
18 that of Nāik, and 6 of Chaudhri.   The section names

2. Sub-
divisions.

---

[1] Dalton's *Ethnology of Bengal*, p. 322.

are very mixed, some being those of eponymous Brāhman *gotras*, as Sāndilya, Kaushik and Bhāradwāj ; others those of Rājpūt septs, as Karchhul ; while others are the names of animals and plants, as Barāh (pig), Baram (the pīpal tree), Nāg (cobra), Kachhapa (tortoise), and a number of other local terms the meaning of which has been forgotten. Each of these sections, however, uses a different mark for branding cows, which it is the religious duty of an Agharia to rear, and though the marks now convey no meaning, they were probably originally the representations of material objects. In the case of names whose meaning is understood, traces of totemism survive in the respect paid to the animal or plant by members of the sept which bears its name. This analysis of the structure of the caste shows that it was a very mixed one. Originally consisting perhaps of a nucleus of immigrant Rājpūts, the offspring of connections with inferior classes have been assimilated ; while the story already quoted is probably intended to signify, after the usual Brāhmanical fashion, that the pedigree of the Agharias at some period included a Chamār.

3. Marriage customs.

Marriage within the exogamous section and also with first cousins is forbidden, though in some places the union of a sister's son with a brother's daughter is permitted. Child marriage is usual, and censure visits a man who allows an unmarried daughter to arrive at adolescence. The bridegroom should always be older than the bride, at any rate by a day. When a betrothal is arranged some ornaments and a cloth bearing the *swastik* or lucky mark are sent to the girl. Marriages are always celebrated during the months of Māgh and Phāgun, and they are held only once in five or six years, when all children whose matches can be arranged for are married off. This custom is economical, as it saves expenditure on marriage feasts. Colonel Dalton also states that the Agharias always employ Hindustāni Brāhmans for their ceremonies, and as very few of these are available, they make circuits over large areas, and conduct all the weddings of a locality at the same period. Before the marriage a kid is sacrificed at the bride's house to celebrate the removal of her status of maidenhood. When the bridegroom arrives at the bride's house he touches with his dagger the string of mango-leaves suspended from the marriage-shed and presents a rupee and a hundred betel-leaves to the bride's *sawāsin* or attendant. Next day the bridegroom's father sends a present of a bracelet and seven small earthen cups to the bride. She is seated in the open, and seven women hold the cups over her head one above the other. Water is then poured from above from one cup into the other, each being filled in turn and the whole finally falling on the bride's head. This probably symbolises the fertilising action of rain. The bride is then bathed and carried in a basket seven times round the marriage-post, after which she is seated in a chair and seven women place their heads together round her while a male relative winds a thread seven times round the heads of the women. The meaning of this ceremony is obscure. The bridegroom makes his appearance alone and is seated with the bride, both being dressed in clothes coloured yellow with turmeric. The bridegroom's party follows, and the feet of the couple are washed with milk. The bride's brother embraces the bridegroom and changes cloths with him. Water is poured over the hands of the couple, the girl's forehead is daubed with vermilion, and a red silk cloth is presented to her and the couple go round the marriage-post. The bride is taken for four days to the husband's house and then returns, and is again sent with the usual *gauna* ceremony, when she is fit for conjugal relations. No price is usually paid for the bride, and each party spends about Rs. 100 on the marriage ceremony. Polygamy and widow marriage are generally allowed, the widow being disposed of by her parents. The ceremony at the marriage of a widow consists in putting vermilion on the parting of her hair and bangles on her wrists. Divorce is allowed on pain of a fine of Rs. 50 if the divorce is sought by the husband, and of Rs. 25 if the wife asks for it. In some localities divorce and also polygamy are said to be forbidden, and in such cases a woman who commits adultery is finally expelled from the caste, and a funeral feast is given to symbolise her death.

The family god of the Agharias is Dulha Deo, who exists in every household. On the Haraiti day or the commencement of the agricultural year they worship the implements

4. Religious and social customs.

of cultivation, and at Dasahra the sword if they have one.
They have a great reverence for cows and feed them sump-
tuously at festivals. Every Agharia has a *guru* or spiritual
guide who whispers the *mantra* or sacred verse into his ear
and is occasionally consulted. The dead are usually burnt,
but children and persons dying of cholera or smallpox are
buried, males being placed on the pyre or in the grave on
their faces and females on their backs, with the feet pointing
to the south. On the third day the ashes are thrown into a
river and the bones of each part of the body are collected
and placed under the pīpal tree, while a pot is slung over
them, through which water trickles continually for a week,
and a lighted lamp, cooked food, a leaf-cup and a tooth-stick
are placed beside them daily for the use of the deceased
during the same period. Mourning ends on the tenth day,
and the usual purification ceremonies are then performed.
Children are mourned for a shorter period. Well-to-do
members of the caste feed a Brāhman daily for a year after
a death, believing that food so given passes to the spirit of
the deceased. On the anniversary of the death the caste-
fellows are feasted, and after that the deceased becomes a
purkha or ancestor and participates in devotions paid at
the *shrādhh* ceremony. When the head of a joint family
dies, his successor is given a turban and betel-leaves, and his
forehead is marked by the priest and other relations with
sandalwood. After a birth the mother is impure for twenty-
one days. A feast is given on the twelfth day, and sometimes
the child is named then, but often children are not named
until they are six years old. The names of men usually
end in *Rām*, *Nāth* or *Singh*, and those of women in *Kunwar*.
Women do not name their husbands, their elderly relations,
nor the sons of their husband's eldest brother. A man does
not name his wife, as he thinks that to do so would tend to
shorten his life in accordance with the Sanskrit saying, ' He
who is desirous of long life should not name himself, his *guru*,
a miser, his eldest son, or his wife.' The Agharias do not
admit outsiders into the caste. They will not take cooked
food from any caste, and water only from a Gaur or Rāwat.
They refuse to take water from an Uriya Brāhman, probably
in retaliation for the refusal of Uriya Brāhmans to accept

water from an Agharia, though taking it from a Kolta. Both the Uriya Brāhmans and Agharias are of somewhat doubtful origin, and both are therefore probably the more concerned to maintain the social position to which they lay claim. But Kewats, Rāwats, Telis and other castes eat cooked food from Agharias, and the caste therefore is admitted to a fairly high rank in the Uriya country. The Agharias do not drink liquor or eat any food which a Rājpūt would refuse.

As cultivators they are considered to be proficient. In the census of 1901 nearly a quarter of the whole caste were shown as mālguzārs or village proprietors and lessees. They wear a coarse cloth of homespun yarn which they get woven for them by Gāndas ; probably in consequence of this the Agharias do not consider the touch of the Gānda to pollute them, as other castes do. They will not grow turmeric, onions, garlic, san-hemp or tomatoes, nor will they rear tasar silk-cocoons. Colonel Dalton says that their women do no out-door work, and this is true in the Central Provinces as regards the better classes, but poor women work in the fields.

5. Occupation.

Aghori, Aghorpanthi.[1]—The most disreputable class of Saiva mendicants who feed on human corpses and excrement, and in past times practised cannibalism. The sect is apparently an ancient one, a supposed reference to it being contained in the Sanskrit drama *Mālati Mādhava*, the hero of which rescues his mistress from being offered as a sacrifice by one named Aghori Ghanta.[2] According to Lassen, quoted by Sir H. Risley, the Aghoris of the present day are closely connected with the Kapālika sect of the Middle Ages, who wore crowns and necklaces of skulls and offered human sacrifices to Chāmunda, a form of Devi. The Aghoris now represent their filthy habits as merely giving practical expression to the abstract doctrine that the whole universe is full of Brahma, and consequently that one thing is as pure as another. By eating the most horrible food they utterly subdue their natural appetites, and hence acquire great power

1. General accounts of the caste.

---

[1] This article is mainly based on a paper on *Aghoris and Aghorpanthis*, by Mr. H. W. Barrow, in the *Journal*   *Anthr. Soc. Bombay*, iii. p. 197.
[2] Bhattachārya, *Hindu Castes and Sects*, p. 392.

over themselves and over the forces of nature. It is believed
that an Aghori can at will assume the shapes of a bird, an
animal or a fish, and that he can bring back to life a corpse
of which he has eaten a part. The principal resort of the
Aghoris appears to be at Benāres and at Girnar near Mount
Abu, and they wander about the country as solitary mendicants. A few reside in Saugor, and they are occasionally
met with in other places. They are much feared and disliked
by the people owing to their practice of extorting alms by
the threat to carry out their horrible practices before the eyes
of their victims, and by throwing filth into their houses.
Similarly they gash and cut their limbs so that the crime of
blood may rest on those who refuse to give. "For the most
part," Mr. Barrow states,[1] "the Aghorpanthis lead a wandering life, are without homes, and prefer to dwell in holes,
clefts of rocks and burning-*ghāts*. They do not cook, but
eat the fragments given them in charity as received, which
they put as far as may be into the cavity of the skull used
as a begging-bowl. The bodies of *chelas* (disciples) who die
in Benāres are thrown into the Ganges, but the dead who
die well off are placed in coffins. As a rule, Aghoris do not
care what becomes of their bodies, but when buried they are
placed in the grave sitting cross-legged. The Aghori *gurus*
keep dogs, which may be of any colour, and are said to be
maintained for purposes of protection. The dogs are not all
pariahs of the streets, although some *gurus* are followed by
three or four when on pilgrimage. Occasionally the dogs
seem to be regarded with real affection by their strange
masters. The Aghori is believed to hold converse with all
the evil spirits frequenting the burning-*ghāts*, and funeral
parties must be very badly off who refuse to pay him something. In former days he claimed five pieces of wood at each
funeral in Benāres ; but the Doms interfere with his perquisites, and in some cases only let him carry off the remains of
the unburned wood from each pyre. When angered and
excited, Aghoris invoke Kāli and threaten to spread devasta-
tion around them. Even among the educated classes, who
should know better, they are dreaded, and as an instance of
the terror which they create among the ignorant, it may be

[1] *Aghoris and Aghorpanthis*, pp. 224, 226.

AGHORI MENDICANT.

mentioned that in the Lucknow District it is believed that if alms are refused them the Aghoris will cause those who refuse to be attacked with fever.

"On the other hand, their good offices may secure benefits, as in the case of a zamīndār of Muzaffarnagar, who at Allahābād refused to eat a piece of human flesh offered to him by an Aghori ; the latter thereupon threw the flesh at the zamīndār's head, on which it stuck. The zamīndār afterwards became so exceedingly wealthy that he had difficulty in storing his wealth."

In former times it is believed that the Aghoris used to kidnap strangers, sacrifice them to the goddess and eat the bodies, and Mr. Barrow relates the following incident of the murder of a boy:[1] "Another horrible case, unconnected with magic and apparently arising from mere blood-thirst, occurred at Neirād in June 1878. An Aghori mendicant of Dwārka staying at the temple of Sitārām Lāldās seized a boy of twelve, named Shankar Rāmdās, who was playing with two other boys, threw him down on the *oatla* of the temple, ripped open his abdomen, tore out part of his entrails, and, according to the poor little victim's dying declaration, began to eat them. The other boys having raised an alarm, the monster was seized. When interrogated by the magistrate as to whether he had committed the crime in order to perform Aghorbidya, the prisoner said that as the boy was Bhakshan he had eaten his flesh. He added that if he had not been interrupted he would have eaten all the entrails. He was convicted, but only sentenced to transportation for life. The High Court, however, altered the sentence and ordered the prisoner to be hanged."

The following instance, quoted by Mr. Barrow from Rewah, shows how an Aghori was hoist with his own petard : "Some years ago, when Mahārāja Bishnāth Singh was Chief of Rewah, a man of the Aghori caste went to Rewah and sat *dharna* on the steps of the palace ; having made ineffectual demands for alms, he requested to be supplied with human flesh, and for five days abstained from food. The Mahārāja was much troubled, and at last, in order to get rid of his unwelcome visitor, sent for Ghansiām Dās,

2. Instances of cannibalism.

---

[1] Page 208.

another Aghori, a Fakīr, who had for some years lived in Rewah. Ghansiām Dās went up to the other Aghori and asked him if it was true that he had asked to be supplied with human flesh. On receiving a reply in the affirmative, Ghansiām Dās said : ' Very well, I too am extremely partial to this form of food ; here is my hand, eat it and I will eat you '; and at the same time he seized hold of the other's hand and began to gnaw at it. The Aghori on this became much alarmed and begged to be excused. He shortly afterwards left Rewah and was not heard of again, while Ghansiām Dās was rewarded for his services."

The following recent instance of an Aghori devouring human corpses is reported from the Punjab : [1] " The loathsome story of a human ghoul from Patiāla shows that the influence of the Aghorpanthi has not yet completely died out in this country. It is said that for some time past human graves have been found robbed of their contents, and the mystery could not be solved until the other day, when the police succeeded in arresting a man in the act of desecrating a child's grave, some forty miles distant from the capital (Patiāla). The ghoul not only did not conceal the undevoured portion of the corpse he had with him, but told his captors the whole story of his gruesome career. He is a low-caste Hindu named Rām Nāth, and is, according to a gentleman who saw him, ' a singularly mild and respectful-looking man, instead of a red-eyed and ravenous savage,' as he had expected to find him from the accounts of his disgusting propensities. He became an orphan at five and fell into the hands of two Sādhus of his own caste, who were evidently Aghorpanthis. They taught him to eat human flesh, which formed the staple of their food. The meat was procured from the graves in the villages they passed through. When Rām Nāth was thoroughly educated in this rank the Sādhus deserted him. Since then he had been living on human carrion only, roaming about the country like a hungry vulture. He cannot eat cooked food, and therefore gets two seers of raw meat from the State every day. It is also reported that the Mahārāja has

[1] *The Tribune* (Lahore), November 29, 1898, quoted in Oman's *Mystics,*   *Ascetics and Saints of India,* pp. 164, 165.

now prohibited his being given anything but cooked food with a view to reforming him."

Sir J. B. Fuller relates the following incident of the employment of an Aghori as a servant :[1] " There are actually ten thousand persons who at census time classed themselves as Aghoris.   All of them do not practise cannibalism and some of them attempt to rise in the world.   One of them secured service as a cook with a British officer of my acquaintance.   My friend was in camp in the jungle with his wife and children, when his other servants came to him in a body and refused to remain in service unless the cook was dismissed, since they had discovered, they declared, that during the night-time he visited cemeteries and dug up the bodies of freshly buried children.   The cook was absent, but they pointed to a box of his that emitted a sickening smell.   The man was incontinently expelled, but for long afterwards the family were haunted by reminiscences of the curries they had eaten."

[1] *Studies of Indian Life and Sentiment,* p. 44.

AHĪR

LIST OF PARAGRAPHS

1. General notice.

Ahīr,[1] **Gaoli, Guāla, Golkar, Gaolān, Rāwat, Gahra, Mahākul.**—The caste of cowherds, milkmen and cattle-breeders. In 1911 the Ahīrs numbered nearly 750,000 persons in the Central Provinces and Berār, being the sixth caste in point of numbers. This figure, however, excludes 150,000 Gowāris or graziers of the Marātha Districts, and if these were added the Ahīrs would out-number the Telis and rank fifth. The name Ahīr is derived from Abhīra, a tribe mentioned several times in inscriptions and the Hindu sacred books. Goāla, a cowherd, from Gopāla,[2] a protector of cows, is the Bengali name for the caste, and Gaoli, with the same signification, is now used in the Central Provinces to signify a dairyman as opposed to a grazier. The Gaolāns appear to be an inferior class of Gaolis in Berār. The Golkars of Chānda may be derived from the Telugu Golars or graziers, with a probable

---

[1] The information about birth customs in this article is from a paper by Mr. Kālika Prasād, Tahsīldār, Rāj-Nandgaon State.

[2] *Go, gau* or *gai*, an ox or cow, and *pāl* or *pālak*, guardian.

18

Bemrose, Collo., Derby.

AHĪRS DECORATED WITH COWRIES FOR THE STICK DANCE AT DIWĀLI.

admixture of Gond blood. They are described as wild-looking people scattered about in the most thickly forested tracts of the District, where they graze and tend cattle. Rāwat, a corruption of Rājpūtra or a princeling, is the name borne by the Ahīr caste in Chhattīsgarh ; while Gahra is their designation in the Uriya country. The Mahākul Ahīrs are a small group found in the Jashpur State, and said to belong to the Nāndvansi division. The name means 'Great family.'

The Abhīras appear to have been one of the immigrant tribes from Central Asia who entered India shortly before or about the commencement of the Christian era. In the Purānas and Mahābhārata they are spoken of as Dasyu or robbers, and Mlechchhas or foreigners, in the story which says that Arjuna, after he had burned the dead bodies of Krishna and Balarām at Dwārka, was proceeding with the widows of the Yādava princes to Mathura through the Punjab when he was waylaid by the Abhīras and deprived of his treasures and beautiful women.[1]   An inscription of the Sāka era 102, or A.D. 180, speaks of a grant made by the Senapati or commander-in-chief of the state, who is called an Abhīra, the locality being Sunda in Kāthiāwār. Another inscription found in Nāsik and assigned by Mr. Enthoven to the fourth century speaks of an Abhīra king, and the Purānas say that after the Andhrabhrityas the Deccan was held by the Abhīras, the west coast tract from the Tāpti to Deogarh being called by their name.[2]   In the time of Samudragupta in the middle of the fourth century the Abhīras were settled in Eastern Rājputana and Mālwa.[3]   When the Kāthis arrived in Gujarāt in the eighth century, they found the greater part of the country in the possession of the Ahīrs.[4]   In the Mīrzāpur District of the United Provinces a tract known as Ahraura is considered to be named after the tribe ; and near Jhānsi another piece of country is called Ahīrwār.[5]   Elliot states that Ahīrs were also Rājas of Nepāl about the commencement of our era.[6]   In Khāndesh, Mr. Enthoven states,

2. Former dominance of the Abhīras.

[1] *Ind. Ant.* (Jan. 1911), 'Foreign Elements in the Hindu Population,' by Mr. D. R. Bhandarkar.
[2] Elliot, *Supplemental Glossary, s.v.* Ahīr.
[3] *Early History of India*, 3rd ed. p. 286.
[4] Elliot, *ibidem.*
[5] *Bombay Monograph on Ahir.*
[6] Elliot, *ibidem.*

the settlements of the Ahīrs were important.   In many castes
there is a separate division of Ahīrs, such as the Ahīr Sunārs,
Sutārs, Lohārs, Shimpīs, Salīs, Guraos and Kolis.   The fort
of Asīrgarh in Nimār bordering on Khāndesh is supposed
to have been founded by one Asa Ahīr, who lived in the
beginning of the fifteenth century.   It is said that his
ancestors had held land here for seven hundred years, and
he had 10,000 cattle, 20,000 sheep and 1000 mares, with
2000 followers ; but was still known to the people, to
whom his benevolence had endeared him, by the simple
name of Asa.   This derivation of Asīrgarh is clearly
erroneous, as it was known as Asīr or Asīrgarh, and held
by the Tāk and Chauhān Rājpūts from the eleventh century.
But the story need not on that account, Mr. Grant says,[1] be
set down as wholly a fable.   Firishta, who records it, has
usually a good credit, and more probably the real existence
of a line of Ahīr chieftains in the Tapti valley suggested a
convenient ethnology for the fortress.   Other traditions of
the past domination of the pastoral tribes remain in the
Central Provinces.   Deogarh on the Chhindwāra plateau
was, according to the legend, the last seat of Gaoli power
prior to its subversion by the Gonds in the sixteenth
century.   Jātba, the founder of the Deogarh Gond
dynasty, is said to have entered the service of the Gaoli
rulers, Mansur and Gansur, and subsequently with the aid
of the goddess Devi to have slain them and usurped their
kingdom.   But a Gaoli chief still retained possession of the
fort of Narnāla for a few years longer, when he also was
slain by the Muhammadans.   Similarly the fort of Gāwilgarh
on the southern crest of the Satpūras is said to be named
after a Gaoli chief who founded it.   The Saugor traditions
bring down the Gaoli supremacy to a much later date, as
the tracts of Etāwa and Khurai are held to have been
governed by their chieftains till the close of the seventeenth
century.

3. Ahīr   Certain dialects called after the Abhīras or Ahīrs still
dialects.   remain.   One, known as Ahīrwati, is spoken in the Rohtak
and Gurgaon Districts of the Punjab and round Delhi.   This
is akin to Mewāti, one of the forms of Rājasthāni or the

[1] *Central Provinces Gazetteer* (1871), Introduction.

language of Rājputāna. The Mālwi dialect of Rājasthāni
is also known as Ahīri ; and that curious form of Gujarāti,
which is half a Bhīl dialect, and is generally known as
Khāndeshi, also bears the name of Ahīrani.[1] The above
linguistic facts seem to prove only that the Abhīras, or their
occupational successors, the Ahīrs, were strongly settled in the
Delhi country of the Punjab, Mālwa and Khāndesh. They
do not seem to throw much light on the origin of the Abhīras
or Ahīrs, and necessarily refer only to a small section of the
existing Ahīr caste, the great bulk of whom speak the Aryan
language current where they dwell. Another authority
states, however, that the Ahīrs of Gujarāt still retain a
dialect of their own, and concludes that this and the other
Ahīr dialects are the remains of the distinct Abhīra language.

It cannot necessarily be assumed that all the above
traditions relate to the Abhīra tribe proper, of which the
modern Ahīr caste are scarcely more than the nominal
representatives. Nevertheless, it may fairly be concluded
from them that the Abhīras were widely spread over India
and dominated considerable tracts of country. They are
held to have entered India about the same time as the
Sakas, who settled in Gujarāt, among other places, and, as
seen above, the earliest records of the Abhīras show them in
Nāsik and Kāthiāwār, and afterwards widely spread in
Khāndesh, that is, in the close neighbourhood of the Sakas.
It has been suggested in the article on Rājpūt that the
Yādava and other lunar clans of Rājpūts may be the
representatives of the Sakas and other nomad tribes who
invaded India shortly before and after the Christian era.
The god Krishna is held to have been the leader of the
Yādavas, and to have founded with them the sacred city of
Dwārka in Gujarāt. The modern Ahīrs have a subdivision
called Jāduvansi or Yāduvansi, that is, of the race of the
Yādavas, and they hold that Krishna was of the Ahīr tribe.
Since the Abhīras were also settled in Gujarāt it is possible
that they may have been connected with the Yādavas, and
that this may be the foundation for their claim that Krishna
was of their tribe. The Dyashraya-Kavya of Hemachandra
speaks of a Chordasama prince reigning near Junagarh as

4. The Yādavas and Krishna.

---

[1] *Linguistic Survey of India*, vol. ix. part ii. p. 50.

an Abhīra and a Yādava. But this is no doubt very con-jectural, and the simple fact that Krishna was a herdsman would be a sufficient reason for the Ahīrs to claim connection with him. It is pointed out that the names of Abhīra chieftains given in the early inscriptions are derived from the god Siva, and this would not have been the case if they had at that epoch derived their origin from Krishna, an incarnation of Vishnu. "If the Abhīras had really been the descendants of the cowherds (Gopas) whose hero was Krishna, the name of the rival god Siva would never have formed components of the names of the Abhīras, whom we find mentioned in inscriptions. Hence the conclusion may safely be drawn that the Abhīras were by no means connected with Krishna and his cowherds even as late as about A.D. 300, to which date the first of the two inscriptions mentioned above is to be assigned. Precisely the same conclusion is pointed to by the contents of the Harivansha and Bhagwat Purāna. The upbringing of Krishna among the cowherds and his flirtations with the milkmaids are again and again mentioned in these works, but the word Abhīra does not occur even once in this connection. The only words we find used are Gopa, Gopi and Vraja. This is indeed remarkable. For the descriptions of the removal of Krishna as an infant to Nanda, the cowherd's hut, of his childhood passed in playing with the cowherd boys, and of his youth spent in amorous sports with the milkmaids are set forth at great length, but the word Abhīra is not once met with. From this only one conclusion is possible, that is, that the Abhīras did not originally represent the Gopas of Krishna. The word Abhīra occurs for the first time in connection with the Krishna legend about A.D. 550, from which it follows that the Abhīras came to be identified with the Gopas shortly before that date."[1]

This argument is interesting as showing that Abhīra was not originally an occupational term for a herdsman, nor a caste name, but belonged to an immigrant tribe. Owing apparently to the fact that the Abhīras, like the Gūjars, devoted them-selves to a pastoral mode of life in India, whereas the previous Aryan immigrants had settled down to cultivation,

[1] *Bombay Ethnographic Survey.*

they gave their name to the great occupational caste of herdsmen which was subsequently developed, and of which they may originally have constituted the nucleus. The Gūjars, who came to India at a later period, form a parallel case ; although the Gūjar caste, which is derived from them, is far less important than the Ahīr, the Gūjars have also been the parents of several Rājpūt clans. The reason why the early Mathura legends of Krishna make no mention of the Ahīrs may be that the deity Krishna is probably compounded of at least two if not more distinct personalities. One is the hero chief of the Yādavas, who fought in the battle of the Pandavas and Kauravas, migrated to Gujarāt and was killed there. As he was chief of the Yādavas this Krishna must stand for the actual or mythical personality of some leader of the immigrant nomad tribes. The other Krishna, the boy cowherd, who grazed cattle and sported with the milkmaids of Brindāban, may very probably be some hero of the indigenous non-Aryan tribes, who, then as now, lived in the forests and were shepherds and herdsmen. His lowly birth from a labouring cowherd, and the fact that his name means black and he is represented in sculpture as being of a dark colour, lend support to this view. The cult of Krishna, Mr. Crooke points out, was comparatively late, and probably connected with the development of the worship of the cow after the decay of Buddhism. This latter Krishna, who is worshipped with his mother as a child-god, was especially attractive to women, both actual and prospective mothers. It is quite probable therefore that as his worship became very popular in Hindustān in connection with that of the cow, he was given a more illustrious origin by identification with the Yādava hero, whose first home was apparently in Gujarāt. In this connection it may also be noted that the episodes connected with Krishna in the Mahābhārata have been considered late interpolations.

But though the Ahīr caste takes its name and is perhaps partly descended from the Abhīra tribe, there is no doubt that it is now and has been for centuries a purely occupational caste, largely recruited from the indigenous tribes. Thus in Bengal Colonel Dalton remarks that the features of the Mathurāvāsi Goālas are high, sharp and delicate, and

5. The modern Ahīrs an occupational caste.

they are of light-brown complexion.   Those of the Magadha subcaste, on the other hand, are undefined and coarse.   They are dark-complexioned, and have large hands and feet. " Seeing the latter standing in a group with some Singhbhūm Kols, there is no distinguishing one from the other.   There has doubtless been much mixture of blood."[1]   Similarly in the Central Provinces the Ahīrs are largely recruited from the Gonds and other tribes.   In Chānda the Gowāris are admittedly descended from the unions of Gonds and Ahīrs, and one of their subcastes, the Gond-Gowāris, are often classed as Gonds.   Again, the Kaonra Ahīrs of Mandla are descended from the unions of Ahīrs either with the Gonds or Kawars, and many of them are probably pure Gonds.   They have Gond sept-names and eat pork.   Members of one of their subdivisions, the Gond-Kaonra, will take water from Gonds, and rank below the other Kaonras, from whom they will accept food and water.   As cattle have to go into the thick jungles to graze in the hot weather, the graziers attending them become intimate with the forest tribes who live there, and these latter are also often employed to graze the cattle, and are perhaps after a time admitted to the Ahīr caste.   Many Ahīrs in Mandla are scarcely considered to be Hindus, living as they do in Gond villages in sole company with the Gonds.

6. Sub-castes.   The principal subcastes of the Ahīrs in northern India are the Jāduvansi, Nāndvansi and Gowālvansi.   The Jādu-vansi claimed to be descended from the Yādavas, who now form the Yādu and Jādon-Bhatti clans of Rājpūts.   The probability of a historical connection between the Abhīras and Yādavas has already been noticed.   The Nāndvansi consider their first ancestor to have been Nānd, the cowherd, the foster-father of Krishna ; while the name of the Gowāl-vansi is simply Goāla or Gauli, a milkman, a common synonym for the caste.   The Kaonra Ahīrs of Mandla and the Kamarias of Jubbulpore are considered to belong to the Nāndvansi group.   Other subcastes in the northern Districts are the Jijhotia, who, like the Jijhotia Brāhmans, take their name from Jajhoti, the classical term for Bundelkhand ; the Bharotia ; and the Narwaria from Narwar.   The Rāwats

[1] Quoted in *Tribes and Castes of Bengal*, art. Goāla.

of Chhattīsgarh are divided into the Jhadia, Kosaria and Kanaujia groups. Of these the Jhadia or 'jungly,' and Kosaria from Kosala, the ancient name of the Chhattīsgarh country, are the oldest settlers, while the Kanaujia are largely employed as personal servants in Chhattīsgarh, and all castes will take water from their hands. The superior class of them, however, refuse to clean household cooking vessels, and are hence known as Thethwār, or exact or pure, as distinguished from the other Rāwats, who will perform this somewhat derogatory work.

The Dauwa or wet-nurse Ahīrs are descended from the illegitimate offspring of Bundela Rājpūt fathers by Ahīr mothers who were employed in this capacity in their families. An Ahīr woman kept by a Bundela was known as Pardwārin, or one coming from another house. This is not considered a disgraceful origin ; though the Dauwa Ahīrs are not re-cognised by the Ahīrs proper, they form a separate section of the caste, and Brāhmans will take water from them. The children of such mothers stood in the relation of foster-brothers to the Rājpūts, whom their mothers had nursed. The giving of milk, in accordance with the common primitive belief in the virtue attaching to an action in itself, was held to constitute a relation of quasi-maternity between the nurse and infant, and hence of fraternity between her own children and her foster-children. The former were called Dhai-bhais or foster-brothers by the Rājpūts ; they were often given permanent grants of land and employed on confidential missions, as for the arrangement of marriages. The minister of a Rāja of Karauli was his Dauwa or foster-father, the husband of his nurse. Similarly, Colonel Tod says that the Dhai-bhai or foster-brother of the Rāja of Boondi, com-mandant of the fortress of Tanagarh, was, like all his class, devotion personified.[1] A parallel instance of the tie of foster-kinship occurs in the case of the foster-brothers of Conachar or Hector in *The Fair Maid of Perth*. Thus the position of foster-brother of a Rājpūt was an honourable one, even though the child might be illegitimate. Ahīr women were often employed as wet-nurses, because domestic service was a profession in which they commonly engaged. Owing

7. The Dauwa or wet-nurse Ahīrs. Fosterage.

[1] *Rājasthān*, ii. p. 639.

to the comparatively humble origin of a large proportion of them they did not object to menial service, while the purity of their caste made it possible to use them for the supply of water and food. In Bengal the Uriya Ahīrs were a common class of servants in European houses.

The Gaolis or milkmen appear to form a distinct branch of the caste with subcastes of their own. Among them are the Nāndvans, common to the Ahīrs, the Mālwi from Mālwa and the Rāghuvansi, called after the Rājpūt clan of that name. The Rānyas take their designation from *rān*, forest, like the Jhādia Rāwats.

8. Exogamy. The caste have exogamous sections, which are of the usual low-caste type, with titular or totemistic names. Those of the Chhattīsgarhi Rāwats are generally named after animals. A curious name among the Mahākul Ahīrs is Mathānkāta, or one who bit his mother's nipples. The marriage of persons belonging to the same section and of first cousins is prohibited. A man may marry his wife's younger sister while his wife is living, but not her elder sister. The practice of exchanging girls between families is permissible.

9. Marriage customs. As a rule, girls may be married before or after puberty, but the Golkars of Chānda insist on infant marriage, and fine the parents if an unmarried girl becomes adolescent. On the other hand, the Kaonra Ahīrs of Mandla make a practice of not getting a girl married till the signs of puberty have appeared. It is said that in Mandla if an unmarried girl becomes pregnant by a man of the caste the *panchāyat* give her to him and fine him Rs. 20 or 30, which they appropriate themselves, giving nothing to the father. If an Ahīr girl is seduced by an outsider, she is made over to him, and a fine of Rs. 40 or 50 is exacted from him if possible. This is paid to the girl's father, who has to spend it on a penalty feast to the caste. Generally, sexual offences within the community are leniently regarded. The wedding ceremony is of the type prevalent in the locality. The proposal comes from the boy's family, and a price is usually given for the bride. The Kaonra Ahīrs of Mandla and the Jharia and Kosaria Rāwats of Chhattīsgarh employ a Brāhman only to write the *lagun* or paper fixing the date of the wedding, and the ceremony is conducted by the *sawāsins* or relatives of

the parties. In Chhattīsgarh the bridegroom is dressed as a girl to be taken to the wedding. In Betūl the weddings of most Gaolis are held in Māgh (January), and that of the Rānya subcaste in the bright fortnight of Kārtik (October). At the ceremony the bride is made to stand on a small stone roller ; the bridegroom then takes hold of the roller facing the bride and goes round in a circle seven times, turning the roller with him. Widow remarriage is permitted, and a widow is often expected to marry the younger brother of her deceased husband. If a bachelor wishes to marry a widow he first goes through the ceremony with a dagger or an earthen vessel. Divorce is freely permitted. In Hoshangābād a strip is torn off the clothes worn by husband and wife as a sign of their divorce. This is presumably in contrast to the knotting of the clothes of the couple together at a wedding.

Among the Rāwats of Chhattīsgarh, when a child is shortly to be born the midwife dips her hand in oil and presses it on the wall, and it is supposed that she can tell by the way in which the oil trickles down whether the child will be a boy or a girl. If a woman is weak and ill during her pregnancy it is thought that a boy will be born, but if she is strong and healthy, a girl. A woman in advanced pregnancy is given whatever she desires to eat, and on one occasion especially delicate kinds of food are served to her, this rite being known as Sidhori. The explanation of the custom is that if the mother does not get the food she desires during pregnancy the child will long for it all through life. If delivery is delayed, a line of men and boys is sometimes made from the door of the house to a well, and a vessel is then passed from hand to hand from the house, filled with water, and back again. Thus the water, having acquired the quality of speed during its rapid transit, will communicate this to the woman and cause her quick delivery. Or they take some of the clay left unmoulded on the potter's wheel and give it her to drink in water ; the explanation of this is exactly similar, the earth having acquired the quality of swiftness by the rapid transit on the wheel. If three boys or three girls have been born to a woman, they think that the fourth should be of the same sex, in order to make up

10. Birth customs.

two pairs. A boy or girl born after three of the opposite sex is called Titra or Titri, and is considered very unlucky. To avert this misfortune they cover the child with a basket, kindle a fire of grass all round it, and smash a brass pot on the floor. Then they say that the baby is the fifth and not the fourth child, and the evil is thus removed. When one woman gives birth to a male and another to a female child in the same quarter of a village on the same day and they are attended by the same midwife, it is thought that the boy child will fall ill from the contagion of the girl child communicated through the midwife. To avoid this, on the following Sunday the child's maternal uncle makes a banghy, which is carried across the shoulders like a large pair of scales, and weighs the child in it against cowdung. He then takes the banghy and deposits it at cross-roads outside the village. The father cannot see either the child or its mother till after the Chathi or sixth-day ceremony of purification, when the mother is bathed and dressed in clean clothes, the males of the family are shaved, all their clothes are washed, and the house is whitewashed ; the child is also named on this day. The mother cannot go out of doors until after the Bārhi or twelfth-day ceremony. If a child is born at an unlucky astrological period its ears are pierced in the fifth month after birth as a means of protection.

11. Funeral rites. Bringing back the soul.   The dead are either buried or burnt. When a man is dying they put basil leaves and boiled rice and milk in his mouth, and a little piece of gold, or if they have not got gold they put a rupee in his mouth and take it out again. For ten days after a death, food in a leaf-cup and a lamp are set out in the house-yard every evening, and every morning water and a tooth-stick. On the tenth day they are taken away and consigned to a river. In Chhattīsgarh on the third day after death the soul is brought back. The women put a lamp on a red earthen pot and go to a tank or stream at night. The fish are attracted towards the light, and one of them is caught and put in the pot, which is then filled with water. It is brought home and set beside a small heap of flour, and the elders sit round it. The son of the deceased or other near relative anoints himself with turmeric and picks up a stone. This is washed with the water from

IMAGE OF KRISHNA AS MURLIDHAR OR THE FLUTE-PLAYER, WITH ATTENDANT DEITIES.

the pot, and placed on the floor, and a sacrifice of a cock or
hen is made to it according as the deceased was a man or a
woman. The stone is then enshrined in the house as a
family god, and the sacrifice of a fowl is repeated annually. It
is supposed apparently that the dead man's spirit is brought
back to the house in the fish, and then transferred to the
stone by washing this with the water.

The Ahīrs have a special relation to the Hindu religion,
owing to their association with the sacred cow, which is itself
revered as a goddess. When religion gets to the anthropomorphic stage the cowherd, who partakes of the cow's sanctity,
may be deified as its representative. This was probably the
case with Krishna, one of the most popular gods of Hinduism,
who was a cowherd, and, as he is represented as being of a
dark colour, may even have been held to be of the indigenous
races. Though, according to the legend, he was really of
royal birth, Krishna was brought up by Nānd, a herdsman of
Gokul, and Jasoda or Dasoda his wife, and in the popular
belief these are his parents, as they probably were in the
original story. The substitution of Krishna, born as a prince,
for Jasoda's daughter, in order to protect him from destruction by the evil king Kānsa of Mathura, is perhaps a later
gloss, devised when his herdsman parentage was considered
too obscure for the divine hero. Krishna's childhood in
Jasoda's house with his miraculous feats of strength and his
amorous sports with Rādha and the other milkmaids of Brindāwan, are among the most favourite Hindu legends. Govind
and Gopāl, the protector or guardian of cows, are names of
Krishna and the commonest names of Hindus, as are also
his other epithets, Murlidhar and Bansidhar, the flute-player ;
for Krishna and Balārām, like Greek and Roman shepherds,
were accustomed to divert themselves with song, to the
accompaniment of the same instrument. The child Krishna
is also very popular, and his birthday, the Janam-Ashtami
on the 8th of dark Bhādon (August), is a great festival. On
this day potsful of curds are sprinkled over the assembled
worshippers. Krishna, however, is not the solitary instance
of the divine cowherd, but has several companions, humble
indeed compared to him, but perhaps owing their apotheosis
to the same reasons. Bhīlat, a popular local godling of the

12. Re-
ligion.
Krishna
and other
deified
cowherds.

Nerbudda Valley, was the son of an Ahīr or Gaoli woman ; she was childless and prayed to Pārvati for a child, and the goddess caused her votary to have one by her own husband, the god Mahādeo. Bhīlat was stolen away from his home by Mahādeo in the disguise of a beggar, and grew up to be a great hero and made many conquests ; but finally he returned and lived with his herdsman parents, who were no doubt his real ones. He performed numerous miracles, and his devotees are still possessed by his spirit. Singāji is another godling who was a Gaoli by caste in Indore. He became a disciple of a holy Gokulastha Gosain or ascetic, and consequently a great observer of the Janam-Ashtami or Krishna's birthday.[1] On one occasion Singāji was late for prayers on this day, and the *guru* was very angry, and said to him, ' Don't show your face to me again until you are dead.' Singāji went home and told the other children he was going to die. Then he went and buried himself alive. The occurrence was noised abroad and came to the ears of the *guru*, who was much distressed, and proceeded to offer his condolences to Singāji's family. But on the way he saw Singāji, who had been miraculously raised from the dead on account of his virtuous act of obedience, grazing his buffaloes as before. After asking for milk, which Singāji drew from a male buffalo calf, the *guru* was able to inform the bereaved parents of their son's joyful reappearance and his miraculous powers ; of these Singāji gave further subsequent demonstration, and since his death, said to have occurred 350 years ago, is widely venerated. The Gaolis pray to him for the protection of their cattle from disease, and make thank-offerings of butter if these prayers are fulfilled. Other pilgrims to Singāji's shrine offer unripe mangoes and sugar, and an annual fair is held at it, when it is said that for seven days no cows, flies or ants are to be seen in the place. In the Betūl district there is a village godling called Dait, represented by a stone under a tree. He is the spirit of any Ahīr who in his lifetime was credited in the locality with having the powers of an exorcist. In Mandla and other Districts when any buffalo herdsman dies at a very advanced

[1] Gokul was the place where Krishna was brought up, and the Gokulastha Gosains are his special devotees.

age the people make a platform for him within the village
and call it Mahashi Deo or the buffalo god. Similarly,
when an old cattle herdsman dies they do the same, and call
it Balki Deo or the bullock god. Here we have a clear
instance of the process of substituting the spirit of the
herdsman for the cow or buffalo as an object of worship.
The occupation of the Ahīr also lends itself to religious
imaginations. He stays in the forest or waste grass-land,
frequently alone from morning till night, watching his herds ;
and the credulous and uneducated minds of the more
emotional may easily hear the voices of spirits, or in a
half-sleeping condition during the heat and stillness of the
long day may think that visions have appeared to them.
Thus they come to believe themselves selected for communication with the unseen deities or spirits, and on occasions of
strong religious excitement work themselves into a frenzy
and are held to be possessed by a spirit or god.

Among the special deities of the Ahīrs is Kharak Deo, 13. Caste
who is always located at the *khirkha,* or place of assembly of deities.
the cattle, on going to and returning from pasture. He appears
to be the spirit or god of the *khirkha.* He is represented by
a platform with an image of a horse on it, and when cattle
fall ill the owners offer flour and butter to him. These
are taken by the Ahīrs in charge, and it is thought that the
cattle will get well. Matar Deo is the god of the pen or
enclosure for cattle made in the jungle. Three days after
the Diwāli festival the Rāwats sacrifice one or more goats to
him, cutting off their heads. They throw the heads into the
air, and the cattle, smelling the blood, run together and
toss them with their horns as they do when they scent a tiger.
The men then say that the animals are possessed by Matar Deo.
Guraya Deo is a deity who lives in the cattle-stalls in the
village and is worshipped once a year. A man holds an egg
in his hand, and walks round the stall pouring liquid over
the egg all the way, so as to make a line round it. The egg
is then buried beneath the shrine of the god, the rite being
probably meant to ensure his aid for the protection of the
cattle from disease in their stalls. A favourite saint of the
Ahīrs is Haridās Bāba. He was a Jogi, and could separate his
soul from his body at pleasure. On one occasion he had

gone in spirit to Benāres, leaving his body in the house of one of his disciples, who was an Ahīr. When he did not return, and the people heard that a dead body was lying there, they came and insisted that it should be burnt. When he came back and found that his body was burnt, he entered into a man and spoke through him, telling the people what had happened. In atonement for their unfortunate mistake they promised to worship him.

14. Other deities.

The Mahākul Ahīrs of Jashpur have three deities, whom they call Mahādeo or Siva, Sahādeo, one of the five Pāndava brothers, and the goddess Lakshmi. They say that the buffalo is Mahādeo, the cow Sahādeo, and the rice Lakshmi. This also appears to be an instance of the personification of animals and the corn into anthropomorphic deities.

15. The Diwāli festival.

The principal festival of the Ahīrs is the Diwāli, falling about the beginning of November, which is also the time when the autumn crops ripen. All classes observe this feast by illuminating their houses with many small saucer-lamps and letting off crackers and fireworks, and they generally gamble with money to bring them good luck during the coming year. The Ahīrs make a mound of earth, which is called Govardhan, that is the mountain in Mathura which Krishna held upside down on his finger for seven days and nights, so that all the people might gather under it and be protected from the devastating storms of rain sent by Indra. After dancing round the mound they drive their cattle over it and make them trample it to pieces. At this time a festival called Marhai is held, at which much liquor is drunk and all classes disport themselves. In Damoh on this day the Ahīrs go to the standing-place for village cattle, and after worshipping the god, frighten the cattle by waving leaves of the basil-plant at them, and then put on fantastic dresses, decorating themselves with cowries, and go round the village, singing and dancing. Elsewhere at the time of the Marhai they dance round a pole with peacock feathers tied to the top, and sometimes wear peacock feathers themselves, as well as aprons sewn all over with cowries. It is said that Krishna and Balārām used to wear peacock feathers when they danced in the jungles of Mathura, but this rite has probably some connection with

Benrose, Colla., Derby.

AHĪR DANCERS IN DIWĀLI COSTUME.

the worship of the peacock. This bird might be venerated by the Ahīrs as one of the prominent denizens of the jungle. In Raipur they tie a white cock to the top of the pole and dance round it. In Mandla, Khila Mutha, the god of the threshing-floor, is worshipped at this time, with offerings of a fowl and a goat. They also perform the rite of *jagāna* or waking him up. They tie branches of a small shrub to a stick and pour milk over the stone which is his emblem, and sing, ' Wake up, Khila Mutha, this is the night of Amāwas ' (the new moon). Then they go to the cattle-shed and wake up the cattle, crying, ' Poraiya, god of the door, watchman of the window, open the door, Nānd Gowāl is coming.' Then they drive out the cattle and chase them with the branches tied to their sticks as far as their grazing-ground. Nānd Gowāl was the foster-father of Krishna, and is now said to signify a man who has a lakh (100,000) of cows. This custom of frightening the cattle and making them run is called *dhor jagāna* or *bichkāna*, that is, to wake up or terrify the cattle. Its meaning is obscure, but it is said to preserve the cattle from disease during the year. In Raipur the women make an image of a parrot in clay at the Diwāli and place it on a pole and go round to the different houses, singing and dancing round the pole, and receiving presents of rice and money. They praise the parrot as the bird who carries messages from a lover to his mistress, and as living on the mountains and among the green verdure, and sing :

" Oh, parrot, where shall we sow *gondla* grass and where shall we sow rice ?

" We will sow *gondla* in a pond and rice in the field.

" With what shall we cut *gondla* grass, and with what shall we cut rice ?

" We shall cut *gondla* with an axe and rice with a sickle."

It is probable that the parrot is revered as a spirit of the forest, and also perhaps because it is destructive to the corn. The parrot is not, so far as is known, associated with any god, but the Hindus do not kill it. In Bilāspur an ear of rice is put into the parrot's mouth, and it is said there that the object of the rite is to prevent the parrots from preying on the corn.

16. Omens. On the night of the full moon of Jesth (May) the Ahīrs stay awake all night, and if the moon is covered with clouds they think that the rains will be good. If a cow's horns are not firmly fixed in the head and seem to shake slightly, it is called Maini, and such an animal is considered to be lucky. If a bullock sits down with three legs under him and the fourth stretched out in front it is a very good omen, and it is thought that his master's cattle will increase and multiply. When a buffalo-calf is born they cover it at once with a black cloth and remove it from the mother's sight, as they think that if she saw the calf and it then died her milk would dry up. The calf is fed by hand. Cow-calves, on the other hand, are usually left with the mother, and many people allow them to take all the milk, as they think it a sin to deprive them of it.

17. Social customs. The Ahīrs will eat the flesh of goats and chickens, and most of them consume liquor freely. The Kaonra Ahīrs of Mandla eat pork, and the Rāwats of Chhattīsgarh are said not to object to field-mice and rats, even when caught in the houses. The Kaonra Ahīrs are also said not to consider a woman impure during the period of menstruation. Nevertheless the Ahīrs enjoy a good social status, owing to their relations with the sacred cow. As remarked by Eha : " His family having been connected for many generations with the sacred animal he enjoys a certain consciousness of moral respectability, like a man whose uncles are deans or canons." [1] All castes will take water from the hands of an Ahīr, and in Chhattīsgarh and the Uriya country the Rāwats and Gahras, as the Ahīr caste is known respectively in these localities, are the only caste from whom Brāhmans and all other Hindus will take water. On this account, and because of their comparative purity, they are largely employed as personal servants. In Chhattīsgarh the ordinary Rāwats will clean the cooking-vessels even of Muhammadans, but the Thethwār or pure Rāwats refuse this menial work. In Mandla, when a man is to be brought back into caste after a serious offence, such as getting vermin in a wound, he is made to stand in the middle of a stream, while some elderly relative pours water over him.

[1] *Behind the Bungalow.*

He then addresses the members of the caste *panchāyat* or committee, who are standing on the bank, saying to them, 'Will you leave me in the mud or will you take me out?' Then they tell him to come out, and he has to give a feast. At this a member of the Meliha sept first eats food and puts some into the offender's mouth, thus taking the latter's sin upon himself. The offender then addresses the *panchāyat* saying, 'Rājas of the Panch, eat.' Then the *panchāyat* and all the caste take food with him and he is readmitted. In Nāndgaon State the head of the caste *panchāyat* is known as Thethwār, the title of the highest subcaste, and is appointed by the Rāja, to whom he makes a present. In Jashpur, among the Mahākul Ahīrs, when an offender is put out of caste he has on readmission to make an offering of Rs. 1-4 to Bālāji, the tutelary deity of the State. These Mahākuls desire to be considered superior to ordinary Ahīrs, and their social rules are hence very strict. A man is put out of caste if a dog, fowl or pig touches his water or cooking-pots, or if he touches a fowl. In the latter case he is obliged to make an offering of a fowl to the local god, and eight days are allowed for procuring it. A man is also put out of caste for beating his father. In Mandla, Ahīrs commonly have the title of Patel or headman of a village, probably because in former times, when the country consisted almost entirely of forest and grass land, they were accustomed to hold large areas on contract for grazing.

18. Ornaments. In Chhattīsgarh the Rāwat women are especially fond of wearing large *churas* or leg-ornaments of bell-metal. These consist of a long cylinder which fits closely to the leg, being made in two halves which lock into each other, while at each end and in the centre circular plates project outwards horizontally. A pair of these *churas* may weigh 8 or 10 lbs., and cost from Rs. 3 to Rs. 9. It is probable that some important magical advantage was expected to come from the wearing of these heavy appendages, which must greatly impede free progression, but its nature is not known.

19. Occupation. Only about thirty per cent of the Ahīrs are still occupied in breeding cattle and dealing in milk and butter. About four per cent are domestic servants, and nearly all the remainder cultivators and labourers. In former times the

Ahīrs had the exclusive right of milking the cow, so that on all occasions an Ahīr must be hired for this purpose even by the lowest castes. Any one could, however, milk the buffalo, and also make curds and other preparations from cow's milk.[1] This rule is interesting as showing how the caste system was maintained and perpetuated by the custom of preserving to each caste a monopoly of its traditional occupation. The rule probably applied also to the bulk of the cultivating and the menial and artisan castes, and now that it has been entirely abrogated it would appear that the gradual decay and dissolution of the caste organisation must follow. The village cattle are usually entrusted jointly to one or more herdsmen for grazing purposes. The grazier is paid separately for each animal entrusted to his care, a common rate being one anna for a cow or bullock and two annas for a buffalo per month. When a calf is born he gets four annas for a cow-calf and eight annas for a she-buffalo, but except in the rice districts nothing for a male buffalo-calf, as these animals are considered useless outside the rice area. The reason is that buffaloes do not work steadily except in swampy or wet ground, where they can refresh themselves by frequent drinking. In the northern Districts male buffalo-calves are often neglected and allowed to die, but the cow-buffaloes are extremely valuable, because their milk is the principal source of supply of *ghī* or boiled butter. When a cow or buffalo is in milk the grazier often gets the milk one day out of four or five. When a calf is born the teats of the cow are first milked about twenty times on to the ground in the name of the local god of the Ahīrs. The remainder of the first day's milk is taken by the grazier, and for the next few days it is given to friends. The village grazier is often also expected to prepare the guest-house for Government officers and others visiting the village, fetch grass for their animals, and clean their cooking vessels. For this he sometimes receives a small plot of land and a present of a blanket annually from the village proprietor. Mālguzārs and large tenants have their private herdsmen. The pasturage afforded by the village waste lands and forest is, as a rule, only sufficient for the plough-

[1] *Eastern India,* ii. p. 467.

bullocks and more valuable milch-animals. The remainder
are taken away sometimes for long distances to the Government forest reserves, and here the herdsmen make stockades
in the jungle and remain there with their animals for months
together.   The cattle which remain in the village are taken
by the owners in the early morning to the *khirkha* or central
standing-ground.   Here the grazier takes them over and
drives them out to pasture.   He brings them back at ten or
eleven, and perhaps lets them stand in some field which
the owner wants manured.   Then he separates the cows
and milch-buffaloes and takes them to their masters' houses,
where he milks them all.   In the afternoon all the cattle
are again collected and driven out to pasture.   The cultivators
are very much in the grazier's hands, as they cannot super-
vise him, and if dishonest he may sell off a cow or calf to
a friend in a distant village and tell the owner that it has
been carried off by a tiger or panther.   Unless the owner
succeeds by a protracted search or by accident in finding the
animal he cannot disprove the herdsman's statement, and the
only remedy is to dispense with the latter's services if such
losses become unduly frequent.   On this account, according to the proverbs, the Ahīr is held to be treacherous and
false to his engagements.   They are also regarded as stupid
because they seldom get any education, retain their rustic
and half-aboriginal dialect, and on account of their solitary
life are dull and slow-witted in company.   'The barber's
son learns to shave on the Ahīr's head.'   'The cow is in
league with the milkman and lets him milk water into the
pail.'   The Ahīrs are also hot-tempered, and their propensity
for drinking often results in affrays, when they break each
other's head with their cattle-staffs.   'A Gaoli's quarrel :
drunk at night and friends in the morning.'

Hindus nearly always boil their milk before using it, as
the taste of milk fresh from the cow is considered unpalat-
able.   After boiling, the milk is put in a pot and a little old
curds added, when the whole becomes *dahi* or sour curds.
This is a favourite food, and appears to be exactly the same
substance as the Bulgarian sour milk which is now considered to have much medicinal value.   Butter is also made
by churning these curds or *dahi*.   Butter is never used

20. Prepar-
ations of
milk.

without being boiled first, when it becomes converted into a sort of oil ; this has the advantage of keeping much better than fresh butter, and may remain fit for use for as long as a year. This boiled butter is known as *ghī*, and is the staple product of the dairy industry, the bulk of the surplus supply of milk being devoted to its manufacture. It is freely used by all classes who can afford it, and serves very well for cooking purposes. There is a comparatively small market for fresh milk among the Hindus, and as a rule only those drink milk who obtain it from their own animals. The acid residue after butter has been made from *dahi* (curds) or milk is known as *matha* or butter-milk, and is the only kind of milk drunk by the poorer classes. Milk boiled so long as to become solidified is known as *khīr*, and is used by confectioners for making sweets. When the milk is boiled and some sour milk added to it, so that it coagulates while hot, the preparation is called *chhana*. The whey is expressed from this by squeezing it in a cloth, and a kind of cheese is obtained.[1] The liquid which oozes out at the root of a cow's horns after death is known as *gaolochan* and sells for a high price, as it is considered a valuable medicine for children's cough and lung diseases.

Andh.[2]—A low cultivating caste of Berār, who numbered 52,000 persons in 1911, and belong to the Yeotmal, Akola and Buldāna Districts. The Andhs appear to be a non-Aryan tribe of the Andhra or Tamil country, from which they derive their name. The territories of the Andhra dynasty extended across southern India from sea to sea in the early part of the Christian era. This designation may, however, have been given to them after migration, emigrants being not infrequently called in their new country by the name of the place from which they came, as Berāri, Purdesi, Audhia (from Oudh), and so on. At present there seems to be no caste called Andh in Madras. Mr. Kitts[3] notes that they still come from Hyderābād across the Penganga river.

---

[1] Buchanan, *Eastern India*, ii. pp. 924, 943.

[2] This article is mainly based on a paper by Mr. W. S. Slaney, E.A.C., Akola.

[3] *Berār Census Report* (1881).

The caste are divided into two groups, Vartāti or pure and Khaltāti or illegitimate, which take food together, but do not intermarry. They have a large number of exogamous septs, most of which appear to have Marāthi names, either taken from villages or of a titular character. A few are called after animals or plants, as Mājiria the cat, Ringni a kind of tree, Dumare from Dumar, an ant-hill, Dukare from Dukar, a pig, and Titawe from Titawa, a bird. Bāghmāre means tiger-killer or one killed by a tiger; members of this sept revere the tiger. Two septs, Bhoyar and Wanjāri, are named after other castes.

Marriage between members of the same sept is prohibited, and also between first cousins, except that a sister's son may marry a brother's daughter. Until recently marriage has been adult, but girls are now wedded as children, and betrothals are sometimes arranged before they are born. The ceremony resembles that of the Kunbis. Betrothals are arranged between October and December, and the weddings take place three or four months later, from January to April. If the bride is mature she goes at once to her husband's house. Polygamy is allowed; and as only a well-to-do man can afford to obtain more than one wife, those who have several are held to be wealthy, and treated with respect. Divorce and the remarriage of widows are permitted, but the widow may not marry her husband's brother nor any member of his clan. If an unmarried girl becomes pregnant by a man of her own or a superior caste she is fined, and can then be married as a widow. Her feet are not washed nor besmeared with red powder at the wedding ceremony like those of other girls. In some localities Andh women detected in a criminal intimacy even with men of such impure castes as the Mahārs and Māngs have been readmitted into the community. A substantial fine is imposed on a woman detected in adultery according to her means and spent on a feast to the caste. All the members thus have a personal interest in the detection and punishment of such offences. The dead are usually buried, and water and sugar are placed in a dying man's mouth instead of the sacred objects used by Hindus; nor are the dying urged to call on Rāma. The dead are buried with the head to the south,

in opposition to the Hindu custom.   The Andhs will eat the
flesh of fowls and pigs, and even cats, rats and snakes in
some localities, though the more civilised have abjured these
latter.   They are very fond of pork, and drink liquor, and
will take food from Kunbis, Mālis and Kolis, but not from
Gonds.   They have a caste *panchāyat* or committee, with
a headman called Mohtaria, and two officers known as
Phopatia and Dukria.   When a caste offence is committed
the Dukria goes to call the offender, and is given the
earthen pots used at the penalty-feast, while the Phopatia
receives a new piece of cloth.   The Mohtaria or headman
goes from village to village to decide cases, and gets a share
of the fine.   The caste are *shikāris* or hunters, and cultivators.   They catch antelope, hares, pig and nilgai in their
nets, and kill them with sticks and stones, and they dam up
streams and net fish.   Birds are not caught.   Generally, the
customs of the Andhs clearly point to an aboriginal origin,
but they are rapidly being Hinduised, and in some tracts can
scarcely be distinguished from Kunbis.

They have Marāthi names ; and though only one name
is given at birth, Mr. Slaney notes that this is frequently
changed for some pet name, and as often as not a man goes
regularly by some name other than his real one.

Arakh.—A small caste of cultivators and labourers
found principally in the Chānda District and Berār and
scattered over other localities.   The Arakhs are considered
to be an offshoot of the Pāsi or Bahelia caste of hunters
and fowlers.   Mr. Crooke [1] writes of them : " All their traditions connect them with the Pāsis and Parasurāma, the
sixth Avatāra of Vishnu.   One story runs that Parasurāma
was bathing in the sea, when a leech bit his foot and caused
it to bleed.   He divided the blood into two parts ; out of
one part he made the first Pāsi and out of the second the
first Arakh.   Another story is that the Pāsis were made
out of the sweat (*pasīna*) of Parasurāma.   While Parasurāma was away the Pāsi shot some animals with his bow,
and the deity was so enraged that he cursed the Pāsi, and
swore that his descendants should keep pigs.   This accounts

[1] *Tribes and Castes*, art. Arakh.

for the degradation of the Pāsis. Subsequently Parasurāma sent for some Pāsis to help him in one of his wars ; but they ran away and hid in an *arhar*[1] field and were hence called Arakhs." This connection with the Pāsis is also recognised in the case of the Arakhs of Berār, of whom Mr. Kitts writes :[2] " The Arakhs found in Morsi are a race akin to the Bahelias. Their regular occupation is bird-catching and *shikār* (hunting). They do not follow Hindu customs in their marriages, but although they keep pigs, eat flesh and drink spirits, they will not touch a Chamār. They appear to be a branch of the Pāsi tribe, and are described as a semi-Hinduised class of aborigines." In the Chānda District, however, the Arakhs are closely connected with the Gond tribe, as is evident from their system of exogamy. Thus they say that they are divided into the Mātia, Tekām, Tesli, Godām, Madai, Sayām and Chorliu septs, worshipping respectively three, four, five, six, seven, eight and twelve gods ; and persons who worship the same number of gods cannot marry with one another. This system of divisions according to the different number of gods worshipped is found in the Central Provinces only among the Gonds and one or two other tribes like the Baigas, who have adopted it from them, and as some of the names given above are also Gondi words, no doubt need be entertained that the Arakhs of Chānda are largely of Gond descent. They are probably, in fact, the offspring of irregular connections between the Gonds and Pāsis, who, being both frequenters of the forests, would naturally come much into contact with each other. And being disowned by the true Pāsis on account of their defective pedigree, they have apparently set up as a separate caste and adopted the name of Arakh to hide the deficiencies of their ancestry.

The social customs of the Arakhs resemble those of other low Hindu castes, and need not be given in detail. Their weddings are held near a temple of Māroti, or if there be none such, then at the place where the Holi fire was lit in the preceding year. A bride-price varying from Rs. 25 to Rs. 40 is usually paid. In the case of the

[1] *Cajanus indicus.*   [2] *Berār Census Report* (1881), p. 157.

marriage of a widow, the second husband goes to the house of the woman, where the couple are bathed and seated on two wooden boards, a branch of a cotton-plant being placed near them. The bridegroom then ties five strings of black glass beads round the woman's neck. The dead are mourned for one day only, and a funeral feast is given to the caste-fellows. The Arakhs are a very low caste, but their touch does not convey impurity.

1. General notice.

Atāri,[1] **Gandhi, Bukekari.**— A small Muhammadan caste of retailers of scent, incense, tooth-powder and *kunku* or pink powder. Atāri is derived from *atar* or *itra*, attar of roses. Gandhi comes from *gandh,* a Sanskrit word for scent. Bukekāri is a Marāthi word meaning a seller of powder. The Atāris number about two hundred persons in Nāgpur, Wardha and Berār. Both Hindus and Muhammadans follow the profession, but the Hindu Atāris are not a separate caste, and belong to the Teli, Gurao and Beldār castes. The Muhammadan Atāris, to whom this article refers, may marry with other Muhammadans, with the exception of low-class tradesmen like the Pinjāras, Kasais and Kunjras. One instance of an Atāri marrying a Rangrez is known, but usually they decline to do so. But since they are not considered to be the equals of ordinary Muhammadans, they constitute more or less a distinct social group. They are of the same position as Muhammadan tin-workers, bangle-makers and pedlars, and sometimes intermarry with them. They admit Hindu converts into the community, but the women refuse to eat with them, and the better-class families will not intermarry with converts. A new convert must be circumcised, but if he is of advanced age, or if his foreskin is wanting, as sometimes happens, they take a rolled-up betel-leaf and cut it in two in substitution for the rite.

2. Marriage customs.

It is essential that a girl should be married before adolescence, as it is said that when the signs of puberty appear in her before wedlock her parents commit a crime equivalent to the shedding of human blood. The father

---

[1] Based on papers by Mr. Bijai Bahādur Royzāda, Naib - Tahsīldār Hinganghāt, and Munshi Kanhya Lāl of the Gazetteer office.

of the boy looks for a bride, and after dropping hints to the girl's family to see if his proposal is acceptable, he sends some female relatives or friends to discuss the marriage. Before the wedding the boy is presented with a *chhāp* or ring of gold or silver with a small cup-like attachment. A *mehar* or dowry must be given to the bride, the amount of which is not below Rs. 50 or above Rs. 250. The bride's parents give her cooking vessels, bedding and a bedstead. After the wedding, the couple are seated on a cot while the women sing songs, and they see each other's face reflected in a mirror. The procession returns after a stay of four days, and is received by the women of the bridegroom's family with some humorous ceremonies bearing on the nature of marriage. A feast called Tāmm Walīma follows, and the couple are shut up together in an inner room, even though they may be under age. The marriage includes some Hindu customs, such as the erection of the *pandal* or shed, rubbing the couple with turmeric and oil, and the tying on of *kankans* or wrist-bands. A girl going wrong before marriage may be wedded with full rites so long as she has not conceived, but after conception until her child is born she cannot go through the ceremony at all. After the birth of the child she may be married simply with the rite for widows. She retains the child, but it has no claim to succeed to her husband's property. A widow may marry again after an interval of forty days from her first husband's death, and she may wed her younger brother-in-law. Divorce is permitted at the instance of either party, and for mere disagreement. A man usually divorces his wife by vowing in the presence of two witnesses that he will in future consider intercourse with her as incestuous in the same degree as with his mother. A divorced woman has a claim to her *mehar* or dowry if not already paid, but forfeits it if she marries again. A man can marry the daughter of his paternal uncle. The services of a Kāzi at weddings are paid for with a fee of Rs. 1-4, and well-to-do persons also give him a pair of turbans.

 The Atāris are Muhammadans of the Sunni sect. They 3. Religion. revere the Muhammadan saints, and on the night of Shabrāt they let off fireworks in honour of their ancestors and make offerings of *halwa*[1] to them and place lamps and scent on their tombs. They swear by the pig and abstain from eating its flesh. The dog is considered an unclean animal and its tail, ears and tongue are especially defiling. If the hair of a dog falls on the ground they cannot pray in that place because the souls of the prophets cannot come there. To see a dog flapping its ears is a bad omen, and a person starting on a journey should postpone his departure. They esteem the spider, because they say it spread its web over the mouth of the cave where Hasan and Husain lay concealed from their enemies and thus prevented it from being searched. Some of them have Pīrs or spiritual preceptors, these being Muhammadan beggars, not necessarily celibate. The ceremony of adhesion is that a man should drink sherbet from the cup from which his preceptor has drunk. They do not observe impurity after a death nor bathe on returning from a funeral.

4. Social customs.   Liquor is of course prohibited to the Atāris as to other Muhammadans, but some of them drink it nevertheless. Some of them eat beef and others abstain. The blood of animals killed must flow before death according to the rite of *halāl*, but they say that fish are an exception, because when Abraham was offering up his son Ishmael and God substituted a goat, the goat bleated before it was killed, and this offended Abraham, who threw his sacrificial knife into the sea : the knife struck and killed a fish, and on this account all fish are considered to be *halāl* or lawful food without any further rite. The Atāris observe the Hindu law of inheritance, and some of them worship Hindu deities, as Māta the goddess of smallpox. As a rule their women are not secluded. The Atāris make *missi* or toothpowder from myrobalans, cloves and cardamoms, and other constituents. This has the effect of blackening the teeth. They also sell the *kunku* or red powder which women rub on their foreheads, its constituents being turmeric, borax and the juice of limes. They sell scent and sometimes deal in tobacco. The scents most in demand are *gulāb-pāni* or rose-water and *phulel* or essence of tilli or sesamum. Scents are usually sold by the tola of 18 annas silver weight,[2] and

---

[1] A preparation of raisins and other fruits and rice.

[2] The ordinary tola is a rupee weight or two-fifths of an ounce.

a tola of attar may vary in price from 8 annas to Rs. 80. Other scents are made from *khas-khas* grass, the mango, henna and musk, the *bela* flower,[1] the champak [2] and cucumber. Scent is manufactured by distillation from the flowers boiled in water, and the drops of congealed vapour fall into sandal-wood oil, which they say is the basis of all scents. Fragrant oils are also sold for rubbing on the hair, made from orange flowers, jasmine, cotton-seed and the flowers of the *aonla* tree.[3] Scent is sold in tiny circular glass bottles, and the oils in little bottles made from thin leather. The Atāris also retail the little black sticks of incense which are set up and burnt at the time of taking food and in temples, so that the smell and smoke may keep off evil spirits. When professional exorcists are called upon to clear any building, such as a hospital, supposed to be haunted by spirits or the ghosts of the dead, they commence operations by placing these sticks of incense at the entrance and setting them alight as in a temple.

Audhelia (Audhalia).—A small hybrid caste found almost exclusively in the Bilāspur District, where they number about 1000 persons. The name is derived from the word Udharia, meaning a person with clandestine sexual intimacies. The Audhelias are a mixed caste and trace their origin from a Daharia Rājpūt ancestor, by one Bhūri Bāndi, a female slave of unknown caste. This couple is supposed to have resided in Ratanpur, the old capital of Chhattīsgarh, and the female ancestors of the Audhelias are said to have been prostitutes until they developed into a caste and began to marry among themselves. Their proper avocation at present is the rearing of pigs, while some of them are also tenants and farm-labourers. Owing to the base descent and impure occupation of the caste they are held in very low esteem, and their touch is considered to convey pollution.

The caste have at present no endogamous divisions and still admit members of other castes with the exception of the very lowest. But social gradations exist to a certain

1. Origin.

2. Marriage.

---

[1] *Jasminum zambac.*   [2] *Michelia champaca.*
[3] *Phyllanthus emblica.*

extent among the members according to the position of their male ancestors, a Daharia Audhelia, for instance, being reluctant to eat or intermarry with a Panka Audhelia. Under these circumstances it has become a rule among the Audhelias not to eat with their caste-fellows excepting their own relations. On the occasion of a caste feast, therefore, each guest prepares his own food, taking only uncooked grain from his host. At present seven *gotras* or exogamous divisions appear to have been formed in the caste with the names of Pachbhaiya, Chhahri, Kālkhor, Bachhāwat, Dhanāwat, Bhainsa and Limuăn. The following story exists as to the origin of these *gotras*: There were formerly three brothers, Sahasmān, Budha and Mangal, who were Sānsis or robbers. One evening the three brothers halted in a forest and went to look for food. One brought back a buffalo-horn, another a peacock's feather and the youngest, Mangal, brought plums. The other brothers asked Mangal to let them share his plums, to which he agreed on condition that one of the brothers should give his daughter to him in marriage. As Mangal and his brothers were of one *gotra* or section, and the marriage would thus involve splitting up the *gotra*, the brothers were doubtful whether it could be performed. They sought about for some sign to determine this difficult question, and decided that if Mangal succeeded in breaking in pieces an iron image of a cat simply by blows of his naked fist, it would be a sufficient indication that they might split up their *gotra*. Mangal was therefore put to the ordeal and succeeded in breaking the image, so the three brothers split up their *gotra*, the eldest assuming the *gotra* name of Bhainsa because he had found a buffalo-horn, the second that of Kālkhor, which is stated to mean peacock, and the third that of Chhahri, which at any rate does not mean a plum. The word Chhahri means either 'shadow,' or 'one who washes the clothes of a woman in confinement.' If we assume it to have the latter meaning, it may be due to the fact that Mangal had to wash the clothes of his own wife, not being able to induce a professional washerman to do so on account of the incestuous nature of the connection. As the eldest brother gave his daughter in an incestuous marriage he was also degraded, and became the ancestor of the Kanjars or prostitutes, who, it is said, to the present day do not solicit Audhelias in consideration of the consanguinity existing between them. The story itself sufficiently indicates the low and mixed descent of the Audhelias, and its real meaning may possibly be that when they first began to form a separate caste they permitted incestuous marriages on account of the paucity of their members. A curious point about the story is that the incestuous nature of the connection is not taken to be the most pressing objection to the marriage of Mangal with his own niece, but the violation of the caste rule prohibiting marriage within the same *gotra*. Bachhāwat and Dhanāwat are the names of sections of the Banjāra caste, and the persons of these *gotras* among the Audhelias are probably the descendants of illicit connections among Banjāras. The word Pachbhaiya means 'five brothers,' and this name possibly commemorates a polyandrous connection of some Audhelia woman. Limuān means a tortoise, which is a section of many castes. Several of the section-names are thus totemistic, and, as in other castes, some reverence is paid to the animal from whom the name is derived. At present the Audhelias forbid marriage within the same *gotra* and also the union of first cousins. Girls are married between five and seven years of age as their numbers are scarce, and they are engaged as early as possible. Unless weddings are arranged by exchanging girls between two families, a high bride-price, often amounting to as much as Rs. 60, is paid. No stigma is incurred, however, if a girl should remain unmarried till she arrives at adolescence, but, on the contrary, a higher price is then obtained for her. Sexual licence either before or after marriage is considered a venial offence, but a woman detected in a *liaison* with a man of one of the lowest castes is turned out of caste. Widow marriage and divorce are freely allowed.

The Audhelias venerate Dulha Deo and Devi, to whom 3. Religion, they usually offer pigs. Their principal festival is the Holi, birth and at which their women were formerly engaged to perform as death. professional dancers. They usually burn their dead and remove the ashes on the third day, throwing them into the nearest stream. A few of the bones are picked up and buried under a pīpal tree, and a pitcher with a hole in the bottom is hung on the tree so that water may trickle down on to them. On the tenth day the caste-people assemble and are shaved and bathe and rub their bodies with oil under the tree. Unmarried men and persons dying of cholera are buried, the head being placed to the north. They consider that if they place the corpse in the reverse position it would be an insult to the Ganges equivalent to kicking the holy river, as the feet of the body would then be turned towards it.

BADHAK

LIST OF PARAGRAPHS

Badhak, Bāgri, Baoria.—A famous tribe of dacoits who flourished up to about 1850, and extended their depredations over the whole of Northern and Central India. The Bāgris and Baorias or Bāwarias still exist and are well known to the police as inveterate criminals; but their operations are now confined to ordinary burglary, theft and cheating, and their more interesting profession of armed gang-robbery on a large scale is a thing of the past. The first part of this article is entirely compiled from the Report on their suppression drawn up by Colonel Sleeman,[1] who may be regarded as the virtual founder of the Thuggee and Dacoity Department. Some mention of the existing Bāgri and Baoria tribes is added at the end. *1. Introductory notice.*

The origin of the Badhaks is obscure, but they seem to have belonged to Gujarāt, as their peculiar dialect, still in use, is a form of Gujarāti. The most striking feature in it is the regular substitution of *kh* for *s*. They claimed to be *2. The Badhak dacoits.*

[1] *Report on the Badhak or Bāgri Dacoits and the Measures adopted by the Government of India for their Suppression,* printed in 1849.

Rājpūts and were divided into clans with the well-known Rājpūt names of Solanki, Panwār, Dhundhel, Chauhān, Rāthor, Gahlot, Bhatti and Chāran. Their ancestors were supposed to have fled from Chitor on one of the historical occasions on which it was assaulted and sacked. But as they spoke Gujarāti it seems more probable that they belonged to Gujarāt, a fertile breeding-place of criminals, and they may have been descended from the alliances of Rājpūts with the primitive tribes of this locality, the Bhīls and Kolis. The existing Bāgris are of short stature, one writer stating that none of them exceed five feet two inches in height ; and this seems to indicate that they have little Rājpūt blood. It may be surmised that the Badhaks rose into importance and found scope for their predatory instincts during the period of general disorder and absence of governing authority through which northern India passed after the decline of the Mughal Empire. And they lived and robbed with the connivance or open support of the petty chiefs and land-holders, to whom they gave a liberal share of their booty. The principal bands were located in the Oudh forests, but they belonged to the whole of northern India including the Central Provinces ; and as Colonel Sleeman's Report, though of much interest, is now practically unknown, I have thought it not out of place to compile an article by means of short extracts from his account of the tribe.

In 1822 the operations of the Badhaks were being conducted on such a scale that an officer wrote : " No District between the Brahmaputra, the Nerbudda, the Satlej and the Himalayas is free from them ; and within this vast field hardly any wealthy merchant or manufacturer could feel himself secure for a single night from the depredations of Badhak dacoits. They had successfully attacked so many of the treasuries of our native Sub-Collectors that it was deemed necessary, all over the North-Western Provinces, to surround such buildings with extensive fortifications. In many cases they carried off our public treasure from strong parties of our regular troops and mounted police ; and none seemed to know whence they came or whither they fled with the booty acquired." [1]

---

[1] Sleeman, p. 10.

Colonel Sleeman thus described a dacoity in the town of 3. In-
Narsinghpur when he was in charge of that District :[1] " In stances of dacoities.
February 1822, in the dusk of the evening, a party of about
thirty persons, with nothing seemingly but walking-sticks in
their hands, passed the piquet of sepoys on the bank of the
rivulet which separates the cantonment from the town of
Narsinghpur.   On being challenged by the sentries they
said they were cowherds and that their cattle were following
close behind.   They walked up the street ; and coming
opposite the houses of the most wealthy merchants, they set
their torches in a blaze by blowing suddenly on pots filled
with combustibles, stabbed everybody who ventured to move
or make the slightest noise, plundered the houses, and in ten
minutes were away with their booty, leaving about twelve
persons dead and wounded on the ground.   No trace of
them was discovered."   Another well-known exploit of the
Badhaks was the attack on the palace of the ex-Peshwa, Bāji
Rao, at Bithūr near Cawnpore.   This was accomplished by a
gang of about eighty men, who proceeded to the locality in
the disguise of carriers of Ganges water.   Having purchased
a boat and a few muskets to intimidate the guard they
crossed the Ganges about six miles below Bithūr, and reached
the place at ten o'clock at night ; and after wounding
eighteen persons who attempted resistance they possessed
themselves of property, chiefly in gold, to the value of more
than two and a half lakhs of rupees ; and retiring without
loss made their way in safety to their homes in the Oudh
forests.   The residence of this gang was known to a British
police officer in the King of Oudh's service, Mr. Orr, and
after a long delay on the part of the court an expedition
was sent which recovered a portion of the treasure and
captured two or three hundred of the Badhaks.   But none of
the recovered property reached the hands of Bāji Rao and
the prisoners were soon afterwards released.[2]   Again in
1839, a gang of about fifty men under a well-known
leader, Gajrāj, scaled the walls of Jhānsi and plundered
the Surāfa or bankers' quarter of the town for two hours,
obtaining booty to the value of Rs. 40,000, which they
carried off without the loss of a man.   The following

[1] Sleeman, p. 10.   [2] Sleeman, p. 57.

account of this raid was obtained by Colonel Sleeman from one of the robbers:[1] "The spy (*hirrowa*) having returned and reported that he had found a merchant's house in Jhānsi which contained a good deal of property, we proceeded to a grove where we took the auspices by the process of *akūt* (counting of grains) and found the omens favourable. We then rested three days and settled the rates according to which the booty should be shared. Four or five men, who were considered too feeble for the enterprise, were sent back, and the rest, well armed, strong and full of courage, went on. In the evening of the fourth day we reached a plain about a mile from the town, where we rested to take breath for an hour; about nine o'clock we got to the wall and remained under it till midnight, preparing the ladders from materials which we had collected on the road. They were placed to the wall and we entered and passed through the town without opposition. A marriage procession was going on before us and the people thought we belonged to it. We found the bankers' shops closed. Thāna and Saldewa, who carried the axes, soon broke them open, while Kulean lighted up his torch. Gajrāj with twenty men entered, while the rest stood posted at the different avenues leading to the place. When all the property they could find had been collected, Gajrāj hailed the god Hanumān and gave orders for the retreat. We got back safely to Mondegri in two days and a half, and then reposed for two or three days with the Rāja of Narwar, with whom we left five or six of our stoutest men as a guard, and then returned home with our booty, consisting chiefly of diamonds, emeralds, gold and silver bullion, rupees and about sixty pounds of silver wire. None of our people were either killed or wounded, but whether any of the bankers' people were I know not."

4. Further instances of dacoities.

Colonel Sleeman writes elsewhere[2] of the leader of the above exploit: "This Gajrāj had risen from the vocation of a *bandarwāla* (monkey showman) to be the Robin Hood of Gwālior and the adjacent States; he was the governor-general of banditti in that country of banditti and kept the whole in awe; he had made himself so formidable that

[1] Sleeman, p. 95.   [2] Sleeman, p. 231.

the Durbar appointed him to keep the *ghāts* or ferries over
the Chambal, which he did in a very profitable manner to
them and to himself, and none entered or quitted the
country without paying blackmail." A common practice of
the Badhaks, when in need of a little ready money, was to
lie in wait for money-changers on their return from the
markets. These men take their bags of money with them
to the important bazārs at a distance from their residence
and return home with them after dusk. The dacoits were
accustomed to watch for them in the darkest and most
retired places on the roads and fell them to the ground
with their bludgeons. This device was often practised and
usually succeeded.[1] Of another Badhak chief, Meherbān, it
is stated [2] that he hired a discharged sepoy to instruct his
followers in the European system of drill, that they might
travel with him in the disguise of regular soldiers, well
armed and accoutred. During the rains Meherbān's spies
(*hirrowa*) were sent to visit the great commercial towns and
report any despatches of money or other valuables, which
were to take place during the following open season. His
own favourite disguise was that of a Hindu prince, while the
remainder of the gang constituted his retinue and escort.
On one occasion, assuming this character, he followed up
a boat laden with Spanish dollars which was being sent from
Calcutta to Benāres ; and having attacked it at its moorings
at Makrai, he killed one and wounded ten men of the guard
and made off with 25,000 Spanish dollars and Rs. 2600
of the Company's coinage. A part of the band were sent
direct to the rendezvous previously arranged, while Meherbān returned to the grove where he had left his women and
proceeded with them in a more leisurely fashion to the same
place. Retaining the character of a native prince he halted
here for two days to celebrate the Holi festival. Marching
thence with his women conveyed in covered litters by hired
bearers who were changed at intervals, he proceeded to his
bivouac in the Oudh forests ; and at Seosāgar, one of his
halting-places, he gave a large sum of money to a gardener
to plant a grove of mango trees near a tank for the benefit
of travellers, in the name of Rāja Meherbān Singh of Gaur

[1] Sleeman, p. 217.   [2] Sleeman, p. 20.

in Oudh ; and promised him further alms on future occasions of pilgrimage if he found the work progressing well, saying that it was a great shame that travellers should be compelled as he had been to halt without shade for themselves or their families during the heat of the day. He arrived safely at his quarters in the forest and was received in the customary fashion by a procession of women in their best attire, who conducted him with dancing and music, like a victorious Roman Proconsul, to his fort.[1]

5. Disguise of religious mendicants.

But naturally not all the Badhaks could do things in the style of Meherbān Singh. The disguise which they most often assumed in the north was that of carriers of Ganges water, while in Central India they often pretended to be Banjāras travelling with pack-bullocks, or pilgrims, or wedding-parties going to fetch the bride or bridegroom. Sometimes also they took the character of religious mendicants, the leader being the high priest and all the rest his followers and disciples. One such gang, described by Colonel Sleeman,[2] had four or five tents of white and dyed cloth, two or three pairs of *nakkāras* or kettle-drums and trumpets, with a great number of buffaloes, cows, goats, sheep and ponies. Some were clothed, but the bodies of the greater part were covered with nothing but ashes, paint and a small cloth waistband. But they always provided themselves with five or six real Bairāgis, whose services they purchased at a very high price. These men were put forward to answer questions in case of difficulty and to bully the landlords and peasantry ; and if the people demurred to the demands of the Badhaks, to intimidate them by tricks calculated to play upon the fears of the ignorant. They held in their hands a preparation of gunpowder resembling common ashes ; and when they found the people very stubborn they repeated their *mantras* over this and threw it upon the thatch of the nearest house, to which it set fire. The explosion was caused by a kind of fusee held in the hand which the people could not see, and taking it for a miracle they paid all that was demanded. Another method was to pretend to be carrying the bones of dead relatives to the Ganges. The bones or ashes of

[1] Sleeman, p. 21.   [2] Sleeman, p. 81.

the deceased, says[1] Colonel Sleeman, are carried to the Ganges in bags, coloured red for females and white for males. These bags are considered holy, and are not allowed to touch the ground upon the way, and during halts in the journey are placed on poles or triangles. The carriers are regarded with respect as persons engaged upon a pious duty, and seldom questioned on the road. When a gang assumed this disguise they proceeded to their place of rendezvous in small parties, some with red and some with white bags, in which they carried the bones of animals most resembling those of the human frame. These were supported on triangles formed of the shafts on which the spear-heads would be fitted when they reached their destination and had prepared for action.

It would have been impossible for the Badhaks to exist and flourish as they did without the protection of the landowners on whose estates they lived ; and this they received in full measure in return for a liberal share of their booty. When the chief of Karauli was called upon to dislodge a gang within his territory, he expressed apprehension that the coercion of the Badhaks might cause a revolution in the State. He was not at all singular, says Colonel Sleeman, in his fear of exasperating this formidable tribe of robbers. It was common to all the smaller chiefs and the provincial governors of the larger ones. They everywhere protected and fostered the Badhaks, as did the landholders ; and the highest of them associated with the leaders of gangs on terms of equality and confidence. It was very common for a chief or the governor of a district in times of great difficulty and personal danger to require from one of the leaders of such gangs a night-guard or *palang ki chauki* : and no less so to entertain large bodies of them in the attack and defence of forts and camps whenever unusual courage and skill were required. The son of the Rāja of Charda exchanged turbans with a Badhak leader, Mangal Singh, as a mark of the most intimate friendship. This episode recalls an alliance of similar character in *Lorna Doone* ; and indeed it would not be difficult to find several points of resemblance between the careers of the more enterprising Badhak leaders and the

6. Countenance and support of landowners.

[1] Sleeman, p. 82.

Doones of Bagworthy ; but India produced no character on the model of John Ridd, and it was reserved for an Englishman, Colonel Sleeman, to achieve the suppression of the Badhaks as well as that of the Thugs. After the fortress and territory of Garhākota in Saugor had been taken by the Mahārāja Sindhia, Zālim Singh, a cousin of the dispossessed Bundela chief, collected a force of Bundelas and Pindāris and ravaged the country round Garhākota in 1813. In the course of his raid he sacked and burnt the town of Deori, and 15,000 persons perished in the flames. Colonel Jean Baptiste, Sindhia's general, obtained a number of picked Badhaks from Rājputāna and offered them a rich reward for the head of Zālim Singh ; and after watching his camp for three months they managed to come on him asleep in the tent of a dancing-girl, who was following his camp, and stabbed him to the heart. For this deed they received Rs. 20,000 from Baptiste with other valuable presents. Their reputation was indeed such that they were frequently employed at this period both by chiefs who desired to take the lives of others and by those who were anxious for the preservation of their own. When it happened that a gang was caught after a robbery in a native State, the custom was not infrequently to make them over to the merchant whose property they had taken, with permission to keep them in confinement until they should refund his money ; and in this manner by giving up the whole or a part of the proceeds of their robbery they were enabled to regain their liberty. Even if they were sent before the courts, justice was at that time so corrupt as to permit of easy avenues of escape for those who could afford to pay ; and Colonel Sleeman records the deposition of a Badhak describing their methods of bribery : " When police officers arrest Badhaks their old women get round them and give them large sums of money ; and they either release them or get their depositions so written that their release shall be ordered by the magistrates. If they are brought to court, their old women, dressed in rags, follow them at a distance of three or four miles with a thousand or two thousand rupees upon ponies ; and these rupees they distribute among the native officers of the court and get the Badhaks released. These old women first ascertain from the people of the villages

who are the Nāzirs and Munshis of influence, and wait
upon them at their houses and make their bargains. If the
officials cannot effect their release, they take money from
the old women and send them off to the Sadar Court, with
letters of introduction to their friends, and advice as to the
rate they shall pay to each according to his supposed influence. This is the way that all our leaders get released, and
hardly any but useless men are left in confinement." [1]

It may be noticed that these robbers took the utmost
pleasure in their calling, and were most averse to the idea of
giving it up and taking to honest pursuits. "Some of the
men with me," one magistrate wrote,[2] "have been in jail for
twenty, and one man for thirty years, and still do not appear
to have any idea of abandoning their illegal vocation ; even
now, indeed, they look on what we consider an honest means
of livelihood with the most marked contempt ; and in relating
their excursions talk of them with the greatest pleasure,
much in the way an eager sportsman describes a boar-chase
or fox-hunt. While talking of their excursions, which were
to me really very interesting, their eyes gleamed with
pleasure ; and beating their hands on their foreheads and
breasts and muttering some ejaculation they bewailed the
hardness of their lot, which now ensured their never again
being able to participate in such a joyous occupation."
Another Badhak, on being examined, said he could not
recall a case of one of the community having ever given up
the trade of dacoity. "None ever did, I am certain of it,"
he continued.[3] "After having been arrested, on our release
we frequently take lands, to make it appear we have left off
dacoity, but we never do so in reality ; it is only done as a
feint and to enable our zamīndārs (landowners) to screen
us." They sometimes paid rent for their land at the rate
of thirty rupees an acre, in return for the countenance and
protection afforded by the zamīndārs. "Our profession,"
another Badhak remarked,[4] "has been a *Pādshāhi Kām*
(a king's trade) ; we have attacked and seized boldly the
thousands and hundreds of thousands that we have freely

7. Pride in
their
profession.

---

[1] Sleeman, p. 152.
[2] Sleeman, p. 127. This passage is
from a letter written by a magistrate,

Mr. Ramsay.
[3] Sleeman, p. 129.
[4] Sleeman, p. 112.

and nobly spent ; we have been all our lives wallowing in wealth and basking in freedom, and find it hard to manage with the few copper pice a day we get from you." At the time when captures were numerous, and the idea was entertained of inducing the dacoits to settle in villages and supporting them until they had been trained to labour, several of them, on being asked how much they would require to support themselves, replied that they could not manage on less than two rupees a day, having earned quite that sum by dacoity. This amount would be more than twenty times the wages of an ordinary labourer at the same period. Another witness put the amount at one to two rupees a day, remarking, ' We are great persons for eating and drinking, and we keep several wives according to our means.' Of some of them Colonel Sleeman had a high opinion, and he mentions the case of one man, Ajīt Singh, who was drafted into the native army and rose to be commander of a company. " I have seldom seen a man," he wrote,[1] "whom I would rather have with me in scenes of peril and difficulty." An attempt of the King of Oudh's, however, to form a regiment of Badhaks had ended in failure, as after a short time they mutinied, beat their commandant and other officers and turned them out of the regiment, giving as their reason that the officers had refused to perform the same duties as the men. And they visited with the same treatment all the other officers sent to them, until they were disbanded by the British on the province of Allahābād being made over to the Company. Colonel Sleeman notes that they were never known to offer any other violence or insult to females than to make them give up any gold ornaments that they might have about their persons. " In all my inquiries into the character, habits and conduct of these gangs, I have never found an instance of a female having been otherwise disgraced or insulted by them. They are all Hindūs, and this reverence for the sex pervades all Hindū society." [2] According to their own account also they never committed murder ; if people opposed them they struck and killed like soldiers, but this was considered to be in fair fight. It may be noted, nevertheless, that they had little idea of clan loyalty, and

[1] Sleeman, p. 124.   [2] Sleeman, p. 125.

informed very freely against their fellows when this course was to their advantage.   They also stated that they could not settle in towns; they had always been accustomed to live in the jungles and commit dacoities upon the people of the towns as a kind of *shikār* (sport); they delighted in it, and they felt living in towns or among other men as a kind of prison, and got quite confused (*ghabrāye*), and their women even more than the men.

The Badhaks had a regular caste organisation, and members of the different clans married with each other like the Rājpūts after whom they were named.   They admitted freely into the community members of any respectable Hindu caste, but not the impure castes or Muhammadans. But at least one instance of the admission of a Muhammadan is given.[1]   The Badhaks were often known to the people as Siārkhawa or jackal-eaters, or Sabkhawa, those who eat everything.   And the Muhammadan in question was given jackal's flesh to eat, and having partaken of it was considered to have become a member of the community.   This indicates that the Badhaks were probably accustomed to eat the flesh of the jackal at a sacrificial meal, and hence that they worshipped the jackal, revering it probably as the deity of the forests where they lived. Such a veneration would account for the importance attached to the jackal's cry as an omen.   The fact of their eating jackals also points to the conclusion that the Badhaks were not Rājpūts, but a low hunting caste like the Pārdhis and Bahelias.   The Pārdhis have Rājpūt sept names as well as the Badhaks.   No doubt a few outcaste Rājpūts may have joined the gangs and become their leaders.   Others, however, said that they abstained from the flesh of jackals, snakes, foxes and cows and buffaloes.   Children were frequently adopted, being purchased in large numbers in time of famine, and also occasionally kidnapped.   They were brought up to the trade of dacoity, and if they showed sufficient aptitude for it were taken out on expeditions, but otherwise left at home to manage the household affairs. They were married to other adopted children and were known as Ghulāmi or Slave Badhaks, like the Jāngar

8. Caste rules and admission of outsiders.

---

[1] Sleeman, p. 147.

Banjāras ; and like them also, after some generations, when
their real origin had been forgotten, they became full
Badhaks. It was very advantageous to a Badhak to have
a number of children, because all plunder obtained was
divided in regularly apportioned shares among the whole
community. Men who were too old to go on dacoity also
received their share, and all children, even babies born
during the absence of the expedition. The Badhaks said
that this rule was enforced because they thought it an
advantage to the community that families should be large
and their numbers should increase ; from which statement
it must be concluded that they seldom suffered any strin-
gency from lack of spoil. They also stated that Badhak
widows would go and find a second husband from among
the regular population, and as a rule would sooner or later
persuade him to join the Badhaks.

9. Reli-
gion :
offerings to
ancestors.

Like other Indian criminals the Badhaks were of a very
religious or superstitious disposition. They considered the
gods of the Hindu creed as favouring their undertakings
so long as they were suitably propitiated by offering to
their temples and priests, and the spirits of the most
distinguished of their ancestors as exercising a vicarious
authority under these deities in guiding them to their prey
and warning them of danger.[1] The following is an account
of a Badhak sacrifice given to Colonel Sleeman by the
Ajīt Singh already mentioned. It was in celebration of a
dacoity in which they had obtained Rs. 40,000, out of
which Rs. 4500 were set aside for sacrifices to the gods
and charity to the poor. Ajīt Singh said : " For offerings
to the gods we purchase goats, sweet cakes and spirits ;
and having prepared a feast we throw a handful of the
savoury food upon the fire in the name of the gods who
have most assisted us ; but of the feast so consecrated
no female but a virgin can partake. The offering is made
through the man who has successfully invoked the god
on that particular occasion ; and, as my god had guided us
this time, I was employed to prepare the feast for him
and to throw the offering upon the fire. The offering must
be taken up before the feast is touched and put upon the

[1] Sleeman, p. 104.

fire, and a little water must be sprinkled on it. The savoury smell of the food as it burns reaches the nostrils of the god and delights him. On this as on most occasions I invoked the spirit of Ganga Singh, my grandfather, and to him I made the offering. I considered him to be the greatest of all my ancestors as a robber, and him I invoked on this solemn occasion. He never failed me when I invoked him, and I had the greatest confidence in his aid. The spirits of our ancestors can easily see whether we shall succeed in what we are about to undertake ; and when we are to succeed they order us on, and when we are not they make signs to us to desist." Their mode [1] of ascertaining which of their ancestors interested himself most in their affairs was commonly this, that whenever a person talked inco-herently in a fever or an epileptic fit, the spirit of one or other of his ancestors was supposed to be upon him. If they were in doubt as to whose spirit it was, one of them threw down some grains of wheat or coloured glass beads, a pinch at a time, saying the name of the ancestor he supposed the most likely to be at work and calling odd or even as he pleased. If the number proved to be as he called it several times running while that name was repeated, they felt secure of their family god, and proceeded at once to sacrifice a goat or something else in his name. When they were being hunted down and arrested by Colonel Sleeman and his assistants, they ascribed their misfortunes to the anger of the goddess Kāli, because they had infringed her rules and disregarded her signs, and said that their forefathers had often told them they would one day be punished for their disobedience.[2]

Whenever one of the gang was wounded and was taken with his wounds bleeding near a place haunted by a spirit, they believed the spirit got angry and took hold of him,[3] in the manner described by Ajīt Singh as follows : " The spirit comes upon him in all kinds of shapes, sometimes in that of a buffalo, at others in that of a woman, some-times in the air above and sometimes from the ground below ; but no one can see him except the wounded person

10. The wounded haunted by spirits.

[1] Sleeman, p. 110.   [2] Sleeman, p. 131.
[3] Sleeman, p. 205.

he is angry with and wants to punish.   Upon such a wounded person we always place a naked sword or some other sharp steel instrument, as spirits are much afraid of weapons of this kind.   If there be any good conjurer at hand to charm away the spirits from the person wounded he recovers, but nothing else can save him." In one case a dacoit named Ghīsa had been severely wounded in an encounter and was seized by the spirit of a banyan tree as he was being taken away : "We made a litter with our ropes and cloaks thrown over them and on this he was carried off by four of our party ; at half a mile distant the road passed under a large banyan tree and as the four men carried him along under the tree, the spirit of the place fell upon him and the four men who carried him fell down with the shock.   They could not raise him again, so much were they frightened, and four other men were obliged to lift him and carry him off." The man died of his wounds soon after they reached the halting-place, and in commenting on this Ajīt Singh continued : "When the spirit seized Ghīsa under the tree we had unfortunately no conjurer, and he, poor fellow, died in consequence.   It was evident that a spirit had got hold of him, for he could not keep his head upright ; it always fell down upon his right or left shoulder as often as we tried to put it right ; and he complained much of a pain in the region of the liver.   We therefore concluded that the spirit had broken his neck and was consuming his liver."

11. Pious funeral observances.
Like pious Hindus as they were, the Badhaks were accustomed, whenever it was possible, to preserve the bones of their dead after the body had been burnt and carry them to the Ganges.   If this was not possible, however, and the exigencies of their profession obliged them to make away with the body without the performance of due funeral rites, they cut off two or three fingers and sent these to the Ganges to be deposited instead of the whole body.[1]   In one case a dacoit, Kundana, was killed in an affray, and the others carried off his body and thrust it into a porcupine's hole after cutting off three of the fingers.   "We gave Kundana's fingers to his mother," Ajīt Singh stated, "and she sent them

[1] Sleeman, p. 106.

with due offerings and ceremonies to the Ganges by the
hands of the family priest. She gave this priest money to
purchase a cow, to be presented to the priests in the name of
her deceased son, and to distribute in charity to the poor and
to holy men. She got from us for these purposes eighty
rupees over and above her son's share of the booty, while
his widow and children continued to receive their usual
share of the takings of the gang so long as they remained
with us."

Before setting out on an expedition it was their regular
custom to take the omens, and the following account may be
quoted of the preliminaries to an expedition of the great
leader, Meherbān Singh, who has already been mentioned :
" In the latter end of that year, Meherbān and his brother set
out and assembled their friends on the bank of the Bisori
river, where the rate at which each member of the party
should share in the spoil was determined in order to secure
to the dependants of any one who should fall in the enterprise their due share, as well as to prevent inconvenient
disputes during and after the expedition. The party
assembled on this occasion, including women and children,
amounted to two hundred, and when the shares had been
determined the goats were sacrificed for the feast. Each
leader and member of the gang dipped his finger in the
blood and swore fidelity to his engagements and his associates under all circumstances. The whole feasted together
and drank freely till the next evening, when Meherbān
advanced with about twenty of the principal persons to a
spot chosen a little way from the camp on the road they
proposed to take in the expedition, and lifting up his hands
in supplication said aloud, ' If it be thy will, O God, and
thine, Kāli, to prosper our undertaking for the sake of the
blind and the lame, *the widow and the orphan*, who depend
upon our exertions for subsistence, vouchsafe, we pray thee,
the call of the female jackal.' All his followers held up
their hands in the same manner and repeated these words
after him. All then sat down and waited in silence for
the reply or spoke only in whispers. At last the cry of
the female jackal was heard three times on the left, and
believing her to have been inspired by the deity for

12. Taking
the omens.

their guidance they were all much rejoiced." The following was another more elaborate method of taking omens
described by Ajīt Singh : " When we speak of seeking
omens from our gods or Devi Deota, we mean the spirits
of those of our ancestors who performed great exploits in
dacoity in their day, gained a great name and established
lasting reputations. For instance, Mahājīt, my grandfather,
and Sāhiba, his father, are called gods and admitted to
be so by us all. We have all of us some such gods to be
proud of among our ancestors ; we propitiate them and ask
for favourable omens from them before we enter upon
any enterprise. We sometimes propitiate the Sūraj Deota
(sun god) and seek good omens from him. We get two
or three goats or rams, and sometimes even ten or eleven,
at the place where we determine to take the auspices,
and having assembled the principal men of the gang we
put water into the mouth of one of them and pray to the
sun and to our ancestors thus : ' O thou Sun God ! And
O all ye other Gods ! If we are to succeed in the enterprise we are about to undertake we pray you to cause
these goats to shake their bodies.' If they do not shake
them after the gods have been thus duly invoked, the enterprise must not be entered upon and the goats are not
sacrificed. We then try the auspices with wheat. We
burn frankincense and scented wood and blow a shell ; and
taking out a pinch of wheat grains, put them on the cloth
and count them. If they come up odd the omen is favourable, and if even it is bad. After this, which we call the
auspices of the Akūt, we take that of the Siārni or female
jackal. If it calls on the left it is good, but if on the right
bad. If the omens turn out favourable in all three trials
then we have no fear whatever, but if they are favourable in only one trial out of the three the enterprise must be
given up."

13. Sup-
pression of
dacoity.

Between 1837 and 1849 the suppression of the regular
practice of armed dacoity was practically achieved by Colonel
Sleeman. A number of officers were placed under his orders,
and with small bodies of military and police were set to hunt
down different bands of dacoits, following them all over
India when necessary. And special Acts were passed to

enable the offence of dacoity, wherever committed, to be tried by a competent magistrate in any part of India as had been done in the case of the Thugs. Many of the Badhaks received conditional pardons, and were drafted into the police in different stations, and an agricultural labour colony was also formed, but does not seem to have been altogether successful. During these twelve years more than 1200 dacoits in all were brought to trial, while some were killed during the operations, and no doubt many others escaped and took to other avocations, or became ordinary criminals when their armed gangs were broken up. In 1825 it had been estimated that the Oudh forests alone contained from 4000 to 6000 dacoits, while the property stolen in 1811 from known dacoities was valued at ten lakhs of rupees.

The Badhaks still exist, and are well known as one of the worst classes of criminals, practising ordinary house-breaking and theft. The name Badhak is now less commonly used than those of Bāgri and Baori or Bāwaria, both of which were borne by the original Badhaks. The word Bāgri is derived from a tract of country in Mālwa which is known as the Bāgar or 'hedge of thorns,' because it is surrounded on all sides by wooded hills.[1] There are Bāgri Jāts and Bāgri Rājpūts, many of whom are now highly respectable landholders. Bāwaria or Baori is derived from *bānwar*, a creeper, or the tendril of a vine, and hence a noose made originally from some fibrous plant and used for trapping animals, this being one of the primary occupations of the tribe.[2] The term Badhak signifies a hunter or fowler, hence a robber or murderer (Platts). The Bāgris and Bāwarias are sometimes considered to be separate communities, but it is doubtful whether there is any real distinction between them. In Bombay the Bāgris are known as Vāghris by the common change of *b* into *v*. A good description of them is contained in Appendix C to Mr. Bhimbhai Kirpārām's volume *Hindus of Gujarat* in the *Bombay Gazetteer*. He divides them into the Chunaria or lime-burners, the Dātonia or sellers of twig tooth-brushes, and two other groups, and states that, " They also keep

14. The Badhaks or Baoris at the present time.

---

[1] Malcolm's *Memoir of Central India*, ii. p. 479.

[2] Crooke's *Tribes and Castes*, art. Bāwaria.

fowls and sell eggs, catch birds and go as *shikāris* or hunters. They traffic in green parrots, which they buy from Bhīls and sell for a profit."

15. Lizard-hunting.

Their strength and powers of endurance are great, the same writer states, and they consider that these qualities are obtained by the eating of the *goh* and *sāndha* or iguana lizards, which a Vāghri prizes very highly. This is also the case with the Bāwarias of the Punjab, who go out hunting lizards in the rains and may be seen returning with baskets full of live lizards, which exist for days without food and are killed and eaten fresh by degrees. Their method of hunting the lizard is described by Mr. Wilson as follows : [1] " The lizard lives on grass, cannot bite severely, and is sluggish in his movements, so that he is easily caught. He digs a hole for himself of no great depth, and the easiest way to take him is to look out for the scarcely perceptible airhole and dig him out ; but there are various ways of saving oneself this trouble. One, which I have seen, takes advantage of a habit the lizard has in cold weather (when he never comes out of his hole) of coming to the mouth for air and warmth. The Chūhra or other sportsman puts off his shoes and steals along the prairie till he sees signs of a lizard's hole. This he approaches on tiptoe, raising over his head with both hands a mallet with a round sharp point, and fixing his eyes intently upon the hole. When close enough he brings down his mallet with all his might on the ground just behind the mouth of the hole, and is often successful in breaking the lizard's back before he awakes to a sense of his danger. Another plan, which I have not seen, is to tie a wisp of grass to a long stick and move it over the hole so as to make a rustling noise. The lizard within thinks, ' Oh here's a snake ! I may as well give in,' and comes to the mouth of the hole, putting out his tail first so that he may not see his executioner. The sportsman seizes his tail and snatches him out before he has time to learn his mistake." This common fondness for lizards is a point in favour of a connection between the Gujarāt Vāghris and the Punjab Bāwarias.

In Sirsa the great mass of the Bāwarias are not given to

[1] *Sirsa Settlement Report.*

crime, and in Gujarāt also they do not appear to have special criminal tendencies.   It is a curious point, however, that Mr. Bhimbhai Kirpārām emphasises the chastity of the women of the Gujarāt Vāghris.[1] "When a family returns home after a money-making tour to Bombay or some other city, the women are taken before Vihāt (Devi), and with the women is brought a buffalo or a sheep that is tethered in front of Vihāt's shrine.   They must confess all, even their slightest shortcomings, such as the following : 'Two weeks ago, when begging in Pārsi Bazār-street, a drunken sailor caught me by the hand.   Another day a Mīyan or Musalmān ogled me, and forgive me, Devi, my looks encouraged him.' If Devi is satisfied the sheep or buffalo shivers, and is then sacrificed and provides a feast for the caste."[2]   On the other hand, Mr. Crooke states[3] that in northern India, "The standard of morality is very low because in Muzaffarnagar it is extremely rare for a Bāwaria woman to live with her husband.   Almost invariably she lives with another man : but the official husband is responsible for the children." The great difference in the standard of morality is certainly surprising.

In Gujarāt[4] the Vāghris have *gurus* or religious preceptors of their own.   These men take an eight-anna silver piece and whisper in the ear of their disciples "Be immortal." . . . "The Bhuvas or priest-mediums play an important part in many Vāghri ceremonies.   A Bhuva is a male child born after the mother has made a vow to the goddess Vihāt or Devi that if a son be granted to her she will devote him to the service of the goddess.   No Bhuva may cut or shave his hair on pain of a fine of ten rupees, and no Bhuva may eat carrion or food cooked by a Muhammadan."

The criminal Bāgris still usually travel about in the disguise of Gosains and Bairāgis, and are very difficult of detection except to real religious mendicants.   Their housebreaking implement or jemmy is known as *Gyān*, but in speaking of it they always add *Dās*, so that it sounds like

16. Social observances.

17. Criminal practices.

---

[1] It would appear that the Gujarāt Vāghris are a distinct class from the criminal section of the tribe.

[2] *Bombay Gazetteer, Gujarāt Hindus*, p. 514.

[3] Art. Bawaria, quoting from *North Indian Notes and Queries*, i. 51.

[4] *Bombay Gazetteer, Hindus of Gujarāt*, p. 574.

the name of a Bairāgi.[1]   They are usually very much afraid
of the *gyān* being discovered on their persons, and are careful
to bury it in the ground at each halting-place, while on the
march it may be concealed in a pack-saddle.   The means of
identifying them, Mr. Kennedy remarks,[2] is by their family
deo or god, which they carry about when wandering with
their families.   It consists of a brass or copper box containing grains of wheat and the seeds of a creeper, both soaked
in *ghī* (melted butter).   The box with a peacock's feather
and a bell is wrapped in two white and then in two red
cloths, one of the white cloths having the print of a man's
hand dipped in goat's blood upon it.   The grains of wheat
are used for taking the omens, a few being thrown up at sun-
down and counted afterwards to see whether they are odd
or even.   When even, two grains are placed on the right
hand of the omen-taker, and if this occurs three times
running the auspices are considered to be favourable.[3]
Mr. Gayer [4] notes that the Badhaks have usually from one to
three brands from a hot iron on the inside of their left wrist.
Those of them who are hunters brand the muscles of the
left wrist in order to steady the hand when firing their
matchlocks.   The customs of wearing a peculiar necklace of
small wooden beads and a kind of gold pin fixed to the front
teeth, which Mr. Crooke [5] records as having been prevalent
some years ago, have apparently been since abandoned, as
they are not mentioned in more recent accounts.   The
Dehliwāl and Mālpura Baorias have, Mr. Kennedy states,[6]
an interesting system of signs, which they mark on the
walls of buildings at important corners, bridges and cross-
roads and on the ground by the roadside with a stick, if no
building is handy.   The commonest is a loop, the straight
line indicating the direction a gang or individual has
taken :

---

[1] Gunthorpe's *Criminal Tribes*.
[2] *Criminal Classes in the Bombay Presidency*, p. 151.
[3] Gunthorpe's *Criminal Tribes*, art. Badhak.
[4] *C. P. Police Lectures*, art. Badhak.
[5] Art. Bāwaria, para. 12.
[6] *Criminal Classes in the Bombay Presidency*, p. 179.

The addition of a number of vertical strokes inside the loop signifies the number of males in a gang. If these strokes are enclosed by a circle it means that the gang is encamped in the vicinity ; while a square inside a circle and line as below means that property has been secured by friends who

have left in the direction pointed by the line. It is said that Baorias will follow one another up for fifty or even a hundred miles by means of these hieroglyphics. The signs are bold marks, sometimes even a foot or more in length, and are made where they will at once catch the eye. When the Mārwāri Baorias desire to indicate to others of their caste, who may follow in their footsteps, the route taken, a member of the gang, usually a woman, trails a stick in the dust as she walks along, leaving a spiral track on the ground. Another method of indicating the route taken is to place leaves under stones at intervals along the road.[1] The form of crime most in favour among the ordinary Baoris is house-breaking by night. Their common practice is to make a hole in the wall beside the door through which the hand passes to raise the latch ; and only occasionally they dig a hole in the base of the wall to admit of the passage of a man, while another favoured alternative is to break in through a barred window, the bars being quickly and forcibly bent and drawn out.[2] One class of Mārwāri Bāgris are also expert coiners.

Bahna, Pinjāra, Dhunia.[3]—The occupational caste of cotton-cleaners. The Bahnas numbered 48,000 persons in the Central Provinces and Berār in 1911. The large increase in the number of ginning-factories has ruined the Bahna's trade of cleaning hand-ginned cotton, and as no distinction attaches to the name of Bahna it is possible that members of the caste who have taken to other occupations may have abandoned it and returned themselves

1. Nomenclature and internal structure.

[1] Kennedy, *loc. cit.* p. 208.
[2] Kennedy, *loc. cit.* p. 185.
[3] This article is partly based on a paper by Munshi Kanhya Lāl of the Gazetteer office.

simply as Muhammadans. The three names Bahna, Pinjāra, Dhunia appear to be used indifferently for the caste in this Province, though in other parts of India they are distinguished. Pinjāra is derived from the word *pinjan* used for a cotton-bow, and Dhunia is from *dhunna*, to card cotton. The caste is also known as Dhunak Pathāni. Though professing the Muhammadan religion, they still have many Hindu customs and ceremonies, and in the matter of inheritance our courts have held that they are subject to Hindu and not Muhammadan law.[1] In Raipur a girl receives half the share of a boy in the division of inherited property. The caste appears to be a mixed occupational group, and is split into many territorial subcastes named after the different parts of the country from which its members have come, as Badharia from Badhas in Mīrzāpur, Sarsūtia from the Sāraswati river, Berāri of Berār, Dakhni from the Deccan, Telangi from Madras, Pardeshi from northern India, and so on. Two groups are occupational, the Newāris of Saugor, who make the thick *newār* tape used for the webbing of beds, and the Kanderas, who make fireworks and generally constitute a separate caste. There is considerable ground for supposing that the Bahnas are mainly derived from the caste of Telis or oil-pressers. In the Punjab Sir D. Ibbetson says[2] that the Penja or cotton-scutcher is an occupational name applied to Telis who follow this profession ; and that the Penja, Kasai and Teli are all of the same caste. Similarly in Nāsik the Telis and Pinjāras are said to form one community, under the government of a single *panchāyat*. In cases of dispute or misconduct the usual penalty is temporary excommunication, which is known as the stopping of food and water.[3] The Telis are an enterprising community of very low status, and would therefore be naturally inclined to take to other occupations ; many of them are shopkeepers, cultivators and landholders, and it is quite probable that in past times they took up the Bahna's profession and changed their religion with the hope of improving their social status.

---

[1] Sir B. Robertson's *C.P. Census Report* (1891), p. 203.
[2] *Punjab Census Report* (1881),
paras. 646, 647.
[3] *Nāsik Gazetteer*, pp. 84, 85.

The Telis are generally considered to be quarrelsome and talkative, and the Bahnas or Dhunias have the same characteristics. If one man abusing another lapses into Billingsgate, the other will say to him, ' *Hamko Julāha Dhunia neh jāno*,' or ' Don't talk to me as if I was a Julāha or a Dhunia.'

Some Bahnas have exogamous sections with Hindu names, while others are without these, and simply regulate their marriages by rules of relationship. They have the primitive Hindu custom of allowing a sister's son to marry a brother's daughter, but not *vice versa*. A man cannot marry his wife's younger sister during her lifetime, nor her elder sister at any time. Children of the same foster-mother are also not allowed to marry. Their marriages are performed by a Kāzi with an imitation of the Nikāh rite. The bridegroom's party sit under the marriage-shed, and the bride with the women of her party inside the house. The Kāzi selects two men, one from the bride's party, who is known as the Nikāhi Bāp or ' Marriage Father,' and the other from the bridegroom's, who is called the Gowāh or ' Witness.' These two men go to the bride and ask her whether she accepts the bridegroom, whose name is stated, for her husband. She answers in the affirmative, and mentions the amount of the dowry which she is to receive. The bridegroom, who has hitherto had a veil (*mukhna*) over his face, now takes it off, and the men go to him and ask him whether he accepts the bride. He replies that he does, and agrees to pay the dowry demanded by her. The Kāzi reads some texts and the guests are given a meal of rice and sugar. Many of the preliminaries to a Hindu marriage are performed by the more backward members of the caste, and until recently they erected a sacred post in the marriage-shed, but now they merely hang the green branch of a mango tree to the roof. The minimum amount of the *mehar* or dowry is said to be Rs. 125, but it is paid to the girl's parents as a bride-price and not to herself, as among the Muhammadans. A widow is expected, but not obliged, to marry her deceased husband's younger brother. Divorce is permitted by means of a written deed known as ' Fārkhati.'

2. Marriage.

The Bahnas venerate Muhammad, and also worship the tombs of Muhammadan saints or *Pīrs*. A green sheet or cloth is spread over the tomb and a lamp is kept burning by it, while offerings of incense and flowers are made. When the new cotton crop has been gathered they lay some new cotton by their bow and mallet and make an offering of *malīda* or cakes of flour and sugar to it. They believe that two angels, one good and one bad, are perched continually on the shoulders of every man to record his good and evil deeds. And when an eclipse occurs they say that the sun and moon have gone behind a pinnacle or tower of the heavens. For exorcising evil spirits they write texts of the Korān on paper and burn them before the sufferer. The caste bury the dead with the feet pointing to the south. On the way to the grave each one of the mourners places his shoulder under the bier for a time, partaking of the impurity communicated by it. Incense is burnt daily in the name of a deceased person for forty days after his death, with the object probably of preventing his ghost from returning to haunt the house. Muhammadan beggars are fed on the tenth day. Similarly, after the birth of a child a woman is unclean for forty days, and cannot cook for her husband during that period. A child's hair is cut for the first time on the tenth or twelfth day after birth, this being known as Jhālar. Some parents leave a lock of hair to grow on the head in the name of the famous saint Sheikh Farīd, thinking that they will thus ensure a long life for the child. It is probably in reality a way of preserving the Hindu *choti* or scalp-lock.

The hereditary calling[1] of the Bahna is the cleaning or scutching of cotton, which is done by subjecting it to the vibration of a bow-string. The seed has been previously separated by a hand-gin, but the ginned cotton still contains much dirt, leaf-fibre and other rubbish, and to remove this is the Bahna's task. The bow is somewhat in the shape of a harp, the wide end consisting of a broad piece of wood over which the string passes, being secured to a straight wooden bar at the back. At the narrow end the bar and string are fixed to an iron ring. The string is made of the

[1] Crooke's *Tribes and Castes*, art. Bahna.

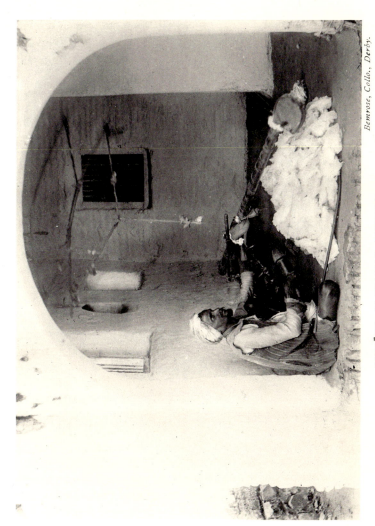

PINJĀRA CLEANING COTTON.

Bemrose, Collo., Derby.

sinew of some animal, and this renders the implement objectionable to Hindus, and may account for the Bahnas being Muhammadans. The club or mallet is a wooden implement shaped like a dumb-bell. The bow is suspended from the roof so as to hang just over the pile of loose cotton ; and the worker twangs the string with the mallet and then draws the mallet across the string, each three or four times. The string strikes a small portion of the cotton, the fibre of which is scattered by the impact and thrown off in a uniform condition of soft fluff, all dirt being at the same time removed. This is the operation technically known as teasing. Buchanan remarked that women frequently did the work themselves at home, using a smaller kind of bow called *dhunkara*. The clean cotton is made up into balls, some of which are passed on to the spinner, while others are used for the filling of quilts and the padded coats worn in the cold weather. The ingenious though rather clumsy method of the Bahna has been superseded by the ginning-factory, and little or no cotton destined for the spindle is now cleaned by him. The caste have been forced to take to cultivation or field labour, while many have become cartmen and others are brokers, peons or constables. Nearly every house still has its *pinjan* or bow, but only a desultory use is made of this during the winter months. As it is principally used by a Muhammadan caste it seems a possible hypothesis that the cotton-bow was introduced into India by invaders of that religion. The name of the bow, *pinjan*, is, however, a Sanskrit derivative, and this is against the above theory. It has already been seen that the fact of animal sinew being used for the string would make it objectionable to Hindus. The Bahnas are subjected to considerable ridicule on account of their curious mixture of Hindu and Muhammadan ceremonies, amounting in some respects practically to a caricature of the rites of Islām ; and further, they share with the weaver class the contempt shown to those who follow a calling considered more suitable for women than men. It is related that when the Mughal general Asaf Khān first made an expedition into the north of the Central Provinces he found the famous Gond-Rājpūt queen Durgāvati of the Garha-Mandla dynasty governing with success a large and prosperous state in this locality. He thought a country ruled by a woman should fall an easy prey to the Muhammadan arms, and to show his contempt for her power he sent her a golden spindle. The queen retorted by a present of a gold cotton-cleaner's bow, and this so enraged the Mughal that he proceeded to attack the Gond kingdom. The story indicates that cotton-carding is considered a Muhammadan profession, and also that it is held in contempt.

5. Proverbs about Bahnas. Various sayings show that the Bahna is not considered a proper Muhammadan, as

> *Turuk to Turuk*
> *Aur Bahna Turuk,*

or ' A Muhammadan (Turk) is a Muhammadan and the Bahna is also a Muhammadan ' ; and again—

> *Achera,[1] Kachera, Pinjāra,*
> *Muhammad se dūr, Dīn se niyāra,*

or ' The Kachera and Pinjāra are lost to Muhammad and far from the faith ' ; and again—

> *Adho Hindu adho Musalmān*
> *Tinkhon kahen Dhunak Pathān,*

or ' Half a Hindu and half a Muhammadan, that is he who is a Dhunak Pathān.' They have a grotesque imitation of the Muhammadan rite of *halāl*, or causing an animal's blood to flow on to the ground with the repetition of the *kalma* or invocation ; thus it is said that when a Bahna is about to kill a fowl he addresses it somewhat as follows :

> *Kāhe karkarāt hai ?*
> *Kāhe barbarāt hai ?*
> *Kāhe jai jai logon ka dāna khāt hāi ?*
> *Tor kiāmat mor niāmat,*
> *Bismillāh hai tuch,*

or " Why do you cackle ? Why do you crow ? Why do you eat other people's grain ? Your death is my feast ; I touch you in the name of God." And saying this he puts a knife to the fowl's throat. The vernacular verse is a good

---

[1] The word Achera is merely a jingle put in to make the rhyme complete. Kachera is a maker of glass bangles.

imitation of the cackling of a fowl. And again, they slice
off the top of an egg as if they were killing an animal and
repeat the formula, "White dome, full of moisture, I know
not if there is a male or female within ; in the name of God
I kill you." A person whose memory is not good enough
to retain these texts will take a knife and proceed to one
who knows them. Such a man will repeat the texts over
the knife, blowing on it as he does so, and the Bahna considers that the knife has been sanctified and retains its virtue
for a week. Others do not think this necessary, but have a
special knife, which having once been consecrated is always
kept for killing animals, and descends as an heirloom in the
family, the use of this sacred knife being considered to make
the repetition of the *kalma* unnecessary. These customs are,
however, practised only by the ignorant members of the
caste in Raipur and Bilāspur, and are unknown in the more
civilised tracts, where the Bahnas are rapidly conforming
to ordinary Muhammadan usage. Such primitive Bahnas
perform their marriages by walking round the sacred post,
keep the Hindu festivals, and feed Brāhmans on the tenth
day after a death. They have a priest whom they call their
Kāzi, but elect him themselves. In some places when a
Bahna goes to the well to draw water he first washes the
parapet of the well to make it ceremonially clean, and then
draws his water. This custom can only be compared with
that of the Rāj-Gonds who wash the firewood with which
they are about to cook their food, in order to make it more
pure. Respectable Muhammadans naturally look down on
the Bahnas, and they retaliate by refusing to take food or
water from any Muhammadan who is not a Bahna. By
such strictness the more ignorant think that they will enhance
their ceremonial purity and hence their social consideration ;
but the intelligent members of the caste know better and
are glad to improve themselves by learning from educated
Muhammadans. The other menial artisan castes among the
Muhammadans have similar ideas, and it is reported that a
Rangrez boy who took food in the house of one of the highest
Muhammadan officers of Government in the Province was
temporarily put out of caste. Another saying about the
Bahnas is—

Sheikhon kī Sheikhi,
Pathānon kī tarr,
Turkon kī Turkshāhi,
Bahnon kī bharrr . . .

or 'Proud as a Sheikh, obstinate as a Pathān, royal as a Turk, buzzing like a Bahna.' This refers to the noise of the cotton-cleaning bow, the twang of which as it is struck by the club is like a quail flying; and at the same time to the Bahna's loquacity. Another story is that a Bahna was once going through the forest with his cotton-cleaning bow and club or mallet, when a jackal met him on the path. The jackal was afraid that the Bahna would knock him on the head, so he said, "With thy bow on thy shoulder and thine arrow in thy hand, whither goest thou, O King of Delhi?" The Bahna was exceedingly pleased at this and replied, 'King of the forest, eater of wild plums, only the great can recognise the great.' But when the jackal had got to a safe distance he turned round and shouted, "With your cotton-bow on your shoulder and your club in your hand, there you go, you sorry Bahna." It is said also that although the Bahnas as good Muhammadans wear beards, they do not cultivate them very successfully, and many of them only have a growth of hair below the chin and none on the under-lip, in the fashion known as a goat's beard. This kind of beard is thus proverbially described as '*Bahna kaisi dārhi*' or 'A Bahna's beard.' It may be repeated in conclusion that much of the ridicule attaching to the Bahnas arises simply from the fact that they follow what is considered a feminine occupation, and the remainder because in their ignorance they parody the rites of Islām. It may seem ill-natured to record the sayings in which they are lampooned, but the Bahnas cannot read English, and these have an interest as specimens of popular wit.

BAIGA

Baiga.[1]—A primitive Dravidian tribe whose home is on the eastern Satpūra hills in the Mandla, Bālāghāt and Bilāspur Districts. The number of the Baigas proper was only 30,000 in 1911. But the Binjhāls or Binjhwārs, a fairly numerous caste in the Chhattīsgarh Division, and especially in the Sambalpur District, appear to have been originally Baigas, though they have dropped the original caste name, become Hinduised, and now disclaim connection with the parent tribe. A reason for this may be found in the fact that Sambalpur contains several Binjhwār zamīndārs, or large landowners, whose families would naturally desire a more respectable pedigree than one giving them the wild Baigas of the Satpūras for their forefathers. And the evolution of the Binjhwār caste is a similar phenomenon to the constitution of the Rāj-Gonds, the Rāj-Korkus, and other aristocratic subdivisions among the forest tribes, who have been admitted to a respectable position in the Hindu social community. The Binjhwārs, however, have been so successful as to cut themselves off almost completely from connection with the original tribe, owing to their adoption of another name. But in Bālāghāt and Mandla the Binjhwār

1. The tribe and its off-shoots.

---

[1] This article is based largely on a monograph by the Rev. J. Lampard, missionary, Baihar, and also on papers by Muhammad Hanīf Siddīqi, forest ranger, Bilāspur, and Mr. Muhammad Ali Haqqāni, B.A., Tahsīldār, Dindori. Some extracts have been made from Colonel Ward's *Mandla Settlement Report* (1869), and from Colonel Bloomfield's *Notes on the Baigas.*

77

subtribe is still recognised as the most civilised subdivision of the Baigas. The Bhainas, a small tribe in Bilāspur, are probably another offshoot, Kath-Bhaina being the name of a subtribe of Baigas in that District, and Rai-Bhaina in Bālāghāt, though the Bhainas too no longer admit identity with the Baigas. A feature common to all three branches is that they have forgotten their original tongue, and now speak a more or less corrupt form of the Indo-Aryan vernaculars current around them. Finally, the term Bhumia or 'Lord of the soil' is used sometimes as the name of a separate tribe and sometimes as a synonym for Baiga. The fact is that in the Central Provinces [1] Bhumia is the name of an office, that of the priest of the village and local deities, which is held by one of the forest tribes. In the tract where the Baigas live, they, as the most ancient residents, are usually the priests of the indigenous gods ; but in Jubbulpore the same office is held by another tribe, the Bharias. The name of the office often attaches itself to members of the tribe, who consider it as somewhat more respectable than their own, and it is therefore generally true to say that the people known as Bhumias in Jubbulpore are really Bharias, but in Mandla and Bilāspur they are Baigas.

In Mandla there is also found a group called Bharia-Baigas. These are employed as village priests by Hindus, and worship certain Hindu deities and not the Gond gods. They may perhaps be members of the Bharia tribe of Jubbulpore, originally derived from the Bhars, who have obtained the designation of Baiga, owing to their employ-ment as village priests. But they now consider themselves a part of the Baiga tribe and say they came to Mandla from Rewah. In Mandla the decision of a Baiga on a boundary dispute is almost always considered as final, and this authority is of a kind that commonly emanates from recognised priority of residence.[2] There seems reason to suppose that the Baigas are really a branch of the primitive Bhuiya tribe of Chota Nāgpur, and that they have taken or been given the name of Baiga, the designation of a village priest, on migration into the Central Provinces. There is reason to

---

[1] In Bengal the Bhumia or Bhumīj are an important tribe.

[2] Colonel Ward's *Mandla Settlement Report* (1868–69), p. 153.

believe that the Baigas were once dominant in the Chhattīsgarh plain and the hills surrounding it which adjoin Chota Nāgpur, the home of the Bhuiyas. The considerations in favour of this view are given in the article on Bhuiya, to which reference may be made.

The Baigas, however, are not without some conceit of themselves, as the following legend will show. In the beginning, they say, God created Nanga Baiga and Nangi Baigin, the first of the human race, and asked them by what calling they would choose to live. They at once said that they would make their living by felling trees in the jungle, and permission being accorded, have done so ever since. They had two sons, one of whom remained a Baiga, while the other became a Gond and a tiller of the soil. The sons married their own two sisters who were afterwards born, and while the elder couple are the ancestors of the Baigas, from the younger are descended the Gonds and all the remainder of the human race. In another version of the story the first Baiga cut down two thousand old *sāl*[1] trees in one day, and God told him to sprinkle a few grains of kutki on the ashes, and then to retire and sleep for some months, when on his return he would be able to reap a rich harvest for his children. In this manner the habit of shifting cultivation is accorded divine sanction. According to Binjhwār tradition Nanga Baiga and Nangi Baigin dwelt on the *kajli ban pahār*, which being interpreted is the hill of elephants, and may well refer to the ranges of Mandla and Bilāspur. It is stated in the *Ain-i-Akbari*[2] that the country of Garha-Mandla abounded in wild elephants, and that the people paid their tribute in these and gold mohurs. In Mandla the Baigas sometimes hang out from their houses a bamboo mat fastened to a long pole to represent a flag which they say once flew from the palace of a Baiga king. It seems likely that the original home of the tribe may have been the Chhattīsgarh plain and the hill-ranges surrounding it. A number of estates in these hills are held by landowners of tribes which are offshoots of the Baigas, as the Bhainas and Binjhwārs. The point is

---

[1] *Shorea robusta.*
[2] Jarrett's *Ain-i-Akbari*, vol. ii. p. 196.

further discussed in the article on Bhuiya. Most of the
Baigas speak a corrupt form of the Chhattīsgarhi dialect.
When they first came under the detailed observation of
English officers in the middle of the nineteenth century, the
tribe were even more solitary and retired than at present.
Their villages, it is said, were only to be found in places
far removed from all cleared and cultivated country. No
roads or well-defined paths connected them with ordinary
lines of traffic and more thickly inhabited tracts, but perched
away in snug corners in the hills, and hidden by convenient
projecting spurs and dense forests from the country round,
they could not be seen except when nearly approached,
and were seldom visited unless by occasional enterprising
Banias and vendors of country liquor. Indeed, without a
Baiga for a guide many of the villages could hardly be discovered, for nothing but occasional notches on the trees
distinguished the tracks to them from those of the sāmbhar
and other wild animals.

3. Tribal sub-divisions.   The following seven subdivisions or subtribes are recognised : Binjhwār, Bharotia, Narotia or Nāhar, Raibhaina,
Kathbhaina, Kondwān or Kundi, and Gondwaina. Of these
the Binjhwār, Bharotia and Narotia are the best-known.
The name of the Binjhwārs is probably derived from the
Vindhyan range, which in turn comes from the Sanskrit
vindhya, a hunter. The rule of exogamy is by no means
strictly observed, and in Kawardha it is said that these
three subcastes intermarry though they do not eat together,
while in Bālāghāt the Bharotias and Narotias both eat together
and intermarry. In both places the Binjhwārs occupy
the highest position, and the other two subtribes will take
food from them. The Binjhwārs consider themselves as
Hindus and abjure the consumption of buffalo's and cow's
flesh and rats, while the other Baigas will eat almost anything. The Bharotias partially shave their heads, and in
Mandla are apparently known as Mundia or Mudia, or
"shaven." The Gondwainas eat both cow's flesh and
monkeys, and are regarded as the lowest subcaste. As
shown by their name they are probably the offspring of
unions between Baigas and Gonds. Similarly the Kondwāns
apparently derive their name from the tract south of the

Mahānadi which is named after the Khond tribe, and was formerly owned by them.

Each subtribe is divided into a number of exogamous septs, the names of which are identical in many cases with those of the Gonds, as Markām, Marāvi, Netām, Tekām and others. Gond names are found most frequently among the Gondwainas and Narotias, and these have adopted from the Gonds the prohibition of marriage between worshippers of the same number of gods. Thus the four septs above mentioned worship seven gods and may not intermarry. But they may marry among other septs such as the Dhurua, Pusām, Bania and Mawār who worship six gods. The Baigas do not appear to have assimilated the further division into worshippers of five, four, three and two gods which exists among the Gonds in some localities, and the system is confined to the lower subtribes. The meanings of the sept names have been forgotten and no instances of totemism are known. And the Binjhwārs and Bharotias, who are more or less Hinduised, have now adopted territorial names for their septs, as Lapheya from Lāpha zamīndāri, Ghugharia from Ghughri village in Mandla, and so on. The adoption of Gond names and septs appears to indicate that Gonds were in former times freely admitted into the Baiga tribe ; and this continues to be the case at present among the lower subtribes, so far that a Gond girl marrying a Baiga becomes a regular member of the community. But the Binjhwārs and Bharotias, who have a somewhat higher status than the others, refuse to admit Gonds, and are gradually adopting the strict rule of endogamy within the subtribe.

A Baiga must not take a wife from his own sept or from another one worshipping the same number of gods. But he may marry within his mother's sept, and in some localities the union of first cousins is permitted. Marriage is adult and the proposal comes from the parents of the bride, but in some places the girl is allowed to select a husband for herself. A price varying from five to twenty rupees is usually paid to the bride's parents, or in lieu of this the prospective husband serves his father-in-law for a period of about two years, the marriage being celebrated after the first year if his conduct is satisfactory. Orphan boys who have no parents to arrange

4. Marriage.

their marriages for them often take service for a wife.   Three
ceremonies should precede the marriage.   The first, which
may take place at any time after the birth of both children,
consists merely in the arrangement for their betrothal.   The
second is only a ratification of the first, feasts being provided
by the boy's parents on both occasions.   While on the approach of the children to marriageable age the final betrothal
or *barokhi* is held.   The boy's father gives a large feast at
the house of the girl and the date of the wedding is fixed.
To ascertain whether the union will be auspicious, two
grains of rice are dropped into a pot of water, after various
preliminary solemnities to mark the importance of the occasion.   If the points of the grains meet almost immediately it
is considered that the marriage will be highly auspicious.   If
they do not meet, a second pair of grains are dropped in,
and should these meet it is believed that the couple will
quarrel after an interval of married life and that the wife
will return to her father's house.   While if neither of the two
first essays are successful and a third pair is required, the
regrettable conclusion is arrived at that the wife will run
away with another man after a very short stay with her husband.   But it is not stated that the betrothal is on that
account annulled.   The wedding procession starts from the
bridegroom's house [1] and is received by the bride's father outside the village.   It is considered essential that he should go
out to meet the bride's party riding on an elephant.   But
as a real elephant is not within the means of a Baiga, two
wooden bedsteads are lashed together and covered with
blankets with a black cloth trunk in front, and this arrangement passes muster for an elephant.   The elephant makes
pretence to charge and trample down the marriage procession,
until a rupee is paid, when the two parties embrace each
other and proceed to the marriage-shed.   Here the bride and
bridegroom throw fried rice at each other until they are tired,
and then walk three or seven times round the marriage-post
with their clothes tied together.   It is stated by Colonel
Ward that the couple always retired to the forest to spend

---

[1] Colonel Ward gives the bride's
house as among the Gonds.   But inquiry in Mandla shows that if this
custom formerly existed it has been
abandoned.

the wedding night, but this custom has now been abandoned. The expenditure on a marriage varies between ten and fifty rupees, of which only about five rupees fall on the bride's parents. The remarriage of widows is permitted, and the widow is expected, though not obliged, to wed her late husband's younger brother, while if she takes another husband he must pay her brother-in-law the sum of five rupees. The ceremony consists merely of the presentation of bangles and new clothes by the suitor, in token of her acceptance of which the widow pours some tepid water stained with turmeric over his head. Divorce may be effected by the husband and wife breaking a straw in the presence of the caste *panchāyat* or committee. If the woman remains in the same village and does not marry again, the husband is responsible for her maintenance and that of her children, while a divorced woman may not remarry without the sanction of the *panchāyat* so long as her husband is alive and remains single. Polygamy is permitted.

A woman is unclean for a month after childbirth, though the Binjhwārs restrict the period to eight days. At the ceremony of purification a feast is given and the child is named, often after the month or day of its birth, as Chaitu, Phāgu, Saoni, and so on, from the months of Chait, Phāgun and Shrāwan. Children who appear to be physically defective are given names accordingly, such as Langra (lame), or Bahira (deaf). The dead are usually buried, the bodies of old persons being burnt as a special honour and to save them from the risk of being devoured by wild animals. Bodies are laid naked in the grave with the head pointing to the south. In the grave of a man of importance two or three rupees and some tobacco are placed. In some places a rupee is thrust into the mouth of the dying man, and if his body is burnt, the coin is recovered from the pyre by his daughter or sister, who wears it as an amulet. Over the grave a platform is made on which a stone is erected. This is called the Bhīri of the deceased and is worshipped by his relatives in time of trouble. If one of the family has to be buried elsewhere, the relatives go to the Bhīri of the great dead and consign his spirit to be kept in their company. At a funeral the mourners take one black

5. Birth and funeral rites.

and one white fowl to a stream and kill and eat them there,
setting aside a portion for the dead man.   Mourning is
observed for a period of from two to nine days, and during
this time labour and even household work are stopped, food
being supplied by the friends of the family.   When a man
is killed by a tiger the Baiga priest goes to the spot and
there makes a small cone out of the blood-stained earth.
This must represent a man, either the dead man or one of
his living relatives.   His companions having retired a few
paces, the priest goes on his hands and knees and performs
a series of antics which are supposed to represent the tiger
in the act of destroying the man, at the same time seizing
the lump of blood-stained earth in his teeth.   One of the
party then runs up and taps him on the back with a small
stick.   This perhaps means that the tiger is killed or otherwise rendered harmless ; and the Baiga immediately lets the
mud cone fall into the hands of one of the party.   It is then
placed in an ant-hill and a pig is sacrificed over it.   The
next day a small chicken is taken to the place, and after a
mark supposed to be the dead man's name is made on its
head with red ochre, it is thrown back into the forest, the
priest exclaiming, ' Take this and go home.'   The ceremony
is supposed to lay the dead man's spirit and at the same
time to prevent the tiger from doing any further damage.
The Baigas believe that the ghost of the victim, if not
charmed to rest, resides on the head of the tiger and incites
him to further deeds of blood, rendering him also secure from
harm by his preternatural watchfulness.[1]

They also think that they can shut up the tiger's *dār* or
jaws, so that he cannot bite them, by driving a nail into a
tree.   The forest track from Kānha to Kisli in the Banjar
forest reserve of Mandla was formerly a haunt of man-
eating tigers, to whom a number of the wood-cutters and
Baiga coolies, clearing the jungle paths, fell victims every
year.   In a large tree, at a dangerous point in the track,
there could recently be seen a nail, driven into the trunk by
a Baiga priest, at some height from the ground.   It was
said that this nail shut the mouth of a famous man-eating
tiger of the locality and prevented him from killing any

[1] Forsyth's *Highlands of Central India*, p. 377.

more victims.   As evidence of the truth of the story there
were shown on the trunk the marks of the tiger's claws,
where he had been jumping up the tree in the effort to pull
the nail out of the trunk and get his man-eating powers
restored.

Although the Binjhwār subcaste now profess Hinduism,   6. Religion.
the religion of the Baigas is purely animistic.   Their principal deity is Bura Deo,[1] who is supposed to reside in a *sāj*
tree (*Terminalia tomentosa*) ; he is worshipped in the month
of Jeth (May), when goats, fowls, cocoanuts, and the liquor
of the new mahua crop are offered to him.   Thākur Deo
is the god of the village land and boundaries, and is propitiated with a white goat.   The Baigas who plough the fields
have a ceremony called Bidri, which is performed before the
breaking of the rains.   A handful of each kind of grain sown
is given by each cultivator to the priest, who mixes the
grains together and sows a little beneath the tree where
Thākur Deo lives.   After this he returns a little to each
cultivator, and he sows it in the centre of the land on which
crops are to be grown, while the priest keeps the remainder.
This ceremony is believed to secure the success of the harvest.   Dulha Deo is the god who averts disease and accident,
and the offering made to him should consist of a fowl or goat
of reddish colour.   Bhīmsen is the deity of rainfall, and
Dharti Māta or Mother Earth is considered to be the wife
of Thākur Deo, and must also be propitiated for the success
of the crops.   The grain itself is worshipped at the threshing floor by sprinkling water and liquor on to it.   Certain
Hindu deities are also worshipped by the Baigas, but not in
orthodox fashion.   Thus it would be sacrilege on the part
of a Hindu to offer animal sacrifices to Nārāyan Deo, the
sun-god, but the Baigas devote to him a special oblation of
the most unclean animal, the pig.   The animal to be sacrificed is allowed to wander loose for two or three years, and
is then killed in a most cruel manner.   It is laid across the
threshold of a doorway on its back, and across its stomach
is placed a stout plank of *sāj*-wood.   Half a dozen men sit
or stand on the ends of this, and the fore and hind feet of
the pig are pulled backwards and forwards alternately over

[1] The Great God.   The Gonds also worship Bura Deo, resident in a *sāj* tree.

the plank until it is crushed to death, while all the men sing
or shout a sacrificial hymn.   The head and feet are cut
off and offered to the deity, and the body is eaten.   The
forests are believed to be haunted by spirits, and in certain
localities *pāts* or shrines are erected in their honour, and
occasional offerings are made to them.   The spirits of married
persons are supposed to live in streams, while trees afford a
shelter to the souls of the unmarried, who become *bhūts* or
malignant spirits after death.   Nāg Deo or the cobra is
supposed to live in an ant-hill, and offerings are made to him
there.   Demoniacal possession is an article of faith, and a
popular remedy is to burn human hair mixed with chillies
and pig's dung near the person possessed, as the horrible
smell thus produced will drive away the spirit.   Many and
weird, Mr. Low writes, are the simples which the Baiga's
travelling scrip contains.   Among these a dried bat has the
chief place ; this the Baiga says he uses to charm his nets
with, that the prey may catch in them as the bat's claws
catch in whatever it touches.   As an instance of the Baiga's
pantheism it may be mentioned that on one occasion when a
train of the new Satpūra railway [1] had pulled up at a wayside forest station, a Baiga was found offering a sacrifice
to the engine.   Like other superstitious people they are
great believers in omens.   A single crow bathing in a stream
is a sign of death.   A cock which crows in the night should
be instantly killed and thrown into the darkness, a custom
which some would be glad to see introduced into much more
civilised centres.   The woodpecker and owl are birds of bad
omen.   The Baigas do not appear to have any idea of a fresh
birth, and one of their marriage songs says, " O girl, take
your pleasure in going round the marriage-post once and for
all, for there is no second birth."   The Baigas are generally
the priests of the Gonds, probably because being earlier residents of the country they are considered to have a more
intimate acquaintance with the local deities.   They have
a wide knowledge of the medicinal properties of jungle
roots and herbs, and are often successful in effecting cures
when the regular native doctors have failed.   Their village
priests have consequently a considerable reputation as skilled

[1] Opened in 1905.

sorcerers and persons conversant with the unseen world.   A case is known of a Brāhman transferred to a jungle station, who immediately after his arrival called in a Baiga priest and asked what forest gods he should worship, and what other steps he should take to keep well and escape calamity. Colonel Ward states that in his time Baigas were commonly called in to give aid when a town or village was attacked by cholera, and further that he had seen the greatest benefit to result from their visit.   For the people had so much confidence in their powers and ceremonies that they lost half their fright at once, and were consequently not so much predisposed to an attack of the disease.   On such an occasion the Baiga priest goes round the village and pulls out a little straw from each house-roof, afterwards burning the whole before the shrine of Khermāta, the goddess of the village, to whom he also offers a chicken for each homestead.   If this remedy fails goats are substituted for chickens, and lastly, as a forlorn hope, pigs are tried, and, as a rule, do not fail, because by this time the disease may be expected to have worked itself out.   It is suggested that the chicken represents a human victim from each house, while the straw stands for the house itself, and the offering has the common idea of a substituted victim.

In stature the Baigas are a little taller than most other tribes, and though they have a tendency to the flat nose of the Gonds, their foreheads and the general shape of their heads are of a better mould.   Colonel Ward states that the members of the tribe inhabiting the Maikal range in Mandla are a much finer race than those living nearer the open country.[1]   Their figures are very nearly perfect, says Colonel Bloomfield,[2] and their wiry limbs, unburdened by superfluous flesh, will carry them over very great distances and over places inaccessible to most human beings, while their compact bodies need no other nutriment than the scanty fare afforded by their native forests.   They are born hunters, hardy and active in the chase, and exceedingly bold and courageous.   In character they are naturally simple, honest and truthful, and when their fear of a stranger has been

7. Appearance and mode of life.

---

[1] *Mandla Settlement Report* (1868–69), p. 153.
[2] *Notes on the Baigas*, p. 4.

dissipated are most companionable folk. A small hut, 6 or 7 feet high at the ridge, made of split bamboos and mud, with a neat veranda in front thatched with leaves and grass, forms the Baiga's residence, and if it is burnt down, or abandoned on a visitation of epidemic disease, he can build another in the space of a day. A rough earthen vessel to hold water, leaves for plates, gourds for drinking-vessels, a piece of matting to sleep on, and a small axe, a sickle and a spear, exhaust the inventory of the Baiga's furniture, and the money value of the whole would not exceed a rupee.[1] The Baigas never live in a village with other castes, but have their huts some distance away from the village in the jungle. Unlike the other tribes also, the Baiga prefers his house to stand alone and at some little distance from those of his fellow-tribesmen. While nominally belonging to the village near which they dwell, so separate and distinct are they from the rest of people that in the famine of 1897 cases were found of starving Baiga hamlets only a few hundred yards away from the village proper in which ample relief was being given. On being questioned as to why they had not caused the Baigas to be helped, the other villagers said, 'We did not remember them'; and when the Baigas were asked why they did not apply for relief, they said, 'We did not think it was meant for Baigas.'

8. Dress and food. Their dress is of the most simple description, a small strip of rag between the legs and another wisp for a head-covering sufficing for the men, though the women are decently covered from their shoulders to half-way between the thighs and knees. A Baiga may be known by his scanty clothing and tangled hair, and his wife by the way in which her single garment is arranged so as to provide a safe sitting-place in it for her child. Baiga women have been seen at work in the field transplanting rice with babies comfortably seated in their cloth, one sometimes supported on either hip with their arms and legs out, while the mother was stooping low, hour after hour, handling the rice plants. A girl is tattooed on the forehead at the age of five, and over her whole body before she is married, both for the sake of ornament and because the practice is considered beneficial to the health.

[1] Mr. Lampard's monograph.

BAIGA VILLAGE, BĀLĀGHĀT DISTRICT.

The Baigas are usually without blankets or warm clothing, and in the cold season they sleep round a wood fire kept burning or smouldering all night, stray sparks from which may alight on their tough skins without being felt. Mr. Lampard relates that on one occasion a number of Baiga men were supplied by the Mission under his charge with large new cloths to cover their bodies with and make them presentable on appearance in church. On the second Sunday, however, they came with their cloths burnt full of small holes ; and they explained that the damage had been done at night while they were sleeping round the fire.

A Baiga, Mr. Lampard continues, is speedily discerned in a forest village bazār, and is the most interesting object in it. His almost nude figure, wild, tangled hair innocent of such inventions as brush or comb, lithe wiry limbs and jungly and uncivilised appearance, mark him out at once. He generally brings a few mats or baskets which he has made, or fruits, roots, honey, horns of animals, or other jungle products which he has collected, for sale, and with the sum obtained (a few pice or annas at the most) he proceeds to make his weekly purchases, changing his pice into cowrie shells, of which he receives eighty for each one. He buys tobacco, salt, chillies and other sundries, besides as much of kodon, kutki, or perhaps rice, as he can afford, always leaving a trifle to be expended at the liquor shop before departing for home. The various purchases are tied up in the corners of the bit of rag twisted round his head. Unlike pieces of cloth known to civilisation, which usually have four corners, the Baiga's headgear appears to be nothing but corners, and when the shopping is done the strip of rag may have a dozen minute bundles tied up in it.

In Baihar of Bālāghāt buying and selling are conducted on perhaps the most minute scale known, and if a Baiga has one or two pice [1] to lay out he will spend no inconsiderable time over it. Grain is sold in small measures holding about four ounces called *baraiyas*, but each of these has a layer of mud at the bottom of varying degrees of thickness, so as to reduce its capacity. Before a purchase can be made it must be settled by whose *baraiya* the grain is to be measured, and

[1] Farthings.

the seller and purchaser each refuse the other's as being unfair to himself, until at length after discussion some neutral person's *baraiya* is selected as a compromise. Their food consists largely of forest fruits and roots with a scanty allowance of rice or the light millets, and they can go without nourishment for periods which appear extraordinary to civilised man. They eat the flesh of almost all animals, though the more civilised abjure beef and monkeys. They will take food from a Gond but not from a Brāhman. The Baiga dearly loves the common country liquor made from the mahua flower, and this is consumed as largely as funds will permit of at weddings, funerals and other social gatherings, and also if obtainable at other times. They have a tribal *panchāyat* or committee which imposes penalties for social offences, one punishment being the abstention from meat for a fixed period. A girl going wrong with a man of the caste is punished by a fine, but cases of unchastity among unmarried Baiga girls are rare. Among their pastimes dancing is one of the chief, and in their favourite dance, known as *karma*, the men and women form long lines opposite to each other with the musicians between them. One of the instruments, a drum called *māndar*, gives out a deep bass note which can be heard for miles. The two lines advance and retire, everybody singing at the same time, and when the dancers get fully into the time and swing, the pace increases, the drums beat furiously, the voices of the singers rise higher and higher, and by the light of the bonfires which are kept burning the whole scene is wild in the extreme.

9. Occupation.   The Baigas formerly practised only shifting cultivation, burning down patches of jungle and sowing seed on the ground fertilised by the ashes after the breaking of the rains. Now that this method has been prohibited in Government forest, attempts have been made to train them to regular cultivation, but with indifferent success in Bālāghāt. An idea of the difficulties to be encountered may be obtained from the fact that in some villages the Baiga cultivators, if left unwatched, would dig up the grain which they had themselves sown as seed in their fields and eat it; while the plough-cattle which were given to them invariably developed diseases in spite of all precautions, as a result of

which they found their way sooner or later to the Baiga's cooking-pot. But they are gradually adopting settled habits, and in Mandla, where a considerable block of forest was allotted to them in which they might continue their destructive practice of shifting sowings, it is reported that the majority have now become regular cultivators. One explanation of their refusal to till the ground is that they consider it a sin to lacerate the breast of their mother earth with a ploughshare. They also say that God made the jungle to produce everything necessary for the sustenance of men and made the Baigas kings of the forest, giving them wisdom to discover the things provided for them. To Gonds and others who had not this knowledge, the inferior occupation of tilling the land was left. The men never become farmservants, but during the cultivating season they work for hire at uprooting the rice seedlings for transplantation ; they do no other agricultural labour for others. Women do the actual transplantation of rice and work as harvesters. The men make bamboo mats and baskets, which they sell in the village weekly markets. They also collect and sell honey and other forest products, and are most expert at all work that can be done with an axe, making excellent woodcutters. But they show no aptitude in acquiring the use of any other implement, and dislike steady continuous labour, preferring to do a few days' work and then rest in their homes for a like period before beginning again. Their skill and dexterity in the use of the axe in hunting is extraordinary. Small deer, hares and peacocks are often knocked over by throwing it at them, and panthers and other large animals are occasionally killed with a single blow. If one of two Baigas is carried off by a tiger, the survivor will almost always make a determined and often successful attempt to rescue him with nothing more formidable than an axe or a stick. They are expert trackers, and are also clever at setting traps and snares, while, like Korkus, they catch fish by damming streams in the hot weather and throwing into the pool thus formed some leaf or root which stupefies them. Even in a famine year, Mr. Low says, a Baiga can collect a large basketful of roots in a single day ; and if the bamboo seeds he is amply provided for. Nowadays Baiga cultivators may occasionally be met with who have taken to regular cultivation and become quite prosperous, owning a number of cattle.

10. Language. As already stated, the Baigas have completely forgotten their own language, and in the Satpūra hills they speak a broken form of Hindi, though they have a certain number of words and expressions peculiar to the caste.

BAIRĀGI

LIST OF PARAGRAPHS

Bairāgi,[1] **Sādhu.**—The general term for members of the Vishnuite religious orders, who formerly as a rule lived by mendicancy. The Bairāgis have now, however, become a caste. In 1911 they numbered 38,000 persons in the Provinces, being distributed over all Districts and States. The name Bairāgi is supposed to come from the Sanskrit Vairāgya and to signify one who is free from human passions. Bairāga is also the term for the crutched stick which such mendicants frequently carry about with them and lean upon, either sitting or standing, and which in case of need would serve them as a weapon. Platts considers[2] that the name of the order comes from the Sanskrit abstract term, and the crutch therefore apparently obtained its name from being used by members of the order. Properly, a religious mendicant of any Vishnuite sect should be called a Bairāgi. But the term is not generally applied to the more distinctive sects as the Kabīrpanthi, Swāmi-Nārāyan, Satnāmi and others, some of which are almost separated from Hinduism,

1. Definition of name and statistics.

---

[1] This article contains material from Sir E. Maclagan's *Punjab Census Report* (1891), and Dr. J. N. Bhattacharya's *Hindu Castes and Sects* (Thacker, Spink & Co., Calcutta).
[2] *Dictionary,* s.v.

93

nor to the Sikh religious orders, nor the Chaitanya sect of Bengal. A proper Bairāgi is one whose principal deity is either Vishnu or either of his great incarnations, Rāma and Krishna.

2. The four Sampradāyas or main orders.

It is generally held that there are four Sampradāyas or main sects of Bairāgis. These are—

(*a*) The Rāmānujis, the followers of the first prominent Vishnuite reformer Rāmānuj in southern India, with whom are classed the Rāmānandis or adherents of his great disciple Rāmānand in northern India. Both these are also called Sri Vaishnava, that is, the principal or original Vaishnava sect.

(*b*) The Nīmānandi, Nīmāt or Nīmbaditya sect, followers of a saint called Nīmānand.

(*c*) The Vishnu-Swāmi or Vallabhachārya sect, worshippers of Krishna and Rādha.

(*d*) The Mādhavachārya sect of southern India.

It will be desirable to give a few particulars of each of these, mainly taken from Wilson's *Hindu Sects* and Dr. Bhattachārya's *Hindu Castes and Sects*.

3. The Rāmānujis.

Rāmānuj was the first great Vishnuite prophet, and lived in southern India in the eleventh or twelfth century on an island in the Kāveri river near Trichinopoly. He preached the worship of a supreme spirit, Vishnu and his consort Lakshmi, and taught that men also had souls or spirits, and that matter was lifeless. He was a strong opponent of the cult of Siva, then predominant in southern India, and of phallic worship. He, however, admitted only the higher castes into his order, and cannot therefore be considered as the founder of the liberalising principle of Vishnuism. The superiors of the Rāmānuja sect are called Achārya, and rank highest among the priests of the Vishnuite orders. The most striking feature in the practice of the Rāmānujis is the separate preparation and scrupulous privacy of their meals. They must not eat in cotton garments, but must bathe, and then put on wool or silk. The teachers allow their select pupils to assist them, but in general all the Rāmānujis cook for themselves, and should the meal during this process, or while they are eating, attract even the look of a stranger, the operation is instantly stopped and the viands buried in the

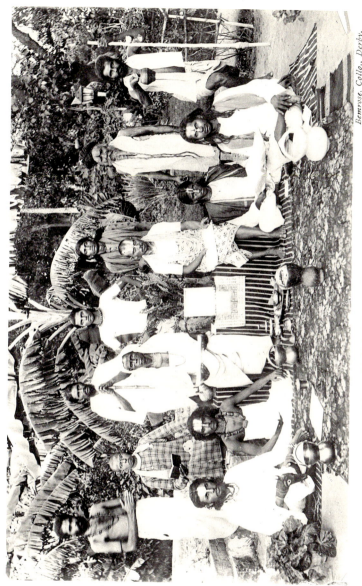

HINDU MENDICANTS WITH SECT MARKS.

Bemrose, Collo., Derby.

ground.   The Rāmānujis address each other with the salutation Dasoham, or 'I am your slave,' accompanied with the
Pranām or slight inclination of the head and the application of joined hands to the forehead.   To the Achāryas or
superiors the other members of the sect perform the Ashtanga
or prostration of the body with eight parts touching the
ground.   The *tilak* or sect-mark of the Rāmānujis consists
of two perpendicular white lines from the roots of the hair
to the top of the eyebrows, with a connecting white line at
the base, and a third central line either of red or yellow.
The Rāmānujis do not recognise the worship of Rādha,
the consort of Krishna.   The mendicant orders of the
Sātanis and Dasaris of southern India are branches of this
sect.

Rāmānand, the great prophet of Vishnuism in northern
India, and the real founder of the liberal doctrines of the
cult, lived at Benāres at the end of the fourteenth century,
and is supposed to have been a follower of Rāmānuj.   He
introduced, however, a great extension of his predecessor's
gospel in making his sect, nominally at least, open to all
castes.   He thus initiated the struggle against the social
tyranny and exclusiveness of the caste system, which was
carried to greater lengths by his disciples and successors,
Kabīr, Nānak, Dādu, Rai Dās and others.   These afterwards
proclaimed the worship of one unseen god who could not be
represented by idols, and the religious equality of all men,
their tenets no doubt being considerably influenced by their
observance of Islām, which had now become a principal
religion of India.   Rāmānand himself did not go so far, and
remained a good Hindu, inculcating the special worship of
Rāma and his consort Sīta.   The Rāmānandis consider the
Rāmāyana as their most sacred book, and make pilgrimages
to Ajodhia and Rāmnath.[1]   Their sect-mark consists of two
white lines down the forehead with a red one between, but
they are continued on to the nose, ending in a loop, instead
of terminating at the line of the eyebrows, like that of the
Rāmānujis.   The Rāmānandis say that the mark on the
nose represents the Singāsun or lion's throne, while the two
white lines up the forehead are Rāma and Lakhshman, and

4. The
Rāmā-
nandis.

---

[1] Sir E. Maclagan's *Punjab Census Report* (1891), p. 122.

the centre red one is Sīta. Some of their devotees wear ochre-coloured clothes like the Sivite mendicants.

The second of the four orders is that of the Nīmānandis, called after a saint Nīmānand. He lived near Mathura Brindāban, and on one occasion was engaged in religious controversy with a Jain ascetic till sunset. He then offered his visitor some refreshment, but the Jain could not eat anything after sunset, so Nīmānand stopped the sun from setting, and ordered him to wait above a *nīm* tree till the meal was cooked and eaten under the tree, and this direction the sun duly obeyed. Hence Nīmānand, whose original name was Bhāskarachārya, was called by his new name after the tree, and was afterwards held to have been an incarnation of Vishnu or the Sun.

The doctrines of the sect, Mr. Growse states,[1] are of a very enlightened character. Thus their tenet of salvation by faith is thought by many scholars to have been directly derived from the Gospels; while another article in their creed is the continuance of conscious individual existence in a future world, when the highest reward of the good will not be extinction, but the enjoyment of the visible presence of the divinity whom they have served while on earth. The Nīmānandis worship Krishna, and were the first sect, Dr. Bhattachārya states,[2] to associate with him as a divine consort Rādha, the chief partner of his illicit loves.

Their headquarters are at Muttra, and their chief festival is the Janam-Ashtami[3] or Krishna's birthday. Their sect-mark consists of two white lines down the forehead with a black patch in the centre, which is called Shiāmbindini. Shiām means black, and is a name of Krishna. They also sometimes have a circular line across the nose, which represents the moon.

The third great order is that of the Mādhavas, named after a saint called Mādhavachārya in southern India. He attempted to reconcile the warring Sivites and Vishnuites by combining the worship of Krishna with that of Siva

---

[1] *Memoir of Mathura.*

[2] *Hindu Castes and Sects*, p. 449.

[3] Lit. the birth on the eighth day, as Krishna was born on the 8th of dark Bhādon.

and Pārvati. The doctrine of the sect is that the human
soul is different from the divine soul, and its members are
therefore called dualists. They admit a distinction between
the divine soul and the universe, and between the human
soul and the material world. They deny also the possibility
of Nirvāna or the absorption and extinction of the human
soul in the divine essence. They destroy their thread at
initiation, and also wear red clothes like the Sivite devotees,
and like them also they carry a staff and water-pot. The
tilak of the Mādhavachāryas is said to consist of two white
lines down the forehead and continued on to the nose
where they meet, with a black vertical line between them.

The fourth main order is the Vishnu-Swāmi, which is
much better known as the Vallabhachārya sect, called after
its founder Vallabha, who was born in A.D. 1479. The
god Krishna appeared to him and ordered him to marry
and set up a shrine to the god at Gokul near Mathura
(Muttra). The sect worship Krishna in his character of
Bāla Gopāla or the cowherd boy. Their temples are
numerous all over India, and especially at Mathura and
Brindāban, where Krishna was brought up as a cowherd.
The temples at Benāres, Jagannāth and Dwārka are rich
and important, but the most celebrated shrine is at Sri
Nāthadwāra in Mewār. The image is said to have trans-
ported itself thither from Mathura, when Aurāngzeb ordered
its temple at Mathura to be destroyed. Krishna is here
represented as a little boy in the act of supporting the
mountain Govardhan on his finger to shelter the people
from the storms of rain sent by Indra. The image is
splendidly dressed and richly decorated with ornaments to
the value of several thousand pounds. The images of
Krishna in the temples are commonly known as Thākurji,
and are either of stone or brass. At all Vallabhachārya
temples there are eight daily services : the Mangala or
morning *levée*, a little after sunrise, when the god is taken
from his couch and bathed ; the Sringāra, when he is
attired in his jewels and seated on his throne ; the Gwāla,
when he is supposed to be starting to graze his cattle in
the woods of Braj ; the Rāj Bhog or midday meal, which,
after presentation, is consumed by the priests and votaries

7. The
Vallabha-
chāryas.

who have assisted at the ceremonies; the Uttāpan, about three o'clock, when the god awakes from his siesta; the Bhog or evening collation; the Sandhiya or disrobing at sunset; and the Sayan or retiring to rest. The ritual is performed by the priests and the lay worshipper is only a spectator, who shows his reverence by the same forms as he would to a human superior.[1]

The priests of the sect are called Gokalastha Gosain or Mahārāja. They are considered to be incarnations of the god, and divine honours are paid to them. They always marry, and avow that union with the god is best obtained by indulgence in all bodily enjoyments. This doctrine has led to great licentiousness in some groups of the sect, especially on the part of the priests or Mahārājas. Women were taught to believe that the service of and contact with the priest were the most real form of worshipping the god, and that intercourse with him was equivalent to being united with the god. Dr. Bhattachārya quotes[2] the following tariff for the privilege of obtaining different degrees of contact with the body of the Mahārāja or priest:

For homage by sight . . .	Rs. 5.
For homage by touch . . .	Rs. 20.
For the honour of washing the Mahārāja's foot	Rs. 35.
For swinging him	Rs. 40.
For rubbing sweet unguents on his body	Rs. 42.
For being allowed to sit with him on the same couch . . .	Rs. 60.
For the privilege of dancing with him	Rs. 100 to 200.
For drinking the water in which he has bathed	Rs. 17.
For being closeted with him in the same room	Rs. 50 to 500.

The public disapprobation caused by these practices

---

[1] Mr. Crooke's *Tribes and Castes*, art. Vallabhachārya.
[2] *Hindu Castes and Sects*, p. 457.

ANCHORITE SITTING ON IRON NAILS.

and their bad effect on the morality of women culminated in the great Mahārāj libel suit in the Bombay High Court in 1862. Since then the objectionable features of the cult have to a large extent disappeared, while it has produced some priests of exceptional liberality and enlightenment. The *tilak* of the Vallabhachāryas is said to consist of two white lines down the forehead, forming a half-circle at its base and a white dot between them. They will not admit the lower castes into the order, but only those from whom a Brāhman can take water.

Besides the main sects as described above, Vaishnavism **8. Minor** has produced many minor sects, consisting of the followers **sects.** of some saint of special fame, and mendicants belonging to these are included in the body of Bairāgis. One or two legends concerning such saints may be given. A common order is that of the Bendiwāle, or those who wear a dot. Their founder began putting a red dot on his forehead between the two white lines in place of the long red line of the Rāmānandis. His associates asked him why he had dared to alter his *tilak* or sect-mark. He said that the goddess Jānki had given him the dot, and as a test he went and bathed in the Sarju river, and rubbed his forehead with water, and all the sect-mark was rubbed out except the dot. So the others recognised the special intervention of the goddess, and he founded a sect. Another sect is called the Chaturbhuji or four-armed, Chaturbhuj being an epithet of Vishnu. He was taking part in a feast when his loin-cloth came undone behind, and the others said to him that as this had happened, he had become impure at the feast. He replied, ' Let him to whom the *dhoti* belongs tie it up,' and immediately four arms sprang from his body, and while two continued to take food, the other two tied up his loin-cloth behind. Thus it was recognised that the Chaturbhuji Vishnu had appeared in him, and he was venerated.

Among the Bairāgis, besides the four Sampradāyas or **9. The** main orders, there are seven Akhāras. These are military **seven** **Akhāras.** divisions or schools for training, and were instituted when the Bairāgis had to fight with the Gosains. Any member of one of the four Sampradāyas can belong to any one of the seven Akhāras, and a man can change his Akhāra as often as he likes, but not his Sampradāya. The Akhāras, with the exception of the Lasgaris, who change the red centre line of the Rāmānandis into a white line, have no special sect-marks. They are distinguished by their flags or standards, which are elaborately decorated with gold thread embroidered on silk or sometimes with jewels, and cost two or three hundred rupees to prepare. These standards were carried by the Nāga or naked members of the Akhāra, who went in front and fought. Once in twelve years a great meeting of all the seven Akhāras is held at Allahābād, Nāsik, Ujjain or Hardwār, where they bathe and wash the image of the god in the water of the holy rivers. The quarrels between the Bairāgis and Gosains usually occurred at the sacred rivers, and the point of con-tention was which sect should bathe first. The following is a list of the seven Akhāras : Digambari, Khāki, Munjia, Kathia, Nirmohi, Nirbāni or Niranjani and Lasgari.

The name of the Digamber or Meghdamber signifies sky-clad or cloud-clad, that is naked. They do penance in the rainy season by sitting naked in the rain for two or three hours a day with an earthen pot on the head and the hands inserted in two others so that they cannot rub the skin. In the dry season they wear only a little cloth round the waist and ashes over the rest of the body. The ashes are produced from burnt cowdung picked up off the ground, and not mixed with straw like that which is prepared for fuel.

The Khāki Bairāgis also rub ashes on the body. During the four hot months they make five fires in a circle, and kneel between them with the head and legs and arms stretched towards the fires. The fires are kindled at noon with little heaps of cowdung cakes, and the penitent stays between them till they go out. They also have a block of wood with a hole through it, into which they insert the organ of generation and suspend it by chains in front and behind. They rub ashes on the body, from which they probably get their name of Khāki or dust-colour.

The Munjia Akhāra have a belt made of *munj* grass round the waist, and a little apron also of grass, which is hung from it, and passed through the legs. Formerly they

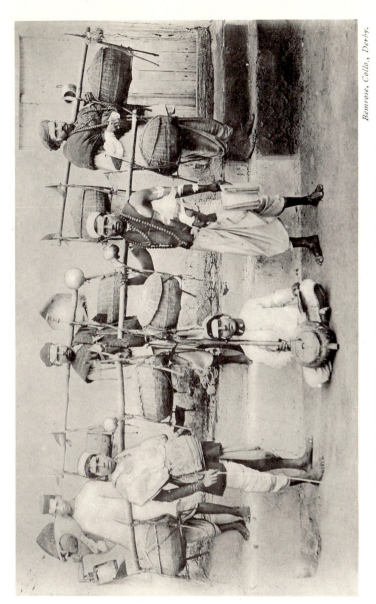

PILGRIMS CARRYING WATER OF THE RIVER NERBUDDA.

wore no other clothes, but now they have a cloth.   They also do penance between the fires.

The Kathias have a waist-belt of bamboo fibre, to which is suspended the wooden block for the purpose already described.   Their name signifies wooden, and is probably given to them on account of this custom.

The Nirmohi carry a *lota* or brass vessel and a little cup, in which they receive alms.

The Nirbāni wear only a piece of string or rope round the waist, to which is attached a small strip of cloth passing through the legs.   When begging, they carry a *kawar* or banghy, holding two baskets covered with cloth, and into this they put all their alms.   They never remove the cloth, but plunge their hands into the basket at random when they want something to eat.   They call the basket Kāmdhenu, the name of the cow which gave inexhaustible wealth. These Bairāgis commonly marry and accumulate property.

The Lasgari are soldiers, as the name denotes.[1]   They wear three straight lines of sandalwood up the forehead. It is said that on one occasion the Bairāgis were suddenly attacked by the Gosains when they had only made the white lines of the sect-mark, and they fought as they were. In consequence of this, they have ever since worn three white lines and no red one.

Others say that the Lasgari are a branch of the Digambari Akhāra, and that the Munjia and Kathia are branches of the Khāki Akhāra.   They give three other Akhāras—Nīralankhi, Mahānirbāni and Santokhi—about which nothing is known.

Besides the Akhāras, the Bairāgis are said to have fifty-two Dwāras or doors, and every man must be a member of a Dwāra as well as of a Sampradāya and Akhāra.   The Dwāras seem to have no special purpose, but in the case of Bairāgis who marry, they now serve as exogamous sections, so that members of the same Dwāra do not inter-marry.

10. The Dwāras.

A candidate for initiation has his head shaved, is invested with a necklace of beads of the *tulsi* or basil, and is taught a *mantra* or text relating to Vishnu by his preceptor.   The initiation text of the Rāmānandis is said to be *Om Rāmāya*

11. Initiation, appearance and customs.

---

[1] From *laskkar*, an army.

Nāmah, or *Om*, Salutation to Rāma. *Om* is a very sacred syllable, having much magical power. Thereafter the novice must journey to Dwārka in Gujarāt and have his body branded with hot iron or copper in the shape of Vishnu's four implements : the *chakra* or discus, the *guda* or club, the *shank* or conch-shell and the *padma* or lotus. Sometimes these are not branded but are made daily on the arms with clay. The sect-mark should be made with Gopichandan or the milkmaid's sandalwood. This is supposed to be clay taken from a tank at Dwārka, in which the Gopis or milk-maids who had been Krishna's companions drowned themselves when they heard of his death. But as this can seldom be obtained any suitable whitish clay is used instead. The Bairāgis commonly let their hair grow long, after being shaved at initiation, to imitate the old forest ascetics. If a man makes a pilgrimage on foot to some famous shrine he may have his head shaved there and make an offering of his hair. Others keep their hair long and shave it only at the death of their *guru* or preceptor. They usually wear white clothes, and if a man has a cloth on the upper part of the body it should be folded over the shoulders and knotted at the neck. He also has a *chimta* or small pair of tongs, and, if he can obtain it, the skin of an Indian antelope, on which he will sit while taking his food. The skin of this animal is held to be sacred. Every Bairāgi before he takes his food should dip a sprig of *tulsi* or basil into it to sanctify it; and if he cannot get this he uses his necklace of *tulsi*-beads for the purpose instead. The caste abstain from flesh and liquor, but are addicted to the intoxicating drugs, *gānja* and *bhāng* or preparations of Indian hemp. A Hindu on meeting a Bairāgi will greet him with the phrase ' Jai Sītārām,' and the Bairāgi will answer, ' Sītārām.' This word is a conjunction of the names of Rāma and his consort Sīta. When a Bairāgi receives alms he will present to the giver a flower and a sprig of *tulsi*.

12. Re-cruitment of the order and its char-acter.
A man belonging to any caste except the impure ones can be initiated as a Bairāgi, and the order is to a large extent recruited from the lower castes. Theoretic-ally all members of the order should eat together ; but the Brāhmans and other high castes belonging to it now eat only

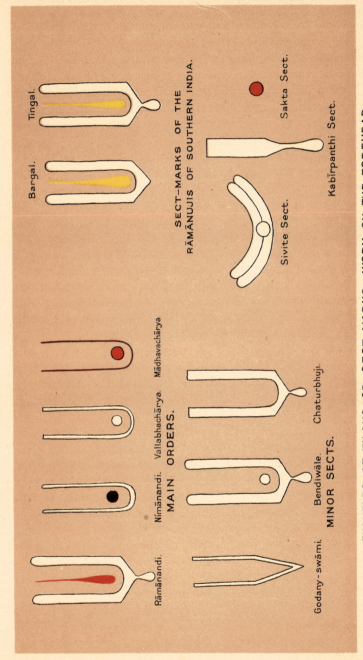

Rāmānandi.   Nīmānandi.   Vallabhachārya.   Mādhavachārya.

MAIN ORDERS.

Godany-swāmi.   Bendiwāle.   Chaturbhuji.

MINOR SECTS.

Bargal.   Tingal.

SECT-MARKS OF THE
RĀMĀNUJIS OF SOUTHERN INDIA.

Sivite Sect.   Sakta Sect.

Kabīrpanthi Sect.

EXAMPLES OF TILAKS OR SECT-MARKS, WORN ON THE FOREHEAD.

among themselves, except on the occasion of a Ghosti or special religious assembly, when all eat in common. As a matter of fact the order is a very mixed assortment of people. Many persons who lost their caste in the famine of 1897 from eating in Government poor-houses, joined the order and obtained a respectable position. Debtors who have become hopelessly involved sometimes find in it a means of escape from their creditors. Women of bad character, who have been expelled from their caste, are also frequently enrolled as female members, and in monasteries live openly with the men. The caste is also responsible for a good deal of crime. Not only is the disguise a very convenient one for thieves and robbers to assume on their travels, but many regular members of the order are criminally disposed. Nevertheless large numbers of Bairāgis are men who have given up their caste and families from a genuine impulse of self-sacrifice, and the desire to lead a religious life.

On account of their sanctity the Bairāgis have a fairly good social position, and respectable Hindu castes will accept cooked food from them. Brāhmans usually, but not always, take water. They act as *gurus* or spiritual guides to the laymen of all castes who can become Bairāgis. They give the Rām and Gopāl Mantras, or the texts of Rāma and Krishna, to their disciples of the three twice-born castes, and the Sheo Mantra or Siva's text to other castes. The last is considered to be of smaller religious efficacy than the others, and is given to the lower castes and members of the higher ones who do not lead a particularly virtuous life. They invest boys with the sacred thread, and make the sect-mark on their foreheads. When they go and visit their disciples they receive presents, but do not ask them to confess their sins nor impose penalties.

If a mendicant Bairāgi keeps a woman it is stated that he is expelled from the community, but this rule does not seem to be enforced in practice. If he is detected in a casual act of sexual intercourse a fine should be imposed, such as feeding two or three hundred Bairāgis. The property of an unmarried Bairāgi descends to a selected *chela* or disciple. The bodies of the dead are usually burnt,

13. Social position and customs.

but those of saints specially famous for their austerities or piety are buried, and salt is put round the body to preserve it. Such men are known as Bhakta.

14. Bairāgi monasteries. The Bairāgis [1] have numerous *maths* or monasteries, scattered over the country and usually attached to temples. The Math comprises a set of huts or chambers for the Mahant or superior and his permanent pupils ; a temple and often the Samādhi or tomb of the founder, or of some eminent Mahant ; and a Dharmsāla or charitable hostel for the accommodation of wandering members of the order, and of other travellers who are constantly visiting the temple. Ingress and egress are free to all, and, indeed, a restraint on personal liberty seems never to have entered into the conception of any Hindu religious legislator. There are, as a rule, a small number of resident *chelas* or disciples who are scholars and attendants on the superiors, and also out-members who travel over the country and return to the monastery as a headquarters. The monastery has commonly some small endowment in land, and the resident *chelas* go out and beg for alms for their common support. If the Mahant is married the headship may descend in his family ; but when he is unmarried his successor is one of his disciples, who is commonly chosen by election at a meeting of the Mahants of neighbouring monasteries. Formerly the Hindu governor of the district would preside at such an election, but it is now, of course, left entirely to the Bairāgis themselves.

15. Married Bairāgis. Large numbers of Bairāgis now marry and have children, and have formed an ordinary caste. The married Bairāgis are held to be inferior to the celibate mendicants, and will take food from them, but the mendicants will not permit the married Bairāgis to eat with them in the *chauka* or place purified for the taking of food. The customs of the married Bairāgis resemble those of ordinary Hindu castes such as the Kurmis. They permit divorce and the remarriage of widows, and burn the dead. Those who have taken to cultivation do not, as a rule, plough with their own hands. Many Bairāgis have acquired property and become

---

[1] This paragraph is taken from Professor Wilson's *Account of Hindu Sects in the Asiatic Researches.*

landholders, and others have extensive moneylending transactions. Two such men who had acquired possession of extensive tracts of zamīndāri land in Chhattīsgarh, in satisfaction of loans made to the Gond zamīndārs, and had been given the zamīndāri status by the Marāthas, were subsequently made Feudatory Chiefs of the Nāndgaon and Chhuikhadan States. These chiefs now marry and the States descend in their families by primogeniture in the ordinary manner. As a rule, the Bairāgi landowners and moneylenders are not found to be particularly good specimens of their class.

Balāhi.[1]—A low functional caste of weavers and village watchmen found in the Nimār and Hoshangābād Districts and in Central India. They numbered 52,000 persons in the Central Provinces in 1911, being practically confined to the two Districts already mentioned. The name is a corruption of the Hindi *bulāhi*, one who calls, or a messenger. The Balāhis seem to be an occupational group, probably an offshoot of the large Kori caste of weavers, one of whose subdivisions is shown as Balāhi in the United Provinces. In the Central Provinces they have received accretions from the spinner caste of Katias, themselves probably a branch of the Koris, and from the Mahārs, the great menial caste of Bombay. In Hoshangābād they are known alternatively as Mahār, while in Burhānpur they are called Bunkar or weaver by outsiders. The following story which they tell about themselves also indicates their mixed origin. They say that their ancestors came to Nimār as part of the army of Rāja Mān of Jodhpur, who invaded the country when it was under Muhammadan rule. He was defeated, and his soldiers were captured and ordered to be killed.[2] One of the Balāhis among them won the favour of the Muhammadan general and asked for his own freedom and that of the other Balāhis from among the prisoners. The Musalmān

1. General notice.

---

[1] This article is based on papers by Mr. Habīb Ullah, Pleader, Burhānpur, Mr. W. Bagley, Subdivisional Officer, and Munsh Kanhya Lāl, of the Gazetteer office.

[2] This legend is probably a vague reminiscence of the historical fact that a Mālwa army was misled by a Gond guide in the Nimār forests and cut up by the local Muhammadan ruler. The well-known Rāja Mān of Jodhpur was, it is believed, never in Nimār.

replied that he would be unable to determine which of
the prisoners were really Balāhis. On this the Balāhi,
whose name was Ganga Kochla, replied that he had an
effective test. He therefore killed a cow, cooked its flesh
and invited the prisoners to partake of it. So many of them
as consented to eat were considered to be Balāhis and
liberated ; but many members of other castes thus obtained
their freedom, and they and their descendants are now included in the community. The subcastes or endogamous
groups distinctly indicate the functional character of the
caste, the names given being Nimāri, Gannore, Katia, Kori
and Mahār. Of these Katia, Kori and Mahār are the
names of distinct castes, Nimāri is a local subdivision indicating those who speak the peculiar dialect of this tract,
and the Gannore are no doubt named after the Rājpūt clan
of that name, of whom their ancestors were not improbably
the illegitimate offspring. The Nimāri Balāhis are said to
rank lower than the rest, as they will eat the flesh of dead
cattle which the others refuse to do. They may not take
water from the village well, and unless a separate one can
be assigned to them, must pay others to draw water for
them. Partly no doubt in the hope of escaping from this
degraded position, many of the Nimāri group became
Christians in the famine of 1897. They are considered to
be the oldest residents of Nimār. At marriages the Balāhi
receives as his perquisite the leaf-plates used for feasts with
the leavings of food upon them ; and at funerals he takes
the cloth which covers the corpse on its way to the burning-
ghāt. In Nimār the Korkus and Balāhis each have a
separate burying-ground which is known as Murghāta.[1] The
Katias weave the finer kinds of cloth and rank a little
higher than the others. In Burhānpur, as already stated,
the caste are known as Bunkar, and they are probably
identical with the Bunkars of Khāndesh ; Bunkar is simply
an occupational term meaning a weaver.

2. Mar-
riage.

The caste have the usual system of exogamous groups,
some of which are named after villages, while the designa-
tions of others are apparently nicknames given to the founder
of the clan, as Bagmār, a tiger-killer, Bhagoria, a runaway,

---

[1] The *ghāt* or river-bank for the disposal of corpses.

and so on. They employ a Brāhman to calculate the horoscopes of a bridal couple and fix the date of their wedding, but if he says the marriage is inauspicious, they merely obtain the permission of the caste *panchāyat* and celebrate it on a Saturday or Sunday. Apparently, however, they do not consult real Brāhmans, but merely priests of their own caste whom they call Balāhi Brāhmans. These Brāhmans are, nevertheless, said to recite the Satya Nārāyan Katha. They also have *gurus* or spiritual preceptors, being members of the caste who have joined the mendicant orders ; and Bhāts or genealogists of their own caste who beg at their weddings. They have the practice of serving for a wife, known as Gharjamai or Lamjhana. When the pauper suitor is finally married at the expense of his wife's father, a marriage-shed is erected for him at the house of some neighbour, but his own family are not invited to the wedding.

After marriage a girl goes to her husband's house for a few days and returns. The first Diwāli or Akha-tīj festival after the wedding must also be passed at the husband's house, but consummation is not effected until the *aina* or *gauna* ceremony is performed on the attainment of puberty. The cost of a wedding is about Rs. 80 to the bridegroom's family and Rs. 20 to the bride's family. A widow is forbidden to marry her late husband's brother or other relatives. At the wedding she is dressed in new clothes, and the foreheads of the couple are marked with cowdung as a sign of purification. They then proceed by night to the husband's village, and the woman waits till morning in some empty building, when she enters her husband's house carrying two water-pots on her head in token of the fertility which she is to bring to it.

Like the Mahārs, the Balāhis must not kill a dog or a cat under pain of expulsion ; but it is peculiar that in their case the bear is held equally sacred, this being probably a residue of some totemistic observance. The most binding form of oath which they can use is by any one of these animals. The Balāhis will admit any Hindu into the community except a man of the very lowest castes, and also Gonds and Korkus. The head and face of the neophyte

3. Other customs.

are shaved clean, and he is made to lie on the ground under a string-cot; a number of the Balāhis sit on this and wash themselves, letting the water drip from their bodies on to the man below until he is well drenched; he then gives a feast to the caste-fellows, and is considered to have become a Balāhi. It is reported also that they will receive back into the community Balāhi women who have lived with men of other castes and even with Jains and Muhammadans. They will take food from members of these religions and of any Hindu caste, except the most impure.

1. Origin and traditions.

Balija, Balji, Gurusthulu, Naidu.—A large trading caste of the Madras Presidency, where they number a million persons. In the Central Provinces 1200 were enumerated in 1911, excluding 1500 Perikis, who though really a sub-caste and not a very exalted one of Balijas,[1] claim to be a separate caste. They are mainly returned from places where Madras troops have been stationed, as Nāgpur, Jubbulpore and Raipur. The caste are frequently known as Naidu, a corruption of the Telugu word Nāyakdu, a prince or leader. Their ancestors are supposed to have been Nāyaks or kings of Madura, Tanjore and Vijayanagar. The traditional occupation of the caste appears to have been to make bangles and pearl and coral ornaments, and they have still a subcaste called Gāzulu, or a bangle-seller. In Madras they are said to be an offshoot of the great cultivating castes of Kamma and Kāpu and to be a mixed community recruited from these and other Telugu castes. Another proof of their mixed descent may be inferred from the fact that they will admit persons of other castes or the descendants of mixed marriages into the community without much scruple in Madras.[2] The name of Balija seems also to have been applied to a mixed caste started by Bāsava, the founder of the Lingāyat sect of Sivites, these persons being known in Madras as Linga Balijas.

2. Marriage.

The Balijas have two main divisions, Desa or Kota, and Peta, the Desas or Kotas being those who claim descent from the old Balija kings, while the Petas are the trading Balijas, and are further subdivided into groups like the Gāzulu or

[1] *Madras Census Report* (1891), p. 277.   [2] *Ibidem* (1891), p. 226.

bangle-sellers and the Periki or salt-sellers.   The subdivisions are not strictly endogamous.   Every family has a surname, and exogamous groups or *gotras* also exist, but these have generally been forgotten, and marriages are regulated by the surnames, the only prohibition being that persons of the same surname may not intermarry.   Instances of such names are : Singiri, Gūdāri, Jadal, Sangnād and Dāsiri.   In fact the rules of exogamy are so loose that an instance is known of an uncle having married his niece.   Marriage is usually infant, and the ceremony lasts for five days.   On the first day the bride and bridegroom are seated on a yoke in the *pandal* or marriage pavilion, where the relatives and guests assemble.   The bridegroom puts a pair of silver rings on the bride's toes and ties the *mangal-sūtram* or flat circular piece of gold round her neck.   On the next three days the bridegroom and bride are made to sit on a plank or cot face to face with each other and to throw flowers and play together for two hours in the mornings and evenings.   On the fourth day, at dead of night, they are seated on a cot and the jewels and gifts for the bride are presented, and she is then formally handed over to the bridegroom's family.   In Madras Mr. Thurston [1] states that on the last day of the marriage ceremony a mock ploughing and sowing rite is held, and during this, the sister of the bridegroom puts a cloth over the basket containing earth, wherein seeds are to be sown by the bridegroom, and will not allow him to go on with the ceremony till she has extracted a promise that his first-born daughter shall marry her son.   No bride-price is paid, and the remarriage of widows is forbidden.

The Balijas bury their dead in a sitting posture.   In the Central Provinces they are usually Lingāyats and especially worship Gauri, Siva's wife.   Jangams serve them as priests. They usually eat flesh and drink liquor, but in Chānda it is stated that both these practices are forbidden.   In the Central Provinces they are mainly cultivators, but some of them still sell bangles and salt.   Several of them are in Government service and occupy a fairly high social position.

In Madras a curious connection exists between the Kāpus and Balijas and the impure Māla caste.   It is said

3. Occupation and social status.

[1] *Ethnographic Notes in Southern India,* p. 16.

that once upon a time the Kāpus and Balijas were flying from the Muhammadans and came to the northern Pallār river in high flood. They besought the river to go down and let them across, but it demanded the sacrifice of a first-born child. While the Kāpus and Balijas were hesitating, the Mālas who had followed them boldly sacrificed one of their children. Immediately the river divided before them and they all crossed in safety. Ever since then the Kāpus and Balijas have respected the Mālas, and the Balijas formerly even deposited the images of the goddess Gauri, of Ganesha, and of Siva's bull with the Mālas, as the hereditary custodians of their gods.[1]

[1] *Madras Census Report* (1891), p. 277.

BANIA

LIST OF PARAGRAPHS

LIST OF SUBORDINATE ARTICLES ON SUBCASTES

Bania, Bāni, Vāni, Mahājan, Seth, Sāhukār.—The occupational caste of bankers, moneylenders and dealers in 1. General notice.

grain, *ghī* (butter), groceries and spices.   The name Bania is
derived from the Sanskrit *vanij*, a merchant.   In western
India the Banias are always called Vānia or Vāni.   Mahājan
literally means a great man, and being applied to successful
Banias as an honorific title has now come to signify a
banker or moneylender ; Seth signifies a great merchant or
capitalist, and is applied to Banias as an honorific prefix.   The
words *Sāhu*, *Sao* and *Sāhukār* mean upright or honest, and
have also, curiously enough, come to signify a moneylender.
The total number of Banias in the Central Provinces in
1911 was about 200,000, or rather over one per cent of
the population.   Of the above total two-thirds were Hindus
and one-third Jains.   The caste is fairly distributed over the
whole Province, being most numerous in Districts with large
towns and a considerable volume of trade.

2. The
Banias a
true
caste : use
of the
name.

There has been much difference of opinion as to whether
the name Bania should be taken to signify a caste, or whether
it is merely an occupational term applied to a number of
distinct castes.   I venture to think it is necessary and
scientifically correct to take it as a caste.   In Bengal the
word Banian, a corruption of Bania, has probably come to
be a general term meaning simply a banker, or person
dealing in money.   But this does not seem to be the case
elsewhere.   As a rule the name Bania is used only
as a caste name for groups who are considered both by
themselves and outsiders to belong to the Bania caste.   It
may occasionally be applied to members of other castes, as
in the case of certain Teli-Banias who have abandoned oil-
pressing for shop-keeping, but such instances are very rare ;
and these Telis would probably now assert that they belonged
to the Bania caste.   That the Banias are recognised as a distinct caste by the people is shown by the number of uncomplimentary proverbs and sayings about them, which is far
larger than in the case of any other caste.[1]   In all these the
name Bania is used and not that of any subdivision, and
this indicates that none of the subdivisions are looked upon
as distinctive social groups or castes.   Moreover, so far as I
am aware, the name Bania is applied regularly to all the
groups usually classified under the caste, and there is no

[1] See para. 19 below.

Benrose, Collo., Derby.

GROUP OF MÃRWÃRI BANIA WOMEN.

group which objects to the name or whose members refuse
to describe themselves by it. This is by no means always
the case with other important castes. The Rāthor Telis of
Mandla entirely decline to answer to the name of Teli,
though they are classified under that caste. In the case of
the important Ahīr or grazier caste, those who sell milk
instead of grazing cattle are called Gaoli, but remain
members of the Ahīr caste. An Ahīr in Chhattīsgarh would
be called Rāwat and in the Marātha Districts Gowāri, but
might still be an Ahīr by caste. The Barai caste of betel-
vine growers and sellers is in some localities called Tamboli
and not Barai ; elsewhere it is known only as Pansāri,
though the name Pansāri is correctly an occupational term,
and, where it is not applied to the Barais, means a grocer or
druggist by profession and not a caste. Bania, on the other
hand, over the greater part of India is applied only to
persons who acknowledge themselves and are generally recognised by Hindu society to be members of the Bania caste,
and there is no other name which is generally applied to any
considerable section of such persons. Certain of the more
important subcastes of Bania, as the Agarwāla, Oswāl and
Parwār, are, it is true, frequently known by the subcaste
name. But the caste name is as often as not, or even more
often, affixed to it. Agarwāla, or Agarwāla Bania, are names
equally applied to designate this subcaste, and similarly with
the Oswāls and Parwārs ; and even so the subcaste name is
only applied for greater accuracy and for compliment, since
these are the best subcastes ; the Bania's quarter of a town
will be called Bania Mahalla, and its residents spoken of as
Banias, even though they may be nearly all Agarwāls or
Oswāls. Several Rājpūt clans are similarly spoken of by their
clan names, as Rāthor, Panwār, and so on, without the addition
of the caste name Rājpūt. Brāhman subcastes are usually
mentioned by their subcaste name for greater accuracy,
though in their case too it is usual to add the caste name.
And there are subdivisions of other castes, such as the Jaiswār
Chamārs and the Somvansi Mehras, who invariably speak
of themselves only by their subcaste name, and discard the
caste name altogether, being ashamed of it, but are nevertheless held to belong to their parent castes. Thus in the

matter of common usage Bania conforms in all respects to the requirements of a proper caste name.

3. Their distinctive occupation.   The Banias have also a distinct and well-defined traditional occupation,[1] which is followed by many or most members of practically every subcaste so far as has been observed. This occupation has caused the caste as a body to be credited with special mental and moral characteristics in popular estimation, to a greater extent perhaps than any other caste. None of the subcastes are ashamed of their traditional occupation or try to abandon it. It is true that a few subcastes such as the Kasaundhans and Kasarwānis, sellers of metal vessels, apparently had originally a somewhat different profession, though resembling the traditional one ; but they too, if they once only sold vessels, now engage largely in the traditional Bania's calling, and deal generally in grain and money. The Banias, no doubt because it is both profitable and respectable, adhere more generally to their traditional occupation than almost any great caste, except the cultivators. Mr. Marten's analysis[2] of the occupations of different castes shows that sixty per cent of the Banias are still engaged in trade ; while only nineteen per cent of Brāhmans follow a religious calling ; twenty-nine per cent of Ahīrs are graziers, cattle-dealers or milkmen ; only nine per cent of Telis are engaged in all branches of industry, including their traditional occupation of oil-pressing ; and similarly only twelve per cent of Chamārs work at industrial occupations, including that of curing hides. In respect of occupation therefore the Banias strictly fulfil the definition of a caste.

4. Their distinctive status.   The Banias have also a distinctive social status. They are considered, though perhaps incorrectly, to represent the Vaishyas or third great division of the Aryan twice-born ; they rank just below Rājpūts and perhaps above all other castes except Brāhmans ; Brāhmans will take food cooked without water from many Banias and drinking-water from all. Nearly all Banias wear the sacred thread ; and the Banias are distinguished by the fact that they abstain more rigorously and generally from all kinds of flesh food than

---

[1] See commencement of article.
[2] *C.P. Census Report* (1911), Occu-   pation Chapter, Subsidiary Table I. p. 234.

any other caste. Their rules as to diet are exceptionally strict, and are equally observed by the great majority of the subdivisions.

Thus the Banias apparently fulfil the definition of a caste, as consisting of one or more endogamous groups or subcastes with a distinct name applied to them all and to them only, a distinctive occupation and a distinctive social status ; and there seems no reason for not considering them a caste. If on the other hand we examine the subcastes of Bania we find that the majority of them have names derived from places,[1] not indicating any separate origin, occupation or status, but only residence in separate tracts. Such divisions are properly termed subcastes, being endogamous only, and in no other way distinctive. No subcaste can be markedly distinguished from the others in respect of occupation or social status, and none apparently can therefore be classified as a separate caste. There are no doubt substantial differences in status between the highest subcastes of Bania, the Agarwāls, Oswāls and Parwārs, and the lower ones, the Kasaundhan, Kasarwāni, Dosar and others. But this difference is not so great as that which separates different groups included in such important castes as Rājpūt and Bhāt. It is true again that subcastes like the Agarwāls and Oswāls are individually important, but not more so than the Marātha, Khedawāl, Kanaujia and Maithil Brāhmans, or the Sesodia, Rāthor, Panwār and Jādon Rājpūts. The higher subcastes of Bania themselves recognise a common relationship by taking food cooked without water from each other, which is a very rare custom among subcastes. Some of them are even said to have intermarried. If on the other hand it is argued, not that two or three or more of the important subdivisions should be erected into independent castes, but that Bania is not a caste at all, and that every subcaste should be treated as a separate caste, then such purely local groups as Kanaujia, Jaiswār, Gujarāti, Jaunpuri and others, which are found in forty or fifty other castes, would have to become separate

5. The endogamous divisions of the Banias.

---

[1] For examples, the subordinate articles on Agarwāl, Oswāl, Maheshri, Khandelwāl, Lād, Agrahari, Ajudhia-bāsi, and Srimāli may be consulted. The census lists contain numerous other territorial names.

castes; and if in this one case why not in all the other castes where they occur? This would result in the impossible position of having forty or fifty castes of the same name, which recognise no connection of any kind with each other, and make any arrangement or classification of castes altogether impracticable. And in 1911 out of 200,000 Banias in the Central Provinces, 43,000 were returned with no subcaste at all, and it would therefore be impossible to classify these under any other name.

6. The Banias derived from the Rājpūts.

The Banias have been commonly supposed to represent the Vaishyas or third of the four classical castes, both by Hindu society generally and by leading authorities on the subject. It is perhaps this view of their origin which is partly responsible for the tendency to consider them as several castes and not one. But its accuracy is doubtful. The important Bania groups appear to be of Rājpūt stock. They nearly all come from Rājputāna, Bundelkhand or Gujarāt, that is from the homes of the principal Rājpūt clans. Several of them have legends of Rājpūt descent. The Agarwālas say that their first ancestor was a Kshatriya king, who married a Nāga or snake princess; the Nāga race is supposed to have signified the Scythian immigrants, who were snake-worshippers and from whom several clans of Rājpūts were probably derived. The Agarwālas took their name from the ancient city of Agroha or possibly from Agra. The Oswāls say that their ancestor was the Rājpūt king of Osnagar in Mārwār, who with his followers was converted by a Jain mendicant. The Nemas state that their ancestors were fourteen young Rājpūt princes who escaped the vengeance of Parasurāma by abandoning the profession of arms and taking to trade. The Khandelwāls take their name from the town of Khandela in Jaipur State of Rājputāna. The Kasarwānis say they immigrated from Kara Mānikpur in Bundelkhand. The origin of the Umre Banias is not known, but in Gujarāt they are also called Bāgaria from the Bāgar or wild country of the Dongarpur and Pertābgarh States of Rājputāna, where numbers of them are still settled; the name Bāgaria would appear to indicate that they are supposed to have immigrated thence into Gujarāt. The Dhūsar Banias ascribe their name to a hill

IMAGE OF THE GOD GANPATI CARRIED IN PROCESSION.

called Dhūsi or Dhosi on the border of Alwar State.   The
Asātis say that their original home was Tīkamgarh State
in Bundelkhand.   The name of the Maheshris is held to
be derived from Maheshwar, an ancient town on the Nerbudda, near Indore, which is traditionally supposed to have
been the earliest settlement of the Yādava Rājpūts.   The
headquarters of the Gahoi Banias is said to have been at
Kharagpur in Bundelkhand, though according to their own
legend they are of mixed origin.   The home of the Srimālis
was the old town of Srimāl, now Bhinmāl in Mārwār.   The
Palliwāl Banias were from the well-known trading town of
Pāli in Mārwār.   The Jaiswāl are said to take their name
from Jaisalmer State, which was their native country.   The
above are no doubt only a fraction of the Bania subcastes,
but they include nearly all the most important and representative ones, from whom the caste takes its status and
character.   Of the numerous other groups the bulk have
probably been brought into existence through the migration
and settlement of sections of the caste in different parts of
the country, where they have become endogamous and
obtained a fresh name.   Other subcastes may be composed
of bodies of persons who, having taken to trade and
prospered, obtained admission to the Bania caste through the
efforts of their Brāhman priests.   But a number of mixed
groups of the same character are also found among the Brāhmans and Rājpūts, and their existence does not invalidate
arguments derived from a consideration of the representative
subcastes.   It may be said that not only the Banias, but
many of the low castes have legends showing them to be of
Rājpūt descent of the same character as those quoted above ;
and since in their case these stories have been adjudged
spurious and worthless, no greater importance should be
attached to those of the Banias.   But it must be remembered
that in the case of the Banias the stories are reinforced by
the fact that the Bania subcastes certainly come from
Rājputāna ; no doubt exists that they are of high caste, and
that they must either be derived from Brāhmans or Rājpūts,
or themselves represent some separate foreign group ; but if
they are really the descendants of the Vaishyas, the main body
of the Aryan immigrants and the third of the four classical

castes, it might be expected that their legends would show some trace of this instead of being unitedly in favour of their Rājpūt origin.

Colonel Tod gives a catalogue of the eighty-four mercantile tribes, whom he states to be chiefly of Rājpūt descent.[1] In this list the Agarwāl, Oswāl, Srimāl, Khandelwāl, Palliwāl and Lād subcastes occur; while the Dhākar and Dhūsar subcastes may be represented by the names Dhākarwāl and Dusora in the lists. The other names given by Tod appear to be mainly small territorial groups of Rājputāna. Elsewhere, after speaking of the claims of certain towns in Rājputāna to be centres of trade, Colonel Tod remarks: "These pretensions we may the more readily admit, when we recollect that nine-tenths of the bankers and commercial men of India are natives of Mārudesh,[2] and these chiefly of the Jain faith. The Oswāls, so termed from the town of Osi, near the Luni, estimate one hundred thousand families whose occupation is commerce. All these claim a Rājpūt descent, a fact entirely unknown to the European inquirer into the peculiarities of Hindu manners."[3]

Similarly, Sir D. Ibbetson states that the Maheshri Banias claim Rājpūt origin and still have subdivisions bearing Rājpūt names.[4] Elliot also says that almost all the mercantile tribes of Hindustān are of Rājpūt descent.[5]

It would appear, then, that the Banias are an offshoot from the Rājpūts, who took to commerce and learnt to read and write for the purpose of keeping accounts. The Chārans or bards are another literate caste derived from the Rājpūts, and it may be noticed that both the Banias and Chārans or Bhāts have hitherto been content with the knowledge of their own rude Mārwāri dialect and evinced no desire for classical learning or higher English education. Matters are now changing, but this attitude shows that they have hitherto not desired education for itself but merely as an indispensable adjunct to their business.

Being literate, the Banias were not infrequently employed

---

[1] *Rājasthān*, i. pp. 76, 109.

[2] That is Mārwār. But perhaps the term here is used in the wider sense of Rājputāna.

[3] *Rājasthān*, ii. p. 145.

[4] *Punjab Census Report* (1881), p. 293.

[5] *Supplemental Glossary*, p. 110.

as ministers and treasurers in Rājpūt states. Forbes says, 7. Banias
in an account of an Indian court : " Beside the king stand the employed
warriors of Rājpūt race or, equally gallant in the field and in Rājpūt
wiser far in council, the Wānia (Bania) Muntreshwars, courts.
already in profession puritans of peace, and not yet drained
enough of their fiery Kshatriya blood. . . . It is remarkable that so many of the officers possessing high rank and
holding independent commands are represented to have
been Wānias."[1] Colonel Tod writes that Nunkurn, the
Kachhwāha chief of the Shekhāwat federation, had a
minister named Devi Das of the Bania or mercantile caste,
and, like thousands of that caste, energetic, shrewd and
intelligent.[2] Similarly, Muhāj, the Jādon Bhātti chief of
Jaisalmer, by an unhappy choice of a Bania minister, completed the demoralisation of the Bhātti state. This minister
was named Sarūp Singh, a Bania of the Jain faith and Mehta
family, whose descendants were destined to be the ex-
terminators of the laws and fortunes of the sons of Jaisal.[3]
Other instances of the employment of Bania ministers are to
be found in Rājpūt history. Finally, it may be noted that
the Banias are by no means the only instance of a mercantile
class formed from the Rājpūts. The two important trading
castes of Khatri and Bhātia are almost certainly of Rājpūt
origin, as is shown in the articles on those castes.

The Banias are divided into a large number of endo- 8. Sub-
gamous groups or subcastes, of which the most important castes.
have been treated in the annexed subordinate articles. The
minor subcastes, mainly formed by migration, vary greatly in
different provinces. Colonel Tod gave a list of eighty-four
in Rājputāna, of which eight or ten only can be identified in
the Central Provinces, and of thirty mentioned by Bhattachārya as the most common groups in northern India, about
a third are unknown in the Central Provinces. The origin
of such subcastes has already been explained. The main
subcastes may be classified roughly into groups coming from
Rājputāna, Bundelkhand and the United Provinces. The
leading Rājputāna groups are the Oswāl, Maheshri, Khandelwāl, Saitwāl, Srimāl and Jaiswāl. These groups are com-

---

[1] *Rāsmāla*, i. pp. 240, 243.
[2] *Rājasthān*, ii. p. 360.   [3] *Ibid.* ii. p. 240.

monly known as Mārwāri Bania or simply Mārwāri. The
Bundelkhand or Central India subcastes are the Gahoi,
Golapūrab, Asāti, Umre and Parwār ;[1] while the Agarwāl,
Dhusar, Agrahari, Ajudhiabāsi and others come from the
United Provinces. The Lād subcaste is from Gujarāt,
while the Lingāyats originally belonged to the Telugu and
Canarese country. Several of the subcastes coming from
the same locality will take food cooked without water from
each other, and occasionally two subcastes, as the Oswāl and
Khandelwāl, even food cooked with water or *katchi.* This
practice is seldom found in other good castes. It is probably due to the fact that the rules about food are less
strictly observed in Rājputāna.

**9. Hindu
and Jain
subcastes :
divisions
among
subcastes.**
Another classification may be made of the subcastes
according as they are of the Hindu or Jain religion ; the
important Jain subcastes are the Oswāl, Parwār, Golapūrab,
Saitwāl and Charnāgar, and one or two smaller ones, as the
Baghelwāl and Samaiya. The other subcastes are principally Hindu, but many have a Jain minority, and similarly
the Jain subcastes return a proportion of Hindus. The
difference of religion counts for very little, as practically all
the non-Jain Banias are strict Vaishnava Hindus, abstain
entirely from any kind of flesh meat, and think it a sin
to take animal life ; while on their side the Jains employ
Brāhmans for certain purposes, worship some of the local
Hindu deities, and observe the principal Hindu festivals.
The Jain and Hindu sections of a subcaste have consequently, as a rule, no objection to taking food together, and
will sometimes intermarry. Several of the important subcastes are subdivided into Bīsa and Dasa, or twenty and ten
groups. The Bīsa or twenty group is of pure descent, or
twenty carat, as it were, while the Dasas are considered
to have a certain amount of alloy in their family pedigree.
They are the offspring of remarried widows, and perhaps
occasionally of still more irregular unions. Intermarriage
sometimes takes place between the two groups, and families
in the Dasa group, by living a respectable life and marrying
well, improve their status, and perhaps ultimately get back

---

[1] The Parwārs probably belonged originally to Rājputāna ; see subordinate
article.

THE ELEPHANT-HEADED GOD GANPATI.

HIS CONVEYANCE IS A RAT, WHICH CAN BE SEEN AS A LITTLE BLOB BETWEEN HIS FEET.

into the Bīsa group. As the Dasas become more respectable
they will not admit to their communion newly remarried
widows or couples who have married within the prohibited
degrees, or otherwise made a *mésalliance*, and hence a third
inferior group, called the Pacha or five, is brought into
existence to make room for these.

Most subcastes have an elaborate system of exogamy. 10. Exo-
They are either divided into a large number of sections, gamy and
rules
or into a few *gotras*, usually twelve, each of which is further regulating
split up into subsections. Marriage can then be regulated marriage.
by forbidding a man to take a wife from the whole of his
own section or from the subsection of his mother, grandmothers and even greatgrandmothers. By this means the
union of persons within five or more degrees of relationship
either through males or females is avoided, and most Banias
prohibit intermarriage, at any rate nominally, up to five
degrees. Such practices as exchanging girls between
families or marrying two sisters are, as a rule, prohibited.
The *gotras* or main sections appear to be frequently named
after Brāhman Rīshis or saints, while the subsections have
names of a territorial or titular character.

There is generally no recognised custom of paying a 11. Mar-
bride- or bridegroom-price, but one or two instances of riage
customs.
its being done are given in the subordinate articles.
On the occasion of betrothal, among some subcastes, the
boy's father proceeds to the girl's house and presents her
with a *māla* or necklace of gold or silver coins or coral, and
a *mundri* or silver ring for the finger. The contract of
betrothal is made at the village temple and the caste-fellows
sprinkle turmeric and water over the parties. Before the
wedding the ceremony of Benaiki is performed ; in this the
bridegroom, riding on a horse, and the bride on a decorated
chair or litter, go round their villages and say farewell to
their friends and relations. Sometimes they have a procession in this way round the marriage-shed. Among the
Mārwāri Banias a *toran* or string of mango-leaves is stretched
above the door of the house on the occasion of a wedding
and left there for six months. And a wooden triangle with
figures perched on it to represent sparrows is tied over
the door. The binding portion of the wedding is the pro-

cession seven times round the marriage altar or post. In some Jain subcastes the bridegroom stands beside the post and the bride walks seven times round him, while he throws sugar over her head at each turn. After the wedding the couple are made to draw figures out of flour sprinkled on a brass plate in token of the bridegroom's occupation of keeping accounts. It is customary for the bride's family to give *sīdha* or uncooked food sufficient for a day's consumption to every outsider who accompanies the marriage party, while to each member of the caste provisions for two to five days are given. This is in addition to the evening feasts and involves great expense. Sometimes the wedding lasts for eight days, and feasts are given for four days by the bridegroom's party and four days by the bride's. It is said that in some places before a Bania has a wedding he goes before the caste *panchāyat* and they ask him how many people he is going to invite. If he says five hundred, they prescribe the quantity of the different kinds of provisions which he must supply. Thus they may say forty maunds (3200 lbs.) of sugar and flour, with butter, spices, and other articles in proportion. He says, 'Gentlemen, I am a poor man ; make it a little less' ; or he says he will give *gur* or cakes of raw cane sugar instead of refined sugar. Then they say, 'No, your social position is too high for *gur* ; you must have sugar for all purposes.' The more guests the host invites the higher is his social consideration ; and it is said that if he does not maintain this his life is not worth living. Sometimes the exact amount of entertainment to be given at a wedding is fixed, and if a man cannot afford it at the time he must give the balance of the feasts at any subsequent period when he has money ; and if he fails to do this he is put out of caste. The bride's father is often called on to furnish a certain sum for the travelling expenses of the bridegroom's party, and if he does not send this money they do not come. The distinctive feature of a Bania wedding in the northern Districts is that women accompany the marriage procession, and the Banias are the only high caste in which they do this. Hence a high-caste wedding party in which women are present can be recognised to be a Bania's. In the Marātha

Districts women also go, but here this custom obtains among other high castes. The bridegroom's party hire or borrow a house in the bride's village, and here they erect a marriage-shed and go through the preliminary ceremonies of the wedding on the bridegroom's side as if they were at home.

Polygamy is very rare among the Banias, and it is generally the rule that a man must obtain the consent of his first wife before taking a second one. In the absence of this precaution for her happiness, parents will refuse to give him their daughter. The remarriage of widows is nominally prohibited, but frequently occurs, and remarried widows are relegated to the inferior social groups in each subcaste as already described. Divorce is also said to be prohibited, but it is probable that women put away for adultery are allowed to take refuge in such groups instead of being finally expelled. *12. Polygamy and widow-marriage.*

The dead are cremated as a rule, and the ashes are thrown into a sacred river or any stream. The bodies of young children and of persons dying from epidemic disease are buried. The period of mourning must be for an odd number of days. On the third day a leaf plate with cooked food is placed on the ground where the body was burnt, and on some subsequent day a feast is given to the caste. Rich Banias will hire people to mourn. Widows and young girls are usually employed, and these come and sit before the house for an hour in the morning and sometimes also in the evening, and covering their heads with their cloths, beat their breasts and make lamentations. Rich men may hire as many as ten mourners for a period of one, two or three months. The Mārwāris, when a girl is born, break an earthen pot to show that they have had a misfortune ; but when a boy is born they beat a brass plate in token of their joy. *13. Disposal of the dead and mourning.*

Nearly all the Banias are Jains or Vaishnava Hindus. An account of the Jain religion has been given in a separate article, and some notice of the retention of Hindu practices by the Jains is contained in the subordinate article on Parwār Bania. The Vaishnava Banias no less than the Jains are strongly averse to the destruction of animal life, and will not kill any living thing. Their principal deity is the god Ganesh *14. Religion : the god Ganpati or Ganesh.*

or Ganpati, the son of Mahādeo and Pārvati, who is the god of good-luck, wealth and prosperity. Ganesh is represented in sculpture with the head of an elephant and riding on a rat, though the rat is now covered by the body of the god and is scarcely visible. He has a small body like a child's with a fat belly and round plump arms. Perhaps his body signifies that he is figured as a boy, the son of Pārvati or Gauri. In former times grain was the main source of wealth, and from the appearance of Ganesh it can be understood why he is the god of overflowing granaries, and hence of wealth and good fortune. The elephant is a sacred animal among Hindus, and that on which the king rides. To have an elephant was a mark of wealth and distinction among Banias, and the Jains harness the cars of their gods to elephants at their great *rath* or chariot festival. Gajpati or ' lord of elephants ' is a title given to a king ; Gajānand or ' elephant-faced ' is an epithet of the god Ganesh and a favourite Hindu name. Gajvīthi or the track of the elephant is a name of the Milky Way, and indicates that there is believed to be a divine elephant who takes this course through the heavens. The elephant eats so much grain that only a comparatively rich man can afford to keep one ; and hence it is easy to understand how the attribute of plenty or of wealth was associated with the divine elephant as his special characteristic. Similarly the rat is connected with overflowing granaries, because when there is much corn in a Hindu house or store-shed there will be many rats ; thus a multitude of rats implied a rich household, and so this animal too came to be a symbol of wealth. The Hindus do not now consider the rat sacred, but they have a tenderness for it, especially in the Marātha country. The more bigoted of them objected to rats being poisoned as a means of checking plague, though observation has fully convinced them that rats spread the plague ; and in the Bania hospitals, formerly maintained for preserving the lives of animals, a number of rats were usually to be found. The rat, in fact, may now be said to stand to Ganpati in the position of a disreputable poor relation. No attempt is made to deny his existence, but he is kept in the background as far as possible. The god Ganpati is also associated with wealth of grain through his parentage. He is the offspring of Siva or Mahādeo and his wife Devi or Gauri. Mahādeo is in this case probably taken in his beneficent character of the deified bull ; Devi in her most important aspect as the great mother-goddess is the earth, but as mother of Ganesh she is probably imagined in her special form of Gauri, the yellow one, that is, the yellow corn. Gauri is closely associated with Ganesh, and every Hindu bridal couple worship Gauri Ganesh together as an important rite of the wedding. Their conjunction in this manner lends colour to the idea that they are held to be mother and son. In Rājputāna Gauri is worshipped as the corn goddess at the Gangore festival about the time of the vernal equinox, especially by women. The meaning of Gauri, Colonel Tod states, is yellow, emblematic of the ripened harvest, when the votaries of the goddess adore her effigies, in the shape of a matron painted the colour of ripe corn. Here she is seen as Ana-pūrna (the corn-goddess), the benefactress of mankind. " The rites commence when the sun enters Aries (the opening of the Hindu year), by a deputation to a spot beyond the city to bring earth for the image of Gauri. A small trench is then excavated in which barley is sown ; the ground is irrigated and artificial heat supplied till the grain germinates, when the females join hands and dance round it, invoking the blessings of Gauri on their husbands. The young corn is then taken up, distributed and presented by the females to the men, who wear it in their turbans." [1] Thus if Ganesh is the son of Gauri he is the offspring of the bull and the growing corn ; and his genesis from the elephant and the rat show him equally as the god of full granaries, and hence of wealth and good fortune. We can understand therefore how he is the special god of the Banias, who formerly must have dealt almost entirely in grain, as coined money had not come into general use.

  At the Diwāli festival the Banias worship Ganpati or Ganesh, in conjunction with Lakshmi, the goddess of wealth. Lakshmi is considered to be the deified cow, and, as such, the other main source of wealth, both as mother of the bull, the tiller of the soil, and the giver of milk from which *ghī*

15. Diwāli festival.

[1] *Rājasthān*, i. p. 491.

(clarified butter) is made ; this is another staple of the Bania's trade, as well as a luxurious food, of which he is especially fond. At Diwāli all Banias make up their accounts for the year, and obtain the signatures of clients to their balances. They open fresh account-books, which they first worship and adorn with an image of Ganesh, and perhaps an invocation to the god on the front page. A silver rupee is also worshipped as an emblem of Lakshmi, but in some cases an English sovereign, as a more precious coin, has been substituted, and this is placed on the seat of the goddess and reverence paid to it. The Banias and Hindus generally think it requisite to gamble at Diwāli in order to bring good luck during the coming year ; all classes indulge in a little speculation at this season.

16. Holi festival.   In the month of Phāgun (February), about the time of the Holi, the Mārwāris make an image of mud naked, calling it Nāthu Rām, who was supposed to be a great Mārwāri. They mock at this and throw mud at it, and beat it with shoes, and have various jests and sports. The men and women are divided into two parties, and throw dirty water and red powder over each other, and the women make whips of cloth and beat the men. After two or three days, they break up the image and throw it away. The Banias, both Jain and Hindu, like to begin the day by going and looking at the god in his temple. This is considered an auspicious omen in the same manner as it is commonly held to be a good omen to see some particular person or class of person the first thing in the morning. Others begin the day by worshipping the sacred *tulsi* or basil.

17. Social customs : rules about food.   The Banias are very strict about food. The majority of them abstain from all kinds of flesh food and alcoholic liquor. The Kasarwānis are reported to eat the flesh of clean animals, and perhaps others of the lower subcastes may also do so, but the Banias are probably stricter than any other caste in their adherence to a vegetable diet. Many of them eschew also onions and garlic as impure food. Banias take the lead in the objection to foreign sugar on account of the stories told of the impure ingredients which it contains, and many of them, until recently, at any

MUD IMAGES, MADE BY WORSHIPPERS AT THE
HOLI FESTIVAL, AND AFTERWARDS DESTROYED.

rate, still adhered to Indian sugar. Drugs are not forbidden, but they are not usually addicted to them. Tobacco is forbidden to the Jains, but both they and the Hindus smoke, and their women sometimes chew tobacco. The Bania while he is poor is very abstemious, and it is said that on a day when he has made no money he goes supperless to bed. But when he has accumulated wealth, he develops a fondness for *ghī* or preserved butter, which often causes him to become portly. Otherwise his food remains simple, and as a rule he confined himself until recently to two daily meals, at midday and in the evening ; but Banias, like most other classes who can afford it, have now begun to drink tea in the morning. In dress the Bania is also simple, adhering to the orthodox Hindu garb of a long white coat and a loin-cloth. He has not yet adopted the cotton trousers copied from the English fashion. Some Banias in their shops wear only a cloth over their shoulders and another round their waist. The *kardora* or silver waist-belt is a favourite Bania ornament, and though plainly dressed in ordinary life, rich Mārwāris will on special festival occasions wear costly jewels. On his head the Mārwāri wears a small tightly folded turban, often coloured crimson, pink or yellow ; a green turban is a sign of mourning and also black, though the latter is seldom seen. The Banias object to taking the life of any animal. They will not castrate cattle even through their servants, but sell the young bulls and buy oxen. In Saugor, a Bania is put out of caste if he keeps buffaloes. It is supposed that good Hindus should not keep buffaloes nor use them for carting or ploughing, because the buffalo is impure, and is the animal on which Yama, the god of death, rides. Thus in his social observances generally the Bania is one of the strictest castes, and this is a reason why his social status is high. Sometimes he is even held superior to the Rājpūt, as the local Rājpūts are often of impure descent and lax in their observance of religious and social restrictions. Though he soon learns the vernacular language of the country where he settles, the Mārwāri usually retains his own native dialect in his account-books, and this makes it more difficult for his customers to understand them.

The Bania has a very distinctive caste character. From early boyhood he is trained to the keeping of accounts and to the view that it is his business in life to make money, and that no transaction should be considered successful or creditable which does not show a profit. As an apprentice, he goes through a severe training in mental arithmetic, so as to enable him to make the most intricate calculations in his head. With this object a boy commits to memory a number of very elaborate tables. For whole numbers he learns by heart the units from one to ten multiplied as high as forty times, and the numbers from eleven to twenty multiplied to twenty times. There are also fractional tables, giving the results of multiplying $\frac{1}{4}$, $\frac{1}{2}$, $\frac{3}{4}$, $1\frac{1}{4}$, $1\frac{1}{2}$, $2\frac{1}{2}$, and $3\frac{1}{2}$ into units from one to one hundred; interest-tables showing the interest due on any sum from one to one thousand rupees for one month, and for a quarter of a month at twelve per cent; tables of the squares of all numbers from one to one hundred, and a set of technical rules for finding the price of a part from the price of the whole.[1] The self-denial and tenacity which enable the Bania without capital to lay the foundations of a business are also remarkable. On first settling in a new locality, a Mārwāri Bania takes service with some shopkeeper, and by dint of the strictest economy puts together a little money. Then the new trader establishes himself in some village and begins to make grain advances to the cultivators on high rates of interest, though occasionally on bad security. He opens a shop and retails grain, pulses, condiments, spices, sugar and flour. From grain he gradually passes to selling cloth and lending money, and being keen and exacting, and having to deal with ignorant and illiterate clients, he acquires wealth; this he invests in purchasing villages, and after a time blossoms out into a big Seth or banker. The Bania can also start a retail business without capital. The way in which he does it is to buy a rupee's worth of stock in a town, and take it out early in the morning to a village, where he sits on the steps of the temple until he has sold it. Up till then he neither eats nor washes his face. He comes back in the evening after

[1] *Bombay Gazetteer, Hindus of Gujarāt*, p. 80.

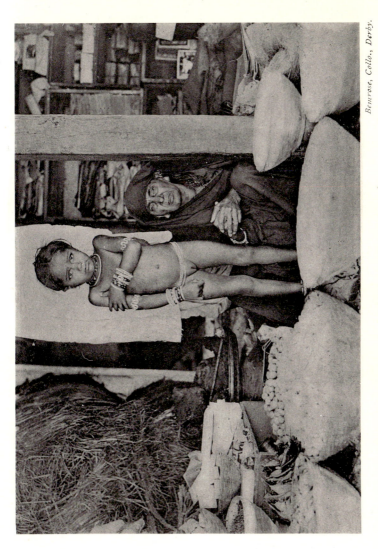

BANIA'S SHOP.

having eaten two or three pice worth of grain, and buys a
fresh stock, which he takes out to another village in the
morning. Thus he turns over his capital with a profit two
or three times a week according to the saying, "If a Bania
gets a rupee he will have an income of eight rupees a
month," or as another proverb pithily sums up the immigrant
Mārwārī's career, 'He comes with a *lota*[1] and goes back with
a lakh.' The Bania never writes off debts, even though his
debtor may be a pauper, but goes on entering them up year
by year in his account-books and taking the debtor's acknow-
ledgment. For he says, '*Purus Pārus*,' or man is like the
philosopher's stone, and his fortune may change any day.

The cultivators rarely get fair treatment from the Banias,
as the odds are too much against them. They must have
money to sow their land, and live while the crops are
growing, and the majority who have no capital are at the
moneylender's mercy. He is of a different caste, and often
of a different country, and has no fellow-feeling towards
them, and therefore considers the transaction merely from
the business point of view of getting as much profit as
possible. The debtors are illiterate, often not even understanding the meaning of figures, or the result of paying
compound interest at twenty-five or fifty per cent ; they can
neither keep accounts themselves nor check their creditor's.
Hence they are entirely in his hands, and in the end their
villages or land, if saleable, pass to him, and they decline
from landlord to tenant, or from tenant to labourer. They
have found vent for their feelings in some of the bitterest
sayings ever current : 'A man who has a Bania for a friend
has no need of an enemy.' 'Borrow from a Bania and you
are as good as ruined.' 'The rogue cheats strangers and
the Bania cheats his friends.' 'Kick a Bania even if he is
dead.' "His heart, we are told, is no bigger than a coriander
seed ; he goes in like a needle and comes out like a sword ;
as a neighbour he is as bad as a boil in the armpit. If a
Bania is on the other side of a river you should leave your
bundle on this side for fear he should steal it. If a Bania
is drowning you should not give him your hand ; he is
sure to have some pecuniary motive for drifting down-stream.

19. Dis-
like of the
cultivators
towards
him.

[1] The common brass drinking-vessel.

A Bania will start an auction in a desert. If a Bania's son tumbles down he is sure to pick up something. He uses light weights and swears that the scales tip up of themselves ; he keeps his accounts in a character that no one but God can read ; if you borrow from him your debt mounts up like a refuse-heap or gallops like a horse ; if he talks to a customer he debits the conversation in his accounts ; and when his own credit is shaky he writes up his transactions on the wall so that they can easily be rubbed out." [1]

20. His virtues. Nevertheless there is a good deal to be said on the other side, and the Bania's faults are probably to a large extent produced by his environment, like other people's. One of the Bania's virtues is that he will lend on security which neither the Government nor the banks would look at, or on none at all. Then he will always wait a long time for his money, especially if the interest is paid. No doubt this is no loss to him, as he keeps his money out at good interest ; but it is a great convenience to a client that his debt can be postponed in a bad year, and that he can pay as much as he likes in a good one. The village moneylender is indispensable to its economy when the tenants are like schoolboys in that money burns a hole in their pocket ; and Sir Denzil Ibbetson states that it is surprising how much reasonableness and honesty there is in his dealings with the people, so long as he can keep his transactions out of a court of justice.[2] Similarly, Sir Reginald Craddock writes : " The village Bania is a much-abused individual, but he is as a rule a quiet, peaceable man, a necessary factor in the village economy. He is generally most forbearing with his clients and customers, and is not the person most responsible for the indebtedness of the ryot. It is the casual moneylender with little or no capital who lives by his wits, or the large firms with shops and agents scattered over the face of the country who work the serious mischief. These latter encourage the people to take loans and discourage repayment until the debt has increased by accumulation of interest to a sum from which the borrower cannot easily free himself." [3]

---

[1] Sir H. H. Risley's *Peoples of India*, p. 127, and Appendix I. p. 8.
[2] *Punjab Census Report* (1881),
p. 291.
[3] *Nāgpur Settlement Report* (1900), para. 54.

The progress of administration, bringing with it easy
and safe transit all over the country ; the institution of a
complete system of civil justice and the stringent enforce-
ment of contracts through the courts ; the introduction of
cash coinage as the basis of all transactions ; and the grant
of proprietary and transferable rights in land, appear to have
at the same time enhanced the Bania's prosperity and
increased the harshness and rapacity of his dealings.   When
the moneylender lived in the village he had an interest in
the solvency of the tenants who constituted his clientèle and
was also amenable to public opinion, even though not of his
own caste.   For it would clearly be an impossibly unpleasant
position for him to meet no one but bitter enemies whenever
he set foot outside his house, and to go to bed in nightly
fear of being dacoited and murdered by a combination of
his next-door neighbours.   He therefore probably adopted
the motto of live and let live, and conducted his transactions
on a basis of custom, like the other traders and artisans who
lived among the village community.   But with the rise of
the large banking - houses whose dealings are conducted
through agents over considerable tracts of country, public
opinion can no longer act.   The agent looks mainly to his
principal, and the latter has no interest in or regard for the
cultivators of distant villages.   He cares only for his profit,
and his business is conducted with a single view to that end.
He himself has no public opinion to face, as he lives in a
town among a community of his caste-fellows, and here
absolutely no discredit is attached to grinding the faces of
the poor, but on the contrary the honour and consideration
accruing to him are in direct proportion to his wealth.   The
agent may have some compunction, but his first aim is to
please his principal, and as he is often a sojourner liable to
early transfer he cares little what may be said or thought
about him locally.

Again the introduction of the English law of contract
and transfer of property, and the increase in the habit of
litigation have greatly altered the character of the moneylending business for the worse.   The debtor signs a bond
sometimes not even knowing the conditions, more often
having heard them but without any clear idea of their effect

21. The money-lender changed for the worse.

22. The enforce-ment of contracts.

or of the consequences to himself, and as readily allows it to be registered. When it comes into court the witnesses, who are the moneylender's creatures, easily prove that it was a genuine and *bona fide* transaction, and the debtor is too ignorant and stupid to be able to show that he did not understand the bargain or that it was unconscionable. In any case the court has little or no power to go behind a properly executed contract without any actual evidence of fraud, and has no option but to decree it in terms of the deed. This evil is likely to be remedied very shortly, as the Government of India have announced a proposal to introduce the recent English Act and allow the courts the discretion to go behind contracts, and to refuse to decree exorbitant interest or other hard bargains. This urgently needed reform will, it may be hoped, greatly improve the character of the civil administration by encouraging the courts to realise that it is their business to do justice between litigants, and not merely to administer the letter of the law ; and at the same time it should have the result, as in England, of quickening the public conscience and that of the money-lenders themselves, which has indeed already been to some extent awakened by other Government measures, including the example set by the Government itself as a creditor.

23. Cash coinage and the rate of interest.   Again the free circulation of metal currency and its adoption as a medium for all transactions has hitherto been to the disadvantage of the debtors. Interest on money was probably little in vogue among pastoral peoples, and was looked upon with disfavour, being prohibited by both the Mosaic and Muhammadan codes. The reason was perhaps that in a pastoral community there existed no means of making a profit on a loan by which interest could be paid, and hence the result of usury was that the debtor ultimately became enslaved to his creditor ; and the enslavement of freemen on any considerable scale was against the public interest. With the introduction of agriculture a system of loans on interest became a necessary and useful part of the public economy, as a cultivator could borrow grain to sow land and support himself and his family until the crop ripened, out of which the loan, principal and interest, could be repaid. If, as seems likely, this was the first occasion

for the introduction of the system of loan-giving on a large scale, it would follow that the rate of interest would be based largely on the return yielded by the earth to the seed. Support is afforded to this conjecture by the fact that in the case of grain loans in the Central Provinces the interest on loans of grain of the crops which yield a comparatively small return, such as wheat, is twenty-five to fifty per cent, while in the case of those which yield a large return, such as juāri and kodon, it is one hundred per cent. These high rates of interest were not of much importance so long as the transaction was in grain. The grain was much less valuable at harvest than at seed time, and in addition the lender had the expense of storing and protecting his stock of grain through the year. It is probable that a rate of twenty-five per cent on grain loans does not yield more than a reasonable profit to the lender. But when in recent times cash came to be substituted for grain it would appear that there was no proportionate reduction in the interest. The borrower would lose by having to sell his grain for the payment of his debt at the most unfavourable rate after harvest, and since the transaction was by a regular deed the lender no longer took any share of the risk of a bad harvest, as it is probable that he was formerly accustomed to do. The rates of interest for cash loans afforded a disproportionate profit to the lender, who was put to no substantial expense in keeping money as he had formerly been in the case of grain. It is thus probable that rates for cash loans were for a considerable period unduly severe in proportion to the risk, and involved unmerited loss to the borrower. This is now being remedied by competition, by Government loans given on a large scale in time of scarcity, and by the introduction of co-operative credit. But it has probably contributed to expedite the transfer of land from the cultivating to the moneylending classes.

Lastly the grant of proprietary and transferable right to land has afforded a new incentive and reward to the success-ful moneylender. Prior to this measure it is probable that no considerable transfers of land occurred for ordinary debt. The village headman might be ousted for non-payment of revenue, or simply through the greed of some Government

24. Proprietary and transferable rights in land.

official under native rule, and of course the villages were continually pillaged and plundered by their own and hostile armies such as the Pindāris, while the population was periodically decimated by famine. But apart from their losses by famine, war and the badness of the central government, it is probable that the cultivators were held to have a hereditary right to their land, and were not liable to ejectment on the suit of any private person. It is doubtful whether they had any conception of ownership of the land, and it seems likely that they may have thought of it as a god or the property of the god ; but the cultivating castes perhaps had a hereditary right to cultivate it, just as the Chamār had a prescriptive right to the hides of the village cattle, the Kalār to the mahua-flowers for making his liquor, the Kumhār to clay for his pots, and the Teli to press the oil-seeds grown in his village. The inferior castes were not allowed to hold land, and it was probably never imagined that the village moneylender should by means of a piece of stamped paper be able to oust the cultivators indebted to him and take their land himself. With the grant of proprietary right to land such as existed in England, and the application of the English law of contract and transfer of property, a new and easy road to wealth was opened to the moneylender, of which he was not slow to take advantage. The Banias have thus ousted numbers of improvident proprietors of the cultivating castes, and many of them have become large landlords. A considerable degree of protection has now been afforded to landowners and cultivators, and the process has been checked, but that it should have proceeded so far is regrettable ; and the operation of the law has been responsible for a large amount of unintentional injustice to the cultivating castes and especially to proprietors of aboriginal descent, who on account of their extreme ignorance and improvidence most readily fall a prey to the moneylender.

25. The Bania as a landlord. As landlords the Banias were not at first a success. They did not care to spend money in improving their property, and ground their tenants to the utmost. Sir R. Craddock remarks of them :[1] " Great or small they are absolutely unfitted by their natural instincts to be landlords.

[1] *Nāgpur Settlement Report* (1900), para. 54.

Shrewdest of traders, most business-like in the matter of bargains, they are unable to take a broad view of the duties of landlord or to see that rack-renting will not pay in the long run."

Still, under the influence of education, and the growth of moral feeling, as well as the desire to stand well with Government officers and to obtain recognition in the shape of some honour, many of the Mārwāri proprietors are developing into just and progressive landlords. But from the cultivator's point of view, residence on their estates, which are managed by agents in charge of a number of villages for an absent owner, cannot compare with the system of the small cultivating proprietor resident among tenants of his own caste, and bound to them by ties of sympathy and caste feeling, which produces, as described by Sir R. Craddock, the ideal village.

As a trader the Bania formerly had a high standard of commercial probity. Even though he might show little kindliness or honesty in dealing with the poorer class of borrowers, he was respected and absolutely reliable in regard to money. It was not unusual for people to place their money in a rich Bania's hands without interest, even paying him a small sum for safe-keeping. Bankruptcy was considered disgraceful, and was visited with social penalties little less severe than those enforced for breaches of caste rules. There was a firm belief that a merchant's condition in the next world depended on the discharge of all claims against him. And the duty of paying ancestral debts was evaded only in the case of helpless or hopeless poverty. Of late, partly owing to the waning power of caste and religious feeling in the matter, and partly to the knowledge of the bankruptcy laws, the standard of commercial honour has greatly fallen. Since the case of bankruptcy is governed and arranged for by law, the trader thinks that so long as he can keep within the law he has done nothing wrong. A banker, when heavily involved, seldom scruples to become a bankrupt and to keep back money enough to enable him to start afresh, even if he does nothing worse. This, however, is probably a transitory phase, and the same thing has happened in England and America at one stage of commercial development. In time it may be expected that the loss of the old

26. Commercial honesty.

religious and caste feeling will be made good by a new standard of commercial honour enforced by public opinion among merchants generally. The Banias are very good to their own caste, and when a man is ruined will have a general subscription and provide funds to enable him to start afresh in a small way. Beggars are very rare in the caste. Rich Mārwāris are extremely generous in their subscriptions to objects of public utility, but it is said that the small Bania is not very charitably inclined, though he doles out handfuls of grain to beggars with fair liberality. But he has a system by which he exacts from those who deal with him a slight percentage on the price received by them for religious purposes. This is called Deodān or a gift to God, and is supposed to go into some public fund for the construction or maintenance of a temple or similar object. In the absence of proper supervision or audit it is to be feared that the Bania inclines to make use of it for his private charity, thus saving himself expense on that score. The system has been investigated by Mr. Napier, Commissioner of Jubbulpore, with a view to the application of these funds to public improvements.

Bania, Agarwāla, Agarwāl.—This is generally considered to be the highest and most important subdivision of the Banias. They numbered about 25,000 persons in the Central Provinces in 1911, being principally found in Jubbulpore and Nāgpur. The name is probably derived from Agroha, a small town in the Hissār District of the Punjab, which was formerly of some commercial importance. Buchanan records that when any firm failed in the city each of the others contributed a brick and five rupees, which formed a stock sufficient for the merchant to recommence trade with advantage. The Agarwālas trace their descent from a Rāja Agar Sen, whose seventeen sons married the seventeen daughters of Bāsuki, the king of the Nāgas or snakes. Elliot considers that the snakes were really the Scythian or barbarian immigrants, the Yueh-chi or Kushāns, from whom several of the Rājpūt clans as the Tāk, Haihāyas and others, who also have the legend of snake ancestry, were probably derived. Elliot also remarks that Rāja Agar Sen, being a king, must have been a Kshatriya, and thus according to the legend the Agarwālas would have Rājpūt ancestry on both sides. Their appearance, Mr. Crooke states, indicates good race and breeding, and would lend colour to the theory of a Rājpūt origin. Rāja Agar Sen is said to have ruled over both Agra and Agroha, and it seems possible that the name of the Agarwālas may also be connected with Agra, which is a much more important place than Agroha. The country round Agra and Delhi is their home, and the shrine of the tutelary goddess of some of the Agarwālas in the Central Provinces is near Delhi. The memory of the Nāga princess who was their ancestor is still, Sir H. Risley states, held in honour by the Agarwālas, and they say, ' Our mother's house is of the race of the snake.' [1] No Agarwāla, whether Hindu or Jain, will kill or molest a snake, and the Vaishnava Agarwālas of Delhi paint pictures of snakes on either side of the outside doors of their houses, and make offerings of fruit and flowers before them.

In the Central Provinces, like other Bania subcastes, they are divided into the Bīsa and Dasa or twenty and ten subdivisions, which marry among themselves. The Bīsa rank higher than the Dasa, the latter being considered to have some flaw in their pedigree, such as descent from a remarried widow. The Dasas are sometimes said to be the descendants of the maidservants who accompanied the seventeen Nāga or snake princesses on their marriages to the sons of Rāja Agar Sen. A third division has now come into existence in the Central Provinces, known as the Pacha or fives; these are apparently of still more doubtful origin than the Dasas. The divisions tend to be endogamous, but if a man of the Bīsa or Dasa cannot obtain a wife from his own group he will sometimes marry in a lower group.

The Agarwālas are divided into seventeen and a half *gotras* or exogamous sections, which are supposed to be descended from the seventeen sons of Rāja Agar Sen. The extra half *gotra* is accounted for by a legend, but it probably has in reality also something to do with illegitimate descent. Some of the *gotras*, as given by Mr. Crooke, are as a matter of fact named after Brāhmanical saints like those of the

[1] *Tribes and Castes of Bengal,* art. Agarwāla.

Brāhmans ; instances of these are Garga, Gautama, Kaushika, Kasyapa and Vasishtha ; the others appear to be territorial or titular names. The prohibitions on marriage between relations are far-reaching among the Agarwālas. The detailed rules are given in the article on Bania, and the effect is that persons descended from a common ancestor cannot intermarry for five generations. When the wedding procession is about to start the Kumhār brings his donkey and the bridegroom has to touch it with his foot, or, according to one version, ride upon it. The origin of this custom is obscure, but the people now say that it is meant to emphasise the fact that the bridegroom is going to do a foolish thing. The remarriage of widows is prohibited, and divorce is not recognised. Most of the Agarwālas are Vaishnava by religion, but a few are Jains. Intermarriage between members of the two religions is permitted in some localities, and the wife adopts that of her husband. The Jain Agarwālas observe the Hindu festivals and employ Brāhmans for their ceremonies. In Nimār the caste have some curious taboos. It is said that a married woman may not eat wheat until a child has been born to her, but only juāri ; and if she has no child she may not eat wheat all her life. If a son is born to her she must go to Mahaur, a village near Delhi where the tutelary goddess of the caste has her shrine. This goddess is called Mohna Devi, and she is the deified spirit of a woman who burnt herself with her husband. After this the woman may eat wheat ; but if a second son is born she must stop eating wheat until she has been to the shrine again. But if she has a daughter she may at once and always eat wheat without visiting the shrine. These rules, as well as the veneration of a snake, from which they believe themselves to be descended on the mother's side, may perhaps, as suggested by Sir H. Risley, be a relic of the system of matriarchal descent. It is said that when Rāja Agar Sen or his sons married the Nāga princesses, he obtained permission as a special favour from the goddess Lakshmi that the children should bear their father's name and not their mother's.[1]

In Nimār some Agarwālas worship Goba Pīr, the god of

[1] *Tribes and Castes of Bengal*, art. Agarwāla.

the sweepers. He is represented by a pole some 30 feet
long on which are hung a cloth and cocoanuts. The
sweepers carry this through the city almost daily during
the month of Shrāwan (July), and people offer cocoanuts,
tying them on to the pole. Some Agarwālas offer vermilion
to the god in token of worship, and a few invite it to the
compounds of their houses and keep it there all night for
the same purpose. When a feast is given in the caste
the Agarwālas do not take their own brass vessels according to the usual practice, but the host gives them little
earthen pots to drink from which are afterwards broken,
and leaf-plates for their food. The Agarwālas will take
food cooked without water (*pakki*) from Oswāl, Maheshri
and Khandelwāl Banias. The Agarwālas of the Central
Provinces hold some substantial estates in Chhattīsgarh ;
these were obtained at the first settlements during 1860–70,
when considerable depression existed, and many of the
village headmen were unwilling to accept the revenue
assessed on their villages. The more enterprising Banias
stepped in and took them, and have profited enormously
owing to the increase in the value of land. Akbar's great
minister, Todar Mal, who first introduced an assessment of
the land-revenue based on the measurement and survey of
the land, is said to have been an Agarwāla.

Bania, Agrahari.[1]—This subcaste numbered nearly 2000
persons in 1911, resident principally in Jubbulpore, Raipur
and Bilāspur, and some of the Feudatory States. Mr.
Crooke states that they claim partly a Vaishya and partly
a Brāhmanical descent, and wear the sacred thread. Like
that of the Agarwāla Banias their name has been connected with the cities of Agra and Agroha. There is
no doubt that they are closely connected with the Agarwālas, and Mr. Nesfield suggests that the two groups must
have been sections of one and the same caste which
quarrelled on some trifling matter connected with cooking
or eating, and have remained separate ever since. The
Agrahari Banias are Hindus, and some of them belong to

[1] The information on this subcaste is taken from Mr. Crooke's article on it
in his *Tribes and Castes*.

the Nānakpanthi sect. They are principally dealers in provisions, and they have acquired some discredit as compared with their kinsfolk the Agarwālas, through not secluding their women and allowing them to attend the shop. They also retail various sweet-smelling woods which are used in religious ceremonies, such as aloe-wood and sandalwood, besides a number of medicines and simples. The richer members of the caste are bankers, dealers in grain and pawnbrokers.

Bania, Ajudhiabāsi, Audhia.—A subcaste of Bania, whose name signifies a resident of Ajodhia, the old name of Oudh. Outsiders often shorten the name to Audhia, but, as will be seen, the name Audhia is regularly applied to a criminal class, who may have been derived from the Ajudhiabāsi Banias, but are now quite distinct from them. The Ajudhiabāsis numbered nearly 2000 persons in 1911, belonging chiefly to the Jubbulpore, Narsinghpur and Hoshangābād Districts. This total includes any persons who may have returned themselves as Audhia. The Ajudhiabāsis are nearly all Hindus with a small Jain minority. Though Oudh was their original home they are now fairly numerous in Cawnpore and Bundelkhand as well, and it may have been from this last locality that they entered the Central Provinces. Here they form a separate endogamous group and do not marry with their caste-fellows in northern India. They have exogamous sections, and marriage is prohibited within the section and also between first cousins. They permit the remarriage of widows, but are said not to recognise divorce, and to expel from the caste a woman guilty of adultery. It may be doubted, however, whether this is correct. Brāhmans serve as their priests, and they invest boys with the sacred thread either at marriage or at a special ceremony known as Gurmukh. The dead are either buried or burnt; in the case of burial men are laid on the face and women on the back, the body being first rubbed with salt, clarified butter, turmeric and milk. A little earth from the grave is carried away and thrown into a sacred river, and when the dead are burnt the ashes are similarly disposed of.

Their principal deity is the goddess Devi, and at the Dasahra festival they offer a goat to her, the flesh of which is distributed among members of the caste.

The Audhias are a well-known criminal tribe, whose headquarters is in the Fatehpur District. They say that they are Banias, and use the name Ajudhiabāsi in speaking of themselves, and from their customs and criminal methods it seems not unlikely that they may originally have been an offshoot from the Ajudhiabāsi Banias. They are now, however, perfectly distinct from this group, and any confusion between them would be very unjust to the latter. In northern India it is said that the Audhias deal largely in counterfeit coin and false jewellery, and never commit crimes of violence;[1] but in Bombay they have taken to housebreaking, though they usually select an empty house.[2] From their homes in the United Provinces they wander over Central India, the Central Provinces, Bengal and Bombay; they are said to avoid the Punjab and Sind owing to difficulties of working, and they have made it a caste offence to commit any crime in the Ganges-Jumna Doāb, probably because this is their home. It is said also that if any one of them is imprisoned he is put out of caste. They wander about disguised as religious mendicants, Brāhmans or Bairāgis. They carry their bedding tied on their back with a cloth, and a large bag slung over the shoulders which contains food, cooking-vessels and other articles. Sometimes they pretend to be Banias and hawk about sweets and groceries, or one of the gang opens a shop, which serves as a rendezvous and centre for collecting information.[3] In the Districts where they reside they are perfectly well-behaved. They are well-to-do and to all appearance respectable in their habits. Their women are well-dressed with plenty of ornaments on their persons. They have no apparent means of support; they neither cultivate land nor trade; and all that appears on the surface is that most of the men and boys go off after the rains and return at the end of

[1] Mr. Crooke's *Tribes and Castes*, art. Audhia.
[2] Kennedy's *Criminal Classes of the*
Bombay Presidency, art. Audhia.
[3] Kennedy, *ibidem*.

the cold weather. If asked how they support themselves they reply by begging. Their marriage rules are those of high-caste Hindus. They are divided into two classes, Unch or high and Nīch or low, the former being of pure blood, and the latter the descendants of kept women. These are practically endogamous. A man may not have more than two wives. If a girl is detected in immorality before marriage, she is permanently excommunicated, and a married woman can be turned out by her husband on proof of adultery. A bridegroom-price is usually paid, the father of the bride visiting the bridegroom and giving him the money in secret. The dead are burnt, and Brāhmans are duly fed. If a man has died through an accident or from cholera, smallpox, poison or leprosy, the corpse, if available, is at once consigned to the Ganges or other river, and during the course of the next twelve months a Mahābrāhman is paid to make an image of the deceased in gram-flour, which is cremated with the usual rites. As in the case of the Ajudhiabāsi Banias, the tribal deity of the Audhias is the goddess Devi.[1]

Bania, Asāthi.—This subcaste numbers about 2500 persons in the Central Provinces, belonging principally to the Damoh and Jubbulpore Districts. They say that their original home was the Tīkamgarh State in Bundelkhand. They do not rank very high, and are sometimes said to be the descendants of an Ahīr who became a Bania. The great bulk are Hindus and a small minority Jains. It is told of the Asāthis that they first bury their dead, in accordance presumably with a former practice, and then exhume and burn the bodies ; and there is a saying—

> *Ārdha jale, ārdha gare*
> *Jinka nām Asāthi pare,*

or, ' He who is an Asāthi is half buried and half burnt.' But this practice, if it ever really existed, has now been abandoned.

Bania, Charnāgri, Channāgri, Samaiya.—The Charnāgris are a small Jain subcaste which numbered about 2500

---

[1] Mr. Crooke's *Tribes and Castes*, art. Audhia.

persons in 1911, residing principally in the Damoh and
Chhīndwāra Districts.   They are the followers of one Taran
Swāmi, who is said to have lived about five centuries ago.
He preached against the worship of the images of the Jain
Tirthakārs, and said that this should be abandoned and only
the sacred books be revered.   The chief sacred place of the
sect is Malhārgarh in Gwalior State ; here the tomb of their
prophet is situated and there is also a large temple in
which the Jain scriptures are enshrined.   In the month of
Phāgun (February) a fair is held here, and Charnāgris dance
in the temples, holding lighted lamps in their hands.
Nowadays the Charnāgris also visit the ordinary Jain
temples when their own are not available.   They are
practically all derived from Parwār Banias, and formerly
would sometimes give their daughters to Parwārs in marriage,
but this practice is said to have stopped.   Like other
Bania subcastes, they are divided into Bīsa and Dasa, or
twenty and ten sections, the Dasa being of irregular descent.
Intermarriage between the two sections occasionally occurs,
and the Dasa will take food from the Bīsa section, but the
latter do not reciprocate except at caste feasts.

Bania, Dhūsar, Bhārgava Dhūsar.—The origin of this
group is much disputed.   They are usually classed as a
subcaste of Bania, but claim to be Brāhmans.   They take
their name from a hill called Dhūsi or Dhosi, near Narnaul
on the border of Alwar State.   The title Bhārgava signifies a
descendant of Bhrigu, one of the famous eponymous Rīshis
or Brāhmanical saints, to whom Manu confided his institutes,
calling him his son.   If this was their original name, it
would show that they were Brāhmans, but its adoption
appears to be somewhat recent.   Their claim to be
Brāhmans is, however, admitted by many members of that
caste, and it is stated that they perform the functions of
Brāhmans in their original home in Rājputāna.   Mr. Burn
wrote of them :[1] " In his book on castes published in 1872
Mr. Sherring does not refer to any claim to kinship with
Brāhmans, though in his description of Dhūsar Banias he
appears to include the people under consideration.   Both

[1] *United Provinces Census Report* (1901), p. 220.

the Dhūsar Bhārgavas and Dhūsar Banias assert that Himu, the capable Vazīr of Muhammad Shāh Suri, belonged to their community, and such a claim by the former is if anything in favour of the view that they are not Brāhmans, since Himu is variously described by Muhammadan writers as a corn-chandler, a weighman and a Bania. Colonel Dow in his history of Hindustān calls him a shopkeeper who was raised by Sher Shāh to be Superintendent of Markets. It is not improbable that Himu's success laid the foundation for a claim to a higher position, but the matter does not admit of absolute proof, and I have therefore accepted the decision of the majority of the caste - committees and considered them as a caste allied to Brāhmans." In the Punjab the Dhūsars appear to be in some places Brāhmans and in others Banias. " They take their food before morning prayer, contrary to the Hindu rule, but of late years they have begun to conform to the orthodox practice. The Brāhman Dhūsar marries with his caste-fellows and the Bania with Banias, avoiding always the same family (*gotra*) or one having the same family deity." [1] From the above accounts it would appear that the Dhūsars may have originally been a class of Brāhmans who took to trade, like the Palliwāl Brāhmans of Mārwār, and have lost their position as Brāhmans and become amalgamated with the Bania caste ; or they may have been Banias, who acted as priests to others of the community, and hence claimed to be Brāhmans. The caste is important and influential, and is now making every effort to recover or substantiate its Brāhman status. One writer states that they combine the office aptitude and hard-heartedness to a debtor characteristic of the Bania. The Dhūsars are rigid in the maintenance of the purity of their order and in the performance of Hindu ceremonies and duties, and neither eat meat nor drink any kind of spirit. In Delhi they were distinguished for their talent as singers, and cultivated a peculiar strain or measure, in which they were unsurpassed. [2] In the Central Provinces the Dhūsars are a flourishing body, their leaders being Rai Bahādur Bihāri Lāl Khizānchi of Jubbulpore and Rai Sāhib

[1] Atkinson, *Himalayan Gazetteer*, article Dhūsar.
ii. p. 473, quoted in Mr. Crooke's   [2] Sherring, *Hindu Castes*, i. p. 293.

Seth Sundar Lāl of Betūl. They have founded the Bhārgava bank of Jubbulpore, and shown considerable public spirit ; to the latter gentleman's generosity a large part of the success of the recent debt-conciliation proceedings in the Betūl District must be attributed.

Bania, Dosar, Dūsra.[1]—This subcaste numbers about 600 persons. The original name is Dūsra or second, and the Dosar or Dūsra are a section of the Ummar Banias, who were so called because they permit widows to make a second marriage. Their home is the Ganges-Jumna Doāb and Oudh, and in the United Provinces they are classed as an inferior subcaste of the Ummars. Here they say that the Ummars are their elder brothers. In the Central Provinces they are said to be forming three local endogamous groups according as their homes were in the Doāb, Oudh or the Allahābād country ; and members of each of these marry among themselves. The Dosars say that they all belong to the Kashyap[2] *gotra* or clan, but for the purpose of marriage they have territorial or titular exogamous sections ; instances of these are Gangapāri, a native of Oudh ; Sāgarah, a resident of Saugor ; Makraha, a seller of *makka* or maize, and Tamākhuha, a tobacco-seller. They pay a bridegroom-price, the full recognised amount of which is Rs. 211, either in cash or brass cooking-vessels. Those who cannot afford this sum give half of it or Rs. 105, and the poorest classes pay anything they can afford. The Dosars are Vaishnava Hindus and employ Sanādhya Brāhmans as their priests. These Brāhmans will take food without water from their clients, but they are an inferior class and are looked down upon by other Brāhmans. The caste are mainly shop-keepers, and they deal in gold and silver ornaments, as well as grain, tobacco and all kinds of groceries.

Bania, Gahoi.[3]—This Hindu subcaste numbered nearly 7000 persons in 1911, belonging principally to the Saugor,

---

[1] This account is based on a paper furnished by Mr. Jeorākhan Lāl, Deputy Inspector of Schools, Bilāspur.

[2] Kashyap was a Brāhman saint,

but the name is perhaps derived from Kachhap, a tortoise.

[3] This article is mainly based on a paper by Mr. Pancham Lāl, Nāib-Tahsīldār Sihora.

Jubbulpore and Narsinghpur Districts. Their home is the Bundelkhand country, which these Districts adjoin, and they say that their original headquarters was at Kharagpur in Bundelkhand, whence they have spread over the surrounding country. They tell a curious story of their origin to the effect that once upon a time there was a certain schoolmaster, one Biya Pānde Brāhman, who could foretell the future. One day he was in his school with his boys when he foresaw that there was about to be an earthquake. He immediately warned his boys to get out of the building, and himself led the way. Only twelve of the boys had followed, and the others were still hesitating, when the earthquake began, the school fell in, and they were all buried in the ruins. The schoolmaster formed the boys who had escaped into one caste, calling them Gahoi, which is supposed to mean that which is left or the residue ; and he determined that he and his descendants would be the priests of the new caste. At the weddings of the Gahois an image of the schoolmaster is painted on the house wall, and the bridegroom worships it with offerings of butter and flowers. The story indicates clearly that the Gahois are of mixed descent from several castes.

The subcaste has twelve *gotras* or sections, and seventy-two *al* or *ānken*, which are subsections of the *gotras*. Several of the *al* names appear to be of a titular or totemistic character, as Mor peacock, Sohania beautiful, Nagaria a drummer, Pahāria a hillman, Matele the name of a village headman in Bundelkhand, Piparvānia from the pīpal tree, Dadaria a singer. The rule of exogamy is said to be that a man must not marry in his own *gotra* nor in the *al* of his mother or either grandmother.[1] Their weddings are held only at the bride's house, no ceremonies being performed at the bridegroom's ; at the ceremony the bridegroom stands in the centre of the shed by the marriage-post and the bride walks seven times round him. At their weddings the Gahois still use the old rupees of the Nāgpur kingdom for presents and payments to menials, and they hoard them up, when they can get them, for this special purpose. The rupee is sacred with the Bania, and this is an instance of the preservation of old accessories for religious ceremonies

---

[1] Mr. Crooke's *Tribes and Castes*, art. Gahoi.

when they have been superseded in ordinary use.   Polygamy
is permitted, but is rare.   The Gahois employ Bhārgava
Brāhmans for their priests, and these are presumably the
descendants of the schoolmaster who founded the caste.
At the thirteenth-day feast after a death the Brāhmans
must be fed first before the members of the caste.   On this
occasion thirteen brass or earthen vessels are filled with
flour, and a piece of money, and presented to thirteen
Brāhmans, while the family priest receives a bed and piece
of cloth.   The priests are said to be greedy, and to raise
quarrels over the value of the presents given to them.   At
the Diwāli festival the Gahois worship the implements of
their trade, pen and ink, and their account-books.   The
Gahois are Vaishnava Hindus, and abstain from all flesh
and alcoholic liquor.   They trade in grain and groceries,
and are bankers and moneylenders.   They are considered
to be cunning in business, and a proverb says that a Gahoi
will deceive even his own father.

Bania, Golapūrab, Golahre.—This Jain subcaste num-
bers about 6000 persons in the Central Provinces, and
belongs mainly to the Saugor, Damoh and Narsinghpur
Districts.   Its distribution is nearly the same as that of the
Gahois, and it is probably also a Bundelkhand group.   The
Golapūrabs are practically all Digambari Jains with a small
Hindu minority.   In some localities they intermarry with
Parwār Banias who are also Digambari Jains ; and they will
take food cooked without water from the Nema subcaste who
are Hindus.   According to one story the Golapūrabs were
the offspring of a Pūrabia, that is probably a Bais Rājpūt, by
a kept woman of the Ahīr caste.   This fits in very well with
the name, as Golak means a bastard, and the termination
pūrab would be from Pūrabia ; but it is probably the name
which has given rise to the story, or at any rate to the supposed descent from a Pūrabia.   In the United Provinces a
small subcaste of Bania called Golahre exists, belonging to
the Jhānsi District, that is the country of the Golapūrabs,
and Jain by religion.   There is no doubt that this group is
the same as the Golapūrabs, and Mr. Crooke derives[1] the

---

[1] *Tribes and Castes*, art. Golahre.

name from *gola*, a grain-mart, which seems more probable than the derivation suggested above. But it is an interesting fact that there is also a caste of cultivators called Golapūrab in the United Provinces, found only in the Agra District. It is suggested that these people are the illegitimate offspring of Sanādhya Brāhmans, with whom they appear to be closely connected. From their sept-names, however, which include those of several Rājpūt clans and also some titular terms of a low-caste type, Mr. Crooke thinks their Brāhmanical origin improbable. It is noticeable that these Golapūrabs though a cultivating caste have, like the Banias, a subcaste called Dasa, comprising persons of irregular descent; they also prohibit the remarriage of widows, and abstain from all flesh and from onions and garlic. Such customs are peculiar in a cultivating caste, and resemble those of Banias. It seems possible that a detailed investigation might give ground for supposing that both the Golahre and Golapūrab subcastes of Banias in the United and Central Provinces respectively are connected with this cultivating caste of Golapūrabs. The latter might have abandoned the Jain religion on taking to cultivation, as a Jain cannot well drive the plough, which involves destruction of animal life; or the Bania section might have adopted Jainism in order to obtain a better social position and differentiate themselves from the cultivators. Unfortunately no detailed information about the Golapūrabs of the Central Provinces is available, from which the probability or otherwise of this hypothesis could be tested.

Bania, Kasarwāni.[1]—This Hindu subcaste numbers about 6500 persons in the Central Provinces, who belong mainly to Saugor, Jubbulpore and the three Chhattīsgarh Districts. The name is probably derived from *kānsa*, bell-metal, as these Banias retail brass and bell-metal vessels. The Kasarwānis may therefore not improbably be an occupational group formed from persons who engaged in the trade, and in that case they may be wholly or partly derived from the Kasārs and Tameras, the castes which work in brass, copper

---

[1] The above notice is partly based on a paper by Mr. Sant Prasād, schoolmaster, Nāndgaon.

and bell-metal. The Kasarwānis are numerous in Allahābād
and Mīrzāpur, and they may have come to Chhattīsgarh
from Mīrzāpur, attracted by the bell-metal industries in
Ratanpur and Drūg. In Saugor and also in the United
Provinces they say that they came from Kara Mānikpur
several generations ago. If the selling of metal vessels was
their original calling, many, or the majority of them, have
now abandoned it, and deal in grain and groceries, and lend
money like other Banias. The Kasarwānis do not observe
the same standard of strictness as the good Bania subcastes
in their social rules. They eat the flesh of goats, sheep,
birds and fish, though they abstain from liquor. They
permit the remarriage of widows and divorce ; and women
who have been divorced can marry again in the caste by the
same rite as widows. They also allow the exchange of girls
in marriage between two families. They do not as a rule
wear the sacred thread. Their priests are Sarwaria Brāhmans,
and these Brāhmans and a few Bania subcastes, such as the
Agarwālas, Umres and Gahois, can take food cooked
without water from them, but other Brāhmans and Rājpūts
will not take any kind of food. Matches are arranged in
the presence of the head of the caste *panchāyat*, who is known
as Chaudhri. The parents on each side give their consent,
and in pledge of it six pice (farthings) are taken from both
of them, mixed together and given to their family priests
and barbers, four pice to the priests and two to the barbers.
The following is a local derivation of the name ; the word
kasar means more or the increase, and *bhata* means less ;
and *Hamāra kya kasar bhata?* means 'How does my
account stand ?' Hence Kasarbāni is one who keeps
accounts, that is a Bania.

Bania, Kasaundhan.—This subcaste numbers about 5500
persons in the Central Provinces and is returned principally
from the Bilāspur, Raipur and Jubbulpore Districts. The
name is derived [1] by Mr. Crooke from *kānsa*, bell-metal, and
dhana, wealth, and it would appear that the Kasaundhans
like the Kasārwanis are an occupational group, made up of
shopkeepers who dealt in metal vessels. Like them also the

[1] *Tribes and Castes*, art. Kasaundhan.

Kasaundhans may have originally been constituted from the metal-working castes, and indeed they may be only a local branch of the Kasarwānis, though no information is available which would decide this point. In the United Provinces both the Kasarwānis and Kasaundhans are divided into the Pūrbia or eastern and Pachhaiyān or western subcastes. Dharam Das, the great disciple of Kabīr, who founded the Kabīrpanthi sect in the Central Provinces, was a Kasaundhan Bania, and the Kabīrpanthi Mahants or high-priests of Kawardha are of this caste. It is probable that a good many of the Kasaundhan Banias in Bilāspur and Raipur belong to the Kabīrpanthi sect. The remainder are ordinary Hindus.

Bania, Khandelwāl.—This subcaste numbers about 1500 persons in the Central Provinces ; they are most numerous in the Hoshangābād and Amraoti Districts, but are scattered all over the Province. They take their name from the town of Khandela in the Jaipur State of Rājputāna, which was formerly the capital of the Shekhāwati federation. There is also a Khandelwāl subcaste of the Brāhman caste, found in the United Provinces.[1] Mr. Bhattachārya says of them :[2] " The Khandelwāl Banias are not inferior to any other division of the caste either in wealth or refinement. There are both Vaishnavites and Jains among them, and the Vaishnavite Khandelwāls wear the sacred thread. The millionaire Seths of Mathura are Khandelwāl Banias."

Bania, Lād.—This subcaste numbers about 5000 persons in the Central Provinces, being settled in Nimār, Nāgpur and all the Berār Districts. The Lād Banias came from Gujarāt, and Lād is derived from Lāt-desh, the old name for Gujarāt. Like other Banias they are divided into the Bīsa and Dasa groups or twenties and tens, the Dasa being of irregular descent. Their family priests are Khedāwal Brāhmans, and their caste deity is Ashāpuri of Ashnai, near Petlād. Lād women, especially those of Baroda, are noted for their taste in dress. The Lād Banias are Hindus of the Vallabhachārya

---

[1] Mr. Crooke's *Tribes and Castes*, art. Khandelwāl.
[2] *Hindu Castes and Sects*, p. 209.

sect, who worship Krishna, and were formerly addicted to sexual indulgence.[1]

Bania, Lingāyat.—The Lingāyat Banias number nearly 8000 persons in the Central Provinces, being numerous in Wardha, Nāgpur and all the Berār Districts. A brief account of the Lingāyat sect has been given in a separate article. The Lingāyat Banias form a separate endogamous group, and they do not eat or intermarry either with other Banias or with members of other castes belonging to the Lingāyat sect. But they retain the name and occupation of Banias. They have five subdivisions, Pancham, Dikshāwant, Chilliwant, Takalkar and Kanade. The Pancham or Panchamsālis are the descendants of the original Brāhman converts to the Lingāyat sect. They are the main body of the community and are initiated by what is known as the eightfold sacrament or *eshta-varna*. The Dikshāwant, from *diksha* or initiation, are a subdivision of the Panchamsālis, who apparently initiate disciples like the Dikshit Brāhmans. The Takalkar are said to take their name from a forest called Takali, where their first ancestress bore a child to the god Siva. The Kanade are from Canara. The meaning of the term Chilliwant is not known; it is said that a member of this subcaste will throw away his food or water if it is seen by any one who is not a Lingāyat, and they shave the whole head. The above form endogamous subcastes. The Lingāyat Banias also have exogamous groups, the names of which are mainly titular, of a low-caste type. Instances of them are Kaode, from *kawa* a crow, Teli an oil-seller, Thubri a dwarf, Ubadkar an incendiary, Gudkari a sugar-seller and Dhāmankar from Dhāmangaon. They say that the *maths* or exogamous groups are no longer regarded, and that marriage is now prohibited between persons having the same surname. It is stated that if a girl is not married before adolescence she is finally expelled from the caste, but this rule has probably become obsolete. The proposal for marriage comes from either the boy's or girl's party, and sometimes the bridegroom receives a small sum for his travelling expenses, while at other times a bride-

[1] See article Bairāgi for some notice of the sect.

price is paid.   At the wedding, rice coloured red is put in
the hands of the bridegroom and juāri coloured yellow in
those of the bride.   The bridegroom places the rice on the
bride's head and she lays the juāri at his feet.   A dish full
of water with a golden ring in it is put between them, and
they lay their hands on the ring together under the water
and walk five times round a decorative little marriage-shed
erected inside the real one.   A feast is given, and the bridal
couple sit on a little dais and eat out of the same dish.
The remarriage of widows is permitted, but the widow may
not marry a man belonging to the section either of her
first husband or of her father.   Divorce is recognised.   The
Lingāyats bury the dead in a sitting posture with the *lingam*
or emblem of Siva, which has never left the dead man during
his lifetime, clasped in his right hand.   Sometimes a platform
is made over the grave with an image of Siva.   They do
not shave the head in token of mourning.   Their principal
festival is Shivrātri or Siva's night, when they offer the
leaves of the bel tree and ashes to the god.   A Lingāyat
must never be without the *lingam* or phallic sign of Siva,
which is carried slung round the neck in a little case of
silver, copper or brass.   If he loses it, he must not eat,
drink nor smoke until he finds it or obtains another.   The
Lingāyats do not employ Brāhmans for any purpose, but are
served by their own priests, the Jangams,[1] who are recruited
both by descent and by initiation from members of the
Pancham group.   The Lingāyat Banias are practically all
immigrants from the Telugu country; they have Telugu
names and speak this language in their homes.   They deal
in grain, cloth, groceries and spices.

Bania, Maheshri.—This important subcaste of Banias
numbered about 14,000 persons in the Central Provinces in
1911, of whom 8000 belonged to the Berār Districts, and the
remainder principally to Hoshangābād, Nimār, Wardha and
Nāgpur.   The name is said to be derived from Maheshwar,
an ancient town on the Nerbudda, near Indore, and one of
the earliest Rājpūt settlements.   But some of them say
that their original home is in Bīkanīr, and tell a story to

---

[1] See separate article on Jangam.

the effect that their ancestor was a Rāja who was turned into stone with his seventy-two followers by some ascetics whose devotions they had interrupted in the forest. But when their wives came to commit *sati* by the stone figures the god Siva intervened and brought them to life again. He told them to give up the profession of arms and take to trade. So the seventy-two followers were the ancestors of the seventy-two *gotras* or sections of the Maheshris, and the Rāja became their tribal *Bhāt* or genealogist, and they were called Maheshri or Maheswari, from Mahesh, a name of Siva. In Gujarāt the term Maheshri or Meshri appears to be used for all Banias who are not Jains, including the other important Hindu subcastes.[1] This is somewhat peculiar, and perhaps tends to show that several of the local subcastes are of recent formation. But though they profess to be named after Siva, the Maheshris, like practically all other Hindu Banias, are Vaishnava by sect, and wear the *kunti* or necklace of beads of basil. A small minority are Jains. It is to be noticed that both the place of their origin, an early Rājpūt settlement of the Yādava clan, and their own legend tend to show that they were derived from the Rājpūt caste ; for as their ancestors were attendants on a Rāja and followed the profession of arms, which they were told to abandon, they could be none other than Rājpūts. The Maheshris also have the Rājpūt custom of sending a cocoa-nut as a symbol of a proposal of marriage. In Nimār the Maheshri Banias say they belong to the Dhākar subcaste, a name which usually means illegitimate, though they themselves explain that it is derived from a place called Dhākargarh, from which they migrated. As already stated they are divided into seventy-two exogamous clans, the names of which appear to be titular or territorial. It is said that at their weddings when the bridegroom gets to the door of the marriage-shed, the bride's mother ties a scarf round his neck and takes hold of his nose and drags him into the shed. Sometimes they make the bridegroom kneel down and pay reverence to a shoe as a joke. They do not observe the custom of the *pangat* or formal festal assembly, which is usual among Hindu castes ; according to this, none

[1] *Bombay Gazetteer, Hindus of Gujarāt*, p. 70.

can begin to eat until all the guests have assembled, when they all sit down at once. Among the Maheshris the guests sit down as they come in, and are served and take their food and go. They only have the *pangat* feast on very rare occasions. The Maheshris are one of the richest, most enterprising and influential classes of Banias. They are intelligent, of high-bred appearance, cleanly habits and courteous manners. The great bankers, Sir Kastūrchand Daga of Kamptee, of the firm of Bansi Lāl Abīrchand, and Rai Bahādur Seth Jīwan Das and Diwān Bahādur Seth Ballabh Das, of Jubbulpore, belong to this subcaste.

Bania, Nema.—This subcaste numbers nearly 4000 persons, the bulk of whom reside in the Saugor, Damoh, Narsinghpur and Seoni Districts. The Nemas are most largely returned from Central India, and are probably a Bundelkhand group; they will eat food cooked without water with Gola-pūrab Banias, who are also found in Bundelkhand. They are mainly Hindus, with a small minority of Jains. The origin of the name is obscure; the suggestion that it comes from Nimār appears to be untenable, as there are very few Nemas in that District. They say that when Parasurāma was slaying the Kshatriyas fourteen young Rājpūt princes, who at the time were studying religion with their family priests, were saved by the latter on renouncing their Kshatriya status and declaring themselves to be Vaishyas. These fourteen princes were the ancestors of the fourteen *gotras* of the Nema subcaste, but the *gotras* actually bear the names of the fourteen Rīshis or saints who saved their lives. These sections appear to be of the usual Brāhmanical type, but marriage is regulated by another set of fifty-two subsections, with names which are apparently titular or territorial. Like other Bania groups the Nemas are divided into Bīsa and Dasa subdivisions or twenties and tens, the Bīsa being of pure and the Dasa of irregular descent. There is also a third group of Pacha or fives, who appear to be the offspring of kept women. After some generations, when the details of their ancestry are forgotten, the Pachas probably obtain promotion into the Dasa group. The Bīsa and Dasa groups take food together, but do not intermarry. The Nemas wear the sacred thread and apparently prohibit the remarriage of widows. The Nemas are considered to be very keen business men, and a saying about them is, " Where a sheep grazes or a Nema trades, what is there left for anybody else ? "

Bania, Oswāl.—This is perhaps the most important subdivision of the Banias after the Agarwāla. The Oswāls numbered nearly 10,000 persons in the Central Provinces in 1911, being found in considerable numbers in all the Berār Districts, and also in Nimār, Wardha and Raipur. The name is derived from the town of Osia or Osnagar in Mārwār. According to one legend of their origin the Rāja of Osnagar had no son, and obtained one through the promise of a Jain ascetic. The people then drove the ascetic from the town, fearing that the Rāja would become a Jain ; but Osadev, the guardian goddess of the place, told the ascetic, Sri Ratan Suri, to convert the Rāja by a miracle. So she took a small hank (*pūni*) of cotton and passed it along the back of the saint, when it immediately became a snake and bit Jaichand, the son of the Rāja, in the toe, while he was asleep beside his wife. Every means was tried to save his life, but he died. As his corpse was about to be burnt, the ascetic sent one of his disciples and stopped the cremation. Then the Rāja came with the body of his son and stood with hands clasped before the saint. He ordered that it was to be taken back to the place where the prince had been bitten, and that the princess was to lie down beside it as before. At midnight the snake returned and licked the bite, when the prince was restored to life. Then the Rāja, with all his Court and people, became a Jain. He and his family founded the *gotra* or section now known as Sri Srimāl or most noble ; his servants formed that known as Srimāl or excellent, while the other Rājpūts of the town became ordinary Oswāls. When the Brāhmans of the place heard of these conversions they asked the saint how they were to live, as all their clients had become Jains. The saint directed that they should continue to be the family priests of the Oswāls and be known as Bhojak or ' eaters.' Thus the Oswāls, though Jains, continue to employ Mārwāri

Brāhmans as their family priests. Another version of the story is that the king of Srimāli[1] allowed no one who was not a millionaire to live within his city walls. In consequence of this a large number of persons left Srimāl, and, settling in Mandovad, called it Osa or the frontier. Among them were Srimāli Banias and also Bhatti, Chauhān, Gahlot, Gaur, Yādava, and several other clans of Rājpūts, and these were the people who were subsequently converted by the Jain ascetic, Sri Ratan Suri, and formed into the single caste of Oswāl.[2] Finally, Colonel Tod states that the Oswāls are all of pure Rājpūt descent, of no single tribe, but chiefly Panwārs, Solankis and Bhattis.[3] From these legends and the fact that their headquarters are in Rājputāna, it may safely be concluded that the Oswāl Banias are of Rājpūt origin.

The large majority of the Oswāls are Jain by religion, but a few are Vaishnava Hindus. Intermarriage between the Hindu and Jain sections is permitted. Like the Agarwālas, the Oswāls are divided into Bīsa, Dasa and Pacha sections or twenties, tens and fives, according to the purity of their lineage. The Pacha subcaste still permit the remarriage of widows. The three groups take food together but do not intermarry. In Bombay, Dasa Oswāls intermarry with the Dasa groups of Srimāli and Parwār Banias,[4] and Oswāls generally can marry with other good Bania subcastes so long as both parties are Jains. The Oswāls are divided into eighty-four *gotras* or exogamous sections for purposes of marriage, a list of which is given by Mr. Crooke.[5] Most of these cannot be recognised, but a few of them seem to be titular, as Lorha a caste which grows hemp, Nunia a salt-refiner, Seth a banker, Daftari an office-boy, Vaid a physician, Bhandāri a cook, and Kukara a dog. These may indicate a certain amount of admixture of foreign elements in the caste. As stated from Benāres, the exogamous rule is that a man cannot marry in his own section, and he cannot marry a girl whose father's or mother's section is the same as that of either his father or mother. This would bar the marriage of first cousins.

---

[1] A town near Jhalor in Mārwār, now called Bhinmāl.

[2] *Bombay Gazetteer, Hindus of Gujarāt,* p. 97.

[3] *Rājasthān,* ii. p. 210, footnote.

[4] *Hindus of Gujarāt, loc. cit.,* and *Bombay Gazetteer,* xvi. 45.

[5] *Tribes and Castes,* art. Oswāl.

Though Jains the Oswāls perform their weddings by walking round the sacred fire and observe certain Hindu rites, including the worship of the god Ganpati.[1] They also revere other Hindu deities and the sun and moon. The dead are burnt, but they do not observe any impurity after a death nor clean the house. On the day after the death the mourning family, both men and women, visit Parasnāth's temple, and lay one seer (2 lbs.) of Indian millet before the god, bow to him and go home. They do not gather the ashes of the dead nor keep the yearly death-day. Their only observance is that on some day between the twelfth day after a death and the end of a year, the caste-people are treated to a dinner of sweetmeats and the dead 'are then forgotten.'[2] The Oswāls will take food cooked with water (*katchi*) only from Brāhmans, and that cooked without water (*pakki*) from Agarwāla and Maheshri Banias. In the Central Provinces the principal deity of the Oswāls is the Jain Tirthakār Parasnāth, and they spend large sums in the erection of splendid temples. The Oswāls are the most prominent trading caste in Rājputāna ; and they have also frequently held high offices, such as Diwān or minister, and paymaster in Rājpūt States.[3]

Bania, Parwār.[4]—This Jain subcaste numbered nearly 1. Origin. 29,000 persons in 1911. They belong almost entirely to the Jubbulpore and Nerbudda Divisions, and the great bulk are found in the Saugor, Damoh and Jubbulpore Districts. The origin of the Parwārs and of their name is not known, but there is some reason to suppose that they are from Rājputāna. Their women wear on the head the *bīj*, a Rājputāna ornament, and use the *chāru*, a deep brass plate for drinking, which also belongs there. Their songs are said to be in the Rājasthāni dialect. It seems likely that the Parwārs may be identical with the Porawāl subcaste found in other Provinces, which, judging from the name, may belong to Rājputāna. In the northern Districts the Parwārs

[1] *Bombay Gazetteer*, vol. xvii. p. 51.
[2] *Ibidem.*
[3] Bhattachārya, *Hindu Castes and Sects*, p. 207.

[4] This article is based on papers by Mr. Pancham Lāl, Naib-Tahsīldār Sihora, and Munshi Kanhya Lāl, of the Gazetteer office.

speak Bundeli, but in the south their language is said to be Mārwāri.

Among the Parwārs the Samaiya or Channāgri form a separate sectarian Jain group. They do not worship the images of the Jain Tirthakārs, but enshrine the sacred books of the Jains in their temples, and worship these. The Parwārs will take daughters in marriage from the Channāgris, and sometimes give their daughters in consideration of a substantial bride-price. Among the Parwārs themselves there is a social division between the Ath Sāke and the Chao Sāke ; the former will not permit the marriage of persons related more nearly than eight degrees, while the latter permit it after four degrees. The Ath Sāke have the higher position, and if one of them marries a Chao Sāke he is degraded to that group. Besides this the Parwārs have an inferior division called Benaikia, which consists of the offspring of irregular unions and of widows who have remarried. Persons who have committed a caste offence and cannot pay the fine imposed on them for it also go into this subcaste. The Benaikias [1] themselves are distributed into four groups of varying degrees of respectability, and families who live correctly and marry as well as they can tend to rise from one to the other until after several generations they may again be recognised as Parwārs proper.

The Parwārs have twelve *gotras* or main sections, and each *gotra* has, or is supposed to have, twelve *muls* or subsections. A Parwār must not marry in his own *gotra* nor in the *mul* of his mother, or any of his grandmothers or greatgrandmothers. This practically bars marriage within seven degrees of relationship. But a man's sister and daughter may be married in the same family, and even to two brothers, and a man can marry two sisters.

As a rule no bride-price is paid, but occasionally an old man desiring a wife will give something substantial to her father in secret. There are two forms of marriage, called Thinga and Dajanha ; in the former, women do not accompany the wedding procession, and they have a separate marriage-shed at the bridegroom's house for their own celebrations ; while in the latter, they accompany it

---

[1] See also notice of Benaikias in article on Vidūr.

and erect such a shed at the house in the bridegroom's village or town where they have their lodging. Before the wedding, the bridegroom, mounted on a horse, and the bride, carried in a litter, proceed together round the marriage-shed. The bridegroom then stands by the sacred post in the centre and the bride walks seven times round him. In the evening there was a custom of dressing the principal male relatives of the bridegroom in women's clothes and making them dance, but this is now being discarded. On the fifth day is held a rite called Palkachār. A new cot is provided by the bride's father, and on it is spread a red cloth. The couple are seated on this with their hands entwined, and their relations come and make them presents. If the bridegroom catches hold of the dress of his mother- or father-in-law, they are expected to make him a handsome present. In other respects the wedding follows the ordinary Hindu ritual. Widow-marriage and divorce are forbidden among the Parwārs proper, and those who practise them go into the lower Benaikia group.

The Parwārs are practically all Jains of the Digambari sect. They build costly and beautiful temples for their Tirthakārs, especially for their favourite Parasnāth. They have also many Hindu practices. They observe the Diwāli, Rakshabandhan and Holi festivals; they say that at the Diwāli the last Tirthakār Mahāvīra attained beatitude and the gods rained down jewels; the little lamps now lighted at Diwāli are held to be symbolic of these jewels. They tie the threads round the wrist on Rakshabandhan to keep off evil spirits. They worship Sītala Devi, the Hindu goddess of smallpox, and employ Brāhmans to choose names for their children and fix the dates of their wedding and other ceremonies, though not at the ceremonies themselves. *5. Religion: Hindu observances.*

The caste burn the dead, with the exception of the bodies of young children, which are buried. The corpse is sometimes placed sitting in a car to be taken to the cremation ground, but often laid on a bier in the ordinary manner. The sitting posture is that in which all the Tirthakārs attained paradise, and their images always represent them in this posture. The corpse is naked save for *6. Disposal of the dead.*

a new piece of cloth round the waist, but it is covered with a sheet. The Jains do not shave their hair in token of mourning, nor do they offer sacrificial cakes to the dead. When the body is burnt they bathe in the nearest water and go home. Neither the bearers nor the mourners are held to be impure. Next day the mourning family, both men and women, visit Parasnāth's temple, lay two pounds of Indian millet before the god and go home.[1] But in the Central Provinces they whitewash their houses, get their clothes washed, throw away their earthen pots and give a feast to the caste.

7. Social rules and customs.

The Parwārs abstain from eating any kind of flesh and from drinking liquor. They have a *panchāyat* and impose penalties for offences against caste rules like the Hindus. Among the offences are the killing of any living thing, unchastity or adultery, theft or other bad conduct, taking cooked food or water from a caste from which the Parwārs do not take them, and violation of any rule of their religion. To get vermin in a wound, or to be beaten by a low-caste man or with a shoe, incidents which entail serious penalties among the Hindus, are not offences with the Parwārs. When an offender is put out of caste the ordinary deprivation is that he is not allowed to enter a Jain temple, and in serious cases he may also not eat nor drink with the caste. The Parwārs are generally engaged in the trade in grain, *ghī*, and other staples. Several of them are well-to-do and own villages.

Bania, Srimāli.—This subcaste takes its name from the town of Srimāl, which is now Bhinmāl in Mārwār. They numbered 600 persons in the Central Provinces in 1911, most of whom belonged to the Hoshangābād District. More than two-thirds were Hindus and the remainder Jains. Colonel Tod writes of Bhinmāl and an adjoining town, Sanchor: "These towns are on the high road to Cutch and Gujarāt, which has given them from the most remote times a commercial celebrity. Bhinmāl is said to contain about 1500 houses and Sanchor half that number. Very wealthy *mahājans* or merchants used to reside here, but insecurity

[1] *Bombay Gazetteer*, vol. xvii. p. 81.

both within and without has much injured these cities."
From Bhinmāl the Srimālis appear to have gone to Gujarāt,
where they are found in considerable numbers. Their
legend of origin is that the goddess Lakshmi created from
a flower-garland 90,000 families to act as servants to the
90,000 Srimāli Brāhmans, and these were the ancestors of
the Srimāli Banias.[1] Both the Jain and Hindu sections
of the Srimāli Banias employ Srimāli Brāhmans as priests.
Like other classes of Banias, the Srimāli are divided into
two sections, the Bīsa and Dasa, or twenty and ten, of which
the Bīsa are considered to be of pure and the Dasa of somewhat mixed descent. In Gujarāt they also have a third
territorial group, known as Lādva, from Lād, the old name
of Gujarāt. All three subdivisions take food together but
do not intermarry.[2] The two highest sections of the Oswāl
Banias are called Sri Srimāl and Srimāl, and it is possible
that further investigation might show the Srimāls and
Oswāls to have been originally of one stock.

Bania, Umre.—This Hindu subcaste belongs to Damoh
and Jubbulpore. They are perhaps the same as the Ummar
Banias of the United Provinces, who reside in the Meerut,
Agra and Kumaon Divisions. The name Umre is found
as a subdivision of several castes in the Central Provinces,
as the Telis and others, and is probably derived from some
town or tract of country in northern or central India, but
no identification has been made. Mr. Bhīmbhai Kirpārām
states that in Gujarāt the Ummar Banias are also known
as Bāgaria from the Bāgar or wild country, comprised in
the Dongarpur and Pertābgarh States of Rājputāna, where
considerable numbers of them are still settled. Their headquarters is at Sāgwāra, near Dongarpur.[3] In Damoh the
Umre Banias formerly cultivated the *al* plant,[4] which yielded
a well-known dye, and hence they lost caste, as in soaking the
roots of the plant to extract the dye the numerous insects in
them are necessarily destroyed. The Dosar subcaste[5] are
a branch of the Umre, who allow widow-remarriage.

---

[1] *Bombay Gazetteer, Hindus of
Gujarāt*, p. 99.
[2] *Ibidem.*

[3] *Ibidem,* p. 98.
[4] *Merinda citrifolia,* see art. Alia.
[5] See article.

BANJĀRA

LIST OF PARAGRAPHS

1. Historical notice of the caste.

Banjāra, Wanjāri, Labhāna, Mukeri.[1] — The caste of carriers and drivers of pack - bullocks. In 1911 the Banjāras numbered about 56,000 persons in the Central Provinces and 80,000 in Berār, the caste being in greater strength here than in any part of India except Hyderābād, where their total is 174,000. Bombay comes next with a figure approaching that of the Central Provinces and Berār, and the caste belongs therefore rather to the Deccan than to northern India. The name has been variously explained, but the most probable derivation is from the Sanskrit

[1] This article is based principally on a *Monograph on the Banjāra Clan*, by Mr. N. F. Cumberlege of the Berār Police, believed to have been first written in 1869 and reprinted in 1882; notes on the Banjāras written by Colonel Mackenzie and printed in the *Berār Census Report* (1881) and the *Pioneer* newspaper (communicated by Mrs. Horsburgh) ; Major Gunthorpe's *Criminal Tribes* ; papers by Mr. M. E. Khare, Extra-Assistant Commissioner, Chānda ; Mr. Nārāyan Rao, Tahr., Betūl ; Mr. Mukund Rao, Manager, Pachmarhi Estate ; and information on the caste collected in Yeotmāl and Nimār.

banijya kara, a merchant.   Sir H. M. Elliot held that the name Banjāra was of great antiquity, quoting a passage from the Dasa Kumara Charita of the eleventh or twelfth century. But it was subsequently shown by Professor Cowell that the name Banjāra did not occur in the original text of this work.[1]   Banjāras are supposed to be the people mentioned by Arrian in the fourth century B.C., as leading a wandering life, dwelling in tents and letting out for hire their beasts of burden.[2]   But this passage merely proves the existence of carriers and not of the Banjāra caste.   Mr. Crooke states[3] that the first mention of Banjāras in Muhammadan history is in Sikandar's attack on Dholpur in A.D. 1504.[4]   It seems improbable, therefore, that the Banjāras accompanied the different Muhammadan invaders of India, as might have been inferred from the fact that they came into the Deccan in the train of the forces of Aurāngzeb.   The caste has indeed two Muhammadan sections, the Turkia and Mukeri.[5]   But both of these have the same Rājpūt clan names as the Hindu branch of the caste, and it seems possible that they may have embraced Islām under the proselytising influence of Aurāngzeb, or simply owing to their having been employed with the Muhammadan troops. The great bulk of the caste in southern India are Hindus, and there seems no reason for assuming that its origin was Muhammadan.

It may be suggested that the Banjāras are derived from the Chāran or Bhāt caste of Rājputāna.   Mr. Cumberlege, whose *Monograph* on the caste in Berār is one of the best authorities, states that of the four divisions existing there the Chārans are the most numerous and by far the most interesting class.[6]   In the article on Bhāt it has been explained how the Chārans or bards, owing to their readiness

2. Banjāras derived from the Chārans or Bhāts.

---

[1] Mr. Crooke's *Tribes and Castes*, art. Banjāra, para. 1.

[2] *Berār Census Report* (1881), p. 150.

[3] *Ibidem*, para. 2, quoting Dowson's Elliot, v. 100.

[4] Khan Bahadur Fazalullah Lutfullah Farīdi in the *Bombay Gazetteer* (*Muhammadans of Gujarat*, p. 86) quoting from General Briggs (*Trans-*

actions Bombay Literary Society, vol. i. 183) says that "as carriers of grain for Muhammadan armies the Banjāras have figured in history from the days of Muhammad Tughlak (A.D. 1340) to those of Aurāngzeb."

[5] Sir H. M. Elliot's *Supplemental Glossary*.

[6] *Monograph on the Banjāra Clan*, p. 8.

to kill themselves rather than give up the property entrusted
to their care, became the best safe-conduct for the passage
of goods in Rājputāna.   The name Chāran is generally held
to mean 'Wanderer,' and in their capacity of bards the
Chārans were accustomed to travel from court to court of
the different chiefs in quest of patronage.   They were first
protected by their sacred character and afterwards by their
custom of *trāga* or *chāndi*, that is, of killing themselves when
attacked and threatening their assailants with the dreaded
fate of being haunted by their ghosts.   Mr. Bhimbhai
Kirparām [1] remarks : " After Parāsurāma's dispersion of the
Kshatris the Chārans accompanied them in their southward
flight.   In those troubled times the Chārans took charge
of the supplies of the Kshatri forces and so fell to their
present position of cattle-breeders and grain-carriers. . . ."
Most of the Chārans are graziers, cattle-sellers and pack-
carriers.   Colonel Tod says : [2] " The Chārans and Bhāts or
bards and genealogists are the chief carriers of these regions
(Mārwār) ; their sacred character overawes the lawless Rājpūt
chief, and even the savage Koli and Bhīl and the plundering
Sahrai of the desert dread the anathema of these singular
races, who conduct the caravans through the wildest and
most desolate regions."   In another passage Colonel Tod
identifies the Chārans and Banjāras [3] as follows : " Murlāh
is an excellent township inhabited by a community of
Chārans of the tribe Cucholia (Kacheli), who are Bunjārris
(carriers) by profession, though poets by birth.   The alliance
is a curious one, and would appear incongruous were not
gain the object generally in both cases.   It was the sanctity
of their office which converted our *bardais* (bards) into
bunjārris, for their persons being sacred, the immunity extended likewise to their goods and saved them from all
imposts ; so that in process of time they became the free-
traders of Rājputāna.   I was highly gratified with the reception I received from the community, which collectively
advanced to meet me at some distance from the town.   The
procession was headed by the village elders and all the fair
Chāranis, who, as they approached, gracefully waved their

[1] *Hindus of Gujarāt*, p. 214 *et seq.*   [2] *Rājasthān*, i. 602.
[3] *Ibidem*, ii. 570, 573.

scarfs over me until I was fairly made captive by the muses of Murlāh! It was a novel and interesting scene. The manly persons of the Chārans, clad in the flowing white robe with the high loose-folded turban inclined on one side, from which the *māla* or chaplet was gracefully suspended ; and the *naiques* or leaders, with their massive necklaces of gold, with the image of the *pitriswar* (*manes*) depending therefrom, gave the whole an air of opulence and dignity. The females were uniformly attired in a skirt of dark-brown camlet, having a bodice of light-coloured stuff, with gold orna-ments worked into their fine black hair ; and all had the favourite *chūris* or rings of *hāthidānt* (elephant's tooth) covering the arm from the wrist to the elbow, and even above it." A little later, referring to the same Chāran community, Colonel Tod writes : " The *tānda* or caravan, consisting of four thousand bullocks, has been kept up amidst all the evils which have beset this land through Mughal and Marātha tyranny. The utility of these caravans as general carriers to conflicting armies and as regular tax-paying subjects has proved their safeguard, and they were too strong to be pillaged by any petty marauder, as any one who has seen a Banjāri encampment will be convinced. They encamp in a square, and their grain-bags piled over each other breast-high, with interstices left for their match-locks, make no contemptible fortification. Even the ruth-less Tūrk, Jamshīd Khān, set up a protecting tablet in favour of the Chārans of Murlāh, recording their exemp-tion from *dīnd* contributions, and that there should be no increase in duties, with threats to all who should injure the community. As usual, the sun and moon are appealed to as witnesses of good faith, and sculptured on the stone. Even the forest Bhīl and mountain Mair have set up their signs of immunity and protection to the chosen of Hinglāz (tutelary deity) ; and the figures of a cow and its *kairi* (calf) carved in rude relief speak the agreement that they should not be slain or stolen within the limits of Murlāh."

In the above passage the community described by Colonel Tod were Chārans, but he identified them with Banjāras, using the name alternatively. He mentions their large herds of pack-bullocks, for the management of which the Chārans, who were graziers as well as bards, would naturally be adapted ; the name given to the camp, *tānda*, is that generally used by the Banjāras ; the women wore ivory bangles, which the Banjāra women wear.[1] In commenting on the way in which the women threw their scarves over him, making him a prisoner, Colonel Tod remarks : "This community had enjoyed for five hundred years the privilege of making prisoner any Rāna of Mewār who may pass through Murlāh, and keeping him in bondage until he gives them a *got* or entertainment. The patriarch (of the village) told me that I was in jeopardy as the Rāna's representative, but not knowing how I might have relished the joke had it been carried to its conclusion, they let me escape." Mr. Ball notes a similar custom of the Banjāra women far away in the Bastar State of the Central Provinces :[2] "To-day I passed through another Banjāra hamlet, from whence the women and girls all hurried out in pursuit, and a brazen-faced powerful-looking lass seized the bridle of my horse as he was being led by the *sais* in the rear. The *sais* and *chaprāsi* were both Muhammadans, and the forward conduct of these females perplexed them not a little, and the former was fast losing his temper at being thus assaulted by a woman." Colonel Mackenzie in his account of the Banjāra caste remarks :[3] "It is certain that the Chārans, whoever they were, first rose to the demand which the great armies of northern India, contending in exhausted countries far from their basis of supply, created, viz. the want of a fearless and reliable transport service. . . . The start which the Chārans then acquired they retain among Banjāras to this day, though in very much diminished splendour and position. As they themselves relate, they were originally five brethren, Rāthor, Turi, Panwār, Chauhān and Jādon. But fortune particularly smiled on Bhīka Rāthor, as his four sons, Mersi, Multāsi, Dheda and Khāmdār, great names among the

---

[1] This custom does not necessarily indicate a special connection between the Banjāras and Chārans, as it is common to several castes in Rājputāna ; but it indicates that the Banjāras came from Rājputāna. Banjāra men also frequently wear the hair long, down to the neck, which is another custom of Rājputāna.

[2] *Jungle Life in India*, p. 517.

[3] *Berār Census Report* (1881), p. 152.

Chārans, rose immediately to eminence as commissariat transporters in the north. And not only under the Delhi Emperors, but under the Satāra, subsequently the Poona Rāj, and the Subāhship of the Nizām, did several of their descendants rise to consideration and power." It thus seems a reasonable hypothesis that the nucleus of the Banjāra caste was constituted by the Chārans or bards of Rājputāna. Mr. Bhimbhai Kirparām [1] also identifies the Chārans and Banjāras, but I have not been able to find the exact passage. The following notice [2] by Colonel Tone is of interest in this connection :

"The vast consumption that attends a Marātha army necessarily superinduces the idea of great supplies ; yet, notwithstanding this, the native powers never concern themselves about providing for their forces, and have no idea of a grain and victualling department, which forms so great an object in a European campaign. The Banias or grain-sellers in an Indian army have always their servants ahead of the troops on the line of march, to purchase in the circumjacent country whatever necessaries are to be disposed of. Articles of consumption are never wanting in a native camp, though they are generally twenty-five per cent dearer than in the town bazārs ; but independent of this mode of supply the Vanjāris or itinerant grain-merchants furnish large quantities, which they bring on bullocks from an immense distance. These are a very peculiar race, and appear a marked and discriminated people from any other I have seen in this country. Formerly they were considered so sacred that they passed in safety in the midst of contending armies ; of late, however, this reverence for their character is much abated and they have been frequently plundered, particularly by Tipu."

The reference to the sacred character attaching to the Banjāras a century ago appears to be strong evidence in favour of their derivation from the Chārans. For it could scarcely have been obtained by any body of commissariat agents coming into India with the Muham-

---

[1] *Bombay Gazetteer, Hindus of Gujarāt.*
[2] *Letter on the Marāthas* (1798), p. 67, *India Office Tracts.*

madans. The fact that the example of disregarding it was first set by a Muhammadan prince points to the same conclusion.

Mr. Irvine notices the Banjāras with the Mughal armies in similar terms:[1] "It is by these people that the Indian armies in the field are fed, and they are never injured by either army. The grain is taken from them, but invariably paid for. They encamp for safety every evening in a regular square formed of the bags of grain of which they construct a breastwork. They and their families are in the centre, and the oxen are made fast outside. Guards with matchlocks and spears are placed at the corners, and their dogs do duty as advanced posts. I have seen them with droves of 5000 bullocks. They do not move above two miles an hour, as their cattle are allowed to graze as they proceed on the march."

One may suppose that the Chārans having acted as carriers for the Rājpūt chiefs and courts, both in time of peace and in their continuous intestinal feuds, were pressed into service when the Mughal armies entered Rājputāna and passed through it to Gujarāt and the Deccan. In adopting the profession of transport agents for the imperial troops they may have been amalgamated into a fresh caste with other Hindus and Muhammadans doing the same work, just as the camp language formed by the superposition of a Persian vocabulary on to a grammatical basis of Hindi became Urdu or Hindustāni. The readiness of the Chārans to commit suicide rather than give up property committed to their charge was not, however, copied by the Banjāras, and so far as I am aware there is no record of men of this caste taking their own lives, though they had little scruple with those of others.

3. Chāran Banjāras employed with the Mughal armies. The Chāran Banjāras, Mr. Cumberlege states,[2] first came to the Deccan with Asaf Khān in the campaign which closed with the annexation by the Emperor Shāh Jahān of Ahmadnagar and Berār about 1630. Their leaders or Nāiks were Bhangi and Jhangi of the Rāthor[3] and

---

[1] *Army of the Indian Mughals*, p. 192.

[2] *Monograph*, p. 14, and *Berār Census Report* (1881) (Kitts), p. 151.

[3] These are held to have been descendants of the Bhīka Rāthor referred to by Colonel Mackenzie above.

Bhagwān Dās of the Jādon clan.   Bhangi and Jhangi had 180,000 pack-bullocks, and Bhagwān Dās 52,000.   It was naturally an object with Asaf Khān to keep his commissariat well up with his force, and as Bhangi and Jhangi made difficulties about the supply of grass and water to their cattle, he gave them an order engraved on copper in letters of gold to the following effect :

Ranjan kā pāni
Chhappar kā ghās
Din ke tīn khūn muāf;
Aur jahān Asaf Jāh ke ghore
Wahān Bhangi Jhangi ke bail,

which may be rendered as follows : " If you can find no water elsewhere you may even take it from the pots of my followers ; grass you may take from the roofs of their huts ; and I will pardon you up to three murders a day, provided that wherever I find my cavalry, Bhangi and Jhangi's bullocks shall be with them." This grant is still in the possession of Bhangi Nāik's descendant who lives at Musi, near Hingoli.   He is recognised by the Hyderābād Court as the head Nāik of the Banjāra caste, and on his death his successor receives a *khillat* or dress-of-honour from His Highness the Nizām.   After Asaf Khān's campaign and settlement in the Deccan, a quarrel broke out between the Rāthor clan, headed by Bhangi and Jhangi, and the Jādons under Bhagwān Dās, owing to the fact that Asaf Khān had refused to give Bhagwān Dās a grant like that quoted above. Both Bhangi and Bhagwān Dās were slain in the feud and the Jādons captured the standard, consisting of eight *thāns* (lengths) of cloth, which was annually presented by the Nizām to Bhangi's descendants.   When Mr. Cumberlege wrote (1869), this standard was in the possession of Hatti Nāik, a descendant of Bhagwān Dās, who had an estate near Muchli Bunder, in the Madras Presidency.   Colonel Mackenzie states [1] that the leaders of the Rāthor clan became so distinguished not only in their particular line but as men of war that the Emperors recognised their carrying distinctive standards, which were known as *dhal*

[1] See note 3, p. 168.

by the Rāthors themselves. Jhangi's family was also represented in the person of Rāmu Nāik, the *patel* or headman of the village of Yaoli in the Yeotmāl District. In 1791–92 the Banjāras were employed to supply grain to the British army under the Marquis of Cornwallis during the siege of Seringapatam,[1] and the Duke of Wellington in his Indian campaigns regularly engaged them as part of the commissariat staff of his army. On one occasion he said of them : " The Banjāras I look upon in the light of servants of the public, of whose grain I have a right to regulate the sale, always taking care that they have a proportionate advantage." [2]

4. Internal structure.

Mr. Cumberlege gives four main divisions of the caste in Berār, the Chārans, Mathurias, Labhānas and Dhāris. Of these the Chārans are by far the most numerous and important, and included all the famous leaders of the caste mentioned above. The Chārans are divided into the five clans, Rāthor, Panwār, Chauhān, Puri and Jādon or Burthia, all of these being the names of leading Rājpūt clans ; and as the Chāran bards themselves were probably Rājpūts, the Banjāras, who are descended from them, may claim the same lineage. Each clan or sept is divided into a number of subsepts ; thus among the Rāthors the principal subsept is the Bhurkia, called after the Bhīka Rāthor already mentioned ; and this is again split into four groups, Mersi, Multāsi, Dheda and Khāmdār, named after his four sons. As a rule, members of the same clan, Panwār, Rāthor and so on, may not intermarry, but Mr. Cumberlege states that a man belonging to the Bānod or Bhurkia subsepts of the Rāthors must not take a wife from his own subsept, but may marry any other Rāthor girl. It seems probable that the same rule may hold with the other subsepts, as it is most unlikely that inter-marriage should still be prohibited among so large a body as the Rāthor Chārans have now become. It may be supposed therefore that the division into subsepts took place when it became too inconvenient to prohibit marriage

[1] General Briggs quoted by Mr. Farīdi in *Bombay Gazetteer, Muhammadans of Gujarāt*, p. 86.

[2] A. Wellesley (1800), quoted in Mr. Crooke's edition of *Hobson-Jobson*, art. Brinjarry.

throughout the whole body of the sept, as has happened in other cases. The Mathuria Banjāras take their name from Mathura or Muttra and appear to be Brāhmans. "They wear the sacred thread,[1] know the *Gayatri Mantra*, and to the present day abstain from meat and liquor, subsisting entirely on grain and vegetables. They always had a sufficiency of Chārans and servants (*Jāngar*) in their villages to perform all necessary manual labour, and would not themselves work for a remuneration otherwise than by carrying grain, which was and still is their legitimate occupation ; but it was not considered undignified to cut wood and grass for the household. Both Mathuria and Labhāna men are fairer than the Chārans ; they wear better jewellery and their loin-cloths have a silk border, while those of the Chārans are of rough, common cloth." The Mathurias are sometimes known as Ahiwāsi, and may be connected with the Ahiwāsis of the Hindustāni Districts, who also drive pack-bullocks and call themselves Brāhmans. But it is naturally a sin for a Brāhman to load the sacred ox, and any one who does so is held to have derogated from the priestly order. The Mathurias are divided according to Mr. Cumberlege into four groups called Pānde, Dube, Tīwari and Chaube, all of which are common titles of Hindustāni Brāhmans and signify a man learned in one, two, three and four Vedas respectively. It is probable that these groups are exogamous, marrying with each other, but this is not stated. The third division, the Labhānas, may derive their name from *lavana*, salt, and probably devoted themselves more especially to the carriage of this staple. They are said to be Rājpūts, and to be descended from Mota and Mola, the cowherds of Krishna. The fourth subdivision are the Dhāris or bards of the caste, who rank below the others. According to their own story[2] their ancestor was a member of the Bhāt caste, who became a disciple of Nānak, the Sikh apostle, and with him attended a feast given by the Mughal Emperor Humayun. Here he ate the flesh of a cow or buffalo, and in consequence became a Muhammadan and was circumcised. He was employed as a musician at the Mughal court, and his sons

---

[1] Cumberlege, *loc. cit.*   [2] Cumberlege, pp. 28, 29.

joined the Chārans and became the bards of the Banjāra caste. " The Dhāris," Mr. Cumberlege continues, "are both musicians and mendicants; they sing in praise of their own and the Chāran ancestors and of the old kings of Delhi; while at certain seasons of the year they visit Chāran hamlets, when each family gives them a young bullock or a few rupees. They are Muhammadans, but worship Sārasvati and at their marriages offer up a he-goat to Gāji and Gandha, the two sons of the original Bhāt, who became a Muhammadan. At burials a Fakīr is called to read the prayers."

5. Minor subcastes.   Besides the above four main divisions, there are a number of others, the caste being now of a very mixed character. Two principal Muhammadan groups are given by Sir H. Elliot, the Tūrkia and Mukeri. The Tūrkia have thirty-six septs, some with Rājpūt names and others territorial or titular. They seem to be a mixed group of Hindus who may have embraced Islam as the religion of their employers. The Mukeri Banjāras assert that they derive their name from Mecca (Makka), which one of their Nāiks, who had his camp in the vicinity, assisted Father Abraham in building.[1] Mr. Crooke thinks that the name may be a corruption of Makkeri and mean a seller of maize. Mr. Cumberlege says of them : " Multānis and Mukeris have been called Banjāras also, but have nothing in common with the caste ; the Multānis are carriers of grain and the Mukeris of wood and timber, and hence the confusion may have arisen between them." But they are now held to be Banjāras by common usage ; in Saugor the Mukeris also deal in cattle. From Chānda a different set of subcastes is reported called Bhūsarjin, Ladjin, Saojin and Kanhejin ; the first may take their name from *bhūsa*, the chaff of wheat, while Lad is the term used for people coming from Gujarāt, and Sao means a banker. In Sambalpur again a class of Thuria Banjāras is found, divided into the Bandesia, Atharadesia, Navadesia and Chhadesia, or the men of the 52 districts, the 18 districts, the 9 districts and the 6 districts respectively. The first and last two of these take food and marry with each other. Other groups are the Guār Banjāras, apparently from Guāra or Gwāla, a milkman, the

---

[1] Elliot's *Races*, quoted by Mr. Crooke, *ibidem*.

Gūguria Banjāras, who may, Mr. Hira Lāl suggests, take their name from trading in *gūgar*, a kind of gum, and the Bahrūp Banjāras, who are Nats or acrobats.   In Berār also a number of the caste have become respectable cultivators and now call themselves Wanjāri, disclaiming any connection with the Banjāras, probably on account of the bad reputation for crime attached to these latter.   Many of the Wanjāris have been allowed to rank with the Kunbi caste, and call themselves Wanjāri Kunbis in order the better to dissociate themselves from their parent caste.   The existing caste is therefore of a very mixed nature, and the original Brāhman and Chāran strains, though still perfectly recognisable, cannot have maintained their purity.

At a betrothal in Nimār the bridegroom and his friends come and stay in the next village to that of the bride. The two parties meet on the boundary of the village, and here the bride-price is fixed, which is often a very large sum, ranging from Rs. 200 to Rs. 1000.   Until the price is paid the father will not let the bridegroom into his house.   In Yeotmāl, when a betrothal is to be made, the parties go to a liquor-shop and there a betel-leaf and a large handful of sugar are distributed to everybody.   Here the price to be paid for the bride amounts to Rs. 40 and four young bullocks.   Prior to the wedding the bridegroom goes and stays for a month or so in the house of the bride's father, and during this time he must provide a supply of liquor daily for the bride's male relatives.   The period was formerly longer, but now extends to a month at the most.   While he resides at the bride's house the bridegroom wears a cloth over his head so that his face cannot be seen.   Probably the prohibition against seeing him applies to the bride only, as the rule in Berār is that between the betrothal and marriage of a Chāran girl she may not eat or drink in the bridegroom's house, or show her face to him or any of his relatives. Mathuria girls must be wedded before they are seven years old, but the Chārans permit them to remain single until after adolescence.

6. Marriage: betrothal.

Banjāra marriages are frequently held in the rains, a season forbidden to other Hindus, but naturally the most convenient to them, because in the dry weather they are usually

7. Marriage.

travelling. For the marriage ceremony they pitch a tent in lieu
of the marriage-shed, and on the ground they place two rice-
pounding pestles, round which the bride and bridegroom
make the seven turns. Others substitute for the pestles
a pack - saddle with two bags of grain in order to symbolise their camp life. During the turns the girl's hand
is held by the Joshi or village priest, or some other Brāhman,
in case she should fall ; such an occurrence being probably a
very unlucky omen. Afterwards, the girl runs away and the
Brāhman has to pursue and catch her. In Bhandāra the girl
is clad only in a light skirt and breast-cloth, and her body is
rubbed all over with oil in order to make his task more
difficult. During this time the bride's party pelt the Brāhman with rice, turmeric and areca-nuts, and sometimes even
with stones ; and if he is forced to cry with the pain, it is
considered lucky. But if he finally catches the girl, he is
conducted to a daïs and sits there holding a brass plate
in front of him, into which the bridegroom's party drop
presents. A case is mentioned of a Brāhman having obtained
Rs. 70 in this manner. Among the Mathuria Banjāras of
Berār the ceremony resembles the usual Hindu type.[1]
Before the wedding the families bring the branches of eight
or ten different kinds of trees, and perform the *hom* or fire
sacrifice with them. A Brāhman knots the clothes of the
couple together, and they walk round the fire. When the
bride arrives at the bridegroom's hamlet after the wedding,
two small brass vessels are given to her ; she fetches water in
these and returns them to the women of the boy's family, who
mix this with other water previously drawn, and the girl, who
up to this period was considered of no caste at all, becomes
a Mathuria.[2] Food is cooked with this water, and the bride
and bridegroom are formally received into the husband's *kuri*
or hamlet. It is possible that the mixing of the water may be
a survival of the blood covenant, whereby a girl was received
into her husband's clan on her marriage by her blood being
mixed with that of her husband.[3] Or it may be simply
symbolical of the union of the families. In some localities
after the wedding the bride and bridegroom are made to

---

[1] Cumberlege, pp. 4, 5.　　　　　[2] Cumberlege, *l.c.*

[3] This custom is noticed in the article on Khairwār.

stand on two bullocks, which are driven forward, and it is believed that whichever of them falls off first will be the first to die.

Owing to the scarcity of women in the caste a widow is seldom allowed to go out of the family, and when her husband dies she is taken either by his elder or younger brother ; this is in opposition to the usual Hindu practice, which forbids the marriage of a woman to her deceased husband's elder brother, on the ground that as successor to the headship of the joint family he stands to her, at least potentially, in the light of a father. If the widow prefers another man and runs away to him, the first husband's relatives claim compensation, and threaten, in the event of its being refused, to abduct a girl from this man's family in exchange for the widow. But no case of abduction has occurred in recent years. In Berār the compensation claimed in the case of a woman marrying out of the family amounts to Rs. 75, with Rs. 5 for the Nāik or headman of the family. Should the widow elope without her brother-in-law's consent, he chooses ten or twelve of his friends to go and sit *dharna* (starving themselves) before the hut of the man who has taken her. He is then bound to supply these men with food and liquor until he has paid the customary sum, when he may marry the widow.[1] In the event of the second husband being too poor to pay monetary compensation, he gives a goat, which is cut into eighteen pieces and distributed to the community.[2]

8. Widow remarriage.

After the birth of a child the mother is unclean for five days, and lives apart in a separate hut, which is run up for her use in the *kuri* or hamlet. On the sixth day she washes the feet of all the children in the *kuri*, feeds them and then returns to her husband's hut. When a child is born in a moving *tānda* or camp, the same rule is observed, and for five days the mother walks alone after the camp during the daily march. The caste bury the bodies of unmarried

9. Birth and death.

[1] Cumberlege, p. 18.

[2] Mr. Hīra Lāl suggests that this custom may have something to do with the phrase *Athāra jāt ke gāyi*, or 'She has gone to the eighteen castes,' used of a woman who has been turned out of the community. This phrase seems, however, to be a euphemism, eighteen castes being a term of indefinite multitude for any or no caste. The number eighteen may be selected from the same unknown association which causes the goat to be cut into eighteen pieces.

persons and those dying of smallpox and burn the others.
Their rites of mourning are not strict, and are observed
only for three days.   The Banjāras have a saying : "Death
in a foreign land is to be preferred, where there are no
kinsfolk to mourn, and the corpse is a feast for birds and
animals"; but this may perhaps be taken rather as an expression of philosophic resignation to the fate which must
be in store for many of them, than a real preference, as with
most people the desire to die at home almost amounts to
an instinct.

10. Reli-
gion :
Banjāri
Devi.

One of the tutelary deities of the Banjāras is Banjāri
Devi, whose shrine is usually located in the forest.   It is
often represented by a heap of stones, a large stone smeared
with vermilion being placed on the top of the heap to represent the goddess.   When a Banjāra passes the place he
casts a stone upon the heap as a prayer to the goddess to
protect him from the dangers of the forest.   A similar
practice of offering bells from the necks of cattle is recorded
by Mr. Thurston :[1] "It is related by Moor that he passed
a tree on which were hanging several hundred bells.   This
was a superstitious sacrifice of the Banjāras (Lambāris), who,
passing this tree, are in the habit of hanging a bell or bells
upon it, which they take from the necks of their sick cattle,
expecting to leave behind them the complaint also.   Our
servants particularly cautioned us against touching these
diabolical bells, but as a few of them were taken for our
own cattle, several accidents which happened were imputed
to the anger of the deity to whom these offerings were
made ; who, they say, inflicts the same disorder on the
unhappy bullock who carries a bell from the tree, as that
from which he relieved the donor."   In their houses the
Banjāri Devi is represented by a pack-saddle set on high in
the room, and this is worshipped before the caravans set
out on their annual tours.

11. Mīthu
Bhūkia.

Another deity is Mīthu Bhūkia, an old freebooter, who
lived in the Central Provinces ; he is venerated by the
dacoits as the most clever dacoit known in the annals of the
caste, and a hut was usually set apart for him in each

[1] *Ethnographic Notes in Southern India*, p. 344, quoting from Moor's
Narrative of Little's Detachment.

hamlet, a staff carrying a white flag being planted before
it. Before setting out for a dacoity, the men engaged would
assemble at the hut of Mīthu Bhūkia, and, burning a lamp
before him, ask for an omen ; if the wick of the lamp
drooped the omen was propitious, and the men present
then set out at once on the raid without returning home.
They might not speak to each other nor answer if challenged ;
for if any one spoke the charm would be broken and the
protection of Mīthu Bhūkia removed ; and they should
either return to take the omens again or give up that
particular dacoity altogether.[1] It has been recorded as a
characteristic trait of Banjāras that they will, as a rule, not
answer if spoken to when engaged on a robbery, and the
custom probably arises from this observance ; but the
worship of Mīthu Bhūkia is now frequently neglected.
After a successful dacoity a portion of the spoil would be
set apart for Mīthu Bhūkia, and of the balance the Nāik or
headman of the village received two shares if he participated
in the crime ; the man who struck the first blow or did most
towards the common object also received two shares, and
all the rest one share. With Mīthu Bhūkia's share a feast
was given at which thanks were returned to him for the
success of the enterprise, a burnt offering of incense being
made in his tent and a libation of liquor poured over the
flagstaff. A portion of the food was sent to the women
and children, and the men sat down to the feast. Women
were not allowed to share in the worship of Mīthu Bhūkia
nor to enter his hut.

Another favourite deity is Siva Bhāia, whose story is 12. Siva
given by Colonel Mackenzie [2] as follows : " The love borne Bhāia.
by Māri Māta, the goddess of cholera, for the handsome Siva
Rāthor, is an event of our own times (1874) ; she proposed
to him, but his heart being pre-engaged he rejected her ;
and in consequence his earthly bride was smitten sick and
died, and the hand of the goddess fell heavily on Siva
himself, thwarting all his schemes and blighting his fortunes
and possessions, until at last he gave himself up to her. She
then possessed him and caused him to prosper exceedingly,
gifting him with supernatural power until his fame was

[1] Cumberlege, p. 35.   [2] *Berār Census Report*, 1881.

noised abroad, and he was venerated as the saintly Siva Bhāia or great brother to all women, being himself unable to marry. But in his old age the goddess capriciously wished him to marry and have issue, but he refused and was slain and buried at Pohur in Berār. A temple was erected over him and his kinsmen became priests of it, and hither large numbers are attracted by the supposed efficacy of vows made to Siva, the most sacred of all oaths being that taken in his name." If a Banjāra swears by Siva Bhāia, placing his right hand on the bare head of his son and heir, and grasping a cow's tail in his left, he will fear to perjure himself, lest by doing so he should bring injury on his son and a murrain on his cattle.[1]

13. Worship of cattle.   Naturally also the Banjāras worshipped their pack-cattle.[2] "When sickness occurs they lead the sick man to the feet of the bullock called Hātadiya.[3] On this animal no burden is ever laid, but he is decorated with streamers of red-dyed silk, and tinkling bells with many brass chains and rings on neck and feet, and silken tassels hanging in all directions ; he moves steadily at the head of the convoy, and at the place where he lies down when he is tired they pitch their camp for the day ; at his feet they make their vows when difficulties overtake them, and in illness, whether of themselves or their cattle, they trust to his worship for a cure."

14. Connection with the Sikhs.   Mr. Balfour also mentions in his paper that the Banjāras call themselves Sikhs, and it is noticeable that the Chāran subcaste say that their ancestors were three Rājpūt boys who followed Guru Nānak, the prophet of the Sikhs. The influence of Nānak appears to have been widely extended over northern India, and to have been felt by large bodies of the people other than those who actually embraced the Sikh religion. Cumberlege states[4] that before starting to his marriage the bridegroom ties a rupee in his turban in honour of Guru Nānak, which is afterwards expended in sweetmeats.

---

[1] Cumberlege, p. 21.

[2] The following instance is taken from Mr. Balfour's article, 'Migratory Tribes of Central India,' in *J.A.S.B.*, new series, vol. xiii., quoted in Mr.

Crooke's *Tribes and Castes*.

[3] From the Sanskrit Hātya-ādhya, meaning 'That which it is most sinful to slay' (Balfour).

[4] *Monograph*, p. 12.

But otherwise the modern Banjāras do not appear to retain any Sikh observances.

"The Banjāras," Sir A. Lyall writes,[1] "are terribly vexed by witchcraft, to which their wandering and precarious existence especially exposes them in the shape of fever, rheumatism and dysentery.   Solemn inquiries are still held in the wild jungles where these people camp out like gipsies, and many an unlucky hag has been strangled by sentence of their secret tribunals."   The business of magic and witchcraft was in the hands of two classes of Bhagats or magicians, one good and the other bad,[2] who may correspond to the European practitioners of black and white magic.   The good Bhagat is called Nimbu-kātna or lemon-cutter, a lemon speared on a knife being a powerful averter of evil spirits. He is a total abstainer from meat and liquor, and fasts once a week on the day sacred to the deity whom he venerates, usually Mahādeo ; he is highly respected and never panders to vice.   But the Jānta, the 'Wise or Cunning Man,' is of a different type, and the following is an account of the devilry often enacted when a deputation visited him to inquire into the cause of a prolonged illness, a cattle murrain, a sudden death or other misfortune. A woman might often be called a Dākun or witch in spite, and when once this word had been used, the husband or nearest male relative would be regularly bullied into consulting the Jānta.   Or if some woman had been ill for a week, an avaricious[3] husband or brother would begin to whisper foul play.   Witchcraft would be mentioned, and the wise man called in.   He would give the sufferer a quid of betel, muttering an incantation, but this rarely effected a cure, as it was against the interest of all parties that it should do so.   The sufferer's relatives would then go to their Nāik, tell him that the sick person was bewitched, and ask him to send a deputation to the Jānta or witch-doctor.   This would be at once despatched, consisting of one male adult from each house in the hamlet, with one of the sufferer's relatives. On the road the party would bury a bone or other article to

15. Witch-
craft.

---

[1] *Asiatic Studies*, i. p. 118 (ed. 1899).
[2] Cumberlege, p. 23 *et seq*.   The description of witchcraft is wholly re-

produced from his *Monograph*.
[3] His motive being the fine inflicted on the witch's family.

test the wisdom of the witch-doctor. But he was not to be caught out, and on their arrival he would bid the deputation rest, and come to him for consultation on the following day. Meanwhile during the night the Jānta would be thoroughly coached by some accomplice in the party. Next morning, meeting the deputation, he would tell every man all particulars of his name and family ; name the invalid, and tell the party to bring materials for consulting the spirits, such as oil, vermilion, sugar, dates, cocoanut, *chironji*,[1] and sesamum. In the evening, holding a lamp, the Jānta would be possessed by Māriai, the goddess of cholera ; he would mention all particulars of the sick man's illness, and indignantly inquire why they had buried the bone on the road, naming it and describing the place. If this did not satisfy the deputation, a goat would be brought, and he would name its sex with any distinguishing marks on the body. The sick person's representative would then produce his *nazar* or fee, formerly Rs. 25, but lately the double of this or more. The Jānta would now begin a sort of chant, introducing the names of the families of the *kuri* other than that containing her who was to be proclaimed a witch, and heap on them all kinds of abuse. Finally, he would assume an ironic tone, extol the virtues of a certain family, become facetious, and praise its representative then present. This man would then question the Jānta on all points regarding his own family, his connections, worldly goods, and what gods he worshipped, ask who was the witch, who taught her sorcery, and how and why she practised it in this particular instance. But the witch-doctor, having taken care to be well coached, would answer everything correctly and fix the guilt on to the witch. A goat would be sacrificed and eaten with liquor, and the deputation would return. The punishment for being proclaimed a Dākun or witch was formerly death to the woman and a fine to be paid by her relatives to the bewitched person's family. The woman's husband or her sons would be directed to kill her, and if they refused, other men were deputed to murder her, and bury the body at once with all the clothing and ornaments then on her person, while a further fine would be exacted from the family for not doing away with her themselves.

[1] The fruit of *Buchanania latifolia*.

But murder for witchcraft has been almost entirely stopped, and nowadays the husband, after being fined a few head of cattle, which are given to the sick man, is turned out of the village with his wife.   It is quite possible, however, that an obnoxious old hag would even now not escape death, especially if the money fine were not forthcoming, and an instance is known in recent times of a mother being murdered by her three sons.   The whole village combined to screen these amiable young men, and eventually they made the Jānta the scapegoat, and he got seven years, while the murderers could not be touched.   Colonel Mackenzie writes that, " Curious to relate, the Jāntas, known locally as Bhagats, in order to become possessed of their alleged powers of divination and prophecy, require to travel to Kazhe, beyond Surat, there to learn and be instructed by low-caste Koli impostors." This is interesting as an instance of the powers of witchcraft being attributed by the Hindus or higher race to the indigenous primitive tribes, a rule which Dr. Tylor and Dr. Jevons consider to hold good generally in the history of magic.

Several instances are known also of the Banjāras having practised human sacrifice.   Mr. Thurston states :[1]   " In former times the Lambādis, before setting out on a journey, used to procure a little child and bury it in the ground up to the shoulders, and then drive their loaded bullocks over the unfortunate victim.   In proportion to the bullocks thoroughly trampling the child to death, so their belief in a successful journey increased."   The Abbé Dubois describes another form of sacrifice :[2]

16. Human sacrifice.

" The Lambādis are accused of the still more atrocious crime of offering up human sacrifices.   When they wish to perform this horrible act, it is said, they secretly carry off the first person they meet.   Having conducted the victim to some lonely spot, they dig a hole in which they bury him up to the neck.   While he is still alive they make a sort of lamp of dough made of flour, which they place on his head ; this they fill with oil, and light four wicks in it.   Having done this, the men and women join hands and, forming a

[1] *Ethnographic Notes in Southern India*, p. 507, quoting from the Rev. J. Cain, *Ind. Ant.* viii. (1879).

[2] *Hindu Manners, Customs and Ceremonies*, p. 70.

circle, dance round their victim, singing and making a great noise until he expires." Mr. Cumberlege records[1] the following statement of a child kidnapped by a Banjāra caravan in 1871. After explaining how he was kidnapped and the tip of his tongue cut off to give him a defect in speech, the Kunbi lad, taken from Sāhungarhi, in the Bhandāra District, went on to say that, " The *tānda* (caravan) encamped for the night in the jungle. In the morning a woman named Gangi said that the devil was in her and that a sacrifice must be made. On this four men and three women took a boy to a place they had made for *pūja* (worship). They fed him with milk, rice and sugar, and then made him stand up, when Gangi drew a sword and approached the child, who tried to run away ; caught and brought back to this place, Gangi, holding the sword with both hands and standing on the child's right side, cut off his head with one blow. Gangi collected the blood and sprinkled it on the idol ; this idol is made of stone, is about 9 inches high, and has something sparkling in its forehead. The camp marched that day, and for four or five days consecutively, without another sacrifice ; but on the fifth day a young woman came to the camp to sell curds, and having bought some, the Banjāras asked her to come in in the evening and eat with them. She did come, and after eating with the women slept in the camp. Early next morning she was sacrificed in the same way as the boy had been, but it took three blows to cut off her head ; it was done by Gangi, and the blood was sprinkled on the stone idol. About a month ago Sitārām, a Gond lad, who had also been kidnapped and was in the camp, told me to run away as it had been decided to offer me up in sacrifice at the next Jiuti festival, so I ran away." The child having been brought to the police, a searching and protracted inquiry was held, which, however, determined nothing, though it did not disprove his story.

17. Admission of outsiders : kidnapped children and slaves.
The Banjāra caste is not closed to outsiders, but the general rule is to admit only women who have been married to Banjāra men. Women of the lowest and impure castes are excluded, and for some unknown reason the Patwas[2] and

[1] *Monograph*, p. 19.
[2] The Patwas are weavers of silk thread and the Nunias are masons and navvies.

Nunias are bracketed with these.   In Nimār it is stated
that formerly Gonds, Korkus and even Balāhis[1] might
become Banjāras, but this does not happen now, because
the caste has lost its occupation of carrying goods, and there
is therefore no inducement to enter it.   In former times
they were much addicted to kidnapping children—these
were whipped up or enticed away whenever an opportunity
presented itself during their expeditions.   The children were
first put into the *gonis* or grain bags of the bullocks and so
carried for a few days, being made over at each halt to the
care of a woman, who would pop the child back into its
bag if any stranger passed by the encampment.   The
tongues of boys were sometimes slit or branded with hot
gold, this last being the ceremony of initiation into the
caste still used in Nimār.   Girls, if they were as old as seven,
were sometimes disfigured for fear of recognition, and for
this purpose the juice of the marking-nut[2] tree would be
smeared on one side of the face, which burned into the
skin and entirely altered the appearance.   Such children
were known as Jāngar.   Girls would be used as concubines
and servants of the married wife, and boys would also be
employed as servants.   Jāngar boys would be married to
Jāngar girls, both remaining in their condition of servitude.
But sometimes the more enterprising of them would
abscond and settle down in a village.   The rule was that
for seven generations the children of Jāngars or slaves
continued in that condition, after which they were recognised as proper Banjāras.   The Jāngar could not draw
in smoke through the stem of the huqqa when it was
passed round in the assembly, but must take off the stem
and inhale from the bowl.   The Jāngar also could not
eat off the bell-metal plates of his master, because these
were liable to pollution, but must use brass plates.   At
one time the Banjāras conducted a regular traffic in
female slaves between Gujarāt and Central India, selling
in each country the girls whom they had kidnapped in
the other.[3]

---

[1] An impure caste of weavers, ranking with the Mahārs.

[2] *Semecarpus Anacardium.*

[3] Malcolm, *Memoir   of   Central
India,* ii. p. 296.

18. Dress.   Up to twelve years of age a Chāran girl only wears a skirt with a shoulder-cloth tucked into the waist and carried over the left arm and the head.   After this she may have anklets and bangles on the forearm and a breast-cloth. But until she is married she may not have the *wānkri* or curved anklet, which marks that estate, nor wear bone or ivory bangles on the upper arm.[1]   When she is ten years old a Labhāna girl is given two small bundles containing a nut, some cowries and rice, which are knotted to two corners of the *dupatta* or shoulder-cloth and hung over the shoulder, one in front and one behind.   This denotes maidenhood. The bundles are considered sacred, are always knotted to the shoulder-cloth in wear, and are only removed to be tucked into the waist at the girl's marriage, where they are worn till death.   These bundles alone distinguish the Labhāna from the Mathuria woman.   Women often have their hair hanging down beside the face in front and woven behind with silver thread into a plait down the back.   This is known as Anthi, and has a number of cowries at the end. They have large bell-shaped ornaments of silver tied over the head and hanging down behind the ears, the hollow part of the ornament being stuffed with sheep's wool dyed red ; and to these are attached little bells, while the anklets on the feet are also hollow and contain little stones or balls, which tinkle as they move.   They have skirts, and separate short cloths drawn across the shoulders according to the northern fashion, usually red or green in colour, and along the skirt-borders double lines of cowries are sewn.   Their breast-cloths are profusely ornamented with needle-work embroidery and small pieces of glass sewn into them, and are tied behind with cords of many colours whose ends are decorated with cowries and beads.   Strings of beads, ten to twenty thick, threaded on horse-hair, are worn round the neck.   Their favourite ornaments are cowries,[2] and they

[1] Cumberlege, p. 16.

[2] Small double shells which are still used to a slight extent as a currency in backward tracts.   This would seem an impossibly cumbrous method of carrying money about nowadays, but I have been informed by a comparatively young official that in his father's time, change for a rupee could not be had in Chhattīsgarh outside the two principal towns.   As the cowries were a form of currency they were probably held sacred, and hence sewn on to clothes as a charm, just as gold and silver are used for ornaments.

Bemrose, Collo., Derby.

BANJĀRA WOMEN WITH THE *SINGH* OR HORN.

have these on their dress, in their houses and on the
trappings of their bullocks.   On the arms they have ten or
twelve bangles of ivory, or in default of this lac, horn or
cocoanut-shell.   Mr. Ball states that he was "at once
struck by the peculiar costumes and brilliant clothing of
these Indian gipsies.   They recalled to my mind the appearance of the gipsies of the Lower Danube and Wallachia." [1]
The most distinctive ornament of a Banjāra married woman
is, however, a small stick about 6 inches long made of the
wood of the *khair* or catechu.   In Nimār this is given to a
woman by her husband at marriage, and she wears it afterwards placed upright on the top of the head, the hair
being wound round it and the head-cloth draped over it in
a graceful fashion.   Widows leave it off, but on remarriage
adopt it again.   The stick is known as *chunda* by the
Banjāras, but outsiders call it *singh* or horn.   In Yeotmāl,
instead of one, the women have two little sticks fixed
upright in the hair.   The rank of the woman is said to be
shown by the angle at which she wears this horn.[2]   The
dress of the men presents no features of special interest.
In Nimār they usually have a necklace of coral beads, and
some of them carry, slung on a thread round the neck, a

[1] *Jungle Life in India*, p. 516.

[2] Brewer's *Dictionary of Phrase and Fable* contains the following notice of horns as an article of dress: "Mr. Buckingham says of a Tyrian lady, 'She wore on her head a hollow silver horn rearing itself up obliquely from the forehead.   It was some four inches in diameter at the root and pointed at the extremity.   This peculiarity re-minded me forcibly of the expression of the Psalmist: "Lift not up your horn on high; speak not with a stiff neck.   All the horns of the wicked also will I cut off, but the horns of the righteous shall be exalted" (Ps. lxxv. 5, 10).'   Bruce found in Abyssinia the silver horns of warriors and distin-guished men.   In the reign of Henry V. the horned headgear was introduced into England and from the effigy of Beatrice, Countess of Arundel, at Arundel Church, who is represented with the horns outspread to a great extent, we may infer that the length of the head-horn, like the length of the shoe-point in the reign of Henry VI., etc., marked the degree of rank. To cut off such horns would be to degrade; and to exalt and extend such horns would be to add honour and dignity to the wearer."   Webb (*Herit-age of Dress*, p. 117) writes: "Mr. Elworthy in a paper to the British Association at Ipswich in 1865 con-sidered the crown to be a development from horns of honour.   He maintained that the symbols found in the head of the god Serapis were the elements from which were formed the composite head-dress called the crown into which horns entered to a very great extent." This seems a doubtful speculation, but still it may be quite possible that the idea of distinguishing by a crown the leader of the tribe was originally taken from the antlers of the leader of the herd.   The helmets of the Vikings were also, I believe, decorated with horns.

tin tooth-pick and ear-scraper, while a small mirror and comb are kept in the head-cloth so that their toilet can be performed anywhere.

Mr. Cumberlege[1] notes that in former times all Chāran Banjāras when carrying grain for an army placed a twig of some tree, the sacred *nīm*[2] when available, in their turban to show that they were on the war-path ; and that they would do the same now if they had occasion to fight to the death on any social matter or under any supposed grievance.

19. Social customs.

The Banjāras eat all kinds of meat, including fowls and pork, and drink liquor. But the Mathurias abstain from both flesh and liquor. Major Gunthorpe states that the Banjāras are accustomed to drink before setting out for a dacoity or robbery and, as they smoke after drinking, the remains of leaf-pipes lying about the scene of action may indicate their handiwork. They rank below the cultivating castes, and Brāhmans will not take water to drink from them. When engaged in the carrying trade, they usually lived in *kuris* or hamlets attached to such regular villages as had considerable tracts of waste land belonging to them. When the *tānda* or caravan started on its long carrying trips, the young men and some of the women went with it with the working bullocks, while the old men and the remainder of the women and children remained to tend the breeding cattle in the hamlet. In Nimār they generally rented a little land in the village to give them a footing, and paid also a carrying fee on the number of cattle present. Their spare time was constantly occupied in the manufacture of hempen twine and sacking, which was much superior to that obtainable in towns. Even in Captain Forsyth's[3] time (1866) the construction of railways and roads had seriously interfered with the Banjāras' calling, and they had perforce taken to agriculture. Many of them have settled in the new ryotwāri villages in Nimār as Government tenants. They still grow *tilli*[4] in preference to other crops, because this oilseed can be raised without much labour or skill, and during their former nomadic life they were accustomed to

---

[1] *Monograph*, p. 40.
[2] *Melia indica.*
[3] Author of the *Nimār Settlement Report.*
[4] *Sesamum.*

sow it on any poor strip of land which they might rent for
a season.   Some of them also are accustomed to leave a
part of their holding untilled in memory of their former and
more prosperous life.   In many villages they have not yet
built proper houses, but continue to live in mud huts
thatched with grass.   They consider it unlucky to inhabit
a house with a cement or tiled roof; this being no doubt a
superstition arising from their camp life.   Their houses
must also be built so that the main beams do not cross,
that is, the main beam of a house must never be in such a
position that if projected it would cut another main beam ;
but the beams may be parallel.   The same rule probably
governed the arrangement of tents in their camps.   In
Nimār they prefer to live at some distance from water,
probably that is of a tank or river ; and this seems to be
a survival of a usage mentioned by the Abbé Dubois : [1]
" Among other curious customs of this odious caste is one
that obliges them to drink no water which is not drawn
from springs or wells.   The water from rivers and tanks
being thus forbidden, they are obliged in case of necessity
to dig a little hole by the side of a tank or river and take
the water filtering through, which, by this means, is supposed
to become spring water."   It is possible that this rule may
have had its origin in a sanitary precaution.   Colonel
Sleeman notes [2] that the Banjāras on their carrying trips
preferred by-paths through jungles to the high roads along
cultivated plains, as grass, wood and water were more
abundant along such paths ; and when they could not avoid
the high roads, they commonly encamped as far as they
could from villages and towns, and upon the banks of rivers
and streams, with the same object of obtaining a sufficient
supply of grass, wood and water.   Now it is well known
that the decaying vegetation in these hill streams renders
the water noxious and highly productive of malaria.   And
it seems possible that the perception of this fact led the
Banjāras to dig shallow wells by the sides of the streams
for their drinking-water, so that the supply thus obtained
might be in some degree filtered by percolation through the

[1] *Hindu Manners, Customs and*   [2] *Report on the Badhak or Bāgri*
Ceremonies, p. 21.   *Dacoits*, p. 310.

intervening soil and freed from its vegetable germs. And the custom may have grown into a taboo, its underlying reason being unknown to the bulk of them, and be still practised, though no longer necessary when they do not travel. If this explanation be correct it would be an interesting conclusion that the Banjāras anticipated so far as they were able the sanitary precaution by which our soldiers are supplied with portable filters when on the march.

20. The Nāik or headman. Banjāra dogs.

Each *kuri* (hamlet) or *tānda* (caravan) had a chief or leader with the designation of Nāik, a Telugu word meaning 'lord' or 'master.' The office of Nāik [1] was only partly hereditary, and the choice also depended on ability. The Nāik had authority to decide all disputes in the community, and the only appeal from him lay to the representatives of Bhangi and Jhangi Nāik's families at Narsi and Poona, and to Burthia Nāik's successors in the Telugu country. As already seen, the Nāik received two shares if he participated in a robbery or other crime, and a fee on the remarriage of a widow outside her family and on the discovery of a witch. Another matter in which he was specially interested was pig-sticking. The Banjāras have a particular breed of dogs, and with these they were accustomed to hunt wild pig on foot, carrying spears. When a pig was killed, the head was cut off and presented to the Nāik or headman, and if any man was injured or gored by the pig in the hunt, the Nāik kept and fed him without charge until he recovered.

The following notice of the Banjāras and their dogs may be reproduced : [2] "They are brave and have the reputation of great independence, which I am not disposed to allow to them. The Wanjāri indeed is insolent on the road, and will drive his bullocks up against a Sāhib or any one else ; but at any disadvantage he is abject enough. I remember one who rather enjoyed seeing his dogs attack me, whom he supposed alone and unarmed, but the sight of a cocked pistol made him very quick in calling them off, and very humble in praying for their lives, which I spared,

---

[1] Colonel Mackenzie's notes.
[2] Mr. W. F. Sinclair, C.S., in *Ind. Ant.* iii. p. 184 (1874).

GROUP OF BANJĀRA WOMEN.

Bemrose, Collo., Derby.

less for his entreaties than because they were really noble animals. The Wanjāris are famous for their dogs, of which there are three breeds. The first is a large, smooth dog, generally black, sometimes fawn-coloured, with a square heavy head, most resembling the Danish boarhound. This is the true Wanjāri dog. The second is also a large, square-headed dog, but shaggy, more like a great underbred spaniel than anything else. The third is an almost tailless greyhound, of the type known all over India by the various names of Lāt, Polygar, Rāmpūri, etc. They all run both by sight and scent, and with their help the Wanjāris kill a good deal of game, chiefly pigs ; but I think they usually keep clear of the old fighting boars. Besides sport and their legitimate occupations the Wanjāris seldom stickle at supplementing their resources by theft, especially of cattle ; and they are more than suspected of infanticide."

The Banjāras are credited with great affection for their dogs, and the following legend is told about one of them : Once upon a time a Banjāra, who had a faithful dog, took a loan from a Bania (moneylender) and pledged his dog with him as security for payment. And some time afterwards, while the dog was with the moneylender, a theft was committed in his house, and the dog followed the thieves and saw them throw the property into a tank. When they went away the dog brought the Bania to the tank and he found his property. He was therefore very pleased with the dog and wrote a letter to his master, saying that the loan was repaid, and tied it round his neck and said to him, ' Now, go back to your master.' So the dog started back, but on his way he met his master, the Banjāra, coming to the Bania with the money for the repayment of the loan. And when the Banjāra saw the dog he was angry with him, not seeing the letter, and thinking he had run away, and said to him, ' Why did you come, betraying your trust ? ' and he killed the dog in a rage. And after killing him he found the letter and was very grieved, so he built a temple to the dog's memory, which is called the Kukurra Mandhi. And in the temple is the image of a dog. This temple is in the Drūg District, five miles from

Bālod.   A similar story is told of the temple of Kukurra Math in Mandla.

The following notice of Banjāra criminals is abstracted from Major Gunthorpe's interesting account : [1] " In the palmy days of the tribe dacoities were undertaken on the most extensive scale.   Gangs of fifty to a hundred and fifty well-armed men would go long distances from their *tāndas* or encampments for the purpose of attacking houses in villages, or treasure-parties or wealthy travellers on the high roads. The more intimate knowledge which the police have obtained concerning the habits of this race, and the detection and punishment of many criminals through approvers, have aided in stopping the heavy class of dacoities formerly prevalent, and their operations are now on a much smaller scale.   In British territory arms are scarcely carried, but each man has a good stout stick (*gedi*), the bark of which is peeled off so as to make it look whitish and fresh.   The attack is generally commenced by stone-throwing and then a rush is made, the sticks being freely used and the victims almost invariably struck about the head or face.   While plundering, Hindustāni is sometimes spoken, but as a rule they never utter a word, but grunt signals to one another.   Their loin-cloths are braced up, nothing is worn on the upper part of the body, and their faces are generally muffled.   In house dacoities men are posted at different corners of streets, each with a supply of well-chosen round stones to keep off any people coming to the rescue.   Banjāras are very expert cattle-lifters, sometimes taking as many as a hundred head or even more at a time.   This kind of robbery is usually practised in hilly or forest country where the cattle are sent to graze.   Secreting themselves they watch for the herdsman to have his usual midday doze and for the cattle to stray to a little distance.   As many as possible are then driven off to a great distance and secreted in ravines and woods.   If questioned they answer that the animals belong to landowners and have been given into their charge to graze, and as this is done every day the questioner thinks nothing more of it.   After a time, the cattle are

---

[1] *Notes on Criminal Tribes frequenting Bombay, Berār and the Central Provinces* (Bombay, 1882).

quietly sold to individual purchasers or taken to markets at a distance.

The Banjāras, however, are far from being wholly criminal, and the number who have adopted an honest mode of livelihood is continually on the increase. Some allowance must be made for their having been deprived of their former calling by the cessation of the continual wars which distracted India under native rule, and the extension of roads and railways which has rendered their mode of transport by pack - bullocks almost entirely obsolete. At one time practically all the grain exported from Chhattīsgarh was carried by them. In 1881 Mr. Kitts noted that the number of Banjāras convicted in the Berār criminal courts was lower in proportion to the strength of the caste than that of Muhammadans, Brāhmans, Koshtis or Sunārs,[1] though the offences committed by them were usually more heinous. Colonel Mackenzie had quite a favourable opinion of them : " A Banjāra who can read and write is unknown. But their memories, from cultivation, are marvellous and very retentive. They carry in their heads, without slip or mistake, the most varied and complicated transactions and the share of each in such, striking a debtor and creditor account as accurately as the best-kept ledger, while their history and songs are all learnt by heart and transmitted orally from generation to generation. On the whole, and taken rightly in their clannish nature, their virtues preponderate over their vices. In the main they are truthful and very brave, be it in war or the chase, and once gained over are faithful and devoted adherents. With the pride of high descent and with the right that might gives in unsettled and troublous times, these Banjāras habitually lord it over and contemn the settled inhabitants of the plains. And now not having foreseen their own fate, or at least not timely having read the warnings given by a yearly diminishing occupation, which slowly has taken their bread away, it is a bitter pill for them to sink into the ryot class or, oftener still, under stern necessity to become the ryot's servant. But they are settling to their fate, and the time must come when

22. Their virtues.

---

[1] *Berār Census Report* (1881), p. 151.

all their peculiar distinctive marks and traditions will be forgotten."

1. Origin and traditions.

Barai,[1] Tamboli, Pansāri.—The caste of growers and sellers of the betel-vine leaf. The three terms are used indifferently for the caste in the Central Provinces, although some shades of variation in the meaning can be detected even here—Barai signifying especially one who grows the betel-vine, and Tamboli the seller of the prepared leaf ; while Pansāri, though its etymological meaning is also a dealer in *pān* or betel-vine leaves, is used rather in the general sense of a druggist or grocer, and is apparently applied to the Barai caste because its members commonly follow this occupation. In Bengal, however, Barai and Tamboli are distinct castes, the occupations of growing and selling the betel-leaf being there separately practised. And they have been shown as different castes in the India Census Tables of 1901, though it is perhaps doubtful whether the distinction holds good in northern India.[2] In the Central Provinces and Berār the Barais numbered nearly 60,000 persons in 1911. They reside principally in the Amraoti, Buldāna, Nāgpur, Wardha, Saugor and Jubbulpore Districts. The betel-vine is grown principally in the northern Districts of Saugor, Damoh and Jubbulpore and in those of Berār and the Nāgpur plain. It is noticeable also that the growers and sellers of the betel-vine numbered only 14,000 in 1911 out of 33,000 actual workers of the Barai caste ; so that the majority of them are now employed in ordinary agriculture, field-labour and other avocations. No very probable derivation has been obtained for the word Barai, unless it comes from *bāri*, a hedge or enclosure, and simply means 'gardener.' Another derivation is from *barāna*, to avert hailstorms, a calling which they still practise in northern India. *Pān*, from the Sanskrit *parna* (leaf), is *the* leaf

---

[1] This notice is compiled principally from a good paper by Mr. M. C. Chatterji, retired Extra Assistant Commissioner, Jubbulpore, and from papers by Professor Sada Shiva Jai Rām, M.A., Government College, Jubbulpore, and Mr. Bhāskar Bāji Rao Desh-mukh, Deputy Inspector of Schools, Nāgpur.

[2] Sherring, *Hindu Tribes and Castes*, i. p. 330. Nesfield, *Brief View*, p. 15. *N.W.P. Census Report* (1891), p 317.

par excellence. Owing to the fact that they produce what is perhaps the most esteemed luxury in the diet of the higher classes of native society, the Barais occupy a fairly good social position, and one legend gives them a Brāhman ancestry. This is to the effect that the first Barai was a Brāhman whom God detected in a flagrant case of lying to his brother. His sacred thread was confiscated and being planted in the ground grew up into the first betel-vine, which he was set to tend. Another story of the origin of the vine is given later in this article. In the Central Provinces its cultivation has probably only flourished to any appreciable extent for a period of about three centuries, and the Barai caste would appear to be mainly a functional one, made up of a number of immigrants from northern India and of recruits from different classes of the population, including a large proportion of the non-Aryan element.

The following endogamous divisions of the caste have been reported : Chaurāsia, so called from the Chaurāsi pargana of the Mīrzāpur District ; Panagaria from Panāgar in Jubbulpore ; Mahobia from Mahoba in Hamīrpur ; Jaiswār from the town of Jais in the Rai Bareli District of the United Provinces ; Gangapāri, coming from the further side of the Ganges ; and Pardeshi or Deshwāri, foreigners. The above divisions all have territorial names, and these show that a large proportion of the caste have come from northern India, the different batches of immigrants forming separate endogamous groups on their arrival here. Other subcastes are the Dūdh Barais, from *dūdh*, milk ; the Kumān, said to be Kunbis who have adopted this occupation and become Barais ; the Jharia and Kosaria, the oldest or jungly Barais, and those who live in Chhattīsgarh ; the Purānia or old Barais ; the Kumhārdhang, who are said to be the descendants of a potter on whose wheel a betel-vine grew ; and the Lahuri Sen, who are a subcaste formed of the descendants of irregular unions. None of the other subcastes will take food from these last, and the name is locally derived from *lahuri*, lower, and *sen* or *shreni*, class. The caste is also divided into a large number of exogamous groups or septs which may be classified according to their names as territorial, titular and totemistic.

2. Caste sub-divisions.

Examples of territorial names are: Kanaujia of Kanauj, Burhānpuria of Burhānpur, Chitoria of Chitor in Rājputāna, Deobijha the name of a village in Chhattīsgarh, and Kharondiha from Kharond or Kālāhandi State. These names must apparently have been adopted at random when a family either settled in one of these places or removed from it to another part of the country. Examples of titular names of groups are: Pandit (priest), Bhandāri (store-keeper), Patharha (hail-averter), Batkāphor (pot-breaker), Bhulya (the forgetful one), Gūjar (a caste), Gahoi (a caste), and so on. While the following are totemistic groups: Katāra (dagger), Kulha (jackal), Bandrele (monkey), Chīkhalkār (from *chīkhal*, mud), Richharia (bear), and others. Where the group is named after another caste it probably indicates that a man of that caste became a Barai and founded a family; while the fact that some groups are totemistic shows that a section of the caste is recruited from the indigenous tribes. The large variety of names discloses the diverse elements of which the caste is made up.

3. Marriage.

Marriage within the *gotra* or exogamous group and within three degrees of relationship between persons connected through females is prohibited. Girls are usually wedded before adolescence, but no stigma attaches to the family if they remain single beyond this period. If a girl is seduced by a man of the caste she is married to him by the *pāt*, a simple ceremony used for widows. In the southern Districts a barber cuts off a lock of her hair on the banks of a tank or river by way of penalty, and a fast is also imposed on her, while the caste-fellows exact a meal from her family. If she has an illegitimate child, it is given away to somebody else, if possible. A girl going wrong with an outsider is expelled from the caste.

Polygamy is permitted and no stigma attaches to the taking of a second wife, though it is rarely done except for special family reasons. Among the Marātha Barais the bride and bridegroom must walk five times round the marriage altar and then worship the stone slab and roller used for pounding spices. This seems to show that the trade of the Pansāri or druggist is recognised as being a proper avocation of the Barai. They subsequently have to worship the potter's

wheel.   After the wedding the bride, if she is a child, goes
as usual to her husband's house for a few days.   In Chhattīsgarh she is accompanied by a few relations, the party being
known as Chauthia, and during her stay in her husband's
house the bride is made to sleep on the ground.   Widow
marriage is permitted, and the ceremony is conducted according to the usage of the locality.   In Betūl the relatives of the
widow take the second husband before Mārotī's shrine, where
he offers a nut and some betel-leaf.   He is then taken to the
mālguzār's house and presents to him Rs. 1-4-0, a cocoanut
and some betel-vine leaf as the price of his assent to the
marriage.   If there is a Deshmukh [1] of the village, a cocoanut
and betel-leaf are also given to him.   The nut offered to
Mārotī represents the deceased husband's spirit, and is subsequently placed on a plank and kicked off by the new
bridegroom in token of his usurping the other's place,
and finally buried to lay the spirit.   The property of the
first husband descends to his children, and failing them his
brother's children or collateral heirs take it before the widow.
A bachelor espousing a widow must first go through the
ceremony of marriage with a swallow-wort plant.   When a
widower marries a girl a silver impression representing the
deceased first wife is made and worshipped daily with the
family gods.   Divorce is permitted on sufficient grounds at
the instance of either party, being effected before the caste
committee or *panchāyat*.   If a husband divorces his wife
merely on account of bad temper, he must maintain her so
long as she remains unmarried and continues to lead a
moral life.

The Barais especially venerate the Nāg or cobra and
observe the festival of Nāg-Panchmi (Cobra's fifth), in connection with which the following story is related.   Formerly
there was no betel-vine on the earth.   But when the five
Pāndava brothers celebrated the great horse sacrifice after
their victory at Hastinapur, they wanted some, and so
messengers were sent down below the earth to the residence
of the queen of the serpents, in order to try and obtain it.
Bāsuki, the queen of the serpents, obligingly cut off the top

4. Reli-
gion and
social
status.

---

[1] The name of a superior revenue officer under the Marāthas, now borne
as a courtesy title by certain families.

joint of her little finger and gave it to the messengers. This was brought up and sown on the earth, and *pān* creepers grew out of the joint. For this reason the betel-vine has no blossoms or seeds, but the joints of the creepers are cut off and sown, when they sprout afresh ; and the betel-vine is called Nāgbel or the serpent-creeper. On the day of Nāg-Panchmi the Barais go to the *bareja* with flowers, cocoanuts and other offerings, and worship a stone which is placed in it and which represents the Nāg or cobra. A goat or sheep is sacrificed and they return home, no leaf of the *pān* garden being touched on that day. A cup of milk is also left, in the belief that a cobra will come out of the *pān* garden and drink it. The Barais say that members of their caste are never bitten by cobras, though many of these snakes frequent the gardens on account of the moist coolness and shade which they afford. The Agarwāla Banias, from whom the Barais will take food cooked without water, have also a legend of descent from a Nāga or snake princess. 'Our mother's house is of the race of the snake,' say the Agarwāls of Bihār.[1] The caste usually burn the dead, with the exception of children and persons dying of leprosy or snake-bite, whose bodies are buried. Mourning is observed for ten days in the case of adults and for three days for children. In Chhattīsgarh if any portion of the corpse remains unburnt on the day following the cremation, the relatives are penalised to the extent of an extra feast to the caste-fellows. Children are named on the sixth or twelfth day after birth either by a Brāhman or by the women of the household. Two names are given, one for ceremonial and the other for ordinary use. When a Brāhman is engaged he gives seven names for a boy and five for a girl, and the parents select one out of these. The Barais do not admit outsiders into the caste, and employ Brāhmans for religious and ceremonial purposes. They are allowed to eat the flesh of clean animals, but very rarely do so, and they abstain from liquor. Brāhmans will take sweets and water from them, and they occupy a fairly good social position on account of the important nature of their occupation.

[1] *Tribes and Castes of Bengal*, art. Agarwāl.

5. Occupation.

"It has been mentioned," says Sir H. Risley,[1] "that the garden is regarded as almost sacred, and the superstitious practices in vogue resemble those of the silk-worm breeder. The Bārui will not enter it until he has bathed and washed his clothes. Animals found inside are driven out, while women ceremonially unclean dare not enter within the gate. A Brāhman never sets foot inside, and old men have a prejudice against entering it. It has, however, been known to be used for assignations." The betel-vine is the leaf of *Piper betel* L., the word being derived from the Malayalam *vettila*, 'a plain leaf,' and coming to us through the Portuguese *betre* and *betle*. The leaf is called *pān*, and is eaten with the nut of *Areca catechu*, called in Hindi *supāri*. The vine needs careful cultivation, the gardens having to be covered to keep off the heat of the sun, while liberal treatment with manure and irrigation is needed. The joints of the creepers are planted in February, and begin to supply leaves in about five months' time. When the first creepers are stripped after a period of nearly a year, they are cut off and fresh ones appear, the plants being exhausted within a period of about two years after the first sowing. A garden may cover from half an acre to an acre of land, and belongs to a number of growers, who act in partnership, each owning so many lines of vines. The plain leaves are sold at from 2 annas to 4 annas a hundred, or a higher rate when they are out of season. Damoh, Rāmtek and Bilahri are three of the best-known centres of cultivation in the Central Provinces. The Bilahri leaf is described in the *Ain-i-Akbari* as follows : "The leaf called Bilahri is white and shining, and does not make the tongue harsh and hard. It tastes best of all kinds. After it has been taken away from the creeper, it turns white with some care after a month, or even after twenty days, when greater efforts are made."[2] For retail sale *bīdas* are prepared, consisting of a rolled betel-leaf containing areca-nut, catechu and lime, and fastened with a clove. Musk and cardamoms are sometimes added. Tobacco should be smoked after eating a *bīda* according to the saying,

---

[1] *Tribes and Castes of Bengal*, art. Bārui.

[2] Blochmann, *Ain-i-Akbari*, i. p.

72, quoted in Crooke's *Tribes and Castes*, art. Tamboli.

'Service without a patron, a young man without a shield, and betel without tobacco are alike savourless.' *Bīdas* are sold at from two to four for a pice (farthing). Women of the caste often retail them, and as many are good-looking they secure more custom ; they are also said to have an indifferent reputation. Early in the morning, when they open their shops, they burn some incense before the bamboo basket in which the leaves are kept, to propitiate Lakshmi, the goddess of wealth.

BARHAI

LIST OF PARAGRAPHS

Barhai, Sutār, Kharādi, Mistri. — The occupational caste of carpenters. The Barhais numbered nearly 110,000 persons in the Central Provinces and Berār in 1911, or about 1 in 150 persons. The caste is most numerous in Districts with large towns, and few carpenters are to be found in villages except in the richer and more advanced Districts. Hitherto such woodwork as the villagers wanted for agriculture has been made by the Lohār or blacksmith, while the country cots, the only wooden article of furniture in their houses, could be fashioned by their own hands or by the Gond woodcutter. In the Mandla District the Barhai caste counts only 300 persons, and about the same in Bālāghāt, in Drūg only 47 persons, and in the fourteen Chhattīsgarh Feudatory States, with a population of more than two millions, only some 800 persons. The name Barhai is said to be from the Sanskrit Vardhika and the root *vardh*, to cut. Sutār is a common name of the caste in the Marātha Districts, and is from Sūtra-kara, one who works by string, or a maker of string. The allusion may be to the Barhai's use of string in planing or measuring timber, or it may possibly indicate a transfer of occupation, the Sutārs having first been mainly string-makers and afterwards abandoned this calling for that of the carpenter. The first wooden implements and articles of furniture may have been held together by string before nails came into use. Kharādi is literally a turner, one who turns woodwork on

1. Strength and local distribution.

a lathe, from *kharāt*, a lathe. Mistri, a corruption of the English Mister, is an honorific title for master carpenters.

2. Internal structure.

The comparatively recent growth of the caste in these Provinces is shown by its subdivisions. The principal sub-castes of the Hindustāni Districts are the Pardeshi or foreigners, immigrants from northern India, and the Pūrbia or eastern, coming from Oudh ; other subcastes are the Sri Gaur Mālas or immigrants from Mālwa, the Berādi from Berār, and the Māhure from Hyderābād. We find also subcastes of Jāt and Teli Barhais, consisting of Jāts and Telis (oil-pressers) who have taken to carpentering. Two other caste-groups, the Chamār Barhais and Gondi Barhais, are returned, but these are not at present included in the Barhai caste, and consist merely of Chamārs and Gonds who work as carpenters but remain in their own castes. In the course of some generations, however, if the cohesive social force of the caste system continues un-abated, these groups may probably find admission into the Barhai caste. Colonel Tod notes that the progeny of one Makūr, a prince of the Jādon Rājpūt house of Jaisalmer, became carpenters, and were known centuries after as Makūr Sutārs. They were apparently considered illegitimate, as he states : " Illegitimate children can never overcome this natural defect among the Rājpūts. Thus we find among all classes of artisans in India some of royal but spurious descent." [1] The internal structure of the caste seems therefore to indicate that it is largely of foreign origin and to a certain degree of recent formation in these Provinces.

3. Marriage customs.

The caste are also divided into exogamous septs named after villages. In some localities it is said that they have no septs, but only surnames, and that people of the same surname cannot intermarry. Well-to-do persons marry their daughters before puberty and others when they can afford the expense of the ceremony. Brāhman priests are employed at weddings, though on other occasions their services are occasionally dis-pensed with. The wedding ceremony is of the type pre-valent in the locality. When the wedding procession reaches the bride's village it halts near the temple of Māroti or Hanumān. Among the Panchāl Barhais the bridegroom does

[1] *Rājasthān*, ii. p. 210.

not wear a marriage crown but ties a bunch of flowers to his turban. The bridegroom's party is entertained for five days. Divorce and the remarriage of widows are permitted. In most localities it is said that a widow is forbidden to marry her first husband's younger as well as his elder brother. Among the Pardeshi Barhais of Betūl if a bachelor desires to marry a widow he must first go through the ceremony with a branch or twig of the *gūlar* tree.[1]

The caste worship Viswakarma, the celestial architect, and venerate their trade implements on the Dasahra festival. They consider the sight of a mongoose and of a light-grey pigeon or dove as lucky omens. They burn the dead and throw the ashes into a river or tank, employing a Mahā-Brāhman to receive the gifts for the dead. *4. Religion.*

In social status the Barhais rank with the higher artisan castes. Brāhmans take water from them in some localities, perhaps more especially in towns. In Betūl for instance Hindustāni Brāhmans do not accept water from the rural Barhais. In Damoh where both the Barhai and Lohār are village menials, their status is said to be the same, and Brāhmans do not take water from Lohārs. Mr. Nesfield says that the Barhai is a village servant and ranks with the Kurmi, with whom his interests are so closely allied. But there seems no special reason why the interests of the carpenter should be more closely allied with the cultivator than those of any other village menial, and it may be offered as a surmise that carpentering as a distinct trade is of comparatively late origin, and was adopted by Kurmis, to which fact the connection noticed by Mr. Nesfield might be attributed ; hence the position of the Barhai among the castes from whom a Brāhman will take water. In some localities well-to-do members of the caste have begun to wear the sacred thread. *5. Social position.*

In the northern Districts and the cotton tract the Barhai works as a village menial. He makes and mends the plough and harrow (*bakhar*) and other wooden implements of agriculture, and makes new ones when supplied with the wood. In Wardha he receives an annual contribution of 100 lbs. of grain from each cultivator. In Betūl he gets 67 lbs. of grain *6. Occupation.*

[1] *Ficus glomerata.*

and other perquisites for each plough of four bullocks. For making carts and building or repairing houses he must be separately paid. At weddings the Barhai often supplies the sacred marriage-post and is given from four annas to a rupee. At the Diwāli festival he prepares a wooden peg about six inches long, and drives it into the cultivator's house inside the threshold, and receives half a pound to a pound of grain.

In cities the carpenters are rapidly acquiring an increased degree of skill as the demand for a better class of houses and furniture becomes continually greater and more extensive. The carpenters have been taught to make English furniture by such institutions as the Friends' Mission of Hoshangābād and other missionaries; and a Government technical school has now been opened at Nāgpur, in which boys from all over the Province are trained in the profession. Very little wood-carving with any pretensions to excellence has hitherto been done in the Central Provinces, but the Jain temples at Saugor and Khurai contain some fair woodwork. A good carpenter in towns can earn from 12 annas to Rs. 1-8 a day, and both his earnings and prospects have greatly improved within recent years. Sherring remarks of the Barhais: "As artisans they exhibit little or no inventive powers: but in imitating the workmanship of others they are perhaps unsurpassed in the whole world. They are equally clever in working from designs and models."[1]

Bāri.—A caste of household servants and makers of leaf-plates, belonging to northern India. The Bāris numbered 1200 persons in the Central Provinces in 1911, residing mainly in Jubbulpore and Mandla. Sir H. Risley remarks of the caste:[2] "Mr. Nesfield regards the Bāri as merely an offshoot from a semi-savage tribe known as Banmānush and Musāhār. He is said still to associate with them at times, and if the demand for leaf-plates and cups, owing to some temporary cause, such as a local fair or an unusual multitude of marriages, happens to become larger than he can at once supply, he gets them secretly made by his ruder kinsfolk and retails them at a higher rate, passing

---

[1] *Hindu Castes*, i. p. 316.
[2] *Tribes and Castes of Bengal*, art. Bāri.

them off as his own production.   The strictest Brāhmans,
those at least who aspire to imitate the self-denying life of
the ancient Indian hermit, never eat off any other plates
than those made of leaves."   " If the above view is correct,"
Sir H. Risley remarks, " the Bāris are a branch of a non-Aryan
tribe who have been given a fairly respectable position in the
social system in consequence of the demand for leaf-plates,
which are largely used by the highest as well as the lowest
castes.   Instances of this sort, in which a non-Aryan or
mixed group is promoted on grounds of necessity or convenience to a higher status than their antecedents would
entitle them to claim, are not unknown in other castes, and
must have occurred frequently in outlying parts of the
country, where the Aryan settlements were scanty and
imperfectly supplied with the social apparatus demanded by
the theory of ceremonial purity."   There is no reason why
the origin of the Bāri from the Banmānush (wild man of the
woods) or Musāhār (mouse-eater), a forest tribe, as suggested
by Mr. Nesfield from his observation of their mutual connection, should be questioned.   The making of leaf-plates is an
avocation which may be considered naturally to pertain to
the tribes frequenting jungles from which the leaves are
gathered ; and in the Central Provinces, though in the north
the Nai or barber ostensibly supplies the leaf-plates, probably
buying the leaves and getting them made up by Gonds and
others, in the Marātha Districts the Gond himself does so,
and many Gonds make their living by this trade.   The
people of the Marātha country are apparently less strict
than those of northern India, and do not object to eat off
plates avowedly the handiwork of Gonds.   The fact that
the Bāri has been raised to the position of a pure caste, so
that Brāhmans will take water from his hands, is one among
several instances of this elevation of the rank of the serving
castes for purposes of convenience.   The caste themselves
have the following legend of their origin : Once upon a time
Parmeshwar [1] was offering rice milk to the spirits of his
ancestors.   In the course of this ceremony the performer has
to present a gift known as Vikraya Dān, which cannot be
accepted by others without loss of position.   Parmeshwar

[1] Vishnu.

offered the gift to various Brāhmans, but they all refused it.
So he made a man of clay, and blew upon the image and
gave it life, and the god then asked the man whom he had
created to accept the gift which the Brāhmans had refused.
This man, who was the first Bāri, agreed on condition that
all men should drink with him and recognise his purity of
caste. Parmeshwar then told him to bring water in a cup,
and drank of it in the presence of all the castes. And in
consequence of this all the Hindus will take water from the
hands of a Bāri. They also say that their first ancestor was
named Sundar on account of his personal beauty ; but if so,
he failed to bequeath this quality to his descendants. The
proper avocation of the Bāris is, as already stated, the
manufacture of the leaf-cups and plates used by all Hindus
at festivals. In the Central Provinces these are made from
the large leaves of the *māhul* creeper (*Bauhinia Vahlii*), or
from the *palās* (*Butea frondosa*). The caste also act as
personal servants, handing round water, lighting and carrying torches at marriages and other entertainments and on
journeys, and performing other functions. Some of them
have taken to agriculture. Their women act as maids to
high-caste Hindu ladies, and as they are always about the
zenāna, are liable to lose their virtue. A curious custom
prevails in Mārwār on the birth of an heir to the throne.
An impression of the child's foot is taken by a Bāri on
cloth covered with saffron, and is exhibited to the native
chiefs, who make him rich presents.[1] The Bāris have the
reputation of great fidelity to their employers, and a
saying about them is, 'The Bāri will die fighting for his
master.'

Basdewa,[2] Wasudeo, Harbola, Kaparia, Jaga, Kapdi.—
A wandering beggar caste of mixed origin, who also
call themselves Sanādhya or Sanaurhia Brāhmans. The
Basdewas trace their origin to Wasudeo, the father of
Krishna, and the term Basdewa is a corruption of Wasudeo
or Wasudeva. Kaparia is the name they bear in the

[1] Sherring, *Tribes and Castes*, i.
pp. 403, 404.
[2] This article is compiled from
papers by Mr. W. N. Maw, Deputy
Commissioner, Damoh, and Murlīdhar,
Munsiff of Khurai in Saugor.

Anterved or country between the Ganges and Jumna, whence they claim to have come. Kaparia has been derived from *kapra*, cloth, owing to the custom of the Basdewas of having several dresses, which they change rapidly like the Bahrūpia, making themselves up in different characters as a show. Harbola is an occupational term, applied to a class of Basdewas who climb trees in the early morning and thence vociferate praises of the deity in a loud voice. The name is derived from *Har*, God, and *bolna*, to speak. As the Harbolas wake people up in the morning they are also called Jaga or Awakener. The number of Basdewas in the Central Provinces and Berār in 1911 was 2500, and they are found principally in the northern Districts and in Chhattīsgarh. They have several territorial subcastes, as Gangāputri or those who dwell on the banks of the Ganges ; Khaltia or Deswāri, those who belong to the Central Provinces ; Parauha, from *para*, a male buffalo calf, being the dealers in buffaloes ; Harbola or those who climb trees and sing the praises of God ; and Wasudeo, the dwellers in the Marātha Districts who marry only among themselves. The names of the exogamous divisions are very varied, some being taken from Brāhman *gotras* and Rājpūt septs, while others are the names of villages, or nicknames, or derived from animals and plants. It may be concluded from these names that the Basdewas are a mixed occupational group recruited from high and low castes, though they themselves say that they do not admit any outsiders except Brāhmans into the community. In Bombay[1] the Wasudevas have a special connection with Kumhārs or potters, whom they address by the term of *kāka* or paternal uncle, and at whose houses they lodge on their travels, presenting their host with the two halves of a cocoanut. The caste do not observe celibacy. A price of Rs. 25 has usually to be given for a bride, and a Brāhman is employed to perform the ceremony. At the conclusion of this the Brāhman invests the bridegroom with a sacred thread, which he thereafter continues to wear. Widow marriage is permitted, and widows are commonly married to widowers. Divorce is also permitted. When a man's wife dies he shaves his moustache and beard, if any,

[1] *Bombay Gazetteer*, xvii. p. 108.

in mourning and a father likewise for a daughter-in-law ; this is somewhat peculiar, as other Hindus do not shave the moustache for a wife or daughter-in-law. The Basdewas are wandering mendicants. In the Marātha Districts they wear a plume of peacock's feathers, which they say was given to them as a badge by Krishna. In Saugor and Damoh instead of this they carry during the period from Dasahra to the end of Māgh or from September to January a brass vessel called *matuk* bound on their heads. It is surmounted by a brass cone and adorned with mango-leaves, cowries and a piece of red cloth, and with figures of Rāma and Lakshman. Their stock-in-trade for begging consists of two *kartāls* or wooden clappers which are struck against each other ; *ghungrus* or jingling ornaments for the feet, worn when dancing ; and a *paijna* or kind of rattle, consisting of two semicircular iron wires bound at each end to a piece of wood with rings slung on to them ; this is simply shaken in the hand and gives out a sound from the movement of the rings against the wires. They worship all these implements as well as their beggar's wallet on the Janam-Ashtami or Krishna's birthday, the Dasahra, and the full moon of Māgh (January). They rise early and beg only in the morning from about four till eight, and sing songs in praise of Sarwan and Karan. Sarwan was a son renowned for his filial piety ; he maintained and did service to his old blind parents to the end of their lives, much against the will of his wife, and was proof against all her machinations to induce him to abandon them. Karan was a proverbially charitable king, and all his family had the same virtue. His wife gave away daily rice and pulse to those who required it, his daughter gave them clothes, his son distributed cows as alms and his daughter-in-law cocoanuts. The king himself gave only gold, and it is related of him that he was accustomed to expend a maund and a quarter [1] weight of gold in alms-giving before he washed himself and paid his morning devotions. Therefore the Basdewas sing that he who gives early in the morning acquires the merit of Karan ; and their presence at this time affords the requisite opportunity to anybody who may be desirous of emulating the

---

[1] About 100 lbs.

king.   At the end of every couplet they cry ' Jai Ganga ' or
' Har Ganga,' invoking the Ganges.

The Harbolas have each a beat of a certain number of
villages which must not be infringed by the others.   Their
method is to ascertain the name of some well-to-do person
in the village.   This done, they climb a tree in the early
morning before sunrise, and continue chanting his praises in
a loud voice until he is sufficiently flattered by their eulogies
or wearied by their importunity to throw down a present of
a few pice under the tree, which the Harbola, descending,
appropriates.   The Basdewas of the northern Districts are
now commonly engaged in the trade of buying and selling
buffaloes.   They take the young male calves from Saugor
and Damoh to Chhattīsgarh, and there retail them at a profit
for rice cultivation, driving them in large herds along the
road.   For the capital which they have to borrow to make
their purchases, they are charged very high rates of interest.
The Basdewas have here a special veneration for the buffalo
as the animal from which they make their livelihood, and
they object strongly to the calves being taken to be tied out
as baits for tiger, refusing, it is said, to accept payment if the
calf should be killed.   Their social status is not high, and
none but the lowest castes will take food from their hands.
They eat flesh and drink liquor, but abstain from pork, fowls
and beef.   Some of the caste have given up animal food.

BASOR

1. Numbers and distribution. **Basor,**[1] **Bansphor, Dhulia, Burud.**—The occupational caste of bamboo-workers, the two first names being Hindi and the last the term used in the Marātha Districts. The cognate Uriya caste is called Kandra and the Telugu one Medara. The Basors numbered 53,000 persons in the Central Provinces and Berār in 1911. About half the total number reside in the Saugor, Damoh and Jubbulpore Districts. The word Basor is a corruption of Bānsphor, ' a breaker of bamboos.' Dhulia, from *dholi,* a drum, means a musician.

2. Caste traditions. The caste trace their origin from Raja Benu or Venu who ruled at Singorgarh in Damoh. It is related of him that he was so pious that he raised no taxes from his subjects, but earned his livelihood by making and selling bamboo fans. He could of course keep no army, but he knew magic, and when he broke his fan the army of the enemy broke up in unison. Venu is a Sanskrit word meaning bamboo. But a mythological Sanskrit king called Vena is mentioned in the Purānas, from whom for his sins was born the first Nishāda, the lowest of human beings, and Manu[2] states that the bamboo-worker is the issue of a

---

[1] Compiled from papers by Mr. Rām Lāl, B.A., Deputy Inspector of Schools, Saugor; Mr. Vishnu Gangādhar Gādgil, Tahsīldār, Narsinghpur ; Mr. Devi Dayal, Tahsīldār, Hatta ; Mr. Kanhya Lāl, B.A., Deputy Inspector of Schools,

Betūl ; Mr. Keshava Rao, Headmaster, Middle School, Seoni ; and Bapu Gulāb Singh, Superintendent, Land Records, Betūl.

[2] Chapter x. 37, and Shūdra Kamlākar, p. 284.

Nishāda or Chandāl father and a Vaideha [1] mother. So
that the local story may be a corruption of the Brāhmanical
tradition. Another legend relates that in the beginning there
were no bamboos, and the first Basor took the serpent which
Siva wore round his neck and going to a hill planted it with
its head in the ground. A bamboo at once sprang up on
the spot, and from this the Basor made the first winnowing
fan. And the snake-like root of the bamboo, which no doubt
suggested the story to its composer, is now adduced in proof
of it.

The Basors of the northern Districts are divided into a   3. Sub-
number of subcastes, the principal of which are : the Purānia divisions.
or Juthia, who perhaps represent the oldest section, Purānia
being from *purāna* old ; they are called Juthia because they
eat the leavings of others ; the Barmaiya or Malaiya,
apparently a territorial group ; the Deshwāri or Bundelkhandi who reside in the *desh* or native place of Bundelkhand ; the Gūdha or Gūrha, the name being derived by
some from *gūda* a pigsty ; the Dumār or Dom Basors ; the
Dhubela, perhaps from the Dhobi caste ; and the Dharkār.
Two or three of the above names appear to be those of
other low castes from which the Basor caste may have been
recruited, perhaps at times when a strong demand existed
for bamboo-workers. The Buruds do not appear to be
sufficiently numerous to have subcastes. But they include
a few Telenga Buruds who are really Medaras, and the caste
proper are therefore sometimes known as Marātha Buruds to
distinguish them from these. The caste has numerous *bainks*
or exogamous groups or septs, the names of which may chiefly
be classified as territorial and totemistic. Among the former
are Mahobia, from the town of Mahoba ; Sirmaiya, from
Sirmau ; Orahia, from Orai, the battlefield of the Banāphar
generals, Alha and Udal ; Tikarahia from Tikāri, and so on.
The totemistic septs include the Sānpero from *sānp* a snake,
the Mangrelo from *mangra* a crocodile, the Morya from *mor*
a peacock, the Titya from the *titehri* bird and the Sarkia
from *sarki* or red ochre, all of which worship their respective
totems. The Katarya or 'dagger' sept worship a real or
painted dagger at their marriage, and the Kemia, a branch

---

[1] A Vaideha was the child of a Vaishya father and a Brāhman mother.

of the *kem* tree (*Stephegyne parvifolia*). The Bandrelo, from *bandar*, worship a painted monkey. One or two groups are named after castes, as Bamhnelo from Brāhman and Bargujaria from Bargūjar Rājpūt, thus indicating that members of these castes became Basors and founded families. One sept is called Marha from Marhai, the goddess of cholera, and the members worship a picture of the goddess drawn in black. The name of the Kulhāntia sept means somersault, and these turn a somersault before worshipping their gods. So strong is the totemistic idea that some of the territorial groups worship objects with similar names. Thus the Mahobia group, whose name is undoubtedly derived from the town of Mahoba, have adopted the mahua tree as their totem, and digging a small hole in the ground place in it a little water and the liquor made from mahua flowers, and worship it. This represents the process of distillation of country liquor. Similarly, the Orahia group, who derive their name from the town of Orai, now worship the *urai* or *khaskhas* grass, and the Tikarahia from Tikāri worship a *tikli* or glass spangle.

4. Marriage.

The marriage of persons belonging to the same *baink* or sept and also that of first cousins is forbidden. The age of marriage is settled by convenience, and no stigma attaches to its postponement beyond adolescence. Intrigues of unmarried girls with men of their own or any higher caste are usually overlooked. The ceremony follows the standard Hindi and Marāthi forms, and presents no special features. A bride-price called *chāri*, amounting to seven or eight rupees, is usually paid. In Betūl the practice of *lamjhana*, or serving the father-in-law for a term of years before marrying his daughter, is sometimes followed. Widow-marriage is permitted, and the widow is expected to wed her late husband's younger brother. The Basors are musicians by profession, but in Betūl the *narsingha*, a peculiar kind of crooked trumpet, is the only implement which may be played at the marriage of a widow. A woman marrying a second time forfeits all interest in the property of her late husband, unless she is without issue and there are no near relatives of her husband to take it. Divorce is effected by the breaking of the woman's bangles in public. If obtained by the wife,

BASORS MAKING BASKETS OF BAMBOO.

Bemrose, Collo., Derby.

she must repay to her first husband the expenditure incurred by him for her marriage when she takes a second. But the acceptance of this payment is considered derogatory and the husband refuses it unless he is poor.

The Basors worship the ordinary Hindu deities and also ghosts and spirits. Like the other low castes they entertain a special veneration for Devi. They profess to exorcise evil spirits and the evil eye, and to cure other disorders and diseases through the agency of their incantations and the goblins who do their bidding. They burn their dead when they can afford it and otherwise bury them, placing the corpse in the grave with its head to the north. The body of a woman is wrapped in a red shroud and that of a man in a white one. They observe mourning for a period of three to ten days, but in Jubbulpore it always ends with the fortnight in which the death takes place ; so that a person dying on the 15th or 30th of the month is mourned only for one day. They eat almost every kind of food, including beef, pork, fowls, liquor and the leavings of others, but abjure crocodiles, monkeys, snakes and rats. Many of them have now given up eating cow's flesh in deference to Hindu feeling. They will take food from almost any caste except sweepers, and one or two others, as Joshi and Jasondhi, towards whom for some unexplained reason they entertain a special aversion. They will admit outsiders belonging to any caste from whom they can take food into the community. They are generally considered as impure, and live outside the village, and their touch conveys pollution, more especially in the Marātha Districts. The ordinary village menials, as the barber and washerman, will not work for them, and services of this nature are performed by men of their own community. As, however, their occupation is not in itself unclean, they rank above sweepers, Chamārs and Dhobis. Temporary exclusion from caste is imposed for the usual offences, and the almost invariable penalty for readmission is a feast to the castefellows. A person, male or female, who has been convicted of adultery must have the head shaved, and is then seated in the centre of the caste-fellows and pelted by them with the leavings of their food. Basor women are not permitted to wear nose-rings on pain of exclusion from caste.

5. Religion and social status.

6. Occupation.

The trade of the Basors is a very essential one to the agricultural community. They make numerous kinds of baskets, among which may be mentioned the *chunka*, a very small one, the *tokni*, a basket of middle size, and the *tokna*, a very large one. The *dauri* is a special basket with a lining of matting for washing rice in a stream. The *jhānpi* is a round basket with a cover for holding clothes; the *tipanna* a small one in which girls keep dolls; and the *bilahra* a still smaller one for holding betel-leaf. Other articles made from bamboo-bark are the *chalni* or sieve, the *khunkhuna* or rattle, the *bānsuri* or wooden flute, the *bijna* or fan, and the *sūpa* or winnowing-fan. All grain is cleaned with the help of the *sūpa* both on the threshing-floor and in the house before consumption, and a child is always laid in one as soon as it is born. In towns the Basors make the bamboo matting which is so much used. The only implement they employ is the *bānka*, a heavy curved knife, with which all the above articles are made. The *bānka* is duly worshipped at the Diwāli festival. The Basors are also the village musicians, and a band of three or four of them play at weddings and on other festive occasions. Some of them work as pig-breeders and others are village watchmen. The women often act as midwives. One subcaste, the Dumār, will do scavenger's work, but they never take employment as *saises*, because the touch of horse-dung is considered as a pollution, entailing temporary excommunication from caste.

1. General notice.

Bedar.[1]—A small caste of about 1500 persons, belonging to Akola, Khāndesh and Hyderābād. Their ancestors were Pindāris, apparently recruited from the different Marātha castes, and when the Pindāris were suppressed they obtained or were awarded land in the localities where they now reside, and took to cultivation. The more respectable Bedars say that their ancestors were Tirole Kunbis, but when Tipu Sultān invaded the Carnatic he took many of them prisoners and ordered them to become Muhammadans. In order to please him they took food with Muhammadans,

---

[1] Based on a paper by Rao Sahib Dhonduji, retired Inspector of Police, Akola, and information collected by Mr. Adurām Chaudhri of the Gazetteer office.

and on this account the Kunbis put them out of caste until they should purify themselves. But as there were a large number of them, they did not do this, and have remained a separate caste. The real derivation of the name is unknown, but the caste say that it is *be-dar* or 'without fear,' and was given to them on account of their bravery. They have now obtained a warrant from the descendant of Shankar Achārya, or the high priest of Sivite Hindus, permitting them to describe themselves as Pūt Kunbi or purified Kunbi.[1] The community is clearly of a most mixed nature, as there are also Dher or Mahār Bedars. They refuse to take food from other Mahārs and consider themselves defiled by their touch. The social position of the caste also presents some peculiar features. Several of them have taken service in the army and police, and have risen to the rank of native officer ; and Rao Sāhib Dhonduji, a retired Inspector of Police, is a prominent member of the caste. The Rāja of Surpur, near Raichur, is also said to be a Bedar, while others are ministerial officials occupying a respectable position. Yet of the Bedars generally it is said that they cannot draw water freely from the public wells, and in Nāsik Bedar constables are not considered suitable for ordinary duty, as people object to their entering houses. The caste must therefore apparently have higher and lower groups, differing considerably in position.

They have three subdivisions, the Marātha, Telugu and Kande Bedars. The names of their exogamous sections are also Marāthi. Nevertheless they retain one or two northern customs, presumably acquired from association with the Pindāris. Their women do not tuck the body-cloth in behind the waist, but draw it over the right shoulder. They wear the *choli* or Hindustāni breast-cloth tied in front, and have a hooped silver ornament on the top of the head, which is known as *dhora*. They eat goats, fowls and the flesh of the wild pig, and drink liquor, and will take food from a Kunbi or a Phulmāli, and pay little heed to the rules of social impurity. But Hindustāni Brāhmans act as their priests.

Before a wedding they call a Brāhman and worship him as a god, the ceremony being known as Deo Brāhman. The

2. Subdivisions and marriage customs.

---

[1] Mr. Marten's *C.P. Census Report* (1911), p. 212.

Brāhman then cooks food in the house of his host.   On the
same occasion a person specially nominated by the Brāhman,
and known as Deokia, fetches an earthen vessel from the
potter, and this is worshipped with offerings of turmeric and
rice, and a cotton thread is tied round it.   Formerly it is
said they worshipped the spent bullets picked up after a
battle, and especially any which had been extracted from the
body of a wounded person.

3. Funeral
rites.

When a man is about tò die they take him down from
his cot and lay him on the ground with his head in the lap
of a relative.   The dead are buried, a person of importance
being carried to the grave in a sitting posture, while others
are laid out in the ordinary manner.   A woman is buried in
a green cloth and a breast-cloth.   When the corpse has been
prepared for the funeral they take some liquor, and after a
few drops have been poured into the mouth of the corpse the
assembled persons drink the rest.   While following to the
grave they beat drums and play on musical instruments and
sing religious songs ; and if a man dies during the night,
since he is not buried till the morning, they sit in the house
playing and singing for the remaining hours of darkness.
The object of this custom must presumably be to keep away
evil spirits.   After the funeral each man places a leafy branch
of some tree or shrub on the grave, and on the thirteenth
day they put food before a cow and also throw some on to
the roof of the house as a portion for the crows.

BELDĀR

Beldār,[1] **Od, Sonkar, Rāj, Larhia, Kārīgar, Matkūda, Chunkar, Munurwār, Thapatkari, Vaddar, Pāthrot, Takāri.**—The term Beldār is generically applied to a number of occupational groups of more or less diverse origin, who work as masons or navvies, build the earthen embankments of tanks or fields, carry lime and bricks and in former times refined salt. Beldār means one who carries a *bel*, a hoe or mattock. In 1911 a total of 25,000 Beldārs were returned from the Central Provinces, being most numerous in the Nimār, Wardha, Nāgpur, Chānda and Raipur districts. The Nunia, Murha and Sānsia (Uriya) castes, which have been treated in separate articles, are also frequently known as Beldār, and cannot be clearly distinguished from the main caste. If they are all classed together the total of the earth- and stone-working castes comes to 35,000 persons.

It is probable that the bulk of the Beldārs and allied castes are derived from the non-Aryan tribes. The Murhas or navvies of the northern Districts appear to be an offshoot of the Bind tribe ; the people known as Matkūda (earth-digger) are usually Gonds or Pardhāns ; the Sānsias and Larhias or Uriyas of Chhattīsgarh and the Uriya country seem to have originated from the Kol, Bhuiya and Oraon

1. General notice.

---

[1] This article is based on papers by Mr. A. K. Smith, C.S., Mr. Khande Rāo, Superintendent of Land Records, Raipur, and Munshi Kanhiya Lāl, of the Gazetteer office.

tribes, the Kols especially making excellent diggers and masons; the Oddes or Vaddars of Madras are a very low caste, and some of their customs point to a similar origin, though the Munurwār masons of Chānda appear to have belonged originally to the Kāpu caste of cultivators.

The term Rāj, which is also used for the Beldārs in the northern Districts, has the distinctive meaning of a mason, while Chūnkar signifies a lime-burner. The Sonkars were formerly occupied in Saugor in carrying lime, bricks and earth on donkeys, but they have now abandoned this calling in Chhattīsgarh and taken to growing vegetables, and have been given a short separate notice. In Hoshangābād some Muhammadan Beldārs are now also found.

2. Beldārs of the northern Districts. The Beldārs of Saugor say that their ancestors were engaged in refining salt from earth. A divine saint named Nona Rīshi (*non*, salt) came down on earth, and while cooking his food mixed some saline soil with it. The bread tasted much better in consequence, and he made the earth into a ball or *goli* and taught his followers to extract the salt from it, whence their descendants are known as Goli Beldārs. The customs of these Beldārs are of the ordinary low-caste type. The wedding procession is accompanied by drums, fireworks and, if means permit, a nautch-girl. If a man puts away his wife without adequate cause the caste *panchāyat* may compel him to support her so long as she remains of good conduct. The party seeking a divorce, whether husband or wife, has to pay Rs. 7 to the caste committee and the other partner Rs. 3, irrespective of where the blame rests, and each remains out of caste until he or she pays.

These Beldārs will not take food from any caste but their own, and will not take water from a Brāhman, though they will accept it from Kurmis, Gūjars and similar castes. Sir H. Risley notes that their women always remove earth in baskets on the head. "The Beldārs regard this mode of carrying earth as distinctive of themselves, and will on no account transport it in baskets slung from the shoulders. They work very hard when paid by the piece, and are notorious for their skill in manipulating the pillars (*sākhi*, witness) left to mark work done, so as to exaggerate the

measurement.   On one occasion while working for me on a
large lake at Govindpur, in the north of the Mānbhum
District, a number of Beldārs transplanted an entire pillar
during the night and claimed payment for several thousand
feet of imaginary earthwork.   The fraud was most skilfully
carried out, and was only detected by accident."[1]   The
Beldārs are often dishonest in their dealings, and will take
large advances for a tank or embankment, and then abscond
with the money without doing the work.   During the open
season parties of the caste travel about in camp looking for
work, their furniture being loaded on donkeys.   They carry
grain in earthen pots encased in bags of netting, neatly and
closely woven, and grind their wheat daily in a small mill
set on a goat-skin.   Butter is made in one of their pots with
a churning-stick, consisting of a cogged wheel fixed on to
the end of a wooden rod.

The Beldārs of Chhattīsgarh are divided into the Odia 3. Odias of
or Uriya, Larhia, Kūchbandhia, Matkūda and Kārīgar Chhattīs-
groups.   Uriya and Larhia are local names, applied to garh.
residents of the Uriya country and Chhattīsgarh respectively.
Odia is the name of a low Madras caste of masons, but
whether it is a corruption of Uriya is not clear.   Kārīgar
means a workman, and Kūchbandhia is the name of a
separate caste, who make loom-combs for weavers.   The
Odias pretend to be fallen Rājpūts.   They say that when
Indra stole the sacrificial horse of Rāja Sāgar and kept it
in the underworld, the Rāja's thousand sons dug great holes
through the earth to get it.   Finally they arrived at the
underworld and were all reduced to ashes by the Rīshi
Kapil Muni, who dwelt there.   Their ghosts besought him
for life, and he said that their descendants should always
continue to dig holes in the earth, which would be used as
tanks ; and that whenever a tank was dug by them, and its
marriage celebrated with a sacrifice, the savour of the sacrifice
would descend to the ghosts and would afford them sustenance.   The Odias say that they are the descendants of
the Rāja's sons, and unless a tank is dug and its marriage
celebrated by them it remains impure.   These Odias have
their tutelary deity in Rewah State, and at his shrine is

---

[1] *Tribes and Castes of Bengal,* art. Beldār.

a flag which none but an Odia of genuine descent from Rāja Sāgar's sons can touch without some injury befalling him. If any Beldār therefore claims to belong to their caste they call on him to touch the flag, and if he does so with impunity they acknowledge him as a brother.

4. Other Chhattīs-garhi Beldārs.　　The other groups of Chhattīsgarhi Beldārs are of lower status, and clearly derived from the non-Aryan tribes. They eat pigs, and at intervals of two or three years they celebrate the worship of Gosain Deo with a sacrifice of pigs, the deity being apparently a deified ascetic or mendicant. On this occasion the Dhīmars, Gonds, and all other castes which eat pig's flesh join in the sacrifice, and consume the meat together after the fashion of the rice at Jagannāth's temple, which all castes may eat together without becoming impure. These Beldārs use asses for the transport of their bricks and stones, and on the Diwāli day they place a lamp before the ass and pay reverence to it. They say that at their marriages a bride-price of Rs. 100 or Rs. 200 must always be paid, but they are allowed to give one or two donkeys and value them at Rs. 50 apiece. They make grindstones (*chakki*), combs for straightening the threads on the loom, and frames for stretching the threads. These frames are called *dongi*, and are made either wholly or partly from the horns of animals, a fact which no doubt renders them impure.

5. Munur-wār and Telenga.　　In Chānda the principal castes of stone-workers are the Telengas (Telugus), who are also known as Thāpatkari (tapper or chiseller), Telenga Kunbi and Munurwār. They occupy a higher position than the ordinary Beldār, and Kunbis will take water from them and sometimes food. They say that they came into Chānda from the Telugu country along the Godāvari and Prānhita rivers to build the great wall of Chānda and the palaces and tombs of the Gond kings. There is no reason to doubt that the Munurwārs are a branch of the Kāpu cultivating caste of the Telugu country. Mr. A. K. Smith states that they refuse to eat the flesh of an animal which has been skinned by a Mahār, a Chamār, or a Gond; the Kunbis and Marāthas also consider flesh touched by a Mahār or Chamār to be impure, but do not object to a Gond. Like the Berār

Kunbis, the Telengas prefer that an animal should be killed by the rite of *halāl* as practised by Muhammadan butchers. The reason no doubt is that the *halāl* is a method of sacrificial slaughter, and the killing of the animal is legitimised even though by the ritual of a foreign religion. The Thāpatkaris appear to be a separate group, and their original profession was to collect and retail jungle fruits and roots having medicinal properties. Though the majority have become stone- and earth-workers some of them still do this.

The Vaddars or Wadewārs are a branch of the Odde 6. Vaddar. caste of Madras. They are almost an impure caste, and a section of them are professional criminals. Their women wear glass bangles only on the left arm, those on the right arm being made of brass or other metal. This rule has no doubt been introduced because glass bangles would get broken when they were supporting loads on the head. The men often wear an iron bangle on the left wrist, which they say keeps off the lightning. Mr. Thurston states that "Women who have had seven husbands are much respected among the Oddes, and their blessing on a bridal pair is greatly prized. They work in gangs on contract, and every one, except very old and very young, shares in the labour. The women carry the earth in baskets, while the men use the pick and spade. The babies are usually tied up in cloths, which are suspended, hammock-fashion, from the boughs of trees. A woman found guilty of immorality is said to have to carry a basketful of earth from house to house before she is readmitted to the caste. The stone-cutting Vaddars are the principal criminals, and by going about under the pretence of mending grindstones they obtain much useful information as to the houses to be looted or parties of travellers to be attacked. In committing a highway robbery or dacoity they are always armed with stout sticks."[1]

In Berār besides the regular Beldārs two castes of stone- 7. Pāthrot. workers are found, the Pathrāwats or Pāthrots (stone-breakers) and the Takāris, who should perhaps be classed as separate castes. Both make and sharpen millstones and grindstones, and they are probably only occupational groups of recent formation. The Takāris are connected with the Pārdhi caste

---

[1] *The Castes and Tribes of Southern India*, art. Odde.

of professional hunters and fowlers and may be a branch of
them.   The social customs of the Pāthrots resemble those
of the Kunbis.   " They will take cooked food from a Sutār
or a Kumbhār.   Imprisonment, the killing of a cow or
criminal intimacy of a man with a woman of another caste
is punished by temporary outcasting, readmission involving
a fine of Rs. 4 or Rs. 5.   Their chief deity is the Devi of
Tuljāpur and their chief festival Dasahra ; the implements
of the caste are worshipped twice a year, on Gudhi Pādwa
and Diwāli.   Women are tattooed with a crescent between
the eyebrows and dots on the right side of the nose, the
right cheek, and the chin, and a basil plant or peacock is
drawn on their wrists." [1]

8. Takāri.   "The Takāris take their name from the verb *tākne*, to
reset or rechisel.   They mend the handmills (*chakkis*) used
for grinding corn, an occupation which is sometimes shared
with them by the Langoti Pārdhis.   The Takāri's avocation
of chiselling grindstones gives him excellent opportunities
for examining the interior economy of houses, and the position of boxes and cupboards, and for gauging the wealth
of the inmates.   They are the most inveterate house-breakers
and dangerous criminals.   A form of crime favoured by
the Takāri, in common with many other criminal classes, is
that of decoying into a secluded spot outside the village
the would-be receiver of stolen property and robbing him
of his cash—a trick which carries a wholesome lesson with
it." [2]   The chisel with which they chip the grindstones
furnishes, as stated by Mr. D. A. Smyth, D.S.P., an excellent implement for breaking a hole through the mud wall
of a house.

Beria, Bedia.

[*Bibliography* : Sir H. Risley's *Tribes and Castes of Bengal* ; Rājendra Lāl
Mitra in *Memoirs, Anthropological Society of London*, iii. p. 122 ; Mr. Crooke's
Tribes and Castes of the North-Western Provinces and Oudh ; Mr. Kennedy's
Criminal Classes of the Bombay Presidency ; Major Gunthorpe's *Criminal
Tribes* ; Mr. Gayer's *Lectures on some Criminal Tribes of the Central Pro-
vinces* ; Colonel Sleeman's *Report on the Badhak or Bāgri Dacoits*.]

1. Histori-   A caste of gipsies and thieves who are closely con-
cal notice.   nected with the Sānsias.   In 1891 they numbered 906

[1] *Akola District Gazetteer* (Mr. C.   [2] *Amraoti District Gazetteer* (Messrs.
Brown), pp. 132, 133.   Nelson and Fitzgerald), p. 146.

persons in the Central Provinces, distributed over the northern Districts; in 1901 they were not separately classified but were identified with the Nats. " They say that some generations ago two brothers resided in the Bhartpur territory, of whom one was named Sains Mūl and the other Mullanur. The descendants of Sains Mūl are the Sānsias and those of Mullanur the Berias or Kolhātis, who are vagrants and robbers by hereditary profession, living in tents or huts of matting, like Nats or other vagrant tribes, and having their women in common without any marriage ceremonies or ties whatsoever. Among themselves or their relatives the Sānsias or descendants of Sains Mūl, they are called Dholi or Kolhāti. The descendants of the brothers eat, drink and smoke together, and join in robberies, but never intermarry." So Colonel Sleeman wrote in 1849, and other authorities agree on the close connection or identity of the Berias and Sānsias of Central India. The Kolhātis belong mainly to the Deccan and are apparently a branch of the Berias, named after the *Kolhān* or long pole with which they perform acrobatic feats. The Berias of Central India differ in many respects from those of Bengal. Here Sir H. Risley considers Beria to be 'the generic name of a number of vagrant, gipsy-like groups'; and a full description of them has been given by Bābu Rājendra Lāl Mitra, who considers them to resemble the gipsies of Europe. " They are noted for a light, elastic, wiry make, very uncommon in the people of this country. In agility and hardness they stand unrivalled. The men are of a brownish colour, like the bulk of Bengalis, but never black. The women are of lighter complexion and generally well-formed; some of them have considerable claims to beauty, and for a race so rude and primitive in their habits as the Berias, there is a sharpness in the features of their women which we see in no other aboriginal race in India. Like the gipsies of Europe they are noted for the symmetry of their limbs; but their offensive habits, dirty clothing and filthy professions give them a repulsive appearance, which is heightened by the reputation they have of kidnapping children and frequenting burial-grounds and places of cremation. . . . Familiar with the use of bows and arrows and great adepts in laying snares and traps, they are seldom without large supplies of game and flesh of wild animals of all kinds. They keep the dried bodies of a variety of birds for medical purposes ; mongoose, squirrels and flying-foxes they eat with avidity as articles of luxury. Spirituous liquors and intoxicating drugs are indulged in to a large extent, and chiefs of clans assume the title of Bhangi or drinkers of hemp (*bhāng*) as a mark of honour. . . . In lying, thieving and knavery the Beria is not a whit inferior to his brother gipsy of Europe. The Beria woman deals in charms for exorcising the devil and palmistry is her special vocation. She also carries with her a bundle of herbs and other real or pretended charms against sickness of body or mind ; and she is much sought after by village maidens for the sake of the philtre with which she restores to them their estranged lovers ; while she foretells the date when absent friends will return and the sex of unborn children. They practise cupping with buffalo horns, pretend to extract worms from decayed teeth and are commonly employed as tattooers. At home the Beria woman makes mats of palm-leaves, while her lord alone cooks. . . . Beria women are even more circumspect than European gipsies. If a wife does not return before the jackal's cry is heard in the evening, she is subject to severe punishment. It is said that a *faux pas* among her own kindred is not considered reprehensible ; but it is certain that no Berini has ever been known to be at fault with any one not of her own caste." This last statement is not a little astonishing, inasmuch as in Central India and in Bundelkhand Berni is an equivalent term for a prostitute. A similar diversity of conjugal morality has been noticed between the Bāgris of northern India and the Vāghris of Gujarāt.[1]

2. Criminal tendencies in the Central Provinces.

In other respects also the Berias of Bengal appear to be more respectable than the remainder of the caste, obtaining their livelihood by means which, if disreputable, are not actually dishonest ; while in Central India the women Berias are prostitutes and the men house-breakers and thieves. These latter are so closely connected with the Sānsias that the account of that caste is also applicable to the Berias.

[1] See article on Badhak.

In Jubbulpore, Mr. Gayer states, the caste are expert house-
breakers, bold and daring, and sometimes armed with swords
and matchlocks.   They sew up stolen property in their bed-
quilts and secrete it in the hollow legs of their sleeping-cots,
and the women habitually conceal jewels and even coins in
the natural passages of the body, in which they make special
saos or receptacles by practice.   The Beria women go about
begging, and often break open the doors of unoccupied
houses in the daytime and steal anything they can find.[1]
Both Sānsia and Beria women wear a *laong* or clove in the
left nostril.

As already stated, the women are professional prostitutes,
but these do not marry, and on arrival at maturity they
choose the life which they prefer.   Mr. Crooke states,[2] however, that regular marriages seldom occur among them,
because nearly all the girls are reserved for prostitution,
and the men keep concubines drawn from any fairly respectable caste.   So far is this the rule that in some localities if
a man marries a girl of the tribe he is put out of caste or
obliged to pay a fine to the tribal council.   This last rule
does not seem to obtain in the Central Provinces, but
marriages are uncommon.   In a colony of Berias in Jubbulpore[3] numbering sixty families it was stated that only eight
weddings could be remembered as having occurred in the
last fifty years.   The boys therefore have to obtain wives as
best they can ; sometimes orphan girls from other castes
are taken into the community, or any outsider is picked up.
For a bride from the caste itself a sum of Rs. 100 is usually
demanded, and the same has to be paid by a Beria man
who takes a wife from the Nat or Kanjar castes, as is sometimes done.   When a match is proposed they ask the
expectant bridegroom how many thefts he has committed
without detection ; and if his performances have been
inadequate they refuse to give him the girl on the ground
that he will be unable to support a wife.   At the betrothal
the boy's parents go to the girl's house, taking with them a
potful of liquor round which a silver ring is placed and a

3. Social customs.

---

[1] Kennedy, p. 247.
[2] Crooke, art. Beria.
[3] The following particulars are taken

from a note by Mr. K. N. Dāte,
Deputy Superintendent, Reformatory
School, Jubbulpore.

pig. The ring is given to the girl and the head of the pig to her father, while the liquor and the body of the pig provide a feast for the caste. They consult Brāhmans at their birth and marriage ceremonies. Their principal deities appear to be their ancestors, whom they worship on the same day of the month and year as that on which their death took place. They make an offering of a pig to the goddess Dadaju or Devi before starting on their annual predatory excursions. Some rice is thrown into the animal's ear before it is killed, and the direction in which it turns its head is selected as the one divinely indicated for their route. Prostitution is naturally not regarded as any disgrace, and the women who have selected this profession mix on perfectly equal terms with those who are married. They occupy, in fact, a more independent position, as they dispose absolutely of their own earnings and property, and on their death it devolves on their daughters or other female relatives, males having no claim to it, in some localities at least. Among the children of married couples daughters inherit equally with sons. A prostitute is regarded as the head of the family so far as her children are concerned. Outsiders are freely admitted into the caste on giving a feast to the community. In Saugor the women of the caste, known as Berni, are the village dancing-girls, and are employed to give performances in the cold weather, especially at the Holi festival, where they dance the whole night through, fortified by continuous potations of liquor. This dance is called *rai*, and is accompanied by most obscene songs and gestures.

BHAINA

LIST OF PARAGRAPHS

Bhaina.[1]—A primitive tribe peculiar to the Central Provinces and found principally in the Bilāspur District and the adjoining area, that is, in the wild tract of forest country between the Satpūra range and the south of the Chota Nāgpur plateau. In 1911 about 17,000 members of the tribe were returned. The tribe is of mixed descent and appears to have been derived principally from the Baigas and Kawars, having probably served as a city of refuge to persons expelled from these and other tribes and the lower castes for irregular sexual relations. Their connection with the Baigas is shown by the fact that in Mandla the Baigas have two subdivisions, which are known as Rai or Rāj-Bhaina, and Kath, or catechu-making Bhaina. The name therefore would appear to have originated with the Baiga tribe. A Bhaina is also not infrequently found to be employed in the office of village priest and magician, which goes by the name of Baiga in Bilāspur. And a Bhaina has the same reputation as a Baiga for sorcery, it being said of him—

Mainhār ki mānjh
Bhaina ki pāng

1. The tribe derived from the Baigas.

---

[1] This article is based principally on a paper by Panna Lāl, Revenue Inspector, Bilāspur, and also on papers by Mr. Syed Sher Ali, Nāib-Tahsīldār, Mr. Hira Lāl and Mr. Adurām Chaudhri of the Gazetteer office.

or 'The magic of a Bhaina is as deadly as the powdered *mainhār* fruit,' this fruit having the property of stupefying fish when thrown into the water, so that they can easily be caught.   This reputation simply arises from the fact that in his capacity of village priest the Bhaina performs the various magical devices which lay the ghosts of the dead, protect the village against tigers, ensure the prosperity of the crops and so on.   But it is always the older residents of any locality who are employed by later comers in this office, because they are considered to have a more intimate acquaintance with the local deities.   And consequently we are entitled to assume that the Bhainas are older residents of the country where they are found than their neighbours, the Gonds and Kawars.   There is other evidence to the same effect ; for instance, the oldest forts in Bilāspur are attributed to the Bhainas, and a chief of this tribe is remembered as having ruled in Bilaigarh ; they are also said to have been dominant in Pendra, where they are still most numerous, though the estate is now held by a Kawar ; and it is related that the Bhainas were expelled from Phuljhar in Raipur by the Gonds.   Phuljhar is believed to be a Gond State of long standing, and the Rāja of Raigarh and others claim to be descended from its ruling family.   A manuscript history of the Phuljhar chiefs records that that country was held by a Bhaina king when the Gonds invaded it, coming from Chānda.   The Bhaina with his soldiers took refuge in a hollow underground chamber with two exits.   But the secret of this was betrayed to the Gonds by an old Gond woman, and they filled up the openings of the chamber with grass and burnt the Bhainas to death.   On this account the tribe will not enter Phuljhar territory to this day, and say that it is death to a Bhaina to do so.   The Binjhwārs are also said to have been dominant in the hills to the east of Raipur District, and they too are a civilised branch of the Baigas. And in all this area the village priest is commonly known as Baiga, the deduction from which is, as already stated, that the Baigas were the oldest residents.[1]   It seems a legitimate conclusion, therefore, that prior to the immigration of the

---

[1] For the meaning of the term Baiga and its application to the tribe, see also article on Bhuiya.

Gonds and Kawars, the ancient Baiga tribe was spread over the whole hill country east and north of the Mahānadī basin.

The Bhainas are also closely connected with the Kawars, who still own many large estates in the hills north of Bilās- pur. It is said that formerly the Bhainas and Kawars both ate in common and intermarried, but at present, though the Bhainas still eat rice boiled in water from the Kawars, the latter do not reciprocate. But still, when a Kawar is cele- brating a birth, marriage or death in his family, or when he takes in hand to make a tank, he will first give food to a Bhaina before his own caste-men eat. And it may safely be assumed that this is a recognition of the Bhaina's position as having once been lord of the land. A Kawar may still be admitted into the Bhaina community, and it is said that the reason of the rupture of the former equal relations between the two tribes was the disgust felt by the Kawars for the rude and uncouth behaviour of the Bhainas. For on one occasion a Kawar went to ask for a Bhaina girl in marriage, and, as the men of the family were away, the women undertook to entertain him. And as the Bhainas had no axes, the daughter proceeded to crack the sticks on her head for kindling a fire, and for grass she pulled out a wisp of thatch from the roof and broke it over her thigh, being unable to chop it. This so offended the delicate susceptibilities of the Kawar that he went away without waiting for his meal, and from that time the Kawars ceased to marry with the Bhainas. It seems possible that the story points to the period when the primitive Bhainas and Baigas did not know the use of iron and to the introduction of this metal by the later-coming Kawars and Gonds. It is further related that when a Kawar is going to make a ceremonial visit he likes always to take with him two or three Bhainas, who are considered as his retainers, though not being so in fact. This enhances his importance, and it is also said that the stupidity of the Bhainas acts as a foil, through which the superior intelligence of the Kawar is made more apparent. All these details point to the same con- clusion that the primitive Bhainas first held the country and were supplanted by the more civilised Kawars, and bears out the theory that the settlement of the Munda tribes was prior to those of the Dravidian family.

3. Internal structure : Totemism.

The tribe has two subdivisions of a territorial nature, Laria or Chhattīsgarhi, and Uriya. The Uriya Bhainas will accept food cooked without water from the Sawaras or Saonrs, and these also from them ; so that they have probably intermarried. Two other subdivisions recorded are the Jhalyāra and Ghantyāra or Ghatyāra ; the former being so called because they live in *jhālas* or leaf huts in the forest, and the latter, it is said, because they tie a *ghanta* or bell to their doors. This, however, seems very improbable. Another theory is that the word is derived from *ghāt*, a slope or descent, and refers to a method which the tribe have of tattooing themselves with a pattern of lines known as *ghāt*. Or it is said to mean a low or despised section. The Jhalyāra and Ghatyāra divisions comprise the less civilised portion of the tribe, who still live in the forests ; and they are looked down on by the Uriya and Laria sections, who belong to the open country. The exogamous divisions of the tribe show clearly enough that the Bhainas, like other subject races, have quite failed to preserve any purity of blood. Among the names of their *gots* or septs are Dhobia (a washerman), Ahera (cowherd), Gond, Mallin (gardener), Panika (from a Panka or Ganda) and others. The members of such septs pay respect to any man belonging to the caste after which they are named and avoid picking a quarrel with him. They also worship the family gods of this caste. The tribe have also a number of totem septs, named after animals or plants. Such are Nāg the cobra, Bāgh the tiger, Chitwa the leopard, Gidha the vulture, Besra the hawk, Bendra the monkey, Kok or Lodha the wild dog, Bataria the quail, Durgachhia the black ant, and so on. Members of a sept will not injure the animal after which it is named, and if they see the corpse of the animal or hear of its death, they throw away an earthen cooking-pot and bathe and shave themselves as for one of the family. Members of the Baghchhāl or tiger sept will, however, join in a beat for tiger though they are reluctant to do so. At weddings the Bhainas have a ceremony known as the *gotra* worship. The bride's father

makes an image in clay of the bird or animal of the groom's
sept and places it beside the marriage-post. The bridegroom worships the image, lighting a sacrificial fire before
it, and offers to it the vermilion which he afterwards smears
upon the forehead of the bride. At the bridegroom's house
a similar image is made of the bride's totem, and on returning there after the wedding she worships this. Women
are often tattooed with representations of their totem
animal, and men swear by it as their most sacred oath. A
similar respect is paid to the inanimate objects after which
certain septs are named. Thus members of the Gawad or
cowdung sept will not burn cowdung cakes for fuel; and
those of the Mircha sept do not use chillies. One sept is
named after the sun, and when an eclipse occurs these
perform the same formal rites of mourning as the others
do on the death of their totem animal. Some of the groups
have two divisions, male and female, which practically rank as
separate septs. Instances of these are the Nāgbans Andura
and the Nāgbans Mai or male and female cobra septs;
the Karsayāl Singhāra and Karsayāl Mundi or stag and doe
deer septs; and the Baghchhāl Andura and Baghchhāl Mai
or tiger and tigress septs. These may simply be instances
of subdivisions arising owing to the boundaries of the sept
having become too large for convenience.

The tribe consider that a boy should be married when 4. Mar-
he has learnt to drive the plough, and a girl when she is riage.
able to manage her household affairs. When a father can
afford a bride for his son, he and his relatives go to the
girl's village, taking with them ten or fifteen cakes of bread
and a bottle of liquor. He stays with some relative and
sends to ask the girl's father if he will give his daughter to
the inquirer's son. If the former agrees, the bread and
liquor are sent over to him, and he drinks three cups of the
spirit as a pledge of the betrothal, the remainder being
distributed to the company. This is known as *Tatia
kholna* or 'the opening of the door,' and is followed some
days afterwards by a similar ceremonial which constitutes
the regular betrothal. On this occasion the father agrees
to marry his daughter within a year and demands the bride-
price, which consists of rice, cloth, a goat and other articles,

the total value being about five rupees. A date is next
fixed for the wedding, the day selected being usually a
Monday or Friday, but no date or month is forbidden. The
number of days to the wedding are then counted, and two
knotted strings are given to each party, with a knot for
each day up to that on which the anointings with oil and
turmeric will commence at the bridegroom's and bride's
houses. Every day one knot is untied at each house up to
that on which the ceremonies begin, and thus the correct
date for them is known. The invitations to the wedding
are given by distributing rice coloured yellow with turmeric
to all members of the caste in the locality, with the intimation that the wedding procession will start on a certain day
and that they will be pleased to attend. During the four
days that they are being anointed the bride and bridegroom
dance at their respective houses to the accompaniment of
drums and other instruments. For the wedding ceremony
a number of Hindu rites have been adopted. The eldest
sister of the bridegroom or bride is known as the *sawāsin*
and her husband as the *sawāsa*, and these persons seem to
act as the representatives of the bridal couple throughout
the marriage and to receive all presents on their behalf.
The custom is almost universal among the Hindus, and it
is possible that they are intended to act as substitutes and
to receive any strokes of evil fortune which may befall the
bridal pair at a season at which they are peculiarly liable to
it. The couple go round the sacred post, and afterwards
the bridegroom daubs the bride's forehead with red lead
seven times and covers her head with her cloth to show
that she has become a married woman. After the wedding
the bridegroom's parents say to him, " Now your parents
have done everything they could for you, and you must
manage your own house." The expenditure on an average
wedding is about fifteen or twenty rupees. A widow is
usually taken in marriage by her late husband's younger
brother or Dewar, or by one of his relatives. If she marries
an outsider, the Dewar realises twelve rupees from him in
compensation for her loss. But if there is no Dewar this
sum is not payable to her first husband's elder brother or
her own father, because they could not have married her

and hence are not held to be injured by a stranger doing so. If a woman is divorced and another man wishes to marry her, he must make a similar payment of twelve rupees to the first husband, together with a goat and liquor for the penal feast. The Bhainas bury or burn the dead according as their means permit.

Their principal deity in Bilāspur is Nakti Devi[1] or the 'Noseless Goddess.' For her ritual rice is placed on a square of the floor washed with cowdung, and *ghī* or preserved butter is poured on it and burnt. A hen is made to eat the rice, and then its head is cut off and laid on the square. The liver is burnt on the fire as an offering to the deity and the head and body of the animal are then eaten. After the death of a man a cock is offered to Nakti Devi and a hen after that of a woman. The fowl is made to pick rice first in the yard of the house, then on the threshold, and lastly inside the house. Thākur Deo is the deity of cultivation and is worshipped on the day before the autumn crops are sown. On this day all the men in the village go to his shrine taking a measure of rice and a ploughshare. At the same time the Baiga or village priest goes and bathes in the tank and is afterwards carried to the assembly on a man's shoulders. Here he makes an offering and repeats a charm, and then kneeling down strikes the earth seven times with the ploughshare, and sows five handfuls of rice, sprinkling water over the seed. After him the villagers walk seven times round the altar of the god in pairs, one man turning up the earth with the ploughshare and the other sowing and watering the seed. While this is going on the Baiga sits with his face covered with a piece of cloth, and at the end the villagers salute the Baiga and go home. When a man wishes to do an injury to another he makes an image of him with clay and daubs it with vermilion and worships it with an offering of a goat or a fowl and liquor. Then he prays the image that his enemy may die. Another way of injuring an enemy is to take rice coloured with turmeric, and after

5. Religious superstitions.

[1] It is or was, of course, a common practice for a husband to cut off his wife's nose if he suspected her of being unfaithful to him. But whether the application of the epithet to the goddess should be taken to imply anything against her moral character is not known.

muttering charms throw it in the direction in which the enemy lives.

6. Admission of outsiders and caste offences.

Outsiders are not usually admitted, but if a Bhaina forms a connection with a woman of another tribe, they will admit the children of such a union, though not the woman herself. For they say : ' The seed is ours and what matters the field on which it was sown.' But a man of the Kawar tribe having intimacy with a Bhaina woman may be taken into the community. He must wait for three or four months after the matter becomes known and will beg for admission and offer to give the penalty feast. A day is fixed for this and invitations are sent to members of the caste. On the appointed day the women of the tribe cook rice, pulse, goat's flesh and urad cakes fried in oil, and in the evening the people assemble and drink liquor and then go to take their food. The candidate for admission serves water to the men and his prospective wife to the women, both being then permitted to take food with the tribe. Next morning the people come again and the woman is dressed in a white cloth with bangles. The couple stand together supported by their brother-in-law and sister-in-law respectively, and turmeric dissolved in water is poured over their heads. They are now considered to be married and go round together and give the salutation or Johār to the people, touching the feet of those who are entitled to this mark of respect, and kissing the others. Among the offences for which a man is temporarily put out of caste is getting the ear torn either accidentally or otherwise, being beaten by a man of very low caste, growing san-hemp (*Crotalaria juncea*), rearing tasar silk-worms or getting maggots in a wound. This last is almost as serious an offence as killing a cow, and, in both cases, before an offender can be reinstated he must kill a fowl and swallow a drop or two of its blood with turmeric. Women commonly get the lobe of the ear torn through the heavy ear-rings which they wear ; and in a squabble another woman will often seize the ear-ring maliciously in order to tear the ear. A woman injured in this way is put out of caste for a year in Jānjgir. To grow turmeric or garlic is also an offence against caste, but a man is permitted to do this for his own use and not for sale. A man who gets leprosy is said to be permanently expelled from caste. The purification of delinquents is conducted by members of the Sonwāni (gold-water) and Patel (headman) septs, whose business it is to give the offender water to drink in which gold has been dipped and to take over the burden of his sins by first eating food with him. But others say that the Hāthi or elephant sept is the highest, and to its members are delegated these duties. And in Jānjgir again the president of the committee gives the gold-water, and is hence known as Sonwān; and this office must always be held by a man of the Bandar or monkey sept.

The Bhainas are a comparatively civilised tribe and have largely adopted Hindu usages. They employ Brāhmans to fix auspicious days for their ceremonies, though not to officiate at them. They live principally in the open country and are engaged in agriculture, though very few of them hold land and the bulk are farm-labourers. They now disclaim any connection with the primitive Baigas, who still prefer the forests. But their caste mark, a symbol which may be affixed to documents in place of a signature or used for a brand on cattle, is a bow, and this shows that they retain the recollection of hunting as their traditional occupation. Like the Baigas, the tribe have forgotten their native dialect and now speak bad Hindi. They will eat pork and rats, and almost anything else they can get, eschewing only beef. But in their intercourse with other castes they are absurdly strict, and will take boiled rice only from a Kawar, or from a Brāhman if it is cooked in a brass and not in an earthen vessel, and this only from a male and not from a female Brāhman; while they will accept baked *chapātis* and other food from a Gond and a Rāwat. But in Sambalpur they will take this from a Savar and not from a Gond. They rank below the Gonds, Kawars and Savars or Saonrs. Women are tattooed with a representation of their sept totem; and on the knees and ankles they have some figures of lines which are known as *ghāts*. These they say will enable them to climb the mountains leading to heaven in the other world, while those who have not such marks will be pierced with spears on their way up the ascent. It has already been suggested that these marks may have given rise to the name of the Ghatyāra division of the tribe.

7. Social customs.

Bhāmta or Bhāmtya.[1]—A caste numbering 4000 persons in the Central Provinces, nearly all of whom reside in the Wardha, Nāgpur and Chānda Districts of the Nāgpur Division. The Bhāmtas are also found in Bombay, Berār and Hyderābād. In Bombay they are known by the names of Uchla or 'Lifter' and Ganthachor or 'Bundle-thief.'[2] The Bhāmtas were and still are notorious thieves, but many of the caste are now engaged in the cultivation of hemp, from which they make ropes, mats and gunny-bags. Formerly it was said in Wardha that a Bhāmta girl would not marry unless her suitor had been arrested not less than fourteen times by the police, when she considered that he had qualified as a man. The following description of their methods does not necessarily apply to the whole caste, though the bulk of them are believed to have criminal tendencies. But some colonies of Bhāmtas who have taken to the manufacture of sacking and gunny-bags from hemp-fibre may perhaps be excepted. They steal only during the daytime, and divide that part of the Province which they frequent into regular beats or ranges. They adopt many disguises. Even in their own cottages one dresses as a Mārwāri Bania, another as a Gujarāt Jain, a third as a Brāhman and a fourth as a Rājpūt. They keep to some particular disguise for years and often travel hundreds of miles, entering and stealing from the houses of the classes of persons whose dress they adopt, or taking service with a merchant or trader, and having gained their employer's confidence, seizing an opportunity to abscond with some valuable property. Sometimes two or three Bhāmtas visit a large fair, and one of them dressed as a Brāhman mingles with the crowd of bathers and worshippers. The false Brāhman notices some ornament deposited by a bather, and while himself entering the water and repeating sacred verses, watches his opportunity and spreads out his cloth near the ornament, which he then catches with his toes, and dragging it with him to a distance as he walks away buries

---

[1] This article is mainly compiled from a paper by Pyāre Lāl Misra, Ethnographic Clerk.

[2] *Bombay Gazetteer* (Campbell), xviii. p. 464.

it in the sand. The accomplices meanwhile loiter near, and when the owner discovers his loss the Brāhman sympathises with him and points out the accomplices as likely thieves, thus diverting suspicion from himself. The victim follows the accomplices, who make off, and the real thief meanwhile digs the ornament out of the sand and escapes at his leisure. Women often tie their ornaments in bundles at such bathing-fairs, and in that case two Bhāmtas will go up to her, one on each side, and while one distracts her attention the other makes off with the bundle and buries it in the sand. A Bhāmta rarely retains the stolen property on his person while there is a chance of his being searched, and is therefore not detected. They show considerable loyalty to one another, and never steal from or give information against a member of the caste. If stolen property is found in a Bhāmta's house, and it has merely been deposited there for security, the real thief comes forward. An escaped prisoner does not come back to his friends lest he should get them into trouble. A Bhāmta is never guilty of house-breaking or gang-robbery, and if he takes part in this offence he is put out of caste. He does not steal from the body of a person asleep. He is, however, expert at the theft of ornaments from the person. He never steals from a house in his own village, and the villagers frequently share directly or indirectly in his gains. The Bhāmtas are now expert railway thieves.[1] Two of them will get into a carriage, and, engaging the other passengers in conversation, find out where they are going, so as to know the time available for action. When it gets dark and the travellers go to sleep, one of the Bhāmtas lies down on the floor and covers himself with a large cloth. He begins feeling some bag under the seat, and if he cannot open it with his hands, takes from his mouth the small curved knife which all Bhāmtas carry concealed between their gum and upper lip, and with this he rips up the seams of the bag and takes out what he finds ; or they exchange bags, according to a favourite device of English railway thieves, and then quickly either leave the train or get into another carriage.

[1] The following particulars are taken from Colonel Portman's *Report on the Bhāmtas of the Deccan* (Bombay, 1887).

If attention is aroused they throw the stolen property out of the window, marking the place and afterwards going back to recover it. Another device is to split open and pick the pockets of people in a crowd. Besides the knife they often have a needle and thread and an iron nut-cutter.

2. Sub-divisions and marriage customs.
Members of other castes, as Chhatri, Kanjar, Rāwat and others, who have taken to stealing, are frequently known as Bhāmtas, but unless they have been specially initiated do not belong to the caste. The Bhāmtas proper have two main divisions, the Chhatri Bhāmtas, who are usually immigrants from Gujarāt, and those of the Marātha country, who are often known as Bhāmtis. The former have a dialect which is a mixture of Hindi, Marāthi and Gujarāti, while the latter speak the local form of Marāthi. The sections of the Chhatri Bhāmtas are named after Rājpūt septs, as Badgūjar, Chauhān, Gahlot, Bhatti, Kachhwāha and others. They may be partly of Rājpūt descent, as they have regular and pleasing features and a fair complexion, and are well built and sturdy. The sections of the Bhāmtis are called by Marātha surnames, as Gudekar, Kaothi, Bailkhade, Sātbhaia and others. The Chhatri Bhāmtas have northern customs, and the Bhāmtis those of the Marātha country. Marriage between persons of the same *gotra* or surname is prohibited. The Chhatris avoid marriage between relations having a common greatgrandparent, but among the Bhāmtis the custom of Mehunchār is prevalent, by which the brother's daughter is married to the sister's son. Girls are usually married at ten and eleven years of age or later. The betrothal and marriage customs of the two subcastes differ, the Chhatris following the ceremonial of the northern Districts and the Bhāmtis that of the Marātha country. The Chhatris do not pay a bride-price, but the Bhāmtis usually do. Widow-marriage is allowed, and while the Chhatris expect the widow to marry her deceased husband's brother, the Bhāmtis do not permit this. Among both subdivisions a price is paid for the widow to her parents. Divorce is only permitted for immoral conduct on the part of the wife. A divorced woman may remarry after giving a feast to the caste *panchāyat* or committee, and obtaining their consent.

The goddess Devi is the tutelary deity of the caste, as of all those who ply a disreputable profession. Animals are sacrificed to her or let loose to wander in her name. The offerings are appropriated by the village washerman. In Bombay the rendezvous of the Bhāmtis is the temple of Devi at Konali, in Akalkot State, near Sholapur, and here the gangs frequently assemble before and after their raids to ask the goddess that luck may attend them and to thank her for success obtained.[1] They worship their rope-making implements on the Dasahra day. They both bury and burn the dead. Ghosts and spirits are worshipped. If a man takes a second wife after the death of his first, the new wife wears a *putli* or image of the first wife on a piece of silver on her neck, and offers it the *hom* sacrifice by placing some *ghī* on the fire before taking a meal. In cases of doubt and difficulty she often consults the *putli* by speaking to it, while any chance stir of the image due to the movement of her body is interpreted as approval or disapproval. In the Central Provinces the Bhāmtis say that they do not admit outsiders into the caste, but this is almost certainly untrue. In Bombay they are said to admit all Hindus[2] except the very lowest castes, and also Muhammadans. The candidate must pass through the two ceremonies of admission into the caste and adoption into a particular family. For the first he pays an admission fee, is bathed and dressed in new clothes, and one of the elders drops turmeric and sugar into his mouth. A feast follows, during which some elders of the caste eat out of the same plate with him. This completes the admission ceremony, but in order to marry in the caste a candidate must also be adopted into a particular family. The Bhāmta who has agreed to adopt him invites the caste people to his house, and there takes the candidate on his knee while the guests drop turmeric and sugar into his mouth. The Bhāmtas eat fish and fowl but not pork or beef, and drink liquor. This last practice is, however, frequently made a caste offence by the Bhāmtis. They take cooked food from Brāhmans and Kunbis and water from Gonds. The keeping of concubines is also an offence entailing temporary excommuni-

[1] Portman, *loc. cit.*   [2] *Bombay Gazetteer* (Campbell), xviii. p. 465.

cation. The morality of the caste is somewhat low and
their women are addicted to prostitution. The occupation
of the Bhāmta is also looked down on, and it is said,
Bhāmta ka kām sub se nikām, or ' The Bhāmta's work is
the worst of all.' This may apply either to his habits of
stealing or to the fact that he supplies a bier made of twine
and bamboo sticks at a death. In Bombay the showy dress
of the Bhāmta is proverbial. Women are tattooed before
marriage on the forehead and lower lip, and on other parts
of the body for purposes of adornment. The men have the
head shaved for three inches above the top of the forehead
in front and an inch higher behind, and they wear the scalp-
lock much thicker than Brāhmans do. They usually have
red head-cloths.

1. General
notice.

Bharbhūnja.[1]—The occupational caste of grain-parchers.
The name is derived from the Sanskrit *bhrāstra*, a frying-pan,
and *bhārjaka*, one who fries. The Bharbhūnjas numbered
3000 persons in 1911, and belong mainly to the northern
Districts, their headquarters being in Upper India. In
Chhattīsgarh the place of the Bharbhūnjas is taken by the
Dhūris. Sir H. Elliot[2] remarks that the caste are traditionally supposed to be descended from a Kahār father and
a Sūdra mother, and they are probably connected with the
Kahārs. In Saugor they say that their ancestors were
Kānkubja Brāhmans who were ordered to parch rice at the
wedding of the great Rāma, and in consequence of this one
of their subcastes is known as Kānbajia. But Kānkubja is
one of the commonest names of subcastes among the people
of northern India, and merely indicates that the bearers
belong to the tract round the old city of Kanauj ; and there
is no reason to suppose that it means anything more in the
case of the Bharbhūnjas. Another group are called Kaitha,
and they say that their ancestors were Kāyasths, who adopted
the profession of grain-parching. It is said that in Bhopāl
proper Kāyasths will take food from Kaitha Bharbhūnjas
and smoke from their huqqa ; and it is noticeable that in

[1] This article contains some information from a paper by Mr. Gopal Parmanand, Deputy Inspector of Schools,
Saugor.

[2] *Memoirs of the Races of the
N.W.P.* vol. i. p. 35.

northern India Mr. Crooke gives [1] not only the Kaitha sub-caste, but other groups called Saksena and Srivāstab, which are the names of well-known Kāyasth subdivisions. It is possible, therefore, that the Kaitha group may really be connected with the Kāyasths. Other subcastes are the Benglāh, who are probably immigrants from Bengal; and the Kāndu, who may also come from that direction, Kāndu being the name of the corresponding caste of grain-parchers in Bengal.

The social customs of the Bharbhūnjas resemble those of Hindustāni castes of fairly good position.[2] They employ Brāhmans for their ceremonies, and the family priest receives five rupees for officiating at a wedding, three rupees for a funeral, one rupee for a birth, and four annas on ordinary occasions. No price is paid for a bride, and at their marriages the greater part of the expense falls on the girl's father, who has to give three feasts as against two provided by the bridegroom's father. After the wedding the bride-groom's father puts on women's clothes given by the bride's father and dances before the family. Rose-coloured water and powder are sprinkled over the guests and the proceeding is known as *Phāg*, because it is considered to have the same significance as the Holi festival observed in Phāgun. This is usually done on the bank of a river or in some garden outside the village. At the *gauna* or going-away ceremony the bride and bridegroom take their seats on two wooden boards and then change places. Divorce and the remarriage of widows are permitted. The union of a widow with her deceased husband's younger brother is considered a suitable match, but is not compulsory. When a bachelor marries a widow, he first goes through the proper ceremony either with a stick or an ear-ring, and is then united to the widow by the simple ritual employed for widow remarriage. A girl who is seduced by a member of the caste may be married to him as if she were a widow, but if her lover is an outsider she is permanently expelled from the caste.

The Bharbhūnjas occupy a fairly high social position,

2. Social customs.

3. Occupation.

---

[1] *Tribes and Castes*, art. Bhār-bhūnja.

[2] See article on Kurmi. The re-mainder of this section is taken from Mr. Gopal Parmanand's notes.

analogous to that of the Barais, Kahārs and other serving castes, the explanation being that all Hindus require the grain parched by them ; this, as it is not cooked with water, may be eaten abroad, on a journey or in the market-place. This is known as *pakki* food, and even Brāhmans will take it from their hands. But Mr. Crooke notes [1] that the work they do, and particularly the sweeping up of dry leaves for fuel, tends to lower them in the popular estimation, and it is a favourite curse to wish of an enemy that he may some day come to stoke the kiln of a grain-parcher. Of their occupation Sir H. Risley states that " Throughout the caste the actual work of parching grain is usually left to the women. The process is a simple one. A clay oven is built, somewhat in the shape of a bee-hive, with ten or twelve round holes at the top. A fire is lighted under it and broken earthen pots containing sand are put on the holes. The grain to be parched is thrown in with the sand and stirred with a flat piece of wood or a broom until it is ready. The sand and parched grain are then placed in a sieve, through which the former escapes. The wages of the parcher are a proportion of the grain, varying from one-eighth to one-fourth. In Bengal the caste was spoken of by early English travellers under the quaint name of the frymen." [2] In the Central Provinces also grain-parching is distinctly a woman's industry, only twenty-two per cent of those shown as working at it being men. There are two classes of tradesmen, those who simply keep ovens and parch grain which is brought to them, and those who keep the grain and sell it ready parched. The rates for parching are a pice a seer or an eighth part of the grain. Gram and rice, husked or unhusked, are the grains usually parched. When parched, gram is called *phutāna* (broken) and rice *lāhi*. The Bharbhūnjas also prepare *sathu*, a flour made by grinding parched gram or wheat, which is a favourite food for a light morning meal, or for travellers. It can be taken without preparation, being simply mixed with water and a little salt or sugar. The following story is told about *sathu* to emphasise its convenience in this respect. Once two travellers were about to take some food before

---

[1] *Ibidem.*

[2] *Tribes and Castes of Bengal*, art. Kāndu.

starting in the morning, of whom one had *sathu* and the other
dhān (unhusked rice).   The one with the *dhān* knew that it
would take him a long time to pound, and then cook and
eat it, so he said to the other, " My poor friend, I perceive
that you only have *sathu*, which will delay you because you
must find water, and then mix it, and find salt, and put it in,
before your *sathu* can be ready, while rice—pound, eat and
go.   But if you like, as you are in a greater hurry than I
am, I will change my rice for your *sathu*."   The other
traveller unsuspectingly consented, thinking he was getting
the best of the bargain, and while he was still looking for
a mortar in which to pound his rice, the first traveller had
mixed and eaten the *sathu* and proceeded on his journey.
In the vernacular the point is brought out by the onoma-
topoeic character of the lines, which cannot be rendered in
English.   The caste are now also engaged in selling tobacco
and sweetmeats and the manufacture of fireworks.   They
stoke their ovens with any refuse they can collect from the
roads, and hence comes the saying, ' *Bhār men dālna*,' ' To
throw into the oven,' meaning to throw away something or
to make ducks and drakes with it ; while *Bhār-jhokna* signifies to light or heat the oven, and, figuratively, to take up
a mean occupation (Platts).   Another proverb quoted by
Mr. Crooke is, ' *Bharbhūnja ka larki kesar ka tīka*,' or ' The
Bharbhūnja's slut with saffron on her forehead,' meaning one
dressed in borrowed plumes.   Another saying is, ' *To tum
kya abhi tak bhār bhunjte rahe*,' or ' Have you been stoking
the oven all this time ? '—meaning to imply that the person
addressed has been wasting his time, because the profits
from grain-parching are so small.   The oven of the Psalmist
into which the grass was cast no doubt closely resembled
that of the Bharbhūnjas.

BHARIA

LIST OF PARAGRAPHS

1. Origin and tribal legend.

Bharia, Bharia - Bhumia.[1] — A Dravidian tribe numbering about 50,000 persons and residing principally in the Jubbulpore District, which contains a half of the total number. The others are found in Chhindwāra and Bilāspur. The proper name of the tribe is Bharia, but they are often called Bharia-Bhumia, because many of them hold the office of Bhumia or priest of the village gods and of the lower castes in Jubbulpore, and the Bharias prefer the designation of Bhumia as being the more respectable. The term Bhumia or 'Lord of the soil' is an alternative for Bhuiya, the name of another Dravidian tribe, and no doubt came to be applied to the office of village priest because it was held by members of this tribe ; the term Baiga has a similar signification in Mandla and Bālāghāt, and is applied to the village priest though he may not belong to the Baiga tribe at all. The Bharias have forgotten their original affinities, and several stories of the origin of the tribe are based on far-fetched derivations of the name. One of these is to the effect that Arjun, when matters were going badly with the Pāndavas in their battle against the Kauravas, took up a handful of *bharru* grass and, pressing it, produced a host of men who fought in the battle and became the ancestors of

[1] This article is compiled from notes taken by Mr. Hīra Lāl, Assistant Gazetteer Superintendent in Jubbul- pore, and from a paper by Rām Lāl Sharma, schoolmaster, Bilāspur.

the Bharias.   And there are others of the same historical
value.   But there is no reason to doubt that Bharia is the
contemptuous form of Bhar, as Telia for Teli, Jugia for Jogi,
Kuria for Kori, and that the Bharias belong to the great
Bhar tribe who were once dominant in the eastern part of
the United Provinces, but are now at the bottom of the
social scale, and relegated by their conquerors to the degrad-
ing office of swineherds.   The Rājjhars, who appear to have
formed a separate caste as the landowning subdivision of the
Bhars, like the Rāj-Gonds among Gonds, are said to be the
descendants of a Rāja and a Bharia woman.   The Rājjhars
form a separate caste in the Central Provinces, and the
Bharias acknowledge some connection with them, but refuse
to take water from their hands, as they consider them to be
of impure blood.   The Bharias also give Mahoba or Bānd-
hogarh as their former home, and these places are in the
country of the Bhars.   According to tradition Rāja Karna
Deva, a former king of Dāhal, the classical name of the
Jubbulpore country, was a Bhar, and it may be that the
immigration of the Bharias into Jubbulpore dates from his
period, which is taken as 1040 to 1080 A.D.   While then it
may be considered as fairly certain that the Bharias are
merely the Bhar tribe with a variant of the name, it is clear
from the titles of their family groups, which will shortly be
given, that they are an extremely mixed class and consist
largely of the descendants of members of other castes, who,
having lost their own social position, have taken refuge among
the Bharias at the bottom of the social scale.   Mr. Crooke
says of the Bhars :[1] " The most probable supposition is that
the Bhars were a Dravidian race closely allied to the Kols,
Cheros and Seoris, who at an early date succumbed to the
invading Aryans.   This is borne out by their appearance
and physique, which closely resemble that of the undoubted
non-Aryan aborigines of the Vindhyan-Kaimūr plateau."   In
the Central Provinces the Bharias have been so closely
associated with the Gonds that they have been commonly
considered to belong to that tribe.   Thus Mr. Drysdale says
of them :[2] ' The Bharias were the wildest of the wild Gonds

---

[1] *Tribes and Castes of the N.W.P.*, art. Bhar.
[2] *C.P. Census Report*, 1881, p. 188.

and were inveterate *dhayā*[1] cutters.' Although, however, they have to some extent intermarried with the Gonds, the Bharias were originally quite a distinct tribe, and would belong to the Kolarian or Munda group but that they have entirely forgotten their own language and speak only Hindi, though with a peculiar intonation especially noticeable in the case of their women.

2. Tribal sub-divisions.   The structure of the tribe is a very loose one, and though the Bharias say that they are divided into subcastes, there are none in reality.   Members of all castes except the very lowest may become Bharias, and one Bharia will recognise another as a fellow-tribesman if he can show relationship to any person admitted to occupy that position.   But a division is in process of formation in Bilāspur based on the practice of eating beef, from which some abstain, and in consequence look down on the others who are addicted to it, and call them Dhur Bharias, the term *dhur* meaning cattle. The abstainers from beef now refuse to marry with the others. The tribe is divided into a number of exogamous groups, and the names of these indicate the very heterogeneous elements of which it consists.   Out of fifty-one groups reported not less than fifteen or sixteen have names derived from other castes or clans, showing almost certainly that such groups were formed by a mixed marriage or the admission of a family of outsiders.   Such names are : Agaria, from the Agarias or iron-workers : this clan worships Loha-Sur, the god of the Agarias ; Ahirwār, or the descendants of an Ahīr : this clan worships the Ahīr gods ; Bamhania, born of a Brāhman ancestor ; Binjhwār or Binjha, perhaps from the tribe of that name ; Chandel, from a Rājpūt clan ; Dagdoha, a synonym of Basor : persons of this sept hang a piece of bamboo and a curved knife to the waist of the bride at their marriages ; Dhurua, born of a Dhurua Gond ; Kuānpa, born of an Ahīr subcaste of that name ; Kurka, of Korku parentage ; Marāvi, the name of a Gond clan ; Rāthor from a Rājpūt clan ; Samarba from a Chamār ; and Yarkara, the name of a Gond clan.   These names sufficiently indicate the diverse elements of which the tribe is made up.   Other

---

[1] *Dhayā* means the system of shifting cultivation, which until prohibited was so injurious to the forests.

group names with meanings are : Gambhele, or those who
seclude their women in a separate house during the menstrual
period ; Kaitha, from the *kaith* tree (*Feronia elephantum*) ;
Karondiha, from the *karonda* plant (*Carissa Carandas*) ;
Magarha, from *magar* a crocodile : members of this group
worship an image of a crocodile made with flour and fried
in oil ; Sonwāni, from *sona* gold : members of this group
perform the ceremony of readmission of persons temporarily
put out of caste by sprinkling on them a little water in
which gold has been dipped.   Any person who does not
know his clan name calls himself a Chandel, and this group,
though bearing the name of a distinguished Rājpūt clan, is
looked upon as the lowest.   But although the rule of
exogamy in marriage is recognised, it is by no means
strictly adhered to, and many cases are known in which
unions have taken place between members of the same
clan.   So long as people can recollect a relationship between
themselves, they do not permit their families to intermarry.
But the memory of the Bharia does not extend beyond the
third generation.

Marriages are adult, and the proposal comes from the
boy's father, who has it conveyed to the girl's father through
some friend in his village.   If a betrothal is arranged the
bride's father invites the father and friends of the bridegroom
to dinner ; on this occasion the boy's father brings some
necklaces of lac beads and spangles and presents them
to the bride's female relatives, who then come out and tie
the necklaces round his neck and those of his friends, place
the spangles on their foreheads, and then, catching hold of
their cheeks, press and twist them violently.   Some turmeric
powder is also thrown on their faces.   This is the binding
portion of the betrothal ceremony.   The date of marriage
is fixed by a Brāhman, this being the only purpose for
which he is employed, and a bride-price varying from six to
twelve rupees is paid.   On this occasion the women draw
caricatures with turmeric or charcoal on the loin-cloth of the
boy's father, which they manage to purloin.   The marriage
ceremony follows generally the Hindu form.   The bridegroom puts on women's ornaments and carries with him an
iron nut-cracker or dagger to keep off evil spirits.   After

3. Mar-
riage.

the wedding, the *midua*, a sort of burlesque dance, is held.
The girl's mother gets the dress of the boy's father and puts
it on, together with a false beard and moustaches, and dances,
holding a wooden ladle in one hand and a packet of ashes in
the other. Every time she approaches the bridegroom's
father on her rounds she spills some of the ashes over him,
and occasionally gives him a crack on the head with her
ladle, these actions being accompanied by bursts of laughter
from the party and frenzied playing by the musicians.
When the party reach the bridegroom's house on their return,
his mother and the other women come out and burn a
little mustard and human hair in a lamp, the unpleasant
smell emitted by these articles being considered potent to
drive away evil spirits. Every time the bride leaves her
father's house she must weep, and must cry separately with
each one of her caste-sisters when taking leave of them.
When she returns home she must begin weeping loudly on
the boundary of the village, and continue doing so until she
has embraced each of her relatives and friends, a performance
which in a village containing a large number of Bharias may
take from three to six hours. These tears are, however,
considered to be a manifestation of joy, and the girl who
cannot produce enough of them is often ridiculed. A prospective son-in-law who serves for his wife is known as
Gharjiān. The work given him is always very heavy, and
the Bharias have a saying which compares his treatment
with that awarded to an ox obtained on hire. If a girl
is seduced by a man of the tribe, she may be married to him
by the ceremony prescribed for the remarriage of a widow,
which consists merely in the placing of bangles on the
wrists and a present of a new cloth, together with a feast
to the caste-fellows. Similarly if she is seduced by a man
of another caste who would be allowed to become a Bharia,
she can be married as a widow to any man of the tribe. A
widow is expected to marry her late husband's younger
brother, but no compulsion is exercised. If a bachelor
espouses a widow, he first goes through the ceremony of
marriage with a ring to which a twig of the date-palm is
tied, by carrying the ring seven times round the marriage
post. This is necessary to save him from the sin of dying

unmarried, as the union with a widow is not reckoned as a true marriage. In Jubbulpore divorce is said to be allowed only for conjugal misbehaviour, and a Bharia will pass over three transgressions on his wife's part before finally turning her out of his house. A woman who wishes to leave her husband simply runs away from him and lives with somebody else. In this case the third party must pay a goat to the husband by way of compensation and give a feast to the caste-fellows.

The carelessness of the Bharias in the matter of child-birth is notorious, and it is said that mothers commonly went on working up to the moment of childbirth and were delivered of children in the fields. Now, however, the woman lies up for three days, and some ceremonies of purification are performed. In Chhattīsgarh infants are branded on the day of their birth, under the impression that this will cause them to digest the food they have taken in the womb. The child is named six months after birth by the father's sister, and its lips are then touched with cooked food for the first time. 4. Child-birth.

The tribe both burn and bury the dead, and observe mourning for an adult for ten days, during which time they daily put out a leaf-cup containing food for the use of the deceased. In the third year after the death, the *mangan* or caste beggar visits the relatives of the deceased, and receives what they call one limb (*ang*), or half his belongings; the *ang* consists of a loin-cloth, a brass vessel and dish, an axe, a scythe and a wrist-ring. 5. Funeral cere-monies.

The Bharias call themselves Hindus and worship the village deities of the locality, and on the day of Diwāli offer a black chicken to their family god, who may be Bura Deo, Dūlha Deo or Karua, the cobra. For this snake they profess great reverence, and say that he was actually born in a Bharia family. As he could not work in the fields he was usually employed on errands. One day he was sent to the house, and surprised one of his younger brother's wives, who had not heard him coming, without her veil. She reproached him, and he retired in dudgeon to the oven, where he was presently burnt to death by another woman, who kindled a fire under it not knowing that he was there. So he has 6. Reli-gion and magic.

been deified and is worshipped by the tribe. The Bharias
also venerate Bāgheshwar, the tiger god, and believe that no
tiger will eat a Bharia. On the Diwāli day they invite the
tiger to drink some gruel which they place ready for him
behind their houses, at the same time warning the other
villagers not to stir out of doors. In the morning they
display the empty vessels as a proof that the tiger has
visited them. They practise various magical devices,
believing that they can kill a man by discharging at him
a *mūth* or handful of charmed objects such as lemons,
vermilion and seeds of urad. This ball will travel through
the air and, descending on the house of the person at whom it
is aimed, will kill him outright unless he can avert its power
by stronger magic, and perhaps even cause it to recoil in the
same manner on the head of the sender. They exorcise the
Sudhiniyas or the drinkers of human blood. A person
troubled by one of these is seated near the Bharia, who
places two pots with their mouths joined over a fire. He
recites incantations and the pots begin to boil, emitting blood.
This result is obtained by placing a herb in the pot whose
juice stains the water red. The blood-sucker is thus successfully exorcised. To drive away the evil eye they burn a
mixture of chillies, salt, human hair and the husks of kodon,
which emits a very evil smell. Such devices are practised by
members of the tribe who hold the office of Bhumia or
village priest. The Bharias are well-known thieves, and
they say that the dark spots on the moon are caused by a
banyan tree, which God planted with the object of diminishing her light and giving thieves a chance to ply their trade.
If a Bhumia wishes to detect a thief, he sits clasping hands
with a friend, while a pitcher is supported on their hands.
An oblation is offered to the deity to guide the ordeal
correctly, and the names of suspected persons are recited
one by one, the name at which the pitcher topples over being
that of the thief. But before employing this method of
detection the Bhumia proclaims his intention of doing so on
a certain date, and in the meantime places a heap of ashes in
some lonely place and invites the thief to deposit the stolen
article in the ashes to save himself from exposure. By
common custom each person in the village is required to visit

the heap and mingle a handful of ashes with it, and not infrequently the thief, frightened at the Bhumia's powers of detection, takes the stolen article and buries it in the ash-heap where it is duly found, the necessity for resorting to the further method of divination being thus obviated.   Occasionally the Bharia in his character of a Hindu will make a vow to pay for a recitation of the Satya Nārāyan Katha or some other holy work.   But he understands nothing of it, and if the Brāhman employed takes a longer time than he had bargained for over the recitation he becomes extremely bored and irritated.

The scantiness of the Bharia's dress is proverbial, and the saying is ' *Bharia bhwāka, pwānda langwāta*,' or ' The Bharia is verily a devil, who only covers his loins with a strip of cloth.'   But lately he has assumed more clothing.   Formerly an iron ring carried on the wrist to exorcise the evil spirits was his only ornament.   Women wear usually only one coarse cloth dyed red, spangles on the forehead and ears, bead necklaces, and cheap metal bracelets and anklets.   Some now have Hindu ornaments, but in common with other low castes they do not usually wear a nose-ring, out of respect to the higher castes.   Women, though they work in the fields, do not commonly wear shoes ; and if these are necessary to protect the feet from thorns, they take them off and carry them in the presence of an elder or a man of higher caste.   They are tattooed with various devices, as a cock, a crown, a native chair, a pitcher stand, a sieve and a figure called *dhandha,* which consists of six dots joined by lines, and appears to be a representation of a man, one dot standing for the head, one for the body, two for the arms and two for the legs. This device is also used by other castes, and they evince reluctance if asked to explain its meaning, so that it may be intended as a representation of the girl's future husband. The Bharia is considered very ugly, and a saying about him is : ' The Bharia came down from the hills and got burnt by a cinder, so that his face is black.'   He does not bathe for months together, and lives in a dirty hovel, infested by the fowls which he loves to rear.   His food consists of coarse grain, often with boiled leaves as a vegetable, and he consumes much whey, mixing it with his scanty portion of

7. Social life and customs.

grain. Members of all except the lowest castes are admitted to the Bharia community on presentation of a *pagri* and some money to the headman, together with a feast to the caste-fellows. The Bharias do not eat monkeys, beef or the leavings of others, but they freely consume fowls and pork. They are not considered as impure, but rank above those castes only whose touch conveys pollution. For the slaughter of a cow the Bilāspur Bharias inflict the severe punishment of nine daily feasts to the caste, or one for each limb of the cow, the limbs being held to consist of the legs, ears, horns and tail. They have an aversion for the horse and will not remove its dung. To account for this they tell a story to the effect that in the beginning God gave them a horse to ride and fight upon. But they did not know how to mount the horse because it was so high. The wisest man among them then proposed to cut notches in the side of the animal by which they could climb up, and they did this. But God, when he saw it, was very angry with them, and ordered that they should never be soldiers, but should be given a winnowing-fan and broom to sweep the grain out of the grass and make their livelihood in that way.

8. Occupation.

The Bharias are usually farmservants and field-labourers, and their services in these capacities are in much request. They are hardy and industrious, and so simple that it is an easy matter for their masters to involve them in perpetual debt, and thus to keep them bound to service from generation to generation. They have no understanding of accounts, and the saying, 'Pay for the marriage of a Bharia and he is your bond-slave for ever,' sufficiently explains the methods adopted by their employers and creditors.

BHĀT

Bhāt, Rao, Jasondhi.—The caste of bards and genea- 1. Origin
logists. In 1911 the Bhāts numbered 29,000 persons in $\frac{\text{of the}}{\text{Bhāts.}}$
the Central Provinces and Berār, being distributed over all
Districts and States, with a slight preponderance in large
towns such as Nāgpur, Jubbulpore and Amraoti. The name
Bhāt is derived from the Sanskrit Bhatta, a lord. The
origin of the Bhāts has been discussed in detail by Sir H.
Risley. Some, no doubt, are derived from the Brāhman
caste as stated by Mr. Nesfield : "They are an offshoot from
those secularised Brāhmans who frequented the courts of
princes and the camps of warriors, recited their praises in
public, and kept records of their genealogies. Such, without much variation, is the function of the Bhāt at the present
day. The Mahābhārata speaks of a band of bards and
eulogists marching in front of Yudishthira as he made his
progress from the field of Kurukshetra towards Hastinapur.
But these very men are spoken of in the same poem as
Brāhmans. Naturally as time went on these courtier priests
became hereditary bards, receded from the parent stem and
founded a new caste." " The best modern opinion," Sir H.

Risley states,[1] "seems disposed to find the germ of the Brāhman caste in the bards, ministers and family priests, who were attached to the king's household in Vedic times. The characteristic profession of the Bhāts has an ancient and distinguished history. The literature of both Greece and India owes the preservation of its oldest treasures to the singers who recited poems in the households of the chiefs, and doubtless helped in some measure to shape the masterpieces which they handed down. Their place was one of marked distinction. In the days when writing was unknown, the man who could remember many verses was held in high honour by the tribal chief, who depended upon the memory of the bard for his personal amusement, for the record of his own and his ancestors' prowess, and for the maintenance of the genealogy which established the purity of his descent. The bard, like the herald, was not lightly to be slain, and even Odysseus in the heat of his vengeance spares the ἀοιδός Phemius, 'who sang among the wooers of necessity.'"[2]

2. Bhāts and Chārans.

There is no reason to doubt that the Birm or Baram Bhāts are an offshoot of Brāhmans, their name being merely a corruption of the term Brāhman. But the caste is a very mixed one, and another large section, the Chārans, are almost certainly derived from Rājpūts. Malcolm states that according to the fable of their origin, Mahādeo first created Bhāts to attend his lion and bull ; but these could not prevent the former from killing the latter, which was a source of infinite vexation and trouble, as it compelled Mahādeo to create new ones. He therefore formed the Chāran, equally devout with the Bhāt, but of bolder spirit, and gave him in charge these favourite animals. From that time no bull was ever destroyed by the lion.[3] This fable perhaps indicates that while the peaceful Bhāts were Brāhmans, the more warlike Chārans were Rājpūts. It is also said that some Rājpūts disguised themselves as bards to escape the vengeance of Parasurāma.[4] The Māru Chārans intermarry with Rājpūts, and their name appears to be derived from Māru, the term for the Rājputāna desert, which is also found in Mārwār.

---

[1] *Tribes and Castes of Bengal*, art. Brāhman.
[3] Malcolm, *Central India*, ii. p. 132.
[2] Art. Bhāt.
[4] *Rājasthān*, ii. p. 406.

Malcolm states [1] that when the Rājpūts migrated from the banks of the Ganges to Rājputāna, their Brāhman priests did not accompany them in any numbers, and hence the Chārans arose and supplied their place. They had to understand the rites of worship, particularly of Siva and Pārvati, the favourite deities of the Rājpūts, and were taught to read and write. One class became merchants and travelled with large convoys of goods, and the others were the bards and genealogists of the Rājpūts. Their songs were in the rudest metre, and their language was the local dialect, understood by all. All this evidence shows that the Chārans were a class of Rājpūt bards.

But besides the Birm or Brāhman Bhāts and the Rājpūt Chārans there is another large body of the caste of mixed origin, who serve as bards of the lower castes and are probably composed to a great extent of members of these castes. These are known as the Brid-dhari or begging Bhāts. They beg from such castes as Lodhis, Telis, Kurmis, Ahīrs and so on, each caste having a separate section of Bhāts to serve it ; the Bhāts of each caste take food from the members of the caste, but they also eat and intermarry with each other. Again, there are Bairāgi Bhāts who beg from Bairāgis, and keep the genealogies of the temple-priests and their successors. Yet another class are the Dasaundhis or Jasondhis, who sing songs in honour of Devi, play on musical instruments and practise astrology. These rank below the cultivating castes and sometimes admit members of such castes who have taken religious vows. *3. Lower-class Bhāts.*

The Brāhman or Birm-Bhāts form a separate subcaste, and the Rājpūts are sometimes called Rājbhāt. These wear the sacred thread, which the Brid-Bhāts and Jasondhis do not. The social status of the Bhāts appears to vary greatly. Sir H. Risley states that they rank immediately below Kāyasths, and Brāhmans will take water from their hands. The Chārans are treated by the Rājpūts with the greatest respect ; [2] the highest ruler rises when one of this class enters or leaves an assembly, and the Chāran is invited to eat first at a Rājpūt feast. He smokes from the same huqqa as Rājpūts, and only caste-fellows can do this, as the smoke *4. Social status of the caste.*

[1] Malcolm, ii. p. 135.   [2] *Rājasthān,* ii. pp. 133, 134.

passes through water on its way to the mouth. In past times the Chāran acted as a herald, and his person was inviolable. He was addressed as Mahārāj,[1] and could sit on the Singhāsan or Lion's Hide, the ancient term for a Rājpūt throne, as well as on the hides of the tiger, panther and black antelope. The Rājpūts held him in equal estimation with the Brāhman or perhaps even greater.[2] This was because they looked to him to enshrine their heroic deeds in his songs and hand them down to posterity. His sarcastic references to a defeat in battle or any act displaying a want of courage inflamed their passions as nothing else could do. On the other hand, the Brid-Bhāts, who serve the lower castes, occupy an inferior position. This is because they beg at weddings and other feasts, and accept cooked food from members of the caste who are their clients. Such an act constitutes an admission of inferior status, and as the Bhāts eat together their position becomes equivalent to that of the lowest group among them. Thus if other Bhāts eat with the Bhāts of Telis or Kalārs, who have taken cooked food from their clients, they are all in the position of having taken food from Telis and Kalārs, a thing which only the lowest castes will do. If the Bhāt of any caste, such as the Kurmis, keeps a girl of that caste, she can be admitted into the community, which is therefore of a very mixed character. Such a caste as the Kurmis will not even take water from the hands of the Bhāts who serve them. This rule applies also where a special section of the caste itself act as bards and minstrels. Thus the Pardhāns are the bards of the Gonds, but rank below ordinary Gonds, who give them food and will not take it from them. And the Sānsias, the bards of the Jāts, and the Mirāsis, who are employed in this capacity by the lower castes generally, occupy a very inferior position, and are sometimes considered as impure.

5. Social customs.

The customs of the Bhāts resemble those of other castes of corresponding status. The higher Bhāts forbid the re-marriage of widows, and expel a girl who becomes pregnant before marriage. They carry a dagger, the special emblem of the Chārans, in order to be distinguished from low-class

---

[1] Great King, the ordinary method of address to Brāhmans.
[2] *Rājasthān*, ii. p. 175.

Bhāts.   The Bhāts generally display the *chaur* or yak-tail
whisk and the *chhadi* or silver-plated rod on ceremonial
occasions, and they worship these emblems of their calling on
the principal festivals.   The former is waved over the bridegroom at a wedding, and the latter is borne before him.
The Brāhman Bhāts abstain from flesh of any kind and
liquor, and other Bhāts usually have the same rules about
food as the caste whom they serve.   Brāhman Bhāts and
Chārans alone wear the sacred thread.   The high status
sometimes assigned to this division of the caste is shown in
the saying :

> *Age Brāhman pīchhe Bhāt*
> *tāke pīchhe aur jāt,*

or, ' First comes the Brāhman, then the Bhāt, and after them
the other castes.'

The business of a Bhāt in former times is thus described
by Forbes :[1] " When the rainy season closes and travelling
becomes practicable, the bard sets off on his yearly tour from
his residence in the Bhātwāra or bard's quarter of some city
or town.   One by one he visits each of the Rājpūt chiefs
who are his patrons, and from whom he has received portions
of land or annual grants of money, timing his arrival, if
possible, to suit occasions of marriage or other domestic
festivals.   After he has received the usual courtesies he produces the Wai, a book written in his own crabbed hieroglyphics or in those of his father, which contains the descent
of the house from its founder, interspersed with many a verse
or ballad, the dark sayings contained in which are chanted
forth in musical cadence to a delighted audience, and are
then orally interpreted by the bard with many an illustrative
anecdote or tale.   The Wai, however, is not merely a source
for the gratification of family pride or even of love of song ;
it is also a record by which questions of relationship are
determined when a marriage is in prospect, and disputes
relating to the division of ancestral property are decided,
intricate as these last necessarily are from the practice of
polygamy and the rule that all the sons of a family are
entitled to a share.   It is the duty of the bard at each
periodical visit to register the births, marriages and deaths

6. The
Bhāt's
business.

[1] *Rāsmāla*, ii. pp. 261, 262.

which have taken place in the family since his last circuit, as well as to chronicle all the other events worthy of remark which have occurred to affect the fortunes of his patron ; nor have we ever heard even a doubt suggested regarding the accurate, much less the honest fulfilment of this duty by the bard. The manners of the bardic tribe are very similar to those of their Rājpūt clients ; their dress is nearly the same, but the bard seldom appears without the *katār* or dagger, a representation of which is scrawled beside his signature, and often rudely engraved upon his monumental stone, in evidence of his death in the sacred duty of *trāga* (suicide)." [1]

7. Their extortionate practices.

The Bhāt thus fulfilled a most useful function as registrar of births and marriages. But his merits were soon eclipsed by the evils produced by his custom of extolling liberal patrons and satirising those who gave inadequately. The desire of the Rājpūts to be handed down to fame in the Bhāt's songs was such that no extravagance was spared to satisfy him. Chand, the great Rājpūt bard, sang of the marriage of Prithwi Rāj, king of Delhi, that the bride's father emptied his coffers in gifts, but he filled them with the praises of mankind. A lakh of rupees [2] was given to the chief bard, and this became a precedent for similar occasions. "Until vanity suffers itself to be controlled," Colonel Tod wrote,[3] "and the aristocratic Rājpūts submit to republican simplicity, the evils arising from nuptial profusion will not cease. Unfortunately those who should check it find their interest in stimulating it, namely, the whole crowd of *māngtas* or beggars, bards, minstrels, jugglers, Brāhmans, who assemble on these occasions, and pour forth their epithalamiums in praise of the virtue of liberality. The bards are the grand recorders of fame, and the volume of precedent is always

[1] See later in this article.

[2] This present of a lakh of rupees is known as Lākh Pasāru, and it is not usually given in cash but in kind. It is made up of grain, land, carriages, jewellery, horses, camels and elephants, and varies in value from Rs. 30,000 to Rs. 70,000. A living bard, Mahamahopadhyaya Murar Dās, has received three Lakh Pasārus from the Rājas of Jodhpur and has refused one from the Rāna of Udaipur in view of the fact that he was made *ayachaka* by the Jodhpur Rāja. *Ayachaka* means literally 'not a beggar,' and when a bard has once been made *ayachaka* he cannot accept gifts from any person other than his own patron. An *ayachaka* was formerly known as *polpat*, as it became his bounden duty to sing the praises of his patron constantly from the gate (*pol*) of the donor's fort or castle. (Mr. Hīra Lāl.)

[3] *Rājasthān*, ii. p. 548.

BHĀT WITH HIS *PUTLA* OR DOLL.

Bemrose, Collo., Derby.

resorted to by citing the liberality of former chiefs ; while the dread of their satire[1] shuts the eyes of the chief to consequences, and they are only anxious to maintain the reputation of their ancestors, though fraught with future ruin." Owing to this insensate liberality in the desire to satisfy the bards and win their praises, a Rājpūt chief who had to marry a daughter was often practically ruined ; and the desire to avoid such obligations led to the general practice of female infanticide, formerly so prevalent in Rājputāna. The importance of the bards increased their voracity ; Mr. Nesfield describes them as " Rapacious and conceited mendicants, too proud to work but not too proud to beg." The Dholis[2] or minstrels were one of the seven great evils which the famous king Sidhrāj expelled from Anhilwāda Pātan in Gujarāt ; the Dākans or witches were another.[3] Malcolm states that " They give praise and fame in their songs to those who are liberal to them, while they visit those who neglect or injure them with satires in which the victims are usually reproached with illegitimate birth and meanness of character. Sometimes the Bhāt, if very seriously offended, fixes an effigy of the person he desires to degrade on a long pole and appends to it a slipper as a mark of disgrace. In such cases the song of the Bhāt records the infamy of the object of his revenge. This image usually travels the country till the party or his friends purchase the cessation of the curses and ridicule thus entailed. It is not deemed in these countries within the power of the prince, much less any other person, to stop a Bhāt or even punish him for such a proceeding. In 1812 Sevak Rām Seth, a banker of Holkar's court, offended one of these Bhāts, pushing him rudely out of the shop where the man had come to ask alms. The man made a figure[4] of him to which he attached a slipper and carried it to court, and everywhere sang the infamy of the Seth. The latter, though a man of wealth and influence, could not prevent him, but obstinately refused to purchase his forbearance. His friends after some months subscribed Rs. 80 and the Bhāt discontinued his execrations, but said it was

---

[1] *Viserva*, lit. poison.
[2] From *dhol*, a drum.
[3] *Rājasthān*, ii. p. 184.
[4] Lit. *putli* or doll.

too late, as his curses had taken effect ; and the superstitious Hindus ascribe the ruin of the banker, which took place some years afterwards, to this unfortunate event." The loquacity and importunity of the Bhāts are shown in the saying, ' Four Bhāts make a crowd ' ; and their insincerity in the proverb quoted by Mr. Crooke, " The bard, the innkeeper and the harlot have no heart ; they are polite when customers arrive, but neglect those leaving (after they have paid) " [1] The Bhāt women are as bold, voluble and ready in retort as the men. When a Bhāt woman passes a male caste-fellow on the road, it is the latter who raises a piece of cloth to his face till the woman is out of sight.[2]

8. The Jasondhis.   Some of the lower classes of Bhāts have become religious mendicants and musicians, and perform ceremonial functions. Thus the Jasondhis, who are considered a class of Bhāts, take their name from the *jas* or hymns sung in praise of Devi. They are divided into various sections, as the Nakīb or flag-bearers in a procession, the Nāzir or ushers who introduced visitors to the Rāja, the Nagāria or players on kettle-drums, the Karaola who pour sesamum oil on their clothes and beg, and the Panda, who serve as priests of Devi, and beg carrying an image of the goddess in their hands. There is also a section of Muhammadan Bhāts who serve as bards and genealogists for Muhammadan castes. Some Bhāts, having the rare and needful qualification of literacy so that they can read the old Sanskrit medical works, have, like a number of Brāhmans, taken to the practice of medicine and are known as Kavirāj.

9. The Chārans as carriers.   As already stated, the persons of the Chārans in the capacity of bard and herald were sacred, and they travelled from court to court without fear of molestation from robbers or enemies. It seems likely that the Chārans may have united the breeding of cattle to their calling of bard ; but in any case the advantage derived from their sanctity was so important that they gradually became the chief carriers and traders of Rājputāna and the adjoining tracts. They further, in virtue of their holy character, enjoyed a partial exemption from the perpetual and harassing imposts levied

---

[1] *Tribes and Castes*, art. Bhāt.
[2] *Ibidem.*   Veiling the face is a sign of modesty.

by every petty State on produce entering its territory ; and the combination of advantages thus obtained was such as to give them almost a monopoly in trade.   They carried merchandise on large droves of bullocks all over Rājputāna and the adjoining countries ; and in course of time the carriers restricted themselves to their new profession, splitting off from the Chārans and forming the caste of Banjāras.

But the mere reverence for their calling would not have sufficed for a permanent safeguard to the Chārans from destitute and unscrupulous robbers.   They preserved it by the customs of *Chandi* or *Trāga* and *Dharna*.   These consisted in their readiness to mutilate, starve or kill themselves rather than give up property entrusted to their care ; and it was a general belief that their ghosts would then haunt the persons whose ill deeds had forced them to take their own lives.   It seems likely that this belief in the power of a suicide or murdered man to avenge himself by haunting any persons who had injured him or been responsible for his death may have had a somewhat wide prevalence and been partly accountable for the reprobation attaching in early times to the murderer and the act of self-slaughter.   The haunted murderer would be impure and would bring ill-fortune on all who had to do with him, while the injury which a suicide would inflict on his relatives in haunting them would cause this act to be regarded as a sin against one's family and tribe.   Even the ordinary fear of the ghosts of people who die in the natural course, and especially of those who are killed by accident, is so strong that a large part of the funeral rites is devoted to placating and laying the ghost of the dead man ; and in India the period of observance of mourning for the dead is perhaps in reality that time during which the spirit of the dead man is supposed to haunt his old abode and render the survivors of his family impure.   It was this fear of ghosts on which the Chārans relied, nor did they hesitate a moment to sacrifice their lives in defence of any obligation they had undertaken or of property committed to their care.   When plunderers carried off any cattle belonging to the Chārans, the whole community would proceed to the spot where the robbers resided ; and in failure of having their property

10. Suicide and the fear of ghosts.

restored would cut off the heads of several of their old men and women.   Frequent instances occurred of a man dressing himself in cotton-quilted cloths steeped in oil which he set on fire at the bottom, and thus danced against the person against whom *trāga* was performed until the miserable creature dropped down and was burnt to ashes.   On one occasion a Cutch chieftain, attempting to escape with his wife and child from a village, was overtaken by his enemy when about to leap a precipice ; immediately turning he cut off his wife's head with his scimitar and, flourishing his reeking blade in the face of his pursuer, denounced against him the curse of the *trāga* which he had so fearfully performed.[1]   In this case it was supposed that the wife's ghost would haunt the enemy who had driven the husband to kill her.

11. Instances of haunting and laying ghosts.

The following account in the *Rāsmāla*[2] is an instance of suicide and of the actual haunting by the ghost : A Chāran asserted a claim against the chief of Siela in Kāthiāwār, which the latter refused to liquidate.   The bard thereupon, taking forty of his caste with him, went to Siela with the intention of sitting *Dharna* at the chief's door and preventing any one from coming out or going in until the claim should be discharged.   However, as they approached the town, the chief, becoming aware of their intention, caused the gates to be closed.   The bards remained outside and for three days abstained from food ; on the fourth day they proceeded to perform *trāga* as follows : some hacked their own arms ; others decapitated three old women of the party and hung their heads up at the gate as a garland ; certain of the women cut off their own breasts.   The bards also pierced the throats of four of their old men with spikes, and they took two young girls by the heels, and dashed out their brains against the town gate.   The Chāran to whom the money was due dressed himself in clothes wadded with cotton which he steeped in oil and then set on fire.   He thus burned himself to death.   But as he died he cried out, "I am now dying ; but I will become a headless ghost (*Kuvīs*) in the palace, and will take the chief's life and cut off his posterity."   After this sacrifice the rest of the bards returned home.

[1] Postans, *Cutch*, p. 172.   [2] Vol. ii. pp. 392-394.

On the third day after the Chāran's death his Bhūt (ghost) threw the Rāni downstairs so that she was very much injured. Many other persons also beheld the headless phantom in the palace. At last he entered the chief's head and set him trembling. At night he would throw stones at the palace, and he killed a female servant outright. At length, in consequence of the various acts of oppression which he committed, none dared to approach the chief's mansion even in broad daylight. In order to exorcise the Bhūt, Jogis, Fakīrs and Brāhmans were sent for from many different places; but whoever attempted the cure was immediately assailed by the Bhūt in the chief's body, and that so furiously that the exorcist's courage failed him. The Bhūt would also cause the chief to tear the flesh off his own arms with his teeth. Besides this, four or five persons died of injuries received from the Bhūt; but nobody had the power to expel him. At length a foreign Jyotishi (astrologer) came who had a great reputation for charms and magic, and the chief sent for him and paid him honour. First he tied all round the house threads which he had charged with a charm; then he sprinkled charmed milk and water all round; then he drove a charmed iron nail into the ground at each corner of the mansion, and two at the door. He purified the house and continued his charms and incantations for forty-one days, every day making sacrifices at the cemetery to the Bhūt's spirit. The Joshi lived in a room securely fastened up; but people say that while he was muttering his charms stones would fall and strike the windows. Finally the Joshi brought the chief, who had been living in a separate room, and tried to exorcise the spirit. The patient began to be very violent, but the Joshi and his people spared no pains in thrashing him until they had rendered him quite docile. A sacrificial fire-pit was made and a lemon placed between it and the chief. The Joshi commanded the Bhūt to enter the lime. The possessed, however, said, 'Who are you; if one of your Deos (gods) were to come, I would not quit this person.' Thus they went on from morning till noon. At last they came outside, and, burning various kinds of incense and sprinkling many charms, the Bhūt was got out into the lemon. When the lemon began to jump about, the whole of the spectators praised the Joshi, crying out : ' The Bhūt has gone into the lemon ! The Bhūt has gone into the lemon ! ' The possessed person himself, when he saw the lemon hopping about, was perfectly satisfied that the Bhūt had left his body and gone out into the lemon. The Joshi then drove the lemon outside the city, followed by drummers and trumpeters ; if the lemon left the road, he would touch it with his stick and put it into the right way again. On the track they sprinkled mustard and salt and finally buried the lemon in a pit seven cubits deep, throwing into the hole above it mustard and salt, and over these dust and stones, and filling in the space between the stones with lead. At each corner, too, the Joshi drove in an iron nail, two feet long, which he had previously charmed. The lemon buried, the people returned home, and not one of them ever saw the Bhūt thereafter. According to the recorder of the tale, the cure was effected by putting quicksilver into the lemon. When a man is attacked with fever or becomes speechless or appears to have lockjaw, his friends conclude from these indications that he is possessed by a Bhūt.

In another case some Bhāts had been put in charge, by the chief of a small State, of a village which was coveted by a neighbouring prince, the Rāna of Dānta. The latter sent for the Bhāts and asked them to guard one or two of his villages, and having obtained their absence by this pretext he raided their village, carrying off hostages and cattle. When the Bhāts got back they collected to the number of a hundred and began to perform *Dharna* against the Rāna. They set out from their village, and at every two miles as they advanced they burned a man, so that by the time they got to the Rāna's territory seven or eight men had been burnt. They were then pacified by his people and induced to go back. The Rāna offered them presents, but they refused to accept them, as they said the guilt of the death of their fellows who had been burned would thereby be removed from the Rāna. The Rāna lost all the seven sons born to him and died childless, and it was generally held to be on account of this sin.[1]

[1] *Rāsmāla*, ii. pp. 143, 144.

Such was the certainty attaching to the Chāran's readiness to forfeit his life rather than prove false to a trust, and the fear entertained of the offence of causing him to do so and being haunted by his ghost, that his security was eagerly coveted in every kind of transaction. " No traveller could journey unattended by these guards, who for a small sum were satisfied to conduct him in safety.[1]   The guards, called Valāvas, were never backward in inflicting the most grievous wounds and even causing the death of their old men and women if the robbers persisted in plundering those under their protection ; but this seldom happened, as the wildest Koli, Kāthi or Rājpūt held the person of a Chāran sacred.   Besides becoming safeguards to travellers and goods, they used to stand security to the amount of many lakhs of rupees.   When rents and property were concerned, the Rājpūts preferred a Chāran's bond to that of the wealthiest banker.   They also gave security for good behaviour, called *chālu zāmin,* and for personal attendance in court called *hāzar zāmin.*   The ordinary *trāga* went no farther than a cut on the arm with the *katār* or crease ; the forearms of those who were in the habit of becoming security had generally several cuts from the elbow downwards.   The Chārans, both men and women, wounded themselves, committed suicide and murdered their relations with the most complete self-devotion.   In 1812 the Marāthas brought a body of troops to impose a payment on the village of Pānchpipla.[2]   The Chārans resisted the demand, but finding the Marāthas determined to carry their point, after a remonstrance against paying any kind of revenue as being contrary to their occupation and principles, they at last cut the throats of ten young children and threw them at the feet of the Marāthas, exclaiming, ' These are our riches and the only payment we can make.'   The Chārans were immediately seized and confined in irons at Jambusar."

As was the case with the Bhāt and the Brāhman, the source of the Chāran's power lay in the widespread fear that a Chāran's blood brought ruin on him who caused the blood to be spilt.   It was also sometimes considered that the

---

[1] *Bombay Gazetteer, Hindus of Gujarāt,* Mr. Bhimbhai Kirparām, pp. 217, 219.
[2] In Broach.

Chāran was possessed by his deity, and the caste were known as Deoputra or sons of God, the favourite dwelling of the guardian spirit.

13. Suicide as a means of revenge. Such a belief enhanced the guilt attaching to the act of causing or being responsible for a Chāran's death. Suicide from motives of revenge has been practised in other countries. "Another common form of suicide which is admired as heroic in China is that committed for the purpose of taking revenge upon an enemy who is otherwise out of reach— according to Chinese ideas a most effective mode of revenge, not only because the law throws the responsibility of the deed on him who occasioned it, but also because the disembodied soul is supposed to be better able than the living man to persecute the enemy."[1] Similarly, among the Hos or Mundas the suicide of young married women is or was extremely common, and the usual motive was that the girl, being unhappy in her husband's house, jumped down a well or otherwise made away with herself in the belief that she would take revenge on his family by haunting them after her death. The treatment of the suicide's body was sometimes directed to prevent his spirit from causing trouble. "According to Jewish custom persons who had killed themselves were left unburied till sunset, perhaps for fear lest the spirit of the deceased otherwise might find its way back to the old home."[2] At Athens the right hand of a person who had taken his own life was struck off and buried apart from the rest of the body, evidently in order to make him harmless after death.[3] Similarly, in England suicides were buried with a spike through the chest to prevent their spirits from rising, and at cross-roads, so that the ghost might not be able to find its way home. This fear appears to have partly underlain the idea that suicide was a crime or an offence against society and the state, though, as shown by Dr. Westermarck, the reprobation attaching to it was far from universal ; while in the cultured communities of ancient Greece and Rome, and among such military peoples as the Japanese suicide was considered at all times a legitimate and, on occasion, a highly meritorious and praiseworthy act.

[1] Westermarck, *Origin and Development of the Moral Ideas*, ii. p. 242.
[2] Westermarck, *ibidem*, p. 246.   [3] Westermarck, *ibidem*, p. 248.

That condition of mind which leads to the taking of one's own life from motives of revenge is perhaps a fruit of ignorance and solitude. The mind becomes distorted, and the sufferer attributes the unhappiness really caused by accident or his own faults or defects to the persecution of a malignant fate or the ill-will of his neighbours and associates. And long brooding over his wrongs eventuates in his taking the extreme step. The crime known as running amok appears to be the outcome of a similar state of mind. Here too the criminal considers his wrongs or misery as the result of injury or unjust treatment from his fellow-men, and, careless of his own life, determines to be revenged on them. Such hatred of one's kind is cured by education, leading to a truer appreciation of the circumstances and environment which determine the course of life, and by the more cheerful temper engendered by social intercourse. And these crimes of vengeance tend to die out with the advance of civilisation.

Analogous to the custom of *trāga* was that of *Dharna*, which was frequently and generally resorted to for the redress of wrongs and offences at a time when the law made little provision for either. The ordinary method of *Dharna* was to sit starving oneself in front of the door of the person from whom redress was sought until he gave it from fear of causing the death of the suppliant and being haunted by his ghost. It was, naturally, useless unless the person seeking redress was prepared to go to extremes, and has some analogy to the modern hunger-strike with the object of getting out of jail. Another common device was to thrust a spear-blade through both cheeks, and in this state to dance before the person against whom *Dharna* was practised. The pain had to be borne without a sign of suffering, which, if displayed, would destroy its efficacy. Or a creditor would proceed to the door of his debtor and demand payment, and if not appeased would stand up in his presence with an enormous weight upon his head, which he had brought with him for the purpose, swearing never to alter his position until satisfaction was given, and denouncing at the same time the most horrible execrations on his debtor, should he suffer him to expire in that situation. This seldom failed to produce the desired effect, but should he actually die

14. *Dharna.*

while in *Dharna*, the debtor's house was razed to the earth
and he and his family sold for the satisfaction of the
creditor's heirs.   Another and more desperate form of
Dharna, only occasionally resorted to, was to erect a large
pile of wood before the house of the debtor, and after the
customary application for payment had been refused the
creditor tied on the top of the pile a cow or a calf, or very
frequently an old woman, generally his mother or other
relation, swearing at the same time to set fire to it if
satisfaction was not instantly given.   All the time the
old woman denounced the bitterest curses, threatening to
persecute the wretched debtor both here and hereafter.[1]

The word *dharna* means 'to place or lay on,' and hence
'a pledge.'   Mr. Hīra Lāl suggests that the standing with
a weight on the head may have been the original form of
the penance, from which the other and severer methods were
subsequently derived.   Another custom known as *dharna*
is that of a suppliant placing a stone on the shrine of
a god or tomb of a saint.   He makes his request and,
laying the stone on the shrine, says, "Here I place this
stone until you fulfil my prayer ; if I do not remove it,
the shame is on you."   If the prayer is afterwards fulfilled,
he takes away the stone and offers a cocoanut.   It seems
clear that the underlying idea of this custom is the same
as that of standing with a stone on the head as described
above, but it is difficult to say which was the earlier or
original form.

15. Casting out spirits.   As a general rule, if the guilt of having caused a suicide
was at a man's door, he should expiate it by going to the
Ganges to bathe.   When a man was haunted by the ghost
of any one whom he had wronged, whether such a person
had committed suicide or simply died of grief at being
unable to obtain redress, it was said of him *Brahm laga*, or
that Brahma had possessed him.   The spirit of a Brāhman
boy, who has died unmarried, is also accustomed to haunt any
person who walks over his grave in an impure condition or
otherwise defiles it, and when a man is haunted in such a
manner it is called *Brahm laga*.   Then an exorcist is called,

---

[1] The above account of *Dharna* is taken from Colonel Tone's *Letter on the
Marāthas* (India Office Tracts).

who sprinkles water over the possessed man, and this burns the Brahm Deo or spirit inside him as if it were burning oil. The spirit cries out, and the exorcist orders him to leave the man.   Then the spirit states how he has been injured by the man, and refuses to leave him.   The exorcist asks him what he requires on condition of leaving the man, and he asks for some good food or something else, and is given it.   The exorcist takes a nail and goes to a *pīpal* tree and orders the Brahm Deo to go into the tree.   Brahm Deo obeys, and the exorcist drives the nail into the tree and the spirit remains imprisoned there until somebody takes the nail out, when he will come out again and haunt him.   The Hindus think that the god Brahma lives in the roots of the *pīpal* tree, Siva in its branches, and Vishnu in the *choti* or scalp-knot, that is the topmost foliage.

Another and mild form of *Dharna* is that known as Khātpāti.   When a woman is angry with her husband on account of his having refused her some request, she will put her bed in a corner of the room and go and lie on it, turning her face to the wall, and remain so, not answering when spoken to nor taking food.   The term Khātpāti signifies keeping to one side of the bed, and there she will remain until her husband accedes to her request, unless indeed he should decide to beat her instead.   This is merely an exaggerated form of the familiar display of temper known as sulking.   It is interesting to note the use of the phrase turning one's face to the wall, with something of the meaning attached to it in the Bible. ^{16. Sulking. Going bankrupt.}

A custom similar to that of *Dharna* was called *Diwāla nikālna* or going bankrupt.   When a merchant had had heavy losses and could not meet his liabilities, he would place the lock of his door outside, reversing it, and sit in the veranda with a piece of sackcloth over him.   Or he wrapped round him the floor-carpet of his room.   When he had displayed these signs of ruin and self-abasement his creditors would not sue him, but he would never be able to borrow money again.

In conclusion a few specimens of Bhāt songs may be given.   The following is an account of the last king of Nāgpur, Raghuji III., commonly known as Bāji Rao : ^{17. Bhāt songs.}

They made a picture of Bāji Rao ;
Bāji Rao was the finest king to see ;
The Brāhmans told lies about him,
They sent a letter from Nāgpur to Calcutta,
They made Bāji Rao go on a pilgrimage.
Brothers ! the great Sirdārs who were with him,
They brought a troop of five hundred horse !
The Tuesday fair in Benāres was held with fireworks,
They made the Ganges pink with rose-petals.
Bāji Rao's gifts were splendid,
His turban and coat were of brocaded silk,
A pair of diamonds and emeralds
He gave to the Brāhmans of Benāres.
Oh brothers ! the Rāja sat in a covered howdah bound on an
    elephant !
Many fans waved over his head ;
How charitable a king he was !

In the above song a note of regret is manifest for the
parade and display of the old court of Nāgpur, English
rule being less picturesque.   The next is a song about the
English :

The English have taken the throne of Nāgpur,
The fear of the English is great.
In a moment's time they conquer countries.
The guns boomed, the English came strong and warlike,
They give wealth to all.
They ram the ramrods in the guns.
They conquered also Tippoo's dominions,
The English are ruling in the fort of Gāwilgarh.

The following is another song about the English, not
quite so complimentary :

The English became our kings and have made current the *kaldār*
    (milled) rupee.
The menials are favoured and the Bhāts have lost their profession,
The mango has lost its taste, the milk has lost its sweetness,
The rose has lost its scent.
Bāji Rao of Nāgpur he also is gone,
No longer are the drums beaten at the palace gate.
Poona customs have come in.
Brāhmans knowing the eighteen Purāns have become Christians ;
The son thinks himself better than his father,
The daughter-in-law no longer respects her mother-in-law,
The wife fights with her husband.
The English have made the railways and telegraphs ;
The people wondered at the silver rupees and all the country
    prospered.

The following is a song about the Nerbudda at Mandla, Rewa being another name for the river:

The stream of the world springs out breaking apart the hills;
The Rewa cuts her path through the soil, the air is darkened with her
　　spray.
All the length of her banks are the seats of saints; hermits and pilgrims
　　worship her.
On seeing the holy river a man's sins fall away as wood is cut by a saw;
By bathing in her he plucks the fruit of holiness.
When boats are caught in her flood, the people pray: 'We are sinners,
　　O Rewa, bring us safely to the bank!'
When the Nerbudda is in flood, Mandla is an island and the people
　　think their end has come:
The rain pours down on all sides, earth and sky become dark as smoke,
　　and men call on Rāma.
The bard says: 'Let it rain as it may, some one will save us as Krishna
　　saved the people of Brindāwan!'

This is a description of a beautiful woman:

A beautiful woman is loved by her neighbours,
But she will let none come to her and answers them not.
They say: 'Since God has made you so beautiful, open your litter and
　　let yourself be seen!'
He who sees her is struck as by lightning, she shoots her lover with the
　　darts of her eyes, invisible herself.
She will not go to her husband's house till he has her brought by the
　　Government.
When she goes her father's village is left empty.
She is so delicate she faints at the sight of a flower,
Her body cannot bear the weight of her cloth,
The garland of jasmine-flowers is a burden on her neck,
The red powder on her feet is too heavy for them.

It is interesting to note that weakness and delicacy in a woman are emphasised as an attraction, as in English literature of the eighteenth century.

The last is a gentle intimation that poets, like other people, have to live:

It is useless to adorn oneself with sandalwood on an empty belly,
Nobody's body gets fat from the scent of flowers;
The singing of songs excites the mind, .
But if the body is not fed all these are vain and hollow.

All Bhāts recite their verses in a high-pitched sing-song tone, which renders it very difficult for their hearers to grasp the sense unless they know it already. The Vedas and all other sacred verses are spoken in this manner, perhaps as a mark of respect and to distinguish them from ordinary speech. The method has some resemblance to intoning. Women use the same tone when mourning for the dead.

BHATRA

Bhatra.[1]—A primitive tribe of the Bastar State and the south of Raipur District, akin to the Gonds. They numbered 33,000 persons in 1891, and in subsequent enumerations have been amalgamated with the Gonds. Nothing is known of their origin except a legend that they came with the Rājas of Bastar from Warangal twenty-three generations ago. The word Bhatra is said to mean a servant, and the tribe are employed as village watchmen and household and domestic servants. They have three divisions, the Pīt, Amnāit and Sān Bhatras, who rank one below the other, the Pīt being the highest and the Sān the lowest. The Pīt Bhatras base their superiority on the fact that they decline to make grass mats, which the Amnāit Bhatras will do, while the Sān Bhatras are considered to be practically identical with the Muria Gonds. Members of the three groups will eat with each other before marriage, but afterwards they will take only food cooked without water from a person belonging to another group. They have the usual set of exogamous septs named after plants and animals. Formerly, it is said, they were tattooed with representations

1. General notice and structure of the caste.

[1] This article is compiled from papers drawn up by Rai Bahādur Panda Baijnāth, Superintendent, Bastar State; Mr. Ravi Shankar, Settlement Officer, Bastar; and Mr. Gopāl Krishna, Assistant Superintendent, Bastar.

271

of the totem plant and animal, and the septs named after the tiger and snake ate the flesh of these animals at a sacrificial meal. These customs have fallen into abeyance, but still if they kill their totem animal they will make apologies to it, and break their cooking-pots, and bury or burn the body. A man of substance will distribute alms in the name of the deceased animal. In some localities members of the Kāchhun or tortoise sept will not eat a pumpkin which drops from a tree because it is considered to resemble a tortoise. But if they can break it immediately on touching the ground they may partake of the fruit, the assumption being apparently that it has not had time to become like a tortoise.

2. Admission of outsiders.

Outsiders are not as a rule admitted. But a woman of equal or higher caste who enters the house of a Bhatra will be recognised as his wife, and a man of the Panāra, or gardener caste, can also become a member of the community if he lives with a Bhatra woman and eats from her hand.

3. Arrangement of marriages.

In Raipur a girl should be married before puberty, and if no husband is immediately available, they tie a few flowers into her cloth and consider this as a marriage. If an unmarried girl becomes pregnant she is debarred from going through the wedding ceremony, and will simply go and live with her lover or any other man. Matches are usually arranged by the parents, but if a daughter is not pleased with the prospective bridegroom, who may sometimes be a well-to-do man much older than herself, she occasionally runs away and goes through the ceremony on her own account with the man of her choice.

If no one has asked her parents for her hand she may similarly select a husband for herself and make her wishes known, but in that case she is temporarily put out of caste until the chosen bridegroom signifies his acquiescence by giving the marriage feast. What happens if he definitely fails to respond is not stated, but presumably the young woman tries elsewhere until she finds herself accepted.

4. The Counter of Posts.

The date and hour of the wedding are fixed by an official known as the Meda Gantia, or Counter of Posts. He is a sort of illiterate village astrologer, who can foretell the character of the rainfall, and gives auspicious dates for sowing and harvest. He goes through some training, and as a test of his capacity is required by his teacher to tell at a glance the number of posts in an enclosure which he has not seen before. Having done this correctly he qualifies as a Meda Gantia. Apparently the Bhatras, being unable at one time to count themselves, acquired an exaggerated reverence for the faculty of counting, and thought that if a man could only count far enough he could reckon into the future ; or it might be thought that as he could count and name future days, he thus obtained power over them, and could tell what would happen on them just as one can obtain power over a man and work him injury by knowing his real name.

At a wedding the couple walk seven times round the sacred post, which must be of wood of the mahua [1] tree, and on its conclusion the post is taken to a river or stream and consigned to the water. The Bhatras, like the Gonds, no doubt revere this tree because their intoxicating liquor is made from its flowers. The couple wear marriage crowns made from the leaves of the date palm and exchange these. A little turmeric and flour are mixed with water in a plate, and the bride, taking the bridegroom's right hand, dips it into the coloured paste and strikes it against the wall. The action is repeated five times, and then the bridegroom does the same with the bride's hand. By this rite the couple pledge each other for their mutual behaviour during married life. From the custom of making an impression of the hand on a wall in token of a vow may have arisen that of clasping hands as a symbol of a bargain assented to, and hence of shaking hands, by persons who meet, as a pledge of amity and the absence of hostile intentions. Usually the hand is covered with red ochre, which is probably a substitute for blood ; and the impression of the hand is made on the wall of a temple in token of a vow. This may be a survival of the covenant made by the parties dipping their hands in the blood of the sacrifice and laying them on the god. A pit about a foot deep is dug close to the marriage-shed, and filled with mud or wet earth. The bride conceals a nut in the mud and the bridegroom has to find it, and

5. Marriage customs.

---

[1] *Bassia latifolia.*

the hiding and finding are repeated by both parties. This rite may have the signification of looking for children. The remainder of the day is spent in eating, drinking and dancing. On the way home after the wedding the bridegroom has to shoot a deer, the animal being represented by a branch of a tree thrown across the path by one of the party. But if a real deer happens by any chance to come by he has to shoot this. The bride goes up to the real or sham deer and pulls out the arrow, and presents her husband with water and a tooth-stick, after which he takes her in his arms and they dance home together. On arrival at the house the bridegroom's maternal uncle or his son lies down before the door covering himself with a blanket. He is asked what he wants, and says he will have the daughter of the bridegroom to wife. The bridegroom promises to give a daughter if he has one, and if he has a son to give him for a friend. The tribe consider that a man has a right to marry the daughter of his maternal uncle, and formerly if the girl was refused by her parents he abducted her and married her forcibly. The bride remains at her husband's house for a few days and then goes home, and before she finally takes up her abode with him the *gauna* or going-away ceremony must be performed. The hands of the bride and bridegroom are tied together, and an arrow is held upright on them and some oil poured over it. The foreheads of the couple are marked with turmeric and rice, this rite being known as *tīka* or anointing, and presents are given to the bride's family.

6. Propitiation of ghosts.
The dead are buried, the corpse being laid on its back with the head to the north. Some rice, cowrie-shells, a winnowing-fan and other articles are placed on the grave. The tribe probably consider the winnowing-fan to have some magical property, as it also forms one of the presents given to the bride at the betrothal. If a man is killed by a tiger his spirit must be propitiated. The priest ties strips of tiger-skin to his arms, and the feathers of the peacock and blue jay to his waist, and jumps about pretending to be a tiger. A package of a hundred seers (200 lbs.) of rice is made up, and he sits on this and finally takes it away with him. If the dead man had any ornaments they must all be given, however valuable, lest his spirit should hanker after

them and return to look for them in the shape of the tiger. The large quantity of rice given to the priest is also probably intended as a provision of the best food for the dead man's spirit, lest it be hungry and come in the shape of the tiger to satisfy its appetite upon the surviving relatives. The laying of the ghosts of persons killed by tigers is thus a very profitable business for the priests.

The tribe worship the god of hunting, who is known as Māti Deo and resides in a separate tree in each village. At the Bījphūtni (threshing) or harvest festival in the month of Chait (March) they have a ceremonial hunting party. All the people of the village collect, each man having a bow and arrow slung to his back and a hatchet on his shoulder. They spread out a long net in the forest and beat the animals into this, usually catching a deer, wild pig or hare, and quails and other birds. They return and cook the game before the shrine of the god and offer to him a fowl and a pig. A pit is dug and water poured into it, and a person from each house must stand in the mud. A little seed taken from each house is also soaked in the mud, and after the feast is over this is taken and returned to the householder with words of abuse, a small present of two or three pice being received from him. The seed is no doubt thus consecrated for the next sowing. The tribe also have joint ceremonial fishing excursions. Their ideas of a future life are very vague, and they have no belief in a place of reward or punishment after death. They propitiate the spirits of their ancestors on the 15th of Asārh (June) with offerings of a little rice and incense.

7. Religion. Ceremonies at hunting.

To cure the evil eye they place a little gunpowder in water and apply it to the sufferer's eyes, the idea perhaps being that the fiery glance from the evil eye which struck him is quenched like the gunpowder. To bring on rain they perform a frog marriage, tying two frogs to a pestle and pouring oil and turmeric over them as in a real marriage. The children carry them round begging from door to door and finally deposit them in water. They say that when rain falls and the sun shines together the jackals are being married. Formerly a woman suspected of being a witch was tied up in a bag and thrown into a river or tank

8. Superstitious remedies.

at various places set apart for the purpose. If she sank she was held to be innocent, and if she floated, guilty. In the latter case she had to defile herself by taking the bone of a cow and the tail of a pig in her mouth, and it was supposed that this drove out the magic-working spirit. In the case of illness of their children or cattle, or the failure of crops, they consult the Pujāri or priest and make an offering. He applies some flowers or grains of rice to the forehead of the deity, and when one of these falls down he diagnoses from it the nature of the illness, and gives it to the sufferer to wear as a charm.

9. Occupation.

The tribe are cultivators and farmservants, and practise shifting cultivation. They work as village watchmen and also as the Mājhi or village headman and the Pujāri or village priest. These officials are paid by contributions of grain from the cultivators. And as already seen, the Bhatras are employed as household servants and will clean cooking-vessels. Since they act as village priests, it may perhaps be concluded that the Bhatras like the Parjas are older residents of Bastar than the bulk of the Gonds, and they have become the household servants of the Hindu immigrants, which the Gonds would probably disdain to do. Some of them wear the sacred thread, but in former times the Bastar Rāja would invest any man with this for a fee of four or five rupees, and the Bhatras therefore purchased the social distinction. They find it inconvenient, however, and lay it aside when proceeding to their work or going out to hunt. If a man breaks his thread he must wait till a Brāhman comes round, when he can purchase another.

10. Names.

Among a list of personal names given by Mr. Baijnāth the following are of some interest: Pillu, one of short stature; Matola, one who learnt to walk late; Phagu, born in Phāgun (February); Ghinu, dirty-looking; Dasru, born on the Dasahra festival; Ludki, one with a fleshy ear; Dalu, big-bellied; Mudi, a ring, this name having been given to a child which cried much after birth, but when its nose was pierced and a ring put in it stopped crying; Chhi, given to a child which sneezed immediately after birth; Nunha, a posthumous child; and Bhuklu, a child which began to play almost as soon as born. The above instances indicate that it is a favourite plan to select the name from any characteristic displayed by the child soon after birth, or from any circumstance or incident connected with its birth. Among names of women are : Cherangi, thin ; Fundi, one with swollen cheeks ; Kandri, one given to crying ; Mahīna (month), a child born a month late ; Batai, one with large eyes ; Gaida, fat ; Pakli, of fair colour ; Boda, one with crooked legs ; Jhunki, one with small eyes ; Rupi, a girl who was given a nose-ring of silver as her brothers had died ; Paro, born on a field-embankment ; Dango, tall. A woman must not call by their names her father-in-law, mother-in-law, her husband's brothers and elder sisters and the sons and daughters of her husband's brothers and sisters.

BHĪL

LIST OF PARAGRAPHS

1. General notice. The Bhīls a Kolarian tribe.

Bhīl.[1]—An indigenous or non-Aryan tribe which has been much in contact with the Hindus and is consequently well known. The home of the Bhīls is the country comprised in the hill ranges of Khāndesh, Central India and Rājpūtāna, west from the Satpūras to the sea in Gujarāt. The total number of Bhīls in India exceeds a million and a half, of which the great bulk belong to Bombay, Rājpūtāna and Central India. The Central Provinces have only about 28,000, practically all of whom reside in the Nimār district, on the hills forming the western end of the Satpūra range and adjoining the Rājpipla hills of Khāndesh. As the southern slopes of these hills lie in Berār, a few Bhīls are also found there. The name Bhīl seems to occur for the first time about A.D. 600. It is supposed to be derived from the Dravidian word for a bow, which is the characteristic weapon of the tribe. It has been suggested that the Bhīls

---

[1] The principal authorities on the Bhīls are: *An Account of the Mewār Bhīls*, by Major P. H. Hendley, *J.A.S.B.* vol. xliv., 1875, pp. 347-385; the *Bombay Gazetteer*, vol. ix., *Hindus of Gujarāt*; and notices in Colonel Tod's *Rājasthān*, Mr. A. L. Forbes's *Rāsmāla*, and *The Khāndesh Bhīl Corps*, by Mr. A. H. A. Simcox, C.S.

GROUP OF BHILS.

Bemrose, Collo., Derby.

are the Pygmies referred to by Ktesias (400 B.C.) and the
Phyllitae of Ptolemy (A.D. 150). The Bhīls are recognised
as the oldest inhabitants of southern Rājputāna and parts of
Gujarāt, and are usually spoken of in conjunction with the
Kolis, who inhabit the adjoining tracts of Gujarāt. The
most probable hypothesis of the origin of the Kolis is that
they are a western branch of the Kol or Munda tribe who
have spread from Chota Nāgpur, through Mandla and
Jubbulpore, Central India and Rājputāna to Gujarāt and
the sea. If this is correct the Kolis would be a Kolarian
tribe. The Bhīls have lost their own language, so that it
cannot be ascertained whether it was Kolarian or Dravidian.
But there is nothing against its being Kolarian in Sir
G. Grierson's opinion ; and in view of the length of residence
of the tribe, the fact that they have abandoned their own
language and their association with the Kolis, this view may
be taken as generally probable. The Dravidian tribes have
not penetrated so far west as Central India and Gujarāt in
appreciable numbers.

The Rājpūts still recognise the Bhīls as the former
residents and occupiers of the land by the fact that some
Rājpūt chiefs must be marked on the brow with a Bhīl's
blood on accession to the *Gaddi* or regal cushion. Tod
relates how Goha,[1] the eponymous ancestor of the Sesodia
Rājpūts, took the state of Idar in Gujarāt from a Bhīl :
" At this period Idar was governed by a chief of the
savage race of Bhīls. The young Goha frequented the
forests in company with the Bhīls, whose habits better
assimilated with his daring nature than those of the Brāhmans. He became a favourite with these *vena-putras* or
sons of the forest, who resigned to him Idar with its woods
and mountains. The Bhīls having determined in sport to
elect a king, their choice fell on Goha ; and one of the young
savages, cutting his finger, applied the blood as the badge
(*tīka*) of sovereignty to his forehead. What was done in
sport was confirmed by the old forest chief. The sequel
fixes on Goha the stain of ingratitude, for he slew his

*2. Rājpūts
deriving
their
title to the
land from
the Bhīls.*

---

[1] The old name of the Sesodia clan,
Gahlot, is held to be derived from this
Goha. See the article Rājpūt Sesodia
for a notice of the real origin of the
clan.

benefactor, and no motive is assigned in the legend for the deed."[1]

The legend is of course a euphemism for the fact that the Rājpūts conquered and dispossessed the Bhīls of Idar. But it is interesting as an indication that they did not consider themselves to derive a proper title to the land merely from the conquest, but wished also to show that it passed to them by the designation and free consent of the Bhīls. The explanation is perhaps that they considered the gods of the Bhīls to be the tutelary guardians and owners of the land, whom they must conciliate before they could hope to enjoy it in quiet and prosperity. This token of the devolution of the land from its previous holders, the Bhīls, was till recently repeated on the occasion of each succession of a Sesodia chief. "The Bhīl landholders of Oguna and Undri still claim the privilege of performing the *tīka* for the Sesodias. The Oguna Bhīl makes the mark of sovereignty on the chief's forehead with blood drawn from his own thumb, and then takes the chief by the arm and seats him on the throne, while the Undri Bhīl holds the salver of spices and sacred grains of rice used in making the badge."[2] The story that Goha killed the old Bhīl chief, his benefactor, who had adopted him as heir and successor, which fits in very badly with the rest of the legend, is probably based on another superstition. Sir J. G. Frazer has shown in *The Golden Bough* that in ancient times it was a common superstition that any one who killed the king had a right to succeed him. The belief was that the king was the god of the country, on whose health, strength and efficiency its prosperity depended. When the king grew old and weak it was time for a successor, and he who could kill the king proved in this manner that the divine power and strength inherent in the late king had descended to him, and he was therefore the fit person to be king.[3] An almost similar story is told of the way in which the Kachhwāha Rājpūts took the territory of Amber State from the Mīna tribe. The infant Rājpūt prince had been deprived of Narwar by

---

[1] *Rājasthān*, i. p. 184.
[2] *Ibidem*, p. 186.
[3] Reference may be made to *The Golden Bough* for the full explanation and illustration of this superstition.

his uncle, and his mother wandered forth carrying him in a basket, till she came to the capital of the Mīnas, where she first obtained employment in the chief's kitchen. But owing to her good cooking she attracted his wife's notice and ultimately disclosed her identity and told her story. The Mīna chief then adopted her as his sister and the boy as his nephew. This boy, Dhola Rai, on growing up obtained a few Rājpūt adherents and slaughtered all the Mīnas while they were bathing at the feast of Diwāli, after which he usurped their country.[1] The repetition both of the adoption and the ungrateful murder shows the importance attached by the Rājpūts to both beliefs as necessary to the validity of their succession and occupation of the land.

The position of the Bhīls as the earliest residents of the country was also recognised by their employment in the capacity of village watchmen. One of the duties of this official is to know the village boundaries and keep watch and ward over them, and it was supposed that the oldest class of residents would know them best. The Bhīls worked in the office of Mānkar, the superior village watchman, in Nimār and also in Berār. Grant Duff states[2] that the Rāmosi or Bhīl was employed as village guard by the Marāthas, and the Rāmosis were a professional caste of village policemen, probably derived from the Bhīls or from the Bhīls and Kolis.

The Rājpūts seem at first to have treated the Bhīls leniently. Intermarriage was frequent, especially in the families of Bhīl chieftains, and a new caste called Bhilāla[3] has arisen, which is composed of the descendants of mixed Rājpūt and Bhīl marriages. Chiefs and landholders in the Bhīl country now belong to this caste, and it is possible that some pure Bhīl families may have been admitted to it. The Bhilālas rank above the Bhīls, on a level with the cultivating castes. Instances occasionally occurred in which the children of a Rājpūt by a Bhīl wife became Rājpūts. When Colonel Tod wrote, Rājpūts would still take food with Ujla Bhīls or those of pure aboriginal descent, and all castes would take water from them.[4] But

3. Historical notice.

---

[1] *Rājasthān*, ii. pp. 320, 321.
[2] *History of the Marāthas*, i. p. 28.
[3] See article.
[4] *Rājasthān*, ii. p. 466.

as Hinduism came to be more orthodox in Rājputāna, the Bhīls sank to the position of outcastes. Their custom of eating beef had always caused them to be much despised. A tradition is related that one day the god Mahādeo or Siva, sick and unhappy, was reclining in a shady forest when a beautiful woman appeared, the first sight of whom effected a cure of all his complaints. An intercourse between the god and the strange female was established, the result of which was many children ; one of whom, from infancy distinguished alike by his ugliness and vice, slew the favourite bull of Mahādeo, for which crime he was expelled to the woods and mountains, and his descendants have ever since been stigmatised by the names of Bhīl and Nishāda.[1] Nishāda is a term of contempt applied to the lowest out-castes. Major Hendley, writing in 1875, states : "Some time since a Thākur (chief) cut off the legs of two Bhīls, eaters of the sacred cow, and plunged the stumps into boiling oil." [2] When the Marāthas began to occupy Central India they treated the Bhīls with great cruelty. A Bhīl caught in a disturbed part of the country was without inquiry flogged and hanged. Hundreds were thrown over high cliffs, and large bodies of them, assembled under promise of pardon, were beheaded or blown from guns. Their women were mutilated or smothered by smoke, and their children smashed to death against the stones.[3] This treatment may to some extent have been deserved owing to the predatory habits and cruelty of the Bhīls, but its result was to make them utter savages with their hand against every man, as they believed that every one's was against them. From their strongholds in the hills they laid waste the plain country, holding villages and towns to ransom and driving off cattle ; nor did any travellers pass with impunity through the hills except in convoys too large to be attacked. In Khāndesh, during the disturbed period of the wars of Sindhia and Holkar, about A.D. 1800, the Bhīls betook themselves to highway robbery and lived in bands either in mountains or in villages immediately beneath them. The revenue contractors were

---

[1] Malcolm, *Memoir of Central India,* i. p. 518.
[2] *An Account of the Bhīls, J.A.S.B.*
(1875), p. 369.
[3] *Hyderābād Census Report* (1891), p. 218.

TANTIA BHĪL, A FAMOUS DACOIT.

unable or unwilling to spend money in the maintenance of soldiers to protect the country, and the Bhīls in a very short time became so bold as to appear in bands of hundreds and attack towns, carrying off either cattle or hostages, for whom they demanded handsome ransoms.[1]   In Gujarāt another writer described the Bhīls and Kolis as hereditary and professional plunderers —'Soldiers of the night,' as they themselves said they were.[2]   Malcolm said of them, after peace had been restored to Central India :[3] "Measures are in progress that will, it is expected, soon complete the reformation of a class of men who, believing themselves doomed to be thieves and plunderers, have been confirmed in their destiny by the oppression and cruelty of neighbouring governments, increased by an avowed contempt for them as outcasts.   The feeling this system of degradation has produced must be changed ; and no effort has been left untried to restore this race of men to a better sense of their condition than that which they at present entertain.   The common answer of a Bhīl when charged with theft or robbery is, ' I am not to blame ; I am the thief of Mahādeo ' ; in other words, ' My destiny as a thief has been fixed by God.' " The Bhīl chiefs, who were known as Bhumia, exercised the most absolute power, and their orders to commit the most atrocious crimes were obeyed by their ignorant but attached subjects without a conception on the part of the latter that they had an option when he whom they termed their Dhunni (Lord) issued the mandates.[4]   Firearms and swords were only used by the chiefs and headmen of the tribe, and their national weapon was the bamboo bow having the bowstring made from a thin strip of its elastic bark.   The quiver was a piece of strong bamboo matting, and would contain sixty barbed arrows a yard long, and tipped with an iron spike either flattened and sharpened like a knife or rounded like a nail ; other arrows, used for knocking over birds, had knob-like heads.   Thus armed, the Bhīls would lie in wait in some deep ravine by the roadside, and an infernal yell announced their attack to the unwary traveller.[5]   Major Hendley states

---

[1] *The Khāndesh Bhīl Corps*, by Mr A. H. A. Simcox.

[2] Forbes, *Rāsmāla*, i. p. 104.

[3] *Memoir of Central India*, i. pp. 525, 526.
[4] *Ibidem*, i. p. 550.
[5] *Hobson-Jobson*, art. Bhīl.

that according to tradition in the Mahābhārata the god Krishna was killed by a Bhīl's arrow, when he was fighting against them in Gujarāt with the Yādavas; and on this account it was ordained that the Bhīl should never again be able to draw the bow with the forefinger of the right hand. "Times have changed since then, but I noticed in examining their hands that few could move the forefinger without the second finger; indeed the fingers appeared useless as independent members of the hands. In connection with this may be mentioned their apparent inability to distinguish colours or count numbers, due alone to their want of words to express themselves." [1]

4. General Outram and the Khāndesh Bhīl Corps. The reclamation and pacification of the Bhīls is inseparably associated with the name of Lieutenant, afterwards Sir James, Outram. The Khāndesh Bhīl Corps was first raised by him in 1825, when Bhīl robber bands were being hunted down by small parties of troops, and those who were willing to surrender were granted a free pardon for past offences, and given grants of land for cultivation and advances for the purchase of seed and bullocks. When the first attempts to raise the corps were made, the Bhīls believed that the object was to link them in line like galley-slaves with a view to extirpate the race, that blood was in high demand as a medicine in the country of their foreign masters, and so on. Indulging the wild men with feasts and entertainments, and delighting them with his matchless urbanity, Captain Outram at length contrived to draw over to the cause nine recruits, one of whom was a notorious plunderer who had a short time before successfully robbed the officer commanding a detachment sent against him. This infant corps soon became strongly attached to the person of their new chief and entirely devoted to his wishes; their goodwill had been won by his kind and conciliatory manners, while their admiration and respect had been thoroughly roused and excited by his prowess and valour in the chase. On one occasion, it is recorded, word was brought to Outram of the presence of a panther in some prickly-pear shrubs on the side of a hill near his station. He went to shoot it with a friend, Outram being on foot and his friend on horseback searching

[1] *An Account of the Bhīls*, p. 369.

through the bushes. When close on the animal, Outram's friend fired and missed, on which the panther sprang forward roaring and seized Outram, and they rolled down the hill together. Being released from the claws of the furious beast for a moment, Outram with great presence of mind drew a pistol which he had with him, and shot the panther dead. The Bhīls, on seeing that he had been injured, were one and all loud in their grief and expressions of regret, when Outram quieted them with the remark, 'What do I care for the clawing of a cat?' and this saying long remained a proverb among the Bhīls.[1] By his kindness and sympathy, listening freely to all that each single man in the corps had to say to him, Outram at length won their confidence, convinced them of his good faith and dissipated their fears of treachery. Soon the ranks of the corps became full, and for every vacant place there were numbers of applicants. The Bhīls freely hunted down and captured their friends and relations who continued to create disturbances, and brought them in for punishment. Outram managed to check their propensity for liquor by paying them every day just sufficient for their food, and giving them the balance of their pay at the end of the month, when some might have a drinking bout, but many preferred to spend the money on ornaments and articles of finery. With the assistance of the corps the marauding tendencies of the hill Bhīls were suppressed and tranquillity restored to Khāndesh, which rapidly became one of the most fertile parts of India. During the Mutiny the Bhīl corps remained loyal, and did good service in checking the local outbursts which occurred in Khāndesh. A second battalion was raised at this time, but was disbanded three years afterwards. After this the corps had little or nothing to do, and as the absence of fighting and the higher wages which could be obtained by ordinary labour ceased to render it attractive to the Bhīls, it was finally converted into police in 1891.[2]

The Bhīls of the Central Provinces have now only two subdivisions, the Muhammadan Bhīls, who were forcibly converted to Islām during the time of Aurāngzeb, and the remainder, who though retaining many animistic beliefs and

5. Subdivisions.

[1] *The Khāndesh Bhīl Corps*, p. 71.   [2] *Ibidem*, p. 275.

superstitions, have practically become Hindus. The
Muhammadan Bhīls only number about 3000 out of 28,000.
They are known as Tadvi, a name which was formerly
applied to a Bhīl headman, and is said to be derived from
tād, meaning a separate branch or section. These Bhīls
marry among themselves and not with any other Muhammadans. They retain many Hindu and animistic usages,
and are scarcely Muhammadan in more than name. Both
classes are divided into groups or septs, generally named
after plants or animals to which they still show reverence.
Thus the Jāmania sept, named after the *jāman* tree,[1] will
not cut or burn any part of this tree, and at their weddings
the dresses of the bride and bridegroom are taken and
rubbed against the tree before being worn. Similarly the
Rohini sept worship the *rohan*[2] tree, the Avalia sept the
aonla[3] tree, the Meheda sept the *bahera*[4] tree, and so on.
The Mori sept worship the peacock. They go into the
jungle and look for the tracks of a peacock, and spreading
a piece of red cloth before the footprint, lay their offerings
of grain upon it. Members of this sept may not be tattooed,
because they think the splashes of colour on the peacock's
feathers are tattoo-marks. Their women must veil themselves if they see a peacock, and they think that if any
member of the sept irreverently treads on a peacock's footprints he will fall ill. The Ghodmārya (Horse-killer) sept
may not tame a horse nor ride one. The Masrya sept will
not kill or eat fish. The Sanyān or cat sept have a tradition
that one of their ancestors was once chasing a cat, which
ran for protection under a cover which had been put over
the stone figure of their goddess. The goddess turned the
cat into stone and sat on it, and since then members of the
sept will not touch a cat except to save it from harm, and
they will not eat anything which has been touched by a cat.
The Ghattaya sept worship the grinding mill at their weddings and also on festival days. The Solia sept, whose name
is apparently derived from the sun, are split up into four
subsepts : the Ada Solia, who hold their weddings at sunrise ;
the Japa Solia, who hold them at sunset ; the Taria Solia,

[1] *Eugenia jambolana.*   [3] *Phyllanthus emblica.*
[2] *Soymida febrifuga.*   [4] *Terminalia belerica.*

who hold them when stars have become visible after sunset ; and the Tar Solia, who believe their name is connected with cotton thread and wrap several skeins of raw thread round the bride and bridegroom at the wedding ceremony.   The Moharia sept worship the local goddess at the village of Moharia in Indore State, who is known as the Moharia Māta ; at their weddings they apply turmeric and oil to the fingers of the goddess before rubbing them on the bride and bridegroom.   The Maoli sept worship a goddess of that name in Barwāni town.   Her shrine is considered to be in the shape of a kind of grain-basket known as *kilia*, and members of the sept may never make or use baskets of this shape, nor may they be tattooed with representations of it. Women of the sept are not allowed to visit the shrine of the goddess, but may worship her at home.   Several septs have the names of Rājpūt clans, as Sesodia, Panwār, Mori, and appear to have originated in mixed unions between Rājpūts and Bhīls.

A man must not marry in his own sept nor in the families of his mothers and grandmothers.   The union of first cousins is thus prohibited, nor can girls be exchanged in marriage between two families.   A wife's sister may also not be married during the wife's lifetime.   The Muhammadan Bhīls permit a man to marry his maternal uncle's daughter, and though he cannot marry his wife's sister he may keep her as a concubine.   Marriages may be infant or adult, but the former practice is becoming prevalent and girls are often wedded before they are eleven.   Matches are arranged by the parents of the parties in consultation with the caste *panchāyat* ; but in Bombay girls may select their own husbands, and they have also a recognised custom of elopement at the Tosina fair in the month of the Mahi Kāntha.   If a Bhīl can persuade a girl to cross the river there with him he may claim her as his wife ; but if they are caught before getting across he is liable to be punished by the bride's father.[1]   The betrothal and wedding ceremonies now follow the ordinary ritual of the middle and lower castes in the Marātha country.[2]   The bride must be

6. Exogamy and marriage customs.

---

[1] *Bombay Gazetteer, Hindus of Gujarāt*, p. 309.
[2] See article Kunbi.

younger than the bridegroom except in the case of a widow. A bride-price is paid which may vary from Rs. 9 to 20 ; in the case of Muhammadan Bhīls the bridegroom is said to give a dowry of Rs. 20 to 25. When the ovens are made with the sacred earth they roast some of the large millet juāri[1] for the family feast, calling this Juāri Māta or the grain goddess. Offerings of this are made to the family gods, and it is partaken of only by the members of the bride's and bridegroom's septs respectively at their houses. No outsider may even see this food being eaten. The leavings of food, with the leaf-plates on which it was eaten, are buried inside the house, as it is believed that if they should fall into the hands of any outsider the death or blindness of one of the family will ensue. When the bridegroom reaches the bride's house he strikes the marriage-shed with a dagger or other sharp instrument. A goat is killed and he steps in its blood as he enters the shed. A day for the wedding is selected by the priest, but it may also take place on any Sunday in the eight fine months. If the wedding takes place on the eleventh day of Kārtik, that is on the expiration of the four rainy months when marriages are forbidden, they make a little hut of eleven stalks of juāri with their cobs in the shape of a cone, and the bride and bridegroom walk round this. The services of a Brāhman are not required for such a wedding. Sometimes the bridegroom is simply seated in a grain basket and the bride in a winnowing-fan ; then their hands are joined as the sun is half set, and the marriage is completed. The bridegroom takes the basket and fan home with him. On the return of the wedding couple, their *kankans* or wristbands are taken off at Hanumān's temple. The Muhammadan Bhīls perform the same ceremonies as the Hindus, but at the end they call in the Kāzi or registrar, who repeats the Muhammadan prayers and records the dowry agreed upon. The practice of the bridegroom serving for his wife is in force among both classes of Bhīls.

7. Widow-marriage, divorce and polygamy. The remarriage of widows is permitted, but the widow may not marry any relative of her first husband. She returns to her father's house, and on her remarriage they

[1] *Sorghum vulgare.*

obtain a bride-price of Rs. 40 or 50, a quarter of which goes in a feast to the tribesmen. The wedding of a widow is held on the Amāwas or last day of the dark fortnight of the month, or on a Sunday. A wife may be divorced for adultery without consulting the *panchāyat.* It is said that a wife cannot otherwise be divorced on any account, nor can a woman divorce her husband, but she may desert him and go and live with a man. In this case all that is necessary is that the second husband should repay to the first as compensation the amount expended by the latter on his marriage with the woman. Polygamy is permitted, and a second wife is sometimes taken in order to obtain children, but this number is seldom if ever exceeded. It is stated that the Bhīl married women are generally chaste and faithful to their husbands, and any attempt to tamper with their virtue on the part of an outsider is strongly resented by the man.

The Bhīls worship the ordinary Hindu deities and the 8. Religion. village godlings of the locality. The favourite both with Hindu and Muhammadan Bhīls is Khande Rao or Khandoba, the war-god of the Marāthas, who is often represented by a sword. The Muhammadans and the Hindu Bhīls also to a less extent worship the Pīrs or spirits of Muhammadan saints at their tombs, of which there are a number in Nimār. Major Hendley states that in Mewār the seats or *sthāns* of the Bhīl gods are on the summits of high hills, and are represented by heaps of stones, solid or hollowed out in the centre, or mere platforms, in or near which are found numbers of clay or mud images of horses.[1] In some places clay lamps are burnt in front of the images of horses, from which it may be concluded that the horse itself is or was worshipped as a god. Colonel Tod states that the Bhīls will eat of nothing white in colour, as a white sheep or goat ; and their grand adjuration is ' By the white ram.'[2] Sir A. Lyall[3] says that their principal oath is by the dog. The Bhīl sepoys told Major Hendley that they considered it of little use to go on worshipping their own gods, as the power of these had declined since the English became supreme. They thought the strong English gods were too much for

[1] *Loc. cit.* p. 347.   [2] *Western India.*
[3] *Asiatic Studies*, 1st series, p. 174.

the weak deities of their country, hence they were desirous of embracing Brāhmanism, which would also raise them in the social scale and give them a better chance of promotion in regiments where there were Brāhman officers.

9. Witch-craft and amulets.

They wear charms and amulets to keep off evil spirits ; the charms are generally pieces of blue string with seven knots in them, which their witch-finder or Badwa ties, reciting an incantation on each ; the knots were sometimes covered with metal to keep them undefiled and the charms were tied on at the Holi, Dasahra or some other festival.[1] In Bombay the Bhīls still believe in witches as the agents of any misfortunes that may befall them. If a man was sick and thought some woman had bewitched him, the suspected woman was thrown into a stream or swung from a tree. If the branch broke and the woman fell and suffered serious injury, or if she could not swim across the stream and sank, she was considered to be innocent and efforts were made to save her. But if she escaped without injury she was held to be a witch, and it frequently happened that the woman would admit herself to be one either from fear of the infliction of a harder ordeal, or to keep up the belief in her powers as a witch, which often secured her a free supper of milk and chickens. She would then admit that she had really bewitched the sick man and undertake to cure him on some sacrifice being made. If he recovered, the animal named by the witch was sacrificed and its blood given her to drink while still warm ; either from fear or in order to keep up the character she would drink it, and would be permitted to stay on in the village. If, on the other hand, the sick person died, the witch would often be driven into the forest to die of hunger or to be devoured by wild animals.[2] These practices have now disappeared in the Central Provinces, though occasionally murders of suspected witches may still occur. The Bhīls are firm believers in omens, the nature of which is much the same as among the Hindus. When a Bhīl is persistently unlucky in hunting, he sometimes says '*Nat laga*,' meaning that some bad spirit is causing his ill-success. Then he will

[1] *Asiatic Studies*, 1st series, p. 352.
[2] *Bombay Gazetteer, Hindus of Gujarāt*, p. 302.

make an image of a man in the sand or dust of the road, or sometimes two images of a man and woman, and throwing straw or grass over the images set it alight, and pound it down on them with a stick with abusive yells.   This he calls killing his bad luck.[1]   Major Hendley notes that the men danced before the different festivals and before battles. The men danced in a ring holding sticks and striking them against each other, much like the Baiga dance.   Before battle they had a war-dance in which the performers were armed and imitated a combat.   To be carried on the shoulders of one of the combatants was a great honour, perhaps because it symbolised being on horseback.   The dance was probably in the nature of a magical rite, designed to obtain success in battle by going through an imitation of it beforehand.   The priests are the chief physicians among the Bhīls, though most old men were supposed to know something about medicine.[2]

The dead are usually buried lying on the back, with the head pointing to the south.   Cooked food is placed on the bier and deposited on the ground half-way to the cemetery. On return each family of the sept brings a wheaten cake to the mourners and these are eaten.   On the third day they place on the grave a thick cake of wheaten flour, water in an earthen pot and tobacco or any other stimulant which the deceased was in the habit of using in his life.

10. Funeral rites.

The Hindu Bhīls say that they do not admit outsiders into the caste, but the Muhammadans will admit a man of any but the impure castes.   The neophyte must be shaved and circumcised, and the Kāzi gives him some holy water to drink and teaches him the profession of belief in Islām.   If a man is not circumcised, the Tadvi or Muhammadan Bhīls will not bury his body.   Both classes of Bhīls employ Brāhmans at their ceremonies.   The tribe eat almost all kinds of flesh and drink liquor, but the Hindus now abjure beef and the Muhammadans pork.   Some Bhīls now refuse to take the skins off dead cattle, but others will do so. The Bhīls will take food from any caste except the impure ones, and none except these castes will now take food from

11. Social customs.

---

[1] *Bombay Gazetteer*, vol. xii. p. 87.
[2] *An Account of the Bhīls*, pp. 362, 363.

them. Temporary or permanent exclusion from caste is imposed for the same offences as among the Hindus.

The typical Bhīl is small, dark, broad-nosed and ugly, but well built and active. The average height of 128 men measured by Major Hendley was 5 feet 6.4 inches. The hands are somewhat small and the legs fairly developed, those of the women being the best. "The Bhīl is an excellent woodsman, knows the shortest cuts over the hills, can walk the roughest paths and climb the steepest crags without slipping or feeling distressed. He is often called in old Sanskrit works Venaputra, 'child of the forest,' or Pāl Indra, 'lord of the pass.' These names well describe his character. His country is approached through narrow defiles (*pāl*), and through these none could pass without his permission. In former days he always levied *rakhwāli* or blackmail, and even now native travellers find him quite ready to assert what he deems his just rights. The Bhīl is a capital huntsman, tracking and marking down tigers, panthers and bears, knowing all their haunts, the best places to shoot them, the paths they take and all those points so essential to success in big-game shooting; they will remember for years the spots where tigers have been disposed of, and all the circumstances connected with their, deaths. The Bhīl will himself attack a leopard, and with his sword, aided by his friends, cut him to pieces."[1] Their agility impressed the Hindus, and an old writer says: "Some Bhīl chieftains who attended the camp of Sidhrāj, king of Gujarāt, astonished him with their feats of activity; in his army they seemed as the followers of Hanumān in attendance upon Rām."[2]

The Bhīls have now had to abandon their free use of the forests, which was highly destructive in its effects, and their indiscriminate slaughter of game. Many of them live in the open country and have become farmservants and field-labourers. A certain proportion are tenants, but very few own villages. Some of the Tadvi Bhīls, however, still retain villages which were originally granted free of revenue on condition of their keeping the hill-passes of the Satpūras

---

[1] *Account of the Mewār Bhīls*, pp. 357, 358.
[2] Forbes, *Rāsmāla*, i. p. 113.

open and safe for travellers.   These are known as Hattiwāla.
Bhīls also serve as village watchmen in Nimār and the
adjoining tracts of the Berār Districts.   Captain Forsyth,
writing in 1868, described the Bhīls as follows : " The
Muhammadan Bhīls are with few exceptions a miserable lot,
idle and thriftless, and steeped in the deadly vice of opium-
eating.   The unconverted Bhīls are held to be tolerably
reliable.   When they borrow money or stock for cultivation
they seldom abscond fraudulently from their creditors, and
this simple honesty of theirs tends, I fear, to keep numbers
of them still in a state little above serfdom." [1]

The Bhīls have now entirely abandoned their own
language and speak a corrupt dialect based on the Aryan
vernaculars current around them.   The Bhīl dialect is
mainly derived from Gujarāti, but it is influenced by Mārwāri
and Marāthi ; in Nimār especially it becomes a corrupt
form of Marāthi.   Bhīli, as this dialect is called, contains a
number of non-Aryan words, some of which appear to come
from the Mundāri, and others from the Dravidian languages ;
but these are insufficient to form any basis for a deduction
as to whether the Bhīls belonged to the Kolarian or
Dravidian race.[2]

14. Language.

Bhilāla.[3]—A small caste found in the Nimār and
Hoshangābād Districts of the Central Provinces and in
Central India.   The total strength of the Bhilālas is
about 150,000 persons, most of whom reside in the
Bhopāwār Agency, adjoining Nimār.   Only 15,000 were
returned from the Central Provinces in 1911.   The
Bhilālas are commonly considered, and the general belief
may in their case be accepted as correct, to be a mixed
caste sprung from the alliances of immigrant Rājpūts with
the Bhīls of the Central India hills.   The original term was
not improbably Bhīlwāla, and may have been applied to
those Rājpūt chiefs, a numerous body, who acquired small
estates in the Bhīl country, or to those who took the daughters
of Bhīl chieftains to wife, the second course being often no

1. General notice.

---

[1] *Nimār Settlement Report*, pp. 246,
247.
[2] Sir G. Grierson, *Linguistic Survey
of India*, vol. ix. part iii. pp. 6-9.

[3] This article is based mainly on
Captain Forsyth's *Nimār Settlement
Report*, and a paper by Mr. T. T.
Korke, Pleader, Khandwa.

doubt a necessary preliminary to the first. Several Bhilāla families hold estates in Nimār and Indore, and their chiefs now claim to be pure Rājpūts. The principal Bhilāla houses, as those of Bhāmgarh, Selāni and Mandhāta, do not inter-marry with the rest of the caste, but only among themselves and with other families of the same standing in Mālwa and Holkar's Nimār. On succession to the *Gaddi* or headship of the house, representatives of these families are marked with a *tīka* or badge on the forehead and sometimes presented with a sword, and the investiture may be carried out by custom by the head of another house. Bhilāla landholders usually have the title of Rao or Rāwat. They do not admit that a Bhilāla can now spring from intermarriage between a Rājpūt and a Bhīl. The local Brāhmans will take water from them and they are occasionally invested with the sacred thread at the time of marriage. The Bhilāla Rao of Mandhāta is hereditary custodian of the great shrine of Siva at Onkār Mandhāta on an island in the Nerbudda. According to the traditions of the family, their ancestor, Bhārat Singh, was a Chauhān Rājpūt, who took Mandhāta from Nāthu Bhīl in A.D. 1165, and restored the worship of Siva to the island, which had been made inaccessible to pilgrims by the terrible deities, Kāli and Bhairava, devourers of human flesh. In such legends may be recognised the propagation of Hinduism by the Rājpūt adventurers and the reconsecration of the aboriginal shrines to its deities. Bhārat Singh is said to have killed Nāthu Bhīl, but it is more probable that he only married his daughter and founded a Bhilāla family. Similar alliances have taken place among other tribes, as the Korku chiefs of the Gāwilgarh and Mahādeo hills, and the Gond princes of Garha Mandla. The Bhilālas generally resemble other Hindus in appearance, showing no marked signs of aboriginal descent. Very probably they have all an infusion of Rājpūt blood, as the Rājpūts settled in the Bhīl country in some strength at an early period of history. The caste have, however, totemistic group names ; they will eat fowls and drink liquor ; and they bury their dead with the feet to the north, all these customs indicating a Dravidian origin. Their subordinate position in past times is shown by the fact that they will accept cooked food from a Kunbi

or a Gūjar ; and indeed the status of all except the chief's
families would naturally have been a low one, as they were
practically the offspring of kept women.   As already stated,
the landowning families usually arrange alliances among
themselves.   Below these comes the body of the caste and
below them is a group known as the Chhoti Tad or bastard
Bhilālas, to which are relegated the progeny of irregular
unions and persons expelled from the caste for social
offences.

The caste, for the purpose of avoiding marriages between
relations, are also divided into exogamous groups called
kul or *kuri*, several of the names of which are of totemistic
origin or derived from those of animals and plants.   Members
of the Jāmra *kuri* will not cut or burn the *jāmun* [1] tree ; those
of the, Saniyār *kuri* will not grow *san*-hemp, while the
Astaryas revere the *sona* [2] tree and the Pipalādya, the *pīpal*
tree.   Some of the *kuris* have Rājpūt sept names, as Mori,
Baghel and Solanki.   A man is forbidden to take a wife
from within his own sept or that of his mother, and the
union of first cousins is also prohibited.   The customs of the
Bhilālas resemble those of the Kunbis and other cultivating
castes.   At their weddings four cart-yokes are arranged in a
square, and inside this are placed two copper vessels filled
with water and considered to represent the Ganges and
Jumna.   When the sun is half set, the bride and the bridegroom clasp hands and then walk seven times round the
square of cart-yokes.   The water of the pots is mixed and
this is considered to represent the mingling of the bride's and
bridegroom's personalities as the Ganges and Jumna meet at
Allahābād.   A sum of about Rs. 60 is usually paid by the
parents of the bridegroom to those of the bride and is
expended on the ceremony.   The ordinary Bhilālas have,
Mr. Korke states, a simple form of wedding which may be
gone through without consulting a Brāhman on the Ekādashi
or eleventh of Kārtik (October) ; this is the day on which
the gods awake from sleep and marks the commencement
of the marriage season.   A cone is erected of eleven plants
of juāri, roots and all, and the couple simply walk round this
seven times at night, when the marriage is complete.   The

2. Mar-
riage.

---

[1] *Eugenia jambolana.*   [2] *Bauhinia racemosa.*

remarriage of widows is permitted. The woman's forehead is marked with cowdung by another widow, probably as a rite of purification, and the cloths of the couple are tied together.

3. Social customs.

The caste commonly bury the dead and erect memorial stones at the heads of graves which they worship in the month of Chait (April), smearing them with vermilion and making an offering of flowers. This may either be a Dravidian usage or have been adopted by imitation from the Muhammadans. The caste worship the ordinary Hindu deities, but each family has a *Kul-devi* or household god, Mr. Korke remarks, to which they pay special reverence. The offerings made to the Kul-devi must be consumed by the family alone, but married daughters are allowed to participate. They employ Nimāri Brāhmans as their priests, and also have *gurus* or spiritual preceptors, who are Gosains or Bairāgis. They will take food cooked with water from Brāhmans, Rājpūts, Munda Gūjars and Tirole Kunbis. The last two groups are principal agricultural castes of the locality and the Bhilālas are probably employed by them as farmservants, and hence accept cooked food from their masters in accordance with a common custom. The local Brāhmans of the Nāgar, Nāramdeo, Baīsa and other subcastes will take water from the hand of a Bhilāla. Temporary excommunication from caste is imposed for the usual offences, such as going to jail, getting maggots in a wound, killing a cow, a dog or a squirrel, committing homicide, being beaten by a man of low caste, selling shoes at a profit, committing adultery, and allowing a cow to die with a rope round its neck ; and further, for touching the corpses of a cow, cat or horse, or a Barhai (carpenter) or Chamār (tanner). They will not swear by a dog, a cat or a squirrel, and if either of the first two animals dies in a house, it is considered to be impure for a month and a quarter. The head of the caste committee has the designation of Mandloi, which is a territorial title borne by several families in Nimār. He receives a share of the fine levied for the *Sarni* or purification ceremony, when a person temporarily expelled is readmitted into caste. Under the Mandloi is the Kotwāl whose business is to summon the members to the caste assemblies ; he also is paid out of the fines and his office is hereditary.

The caste are cultivators, farmservants and field-labourers, and a Bhilāla also usually held the office of Mānkar, a superior kind of Kotwār or village watchman. The Mānkar did no dirty work and would not touch hides, but attended on any officer who came to the village and acted as a guide. Where there was a village *sarai* or rest-house, it was in charge of the Mānkar, who was frequently also known as zamīndār. This may have been a recognition of the ancient rights of the Bhilālas and Bhīls to the country.

Captain Forsyth, Settlement Officer of Nimār, had a very unfavourable opinion of the Bhilālas, whom he described as proverbial for dishonesty in agricultural engagements and worse drunkards than any of the indigenous tribes.[1] This judgment was probably somewhat too severe, but they are poor cultivators, and a Bhilāla's field may often be recognised by its slovenly appearance.[2]

A century ago Sir J. Malcolm also wrote very severely of the Bhilālas : " The Bhilāla and Lundi chiefs were the only robbers in Mālwa whom under no circumstances travellers could trust. There are oaths of a sacred but obscure kind among those that are Rājpūts or who boast their blood, which are almost a disgrace to take, but which, they assert, the basest was never known to break before Mandrup Singh, a Bhilāla, and some of his associates, plunderers on the Nerbudda, showed the example. The vanity of this race has lately been flattered by their having risen into such power and consideration that neighbouring Rājpūt chiefs found it their interest to forget their prejudices and to condescend so far as to eat and drink with them. Hatti Singh, Grassia chief of Nowlāna, a Khīchi Rājpūt, and several others in the vicinity cultivated the friendship of Nādir, the late formidable Bhilāla robber-chief of the Vindhya range ; and among other sacrifices made by the Rājpūts, was eating and drinking with him. On seeing this take place in my camp, I asked Hatti Singh whether he was not degraded by doing so ; he said no, but that Nādir was elevated." [3]

[1] *Settlement Report* (1869), para. 411.
[2] Mr. Montgomerie's *Nimār Settle-* *ment Report.*
[3] *Memoir of Central India*, ii. p. 156.

Bhishti.—A small Muhammadan caste of water-bearers.
Only 26 Bhishtis were shown in the Central Provinces in
1901 and 278 in 1891. The tendency of the lower
Muhammadan castes, as they obtain some education, is to
return themselves simply as Muhammadans, the caste name
being considered derogatory. The Bhishtis are, however,
a regular caste numbering over a lakh of persons in India,
the bulk of whom belong to the United Provinces. Many
of them are converts from Hinduism, and they combine
Hindu and Muhammadan practices. They have *gotras*
or exogamous sections, the names of which indicate the
Hindu origin of their members, as Huseni Brāhman, Samri
Chauhān, Bahmangour and others. They prohibit marriage
within the section and within two degrees of relationship on
the mother's side. Marriages are performed by the Muhammadan ritual or Nikāh, but a Brāhman is sometimes asked
to fix the auspicious day, and they erect a marriage-shed.
The bridegroom goes to the bride's house riding on a horse,
and when he arrives drops Rs. 1-4 into a pot of water held
by a woman. The bride whips the bridegroom's horse
with a switch made of flowers. During the marriage the
bride sits inside the house and the bridegroom in the shed
outside. An agent or Vakīl with two witnesses goes
to the bride and asks her whether she consents to
marry the bridegroom, and when she gives her consent,
as she always does, they go out and formally communicate it to the Kāzi. The dowry is then settled, and the
bond of marriage is sealed. But when the parents of
the bride are poor they receive a bride-price of Rs. 30,
from which they pay the dowry. The Bhishtis worship
their leather bag (*mashk*) as a sort of fetish, and burn
incense before it on Fridays.[1] The traditional occupation
of the Bhishti is to supply water, and he is still engaged in
this and other kinds of domestic service. The name is said
to be derived from the Persian *bihisht*, 'paradise,' and to have
been given to them on account of the relief which their
ministrations afforded to the thirsty soldiery.[2] Perhaps,
too, the grandiloquent name was applied partly in derision,

[1] Crooke's *Tribes and Castes*, art. Bhishti.
[2] Elliott's *Memoirs of the North-Western Provinces*, i. p. 191.

like similar titles given to other menial servants. They
are also known as Mashki or Pakhāli, after their leathern
water-bag. The leather bag is a distinctive sign of the
Bhishti, but when he puts it away he may be recognised
from the piece of red cloth which he usually wears round
his waist. There is an interesting legend to the effect
that the Bhishti who saved the Emperor Humayun's life at
Chausa, and was rewarded by the tenure of the Imperial
throne for half a day, employed his short lease of power by
providing for his family and friends, and caused his leather
bag to be cut up into rupees, which were gilded and stamped
with the record of his date and reign in order to perpetuate
its memory.[1] The story of the Bhishti obtaining his name on
account of the solace which he afforded to the Muhammadan
soldiery finds a parallel in the case of the English army :

> The uniform 'e wore
> Was nothin' much before,
> An' rather less than 'arf o' that be'ind,
> For a piece o' twisty rag
> An' a goatskin water-bag
> Was all the field-equipment 'e could find.
>
> .   .   .   .   .
>
> With 'is mussick on 'is back,
> 'E would skip with our attack,
> An' watch us till the bugles made 'Retire,'
> An' for all 'is dirty 'ide
> 'E was white, clear white, inside
> When 'e went to tend the wounded under fire.[2]

An excellent description of the Bhishti as a household
servant is contained in Eha's *Behind the Bungalow*,[3] from
which the following extract is taken : " If you ask : Who
is the Bhishti ? I will tell you. Bihisht in the Persian
tongue means Paradise, and a Bihishtee is therefore an
inhabitant of Paradise, a cherub, a seraph, an angel of mercy.
He has no wings ; the painters have misconceived him ; but
his back is bowed down with the burden of a great goat-skin
swollen to bursting with the elixir of life. He walks the
land when the heaven above him is brass and the earth iron,
when the trees and shrubs are languishing and the last blade

---

[1] Crooke's *Tribes and Castes*, ii. p.
100.
[2] Rudyard Kipling, *Barrack-Room*

Ballads, 'Gunga Din.'
[3] Thacker and Co., London.

of grass has given up the struggle for life, when the very roses smell only of dust, and all day long the roaming dust-devils waltz about the fields, whirling leaf and grass and corn-stalk round and round and up and away into the regions of the sky; and he unties a leather thong which chokes the throat of his goat-skin just where the head of the poor old goat was cut off, and straightway, with a life-reviving gurgle, the stream called *thandha pāni* gushes forth, and plant and shrub lift up their heads and the garden smiles again. The dust also on the roads is laid, and a grateful incense rises from the ground, the sides of the water *chatti* grow dark and moist and cool themselves in the hot air, and through the dripping interstices of the *khaskhas* tattie a chilly fragrance creeps into the room, causing the mercury in the thermometer to retreat from its proud place. I like the Bhishti and respect him. As a man he is temperate and contented, eating *bājri* bread and slaking his thirst with his own element. And as a servant he is laborious and faithful, rarely shirking his work, seeking it out rather. For example, we had a bottle-shaped filter of porous stoneware, standing in a bucket of water which it was his duty to fill daily; but the good man, not content with doing his bare duty, took the plug out of the filter and filled it too. And all the station knows how assiduously he fills the rain-gauge." With the construction of water-works in large stations the Bhishti is losing his occupation, and he is a far less familiar figure to the present generation of Anglo-Indians than to their predecessors.

1. Origin and traditions.

Bhoyar,[1] **Bhoir** (Honorific titles, Mahājan and Patel).— A cultivating caste numbering nearly 60,000 persons in 1911, and residing principally in the Betūl and Chhīndwāra Districts. The Bhoyars are not found outside the Central Provinces. They claim to be the descendants of a band of Panwār Rājpūts, who were defending the town of Dhārānagri or Dhār in Central India when it was besieged by Aurāngzeb. Their post was on the western part of the wall, but they gave way and fled into the town as the sun was rising, and it

---

[1] This article is mainly compiled from papers by Mr. Pāndurang Laksh- man Bākre, pleader, Betūl, and Munshi Pyāre Lāl, ethnographic clerk.

shone on their faces.   Hence they were called Bhoyar from
a word *bhor* meaning morning, because they were seen
running away in the morning.   They were put out of caste by
the other Rājpūts, and fled to the Central Provinces.   The
name may also be a variant of that of the Bhagore Rājpūts.
And another derivation is from *bhora*, a simpleton or timid
person.   Their claim to be immigrants from Central India
is borne out by the fact that they still speak a corrupt form
of the Mālwi dialect of Rājputāna, which is called after them
Bhoyari, and their Bhāts or genealogists come from Mālwa.
But they have now entirely lost their position as Rājpūts.

The Bhoyars are divided into the Panwāri, Dholewār, 2. Sub-
Chaurāsia and Daharia subcastes.   The Panwārs are the castes and
most numerous and the highest, as claiming to be directly sections.
descended from Panwār Rājpūts.   They sometimes called
themselves Jagdeo Panwārs, Jagdeo being the name of the
king under whom they served in Dhārānagri.   The Dholewārs
take their name from Dhola, a place in Mālwa, or from *dhol*,
a drum.   They are the lowest subcaste, and some of them
keep pigs.   It is probable that these subcastes immigrated
with the Mālwa Rājas in the fifteenth century, the Dholewārs
being the earlier arrivals, and having from the first intermarried
with the local Dravidian tribes.   The Daharias take their
name from Dāhar, the old name of the Jubbulpore country,
and may be a relic of the domination of the Chedi kings of
Tewar.   The name of the Chaurāsias is probably derived
from the Chaurāsi or tract of eighty-four villages formerly
held by the Betūl Korku family of Chāndu.   The last two
subdivisions are numerically unimportant.   The Bhoyars
have over a hundred *kuls* or exogamous sections.   The
names of most of these are titular, but some are territorial
and a few totemistic.   Instances of such names are Onkār
(the god Siva), Deshmukh and Chaudhari, headman, Hazāri
(a leader of 1000 horse), Gore (fair-coloured), Dongardiya
(a lamp on a hill), Pinjāra (a cotton-cleaner), Gādria (a
shepherd), Khaparia (a tyler), Khawāsi (a barber), Chiknyā
(a sycophant), Kinkar (a slave), Dukhi (penurious), Suplya
toplya (a basket and fan maker), Kasai (a butcher), Gohattya
(a cow-killer), and Kālebhūt (black devil).   Among the
territorial sections may be mentioned Sonpūria, from Sonpur,

and Pathāria, from the hill country. The name Badnagrya is also really territorial, being derived from the town of Badnāgar, but the members of the section connect it with the *bad* or banyan tree, the leaves of which they refrain from eating. Two other totemistic gotras are the Bāranga and Baignya, derived from the *bārang* plant (*Kydia calycina*) and from the brinjal respectively. Some sections have the names of Rājpūt septs, as Chauhān, Parihār and Panwār. This curiously mixed list of family names appears to indicate that the Bhoyars originate from a small band of Rājpūts who must have settled in the District about the fifteenth century as military colonists, and taken their wives from the people of the country. They may have subsequently been recruited by fresh bands of immigrants who have preserved a slightly higher status. They have abandoned their old high position, and now rank below the ordinary cultivating castes like Kunbis and Kurmis who arrived later; while the caste has probably in times past also been recruited to a considerable extent by the admission of families of outsiders.

3. Marriage.

Marriage within the *kul* or family group is forbidden, as also the union of first cousins. Girls are usually married young, and sometimes infants of one or two months are given in wedlock, while contracts of betrothal are made for unborn children if they should be of the proper sex, the mother's womb being touched with *kunku* or red powder to seal the agreement. A small *dej* or price is usually paid for the bride, amounting to Rs. 5 with 240 lbs. of grain, and 8 seers of *ghī* and oil. At the betrothal the Joshi or astrologer is consulted to see whether the names of the couple make an auspicious conjunction. He asks for the names of the bride and bridegroom, and if these are found to be inimical another set of names is given, and the experiment is continued until a union is obtained which is astrologically auspicious. In order to provide for this contingency some Bhoyars give their children ten or twelve names at birth. If all the names fail, the Joshi invents new ones of his own, and in some way brings about the auspicious union to the satisfaction of both parties, who consider it no business of theirs to pry into the Joshi's calculations or to question his methods. After the marriage-shed is erected

the family god must be invoked to be present at the
ceremony.   He is asked to come and take his seat in an
earthen pot containing a lighted wick, the pot being supported on a toy chariot made of sticks.   A thread is coiled
round the neck of the jar, and the Bhoyars then place it in
the middle of the house, confident that the god has entered
it, and will ward off all calamities during the marriage.
This is performed by the *bhānwar* ceremony, seven earthen
pots being placed in a row, while the bride and bridegroom
walk round in a circle holding a basket with a lighted lamp
in it.   As each circle is completed, one pot is removed.
This always takes place at night.   The Dholewārs do not
perform the *bhānwar* ceremony, and simply throw sacred
rice on the couple, and this is also done in Wardha.
Sometimes the Bhoyars dispense with the presence of the
Brāhman and merely get some rice and juāri consecrated by
him beforehand, which they throw on the heads of the
couple, and thereupon consider the marriage complete.
Weddings are generally held in the bright fortnight of
Baisākh (April–May), and sometimes can be completed in a
single day.   Widow-marriage is allowed, but it is considered
that the widow should marry a widower and not a bachelor.

The regular occupation of the Bhoyars is agriculture, 4. Occupa-
and they are good cultivators, growing much sugar-cane tion.
with well - irrigation.   They are industrious, and their
holdings on the rocky soils of the plateau Districts are
often cleared of stones at the cost of much labour.   Their
women work in the fields.   In Betūl they have the reputation
of being much addicted to drink.

They do not now admit outsiders, but their family 5. Social
names show that at one time they probably did so, and this status.
laxity of feeling survives in the toleration with which they
readmit into caste a woman who has gone wrong with an
outsider.   They eat flesh and fowls, and the Dholewārs eat
pork, while as already stated they are fond of liquor.   To
have a shoe thrown on his house by a caste-fellow is a
serious degradation for a Bhoyar, and he must break his
earthen pots, clean his house and give a feast.   To be
beaten with a shoe by a low caste like Mahār entails shaving
the moustaches and paying a heavy fine, which is spent on a

feast. The Bhoyars do not take food from any caste but Brāhmans, but no caste higher than Kunbis and Mālis will take water from them. In social status they rank somewhat below Kunbis. In appearance they are well built, and often of a fair complexion. Unmarried girls generally wear skirts instead of *sāris* or cloths folding between the legs ; they also must not wear toe-rings. Women of the Panwār subcaste wear glass bangles on the left hand, and brass ones on the right. All women are tattooed. They both burn and bury the dead, placing the corpse on the pyre with its head to the south or west, and in Wardha to the north. Here they have a peculiar custom as regards mourning, which is observed only till the next Monday or Thursday whichever falls first. Thus the period of mourning may extend from one to four days. The Bhoyars are considered in Wardha to be more than ordinarily timid, and also to be considerable simpletons, while they stand in much awe of Government officials, and consider it a great misfortune to be brought into a court of justice. Very few of them can read and write.

BHUIYA

LIST OF PARAGRAPHS

Bhuiya, Bhuinhār, Bhumia.[1]—The name of a very important tribe of Chota Nāgpur, Bengal and Orissa. The Bhuiyas numbered more than 22,000 persons in the Central Provinces in 1911, being mainly found in the Sargūja and Jashpur States. In Bengal and Bihār the Bhuiyas proper count about half a million persons, while the Mūsahar and Khandait castes, both of whom are mainly derived from the Bhuiyas, total together well over a million.

1. The tribe and its name.

The name Bhuiya means 'Lord of the soil,' or 'Belonging to the soil,' and is a Sanskrit derivative. The tribe have completely forgotten their original name, and adopted this designation conferred on them by the immigrant Aryans. The term Bhuiya, however, is also employed by other tribes and by some Hindus as a title for landholders, being practically equivalent to zamīndār. And hence a certain confusion arises, and classes or individuals may have the name of Bhuiya without belonging to the tribe at all. " In most

---

[1] This article is compiled partly from Colonel Dalton's *Ethnology of Bengal* and Sir H. Risley's *Tribes and Castes of Bengal*; a monograph has also been furnished by Mr. B. C. Mazumdār, pleader, Sambalpur, and papers by Mr. A. B. Napier, Deputy Commissioner, Raipur, and Mr. Hīra Lāl.

parts of Chota Nāgpur," Sir H. Risley says, "there is a well-
known distinction between a Bhuiya by tribe and a Bhuiya
by title.   The Bhuiyas of Bonai and Keonjhar described by
Colonel Dalton belong to the former category ; the Bhuiya
Mundas and Oraons to the latter.   The distinction will be
made somewhat clearer if it is explained that every 'tribal
Bhuiya' will as a matter of course describe himself as
Bhuiya, while a member of another tribe will only do so if
he is speaking with reference to a question of land, or desires
for some special reason to lay stress on his status as a landholder or agriculturist."

We further find in Bengal and Benāres a caste of landholders known as Bhuinhār or Bābhan, who are generally
considered as a somewhat mixed and inferior group of
Brāhman and Rājpūt origin.   Both Sir H. Risley and Mr.
Crooke adopt this view and deny any connection between
the Bhuinhārs and the Bhuiya tribes.   Bābhan appears to
be a corrupt form of Brāhman.   Mr. Mazumdār, however,
states that Bhuiya is never used in Bengali as an equivalent
for zamīndār or landholder, and he considers that the
Bhuinhārs and also the Bārah Bhuiyas, a well-known group
of twelve landholders of Eastern Bengal and Assam, belonged
to the Bhuiya tribe.   He adduces from Sir E. Gait's *History
of Assam* the fact that the Chutias and Bhuiyas were
dominant in that country prior to its conquest by the
Ahoms in the thirteenth century, and considers that these
Chutias gave their name to Chutia or Chota Nāgpur.   I am
unable to express any opinion on Mr. Mazumdār's argument,
and it is also unnecessary as the question does not concern
the Central Provinces.

2. Distribu-
tion of the
tribe.

The principal home of the Bhuiya tribe proper is the
south of the Chota Nāgpur plateau, comprised in the Gāng-
pur, Bonai, Keonjhar and Bāmra States.   "The chiefs of
these States," Colonel Dalton says, " now call themselves
Rājpūts ; if they be so, they are strangely isolated families
of Rājpūts.   The country for the most part belongs to the
Bhuiya sub-proprietors.   They are a privileged class, holding
as hereditaments the principal offices of the State, and are
organised as a body of militia.   The chiefs have no right to
exercise any authority till they have received the *tilak* or

token of investiture from their powerful Bhuiya vassals. Their position altogether renders their claim to be considered Rājpūts extremely doubtful, and the stories told to account for their acquisition of the dignity are palpable fables. They were no doubt all Bhuiyas originally; they certainly do not look like Rājpūts." Members of the tribe are the household servants of the Bāmra Rāja's family, and it is said that the first Rāja of Bāmra was a child of the Patna house, who was stolen from his home and anointed king of Bāmra by the Bhuiyas and Khonds. Similarly Colonel Dalton records the legend that the Bhuiyas twenty-seven generations ago stole a child of the Moharbhanj Rāja's family, brought it up amongst them and made it their Rāja. He was freely admitted to intercourse with Bhuiya girls, and the children of this intimacy are the progenitors of the Rājkuli branch of the tribe. But they are not considered first among Bhuiyas because they are not of pure Bhuiya descent. Again the Rāja of Keonjhar is always installed by the Bhuiyas. These facts indicate that the Bhuiyas were once the rulers of Chota Nāgpur and are recognised as the oldest inhabitants of the country. From this centre they have spread north through Lohardaga and Hazāribāgh and into southern Bihār, where large numbers of Bhuiyas are encountered on whom the opprobrious designation of Mūsahar or 'rat-eater' has been conferred by their Hindu neighbours. Others of the tribe who travelled south from Chota Nāgpur experienced more favourable conditions, and here the tendency has been for the Bhuiyas to rise rather than to decline in social status. "Some of their leading families," Sir H. Risley states, "have come to be chiefs of the petty States of Orissa, and have now sunk the Bhuiya in the Khandait or swordsman, a caste of admitted respectability in Orissa and likely in course of time to transform itself into some variety of Rājpūt."

The varying status of the Bhuiyas in Bihār, Chota Nāgpur and Orissa is a good instance of the different ways in which the primitive tribes have fared in contact with the immigrant Aryans. Where the country has been completely colonised and populated by Hindus, as in Bihār, the aboriginal residents have commonly become transformed into village

3. Example of the position of the aborigines in Hindu society.

drudges, relegated to the meanest occupations, and despised as impure by the Hindu cultivators, like the Chamārs of northern India and the Mahārs of the Marātha Districts. Where the Hindu immigration has only been partial and the forests have not been cleared, as in Chota Nāgpur and the Central Provinces, they may keep their old villages and tribal organisation and be admitted as a body into the hierarchy of caste, ranking above the impure castes but below the Hindu cultivators. This is the position of the Gonds, Baigas and other tribes in these tracts. While, if the Hindus come only as colonists and not as rulers, the indigenous residents may retain the overlordship of the soil and the landed proprietors among them may be formed into a caste ranking with the good cultivating castes of the Aryans. Instances of such are the Khandaits of Orissa, the Binjhwārs of Chhattīsgarh and the Bhilālas of Nimār and Indore.

4. The Bhuiyas a Kolarian tribe. The Bhuiyas have now entirely forgotten their own language and speak Hindi, Uriya and Bengali, according as each is the dominant vernacular of their Hindu neighbours. They cannot therefore on the evidence of language be classified as a Munda or Kolarian or as a Dravidian tribe. Colonel Dalton was inclined to consider them as Dravidian : [1] " Mr. Stirling in his account of Orissa classes them among the Kols ; but there are no grounds that I know of for so connecting them. As I have said above, they appear to me to be linked with the Dravidian rather than with the Kolarian tribes." His account, however, does not appear to contain any further evidence in support of this view ; and, on the other hand, he identifies the Bhuiyas with the Savars or Saonrs. Speaking of the Bendkars or Savars of Keonjhar, he says : " It is difficult to regard them otherwise than as members of the great Bhuiya family, and thus connecting them we link the Bhuiyas and Savaras and give support to the conjecture that the former are Dravidian." But it is now shown in the *Linguistic Survey* that the Savars have a Munda dialect. In Chota Nāgpur this has been forgotten, and the tribe speak Hindi or Uriya like the Bhuiyas, but it remains in the hilly tracts of Ganjām and

[1] *Ethnology of Bengal*, p. 140.

Vizagapatām.[1] Savara is closely related to Kharia and
Juāng, the dialects of two of the most primitive Munda
tribes.   The Savars must therefore be classed as a Munda
or Kolarian tribe, and since Colonel Dalton identified the
Bhuiyas with the Savars of Chota Nāgpur, his evidence
appears really to be in favour of the Kolarian origin of the
Bhuiyas.   He notes further that the ceremony of naming
children among the Bhuiyas is identical with that of the
Mundas and Hos.[2]   Mr. Mazumdār writes : " Judging
from the external appearance and general physical type one
would be sure to mistake a Bhuiya for a Munda.   Their
habits and customs are essentially Mundāri.   The Bhuiyas
who live in and around the District of Mānbhūm are not
much ashamed to admit that they are Kol people ; and
Bhumia Kol is the name that has been given them there
by the Hindus.   The Mundas and Larka-Kols of Chota
Nāgpur tell us that they first established themselves there
by driving out the Bhuiyas ; and it seems likely that the
Bhuiyas formed the first batch of the Munda immigrants in
Chota Nāgpur and became greatly Hinduised there, and on
that account were not recognised by the Mundas as people
of their kin."   If the tradition of the Mundas and Kols that
they came to Chota Nāgpur after the Bhuiyas be accepted,
and tradition on the point of priority of immigration is
often trustworthy, then it follows that the Bhuiyas must be
a Munda tribe.   For the main distinction other than that of
language between the Munda and Dravidian tribes is that
the former were the earlier and the latter subsequent
immigrants.   The claim of the Bhuiyas to be the earliest
residents of Chota Nāgpur is supported by the fact that
they officiate as priests in certain temples.   Because in
primitive religion the jurisdiction of the gods is entirely
local, and foreigners bringing their own gods with them are
ignorant of the character and qualities of the local deities,
with which the indigenous residents are, on the other hand,
well acquainted.   Hence the tendency of later comers to
employ these latter in the capacity of priests of the godlings
of the earth, corn, forests and hills.   Colonel Dalton writes :[3]

---

[1] *Linguistic Survey*, vol. xiv. *Munda and Dravidian Languages*, p. 217.
[2] Page 142.   [3] *Ibidem*, p. 141.

"It is strange that these Hinduised Bhuiyas retain in their own hands the priestly duties of certain old shrines to the exclusion of Brāhmans. This custom has no doubt descended in Bhuiya families from the time when Brāhmans were not, or had obtained no footing amongst them, and when the religion of the land and the temples were not Hindu ; they are now indeed dedicated to Hindu deities, but there are evidences of the temples having been originally occupied by other images. At some of these shrines human sacrifices were offered every third year and this continued till the country came under British rule." And again of the Pauri Bhuiyas of Keonjhar : "The Pauris dispute with the Juāngs the claim to be the first settlers in Keonjhar, and boldly aver that the country belongs to them. They assert that the Rāja is of their creation and that the prerogative of installing every new Rāja on his accession is theirs, and theirs alone. The Hindu population of Keonjhar is in excess of the Bhuiya and it comprises Gonds and Kols, but the claim of the Pauris to the dominion they arrogate is admitted by all ; even Brāhmans and Rājpūts respectfully acknowledge it, and the former by the addition of Brāhmanical rites to the wild ceremonies of the Bhuiyas affirm and sanctify their installation." In view of this evidence it seems a probable hypothesis that the Bhuiyas are the earliest residents of these parts of Chota Nāgpur and that they are a Kolarian tribe.

5. The Baigas and the Bhuiyas. Chhattīsgarh the home of the Baigas.   There appears to be considerable reason for supposing that the Baiga tribe of the Central Provinces are really a branch of the Bhuiyas. Though the Baigas are now mainly returned from Mandla and Bālāghāt, it seems likely that these Districts were not their original home, and that they emigrated from Chhattīsgarh into the Satpūra hills on the western borders of the plain. The hill country of Mandla and the Maikal range of Bālāghāt form one of the wildest and most inhospitable tracts in the Province, and it is unlikely that the Baigas would have made their first settlements here and spread thence into the fertile plain of Chhattīsgarh. Migration in the opposite direction would be more natural and probable. But it is fairly certain that the Baiga tribe were among the earliest if not the earliest

residents of the Chhattīsgarh plain and the hills north and east of it.   The Bhaina, Bhunjia and Binjhwār tribes who still reside in this country can all be recognised as offshoots of the Baigas.   In the article on Bhaina it is shown that some of the oldest forts in Bilāspur are attributed to the Bhainas and a chief of this tribe is remembered as having ruled in Bilaigarh south of the Mahānadi.   They are said to have been dominant in Pendra where they are still most numerous, and to have been expelled from Phuljhar in Raipur by the Gonds.   The Binjhwārs or Binjhāls again are an aristocratic subdivision of the Baigas, belonging to the hills east of Chhattīsgarh and the Uriya plain country of Sambalpur beyond them.   The zamīndārs of Bodāsāmar, Rāmpur, Bhatgaon and other estates to the south and east of the Chhattīsgarh plain are members of this tribe.   Both the Bhainas and Binjhwārs are frequently employed as priests of the village deities all over this area, and may therefore be considered as older residents than the Gond and Kawar tribes and the Hindus.   Sir G. Grierson also states that the language of the Baigas of Mandla and Bālāghāt is a form of Chhattīsgarhi, and this is fairly conclusive evidence of their first having belonged to Chhattīsgarh.[1]   It seems not unlikely that the Baigas retreated into the hills round Chhattīsgarh after the Hindu invasion and establishment of the Haihaya Rājpūt dynasty of Ratanpur, which is now assigned to the ninth century of the Christian era ; just as the Gonds retired from the Nerbudda valley and the Nāgpur plain before the Hindus several centuries later.   Sir H. Risley states that the Binjhias or Binjhwārs of Chota Nāgpur say that their ancestors came from Ratanpur twenty generations ago.[2]

But the Chhattīsgarh plain and the hills north and east of it are adjacent to and belong to the same tract of country as the Chota Nāgpur States, which are the home of the Bhuiyas.   Sir H. Risley gives Baiga as a name for a sorcerer, and as a synonym or title of the Khairwār tribe in Chota Nāgpur, possibly having reference to the idea that

6. The Baigas a branch of the Bhuiyas.

---

[1] In the article on Binjhwār, it was supposed that the Baigas migrated east from the Satpūra hills into Chhattīsgarh.   But the evidence adduced above appears to show that this view is incorrect.

[2] *Tribes and Castes*, art. Binjhia.

they, being among the original inhabitants of the country, are best qualified to play the part of sorcerer and propitiate the local gods. It has been suggested in the article on Khairwār that that tribe are a mongrel offshoot of the Santāls and Cheros, but the point to be noticed here is the use of the term Baiga in Chota Nāgpur for a sorcerer ; and a sorcerer may be taken as practically equivalent for a priest of the indigenous deities, all tribes who act in this capacity being considered as sorcerers by the Hindus. If the Bhuiyas of Chota Nāgpur had the title of Baiga, it is possible that it may have been substituted for the proper tribal name on their migration to the Central Provinces. Mr. Crooke distinguishes two tribes in Mīrzāpur whom he calls the Bhuiyas and Bhuiyārs. The Bhuiyas of Mīrzāpur seem to be clearly a branch of the Bhuiya tribe of Chota Nāgpur, with whom their section-names establish their identity.[1] Mr. Crooke states that the Bhuiyas are distinguished with very great difficulty from the Bhuiyārs with whom they are doubtless very closely connected.[2] Of the Bhuiyārs[3] he writes that the tribe is also known as Baiga, because large numbers of the aboriginal local priests are derived from this caste. He also states that " Most Bhuiyārs are Baigas and officiate in their own as well as allied tribes ; in fact, as already stated, one general name for the tribe is Baiga."[4] It seems not unlikely that these Bhuiyārs are the Baigas of the Central Provinces and that they went to Mīrzāpur from here with the Gonds. Their original name may have been preserved or revived there, while it has dropped out of use in this Province. The name Baiga in the Central Provinces is sometimes applied to members of other tribes who serve as village priests, and, as has already been seen, it is used in the same sense in Chota Nāgpur. The Baigas of Mandla are also known as Bhumia, which is only a variant of Bhuiya, having the same meaning of lord of the soil or belonging to the soil. Both Bhuiya and Bhumia are in fact nearly equivalent to our word ' aboriginal,' and both are names given to the tribe by the

---

[1] Crooke, *Tribes and Castes*, art. Bhuiya, para. 4.

[2] *Ibidem*, para. 3.

[3] *Ibidem*, art. Bhuiyār, para. 1.

[4] *Ibidem*, para. 16.

Hindus and not originally that by which its members called themselves.   It would be quite natural that a branch of the Bhuiyas, who settled in the Central Provinces and were commonly employed as village priests by the Hindus and Gonds should have adopted the name of the office, Baiga, as their tribal designation ; just as the title of Munda or village headman has become the name of one branch of the Kol tribe, and Bhumij, another term equivalent to Bhuiya, of a second branch.   Mr. A. F. Hewitt, Settlement Officer of Raipur, considered that the Buniyas of that District were the same tribe as the Bhuiyas of the Garhjāt States.[1]   By Buniya he must apparently have meant the Bhunjia tribe of Raipur, who as already stated are an offshoot of the Baigas. Colonel Dalton describes the dances of the Bhuiyas of Chota Nāgpur as follows :[2] " The men have each a wide kind of tambourine.   They march round in a circle, beating these and singing a very simple melody in a minor key on four notes.   The women dance opposite to them with their heads covered and bodies much inclined, touching each other like soldiers in line, but not holding hands or wreathing arms like the Kols."   This account applies very closely to the Sela and Rīna dances of the Baigas.   The Sela dance is danced by men only who similarly march round in a circle, though they do not carry tambourines in the Central Provinces. Here, however, they sometimes carry sticks and march round in opposite directions, passing in and out and hitting their sticks against each other as they meet, the movement being exactly like the grand chain in the Lancers.   Similarly the Baiga women dance the Rīna dance by themselves, standing close to each other and bending forward, but not holding each other by the hands and arms, just as described by Colonel Dalton.   The Gonds now also have the Sela and Rīna dances, but admit that they are derived from the Baigas.   Another point of some importance is that the Bhuiyas of Chota Nāgpur and the Baigas and the tribes derived from them in the Central Provinces have all completely abandoned their own language and speak a broken form of that of their Hindu neighbours.   As has been seen, too, the Bhuiyas are commonly employed as priests in Chota

[1] Dalton, p. 147.   [2] Page 142.

Nāgpur, and there seems therefore to be a strong case for the original identity of the two tribes.[1]   Both the Baigas and Bhuiyas, however, have now become greatly mixed with the surrounding tribes, the Baigas of Mandla and Bālāghāt having a strong Gond element.

7. Tribal sub-divisions.   In Singhbhūm the Bhuiyas call themselves *Pāwan-bans* or 'The Children of the Wind,' and in connection with Hanumān's title of *Pāwan-ka-pūt* or 'The Son of the Wind,' are held to be the veritable apes of the Rāmāyana who, under the leadership of Hanumān, the monkey-god, assisted the Aryan hero Rāma on his expedition to Ceylon.   This may be compared with the name given to the Gonds of the Central Provinces of Rāwanbansi, or descendants of Rāwan, the idea being that their ancestors were the subjects of Rāwan, the demon king of Ceylon, who was conquered by Rāma.   "All Bhuiyas," Sir H. Risley states, "affect great reverence for the memory of Rikhmun or Rikhiasan, whom they regard, some as a patron deity, others as a mythical ancestor, whose name distinguishes one of the divisions of the tribe.   It seems probable that in the earliest stage of belief Rikhmun was the bear-totem of a sept of the tribe, that later on he was transformed into an ancestral hero, and finally promoted to the rank of a tribal god."   The Rikhiasan Mahatwār subtribe of the Bhuiyas in the Central Provinces are named after this hero Rikhmun ; the designation of Mahatwār signifies that they are the Mahtos or leaders of the Bhuiyas.   The Khandaits or Pāiks are another subcaste formed from those who became soldiers ; in Orissa they are now, as already stated, a separate caste of fairly high rank. The Parja or 'subject people' are the ordinary Bhuiyas, probably those living in Hindu tracts.   The Dhur or 'dust' Gonds, and the Parja Gonds of Bastar may be noted as a parallel in nomenclature.   The Rautadi are a territorial group, taking their name from a place called Raotal.   The Khandaits practise hypergamy with the Rautadi, taking daughters from them, but not giving their daughters to them. The Pābudia or Mādhai are the hill Bhuiyas, and are the

---

[1] The question of the relation of the Baiga tribe to Mr. Crooke's Bhuiyārs was first raised by Mr. E. A. H. Blunt, Census Superintendent, United Provinces.

most wild and backward portion of the tribe.   Dalton writes
of them in Keonjhar: " They are not bound to fight for
the Rāja, though they occasionally take up arms against
him.   Their duty is to attend on him and carry his loads
when he travels about, and so long as they are satisfied with
his person and his rule, no more willing or devoted subjects
could be found.   They are then in Keonjhar, as in Bonai, a
race whom you cannot help liking and taking an interest in
from the primitive simplicity of their customs, their amena-
bility and their anxiety to oblige ; but unsophisticated as
they are they wield an extraordinary power in Keonjhar,
and when they take it into their heads to use that power,
the country may be said to be governed by an oligarchy
composed of the sixty chiefs of the Pawri Desh, the Bhuiya
Highlands.   A knotted string passed from village to village
in the name of the sixty chiefs throws the entire country into
commotion, and the order verbally communicated in connection with it is as implicitly obeyed as if it emanated from
the most potent despot." This knotted string is known as
Gānthi.   The Pābudias say that their ancestors were twelve
brothers belonging to Keonjhar, of whom eight went to an
unknown country, while the remaining four divided among
themselves all the territory of which they had knowledge,
this being comprised in the four existing states of Keonjhar,
Bāmra, Palahāra and Bonai.   Any Pābudia who takes up his
residence permanently beyond the boundaries of these four
states is considered to lose his caste, like Hindus in former
times who went to dwell in the foreign country beyond the
Indus.[1]   But if the wandering Pābudia returns in two years,
and proves that he has not drunk water from any other caste,
he is taken back into the fold.   Other subdivisions are the
Kāti or Khatti and the Bāthudia, these last being an inferior
group who are said to be looked down on because they have
taken food from other low castes.   No doubt they are really
the offspring of irregular unions.

In Raigarh the Bhuiyas appear to have no exogamous   8. Exo-
divisions.   When they wish to arrange a marriage they   gamous
compare the family gods of the parties, and if these are not   septs.
identical and there is no recollection of a common ancestor

---

[1] Mr. Mazumdār's monograph.

for three generations, the union is permitted.　In Sambalpur, however, Mr. Mazumdār states, all Bhuiyas are divided into the following twelve septs :　Thākur, or the clan of royal blood ; Saont, from *sāmanta*, a viceroy ; Padhān, a village headman ; Nāik, a military leader ; Kālo, a wizard or priest ; Dehri, also a priest ; Chatria, one who carried the royal umbrella ; Sāhu, a moneylender ; Mājhi, a headman ; Behra, manager of the household ; Amāta, counsellor ; and Dandsena, a police official.　The Dehrin sept still worship the village gods on behalf of the tribe.

9. Marriage customs.

Marriage is adult, but the more civilised Bhuiyas are gradually adopting Hindu usages, and parents arrange matches for their children while they are still young. Among the Pābudias some primitive customs survive.　They have the same system as the Oraons, by which all the bachelors of the village sleep in one large dormitory ; this is known as Dhāngarbāsa, *dhāngar* meaning a farmservant or young man, or Māndarghar, the house of the drums, because these instruments are kept in it.　" Some villages," Colonel Dalton states, " have a Dhāngaria bāsa, or house for maidens, which, strange to say, they are allowed to occupy without any one to look after them.　They appear to have very great liberty, and slips of morality, so long as they are confined to the tribe, are not much heeded."　This intimacy between boys and girls of the same village does not, however, commonly end in marriage, for which a partner should be sought from another village.　For this purpose the girls go in a body, taking with them some ground rice decorated with flowers.　They lay this before the elders of the village they have entered, saying, ' Keep this or throw it into the water, as you prefer.'　The old men pick up the flowers, placing them behind their ears.　In the evening all the boys of the village come and dance with the girls, with intervals for courtship, half the total number of couples dancing and sitting out alternately.　This goes on all night, and in the morning any couples who have come to an understanding run away together for a day or two.　The boy's father must present a rupee and a piece of cloth to the girl's mother, and the marriage is considered to be completed.

Among the Pābudia or Madhai Bhuiyas the bride-price

consists of two bullocks or cows, one of which is given to the girl's father and the other to her brother.   The boy's father makes the proposal for marriage, and the consent of the girl is necessary.   At the wedding turmeric and rice are offered to the sun ; some rice is then placed on the girl's head and turmeric rubbed on her body, and a brass ring is placed on her finger.   The bridegroom's father says to him, " This girl is ours now : if in future she becomes one-eyed, lame or deaf, she will still be ours."   The ceremony concludes with the usual feast and drinking bout.   If the boy's father cannot afford the bride-price the couple sometimes run away from home for two or three days, when their parents go in search of them and they are brought back and married in the boy's house.

A widow is often taken by the younger brother of the deceased husband, though no compulsion is exerted over her.   But the match is common because the Bhuiyas have the survival of fraternal polyandry, which consists in allowing unmarried younger brothers to have access to an elder brother's wife during his lifetime.[1]   Divorce is allowed for misconduct on the part of the wife or mutual disagreement.

10. Widow-marriage and divorce.

The Bhuiyas commonly take as their principal deity the spirit of the nearest mountain overlooking their village, and make offerings to it of butter, rice and fowls.   In April they present the first-fruits of the mango harvest.   They venerate the sun as Dharam Deota, but no offerings are made to him.   Nearly all Bhuiyas worship the cobra, and some of them call it their mother and think they are descended from it.   They will not touch or kill a cobra, and do not swear by it.   In Rairakhol they venerate a goddess, Rambha Devi, who may be a corn-goddess, as the practice of burning down successive patches of jungle and sowing seed on each for two or three years is here known as *rambha*.   They think that the sun and moon are sentient beings, and that fire and lightning are the children of the sun, and the stars the children of the moon.   One day the moon invited the sun to dinner and gave him very nice food, so that the sun asked what it was.   The moon said she had cooked her own children, and on this the sun went home and cooked all

11. Religion.

[1] From Mr. Mazumdār's monograph.

his children and ate them, and this is the reason why there are no stars during the day. But his eldest son, fire, went and hid in a *rengal* tree, and his daughter, the lightning, darted hither and thither so that the sun could not catch her. And when night came again, and the stars came out, the sun saw how the moon had deceived him and cursed her, saying that she should die for fifteen days in every month. And this is the reason for the waxing and waning of the moon. Ever since this event fire has remained hidden in a *rengal* tree, and when the Bhuiyas want him they rub two pieces of its wood together and he comes out. This is the Bhuiya explanation of the production of fire from the friction of wood.

12. Religious dancing.

In the month of Kārtik (October), or the next month, they bring from the forest a branch of the *karm* tree and venerate it and perform the *karma* dance in front of it. They think that this worship and dance will cause the *karma* tree, the mango, the jack-fruit and the mahua to bear a full crop of fruit. Monday, Wednesday and Friday are considered the proper days for worshipping the deities, and children are often named on a Friday.

13. Funeral rites and inheritance.

The dead are either buried or burnt, the corpse being placed always with the feet pointing to its native village. On the tenth day the soul of the dead person is called back to the house. But if a man is killed by a tiger or by falling from a tree no mourning is observed for him, and his soul is not brought back. To perish from snake-bite is considered a natural death, and in such cases the usual obsequies are awarded. This is probably because they revere the cobra as their first mother. The Pābudia Bhuiyas throw four to eight annas' worth of copper on to the pyre or into the grave, and if the deceased had a cow some *ghī* or melted butter. No division of property can take place during the lifetime of either parent, but when both have died the children divide the inheritance, the eldest son taking two shares and the others one equal share each.

14. Physical appearance and occupation.

Colonel Dalton describes the Bhuiyas as, " A dark-brown, well-proportioned race, with black, straight hair, plentiful on the head, but scant on the face, of middle height, figures well knit and capable of enduring great fatigue, but light-framed like the Hindu rather than presenting the usual muscular development of the hillman." Their dress is scanty, and in the Tributary States Dalton says that the men and women all wear dresses of brown cotton cloth. This may be because white is a very conspicuous colour in the forests. They wear ornaments and beads, and are distinctive in that neither men nor women practise tattooing, though in some localities this rule is not observed by the women. To keep themselves warm at night they kindle two fires and sleep between them, and this custom has given rise to the saying, ' Wherever you see a Bhuiya he always has a fire.' In Bāmra the Bhuiyas still practise shifting cultivation, for which they burn the forest growth from the hillsides and sow oilseeds in the fresh soil. This method of agriculture is called locally Khasrathumi. They obtain their lands free from the Rāja in return for acting as luggage porters and coolies. In Bāmra they will not serve as farm-servants or labourers for hire, but elsewhere they are more docile.

A woman divorced for adultery is not again admitted 15. Social to caste intercourse. Her parents take her to their village, customs. where she has to live in a separate hut and earn her own livelihood. If any Bhuiya steals from a Kol, Gānda or Ghasia he is permanently put out of caste, while for killing a cow the period of expulsion is twelve years. The emblem of the Bhuiyas is a sword, in reference to their employment as soldiers, and this they affix to documents in place of their signature.

Bhulia,[1] **Bholia, Bhoriya, Bholwa, Mihir, Mehar.**—A caste of weavers in the Uriya country. In 1901 the Bhulias numbered 26,000 persons, but with the transfer of Sambalpur and the Uriya States to Bengal this figure has been reduced to 5000. A curious fact about the caste is that though solely domiciled in the Uriya territories, many families belonging to it talk Hindi in their own houses. According to one of their traditions they immigrated to this part of the country with the first Chauhān Rāja of Patna, and it may be that they are members of some

---

[1] This article is compiled from a paper taken by Mr. Hīra Lāl at Sonpur.

northern caste who have forgotten their origin and taken to a fresh calling in the land of their adoption. The Koshtas of Chhattīsgarh have a subcaste called Bhoriya, and possibly the Bhulias have some connection with these. The caste sometimes call themselves Devāng, and Devāng or Devāngan is the name of another subcaste of Koshtis. Various local derivations of the name are current, generally connecting it with *bhūlna*, to forget. The Bhulias occupy a higher rank than the ordinary weavers, corresponding with that of the Koshtis elsewhere, and this is to some extent considered to be an unwarranted pretension. Thus one saying has it: "Formerly a son was born from a Chandāl woman; at that time none were aware of his descent or rank, and so he was called Bhulia (one who is forgotten). He took the loom in his hands and became the brother-in-law of the Gānda." The object here is obviously to relegate the Bhulia to the same impure status as the Gānda. Again the Bhulias affect the honorific title of Meher, and another saying addresses them thus: "Why do you call yourself Meher? You make a hole in the ground and put your legs into it and are like a cow with foot-and-mouth disease struggling in the mud." The allusion here is to the habit of the weaver of hollowing out a hole for his feet as he sits before the loom, while cattle with foot-and-mouth disease are made to stand in mud to cool and cleanse the feet.

The caste have no subcastes, except that in Kālāhandi a degraded section is recognised who are called Sānpāra Bhulias, and with whom the others refuse to intermarry. These are, there is little reason to doubt, the progeny of illicit unions. They say that they have two *gotras*, Nāgas from the cobra and Kachhap from the tortoise. But these have only been adopted for the sake of respectability, and exercise no influence on marriage, which is regulated by a number of exogamous groups called *vansa*. The names of the *vansas* are usually either derived from villages or are titles or nicknames. Two of them, Bāgh (tiger) and Kimir (crocodile), are totemistic, while two more, Kumhār (potter) and Dhuba (washerman), are the names of other castes. Examples of titular names are Bānkra (crooked),

Ranjūjha (warrior), Kodjit (one who has conquered a score
of people) and others. The territorial names are derived
from those of villages where the caste reside at present.
Marriage within the *vansa* is forbidden, but some of the
vansas have been divided into *bad* and *sān*, or great and
small, and members of these may marry with each other,
the subdivision having been adopted when the original
group became so large as to include persons who were
practically not relations. The binding portion of the
wedding ceremony is that the bridegroom should carry the
bride in a basket seven times round the *hom* or sacrificial
fire. If he cannot do this, the girl's grandfather carries
them both. After the ceremony the pair return to the
bridegroom's village, and are made to sleep on the same
bed, some elder woman of the family lying between them.
After a few days the girl goes back to her parents and does
not rejoin her husband until she attains maturity. The
remarriage of widows is permitted, and in Native States is
not less costly to the bridegroom than the regular ceremony.
In Sonpur the suitor must proceed to the Rāja and pay
him twenty rupees for his permission, which is given in the
shape of a present of rice and nuts. Similar sums are paid
to the caste-fellows and the parents of the girl, and the
Rāja's rice and nuts are then placed on the heads of the
couple, who become man and wife. Divorce may be effected
at the instance of the husband or the wife's parents on the
mere ground of incompatibility of temper. The position of
the caste corresponds to that of the Koshtas ; that is, they
rank below the good cultivating castes, but above the menial
and servile classes. They eat fowls and the flesh of wild
pig, and drink liquor. A *liaison* with one of the impure
castes is the only offence entailing permanent expulsion
from social intercourse. A curious rule is that in the case
of a woman going wrong with a man of the caste, the man
only is temporarily outcasted and forced to pay a fine
on readmission, while the woman escapes without penalty.
They employ Brāhmans for ceremonial purposes. They
are considered proverbially stupid, like the Koris in the
northern Districts, but very laborious. One saying about
them is : " The Kewat catches fish but himself eats crabs,

and the Bhulia weaves loin-cloths but himself wears only a rag"; and another: "A Bhulia who is idle is as useless as a confectioner's son who eats sweetmeats, or a money-lender's son with a generous disposition, or a cultivator's son who is extravagant."

1. Origin and traditions.

Bhunjia.[1]—A small Dravidian tribe residing in the Bindrānawāgarh and Khariār zamīndāris of the Raipur District, and numbering about 7000 persons. The tribe was not returned outside this area in 1911, but Sherring mentions them in a list of the hill tribes of the Jaipur zamīndāri of Vizagapatam, which touches the extreme south of Bindrānawāgarh. The Bhunjias are divided into two branches, Chaukhutia and Chinda, and the former have the following legend of their origin. On one occasion a Bhatra Gond named Bāchar cast a net into the Pairi river and brought out a stone. He threw the stone back into the river and cast his net again, but a second and yet a third time the stone came out. So he laid the stone on the bank of the river and went back to his house, and that night he dreamt that the stone was Bura Deo, the great God of the Gonds. So he said: 'If this dream be true let me draw in a deer in my net to-morrow for a sign'; and the next day the body of a deer appeared in his net. The stone then called upon the Gond to worship him as Bura Deo, but the Gond demurred to doing so himself, and said he would provide a substitute as a devotee. To this Bura Deo agreed, but said that Bāchar, the Gond, must marry his daughter to the substituted worshipper. The Gond then set out to search for somebody, and in the village of Lafandi he found a Halba of the name of Konda, who was a cripple, deaf and dumb, blind, and a leper. He brought Konda to the stone, and on reaching it he was miraculously cured of all his ailments and gladly began to worship Bura Deo. He afterwards married the Gond's daughter and they had a son called Chaukhutia Bhunjia, who was the ancestor of the Chaukhutia division of the tribe. Now the term Chaukhutia in

---

[1] This article is based on papers by Mr. Hīra Lāl, Mr. Gokul Prasād, Tahsīldār, Dhamtarī, Mr. Pyāre Lāl Misra of the Gazetteer office, and Munshi Ganpati Gīri, Superintendent, Bindrānawāgarh estate.

Chhattīsgarhi signifies a bastard, and the story related above is obviously intended to signify that the Chaukhutia Bhunjias are of mixed descent from the Gonds and Halbas. It is clearly with this end in view that the Gond is made to decline to worship the stone himself and promise to find a substitute, an incident which is wholly unnatural and is simply dragged in to meet the case. The Chaukhutia sub-tribe especially worship Bura Deo, and sing a song relating to the finding of the stone in their marriage ceremony as follows :

> *Johār, johār Thākur Deota, Tumko lāgon,*
> *Do matia ghar men dīne tumhāre nām.*
> *Johār, johār Konda, Tumko lāgon,*
> *Do matia ghar men, etc.*
> *Johār, johār Bāchar Jhākar Tumko lāgon, etc.*
> *Johār, johār Būdha Rāja Tumko lāgon, etc.*
> *Johār, johār Lafandi Māti Tumko lāgon, etc.*
> *Johār, johār Ānand Māti Tumko lāgon, etc.*

which may be rendered :

> I make obeisance to thee, O Thākur Deo, I bow down to thee !
> In thy name have I placed two pots in my house (as a mark of respect).
> I make obeisance to thee, O Konda Pujāri, I bow down to thee !
> In thy name have I placed two pots in my house.
> I make obeisance to thee, O Bāchar Jhākar !
> In thy name have I placed two pots in my house.
> I make obeisance to thee, O Būdha Rāja !
> In thy name have I placed two pots in my house.
> I make obeisance to thee, O Soil of Lafandi !
> In thy name have I placed two pots in my house.
> I make obeisance to thee, O Happy Spot !
> In thy name have I placed two pots in my house.

The song refers to the incidents in the story. Thākur Deo is the title given to the divine stone, Konda is the Halba priest, and Bāchar the Gond who cast the net. Būdha Rāja, otherwise Singh Sei, is the Chief who was ruling in Bindrānawāgarh at the time, Lafandi the village where Konda Halba was found, and the Ānand Māti or Happy Spot is that where the stone was taken out of the river. The majority of the sept-names returned are of Gond origin, and there seems no doubt that the Chaukhutias are, as the story says, of mixed descent from the Halbas and Gonds. It is noticeable, however, that the Bhunjias, though surrounded by Gonds on all sides, do not speak Gondi but a dialect of Hindi, which Sir G. Grierson considers to resemble that of the Halbas, and also describes as "A form of Chhattīsgarhi which is practically the same as Baigāni. It is a jargon spoken by Binjhwārs, Bhumias and Bhunjias of Raipur, Raigarh, Sārangarh and Patna in the Central Provinces."[1] The Binjhwārs also belong to the country of the Bhunjias, and one or two estates close to Bindrānawāgarh are held by members of this tribe. The Chinda division of the Bhunjias have a saying about themselves: ' *Chinda Rāja, Bhunjia Pāik*'; and they say that there was originally a Kamār ruler of Bindrānawāgarh who was dispossessed by Chinda. The Kamārs are a small and very primitive tribe of the same locality. *Pāik* means a foot-soldier, and it seems therefore that the Bhunjias formed the levies of this Chinda, who may very probably have been one of themselves. The term Bhunjia may perhaps signify one who lives on the soil, from *bhūm*, the earth, and *jia*, dependent on. The word *Birjia*, a synonym for Binjhwār, is similarly a corruption of *bewar jia*, and means one who is dependent on *dahia* or patch cultivation. Sir H. Risley gives Birjia, Binjhia and Binjhwār[2] as synonymous terms, and Bhunjia may be another corruption of the same sort. The Binjhwārs are a Hinduised offshoot of the ancient Baiga tribe, who may probably have been in possession of the hills bordering the Chhattīsgarh plain as well as of the Satpūra range before the advent of the Gonds, as the term Baiga is employed for a village priest over a large part of this area. It thus seems not improbable that the Chinda Bhunjias may have been derived from the Binjhwārs, and this would account for the fact that the tribe speaks a dialect of Hindi and not Gondi. As already seen, the Chaukhutia subcaste appear to be of mixed origin from the Gonds and Halbas, and as the Chindas are probably descended from the Baigas, the Bhunjias may be considered to be an offshoot from these three important tribes.

2. Sub-divisions.   Of the two subtribes already mentioned the Chaukhutia

---

[1] From the *Index of Languages and Dialects*, furnished by Sir G. Grierson for the census.

[2] *Tribes and Castes of Bengal*, art. Binjhia.

are recognised to be of illegitimate descent. As a consequence
of this they strive to obtain increased social estimation by
a ridiculously strict observance of the rules of ceremonial
purity. If any man not of his own caste touches the hut
where a Chaukhutia cooks his food, it is entirely abandoned
and a fresh one built. At the time of the census they
threatened to kill the enumerator if he touched their huts
to affix the census number. Pegs had therefore to be
planted in the ground a little in front of the huts and marked
with their numbers. The Chaukhutia will not eat food
cooked by other members of his own community, and this
is a restriction found only among those of bastard descent,
where every man is suspicious of his neighbour's parentage.
He will not take food from the hands of his own daughter
after she is married ; as soon as the ceremony is over her
belongings are at once removed from the hut, and even the
floor beneath the seat of the bride and bridegroom during
the marriage ceremony is dug up and the surface earth
thrown away to avoid any risk of defilement. Only when it
is remembered that these rules are observed by people who
do not wash themselves from one week's end to the other,
and wear the same wisp of cloth about their loins until it
comes to pieces, can the full absurdity of such customs as the
above be appreciated. But the tendency appears to be of
the same kind as the intense desire for respectability so often
noticed among the lower classes in England. The Chindas,
whose pedigree is more reliable, are far less particular about
their social purity.

As already stated, the exogamous divisions of the
Bhunjias are derived from those of the Gonds. Among
the Chaukhutias it is considered a great sin if the signs of
puberty appear in a girl before she is married, and to avoid
this, if no husband has been found for her, they perform a
'Kānd Byāh' or 'Arrow Marriage' : the girl walks seven
times round an arrow fixed in the ground, and is given away
without ceremony to the man who by previous arrangement
has brought the arrow. If a girl of the Chinda group goes
wrong with an outsider before marriage and becomes
pregnant, the matter is hushed up, but if she is a Chaukhutia
it is said that she is finally expelled from the community,

3. Marriage.

the same severe course being adopted even when she is not pregnant if there is reason to suppose that the offence has been committed. A proposal for marriage among the Chaukhutias is made on the boy's behalf by two men who are known as Mahālia and Jangālia, and are supposed to represent a Nai (barber) and Dhīmar (water-carrier), though they do not actually belong to these castes. As among the Gonds, the marriage takes place at the bridegroom's village, and the Mahālia and Jangālia act as stewards of the ceremony, and are entrusted with the rice, pulse, salt, oil and other provisions, the bridegroom's family having no function in the matter except to pay for them. The provisions are all stored in a separate hut, and when the time for the feast has come they are distributed raw to all the guests, each family of whom cook for themselves. The reason for this is, as already explained, that each one is afraid of losing status by eating with other members of the tribe. The marriage is solemnised by walking round the sacred post, and the ceremony is conducted by a hereditary priest known as Dīnwāri, a member of the tribe, whose line it is believed will never become extinct. Among the Chinda Bhunjias the bride goes away with her husband, and in a short time returns with him to her parents' house for a few days, to make an offering to the deities. But the Chaukhutias will not allow her, after she has lived in her father-in-law's house, to return to her home. In future if she goes to visit her parents she must stay outside the house and cook her food separately. Widow-marriage and divorce are permitted, but a husband will often overlook transgressions on the part of his wife and only put her away when her conduct has become an open scandal. In such a case he will either quietly leave house and wife and settle alone in another village, or have his wife informed by means of a neighbour that if she does not leave the village he will do so. It is not the custom to bring cases before the tribal committee or to claim damages. A special tie exists between a man and his sister's children. The marriage of a brother's son or daughter to a sister's daughter or son is considered the most suitable. A man will not allow his sister's children to eat the leavings of food on his plate, though his own children may do so. This is a special token of respect to his sister's children. He will not chastise his sister's children, even though they deserve it. And it is considered especially meritorious for a man to pay for the wedding ceremony of his sister's son or daughter.

Every third year in the month of Chait (March) the tribe offer a goat and a cocoanut to Māta, the deity of cholera and smallpox. They bow daily to the sun with folded hands, and believe that he is of special assistance to them in the liquidation of debt, which the Bhunjias consider a primary obligation. When a debt has been paid off they offer a cocoanut to the sun as a mark of gratitude for his assistance. They also pay great reverence to the tortoise. They call the tortoise the footstool (*pīdha*) of God, and have adopted the Hindu theory that the earth is supported by a tortoise swimming in the midst of the ocean. Professor Tylor explains as follows how this belief arose :[1] " To man in the lower levels of science the earth is a flat plain over which the sky is placed like a dome as the arched upper shell of the tortoise stands upon the flat plate below, and this is why the tortoise is the symbol or representative of the world." It is said that Bhunjia women are never allowed to sit either on a footstool or a bed-cot, because these are considered to be the seats of the deities. They consider it disrespectful to walk across the shadow of any elderly person, or to step over the body of any human being or revered object on the ground. If they do this inadvertently, they apologise to the person or thing. If a man falls from a tree he will offer a chicken to the tree-spirit.

The tribe will eat pork, but abstain from beef and the flesh of monkeys. Notwithstanding their strictness of social observance, they rank lower than the Gonds, and only the Kamārs will accept food from their hands. A man who has got maggots in a wound is purified by being given to drink water, mixed with powdered turmeric, in which silver and copper rings have been dipped. Women are secluded during the menstrual period for as long as eight days, and during this time they may not enter the dwelling-hut nor touch any article belonging to it. The Bhunjias take their

4. Religion.

5. Social rules.

[1] *Early History of Mankind*, p. 341.

food on plates of leaves, and often a whole family will have only one brass vessel, which will be reserved for production on the visit of a guest. But no strangers can be admitted to the house, and a separate hut is kept in the village for their use. Here they are given uncooked grain and pulse, which they prepare for themselves. When the women go out to work they do not leave their babies in the house, but carry them tied up in a small rag under the arm. They have no knowledge of medicine and are too timid to enter a Government dispensary. Their panacea for most diseases is branding the skin with a hot iron, which is employed indifferently for headache, pains in the stomach and rheumatism. Mr. Pyāre Lāl notes that one of his informants had recently been branded for rheumatism on both knees and said that he felt much relief.

BINJHWĀR

Binjhwār, Binjhāl.[1]—A comparatively civilised Dravidian tribe, or caste formed from a tribe, found in the Raipur and Bilāspur Districts and the adjoining Uriya country. In 1911 the Binjhwārs numbered 60,000 persons in the Central Provinces. There is little or no doubt that the Binjhwārs are an offshoot of the primitive Baiga tribe of Mandla and Bālāghāt, who occupy the Satpūra or Maikal hills to the north of the Chhattīsgarh plain. In these Districts a Binjhwār subdivision of the Baigas exists ; it is the most civilised and occupies the highest rank in the tribe. In Bhandāra is found the Injhwār caste who are boatmen and cultivators. This caste is derived from the Binjhwār subdivision of the Baigas, and the name Injhwār is simply a corruption of Binjhwār. Neither the Binjhwārs nor the Baigas are found except in the territories above mentioned, and it seems clear that the Binjhwārs are a comparatively civilised section of the Baigas, who have become a distinct caste. They are in fact the landholding section of the Baigas, like the Rāj-Gonds among the Gonds and the Bhilālas among Bhīls. The zamīndārs of Bodāsāmar, Rāmpur, Bhatgāon and other estates to the south and east of the Chhattīsgarh plain belong to this tribe. But owing

1. Origin and tradition.

---

[1] This article is based on a paper by Mr. Miān Bhai Abdul Hussain, Extra Assistant Commissioner, Sambalpur.

to the change of name their connection with the parent Baigas has now been forgotten. The name Binjhwār is derived from the Vindhya hills, and the tribe still worship the goddess Vindhyabāsini of these hills as their tutelary deity. They say that their ancestors migrated from Binjha-kop to Lāmpa, which may be either Lāmta in Bālāghāt or Lāphāgarh in Bilāspur. The hills of Mandla, the home of perhaps the most primitive Baigas, are quite close to the Vindhya range. The tribe say that their original ancestors were *Bārah bhai betkār*, or the twelve Brother Archers. They were the sons of the goddess Vindhyabāsini. One day they were out shooting and let off their arrows, which flew to the door of the great temple at Puri and stuck in it. Nobody in the place was able to pull them out, not even when the king's elephants were brought and harnessed to them; till at length the brothers arrived and drew them forth quite easily with their hands, and the king was so pleased with their feat that he gave them the several estates which their descendants now hold. The story recalls that of Arthur and the magic sword. According to another legend the mother of the first Rāja of Patna, a Chauhān Rājpūt, had fled from northern India to Sambalpur after her husband and relations had been killed in battle. She took refuge in a Binjhwār's hut and bore a son who became Rāja of Patna; and in reward for the protection afforded to his mother he gave the Binjhwār the Bodāsāmar estate, requiring only of him and his descendants the tribute of a silk cloth on accession to the zamīndāri; and this has been rendered ever since by the zamīndārs of Bodāsāmar to the Rājas of Patna as a mark of fealty. It is further stated that the twelve archers when they fired the memor-able arrows in the forest were in pursuit of a wild boar; and the landholding class of Binjhwārs are called Bāriha from *bārāh*, a boar. As is only fitting, the Binjhwārs have taken the arrow as their tribal symbol or mark; their cattle are branded with it, and illiterate Binjhwārs sign it in place of their name. If a husband cannot be found for a girl she is sometimes married to an arrow. At a Binjhwār wedding an arrow is laid on the trunk of mahua [1] which forms the

---

[1] *Bassia latifolia.*

marriage-post, and honours are paid to it as representing the bridegroom.

The tribe have four subdivisions, the Binjhwārs proper, the Sonjharas, the Birjhias and the Binjhias. The Sonjharas consist of those who took to washing for gold in the sands of the Mahānadi, and it may be noted that a separate caste of Sonjharas is also in existence in this locality besides the Binjhwār group. The Birjhias are those who practised *bewar* or shifting cultivation in the forests, the name being derived from *bewarjia*, one living by *bewar*-sowing. Binjhia is simply a diminutive form of Binjhwār, but in Bilāspur it is sometimes regarded as a separate caste. The zamīndār of Bhatgaon belongs to this group. The tribe have also exogamous divisions, the names of which are of a diverse character, and on being scrutinised show a mixture of foreign blood. Among totemistic names are Bāgh, a tiger; Pod, a buffalo; Kamalia, the lotus flower; Panknāli, the water-crow; Tār, the date-palm; Jāl, a net, and others. Some of the sections are nicknames, as Udhār, a debtor; Marai Meli Bāgh, one who carried a dead tiger; Ultum, a talker; Jālia, a liar; Kessal, one who has shaved a man, and so on. Several are the names of other castes, as Lohār, Dūdh Kawaria, Bhīl, Bānka and Mājhi, indicating that members of these castes have become Binjhwārs and have founded families. The sept names also differ in different localities; the Birjhia subtribe who live in the same country as the Mundas have several Munda names among their septs, as Munna, Son, Solai; while the Binjhwārs who are neighbours of the Gonds have Gond sept names, as Tekām, Sonwāni, and others. This indicates that there has been a considerable amount of intermarriage with the surrounding tribes, as is the case generally among the lower classes of the population in Chhattīsgarh. Even now if a woman of any caste from whom the Binjhwārs will take water to drink forms a connection with a man of the tribe, though she herself must remain in an irregular position, her children will be considered as full members of it. The Bārhias or landowning group have now adopted names of Sanskrit formation, as Gajendra, an elephant, Rāmeswar, the god Rāma, and Nāgeshwar, the cobra deity. Two of their septs are named Lohār (black-

2. Tribal subdivisions.

smith) and Kumhār (potter), and may be derived from members of these castes who became Binjhwārs or from Binjhwārs who took up the occupations. At a Binjhwār wedding the presence of a person belonging to each of the Lohār and Kumhār septs is essential, the reason being probably the estimation in which the two handicrafts were held when the Binjhwārs first learnt them from their Hindu neighbours.

3. Marriage.

In Sambalpur there appears to be no system of exogamous groups, and marriage is determined simply by relationship. The union of agnates is avoided as long as the connection can be traced between them, but on the mother's side all except first cousins may marry. Marriage is usually adult, and girls are sometimes allowed to choose their own husbands. A bride-price of about eight *khandis* (1400 lbs.) of unhusked rice is paid. The ceremony is performed at the bridegroom's house, to which the bride proceeds after bidding farewell to her family and friends in a fit of weeping. Weddings are avoided during the four months of the rainy season, and in Chait (March) because it is inauspicious, Jeth (May) because it is too hot, and Pūs (December) because it is the last month of the year among the Binjhwārs. The marriage ceremony should begin on a Sunday, when the guests are welcomed and their feet washed. On Monday the formal reception of the bride takes place, the Gandsān or scenting ceremony follows on Tuesday, and on Wednesday is the actual wedding. At the scenting ceremony seven married girls dressed in new clothes dyed yellow with turmeric conduct the bridegroom round the central post ; one holds a dish containing rice, mango leaves, myrobalans and betel-nuts, and a second sprinkles water from a small pot. At each round the bridegroom is made to throw some of the condiments from the dish on to the wedding-post, and after the seven rounds he is seated and is rubbed with oil and turmeric.

4. The marriage ceremony.

Among the Birjhias a trunk of mahua with two branches is erected in the marriage-shed, and on this a dagger is placed in a winnowing-fan filled with rice, the former representing the bridegroom and the latter the bride. The bride first goes round the post seven times alone, and then the bridegroom, and after this they go round it together. A plough is brought and they stand upon the yoke, and seven cups of water having been collected from seven different houses, four are poured over the bridegroom and three over the bride. Some men climb on to the top of the shed and pour pots of water down on to the couple. This is now said to be done only as a joke. Next morning two strong men take the bridegroom and bride, who are usually grown up, on their backs, and the parties pelt each other with unhusked rice. Then the bridegroom holds the bride in his arms from behind and they stand facing the sun, while some old man ties round their feet a thread specially spun by a virgin. The couple stand for some time and then fall to the ground as if dazzled by his rays, when water is again poured over their bodies to revive them. Lastly, an old man takes the arrow from the top of the marriage-post and draws three lines with it on the ground to represent the Hindu trinity, Brahma, Vishnu and Siva, and the bridegroom jumps over these holding the bride in his arms. The couple go to bathe in a river or tank, and on the way home the bridegroom shoots seven arrows at an image of a sāmbhar deer made with straw. At the seventh shot the bride's brother takes the arrow, and running away and hiding it in his cloth lies down at the entrance of the bridegroom's house. The couple go up to him, and the bridegroom examines his body with suspicion, pretending to think that he is dead. He draws the arrow out of his cloth and points to some blood which has been previously sprinkled on the ground. After a time the boy gets up and receives some liquor as a reward. This procedure may perhaps be a symbolic survival of marriage by capture, the bridegroom killing the bride's brother before carrying her off, or more probably, perhaps, the boy may represent a dead deer. In some of the wilder tracts the man actually waylays and seizes the girl before the wedding, the occasion being previously determined, and the women of her family trying to prevent him. If he succeeds in carrying her off they stay for three or four days in the forest and then return and are married.

If a Binjhwār girl is seduced and rendered pregnant by a man of the tribe, the people exact a feast and compel them to join their hands in an informal manner before the   5. Sexual morality.

caste committee, the tie thus formed being considered as indissoluble as a formal marriage. Polygamy is permitted ; a Binjhwār zamīndār marries a new wife, who is known as Pāt Rāni, to celebrate his accession to his estates, even though he may have five or six already.

Divorce is recognised but is not very common, and a married woman having an intrigue with another Binjhwār is often simply made over to him and they live as husband and wife. If this man does not wish to take her she can live with any other, conjugal morality being very loose in Sambalpur. In Bodāsāmar a fine of from one to ten rupees is payable to the zamīndār in the case of each divorce, and a feast must also be given to the caste-fellows.

6. Disposal of the dead.

The tribe usually bury the dead, and on the third day they place on the grave some uncooked rice and a lighted lamp. As soon as an insect flies to the lamp they catch it, and placing it in a cake of flour carry this to a stream, where it is worshipped with an offering of coloured rice. It is then thrust into the sand or mud in the bed of the stream with a grass broom. This ceremony is called Khārpāni or 'Grass and Water,' and appears to be a method of disposing of the dead man's spirit. It is not performed at all for young children, while, on the other hand, in the case of respected elders a second ceremony is carried out of the same nature, being known as Badāpāni or 'Great Water.' On this occasion the *jīva* or soul is worshipped with greater pomp. Except in the case of wicked souls, who are supposed to become malignant ghosts, the Binjhwārs do not seem to have any definite belief in a future life. They say, '*Je maris te saris*,' or 'That which is dead is rotten and gone.'

7. Religion.

The tribe worship the common village deities of Chhattīsgarh, and extend their veneration to Bura Deo, the principal god of the Gonds. They venerate their daggers, spears and arrows on the day of Dasahra, and every third year their tutelary goddess Vindhyabāsini is carried in procession from village to village. Mr. Miān Bhai gives the following list of precepts as forming the Binjhwār's moral code :—Not to commit adultery outside the caste ; not to eat beef ; not to murder ; not to steal ; not to swear falsely before the caste committee. The tribe have *gurus* or spiritual preceptors, whom he describes as the most ignorant Bairāgis, very little better than impostors.   When a boy or girl grows up the Bairāgi comes and whispers the *Karn mantra* or spell in his ear, also hanging a necklace of *tulsi* (basil) beads round his neck ; for this the *guru* receives a cloth, a cocoanut and a cash payment of four annas to a rupee.   Thereafter he visits his disciples annually at harvest time and receives a present of grain from them.

On the 11th of Bhādon (August) the tribe celebrate the *karma* festival, which is something like May-Day or a harvest feast.   The youths and maidens go to the forest and bring home a young *karma* tree, singing, dancing and beating drums.   Offerings are made to the tree, and then the whole village, young and old, drink and dance round it all through the night.   Next morning the tree is taken to the nearest stream or tank and consigned to it.   After this the young girls of five or six villages make up a party and go about to the different villages accompanied by drummers and Gānda musicians.   They are entertained for the night, and next morning dance for five or six hours in the village and then go on to another. *8. Festivals.*

The tribe are indiscriminate in their diet, which includes pork, snakes, rats, and even carnivorous animals, as panthers. They refuse only beef, monkeys and the leavings of others. The wilder Binjhwārs of the forests will not accept cooked food from any other caste, but those who live in association with Hindus will take it when cooked without water from a few of the higher ones.   The tribe are not considered as impure.   Their dress is very simple, consisting as a rule only of one dirty white piece of cloth in the case of both men and women.   Their hair is unkempt, and they neither oil nor comb it.   A genuine Binjhwār of the hills wears long frizzled hair with long beard and moustaches, but in the open country they cut their hair and shave the chin.   Every Binjhwār woman is tattooed either before or just after her marriage, when she has attained to the age of adolescence. A man will not touch or accept food from a woman who is not tattooed on the feet.   The expenses must be paid either by the woman's parents or her brothers and not by her husband.   The practice is carried to an extreme, and many *9. Social customs.*

women have the upper part of the chest, the arms from shoulder to wrist, and the feet and legs up to the knee covered with devices. On the chest and arms the patterns are in the shape of flowers and leaves, while along the leg a succession of zigzag lines are pricked. The Binjhwārs are usually cultivators and labourers, while, as already stated, several zamīndāri and other estates are owned by members of the tribe. Binjhwārs also commonly hold the office of Jhānkar or priest of the village gods in the Sambalpur District, as the Baigas do in Mandla and Bālāghāt. In Sambalpur the Jhānkar or village priest is a universal and recognised village servant of fairly high status. His business is to conduct the worship of the local deities of the soil, crops, forests and hills, and he generally has a substantial holding, rent free, containing some of the best land in the village. It is said locally that the Jhānkar is looked on as the founder of the village, and the representative of the old owners who were ousted by the Hindus. He worships on their behalf the indigenous deities, with whom he naturally possesses a more intimate acquaintance than the later immigrants ; while the gods of these latter cannot be relied on to exercise a sufficient control over the works of nature in the foreign land to which they have been imported, or to ensure that the earth and the seasons will regularly perform their necessary functions in producing sustenance for mankind.

BISHNOI

LIST OF PARAGRAPHS

Bishnoi.[1]—A Hindu sect which has now developed into a caste. The sect was founded in the Punjab, and the Bishnois are immigrants from northern India. In the Central Provinces they numbered about 1100 persons in 1911, nearly all of whom belonged to the Hoshangābād District. The best description of the sect is contained in Mr. Wilson's *Sirsa Settlement Report* (quoted in Sir E. Maclagan's *Census Report of the Punjab* for 1891), from which the following details are taken : " The name Bishnoi means a worshipper of Vishnu. The founder of the sect was a Panwār Rājpūt named Jhāmbāji, who was born in a village of Bikaner State in A.D. 1451. His father had hitherto remained childless, and being greatly oppressed by this misfortune had been promised a son by a Muhammadan Fakīr. After nine months Jhāmbāji was born and showed his miraculous origin in various ways, such as producing sweets from nothing for the delectation of his companions. Until he was thirty-four years old he spoke no word and was employed in tending his father's cattle. At this time a Brāhman was sent for to get him to speak, and on confessing his failure, Jhāmbāji showed his power by lighting a

1. Origin of the sect.

---

[1] This article is compiled from Mr. Wilson's account of the Bishnois as reproduced in Mr. Crooke's *Tribes and Castes*, and from notes taken by Mr. Adurām Chaudhri in the Hoshangābād District.

lamp with a snap of his fingers and spoke his first word. He adopted the life of a teacher and went to reside on a sand-hill some thirty miles south of Bikaner. In 1485 a fear-ful famine desolated the country, and Jhāmbāji gained an enormous number of disciples by providing food for all who would declare their belief in him. He is said to have died on his sandhill at the good old age of eighty-four, and to have been buried at a spot about a mile distant from it. A further account says that his body remained suspended for six months in the bier without decomposing. His name Jhāmbāji was a contraction of Achambha (The Wonder), with the honorific suffix *ji*.

2. Precepts of Jhām-bāji.

"The sayings (*shabd*) of Jhāmbāji, to the number of one hundred and twenty, were recorded by his disciples, and have been handed down in a book (*pothi*) which is written in the Nāgari character, and in a Hindu dialect similar to Bāgri and therefore probably a dialect of Rājasthāni. The following is a translation of the twenty-nine precepts given by him for the guidance of his followers : ' For thirty days after childbirth and five days after a menstrual discharge a woman must not cook food. Bathe in the morning. Commit no adultery. Be content. Be abstemious and pure. Strain your drinking-water. Be careful of your speech. Examine your fuel in case any living creature be burnt with it. Show pity to living creatures. Keep duty present to your mind as the teacher bade. Do not steal. Do not speak evil of others. Do not tell lies. Never quarrel. Avoid opium, tobacco, *bhāng* and blue clothing. Flee from spirits and flesh. See that your goats are kept alive (not sold to Musalmāns, who will kill them for food). Do not plough with bullocks. Keep a fast on the day before the new moon. Do not cut green trees. Sacrifice with fire. Say prayers ; meditate. Perform worship and attain heaven.' And the last of the twenty-nine duties pre-scribed by the teacher : ' Baptise your children if you would be called a true Bishnoi.' [1]

"Some of these precepts are not strictly obeyed. For

---

[1] The total number of precepts as given above is only twenty-five, but can be raised to twenty-nine by counting the prohibition of opium, tobacco, *bhāng*, blue clothing, spirits and flesh separately.

instance, though ordinarily they allow no blue in their
clothing, yet a Bishnoi, if he is a police constable, is allowed
to wear a blue uniform ; and Bishnois do use bullocks,
though most of their farming is done with camels.   They
also seem to be generally quarrelsome (in words) and given to
use bad language.   But they abstain from tobacco, drugs
and spirits, and are noted for their regard for animal life,
which is such that not only will they not themselves kill any
living creature, but they do their utmost to prevent others
from doing so.   Consequently their villages are generally
swarming with antelope and other animals, and they forbid
their Musalmān neighbours to kill them, and try to dissuade
European sportsmen from interfering with them.   They
wanted to make it a condition of their settlement that no
one should be allowed to shoot on their land, but at the
same time they asked that they might be assessed at lower
rates than their neighbours, on the ground that the antelope,
being thus left undisturbed, did more damage to their crops ;
but I told them that this would lessen the merit (*pun*) of
their actions in protecting the animals, and they must be
treated just as the surrounding villages were.   They consider
it a good deed to scatter grain to pigeons and other birds,
and often have a large number of half-tame birds about
their villages.   The day before the new moon (Amāwas)
they observe as a Sabbath and fast-day, doing no work in
the fields or in the house.   They bathe and pray three times
a day, in the morning, afternoon and evening, saying ' Bishnu !
Bishnu ! ' instead of the ordinary Hindu ' Rām ! Rām.'   Their
clothing is the same as that of other Bāgris, except that their
women do not allow the waist to be seen, and are fond of
wearing black woollen clothing.   They are more particular
about ceremonial purity than ordinary Hindus are, and it is
a common saying that if a Bishnoi's food is on the first of a
string of twenty camels and a man of another caste touches
the last camel of the string, the Bishnoi would consider his
food defiled and throw it away."

The ceremony of initiation is as follows: " A number
of representative Bishnois assemble, and before them a Sādh
or Bishnoi priest, after lighting a sacrificial fire (*hom*),
instructs the novice in the duties of the faith.   He then

3. Customs
of the
Bishnois in
the Punjab.

4. Initia-
tion and
baptism,

takes some water in a new earthen vessel, over which he
prays in a set form (*Bishno gāyatri*), stirring it the while
with his string of beads (*māla*), and after asking the consent
of the assembled Bishnois he pours the water three times
into the hands of the novice, who drinks it off. The
novice's scalp-lock (*choti*) is then cut off and his head shaved,
for the Bishnois shave the whole head and do not leave
a scalp-lock like the Hindus, but they allow the beard to
grow, only shaving the chin on the father's death. Infant
baptism is also practised, and thirty days after birth the
child, whether boy or girl, is baptised by the priest (Sādh)
in much the same way as an adult; only the set form of
prayer is different, and the priest pours a few drops of water
into the child's mouth, and gives the child's relatives each
three handfuls of the consecrated water to drink; at the
same time the barber clips off the child's hair. The
baptismal ceremony has the effect of purifying the house,
which has been made impure by the birth (*sūtak*).

"The Bishnois do not revere Brāhmans, but have priests
of their own known as Sādh, who are chosen from among
the laity. The priests are a hereditary class, and do not
intermarry with other Bishnois, from whom, like Brāhmans,
they receive food and offerings. The Bishnois do not burn
their dead, but bury them below the cattle-shed or in some
place like a pen frequented by cattle. They make pilgrimages to the place where Jhāmbāji is buried to the south of
Bikaner; here a tomb and temple have been erected to his
memory, and gatherings are held twice a year. The sect
observe the Holi in a different way from other Hindus.
After sunset on that day they fast till the next forenoon
when, after hearing read the account of how Prahlād was
tortured by his infidel father, Hrianya Kasipu, for believing
in the god Vishnu, until he was delivered by the god himself
in his incarnation of Narsingh, the Man-lion, and mourning
over Prahlād's sufferings, they light a sacrificial fire and
partake of consecrated water, and after distributing sugar
(*gur*) in commemoration of Prahlād's delivery from the fire
into which he was thrown, they break their fast."

5. Nature   The above interesting account of the Bishnois by Mr.
of the sect. Wilson shows that Jhāmbāji was a religious reformer, who

attempted to break loose from the debased Hindu polytheism
and arrogant supremacy of the Brāhmans by choosing one
god, Vishnu, out of the Hindu pantheon and exalting him into
the sole and supreme deity.   In his method he thus differed
from Kabīr and other reformers, who went outside Hinduism
altogether, preaching a monotheistic faith with one unseen
and nameless deity.   The case of the Mānbhaos, whose
unknown founder made Krishna the one god, discarding the
Vedas and the rest of Hinduism, is analogous to Jhāmbāji's
movement.   His creed much resembles that of the other
Hindu reformers and founders of the Vaishnavite sects.
The extreme tenderness for animal life is a characteristic
of most of them, and would be fostered by the Hindu belief
in the transmigration of souls.   The prohibition of liquor
is another common feature, to which Jhāmbāji added that
of all kinds of drugs.   His mind, like those of Kabīr and
Nānak, was probably influenced by the spectacle of the
comparatively liberal creed of Islām, which had now taken
root in northern India.   Mr. Crooke remarks that the
Bishnois of Bijnor appear to differ from those of the Punjab
in using the Muhammadan form of salutation, *Salām alaikum*,
and the title of Shaikhji.   They account for this by saying
they murdered a Muhammadan Kāzi, who prevented them
from burning a widow, and were glad to compound the
offence by pretending to adopt Islām.   But it seems
possible that on their first rupture with Hinduism they
were to some extent drawn towards the Muhammadans,
and adopted practices of which, on tending again to conform to their old religion, they have subsequently become
ashamed.

In northern India the members of different castes who
have become Bishnois have formed separate endogamous
groups, of which Mr. Crooke gives nine ; among these are
the Brāhman, Bania, Jāt, Sunār, Ahīr and Nai Bishnois.
Only members of comparatively good castes appear to have
been admitted into the community, and in the Punjab they
are nearly all Jāts and Banias.   In the Central Provinces
the caste forms only one endogamous group.   They have
gotras or exogamous sections, the names of which appear
to be of the titular or territorial type.   Some of the *gotras*,

6. Bishnois in the Central Provinces.

Jhuria, Ajna, Sain and Ahīr,[1] are considered to be lower than the others, and though they are not debarred from intermarriage, a connection with them is looked upon as something of a *mésalliance*. They are not consulted in the settlement of tribal disputes. No explanation of the comparatively degraded position of these septs is forthcoming, but it may probably be attributed to some blot in their ancestral escutcheon. The Bishnois celebrate their marriages at any period of the year, and place no reliance on astrology. According to their saying, "Every day is as good as Sankrānt,[2] every day is as good as Amāwas.[3] The Ganges flows every day, and he whose preceptor has taught him the most truth will get the most good from bathing in it."

7. Marriage.

Before a wedding the bride's father sends, by the barber, a cocoanut and a silver ring tied round it with a yellow thread. On the thread are seven, nine, eleven or thirteen knots, signifying the number of days to elapse before the ceremony. The barber on his arrival stands outside the door of the house, and the bridegroom's father sends round to all the families of his caste. The men go to the house and the women come singing to the barber, and rub turmeric on the boy. A married woman touches the cocoanut and waves a lighted lamp seven times round the bridegroom's head. This is meant to scare off evil spirits. On arrival at the bride's village the bridegroom touches the marriage-shed with the branch of a *ber* or wild plum tree. The mother of the bride gives him some sugar, rubs lamp-black on his eyes and twists his nose. The bride and bridegroom are seated side by side on wooden boards, and after the caste priest (Sādh) has chanted some sacred verses, water is poured nine times on to the palms of the bridegroom, and he drinks it. They do not perform the ceremony of walking round the sacred pole. Girls are usually married at a very early age, sometimes when they are only a few months old. Subsequently, when the bride-

---

[1] Jhuria may be Jharia, jungly; Sain is a term applied to beggars; the Ahīr or herdsman sept may be descended from a man of this caste who became a Bishnoi.

[2] The day when the sun passes from one zodiacal sign into another.

[3] The New Moon day or the day before.

groom comes to take his bride, her family present her with clothing and a spinning-wheel, this implement being still in favour among the Bishnois.   When a widow is to be married again she is taken to her new husband's house at night, and there grinds a flour-mill five times, being afterwards presented with lac bangles.

The dead are never burnt, but their bodies are weighted 8. Disposal with sand-bags and thrown into a stream.   The practice of the dead. which formerly prevailed among the Bishnois of burying their dead in the courtyard of the house by the cattle-stalls has now fallen into desuetude as being insanitary.   A red cloth is spread over the body of a woman, and if her maternal relatives are present each of them places a piece of cloth on the bier.   After the funeral the mourning party proceed to a river to bathe, and then cook and eat their food on the bank.   This custom is also followed by the Panwār Rājpūts of the Wainganga Valley, but is forbidden by most of the good Hindu castes.   No period of impurity is observed after a death, but on some day between the fourth and tenth days afterwards a feast is given to the caste-fellows.

The Bishnois of the Central Provinces are gradually 9. Develop-becoming an ordinary Hindu caste, a fate which has several ment into a caste. times befallen the adherents of Hindu reformers.   Many of the precepts of Jhāmbāji are neglected.   They still usually strain their water and examine their fuel before burning it to remove insects, and they scatter flour to feed the ants and grain for peacocks and pigeons.   The wearing of blue cloth is avoided by most, blue being for an obscure reason a somewhat unlucky colour among the Hindus.   But they now use bullocks for ploughing, and cut green trees except on the Amāwas day.   Many of them, especially the younger generation, have begun to grow the Hindu *choti* or scalp-lock.   They go on pilgrimage to all the Hindu sacred places, and no doubt make presents there to Brāhman priests. They offer *pindas* or sacrificial cakes to the spirits of their deceased ancestors.   They observe some of the ordinary Hindu festivals, as the Anant Chaturthi, and some of them employ Brāhmans to read the Satya Nārāyan Katha, the favourite Hindu sacred book.   They still retain their special observance of the Holi. The admission of proselytes has practically ceased, and they marry among themselves like an ordinary Hindu caste, in which light they are gradually coming to be regarded. The Bishnois are usually cultivators or moneylenders by calling.

BOHRA

Bohra, Bohora.[1]—A Muhammadan caste of traders who come from Gujarāt and speak Gujarāti. At the last census they numbered nearly 5000 persons, residing principally in the Nimār, Nāgpur and Amraoti Districts, Burhānpur being the headquarters of the sect in the Central Provinces. The name is probably derived from the Hindi *byohāra*, a trader. Members of the caste are honorifically addressed as Mullāji. According to the received account of the rise of the Bohras in Gujarāt a missionary, Abdulla, came from Yemen to Cambay in A.D. 1067. By his miracles he converted the great king Sidhrāj of Anhilvāda Pātan in Gujarāt, and he with numbers of his subjects embraced the new faith. For two centuries and a half the Bohras flourished, but with the establishment of Muzaffar Shāh's power (A.D. 1390–1413) in that country the spread of Sunni doctrines was encouraged and the Bohra and other Shia sects suppressed. Since then, with gradually lessening numbers, they have passed through several bitter persecutions, meeting with little favour or protection, till at the close of the eighteenth century they found shelter under British rule. In 1539 the members of the sect living in Arabia were expelled from there and came to Gujarāt, where they were hospitably received by their brethren, the headquarters of the sect being thenceforward

---

[1] This article is largely based on Mr. F. L. Farīdi's full description of the sect in the *Bombay Gazetteer*, *Muhammadans of Gujarāt*, and on a paper by Mr. Habib Ullah, pleader, Burhānpur.

345

fixed at Surat. The Bohras are Shias of the great Ismailia sect of Egypt. The Ismailia sect split off from the orthodox Shias on the question of the succession to the sixth Imām, Jāfar Sādik, in A.D. 765. The dispute was between his eldest son's son Ismail and his second son Musi, the Ismailias being those who supported the former and the orthodox Shias the latter. The orthodox Shias are distinguished as believers in twelve Imāms, the last of whom is still to come. The Ismailias again divided on a similar dispute as to the succession to the Khalīfa Almustansir Billah by his eldest son Nazār or his younger son Almustaāli. The Bohras are descended from the Mustaālians or supporters of the younger son and the Khojas from the Nazārians who supported the elder son.[1] All these distinctions appear somewhat trivial.

2. Their religious tenets.

Gujarāt contains two classes of Bohras : the traders who are all Shias and are the only immigrants into the Central Provinces, and a large class of cultivating Bohras who are Sunnis. The latter may be the descendants of the earliest converts and may have been forced to become Sunnis when this sect was dominant in Gujarāt as noticed above, while the Shias are perhaps descended from the later immigrants from Arabia. The Shia Bohras themselves are further divided into several sects of which the Dāudi are the principal.

Mr. Farīdi writes of them :[2] " They are attentive to their religious duties, both men and women knowing the Korān. They are careful to say their prayers, to observe Muharram as a season of mourning and to go on pilgrimage to Mecca and Kerbala. They strictly abstain from music and dancing and from using or dealing in intoxicating drinks or drugs. Though fierce sectarians, keenly hating and hated by the regular Sunnis and other Muhammadans than those of their own sect, their reverence for Ali and for their high priest seems to be further removed from adoration than among the Khojahs. They would appear to accept the ordinary distinctions of right and wrong, punishing drunkenness, adultery and other acts generally considered

---

[1] *Bombay Gazetteer, Muhammadans of Gujarāt*, p. 30. Sir H. T. Colebrooke and Mr. Conolly thought that the Bohras were true Shias and not Ismailias.

[2] *Ibidem*, pp. 30-32.

GROUP OF BOHRAS AT BURHÁNPUR (NIMÁR).

Remrose, Collo., Derby.

disgraceful.   Of the state beyond death they hold that, after
passing a time of freedom as evil spirits, unbelievers go to a
place of torment.   Believers, but apparently only believers
of the Ismaili faith, after a term of training enter a state of
perfection.   Among the faithful each disembodied spirit
passes the term of training in communion with the soul of
some good man.   The spirit can suggest good or evil to
the man and may learn from his good deeds to love the
right ; when the good man dies the spirits in communion
with his soul are, if they have gained by their training,
attached to some more perfect man, or if they have lost by
their opportunities are sent back to learn ; spirits raised to
a higher degree of knowledge are placed in communion with
the High Priest on earth ; and on his death are with him
united to the Imāms, and when through the Imāms they
have learnt what they still require to know they are absorbed
in perfection.   Except for some peculiarities in their names ;
that they attach special importance to circumcision ; that
the sacrifice or *alsikah* ceremony is held in the Mullah's
house ; that at marriage the bride and bridegroom when
not of age are represented by sponsors or *walis* ; that at
death a prayer for pity on his soul and body is laid in the
dead man's hands ; and that on certain occasions the High
Priest feeds the whole community—Bohra customs do not
so far as has been ascertained differ from those of ordinary
Muhammadans.

"Their leader, both in things religious and social, is the
head Mullah of Surat.   The ruling Mullah names his
successor, generally, but it is said not always, from among
the members of his own family.   Short of worship the head
Mullah is treated with the greatest respect.   He lives in
much state and entertains with the most profuse liberality.
On both religious and civil questions his authority is final.
Discipline is enforced in religious matters by fine, and in
case of adultery, drunkenness and other offences, by fine,
excommunication and rarely by flogging.   On ceremonial
occasions the head Mullah sits on his throne, and in token
of his power has the flyflapper, *chauri*, held before him.   As
the Bohras enter they make three prostrations, *salaams*, close
their hands and stand before him.   To such as are worthy

3. The
Mullahs.

he says ' Be seated,' to others ' Stand.' Once a year, on
the 18th Rajjab, every Dāudi lays his palm within the head
Mullah's hand and takes an oath to be faithful. On this
day when he goes to the mosque the Bohras are said to kiss
the Mullah's footsteps and to apply the dust he treads to
their heads and eyes." Each considerable settlement of the
sect has a deputy Mullah of its own.

4. Bohra
graveyards.
The Sahadra or burial-place of the Bohras at Burhānpur
contains the tombs of three of the Surat Mullahs who
happened to die when they were at Burhānpur. The tombs
are in shell-lime and are fairly handsome erections. The
Bohras support here by voluntary subscription a rest-house,
where members of the sect coming to the city can obtain free
board and lodging for as long as they like to stay. Mr.
Conolly says of their graveyards : [1]

" Their burial-grounds have a pleasing appearance, the
tombs being regularly arranged in streets, east and west.
The tombs themselves, which are, of course, north and south,
the corpse resting on its right side, differ in no respect from
those of Sunnis, with the exception of a small *chirāgh takia*
or lamp-socket, cut out of the north face, just like the cavity
for the inscription of our own tombs."

5. Reli-
gious
customs.
Of their religion Mr. Kitts writes : [2] " In prayers they
differ both from Shias and Sunnis in that they follow their
Mullah, praying aloud after him, but without much regularity
of posture. The times for commencing their devotions are
about five minutes later than those observed by Sunnis.
After the midday and sunset supplications they allow a
short interval to elapse, remaining themselves in the mosque
meanwhile. They then commence the afternoon and evening prayers and thus run five services into three."

Mr. Thurston notes that the Bohras consider themselves
so superior to other sects that if another Muhammadan
enters their mosque they afterwards clean the spot which he
has occupied during his prayers.[3] They show strictness in
other ways, making their own sweetmeats at home and
declining to eat those of the Halwai (confectioner). It is said

[1] *J.A.S.B.* vol. vi. (1837), part ii.
p. 847.
[2] *Berar Census Report* (1818), p. 70.
[3] *Castes and Tribes of Southern
India*, art. Bohra.

also that they will not have their clothes washed by a Dhobi, nor wear shoes made by a Chamār, nor take food touched by any Hindu. They are said to bathe only on Fridays, and some of them not on every Friday. If a dog touches them they are unclean and must change their clothes. They celebrate the Id and Ramazān a day before other Muhammadans. At the Muharram their women break all their bangles and wear new bangles next day to show that they have been widowed, and during this period they observe mourning by going without shoes and not using umbrellas. Mr. Conolly says of them : " I must not omit to notice that a fine of 20 cowries (equally for rich and poor) punishes the non-attendance of a Bohra at the daily prayers. A large sum is exacted for remissness during the Ramazān, and it is said that the dread of loss operates powerfully upon a class of men who are particularly penny-wise. The money collected thus is transmitted by the Ujjain Mullah to his chief at Surat, who devotes it to religious purposes such as repairing or building mosques, assisting the needy of his subjects and the like. Several other offences have the same characteristic punishment, such as fornication, drunkenness, etc. But the cunning Bohras elude many of the fines and daily indulge in practices not sanctioned by their creed ; thus in their shops pictures and figures may be purchased though it is against the commandments to sell the likeness of any living thing."

It has been seen that when a Bohra is buried a prayer for pity on his soul and body is laid in the dead man's hands, of which Mr. Farīdi gives the text. But other Muhammadans tell a story to the effect that the head Mullah writes a letter to the archangel Gabriel in which he is instructed to supply a stream of honey, a stream of milk, water and some fruit trees, a golden building and a number of houris, the extent of the order depending on the amount of money which has been paid to the Mullah by the departed in his lifetime ; and this letter is placed beneath the dead man's head in the grave, the Bohras having no coffins. The Bohras indignantly repudiate any such version of the letter, and no doubt if the custom ever existed it has died out.

The Bohras, Captain Forsyth remarks, though bigoted

6. Occupa-
tion.

religionists, are certainly the most civilised and enterprising and perhaps also the most industrious class in the Nimār District. They deal generally in hardware, piece-goods and drugs, and are very keen traders. There is a proverb, " He who is sharper than a Bohra must be mad, and he who is fairer than a Khatri must be a leper." Some of them are only pedlars and hawkers, and in past times their position seems to have been lower than at present. An old account says : [1] " The Bohras are an inferior set of travelling merchants. The inside of a Bohra's box is like that of an English country shop ; spelling-books, prayer-books, lavender-water, soap, tapes, scissors, knives, needles and thread make but a small part of the variety." And again : " In Bombay the Bohras go about the town as the dirty Jews do in London early and late, carrying a bag and inviting by the same nasal tone servants and others to fill it with old clothes, empty bottles, scraps of iron, etc." [2]

7. Houses
and dress.

Of their method of living Malcolm wrote : [3] " I visited several of the houses of this tribe at Shāhjahānpur, where a colony of them are settled, and was gratified to find not only in their apartments, but in the spaciousness and cleanliness of their kitchens, in the well-constructed chimney, the neatly arranged pantries, and the polished dishes and plates as much of real comfort in domestic arrangements as could be found anywhere. We took the parties we visited by surprise and there could have been no preparation." The Bohras do not charge interest on loans, and they combine to support indigent members of the community, never allowing one of their caste to beg. The caste may easily be known from other Muhammadans by their small, tightly wound turbans and little skull-caps, and their long flowing robes, and loose trousers widening from the ankle upwards and gathered in at the waist with a string. The women dress in a coloured cotton or silk petticoat, a short-sleeved bodice and a coloured cotton head-scarf. When they go out of doors they throw a dark cloak over the head which covers the body to the ankles, with gauze openings for the eyes.

[1] Crooke's edition of *Hobson-Jobson*, art. Bohra.
[2] Moor's *Hindu Infanticide*, p. 168.
[3] *Memoir of Central India*, ii. p. 111.

BRĀHMAN [1]

LIST OF PARAGRAPHS

LIST OF SUBORDINATE ARTICLES ON SUBCASTES

Brāhman, Bāman.—The well-known priestly caste of India and the first of the four traditional castes of the Hindu scriptures. In 1911 the Brāhmans numbered about 450,000 persons in the Central Provinces and Berār, or

1. Origin and development of the caste.

[1] This article is mainly compiled from a full and excellent account of the caste by Mr. Gopal Datta Joshi, Civil Judge, Saugor, C.P., to whom the writer is much indebted. Extracts have also been taken from Mr. W. Crooke's and Sir H. Risley's articles on the caste in their works on the *Tribes and Castes* of the United Provinces and Bengal respectively; from Mr. J. N. Bhattachārya's *Hindu Castes and Sects* (Thacker, Spink & Co., Calcutta, 1896), and from the Rev. W. Ward's *View of the History*, *Literature and Religion of the Hindus* (London, 1817).

nearly 3 per cent of the population. This is less than the average strength for India as a whole, which is about $4\frac{1}{2}$ per cent. The caste is spread over the whole Province, but is in greatest numbers in proportion to the population in Saugor and Jubbulpore, and weakest in the Feudatory States.

The name Brāhman or Brahma is said to be from the root *brih* or *vrih*, to increase. The god Brahma is considered as the spirit and soul of the universe, the divine essence and source of all being. Brāhmana, the masculine numerative singular, originally denoted one who prays, a worshipper or the composer or reciter of a hymn.[1] It is the common term used in the Vedas for the officiating priest. Sir H. Risley remarks on the origin of the caste:[2] " The best modern opinion seems disposed to find the germ of the Brāhman caste in the bards, ministers and family priests who were attached to the king's household in Vedic times. Different stages of this institution may be observed. In the earliest ages the head of every Aryan household was his own priest, and even a king would himself perform the sacrifices which were appropriate to his rank. By degrees families or guilds of priestly singers arose, who sought service under the kings, and were rewarded by rich presents for the hymns or praise and prayer recited and sacrifices offered by them on behalf of their masters. As time went on the sacrifices became more numerous and more elaborate, and the mass of ritual grew to such an extent that the king could no longer cope with it unaided. The employment of *purohits* or family priests, formerly optional, now became a sacred duty if the sacrifices were not to fall into disuse. The Brāhman obtained a monopoly of priestly functions, and a race of sacerdotal specialists arose which tended continually to close its ranks against the intrusion of outsiders." Gradually then from the household priests and those who made it their business to commit to memory and recite the sacred hymns and verses handed down orally from generation to generation through this agency, an

[1] Crooke's *Tribes and Castes*, art. Brāhman, quoting Professor Eggeling in *Encyclopædia Britannica*, s.v. Brāhmanism.

[2] *Tribes and Castes of Bengal*, art. Brāhman.

occupational caste emerged, which arrogated to itself the monopoly of these functions, and the doctrine developed that nobody could perform them who was not qualified by birth, that is, nobody could be a Brāhman who was not the son of a Brāhman. When religious ritual became more important, as apparently it did, a desire would naturally arise among the priests to make their revered and lucrative profession a hereditary monopoly ; and this they were easily and naturally able to do by only teaching the sacred songs and the sacrificial rules and procedure to their own descendants. The process indeed would be to a considerable extent automatic, because the priests would always take their own sons for their pupils in the first place, and in the circumstances of early Indian society a married priesthood would thus naturally evolve into a hereditary caste. The Levites among the Jews and the priests of the Pārsis formed similar hereditary orders, and the reason why they did not arise in other great religions would appear to have been the prescription or encouragement of the rule of celibacy for the clergy and the foundation of monasteries, to which admission was free. But the military landed aristocracies of Europe practically formed hereditary castes which were analogous to the Brāhman and Rājpūt castes, though of a less stereotyped and primitive character. The rise of the Brāhman caste was thus perhaps a comparatively simple and natural product of religious and social evolution, and might have occurred independently of the development of the caste system as a whole. The former might be accounted for by reasons which would be inadequate to explain the latter, even though as a matter of fact the same factors were at work in both cases.

The hereditary monopoly of the sacred scriptures would be strengthened and made absolute when the Sanskrit language, in which they had been composed and handed down, ceased to be the ordinary spoken language of the people. Nobody then could learn them unless he was taught by a Brāhman priest. And by keeping the sacred literature in an unknown language the priesthood made their own position absolutely secure and got into their own hands the allocation of the penalties and rewards promised

2. Their monopoly of literature.

by religion, for which these books were the authority, that is to say, the disposal of the souls of Hindus in the after-life. They, in fact, held the keys of heaven and hell. The jealousy with which they guarded them is well shown by the Abbé Dubois :[1] "To the Brāhmans alone belongs the right of reading the Vedas, and they are so jealous of this, or rather it is so much to their interest to prevent other castes obtaining any insight into their contents, that the Brāhmans have inculcated the absurd theory, which is implicitly believed, that should anybody of any other caste be so highly imprudent as even to read the title-page his head would immediately split in two. The very few Brāhmans who are able to read those sacred books in the original, only do so in secret and in a whisper. Expulsion from caste, without the smallest hope of re-entering it, would be the lightest punishment of a Brāhman who exposed those books to the eyes of the profane." It would probably be unfair, however, to suppose that the Vedas were kept in the original Sanskrit simply from motives of policy. It was probably thought that the actual words of the sacred text had themselves a concrete force and potency which would be lost in a translation. This is the idea underlying the whole class of beliefs in the virtue of charms and spells.

But the Brāhmans had the monopoly not only of the sacred Sanskrit literature, but practically of any kind of literacy or education. They were for long the only literate section of the people. Subsequently two other castes learnt to read and write in response to an economic demand, the Kāyasths and the Banias. The Kāyasths, it has been suggested in the article on that caste, were to a large extent the offspring and inmates of the households of Brāhmans, and were no doubt taught by them, but only to read and write the vernacular for the purpose of keeping the village records and accounts of rent. They were excluded from any knowledge of Sanskrit, and the Kāyasths subsequently became an educated caste in spite of their Brāhman pre-ceptors, by learning Persian under their Muhammadan, and English under their European employers. The Banias never desired nor were encouraged to attain to any higher

[1] *Hindu Manners, Customs, and Ceremonies*, 3rd ed. p. 172.

degree of literacy than that necessary for keeping accounts of sale and loan transactions. The Brāhmans thus remained the only class with any real education, and acquired a monopoly not only of intellectual and religious leadership, but largely of public administration under the Hindu kings. No literature existed outside their own, which was mainly of a sacerdotal character; and India had no heritage such as that bequeathed by Greece and Rome to mediaeval Europe which could produce a Renaissance or revival of literacy, leading to the Reformation of religion and the breaking of the fetters in which the Roman priesthood had bound the human mind. The Brāhmans thus established, not only a complete religious, but also a social ascendancy which is only now beginning to break down since the British Government has made education available to all.

The Brāhman body, however, lacked one very important element of strength. They were apparently never organised nor controlled by any central authority such as that which made the Roman church so powerful and cohesive. Colleges and seats of learning existed at Benāres and other places, at which their youth were trained in the knowledge of religion and of the measure of their own pretensions, and the means by which these were to be sustained. But probably only a small minority can have attended them, and even these when they returned home must have been left practically to themselves, spread as the Brāhmans were over the whole of India with no means of postal communication or rapid transit. And by this fact the chaotic character of the Hindu religion, its freedom of belief and worship, its innumerable deities, and the almost complete absence of dogmas may probably be to a great extent explained. And further the Brāhman caste itself cannot have been so strictly organised that outsiders and the priests of the lower alien religions never obtained entrance to it. As shown by Mr. Crooke, many foreign elements, both individuals and groups, have at various times been admitted into the caste.

3. Absence of central authority.

The early texts indicate that Brāhmans were in the habit of forming connections with the widows of Rājanyas and Vaishyas, even if they did not take possession of the

4. Mixed elements in the caste.

wives of such men while they were still alive.[1]   The sons
of Angiras, one of the great ancestral sages, were Brāhmans
as well as Kshatriyas.   The descendants of Garga, another
well-known eponymous ancestor, were Kshatriyas by birth
but became Brāhmans.   Visvāmitra was a Kshatriya, who,
by the force of his austerities, compelled Brahma to admit
him into the Brāhmanical order, so that he might be on a
level with Vasishtha with whom he had quarrelled.   According to a passage in the Mahābhārata all castes become
Brāhmans when once they have crossed the Gomti on a
pilgrimage to the hermitage of Vasishtha.[2]   In more recent
times there are legends of persons created Brāhmans by
Hindu Rājas.   Sir J. Malcolm in Central India found many
low-caste female slaves in Brāhman houses, the owners of
which had treated them as belonging to their own caste.[3]

It would appear also that in some cases the caste priests of
different castes have become Brāhmans.   Thus the Sāraswat
Brāhmans of the Punjab are the priests of the Khatri caste.
They have the same complicated arrangement of exogamy
and hypergamy as the Khatris, and will take food from
that caste.   It seems not improbable that they are really
descendants of Khatri priests who have become Brāhmans.[4]

Similarly such groups as the Oswāl, Srimāl and Palliwāl
Brāhmans of Rājputāna, who are priests of the subcastes of
Banias of the same name, may originally have been caste
priests and become Brāhmans.   The Nāramdeo Brāhmans,
or those living on the Nerbudda River, are said to be
descendants of a Brāhman father by a woman of the Naoda
or Dhīmar caste ; and the Golapūrab Brāhmans similarly of
a Brāhman father and Ahīr mother.   In many cases, such
as the island of Onkar Mandhāta in the Nerbudda in Nimār,
and the Mahādeo caves at Pachmarhi, the places of worship
of the non-Aryan tribes have been adopted by Hinduism
and the old mountain or river gods transformed into Hindu
deities.   At the same time it is not improbable that the
tribal priests of the old shrines have been admitted into the
Brāhman caste.

---

[1] Muir, *Ancient Sanskrit Texts*, i.
282 *sq.*

[2] Quoted in Mr. Crooke's *Tribes
and Castes*, art. Brāhman.

[3] Quoted by Mr. Crooke.

[4] *Tribes and Castes of the Punjāb*,
by Mr. H. A. Rose, vol. ii. p. 123.

The Brāhman caste has ten main territorial divisions, forming two groups, the Pānch-Gaur or five northern, and the Pānch-Drāvida or five southern. The boundary line between the two groups is supposed to be the Nerbudda River, which is also the boundary between Hindustān and the Deccan. But the Gujarāti Brāhmans belong to the southern group, though Gujarāt is north of the Nerbudda. The five northern divisions are :

5. Caste subdivisions.

(*a*) *Sāraswat.*—These belong to the Punjab and are named after the Sāraswati river of the classical period, on whose banks they are supposed to have lived.

(*b*) *Gaur.*—The home of these is the country round Delhi, but they say that the name is from the old Gaur or Lakhnauti kingdom of Bengal. If this is correct, it is difficult to understand how they came from Bengal to Delhi contrary to the usual tendency of migration. General Cunningham has suggested that Gaura was also the name of the modern Gonda District, and it is possible that the term was once used for a considerable tract in northern India as well as Bengal, since it has come to be applied to all the northern Brāhmans.[1]

(*c*) *Kānkubja or Kanaujia.*—These are named after the old town of Kanauj on the Ganges near Cawnpore, once the capital of India. The Kanaujia are the most important of the northern groups and extend from the west of Oudh to beyond Benāres and into the northern Districts of the Central Provinces. Here they are subdivided into four principal groups—the Kanaujia, Jijhotia, Sarwaria and Sanādhya, which are treated in annexed subordinate articles.

(*d*) *Maithil.*—They take their name from Mithila, the old term for Bihār or Tirhūt, and belong to this tract.

(*e*) *Utkal.*—These are the Brāhmans of Orissa.

The five groups of the Pānch-Drāvida are as follows :

(*a*) *Maharāshtra.*—These belong to the Marātha country or Bombay. They are subdivided into three main territorial groups—the Deshasth, or those of the home country, that is the Poona tract above the Western Ghāts ; the Konkonasth, who belong to the Bombay Konkan or littoral ;

---

[1] See also article Rājpūt-Gaur.

and the Karhāra, named after a place in the Satāra District.[1]

(*b*) *Tailanga or Andhra.*—The Brāhmans of the Telugu country, Hyderābād and the northern part of Madras. This territory was known as Andhra and governed by an important dynasty of the same name in early times.

(*c*) *Drāvida.*—The Brāhmans of the Tamil country or the south of Madras.

(*d*) *Karnāta.*—The Brāhmans of the Carnatic, or the Canarese country. The Canarese area comprises the Mysore State, and the British Districts of Canara, Dharwar and Belgaum.

(*e*) *Gurjara.*—The Brāhmans of Gujarāt, of whom two subcastes are found in the Central Provinces. The first consists of the Khedāwāls, named after Kheda, a village in Gujarāt, who are a strictly orthodox class holding a good position in the caste. And the second are the Nāgar Brāhmans, who have been long settled in Nimār and the adjacent tracts, and act as village priests and astrologers. Their social status is somewhat lower.

There are, however, a large number of other subcastes, and the tendency to fissure in a large caste, and to the formation of small local groups which marry among themselves, is nowhere more strikingly apparent than among the Brāhmans. This is only natural, as they, more than any other caste, attach importance to strict ceremonial observance in matters of food and the daily ritual of prayer, and any group which was suspected of backsliding in respect of these on emigration to a new locality would be debarred from intermarriage with the parent caste at home. An instance of this is found among the Chhattīsgarhi Brāhmans, who have been long settled in this backward tract and cut off from communication with northern India. They are mainly of the Kanaujia division, but the Kanaujias of Oudh will neither take food nor intermarry with them, and they now constitute a separate subcaste of Kanaujias. Similarly the Mālwi Brāhmans, whose home is in Mālwa, whence they have spread to Hoshangābād and Betul, are believed to have been originally a branch of the Gaur or Kanaujia,

---

[1] See subordinate articles.

but have now become a distinct subcaste, and have adopted
many of the customs of Marātha Brāhmans.   Mandla
contains a colony of Sarwaria[1] Brāhmans who received
grants of villages from the Gond kings and have settled
down there.   They are now cultivators, and some have
taken to the plough, while they also permit widow-remarriage
in all but the name.   They are naturally cut off from
intercourse with the orthodox Sarwarias and marry among
themselves.   The Harenia Brāhmans of Saugor are believed
to have immigrated from Hariāna some generations ago and
form a separate local group ; and also the Laheria Brāhmans
of the same District, who, like the Mandla Sarwarias, permit
widows to marry.   In Hoshangābād there is a small subcaste of Bawīsa or ' Twenty-two ' Brāhmans, descended from
twenty-two families from northern India, who settled here
and have since married among themselves.   A similar diversity
of subcastes is found in other Provinces.   The Brāhmans
of Bengal are also mainly of the Kanaujia division, but they
are divided into several local subcastes, of which the principal
are Rārhi and Barendra, named after tracts in Bengal, and
quite distinct from the subdivisions of the Kanaujia group in
the Central Provinces.

Another class of local subdivisions consists of those 6. Miscel-
Brāhmans who live on the banks of the various sacred rivers laneous
or at famous shrines, and earn their livelihood by conducting groups.
pilgrims through the series of ceremonies and acts of worship which are performed on a visit to such places ; they
receive presents from the pilgrims and the offerings made
at the shrines.   The most prominent among these are the
Gayawāls of Gaya, the Prayāgwāls of Allahābād (Prayāg), the
Chaubes of Mathura, the Gangapūtras (Sons of the Ganges)
of Benāres, the Pandarāms of southern India and the
Nāramdeo Brāhmans who hold charge of the many temples
on the Nerbudda.   As such men accept gifts from pilgrims
they are generally looked down on by good Brāhmans and
marry among themselves.   Many of them have a character
for extortion and for fleecing their clients, a propensity
commonly developed in a profession of this kind.   Such a
reputation particularly attaches to the Chaubes of Mathura

[1] A section of the Kanaujia.   See above.

and Brindāban, the holy places of the god Krishna. They
are strong and finely built men, but gluttonous, idle and
dissolute. Some of the Benāres Brāhmans are known as
Sawalākhi, or having one and a quarter lakhs, apparently
on account of the wealth they amass from pilgrims. A
much lower group are the Mahā-Brāhmans (great Brāhmans), who are also known as Patīt (degraded) or Katia.
These accept the gifts offered by the relatives after a death
for the use of the dead man in the next world during
the period of mourning; they also eat food which it is
supposed will benefit the dead man, and are considered to
represent him. Probably on this account they share in the
impurity attaching to the dead, and are despised by all
castes and sometimes not permitted to live in the village.
Other Brāhmans are degraded on account of their having
partly adopted Muhammadan practices. The Husaini
Brāhmans of western India are so called as they combine
Muhammadan with Hindu rites. They are principally
beggars. And the Kalanki Brāhmans of Wardha and other
Districts are looked down upon because, it is said, that at
the bidding of a Muhammadan governor they make a figure
of a cow from sugar and eat it up. Probably they may have
really acted as priests to Muhammadans who were inclined
to adopt certain Hindu rites on the principle of imitation,
and with a view to please their disciples conformed to some
extent to Islām.

7. Sect-
arian divi-
sions.　　　Brāhmans have also sectarian divisions according to the
different Vedas, which they especially study. It is held
that the ancient Rishis or saints, like the Jewish patriarchs,
lived far beyond the ordinary span of existence, and hence
had time to learn all the Vedas and their commentaries.
But this was impossible for their shorter-lived descendants,
and hence each Veda has been divided into a number of
Shākhas or branches, and the ordinary Brāhman only learns
one Shākha of one Veda. Most Brāhmans of the Central
Provinces are either Rigvedis or Yajurvedis, and these
commonly marry only followers of their own Veda, thus
forming a sort of cross set of endogamous divisions. The
restriction on marriage may also extend to the Shākha, so
that a man can only marry in a family of the same Shākha

as himself.   This applies in the Central Provinces mainly
to the Yajurvedis, who have three well-known Shākhas or
branches called Kānnava, Apastambha and Mādhyandina.
These are derived from the Shukla or White Yajurveda,
which can be understood, while the Black Yajurveda is
obscure and unintelligible.   The Rigvedis and Yajurvedis
have some differences in their methods of recitation.   The
Rigvedis are said to move the head up and down when they
recite and not to use the hands; while the Yajurvedis swing
the hands and body from side to side.   It is said that a
Mādhyandina cannot say his prayers nor take his food
before midday, and hence the name, which means half the
day.   These points of distinction are given as stated by the
local Brāhmans, and it is not known whether they would be
endorsed by the Pandits.   The Marātha Brāhmans of the
Central Provinces are usually Rigvedis and the Kanaujia
Brāhmans Yajurvedis.   Followers of the other two Vedas
are practically not found.   Among Kanaujia Brāhmans it is
also customary to ask the head of a family with which a
marriage is proposed whether he ties a knot in the right or
left half of his Shikha or scalp-lock during his prayers and
whether he washes his right or left foot first in the performance of a religious ceremony.

The exogamous arrangements of the Brāhmans are also   8. Exo-
very complex.   It is said that the Brāhmans are descended   gamy.
from the seven sons of the god Brahma, who were Bhrigu,
Angirasa, Marichi, Atri, Pulaha, Pulastya and Vasishtha.
But Pulaha only begot demons and Pulastya giants, while
Vasishtha died and was born again as a descendant of
Marichi.   Consequently the four ancestors of the Brāhmans
were Bhrigu, Angirasa, Marichi and Atri.   But according
to another account the ancestors of the Brāhmans were the
seven Rishis or saints who form the constellation of the
Great Bear.   These were Jamadagni, Bhāradwāj, Gautam,
Kashyap, Vasishtha, Agastya, Atri and Visvāmitra, who
makes the eighth and is held to be descended from Atri.
These latter saints are also said to be the descendants of
the four original ones, Atri appearing in both lists.   But the
two lists taken together make up eleven great saints, who
were the eponymous ancestors of the Brāhmans.   All the

different subcastes have as a rule exogamous classes tracing their descent from these saints. But each group, such as that of Bhrigu or Angirasa, contains a large number of exogamous sections usually named after other more recent saints, and intermarriage is sometimes prohibited among the different sections, which are descended from the same son of Brahma or star of the Great Bear. The arrangement thus bears a certain resemblance to the classification system of exogamy found among primitive races, only that the number of groups is now fairly large ; but it is said that originally there were only four, from the four sons of Brahma who gave birth to Brâhmans. The names of other important saints, after whom exogamous sections are most commonly called, are Garg, Sandilya, Kaushik, Vatsya and Bhârgava. These five appear sometimes to be held as original ancestors in addition to the eleven already mentioned. It may be noted that some of the above names of saints have a totemistic character ; for instance, Bhâradwâj means a lark ; Kashyap resembles Kachhap, the name for a tortoise ; Kaushik may come from the *kusha* grass ; Agastya from the *agasti* flower, and so on. Within the main group exogamy sometimes also goes by titles or family names. Thus the principal titles of the Kanaujias are: Pânde, a wise man ; Dube, learned in two Vedas ; Tiwâri, learned in three Vedas ; Chaube, learned in four Vedas ; Sukul, white or pure ; Upâdhya, a teacher ; Agnihotri, the priest who performs the fire-sacrifice ; Dikshit, the initiator, and so on. Marriage between persons bearing the same family name tends to be prohibited, as they are considered to be relations.

9. Restrictions on marriage.
The prohibition of marriage within the *gotra* or exogamous section bars the union of persons related solely through males. In addition to this, according to Hindu law a Brâhman must not marry a girl of his mother's or maternal grandfather's *gotra*, or one who is a *sapinda* of his father or maternal grandfather. Mr. Joshi states that *sapindas* are persons related through being particles of the same body. It is also understood that two persons are said to be *sapindas* when they can offer *pindas* or funeral cakes to the same ancestor. The rule barring the marriage of *sapindas* is that two persons cannot marry if they are

both as near as fourth in descent from a common ancestor, and the relationship is derived through the father of either party. If either is more remote than fourth in descent they apparently could marry. If the relationship of the couple is through their mothers in each case, then they cannot marry if they are third in descent from the same ancestor, but may do so in the fourth or subsequent generations. It is of no importance whether the intervening links between the common ancestor and the proposed couple are male or female ; descent is considered to be male if through the father, and female if through the mother. In practice, marriages are held to be valid between persons fourth in descent from a common ancestor in the case of male relationship, and third in the case of female relationship, that is, persons having a common greatgrandparent in the male line or a common grandparent in the female line can marry.

Other rules are that girls must not be exchanged in marriage between two families, and a man may not marry two sisters, though he can marry his deceased wife's sister. The bride should be both younger in age and shorter in stature than the bridegroom. A younger sister should not be married while her elder sister is single.

The practice of hypergamy is, or was until recently, 10. Hypergamy. common among Brāhmans. This is the rule by which the social estimation of a family is raised if its girls are married into a class of higher social status than its own. Members of the superior classes will take daughters from the lower classes on payment usually of a substantial bride-price, but will not give their daughters to them. According to Manu, men of the higher castes were allowed to take wives from the lower ones but not to give daughters to them. The origin of the custom is obscure. If caste was based on distinctions of race, then apparently the practice of hypergamy would be objectionable, because it would destroy the different racial classes. If, on the other hand, the castes consisted of groups of varying social status, the distinction being that those of the lower ones could not participate in the sacramental or communal meals of the higher ones, then the marriage of a daughter into a higher group, which would carry with it participation at the sacramental marriage feast of this group, might well be a coveted distinction. The custom of hypergamy prevails somewhat largely in northern India between different subcastes, groups of different social status in the same subcaste, and occasionally even between different castes. The social results of hypergamy, when commonly practised, are highly injurious. Men of the higher subcastes get paid for marrying several wives, and indulge in polygamy, while the girls of the higher subcastes and the boys of the lower ones find it difficult and sometimes even impossible to obtain husbands and wives. The custom attained its most absurd development among the Kulin Brāhmans of eastern Bengal, as described by Sir H. Risley.[1] Here the Brāhmans were divided by a Hindu king, Ballāl Sen, into two classes, the Kulin (of good family), who had observed the entire nine counsels of perfection ; and the Srotriya, who, though regular students of the Vedas, had lost sanctity by intermarrying with families of inferior birth. The latter were further sub-divided into three classes according to their degree of social purity, and each higher class could take daughters from the next one or two lower ones. The doctrine known as Kula-gotra was developed, whereby the reputation of a family depended on the character of the marriages made by its female members. In describing the results of the system Sir H. Risley states : " The rush of competition for Kulin husbands on the part of the inferior classes became acute. In order to dispose of the surplus of women in the higher groups polygamy was resorted to on a very large scale : it was popular with the Kulins because it enabled them to make a handsome income by the accident of their birth ; and it was accepted by the parents of the girls concerned as offering the only means of complying with the requirements of the Hindu religion. Tempted by a *pān* or premium, which often reached the sum of two thousand rupees, Swābhava Kulins made light of their *kul* and its obligations, and married girls, whom they left after the ceremony to be taken care of by their parents. Matrimony became a sort of profession, and the honour of marrying a girl to a Kulin is said to have been so highly valued in

[1] *Tribes and Castes*, art. Brāhman.

eastern Bengal that as soon as a boy was ten years old his friends began to discuss his matrimonial prospects, and before he was twenty he had become the husband of many wives of ages varying from five to fifty." The wives were commonly left at home to be supported by their parents, and it is said that when a Kulin Brāhman had a journey to make he usually tried to put up for the night at the house of one of his fathers-in-law. All the marriages were recorded in the registers of the professional Ghātaks or marriage-brokers, and each party was supplied with an extract. On arrival at his father-in-law's house the Kulin would produce his extract showing the date on which his marriage took place ; and the owner of the house, who was often unfamiliar with the bridegroom's identity, would compare it with his own extract. When they agreed he was taken in and put up for the night, and enjoyed the society of his wife. The system thus entailed the greatest misery to large numbers of women, both those who were married to husbands whom they scarcely ever saw, and those of the higher classes who got no husbands at all. It is now rapidly falling into abeyance. Hypergamy is found in the Central Provinces among the subcastes of Kanaujia Brāhmans. The Sarwaria subcaste, which is the highest, takes daughters from Kanaujias and Jijhotias, and the Kanaujias take them from the Jijhotias. These and other subcastes such as the Khedāwāls are also often divided into two groups of different status, the higher of which takes daughters from the lower. Usually the parents of the girl pay a liberal bridegroom-price in money or ornaments. It has never, however, been carried to the same length here as in Bengal, and two, or in some cases three, wives are the limit for a man of the higher classes. One division of Kanaujias is called the Sātkul or seven families, and is the highest. Other Kanaujias, who are known as Pachhādar, pay substantial sums for husbands for this group, and it is reported that if such a marriage takes place and the bridegroom-price is not paid up, the husband will turn his wife out and send her home to her father. Certain subcastes of Sunārs also have hypergamy and, as between different castes, it exists between the Dāngis and Rājpūts, pure Rājpūts being held willing to take daughters in marriage from the highest clans of Dāngis.

11. Mar-
riage
customs.
A text of Manu prescribes : [1] "If a young woman marry while she is pregnant, whether her pregnancy be known or unknown, the male child in her womb belongs to the bridegroom and is called a son received with his bride." But at present a Brāhman girl who is known to be pregnant will be wholly debarred from the sacrament of marriage. An invitation to a wedding is sent by means of grains of rice coloured yellow with turmeric and placed in a brass bowl with areca-nuts over them. All the members of the caste or subcaste who eat food with the host and are resident in the same town or close at hand are as a rule invited, and all relatives of the family who reside at a distance. The head of the family goes himself to the residence of the guests and invites them with expressions of humility to honour his home. Before the wedding the ancestors of the family and also the divine mothers are worshipped, these latter consisting of the consorts of the principal gods. In front of the wedding procession are carried *kalashas* or earthen jars filled to the brim with water, and with green shoots and branches floating on the top. The *kalasha* is said to represent the universe and to contain the principal gods and divine mothers, while the waters in it are the seven seas. All these are witnesses to the wedding. Among other ceremonies, presents of fruit, food, ornaments and jewellery are exchanged between the parties, and these are called *choli-ka-bharāna* or filling the bride's breast-cloth. The original object of giving these presents was thus, it would appear from the name, to render the bride fertile. The father then gives his daughter away in a set form of speech. After reciting the exact moment of time, the hour, the day, the minute according to solar and lunar reckoning, the year and the epoch, he proceeds : " In the name of Vishnu (repeating the name three times), the supreme spirit, father and creator of the universe, and in furtherance of his wish for the propagation of the human species, I (specifying his full name and section, etc.), in the company of my married wife, do hereby offer the hand of my daughter—may she live

[1] Chap. ix. v. 173.

long—full of all virtuous qualities, image of Lakshmi, wife of Vishnu, anxious of union in lawful wedlock, ornamented and dressed, brought up and instructed according to the best of my means, by name (naming her and repeating the full description of ancestors, class, etc.) in the solemn presence of the Brāhmans, Gurus, fire and deities, to you—may you live long—(repeating the bridegroom's name and full description), anxious to obtain a wife with a view to secure the abode of bliss and eternal happiness in the heaven of Brahma. Accept her with *kusha* grass, grains of rice, water and presents of money." Afterwards the father asks the bridegroom never to disregard the feelings and sentiments of his wife in matters of religion, social pleasures and the acquisition of money, and the bridegroom agrees. The binding portion of the ceremony consists in walking seven times round the sacred post, and when the seventh round is completed the marriage is irrevocable. Among the Marātha Brāhmans the bridegroom is called Nawar Deo or the new god. During the five days of the wedding he is considered to be a sort of king, and is put in the highest place, and everybody defers to him. They make the bridegroom and bride name each other for a joke, as they are ashamed to do this, and will not untie their clothes to let them bathe until they have done it. At all the feasts the bride and bridegroom are made to eat out of the same plate, and they put pieces of food in each other's mouth, which is supposed to produce affection between them. The wedding expenses in an ordinary Kanaujia Brāhman's family, whose income is perhaps Rs. 20 to 40 a month, are estimated at Rs. 200 for the bridegroom's party and Rs. 175 for the bride's, exclusive of any bride- or bridegroom-price. The bulk of the expenditure is on feasts to the caste. The bride does not live with her husband until after she arrives at puberty, but it is thought desirable that she should spend long visits with his family before this, in order that she may assimilate their customs and be trained by her mother-in-law, according to the saying, 'Tender branches are easily bent.' Among some Marātha Brāhmans, when the bride arrives at puberty a ceremony called Garhbhadān is performed, and the husband confesses whether he has cohabited with his wife before her puberty, and if so, he is fined a small sum.   Such instances usually occur when the signs of puberty are delayed.   If the planet Mangal or Mars is adverse to a girl in her horoscope, it is thought that her husband will die. The women of her family will, therefore, first marry her secretly to a pīpal-tree, so that the tree may die instead. But they do not tell this to the bridegroom.   In Saugor, girls whose horoscope is unfavourable to the husband are first married to the *arka* or swallow-wort plant.   If a Brāhman has not sufficient funds to arrange for the marriage of his daughter he will go about and beg, and it is considered that alms given for this purpose acquire special merit for the donor, nor will any good Brāhman refuse a contribution according to his means.

12. Polygamy, divorce and treatment of widows. Polygamy conveys no stigma among Brāhmans, but is uncommon.   Divorce is not recognised, a woman who is put away by her husband being turned out of the caste.   The remarriage of widows is strictly prohibited.   It is said that marriage is the only sacrament (Sanskār) for a woman, and she can only go through it once.   The holy nuptial texts may not be repeated except for a virgin.   The prohibition of the remarriage of widows has become a most firmly rooted prejudice among the higher classes of Hindus, and is the last to give way before the inroads of liberal reform.   Only a small minority of the most advanced Brāhmans have recognised widow-remarriage, and these are generally held to be excluded from the caste, though breaches of the rules against the consumption of prohibited kinds of meat, and the drinking of aerated waters and even alcoholic liquor, are now winked at and not visited with the proper penalty. Nevertheless, many classes of Brāhmans, who live in the country and have taken to cultivation, allow widows to live with men without putting the family out of caste.   Where this is not permitted, surreptitious intercourse may occasionally take place with members of the family.   The treatment of widows is also becoming more humane.   Only Marātha and Khedawāl Brāhmans in the Central Provinces still force them to shave their heads, and these will permit a child-widow to retain her hair until she grows up, though they regard her as impure while she has it.   A widow is usually

forbidden to have a cot or bed, and must sleep on the
ground or on a plank. She may not chew betel-leaves,
should eat only once a day, and must rigorously observe all
the prescribed fasts. She wears white clothes only, no glass
bangles, and no ornaments on her feet. She is subject to
other restrictions and is a general drudge in the family. It
is probable that the original reason for such treatment of a
widow was that she was considered impure through being
perpetually haunted by her husband's ghost. Hindus say
that a widow is half-dead. She should not be allowed to
cook the household food, because while cooking it she will
remember her husband and the food will become like a
corpse. The smell of such food will offend the gods, and it
cannot be offered to them. A widow is not permitted to
worship the household god or the ancestors of the family.
It was no doubt an advantage under the joint family system
that a widow should not claim any life-interest in her
husband's property. The modern tendency of widows, who
are left in possession, to try and alienate the property from
the husband's relatives has been a fruitful cause of litigation
and the ruin of many old landed families. The severe
treatment of widows was further calculated to suppress any
tendency on the part of wives to poison their husbands.
These secondary grounds may have contributed something
to the preservation and enforcement of an idea based originally on superstitious motives.

For a widow to remain single and lead an austere and 13. *Sati* or
joyless life was held to confer great honour on her family ; burning of widows.
and this was enormously enhanced when she decided to
become *sati* and die with her husband on the funeral pyre.
Though it is doubtful whether this practice is advocated by
the Vedas, subsequent Hindu scriptures insist strongly on it.
It was said that a widow who was burnt with her husband
would enjoy as many years in paradise as there are hairs on
the human head, that is to say, thirty-five million. Con-
versely, one who insisted on surviving him would in her
next birth go into the body of some animal. By the act of
sati she purified all her husband's ancestors, even from the
guilt of killing a Brāhman, and also those of her own family.
If a man died during an absence from home in another

country his wife was recommended to take his slippers or any other article of dress and burn herself with them tied to her breast.[1]

Great honour was paid to a Sati, and a temple or memorial stone was always erected to her at which her spirit was venerated, and this encouraged many pious women not only to resign themselves to this terrible death but ardently to desire it. The following account given by Mr. Ward of the method of a *sati* immolation in Bengal may be reproduced : [2]

"When the husband's life is despaired of and he is carried to the bank of the Ganges, the wife declares her resolution to be burnt with him. In this case she is treated with great respect by her neighbours, who bring her delicate food, and when her husband is dead she again declares her resolve to be burnt with his body. Having broken a small branch from a mango tree she takes it with her and proceeds to the body, where she sits down. The barber then paints the sides of her feet red, after which she bathes and puts on new clothes. During these preparations the drum beats a certain sound by which it is known that a widow is about to be burnt with the corpse of her husband. A hole is dug in the ground round which posts are driven into the earth, and thick green stakes laid across to form a kind of bed ; and upon these are laid in abundance dry faggots, hemp, clarified butter and pitch. The officiating Brāhman now causes the widow to repeat the prayer that as long as fourteen Indras reign, or as many years as there are hairs on her head, she may abide in heaven with her husband; that during this time the heavenly dancers may wait on her and her husband ; and that by this act of merit all the ancestors of her mother and husband may ascend to heaven. She now presents her ornaments to her friends, ties some red cotton on both wrists, puts two new combs in her hair, paints her forehead, and takes into the end of the cloth that she wears some parched rice and cowries. The dead body is bathed, anointed with butter, and dressed in new clothes. The son takes a handful of boiled rice and offers it in the name of his deceased father. Ropes and another piece of

---

[1] Ward's *Hindus*, vol. ii. p. 97. [2] *Ibidem*, pp. 98, 100.

cloth are spread on the wood, and the dead body is laid upon the pile.   The widow next walks round the pyre seven times, as she did round the marriage-post at her wedding, strewing parched rice and cowries as she goes, which the spectators catch and keep under the belief that they will cure diseases.   The widow then lies down on the fatal pile by the side of the dead body.   The bodies are bound together with ropes and the faggots placed over them.   The son, averting his head, puts fire to the face of his father, and at the same moment several persons light the pile at different sides, when the women and mourners set up cries.   More faggots are hastily brought and thrown over the pile, and two bamboo levers are pressed over them to hold down the bodies and the pile.   Several persons are employed in holding down these levers.   More clarified butter, pitch and faggots are thrown on to the pile till the bodies are consumed.   This may take about two hours, but I conceive the woman must be dead in a few minutes after the fire has been kindled."

As showing the tenacity with which women sometimes adhered to their resolve to be burned with their husbands, and thus, as they believed, resume their conjugal life in heaven, the following account by Sir William Sleeman, in his *Rambles and Recollections*, of a *sati* at Jubbulpore may be given :

" At Gopālpur on the Nerbudda are some very pretty temples built for the most part to the memory of women who have burned themselves with the remains of their husbands, and on the very spot where the cremation occurred.   Among them was one recently raised over the ashes of one of the most extraordinary old bodies I had ever seen, who burned herself in my presence in 1829.   In March 1828 I had issued a proclamation prohibiting any one from aiding or assisting in *sati*, and distinctly stating that to bring one ounce of wood for the purpose would be considered as so doing.   Subsequently, on Tuesday, 24th November, I had an application from the heads of the most respectable and most extensive family of Brāhmans in the District, to suffer this old woman to burn herself with the remains of her husband, Umeid Singh Upādhya, who had that morning died upon the banks of the Nerbudda.   I threatened to

enforce my order and punish severely any man who assisted ;
and placed a police guard for the purpose of seeing that
no one did so.   The old woman remained by the edge of the
water without eating or drinking.   Next day the body of
her husband was burned in the presence of several thousand
spectators, who had assembled to see the *sati*.   The sons
and grandsons of the old woman remained with her, urging
her to desist from her resolve, while her other relatives
surrounded my house urging me to allow her to burn.   All
the day she remained sitting upon a bare rock in the bed
of the Nerbudda, refusing every kind of sustenance, and
exposed to the intense heat of the sun by day and the severe
cold of the night, with only a thin sheet thrown over her
shoulders.   On the next day, Thursday, to cut off all hope
of her being moved from her purpose, she put on the *dhujja*
or coarse red turban and broke her bracelets in pieces, by
which she became dead in law and for ever excluded from
caste.   Should she choose to live after this she could never
return to her family.   On the morning of Saturday, the
fourth day after the death, I rode out ten miles to the spot,
and found the poor old widow sitting with the *dhujja* round
her head, a brass plate before her with undressed rice and
flowers, and a cocoanut in each hand.   She talked very
collectedly, telling me that she had determined to mix her
ashes with those of her departed husband, and should
patiently await my permission to do so, assured that God
would enable her to sustain life till that was given, though
she dared not eat or drink.   Looking at the sun, then rising
before her over a long and beautiful reach of the Nerbudda,
she said calmly : ' My soul has been for five days with my
husband's near that sun ; nothing but my earthly frame is
left, and this I know you will in time suffer to be mixed
with the ashes of his in yonder pit, because it is not in your
nature wantonly to prolong the miseries of a poor old woman.'
I told her that my object and duty was to save and preserve
her ; I was come to urge her to live and keep her family
from the disgrace of being thought her murderers.   I tried
to work upon her pride and fears.   I told her that the rent-
free lands on which her family had long subsisted might be
resumed by Government if her children permitted her to do

this act; and that no brick or stone should ever mark the place of her death; but if she would live, a splendid habitation should be made for her among the temples, and an allowance given her from the rent-free lands. She smiled, but held out her arm and said, ' My pulse has long ceased to beat, for my spirit has departed, and I have nothing left but a little earth that I wish to mix with the ashes of my husband. I shall suffer nothing in burning, and if you wish proof order some fire, and you shall see this arm consumed without giving me any pain.' I did not attempt to feel her pulse, but some of my people did, and declared that it had ceased to be perceptible. At this time every native present believed that she was incapable of suffering pain, and her end confirmed them in their opinion. Satisfied myself that it would be unavailing to attempt to save her life, I sent for all the principal members of the family, and consented that she should be suffered to burn herself if they would enter into engagements that no other member of their family should ever do the same. This they all agreed to, and the papers having been drawn out in due form about midday, I sent down notice to the old lady, who seemed extremely pleased and thankful. The ceremonies of bathing were gone through before three, while the wood and other combustible materials for a strong fire were collected and put into the pit. After bathing she called for a *pān* (betel-leaf) and ate it, then rose up, and with one arm on the shoulder of her eldest son, and the other on that of her nephew, approached the fire. As she rose up fire was set to the pile, and it was instantly in a blaze. The distance was about one hundred and fifty yards; she came on with a calm and cheerful countenance, stopped once, and casting her eyes upwards said, ' Why have they kept me five days from thee, my husband ? ' On coming to the sentries her supports stopped, she walked round the pit, paused a moment; and while muttering a prayer threw some flowers into the fire. She then walked deliberately and steadily to the brink, stepped into the centre of the flame, sat down, and leaning back in the midst as if reposing upon a couch, was consumed without uttering a shriek or betraying one sign of agony."

In cases, however, where women shrank from the flames

they were frequently forced into them, as it was a terrible disgrace to their families that they should recoil on the scene of the sacrifice. Opium and other drugs were also administered to stupefy the woman and prevent her from feeling pain. Widows were sometimes buried alive with their dead husbands. The practice of *sati* was finally prohibited in 1829, without exciting the least discontent.

14. Funeral rites and mourning.
The bodies of children dying before they are named, or before the tonsure ceremony is performed on them, are buried, and those of other persons are burnt. In the grave of a small child some of its mother's milk, or, if this is not available, cow's milk in a leaf-cup or earthen vessel, is placed. Before a body is burnt cakes of wheat-flour are put on the face, breast and both shoulders, and a coin is always deposited for the purchase of the site. Mourning or impurity is observed for varying periods, according to the nearness of relationship. For a child, relatives other than the parents have only to take a bath to remove the impurity caused by the death. In a small town or village all Brähmans of the same subcaste living in the place are impure from the time of the death until cremation has taken place. After the funeral the chief mourner performs the *shräddh* ceremony, offering *pindas* or cakes of rice, with libations of water, to the dead. Presents are made to Brähmans for the use of the dead man in the other world, and these are sometimes very valuable, as it is thought that the spirit will thereby be profited. Such presents are taken by the Mahä-Brähman, who is much despised. When a late zamïndär of Khariär died, Rs. 2000 were given to the Mahä-Brähman for the use of his soul in the next world. The funeral rites are performed by an ordinary Brähman, known as Malai, who may receive presents after the period of impurity has expired. Formerly a calf was let loose in the name of the deceased after being branded with the mark of a trident to dedicate it to Siva, and allowed to wander free thenceforth. Sometimes it was formally married to three or four female calves, and these latter were presented to Brähmans. Sometimes the calf was brought to stand over the dying man and water poured down its tail into his mouth. The practice of letting loose a male calf is now declining, as these animals

are a great nuisance to the crops, and cultivators put them
in the pound. The calf is therefore also presented to a
Brāhman. It is believed that the *shrāddh* ceremony is
necessary to unite the dead man's spirit with the Pitris or
ancestors, and without this it wanders homeless. Some
think that the ancestors dwell on the under or dark side of
the moon. Those descendants who can offer the *pindas* or
funeral cakes to the same ancestor are called Sapindas or
relatives, and the man who fills the office of chief mourner
thereby becomes the dead man's heir. Persons who have
died a violent death or have been executed are not entitled
to the ordinary funeral oblations, and cannot at once be
united with the ancestors. But one year after the death
an effigy of the deceased person is made in *kusha* grass and
burnt, with all the ordinary funeral rites, and offerings are
made to his spirit as if he had died on this occasion. If
the death was caused by snake-bite a gold snake is made
and presented to a Brāhman before this ceremony is begun.
This is held to be the proper funeral ceremony which unites
his spirit with the ancestors. Formerly in Madras if a man
died during the last five days of the waning of the moon it
was considered very unlucky. In order to escape evil effects
to the relatives a special opening was made in the wall of
the house, through which the body was carried, and the
house itself was afterwards abandoned for three to six
months.[1] A similar superstition prevails in the Central
Provinces about a man dying in the Mul Nakshatra or
lunar asterism, which is perhaps the same or some similar
period. In this case it is thought that the deaths of four other
members of the household are portended, and to avert this four
human figures are made of flour or grass and burnt with the
corpse. According to the Abbé Dubois if a man died on a
Saturday it was thought that another death would occur
in the family, and to avert this a living animal, such as a
ram, goat or fowl, was offered with the corpse.[2]

The religion of the Brāhmans is Hinduism, of which
they are the priests and exponents. Formerly the Brāhman
considered himself as a part of Brahma, and hence a god.

15. Religion.

---

[1] *Hindu Manners, Customs and Ceremonies*, by the Abbé Dubois, 3rd ed. p. 499.
[2] *Ibidem*, p. 500.

This belief has decayed, but the gods are still held to reside in the body ; Siva in the crown of the head, Vishnu in the chest, Brahma in the navel, Indra in the genitals and Ganesh in the rectum. Most Brāhmans belong to a sect worshipping especially Siva or Vishnu, or Rāma and Krishna, the incarnations of the latter god, or Sakti, the female principle of energy of Siva. But as a rule Brāhmans, whether of the Sivite or Vishnuite sects, abstain from flesh meat and are averse to the killing of any living thing. The following account of the daily ritual prayers of a Benāres Brāhman may be reproduced from M. André Chevrillon's *Romantic India*,[1] as, though possibly not altogether accurate in points of detail, it gives an excellent idea of their infinitely complicated nature :

16. Daily ritual.

" Here is the daily life of one of the twenty-five thousand Brāhmans of Benāres. He rises before the dawn, and his first care is to look at an object of good omen. If he sees a crow at his left, a kite, a snake, a cat, a hare, a jackal, an empty jar, a smoking fire, a wood-pile, a widow, a man blind of one eye, he is threatened with great dangers during the day. If he intended to make a journey, he puts it off. But if he sees a cow, a horse, an elephant, a parrot, a lizard, a clear-burning fire, a virgin, all will go well. If he should sneeze once, he may count upon some special good fortune ; but if twice some disaster will happen to him. If he yawns some demon may enter his body. Having avoided all objects of evil omen, the Brāhman drops into the endless routine of his religious rites. Under penalty of rendering all the day's acts worthless, he must wash his teeth at the bank of a sacred stream or lake, reciting a special *mantra*, which ends in this ascription : ' O Ganges, daughter of Vishnu, thou springest from Vishnu's foot, thou art beloved by him ! Remove from us the stains of sin and birth, and until death protect us thy servants ! ' He then rubs his body with ashes, saying : ' Homage to Siva, homage to the source of all birth ! May he protect me during all births ! ' He traces the sacred signs upon his forehead—the three vertical lines representing the foot of Vishnu, or the three ' horizontal lines which symbolise the

[1] London, Heinemann (1897), pp. 84-91.

trident of Siva—and twists into a knot the hair left by the
razor on the top of his head, that no impurity may fall
from it to pollute the sacred river.

" He is now ready to begin the ceremonies of the morning
(*sandhya*), those which I have just observed on the banks
of the river.   Minutely and mechanically each Brāhman
performs by himself these rites of prescribed acts and
gestures.   First the internal ablution : the worshipper takes
water in the hollow of his hand, and, letting it fall from
above into his mouth, cleanses his body and soul.   Meanwhile he mentally invokes the names of Vishnu, saying,
' Glory to Keshava, to Narāyana, to Mādhava, to Govinda,'
and so on.

" The second rite is the exercise or ' discipline ' of the
respiration (*prajayama*).   Here there are three acts : first,
the worshipper compresses the right nostril with the thumb,
and drives the breath through the left ; second, he inhales
through the left nostril, then compresses it, and inhales
through the other ; third, he stops the nose completely with
thumb and forefinger, and holds his breath as long as
possible.   All these acts must be done before sunrise, and
prepare for what is to follow.   Standing on the water's edge,
he utters solemnly the famous syllable OM, pronouncing it
aum, with a length equalling that of three letters.   It recalls
to him the three persons of the Hindu trinity : Brahma,
who creates ; Vishnu, who preserves ; Siva, who destroys.
More noble than any other word, imperishable, says Manu,
it is eternal as Brahma himself.   It is not a sign, but a being,
a force ; a force which constrains the gods, superior to them,
the very essence of all things.   Mysterious operations of the
mind, strange associations of ideas, from which spring
conceptions like these !   Having uttered this ancient and
formidable syllable, the man calls by their names the three
worlds : earth, air, sky ; and the four superior heavens.   He
then turns towards the east, and repeats the verse[1] from the
Rig-Veda : ' Let us meditate upon the resplendent glory of
the divine vivifier, that it may enlighten our minds.'   As he
says the last words he takes water in the palm of his hand
and pours it upon the top of his head.   ' Waters,' he says,

[1] This is the famous Gayatri.

'give me strength and vigour that I may rejoice. Like
loving mothers, bless us, penetrate us with your sacred
essence. We come to wash ourselves from the pollution of
sins : make us fruitful and prosperous.' Then follow other
ablutions, other *mantras*, verses from the Rig-Veda, and this
hymn, which relates the origin of all things : 'From the
burning heat came out all things. Yes, the complete order
of the world ; Night, the throbbing Ocean, and after the
throbbing Ocean, Time, which separates Light from
Darkness. All mortals are its subjects. It is this which
disposes of all things, and has made, one after another, the
sun, the sky, the earth, the intermediate air.' This hymn,
says Manu, thrice repeated, effaces the gravest sins.

" About this time, beyond the sands of the opposite shore
of the Ganges, the sun appears. As soon as its brilliant
disc becomes visible the multitude welcome it, and salute it
with 'the offering of water.' This is thrown into the air,
either from a vase or from the hand. Thrice the worshipper,
standing in the river up to his waist, flings the water towards
the sun. The farther and wider he flings it, the greater the
virtue attributed to this act. Then the Brāhman, seated
upon his heels, fulfils the most sacred of his religious duties :
he meditates upon his fingers. For the fingers are sacred,
inhabited by different manifestations of Vishnu ; the thumb
by Govinda, the index-finger by Mādhava, the middle finger
by Hrikesa, the third by Trivikama and the little finger by
Vishnu himself. 'Homage to the two thumbs,' says the
Brāhman, 'to the two index-fingers, to the two middle
fingers, to the two "unnamed fingers," to the two little fingers,
to the two palms, to the two backs of the hands.' Then he
touches the various parts of the body, and lastly, the right
ear, the most sacred of all, where reside fire, water, the sun
and the moon. He then takes a red bag (*gomukhi*), into
which he plunges his hand, and by contortions of the fingers
rapidly represents the chief incarnations of Vishnu : a fish,
a tortoise, a wild boar, a lion, a slip-knot, a garland.[1]

" The second part of the service is no less rich than the
first in ablutions and *mantras*. The Brāhman invokes the

---

[1] It is not known how a slip-knot
and a garland are connected with any
incarnation of Vishnu. For the incarnations see articles Vaishnava sect.

sun, ' Mitra, who regards all creatures with unchanging
gaze,' and the Dawns, ' brilliant children of the sky,' the
earliest divinities of our Aryan race.   He extols the world
of Brahma, that of Siva, that of Vishnu ; recites passages
from the Mahābhārata, the Purānas, all the first hymn of the
Rig-Veda, the first lines of the second, the first words of the
principal Vedas, of the Yajur, the Sama, and the Atharva,
then fragments of grammar, inspired prosodies, and, in
conclusion, the first words of the book of the Laws of
Yajnavalkya, the philosophic Sutras : and finally ends the
ceremony with three kinds of ablutions, which are called the
refreshing of the gods, of the sages and of the ancestors.

" First, placing his sacred cord upon the left shoulder, the
Brāhman takes up water in the right hand, and lets it run
off his extended fingers.   To refresh the sages, the cord
must hang about the neck, and the water run over the side
of the hand between the thumb and the forefinger, which is
bent back.   For the ancestors, the cord passes over the
right shoulder, and the water falls from the hand in the
same way as for the sages.   ' Let the fathers be refreshed,'
says the prayer, ' may this water serve all those who inhabit
the seven worlds, as far as to Brahma's dwelling, even
though their number be greater than thousands of millions
of families.   May this water, consecrated by my cord, be
accepted by the men of my race who have left no sons.'

" With this prayer the morning service ends.   Now,
remember that this worship is daily, that these formulas
must be pronounced, these movements of the hands made with
mechanical precision ; that if the worshipper forgets one of
the incarnations of Vishnu which he is to figure with his
fingers, if he stop his left nostril when it should be the right,
the entire ceremony loses its efficacy ; that, not to go astray
amid this multitude of words and gestures required for each
rite, he is obliged to use mnemotechnic methods ; that there
are five of these for each series of formulas ; that his attention always strained and always directed toward the externals
of the cult, does not leave his mind a moment in which to
reflect upon the profound meaning of some of these prayers,
and you will comprehend the extraordinary scene that the
banks of the Ganges at Benāres present every morning ;

this anxious and demented multitude, these gestures, eager and yet methodical, this rapid movement of the lips, the fixed gaze of these men and women who, standing in the water, seem not even to see their neighbours, and count mentally like men in the delirium of a fever. Remember that there are ceremonies like these in the afternoon and also in the evening, and that in the intervals, in the street, in the house at meals, when going to bed, similar rites no less minute pursue the Brāhman, all preceded by the exercises of respiration, the enunciation of the syllable OM, and the invocation of the principal gods. It is estimated that between daybreak and noon he has scarcely an hour of rest from the performance of these rites. After the great powers of nature, the Ganges, the Dawn, and the Sun, he goes to worship in their temples the representations of divinity, the sacred trees, finally the cows, to whom he offers flowers. In his own dwelling other divinities await him, five black stones,[1] representing Siva, Ganesa, Surya, Devi and Vishnu, arranged according to the cardinal points : one towards the north, a second to the south-east, a third to the south-west, a fourth to the north-west, and one in the centre, this order changing according as the worshipper regards one god or another as most important ; then there is a shell, a bell— to which, kneeling, he offers flowers—and, lastly, a vase, whose mouth contains Vishnu, the neck Rudra, the paunch Brahma, while at the bottom repose the three divine mothers, the Ganges, the Indus, and the Jumna.

" This is the daily cult of the Brāhman of Benāres, and on holidays it is still further complicated. Since the great epoch of Brāhmanism it has remained the same. Some details may alter, but as a whole it has always been thus tyrannical and thus extravagant. As far back as the Upanishads appears the same faith in the power of articulate speech, the same imperative and innumerable prescriptions, the same singular formulas, the same enumeration of grotesque

[1] In the Central Provinces Ganpati is represented by a round red stone, Surya by a rock crystal or the Swastik sign, Devi by an image in brass or by a stone brought from her famous temple at Mahur, and Vishnu by the round black stone or Sāligrām. Besides these every Brāhman will have a special family god, who may be one of the above or another deity, as Rāma or Krishna.

BRÃHMAN WORSHIPPING HIS HOUSEHOLD GODS.

Bemrose, Collo., Derby.

gestures. Every day, for more than twenty-five hundred years, since Buddhism was a protest against the tyranny and absurdity of rites, has this race mechanically passed through this machinery, resulting in what mental malformations, what habitual attitudes of mind and will, the race is now too different from ourselves for us to be able to conceive."

Secular Brāhmans now, however, greatly abridge the length of their prayers, and an hour or an hour and a half in the morning suffices for the daily bath and purification, the worship of the household deities and the morning meal.

Brāhman boys are invested with the sacred thread between the ages of five and nine.   The ceremony is called Upanayana or the introduction to knowledge, since by it the boy acquires the right to read the sacred books.   Until this ceremony he is not really a Brāhman, and is not bound to observe the caste rules and restrictions.   By its performance he becomes Dvija or twice-born, and the highest importance is attached to the change or initiation.   He may then begin to acquire divine knowledge, and perhaps in past times it was thought that he obtained the divine character belonging to a Brāhman.   The sacred thread is made of three strands of cotton, which should be obtained from the cotton tree growing wild.   Sometimes a tree is grown in the yard of the house for the provision of the threads.   It has several knots in it, to which great importance is attached, the number of knots being different for a Brāhman, a Kshatriya and a Vaishya, the three twice-born castes.   The thread hangs from the left shoulder, falling on to the right hip.   Sometimes, when a man is married, he wears a double thread of six strands, the second being for his wife ; and after his father dies a treble one of nine strands.   At the investiture the boy's nails are cut and his hair is shaved, and he performs the *hom* or fire sacrifice for the first time.   He then acquires the status of a Brahmachari or disciple, and in former times he would proceed to some religious centre and begin to study the sacred books.   The idea of this is preserved by a symbolic ritual.   Some Brāhmans shave the boy's head completely, make a girdle of *kusha* or *munj* grass round his waist, provide him with a begging-bowl and tongs and the skin of an antelope to sit on and make him go and beg

17. The sacred thread.

from four houses. Among others the boy gets on to a wooden horse and announces his intention of going off to Benāres to study. His mother then sits on the edge of a well and threatens to throw herself in if he will not change his mind, or the maternal uncle promises to give the boy his daughter in marriage. Then the boy relinquishes his intention and agrees to stay at home. The sacred thread must always be passed through the hand before saying the Gayatri text in praise of the sun, the most sacred Brāhmanical text. The sacred thread is changed once a year on the day of Rakshabandhan ; the Brāhman and all his family change it together. The word Rakshabandhan means binding or tying up the devils, and it would thus appear that the sacred thread and the knots in it may have been originally intended to some extent to be a protection against evil spirits. It is also changed on the occasion of a birth or death in the family, or of an eclipse, or if it breaks. The old threads are torn up or sewn into clothes by the very poor in the Marātha districts. It is said that the Brāhmans are afraid that the Kunbis will get hold of their old threads, and if they do get one they will fold it into four strings, holding a lamp in the middle, and wave it over any one who is sick. The Brāhmans think that if this is done all the accumulated virtue which they have obtained by many repetitions of the Gayatri or sacred prayer will be transferred to the sick Kunbi. Many castes now wear the sacred thread who have no proper claim to do so, especially those who have become landholders and aspire to the status of Rājpūts.

18. Social position.   The Brāhman is of course supreme in Hindu society. He never bows his head in salutation to any one who is not a Brāhman, and acknowledges with a benediction the greetings of all other classes. No member of another caste, Dr. Bhattachārya states, can, consistently with Hindu etiquette and religious beliefs, refuse altogether to bow to a Brāhman. " The more orthodox Sūdras carry their veneration for the priestly caste to such an extent that they will not cross the shadow of a Brāhman, and it is not unusual for them to be under a vow not to eat any food in the morning before drinking Brāhman nectar,[1] or water in which the toe of a

[1] *Bipracharanamrita.*

Brāhman has been dipped.   On the other hand, the pride of the Brāhman is such that he does not bow even to the images of the gods in a Sūdra's house.   When a Brāhman invites a Sūdra the latter is usually asked to partake of the host's *prasāda* or favour in the shape of the leavings of his plate.   Orthodox Sūdras actually take offence if invited by the use of any other formula.   No Sūdra is allowed to eat in the same room or at the same time with Brāhmans." [1]

A man of low caste meeting a Brāhman says ' Pailagi ' or ' I fall at your feet,' and touches the Brāhman's foot with his hand, which he then carries to his own forehead to signify this.   A man wishing to ask a favour in a humble manner stands on one leg and folds his cloth round his neck to show that his head is at his benefactor's disposal ; and he takes a piece of grass in his mouth by which he means to say, ' I am your cow.'   Brāhmans greeting each other clasp the hands and say ' Salaam,' this method of greeting being known as Namaskar.   Since most Brāhmans have abandoned the priestly calling and are engaged in Government service and the professions, this exaggerated display of reverence is tending to disappear, nor do the educated members of the caste set any great store by it, preferring the social estimation attaching to such a prominent secular position as they often attain for themselves.

Any Brāhman is, however, commonly addressed by other castes as Mahārāj, great king, or else as Pandit, a learned man.   I had a Brāhman chuprāssie, or orderly, who was regularly addressed by the rest of the household as Pandit, and on inquiring as to the literary attainments of this learned man, I found he had read the first two class-books in a primary school.   Other titles of Brāhmans are Dvija, or twice-born, that is, one who has had the thread ceremony performed ; Bipra, applied to a Brāhman learned in the Shāstras or scriptures ; and Srotriya, a learned Brāhman who is engaged in the performance of Vedic rites. 19. Titles.

The Brāhmans have a caste *panchāyat*, but among the educated classes the tendency is to drop the *panchāyat* procedure and to refer matters of caste rules and etiquette to the informal decision of a few of the most respected local 20. Caste *panchāyat* and offences.

[1] *Hindu Castes and Sects*, pp. 19-21.

members. In northern India there is no supreme authority for the caste, but the five southern divisions acknowledge the successor of the great reformer Shankar Achārya as their spiritual head, and important caste questions are referred to him. His headquarters are at the monastery of Sringeri on the Cauvery river in Mysore. Mr. Joshi gives four offences as punishable with permanent exclusion from caste : killing a Brāhman, drinking prohibited wine or spirits, committing incest with a mother or step-mother or with the wife of one's spiritual preceptor, and stealing gold from a priest. Some very important offences, therefore, such as murder of any person other than a Brāhman, adultery with a woman of impure caste and taking food from her, and all offences against property, except those mentioned, do not involve permanent expulsion. Temporary exclusion is inflicted for a variety of offences, among which are teaching the Vedas for hire, receiving gifts from a Sūdra for performing fire-worship, falsely accusing a spiritual preceptor, subsisting by the harlotry of a wife, and defiling a damsel. It is possible that some of the offences against morality are comparatively recent additions. Brāhmans who cross the sea to be educated in England are readmitted into caste on going through various rites of purification ; the principal of these is to swallow the five products of the sacred cow, milk, *ghī* or preserved butter, curds, dung and urine. But the small minority who have introduced widow-marriage are still banned by the orthodox.

21. Rules about food.

Brāhmans as a rule should not eat meat nor drink intoxicating liquor. But it is said that the following indulgences have been recognised : for residents in eastern India the eating of flesh and drinking liquor ; for those of northern India the eating of flesh ; for those in the west the use of water out of leather buckets ; and in the south marriage with a first cousin on the mother's side. Hindustāni Brāhmans eat meat, according to Mr. Joshi, and others are now also adopting this custom. The kinds of meat permitted are mutton and venison, scaly, but not scaleless, fish, hares, and even the tortoise, wild boar, wild buffalo and rhinoceros. Brāhmans are said even to eat domestic fowls, though not openly, and wild jungle

BRĀHMAN BATHING PARTY.

Bemrose, Collo., Derby.

fowls are preferred, but are seldom obtainable.   Marātha
Brāhmans will not eat meat openly.   Formerly only the
flesh of animals offered in sacrifice could be eaten, but this
rule is being disregarded and some Brāhmans buy mutton
from the butchers.   A Brāhman should not eat even *pakki
rasoi* or food cooked without water, such as sweetmeats and
cakes fried in butter or oil, except when cooked by his own
family and in his own home.   But these are now partaken
of abroad, and also purchased from the Halwai or confectioner
on the assumption that he is a Brāhman.   A Brāhman
should take food cooked with water only from his own
relations and in his own home after the place has been
purified and spread with cowdung.   He bathes before
eating, and wears only a yellow silk or woollen cloth round
his waist, which is kept specially for this purpose, cotton
being regarded as impure.   But these rules are tending to
become obsolete, as educated Brāhmans recognise more and
more what a hindrance they cause to any social enjoyment.
Boys especially who receive an English education in high
schools and universities are rapidly becoming more liberal.
They will drink soda-water or lemonade of which they
are very fond, and eat European sweets and sometimes
biscuits.   The social intercourse of boys of all castes and
religions in school and games, and in the latter the frequent
association with Europeans, are having a remarkable effect
in breaking down caste prejudice, the results of which
should become very apparent in a few years.   A Brāhman
also should not smoke, but many now do so, and when
they go to see a friend will take their own huqqa with
them as they cannot smoke out of his.   Marātha and
Khedawāl Brāhmans, however, as a rule do not smoke, but
only chew tobacco.

A Brāhman's dress should be white, and he can have a   22. Dress.
coloured turban, preferably red.   Marātha Brāhmans were
very particular about the securing of their *dhoti* or loin-
cloth, which always had to have five tucks, three into the
waistband at the two sides and in front, while the loose
ends were tucked in in front and behind.   Buttons had to
be avoided as they were made of bone, and shoes were
considered to be impure as being of leather.   Formerly a

Brāhman never entered a house with his shoes on, as he would consider the house to be defiled. According to the old rule, if a Brāhman touches a man of an impure caste, as a Chamār (tanner) or Basor (basket-maker), he should bathe and change his loin-cloth, and if he touches a sweeper he should change his sacred thread. Now, however, educated Brāhmans usually wear white cotton trousers and black or brown coats of cloth, alpaca or silk with the normal allowance of buttons, and European shoes and boots which they keep on indoors. Boys are even discarding the *choti* or scalp-lock and simply cut their hair short in imitation of the English. For the head small felt caps have become fashionable in lieu of turbans.

23. Tattooing.

Men are never tattooed, but women are freely tattooed on the face and body. One dot is made in the centre of the forehead and three on the left nostril in the form of a triangle. All the limbs and the fingers and toes may also be tattooed, the most common patterns being a peacock with spread wings, a fish, cuckoo, scorpion, a child's doll, a sieve, a pattern of Sīta's cookroom and representations of all female ornaments. Some women think that they will be able to sell the ornaments tattooed on their bodies in the next world and subsist on the proceeds.

24. Occupation.

In former times the Brāhman was supposed to confine himself to priestly duties, learning the Vedas and giving instruction to the laity. His subsistence was to be obtained from gleaning the fields after the crop had been cut and from unsolicited alms, as it was disgraceful for him to beg. But if he could not make a living in this manner he was at liberty to adopt a trade or profession. The majority of Brāhmans have followed the latter course with much success. They were the ministers of Hindu kings, and as these were usually illiterate, most of the power fell into the Brāhmans' hands. In Poona the Marātha Brāhmans became the actual rulers of the State. They have profited much from gifts and bequests of land for charitable purposes and are one of the largest landholding castes. In Mewār it was recorded that a fifth of the State revenue from land was assigned in religious grants,[1] and in the deeds of gift, drawn

[1] *Rājasthān*, i. p. 487.

up no doubt by the Brāhmans themselves, the most terrible
penalties were invoked on any one who should interfere with
the grant.   One of these was that such an impious person
would be a caterpillar in hell for sixty thousand years.[1]
Plots of land and mango groves are also frequently given to
Brāhmans by village proprietors.   A Brāhman is forbidden
to touch the plough with his own hands, but this rule is
falling into abeyance and many Brāhman cultivators plough
themselves.   Brāhmans are also prohibited from selling a
large number of articles, as milk, butter, cows, salt and so
on.   Formerly a Brāhman village proprietor refused payment for the supplies of milk and butter given to travellers,
and some would expend the whole produce of their cattle in
feeding religious mendicants and poor Brāhmans.   But these
scruples, which tended to multiply the number of beggars
indefinitely, have happily vanished, and Brāhmans will even
sell cows to a butcher.   Mr. Joshi relates that a suit was
brought by a Brāhman in his court for the hide of a cow
sold by him for slaughter.   A number of Brāhmans are
employed as personal servants, and these are usually cooks,
a Brāhman cook being very useful, since all Hindus can eat
the food which he prepares.   Nor has this calling hitherto
been considered derogatory, as food is held to be sacred,
and he who prepares it is respected.   Many live on
charitable contributions, and it is a rule among Hindus
that a Brāhman coming into the house and asking for
a present must be given something or his curse will ruin
the family.   Liberality is encouraged by the recitation of
legends, such as that of the good king Harischandra who
gave away his whole kingdom to the great Brāhman saint
Visvamitra, and retired to Benāres with a loin-cloth which
the recipient allowed him to retain from his possessions.
But Brāhmans who take gifts at the time of a death, and
those who take them from pilgrims at the sacred shrines,
are despised and considered as out of caste, though not the
priests in charge of temples.   The rapacity of all these classes
is proverbial, and an instance may be given of the conduct of
the Pandas or temple-priests of Benāres.   These men were
so haughty that they never appeared in the temple unless

[1] *Rājasthān*, i. p. 698.

some very important visitor was expected, who would be able to pay largely. It is related that when the ex-Peshwa of Poona came to Benāres after the death of his father he solicited the Panda of the great temple of Viseshwar to assist him in the performance of the ceremonies necessary for the repose of his father's soul. , But the priest refused to do so until the Mahārāja had filled with coined silver the *hauz* or font of the temple. The demand was acceded to and Rs. 125,000 were required to fill the font.[1] Those who are very poor adopt the profession of a Mahā-Brāhman or Mahāpātra, who takes gifts for the dead. Respectable Brāhmans will not accept gifts at all, but when asked to a feast the host usually gives them one to four annas or pence with betel-leaf at the time of their departure, and there is no shame in accepting this. A very rich man may give a gold mohar (guinea) to each Brāhman. Other Brāhmans act as astrologers and foretell events. They pretend to be able to produce rain in a drought or stop excessive rainfall when it is injuring the crops. They interpret dreams and omens. In the case of a theft the loser will go to a Brāhman astrologer, and after learning the circumstances the latter will tell him what sort of person stole the property and in what direction the property is concealed. But the large majority of Brāhmans have abandoned all priestly functions, and are employed in all grades of Government service, the professions and agriculture. In 1911 about fifty-three per cent of Brāhmans in the Central Provinces were supported by agriculture as landowners, cultivators and labourers. About twenty-two per cent were engaged in the arts and professions, seven per cent in Government service, including the police which contains many Brāhman constables, and only nineteen per cent were returned under all occupations connected with religion.

25. Character of Brāhmans.   Many hard things have been said about the Brāhman caste and have not been undeserved. The Brāhman priesthood displayed in a marked degree the vices of arrogance, greed, hypocrisy and dissimulation, which would naturally be engendered by their sacerdotal pretensions and the position they claimed at the head of Hindu society. But the priests

---

[1] At that time £12,500 or more, now about £8000.

and mendicants now, as has been seen, contribute only a comparatively small minority of the whole caste.   The majority
of the Brāhmans are lawyers, doctors, executive officers of
Government and clerks in all kinds of Government, railway
and private offices.   The defects ascribed to the priesthood
apply to these, if at all, only in a very minor degree.   The
Brāhman official has many virtues.   He is, as a rule, honest,
industrious and anxious to do his work creditably.   He
spends very little on his own pleasures, and his chief aim in
life is to give his children as good an education as he can
afford.   A half or more of his income may be devoted to
this object.   If he is well-to-do he helps his poor relations
liberally, having the strong fellow-feeling for them which is
a relic of the joint family system.   He is a faithful husband
and an affectionate father.   If his outlook on life is narrow
and much of his leisure often devoted to petty quarrels and
intrigues, this is largely the result of his imperfect, parrot-
like education and lack of opportunity for anything better.
In this respect it may be anticipated that the excellent
education and training now afforded by Government in
secondary schools for very small fees will produce a great
improvement ; and that the next generation of educated
Hindus will be considerably more manly and intelligent,
and it may be hoped at the same time not less honest,
industrious and loyal than their fathers. ·

Brāhman, Ahivāsi.— A class of persons who claim to
be Brāhmans, but are generally engaged in cultivation and
pack-carriage.   They are looked down upon by other
Brāhmans, and permit the remarriage of widows.   The
name means the abode of the snake or dragon, and the
caste are said to be derived from a village Sunrakh in
Muttra District, where a dragon once lived.   For further
information Mr. Crooke's article on the caste,[1] from which
the above details are taken, may be consulted.

Brāhman, Jijhotia.—This is a local subdivision of the
Kanaujia subcaste, belonging to Bundelkhand.   They take
their name from Jajhoti, the classical term for Bundelkhand,

[1] *Tribes and Castes of the North-West Provinces and Oudh*, s.v.

and reside in Saugor and the adjoining Districts, where they usually act as priests to the higher castes. The Jijhotia Brāhmans rank a little below the Kanaujias proper and the Sarwarias, who are also a branch of the Kanaujia division. The two latter classes take daughters in marriage from Jijhotias, but do not give their daughters to them. But these hypergamous marriages are now rare. Jijhotia Brāhmans will plough with their own hands in Saugor.

Brāhman, Kanaujia, Kanyakubja.—This, the most important division of the northern Brāhmans, takes its name from the ancient city of Kanauj in the Farukhābād District on the Ganges, which was on two occasions the capital of India. The great king Harsha Vardhana, who ruled the whole of northern India in the seventh century, had his headquarters here, and when the Chinese pilgrim Hiuen Tsang stayed at Kanauj in A.D. 638 and 643 he found upwards of a hundred monasteries crowded by more than 10,000 Buddhist monks. " Hinduism flourished as well as Buddhism, and could show more than two hundred temples with thousands of worshippers. The city, which was strongly fortified, extended along the east bank of the Ganges for about four miles, and was adorned with lovely gardens and clear tanks. The inhabitants were well-to-do, including some families of great wealth ; they dressed in silk, and were skilled in learning and the arts." [1]   When Mahmūd of Ghazni appeared before Kanauj in A.D. 1018 the number of temples is said to have risen to 10,000. The Sultan destroyed the temples, but seems to have spared the city. Thereafter Kanauj declined in importance, though still the capital of a Rājpūt dynasty, and the final sack by Shihāb-ud-Dīn in A.D. 1194 reduced it to desolation and insignificance for ever. [2]

The Kanaujia Brāhmans include the principal body of the caste in Bengal and in the Hindi Districts of the Central Provinces. They are here divided into four subgroups, the Kanaujia proper, Sarwaria, Jijhotia and Sanādhya, which are separately noticed. The Sarwarias are sometimes considered to rank a little higher than the proper Kanaujias. It is said that the two classes are the

[1] *Early History of India*, 3rd ed. p. 376.   [2] *Ibidem*, p. 385.

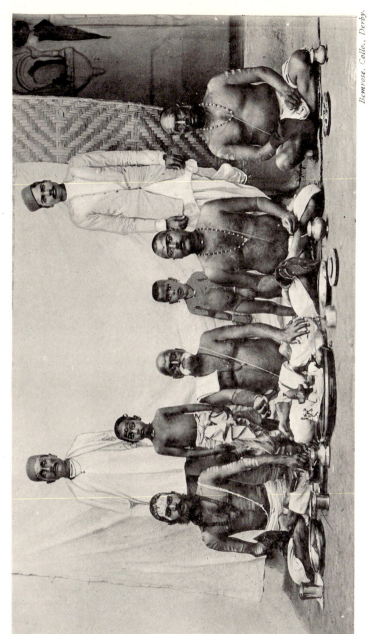

Bemrose. Collo., Derby.

BRÃHMAN PUJÃRIS OR PRIESTS.

descendants of two brothers, Kanya and Kubja, of whom the former accepted a present from the divine king Rāma of Ayodhya when he celebrated a sacrifice on his return from Ceylon, while the latter refused it. The Sarwarias are descended from Kubja who refused the present and therefore are purer than the Kanaujias, whose ancestor, Kanya, accepted it. Kanya and Kubja are simply the two parts of Kanyakubja, the old name for Kanauj. It may be noted that Kanya means a maiden and also the constellation Virgo, while Kubja is a name of the planet Mars; but it is not known whether the words in this sense are connected with the name of the city. The Kanaujia Brāhmans of the Central Provinces practise hypergamy, as described in the general article on Brāhman. Mr. Crooke states that in the United Provinces the children of a man's second wife can intermarry with those of his first wife, provided that they are not otherwise related or of the same section. The practice of exchanging girls between families is also permitted there.[1] In the Central Provinces the Kanaujias eat meat and sometimes plough with their own hands. The Chhattīsgarhi Kanaujias form a separate group, who have been long separated from their brethren elsewhere. As a consequence other Kanaujias will neither eat nor intermarry with them. Similarly in Saugor those who have come recently from the United Provinces will not marry with the older settlers. A Kanaujia Brāhman is very strict in the matter of taking food, and will scarcely eat it unless cooked by his own relations, according to the saying, '*Ath Kanaujia, nau chulha*,' or 'Eight Kanaujias will want nine places to cook their food.'

Brāhman, Khedāwāl.—The Khedāwāls are a class of Gujarāti Brāhmans, who take their name from Kheda or Kaira, the headquarters of the Kaira District, where they principally reside. They have two divisions, known as Inside and Outside. It is said that once the Kaira chief was anxious to have a son and offered them gifts. The majority refused the gifts, and leaving Kaira settled in villages outside the town; while a small number accepted the gifts and

---

[1] *Tribes and Castes*, art. Kanaujia.

remained inside, and hence two separate divisions arose, the outside group being the higher.[1] It is said that the first Khedāwāl who came to the Central Provinces was on a journey from Gujarāt to Benāres when, on passing through Panna State, he saw some diamonds lying in a field. He stopped and picked up as many as he could and presented them to the Rāja of Panna, who made him a grant of an estate, and from this time other Khedāwāls came and settled. A considerable colony of them now exists in Saugor and Damoh. The Khedāwāls are clever and astute, and many of them are the agents of landowners and moneylenders, while a large proportion are in the service of the Government. They do not as a rule perform priestly functions in the Central Provinces. Their caste observances are strict. Formerly it is said that a Khedāwāl who was sent to jail was permanently expelled from caste, and though the rule has been relaxed the penalties for readmission are still very heavy. They do not smoke, but only chew tobacco. Widows must dress in white, and their heads are sometimes shaved. They are said to consider a camel as impure as a donkey, and will not touch either animal. One of their common titles is Mehta, meaning great. The Khedāwāls of the Central Provinces formerly married only among themselves, but since the railway has been opened intermarriage with their caste-fellows in Gujarāt has been resumed.

Brāhman, Mahārāshtra, Marātha.—The Marātha Brāhmans, or those of the Bombay country, are numerous and important in the Central Provinces. The northern Districts were for a period governed by Marātha Brāhmans on behalf of the Peshwa of Poona, and under the Bhonsla dynasty of Nāgpur in the south they took a large part in the administration. The Marātha Brāhmans have three main subcastes, the Deshasth, Konkonasth and Karhāda. The Deshasth Brāhmans belong to the country of Poona above the Western Ghats, which is known as the *desh* or home country. They are numerous in Berār and Nāgpur. The Konkonasth are so called because they reside in the Konkan country along the Bombay coast. They have noticeably fair complexions,

[1] *Bombay Gazetteer, Hindus of Gujarāt*, p. 11.

Benrose, Collo., Derby.

GROUP OF MARĀTHA BRĀHMAN MEN.

good features and often grey eyes. According to a legend they were sprung from the corpses of a party of shipwrecked foreigners, who were raised to life by Parasurāma.[1] This story and their fine appearance have given rise to the hypothesis that their ancestors were shipwrecked sailors from some European country, or from Arabia or Persia. They are also known as Chitpāvan, which is said to mean the pure in heart, but a derivation suggested in the *Bombay Gazetteer* is from Chiplun or Chitāpolan, a place in the Konkan which was their headquarters. The Peshwa of Poona was a Konkonasth Brāhman, and there are a number of them in Saugor. The Karhāda Brāhmans take their name from the town of Karhād in the Satāra District. They show little difference from the Deshasths in customs and appearance.

Formerly the above three subcastes were endogamous and married only among themselves. But since the railway has been opened they have begun to intermarry with each other to a limited extent, having obtained sanction to this from the successor of Shankar Achārya, whom they acknowledge as their spiritual head.

The Marātha Brāhmans are also divided into sects, according to the Veda which they follow. Most of them are either Rigvedis or Yajurvedis, and these two sects marry among themselves. These Brāhmans are strict in the observance of caste rules. They do not take water from any but other Brāhmans, and abstain from flesh and liquor. They will, however, eat with any of the Pānch-Drāvid or southern divisions of Brāhmans except those of Gujarāt. They usually abstain from smoking, and until recently have made widows shave their heads ; but this rule is perhaps now relaxed. As a rule they are well educated, and the majority of them look to Government service for a career, either as clerks in the public offices or as officers of the executive and judicial services. They are intelligent and generally reliable workers. The full name of a Marātha or Gujarāti Brāhman consists of his own name, his father's name and a surname. But he is commonly addressed by his own name, followed by the honorific termination Rao for Rāja, a king, or Pant for Pandit, a wise man.

[1] *Bombay Gazetteer, Satāra,* p. 54.

Brāhman, Maithil.—One of the five Pānch-Gaur or
northern divisions, comprising the Brāhmans of Bihār or
Tirhūt. There are some Maithil Brāhman families settled in
Mandla, who were formerly in the service of the Gond kings.
They have the surname of Ojha, which is one of those borne by
the caste and signifies a soothsayer. The Maithil Brāhmans
are said to have at one time practised magic. Mithila or
Bihār has also, from the earliest times, been famous for the
cultivation of Sanskrit, and the great lawgiver Yajnavalkya
is described as a native of this country.[1] The head of the
subcaste is the Mahārāja of Darbhanga, to whom family
disputes are sometimes referred for decision. The Maithil
Brāhmans are said to be mainly Sakti worshippers. They
eat flesh and fish, but do not drink liquor or smoke
tobacco.[2]

Brāhman, Mālwi.—This is a local class of Brāhmans from
Mālwa in Central India, who are found in the Hoshangābād
and Betūl Districts. They are said to have been invited
here by the Gond kings of Kherla in Betūl six or more
centuries ago, and are probably of impure descent. Mālwa
is north of the Nerbudda, and they should therefore properly
belong to the Pānch-Gaur division, but they speak Marāthi
and their customs resemble those of Marātha Brāhmans,
who will take food cooked without water from them. The
Mālwi Brāhmans usually belong to the Madhyandina branch
of the Yajurvedi sect. They work as village accountants
(*patwāris*) and village priests, and also cultivate land.

Brāhman, Nāgar.—A class of Gujarāti Brāhmans found
in the Nimār District. The name is said to be derived
from the town of Vadnagar of Gujarāt, now in Baroda State.
According to one account they accepted grants of land from
a Rājpūt king, and hence were put out of caste by their
fellows. Another story is that the Nāgar Brāhman women
were renowned for their personal beauty and also for their
skill in music. The emperor Jahāngir, hearing of their
fame, wished to see them and sent for them, but they refused

---

[1] Bhattachārya, *Hindu Castes and Sects*, p. 47.
[2] *Ibidem*, p. 48.

to go.   The emperor then ordered that all the men should
be killed and the women be taken to his Court.   A terrible
struggle ensued, and many women threw themselves into
tanks and rivers and were drowned, rather than lose their
modesty by appearing before the emperor.   A body of
Brāhmans numbering 7450 (or 74½ hundred) threw away
their sacred threads and became Sūdras in order to save
their lives.   Since this occurrence the figure 74½ is considered very unlucky.   Banias write 74½ in the beginning
of their account-books, by which they are held to take a
vow that if they make a false entry in the book they will be
guilty of the sin of having killed this number of Brāhmans.
The same figure is also written on letters, so that none but
the person to whom they are addressed may dare to open
them.[1]

The above stories seem to show that the Nāgar Brāhmans
are partly of impure descent.   In Gujarāt it is said that one
section of them called Bārud are the descendants of Nāgar
Brāhman fathers who were unable to get wives in their own
caste and took them from others.   The Bārud section also
formerly permitted the remarriage of widows.[2]   This seems
a further indication of mixed descent.   The Nāgars settled
in the Central Provinces have for a long time ceased to
marry with those of Gujarāt owing to difficulties in communication.   But now that the railway has been opened
they have petitioned the Rao of Bhaunagar, who is the
head of the caste, and a Nāgar Brāhman, to introduce intermarriage again between the two sections of the caste.   Many
Nāgar Brāhmans have taken to secular occupations and are
land-agents and cultivators.

Formerly the Nāgar Brāhmans observed very strict rules
about defilement when in the state called *Nuven*, that is,
having bathed and purified themselves prior to taking food.
A Brāhman in this condition was defiled if he touched an
earthen vessel unless it was quite new and had never held
water.   If he sat down on a piece of cotton cloth or a scrap
of leather or paper he became impure unless Hindu letters
had been written on the paper ; these, as being the goddess

---

[1] From Mr. Gopal Datta Joshi's paper.
[2] *Rāsmāla*, ii. p. 233.

Sāraswati, would preserve it from defilement. But cloth or leather could not be purified through being written on. Thus if the Brāhman wished to read any book before or at his meal it had to be bound with silk and not with cotton ; leather could not be used, and instead of paste of flour and water the binder had to employ paste of pounded tamarind seed. A printed book could not be read, because printing-ink contained impure matter. Raw cotton did not render the Brāhman impure, but if it had been twisted into the wick of a lamp by any one not in a state of purity he became impure. Bones defiled, but women's ivory armlets did not, except in those parts of the country where they were not usually worn, and then they did. The touch of a child of the same caste who had not learned to eat grain did not defile, but if the child ate grain it did. The touch of a donkey, a dog or a pig defiled ; some said that the touch of a cat also defiled, but others were inclined to think it did not, because in truth it was not easy to keep the cat out.[1]

If a Brāhman was defiled and rendered impure by any of the above means he could not proceed with his meal.

Brāhman, Nāramdeo.—A class of Brāhmans who live in the Hoshangābād and Nimār Districts near the banks of the Nerbudda, from which river their name is derived. According to their own account they belong to the Gurjara or Gujarāti division, and were expelled from Gujarāt by a Rāja who had cut up a golden cow and wished them to accept pieces of it as presents. This they refused to do on account of the sin involved, and hence were exiled and came to the Central Provinces. A local legend about them is to the effect that they are the descendants of a famous Rishi or saint, who dwelt beside the Nerbudda, and of a Naoda or Dhīmar woman who was one of his disciples. The Nāramdeo Brāhmans have for the most part adopted secular occupations, though they act as village priests or astrologers. They are largely employed as village accountants (*patwāris*), clerks in Government offices, and agents to landowners, that is, in very much the same capacity

[1] *Rāsmāla*, ii. p. 259.

Benrose, Collo., Derby.

GROUP OF NÁRAMDEO BRÁHMAN WOMEN.

as the Kāyasths.   As land-agents they show much astute-
ness, and are reputed to have enriched themselves in many
cases at the expense of their masters.   Hence they are
unpopular with the cultivators just as the Kāyasths are, and
very uncomplimentary proverbs are current about them.

Brāhman, Sanādhya, Sanaurhia.—The Sanādhyas are
considered in the Central Provinces to be a branch of the
Kanaujia division.   Their home is in the Ganges-Jumna Doāb
and Rohilkhand, between the Gaur Brāhmans to the north-
west and the Kanaujias to the east.   Mr. Crooke states that
in some localities the Sanādhyas intermarry with both the
Kanaujia and Gaur divisions.   But formerly both Kanaujias
and Gaurs practised hypergamy with the Sanādhyas, taking
daughters from them in marriage but not giving their
daughters to them.[1]   This fact indicates the inferiority of
the Sanādhya group, but marriage is now becoming reciprocal.
In Bengal the Sanādhyas account for their inferiority to
the other Kanaujias by saying that their ancestors on one
occasion at the bidding of a Rāja partook of a sacrificial
feast with all their clothes on, instead of only their loin-
cloths according to the rule among Brāhmans, and were
hence degraded.   The Sanādhyas themselves have two
divisions, the *Sārhe-tīn ghar* and *Dasghar*, or Three-and-a-
half houses and Ten houses, of whom the former are superior,
and practise hypergamy with the latter.   Further, it is said
that the Three-and-a-half group were once made to intermarry with the degraded Kataha or Mahā-Brāhmans, who
are funeral priests.[2]   This further indicates the inferior
status of the Sanādhyas.   The Sanaurhia criminal caste of
pickpockets are supposed to be made up of a nucleus of
Sanādhya Brāhmans with recruits from all other castes,
but this is not certain.   In the Central Provinces a number
of Sanādhyas took to carrying grain and merchandise on
pack-bullocks, and are hence known as Belwār.   They form
a separate subcaste, ranking below the other Sanādhyas and
marrying among themselves.   Mr. Crooke notes that at
their weddings the Sanādhyas worship a potter's wheel.
Some make an image of it on the wall of the house, while

---

[1] *Tribes and Castes*, art. Sanādhya.   [2] Crooke, *ibidem*, paras. 3 and 6.

others go to the potter's house and worship his wheel there. In the Central Provinces after the wedding they get a bed newly made with *newār* tape and seat the bride and bridegroom on it, and put a large plate at their feet, in which presents are placed. The Sanādhyas differ from the Kanaujias in that they smoke tobacco but do not eat meat, while the Kanaujias eat meat but do not smoke. They greet each other with the word Dandāwat, adding Mahārāj to an equal or superior.

Brāhman, Sarwaria.—This is the highest class of the Kanaujia Brāhmans, who take their name from the river Sarju or Gogra in Oudh, where they have their home. They observe strict rules of ceremonial purity, and do not smoke tobacco nor plough with their own hands. An orthodox Sarwaria Brāhman will not give his daughter in marriage in a village from which his family has received a girl, and sometimes will not even drink the water of that village. The Sarwarias make widows dress in white and sometimes shave their heads. In some tracts they intermarry with the Kanaujia Brāhmans, and in others take daughters in marriage but do not give their own daughters to them. In Dr. Buchanan's time, a century ago, the Sarwaria Brāhmans would not eat rice sold in the bazār which had been cleaned in boiling water, as they considered that it had thereby become food cooked with water; and they carried their own grain to the grain-parcher to be prepared for them. When they ate either parched grain or sweetmeats from a confectioner in public they must purify the place on which they sat down with cowdung and water.[1] This may be compared with a practice observed by very strict Brāhmans even now, of adding water to the medicine which they obtain from a Government dispensary, to purify it before drinking it.

Brāhman, Utkal.—These are the Brāhmans of Orissa and one of the Pānch-Gaur divisions. They are divided into two groups, the Dākshinatya or southern and the Jajpuria or northern clan. The Utkal Brāhmans, who first settled in Sambalpur, are known as Jharia or jungly, and form a

---

[1] *Eastern India,* ii. 472, quoted in Mr. Crooke's art. Sarwaria.

GROUP OF NĀRAMDEO BRĀHMAN MEN.

Bemrose, Collo., Derby.

separate subcaste, marrying among themselves, as the later immigrants refuse to intermarry with them. Another group of Orissa Brāhmans have taken to cultivation, and are known as Halia, from *hal*, a plough. They grow the betel-vine, and in Orissa the areca and cocoanuts, besides doing ordinary cultivation. They have entirely lost their sacerdotal character, but glory in their occupation, and affect to despise the Bed or Veda Brāhmans, who live upon alms.[1] A third class of Orissa Brāhmans are the Pandas, who serve as priests and cooks in the public temples and also in private houses, and travel about India touting for pilgrims to visit the temple at Jagannāth. Dr. Bhattachārya describes the procedure of the temple-touts as follows : [2]

" Their tours are so organised that during their campaigning season, which commences in November and is finished by the car-festival at the beginning of the rains, very few villages of the adjoining Provinces escape their visits and taxation. Their appearance causes a disturbance in every household. Those who have already visited ' The Lord of the World ' at Puri are called upon to pay an instalment towards the debt contracted by them while at the sacred shrine, which, though paid many times over, is never completely satisfied. That, however, is a small matter compared with the misery and distraction caused by the ' Jagannāth mania,' which is excited by the preachings and pictures of the Panda. A fresh batch of old ladies become determined to visit the shrine, and neither the wailings and protestations of the children nor the prospect of a long and toilsome journey can dissuade them. The arrangements of the family are for the time being altogether upset, and the grief of those left behind is heightened by the fact that they look upon the pilgrims as going to meet almost certain death. . . ."

This vivid statement of the objections to the habit of pilgrimage from a Brāhman writer is very interesting. Since the opening of the railway to Puri the danger and expense as well as the period of absence have been greatly reduced ; but the pilgrimages are still responsible for a large

---

[1] Stirling's description of Orissa in *As. Res.* vol, xv. p. 199, quoted in *Hindu Castes and Sects.*

[2] *Hindu Castes and Sects*, p. 63.

mortality, as cholera frequently breaks out among the vast assembly at the temple, and the pilgrims, hastily returning to all parts of India, carry the disease with them, and cause epidemics in many localities. All castes now eat the rice cooked at the temple of Jagannāth together without defilement, and friendships are cemented by eating a little of this rice together as a sacred bond.

Chadār,[1] Kotwar.—A small caste of weavers and village watchmen resident in the Districts of Saugor, Damoh, Jubbulpore and Narsinghpur. They numbered 28,000 persons in 1911. The caste is not found outside the northern Districts of the Central Provinces. The name is derived from the Sanskrit *chirkar*, a weaver, and belongs to Bundelkhand, but beyond this the Chadārs have no knowledge or traditions of their origin. They are probably an occupational group formed from members of the Dravidian tribes and others who took to the profession of village watchmen. A number of other occupational castes of low status are found in the northern Districts, and their existence is probably to be accounted for by the fact that the forest tribes were subjected and their tribal organisation destroyed by the invading Bundelas and other Hindus some centuries ago. They were deprived of the land and relegated to the performance of menial and servile duties in the village, and they have formed a new set of divisions into castes arising from the occupations they adopted. The Chadārs have two subcastes based on differences of religious practice, the Parmesuria or worshippers of Vishnu, and Athia or devotees of Devi. It is doubtful, however, whether these are strictly endogamous. They have a large number of exogamous septs or *bainks*, which are named after all sorts of animals, plants and natural objects. Instances of these names are Dhāna (a leaf of the rice plant), Kāsia (bell-metal), Gohia (a kind of lizard), Bachhulia (a calf), Gujaria (a milkmaid), Moria (a peacock), Laraiya (a jackal), Khatkīra (a bug), Sugaria (a pig), Barraiya (a wasp), Neora (a mongoose), Bhartu Chiraiya (a sparrow), and so on. Thirty-nine names

---

[1] This article is compiled from papers by Mr. Wali Muhammad, Tahsīldār of Khurai, and Kanhya Lāl, clerk in the Gazetteer office.

in all are reported. Members of each sept draw the figure of the animal or plant after which it is named on the wall at marriages and worship it. They usually refuse to kill the totem animal, and the members of the Sugaria or pig sept throw away their earthen vessels if a pig should be killed in their sight, and clean their houses as if on the death of a member of the family. Marriage between members of the same sept is forbidden and also between first cousins and other near relations. The Chadārs say that the marriages of persons nearly related by blood are unhappy, and occasion serious consequences to the parties and their families. Girls are usually wedded in the fifth, seventh, ninth, or eleventh year of their age and boys between the ages of eight and sixteen. If an unmarried girl is seduced by a member of the caste she is married to him by the simple form adopted for the wedding of a widow. But if she goes wrong with an outsider of low caste she is permanently expelled. The remarriage of widows is permitted and divorce is also allowed, a deed being executed on stamped paper before the *panchāyat* or caste committee. If a woman runs away from her husband to another man he must repay to the husband the amount expended on her wedding and give a feast to the caste. A Brāhman is employed to fix the date of a wedding and sometimes for the naming of children, but he is only consulted and is never present at the ceremony. The caste venerate the goddess Devi, offering her a virgin she-goat in the month of Asārh (June-July). They worship their weaving implements at the Diwāli and Holi festivals, and feed the crows in Kunwār (September-October) as representing the spirits of their ancestors. This custom is based on the superstition that a crow does not die of old age or disease, but only when it is killed. To cure a patient of fever they tie a blue thread, irregularly knotted, round his wrist. They believe that thunder-bolts are the arrows shot by Indra to kill his enemies in the lower world, and that the rainbow is Indra's bow ; any one pointing at it will feel pain in his finger. The dead are mourned for ten days, and during that time a burning lamp is placed on the ground at some distance from the house, while on the tenth day a tooth-stick and water and food are set out for the

soul of the dead.   They will not throw the first teeth of a
child on to a tiled roof, because they believe that if this
is done his next teeth will be wide and ugly like the tiles.
But it is a common practice to throw the first teeth on to
the thatched roof of the house.   The Chadārs will admit
members of most castes of good standing into the community, and they eat flesh, including pork and fowls, and
drink liquor, and will take cooked food from most of the
good castes and from Kalārs, Khangārs and Kumhārs.   The
social status of the caste is very low, but they rank above
the impure castes and are of cleanly habits, bathing daily
and cleaning their kitchens before taking food.   They are
employed as village watchmen and as farmservants and
field-labourers, and also weave coarse country cloth.

CHAMĀR

LIST OF PARAGRAPHS

Chamār, Chambhār.[1]—The caste of tanners and menial labourers of northern India. In the Central Provinces the Chamārs numbered about 900,000 persons in 1911. They are the third caste in the Province in numerical strength, being exceeded by the Gonds and Kunbis. About 600,000 persons, or two-thirds of the total strength of the caste in the Province, belong to the Chhattīsgarh Division and adjacent Feudatory States. Here the Chamārs have to some extent emancipated themselves from their servile status and have become cultivators, and occasionally even mālguzārs or landed proprietors ; and between them and

1. General notice of the caste.

---

[1] This article is based on the Rev. E. M. Gordon's *Indian Folk-Tales* (London, Elliott & Stock, 1908), and the Central Provinces *Monograph on the Leather Industry*, by Mr. C. G. Chenevix Trench, C.S. ; with extracts from Sir H. H. Risley's and Mr. Crooke's descriptions of the caste, and from the *Berār Census Report* (1881) ; on information collected for the District Gazetteers ; and papers by Messrs. Durga Prasād Pānde, Tahsīldār, Raipur ; Rām Lāl, Deputy Inspector of Schools, Saugor ; Govind Vithal Kāne, Naib-Tahsīldār, Wardha ; Bālkrishna Rāmchandra Bakhle, Tahsīldār, Mandla ; Sitārām, schoolmaster, Bālāghāt ; and Kanhya Lāl of the Gazetteer office. Some of the material found in Mr. Gordon's book was obtained independently by the writer in Bilāspur before its publication and is therefore not specially acknowledged.

the Hindus a bitter and long-standing feud is in progress. Outside Chhattīsgarh the Chamārs are found in most of the Hindi-speaking Districts whose population has been recruited from northern and central India, and here they are perhaps the most debased class of the community, consigned to the lowest of menial tasks, and their spirit broken by generations of servitude. In the Marātha country the place of the Chamārs is taken by the Mehras or Mahārs. In the whole of India the Chamārs are about eleven millions strong, and are the largest caste with the exception of the Brāhmans. The name is derived from the Sanskrit Charmakāra, a worker in leather ; and, according to classical tradition, the Chamār is the offspring of a Chandāl or sweeper woman by a man of the fisher caste.[1] The superior physical type of the Chamār has been noticed in several localities. Thus in the Kanara District of Bombay[2] the Chamār women are said to be famed for their beauty of face and figure, and there it is stated that the Padminis or perfect type of women, middle-sized with fine features, black lustrous hair and eyes, full breasts and slim waists,[3] are all Chamārins. Sir D. Ibbetson writes[4] that their women are celebrated for beauty, and loss of caste is often attributed to too great a partiality for a Chamārin. In Chhattīsgarh the Chamārs are generally of fine stature and fair complexion ; some of them are lighter in colour than the Chhattīsgarhi Brāhmans, and it is on record that a European officer mistook a Chamār for a Eurasian and addressed him in English. This, however, is by no means universally the case, and Sir H. Risley considers[5] that " The average Chamār is hardly distinguishable in point of features, stature or complexion from the members of those non-Aryan races from whose ranks we should primarily expect the profession of leather-dressers to be recruited." Again, Sir Henry Elliot, writing of the Chamārs of the North-Western Provinces, says : " Chamārs

[1] There are other genealogies showing the Chamār as the offspring of various mixed unions.

[2] *Bombay Gazetteer*, vol. xv. Kanara, p. 355.

[3] The Hindus say that there are five classes of women, Padmini, Hastini, Chitrani and Shunkhini being the first

four, and of these Padmini is the most perfect. No details of the other classes are given. *Rāsmāla*, i. p. 160.

[4] *Punjab Census Report* (1881), p. 320.

[5] *Tribes and Castes of Bengal*, art. Chamār.

are reputed to be a dark race, and a fair Chamār is said to be as rare an object as a black Brāhman :

Karia Brāhman, gor Chamār,
Inke sāth nā utariye pār,

that is, 'Do not cross a river in the same boat with a black Brāhman or a fair Chamār,' both being of evil omen." The latter description would certainly apply to the Chamārs of the Central Provinces outside the Chhattīsgarh Districts, but hardly to the caste as a whole within that area. No satisfactory explanation has been offered of this distinction of appearance of some groups of Chamārs. It is possible that the Chamārs of certain localities may be the descendants of a race from the north-west, conquered and enslaved by a later wave of immigrants ; or that their physical development may owe something to adult marriage and a flesh diet, even though consisting largely of carrion. It may be noticed that the sweepers, who eat the broken food from the tables of the Europeans and wealthy natives, are sometimes stronger and better built than the average Hindu. Similarly, the Kasais or Muhammadan butchers are proverbially strong and lusty. But no evidence is forthcoming in support of such conjectures, and the problem is likely to remain insoluble.

"The Chamārs," Sir H. Risley states,[1] "trace their own pedigree to Ravi or Rai Dās, the famous disciple of Rāmānand at the end of the fourteenth century, and whenever a Chamār is asked what he is, he replies a Ravi Dās. Another tradition current among them alleges that their original ancestor was the youngest of four Brāhman brethren who went to bathe in a river and found a cow struggling in a quicksand. They sent the youngest brother in to rescue the animal, but before he could get to the spot it had been drowned. He was compelled, therefore, by his brothers to remove the carcase, and after he had done this they turned him out of their caste and gave him the name of Chamār." Other legends are related by Mr. Crooke in his article on the caste.

The Chamārs are broken up into a number of endogamous subcastes. Of these the largest now consists of the

2. Endogamous divisions.

---

[1] *Loc. cit.*

members of the Satnāmi sect in Chhattīsgarh, who do not
intermarry with other Chamārs. They are described in the
article on that sect. The other Chamārs call the Satnāmis
Jharia or 'jungly,' which implies that they are the oldest
residents in Chhattīsgarh. The Satnāmis are all cultivators,
and have given up working in leather. The Chungias (from
chungi, a leaf-pipe) are a branch of the Satnāmis who have
taken to smoking, a practice which is forbidden by the rules
of the sect. In Chhattīsgarh those Chamārs who still cure
hides and work in leather belong either to the Kanaujia or
Ahirwār subcastes, the former of whom take their name
from the well-known classical town of Kanauj in northern
India, while the latter are said to be the descendants of
unions between Chamār fathers and Ahīr mothers. The
Kanaujias are much addicted to drink, and though they eat
pork they do not rear pigs. The Ahirwārs, or Erwārs as
they are called outside Chhattīsgarh, occupy a somewhat
higher position than the Kanaujias. They consider themselves to be the direct descendants of the prophet Raidās or
Rohidās, who, they say, had seven wives of different castes;
one of them was an Ahīr woman, and her offspring were
the ancestors of the Ahirwār subcaste. Both the Kanaujias
and Ahirwārs of Chhattīsgarh are generally known to outsiders as Paikaha, a term which indicates that they still
follow their ancestral calling of curing hides, as opposed to
the Satnāmis, who have generally eschewed it. Those
Chamārs who are curriers have, as a rule, the right to receive
the hides of the village cattle in return for removing the
carcases, each family of Chamārs having allotted to them a
certain number of tenants whose dead cattle they take,
while their women are the hereditary midwives of the village.
Such Chamārs have the designation of Meher. The Kanaujias make shoes out of a single piece of leather, while the
Ahirwārs cut the front separately. The latter also ornament
their shoes with fancy work consisting of patterns of silver
thread on red cloth. No Ahirwār girl is married until she
has shown herself proficient in this kind of needlework.[1]
Another well-known group, found both in Chhattīsgarh and
elsewhere, are the Jaiswāras, who take their name from the

[1] From Mr. Gordon's paper.

old town of Jais in the United Provinces. Many of them
serve as grooms, and are accustomed to state their caste as
Jaiswāra, considering it a more respectable designation than
Chamār. The Jaiswāras must carry burdens on their heads
only and not on their shoulders, and they must not tie up
a dog with a halter or neck-rope, this article being venerated
by them as an implement of their calling. A breach of
either of these rules entails temporary excommunication
from caste and a fine for readmission. Among a number
of territorial groups may be mentioned the Bundelkhandi
or immigrants from Bundelkhand; the Bhadoria from the
Bhadāwar State; the Antarvedi from Antarved or the
Doāb, the country lying between the Ganges and Jumna;
the Gangāpāri or those from the north of the Ganges; and
the Pardeshi (foreigners) and Desha or Deswār (belonging
to the country), both of which groups come from Hindustān.
The Deswār Chamārs of Narsinghpur [1] are now all agriculturists and have totally abjured the business of working
in leather. The Mahobia and Khaijrāha take their names
from the towns of Mahoba and Khaijra in Central India.
The Lādse or Lādvi come from south Gujarāt, which in
classical times was known as Lāt; while the Marātha,
Berāria and Dakhini subdivisions belong to southern India.
There are a number of other territorial groups of less
importance.

Certain subcastes are of an occupational nature, and
among these may be mentioned the Budalgirs of Chhindwāra, who derive their name from the *budla*, or leather bag
made for the transport and storage of oil and *ghī*. The
budla, Mr. Trench remarks,[2] has been ousted by the kerosene
oil tin, and the industry of the Budalgirs has consequently
almost disappeared; but the *budlas* are still used by barbers
to hold oil for the torches which they carry in wedding
processions. The Daijanya subcaste are so named because
their women act as midwives (*dai*), but this business is by
no means confined to one particular group, being undertaken
generally by Chamār women. The Kataua or Katwa are
leather-cutters, the name being derived from *kātna*, to cut.
And the Gobardhua (from *gobar*, cowdung) collect the

3. Sub-
castes
continued.

---

[1] *Monograph on Leather Industries*, p. 9.   [2] *Ibidem.*

droppings of cattle on the threshing-floors and wash out and eat the undigested grain. The Mochis or shoemakers and Jīngars [1] or saddlemakers and bookbinders have obtained a better position than the ordinary Chamārs, and have now practically become separate castes ; while, on the other hand, the Dohar subcaste of Narsinghpur have sunk to the very lowest stage of casual labour, grass-cutting and the like, and are looked down on by the rest of the caste.[2] The Korchamārs are said to be the descendants of alliances between Chamārs and Koris or weavers, and the Turkanyas probably have Turk or Musalmān blood in their veins. In Berār the Romya or Haralya subcaste claim the highest rank and say that their ancestor Harlya was the primeval Chamār who stripped off a piece of his own skin to make a pair of shoes for Mahādeo.[3] The Māngya [4] Chamārs of Chānda and the Nona Chamārs of Damoh are groups of beggars, who are the lowest of the caste and will take food from the hands of any other Chamār. The Nona group take their name from Nona or Lona Chamārin, a well-known witch about whom Mr. Crooke relates the following story : [5] " Her legend tells how Dhanwantari, the physician of the gods, was bitten by Takshaka, the king of the snakes, and knowing that death approached he ordered his sons to cook and eat his body after his death, so that they might thereby inherit his skill in medicine. They accordingly cooked his body in a cauldron, and were about to eat it when Takshaka appeared to them in the form of a Brāhman and warned them against this act of cannibalism. So they let the cauldron float down the Ganges, and as it floated down, Lona the Chamārin, who was washing on the bank of the river, took the vessel out in ignorance of its contents, and partook of the ghastly food. She at once obtained power to cure diseases, and especially snake-bite. One day all the women were transplanting rice, and it was found that Lona could do as much work as all her companions put together. So they watched her, and when she thought she was alone she stripped off her clothes (nudity being an

---

[1] See articles on these castes.

[2] *Monograph on Leather Industries*, p. 3.

[3] *Berār Census Report* (1881), p. 149.

[4] From *māngna*, to beg.

[5] *Tribes and Castes*, art. Chamār.

essential element in magic), muttered some spells, and threw the plants into the air, when they all settled down in their proper places.   Finding she was observed, she tried to escape, and as she ran the earth opened, and all the water of the rice-fields followed her and thus was formed the channel of the Loni River in the Unao District."   This Lona or Nona has obtained the position of a nursery bogey, and throughout Hindustān, Sir H. Risley states, parents frighten naughty children by telling them that Nona Chamārin will carry them off.   The Chamārs say that she was the mother or grandmother of the prophet Ravi Dās, or Rai Dās already referred to.

The caste is also divided into a large number of exoga- 4. Exo-
mous groups or sections, whose names, as might be expected, gamous
divisions.
present a great diversity of character.   Some are borrowed from Rājpūt clans, as Sūrajvansi, Gaharwār and Rāthor ; while others, as Marai, are taken from the Gonds.   Instances of sections named after other castes are Banjar (Banjāra), Jogi, Chhipia (Chhipi, a tailor) and Khairwār (a forest tribe). The Chhipia section preserve the memory of their compara- tively illustrious descent by refusing to eat pork.   Instances of sections called after a title or nickname of the reputed founder are Mālādhāri, one who wears a garland ; Māchhi- Mundia or fly-headed, perhaps the equivalent of feather- brained ; Hathīla, obstinate ; Bāghmār, a tiger-killer ; Mān- gaya, a beggar ; Dhuliya, a drummer ; Jadkodiha, one who digs for roots, and so on.   There are numerous territorial groups named after the town or village where the ancestor of the clan may be supposed to have lived ; and many names also are of a totemistic nature, being taken from plants, animals or natural objects.   Among these are Khunti, a peg ; Chandaniha, sandalwood ; Tarwāria, a sword ; Borbans, plums ; Miri, chillies ; Chauria, a whisk ; Baraiya, a wasp ; Khalaria, a hide or skin ; Kosni, *kosa* or tasar silk ; and Purain, the lotus plant.   Totemistic observances survive only in one or two isolated instances.

A man must not take a wife from his own section, nor in 5. Mar-
some localities from that of his mother or either of his grand- riage.
mothers.   Generally the union of first cousins is prohibited. Adult marriage is the rule, but those who wish to improve

their social position have taken to disposing of their daughters
at an early age. Matches are always arranged by the
parents, and it is the business of the boy's father to find a
bride for his son. A bride-price is paid which may vary
from two pice (farthings) to a hundred rupees, but usually
averages about twenty rupees. In Chānda the amount is
fixed at Rs. 13 and it is known as *hunda*, but if the bride's
grandmother is alive it is increased to Rs. 15-8, and the
extra money is given to her. The marriage ceremony
follows the standard type prevalent in the locality. On his
journey to the girl's house the boy rides on a bullock and is
wrapped up in a blanket. In Bilāspur a kind of sham fight
takes place between the parties, which is a reminiscence of
the former practice of marriage by capture and is thus
described as an eye-witness by the Rev. E. M. Gordon of
Mungeli : [1]

" As the bridegroom's party approached the home of the
bride the boy's friends lifted him up on their shoulders, and,
surrounding him on every side, they made their way to the
bride's house, swinging round their sticks in a threatening
manner. On coming near the house they crossed sticks
with the bride's friends, who gradually fell back and allowed
the bridegroom's friends to advance in their direction. The
women of the house gathered with baskets and fans and
some threw about rice in pretence of self-defence. When
the sticks of the bridegroom's party struck the roof of the
bride's house or of the marriage-shed her friends considered
themselves defeated and the sham fight was at an end."
Among the Marātha Chamārs of Betūl two earthen pots full
of water are half buried in the ground and worship is paid to
them. The bride and bridegroom then stand together and
their relatives take out water from the pots and pour it on to
their heads from above. The idea is that the pouring of the
sacred water on to them will make them grow, and if the
bride is much smaller than the bridegroom more water is
poured on to her in order that she may grow faster. The
practice may symbolise the fertilising influence of rain.
Among the Dohar Chamārs of Narsinghpur the bride and
bridegroom are seated on a plough-yoke while the marriage

[1] *Indian Folk-Tales.*

ceremony is performed.   Before the wedding the bride's party
take a goat's leg in a basket with other articles to the
janwāsa or bridegroom's lodging and present it to his father.
The bride and bridegroom take the goat's leg and beat each
other with it alternately.   Another ceremony, known as
Pendpūja, consists in placing pieces of stick with cotton stuck
to the ends in an oven and burning them in the name of
the deceased ancestors ; but the significance, if there be any,
of this rite is obscure.   Some time after the wedding the bride
is taken to her husband's house to live with him, and on this
occasion a simple ceremony known as Chauk or Pathoni is
performed.

Widows commonly remarry, and may take for their
second husband anybody they please, except their own
relatives and their late husband's elder brother and ascendant
relations.   In Chhattīsgarh widows are known either as
barandi or *randi*, the *randi* being a widow in the ordinary
sense of the term and the *barandi* a girl who has been
married but has not lived with her husband.   Such a girl is
not required to break her bangles on her husband's death, and,
being more in demand as a second wife, her father naturally
obtains a good price for her.   To marry a woman whose
husband is alive is known as *chhandwe banāna*, the term
chhandwe implying that the woman has discarded, or has been
discarded by, her husband.   The second husband must in
this case repay to the first husband the expenses incurred by
him on his wedding.   The marriage ceremony for a widow
is of the simplest character, and consists generally of the
presentation to her by her new husband of those articles which
a married woman may use, but which should be forsworn by
a widow, as representing the useless vanities of the world.
Thus in Saugor the bridegroom presents his bride with new
clothes, vermilion for the parting of her hair, a spangle for
her forehead, lac dye for her feet, antimony for the eyes, a
comb, glass bangles and betel-leaves.   In Mandla and Seoni
the bridegroom gives a ring, according to the English custom,
instead of bangles.   When a widow marries a second time
her first husband's property remains with his family and also
the children, unless they are very young, when the mother
may keep them for a few years and subsequently send them

6. Widow-
marriage
and
divorce.

back to their father's relatives. Divorce is permitted for
a variety of causes, and is usually effected in the presence of
the caste *panchāyat* or committee by the husband and wife
breaking a straw as a symbol of the rupture of the union.
In Chānda an image of the divorced wife is made of grass
and burnt to indicate that to her husband she is as good as
dead ; if she has children their heads and faces are shaved in
token of mourning, and in the absence of children the
husband's younger brother has this rite performed ; while the
husband gives a funeral feast known as *Marti Jīti kā Bhāt*,
or ' The feast of the living dead woman.'   In Chhattīsgarh
marriage ties are of the loosest description, and adultery is
scarcely recognised as an offence.   A woman may go and
live openly with other men and her husband will take her
back afterwards.   Sometimes, when two men are in the
relation of Mahāprasād or nearest friend to each other, that
is, when they have vowed friendship on rice from the temple
of Jagannāth, they will each place his wife at the other's disposal.   The Chamārs justify this carelessness of the fidelity
of their wives by the saying, ' If my cow wanders and comes
home again, shall I not let her into her stall ? '   In Seoni, if
a Chamār woman is detected in a misdemeanour with a
man of the caste, both parties are taken to the bank of
a tank or river, where their heads are shaved in the presence of the caste *panchāyat* or committee.   They are then
made to bathe, and the shoes of all the assembled Chamārs
made up into two bundles and placed on their heads, while
they are required to promise that they will not repeat the
offence.

7. Funeral
customs.
         The caste usually bury the dead with the feet to the
north, like the Gonds and other aboriginal tribes.   They say
that heaven is situated towards the north, and the dead man
should be placed in a position to start for that direction.
Another explanation is that the head of the earth lies
towards the north, and yet another that in the Satyug or
beginning of time the sun rose in the north ; and in each
succeeding Yug or era it has veered round the compass until
now in the Kali Yug or Iron Age it rises in the east.   In
Chhattīsgarh, before burying a corpse, they often make a mark
on the body with butter, oil or soot ; and when a child is

subsequently born into the same family they look for any kind of mark on the corresponding place on its body. If any such be found they consider the child as a reincarnation of the deceased person. Still-born children, and those who die before the Chathi or sixth-day ceremony of purification, are not taken to the burial-ground, but their bodies are placed in an earthen pot and interred below the doorway or in the courtyard of the house. In such cases no funeral feast is demanded from the family, and some people believe that the custom tends in favour of the mother bearing another child ; others say, however, that its object is to prevent the *tonhi* or witch from getting hold of the body of the child and rousing its spirit to life to do her bidding as Matia Deo.[1] In Seoni a curious rule obtains to the effect that the bodies of those who eat carrion or the flesh of animals dying a natural death should be cremated. In the northern Districts a bier painted white is used for a man and a red one for a woman.

Among the better-class Chamārs it is customary to place a newborn child in a winnowing-fan on a bed of rice. The nurse receives the rice and she also goes round to the houses of the headman of the village and the relatives of the family and makes a mark with cowdung on their doors as an announcement of the birth, for which she receives a small present. In Chhattīsgarh a woman is given nothing to eat or drink on the day that a child is born and for two days afterwards. On the fourth day she receives a liquid decoction of ginger, the roots of the *orai* or *khaskhas* grass, areca-nut, coriander and turmeric and other hot substances, and in some places a cake of linseed or sesamum. She sometimes goes on drinking this mixture for as long as a month, and usually receives solid food for the first time on the sixth day after the birth, when she bathes and her impurity is removed. The child is not permitted to suckle its mother until the third day after it is born, but before this it receives a small quantity of a mixture made by boiling the urine of a calf with some medicinal root. In Chhattīsgarh it is a common practice to brand a child on the stomach on the name-day or sixth day after its birth ; twenty or more small burns may be made with the point of a *hansia* or sickle on the

8. Childbirth.

_____
[1] *Indian Folk-Tales*, pp. 49, 50.

stomach, and it is supposed that this operation will prevent it from catching cold. Another preventive for convulsions and diseases of the lungs is the rubbing of the limbs and body with castor-oil ; the nurse wets her hands with the oil and then warms them before a fire and rubs the child. It is also held in the smoke of burning *ajwāin* plants (*Carum copticum*). Infants are named on the Chathi or sixth day, or sometimes on the twelfth day after birth. The child's head is shaved, and the hair, known as Jhālar, thrown away, the mother and child are washed and the males of the family are shaved. The mother is given her first regular meal of grain and pulse cooked with pumpkins. A pregnant woman who is afraid that her child will die will sometimes sell it to a neighbour before its birth for five or six cowries.[1] The baby will then be named Pachkouri or Chhekouri, and it is thought that the gods, who are jealous of the lives of children, will overlook one whose name shows it to be valueless. Children are often nicknamed after some peculiarity as Kānwa (one-eyed), Behra (deaf), Konda (dumb), Khurwa (lame), Kāri (black), Bhūri (fair). It does not follow that a child called Konda is actually dumb, but it may simply have been late in learning to speak. Parents are jealous of exposing their children to the gaze of strangers and especially of a crowd, in which there will almost certainly be some malignant person to cast the evil eye upon them. Young children are therefore not infrequently secluded in the house and deprived of light and air to an extent which is highly injurious to them.

9. Religion.

The caste worship the ordinary Hindu and village deities of the localities in which they reside, and observe the principal festivals. In Saugor the Chamārs have a family god, known as Marri, who is represented by a lump of clay kept in the cooking-room of the house. He is supposed to represent the ancestors of the family. The Seoni Chamārs especially worship the castor-oil plant. Generally the caste revere the *rāmpi* or skinning-knife with offerings of flour-cakes and cocoanuts on festival days. In Chhattīsgarh more than half the Chamārs belong to the reformed Satnāmi sect, by which the worship of images is at least nominally abolished. This

[1] Shells which were formerly used as money.

is separately treated.   Mr. Gordon states[1] that it is impossible to form a clear conception of the beliefs of the
village Chamārs as to the hereafter : " That they have the
idea of hell as a place of punishment may be gathered from
the belief that if salt is spilt the one who does this will in
Patāl—or the infernal region—have to gather up each grain
of salt with his eyelids.   Salt is for this reason handed round
with great care, and it is considered unlucky to receive it in
the palm of the hand ; it is therefore invariably taken in a
cloth or in a vessel.   There is a belief that the spirit of the
deceased hovers round familiar scenes and places, and on
this account, whenever it is possible, it is customary to
destroy or desert the house in which any one has died.   If
a house is deserted the custom is to sweep and plaster the
place, and then, after lighting a lamp, to leave it in the
house and withdraw altogether.   After the spirit of the dead
has wandered around restlessly for a certain time it is said
that it will again become incarnate and take the form of
man or of one of the lower animals."

The curing and tanning of hides is the primary occupation of the Chamār, but in 1911 only 80,000 persons, or
about a seventh of the actual workers of the caste, were
engaged in it, and by Satnāmis the trade has been entirely
eschewed.   The majority of the Chhattīsgarhi Chamārs are
cultivators with tenant right, and a number of them have
obtained villages.   In the northern Districts, however, the
caste are as a rule miserably poor, and none of them own
villages.   A very few are tenants, and the vast majority
despised and bullied helots.   The condition of the leather-
working Chamārs is described by Mr. Trench as lamentable.[2]
Chief among the causes of their ruin has been the recently
established trade in raw hides.   Formerly the bodies of all
cattle dying within the precincts of the village necessarily
became the property of the Chamārs, as the Hindu owners
could not touch them without loss of caste.   But since
the rise of the cattle-slaughtering industry the cultivator has
put his religious scruples in his pocket, and sells his old and
worn-out animals to the butchers for a respectable sum.
" For a mere walking skeleton of a cow or bullock from

10. Occu-
pation.

---

[1] *Indian Folk-Tales*, pp. 49, 50.   [2] *Monograph*, p. 3.

two to four rupees may be had for the asking, and so long as he does not actually see or stipulate for the slaughter of the sacred animal, the cultivator's scruples remain dormant. No one laments this lapse from ortho- doxy more sincerely than the outcaste Chamār. His situation may be compared with that of the Cornish pilchard-fishers, for whom the growing laxity on the part of continental Roman Catholic countries in the observance of Lent is already more than an omen of coming disaster." [1]

11. The tanning process. When a hide is to be cured the inside is first cleaned with the *rāmpi*, a chisel-like implement with a short-blade four inches broad and a thick short handle. It is then soaked in a mixture of water and lime for ten or twelve days, and at intervals scraped clean of flesh and hair with the *rāmpi*. "The skill of a good tanner appears in the absence of superfluous inner skin, fat or flesh, remaining to be removed after the hide is finally taken out of the lime- pit. Next the hard berries of the *ghont* [2] tree are poured into a large earthen vessel sunk in the ground, and water added till the mixture is so thick as to become barely liquid. In this the folded hide is dipped three or four times a day, undergoing meanwhile a vigorous rubbing and kneading. The average duration of this process is eight days, and it is followed by what is according to European ideas the real tanning. Using as thread the roots of the ubiquitous *palās* [3] tree, the Chamār sews the hide up into a mussack-shaped bag open at the neck. The sewing is admirably executed, and when drawn tight the seams are nearly, but purposely not quite, water-tight. The hide is then hung on low stout scaffolding over a pit and filled with a decoction of the dried and semi-powdered leaves of the *dhaura* [4] tree mixed with water. As the decoction trickles slowly through the seams below, more is poured on from above, and from time to time the position of the hide is reversed in such a way that the tanning permeates each part in turn. Sometimes only one reversal of the hide takes place half-way through the process, which occupies as a rule some

---

[1] *Monograph on Leather Industries*, p. 5.
[2] *Zizyphus xylopera.*   [3] *Butea frondosa.*   [4] *Anogeissus latifolia.*

Bemrose, Collo., Derby.

CHAMĀRS TANNING AND WORKING IN LEATHER.

eight days. But energetic Chamārs continually turn and refill the skin until satisfied that it is thoroughly saturated with the tanning. After a washing in clean water the hide is now considered to be tanned." [1]

In return for receiving the hides of the village cattle the Chamār had to supply the village proprietor and his family with a pair of shoes each free of payment once a year, and sometimes also the village accountant and watchman; but the cultivators had usually to pay for them, though nowadays they also often insist on shoes in exchange for their hides. Shoes are usually worn in the wheat and cotton growing areas, but are less common in the rice country, where they would continually stick in the mud of the fields. The Saugor or Bundelkhandi shoe is a striking specimen of footgear. The sole is formed of as many as three layers of stout hide, and may be nearly an inch thick. The uppers in a typical shoe are of black soft leather, inlaid with a simple pattern in silver thread. These are covered by flaps of stamped yellow goat-skin cut in triangular and half-moon patterns, the interstices between the flaps being filled with red cloth. The heel-piece is continued more than half-way up the calf behind. The toe is pointed, curled tightly over backwards and surmounted by a brass knob. The high frontal shield protects the instep from mud and spear-grass, and the heel-piece ensures the retention of the shoe in the deepest quagmire. Such shoes cost one or two rupees a pair. [2] In the rice Districts sandals are often worn on the road, and laid aside when the cultivator enters his fields. Women go bare-footed as a rule, but sometimes have sandals. Up till recently only prostitutes wore shoes in public, and no respectable woman would dare to do so. In towns boots and shoes made in the English fashion at Cawnpore and other centres have now been generally adopted, and with these socks are worn. The Mochis and Jīngars, who are offshoots from the Chamār caste, have adopted the distinctive occupations of making shoes and horse furniture with prepared leather, and no longer cure hides. They have

12. Shoes.

[1] The above is an abridgment of the description in Mr. Trench's *Monograph*, to which reference may be made for further details.

[2] *Monograph on the Leather Industries*, pp. 10, 11.

thus developed into a separate caste, and consider themselves greatly superior to the Chamārs.

13. Other articles made of leather.   Other articles made of leather are the thongs and nose-strings for bullocks, the buckets for irrigation wells, rude country saddlery, and *mussacks* and *pakhāls* for carrying water.   These last are simply hides sewn into a bag and provided with an orifice.   To make a pair of bellows a goat-skin is taken with all four legs attached, and wetted and filled with sand.   It is then dried in the sun, the sand shaken out, the sticks fitted at the hind-quarters for blowing, and the pair of bellows is complete.

14. Customs connected with shoes.   The shoe, as everybody in India knows, is a symbol of the greatest degradation and impurity.   This is partly on account of its manufacture from the impure leather or hide, and also perhaps because it is worn and trodden under foot. All the hides of tame animals are polluted and impure, but those of certain wild animals, such as the deer and tiger, are not so, being on the contrary to some extent sacred.   This last feeling may be due to the fact that the old anchorites of the forests were accustomed to cover themselves with the skins of wild animals, and to use them for sitting and kneeling to pray.   A Bairāgi or Vaishnava religious mendicant much likes to carry a tiger-skin on his body if he can afford one ; and a Brāhman will have the skin of a black-buck spread in the room where he performs his devotions.   Possibly the sin involved in killing tame animals has been partly responsible for the impurity attaching to their hides, to the obtaining of which the death of the animal must be a preliminary.   Every Hindu removes his shoes before entering a house, though with the adoption of English boots a breach is being made in this custom.   So far as the houses of Europeans are concerned, the retention of shoes is not, as might be imagined, of recent origin, but was noticed by Buchanan a hundred years ago : " Men of rank and their attendants continue to wear their shoes loose for the purpose of throwing them off whenever they enter a room, which they still continue to do everywhere except in the houses of Europeans, in which all natives of rank now imitate our example."   In this connection it must be remembered that a Hindu house is always sacred as the shrine of the

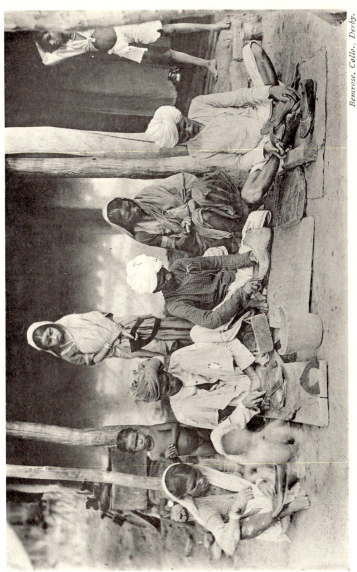

CHAMÂRS CUTTING LEATHER AND MAKING SHOES.

household god, and shoes are removed before stepping across the threshold on to the hallowed ground. This consideration does not apply to European houses, and affords ground for dispensing with the removal of laced shoes and boots.

To be beaten or sometimes even touched with a shoe by a man of low caste entails temporary social excommunication to most Hindus, and must be expiated by a formal purification and caste feast. The outcaste Mahārs punish a member of their community in the same manner even if somebody should throw a shoe on to the roof of his house, and the Pharasaical absurdities of the caste system surely find their culminating point in this rule. Similarly if a man touches his shoe with his hand and says ' I have beaten you,' to a member of any of the lower castes in Seoni, the person so addressed is considered as temporarily out of caste. If he then immediately goes and informs his caste-fellows he is reinstated with a nominal fine of grain worth one or two pice. But if he goes back to his house and takes food, and the incident is subsequently discovered, a penalty of a goat is levied. A curious exception recognised is that of the *Sirkāri jūta*, or shoe belonging to a Government servant, and to be beaten with this shoe does not entail social punishment.

In return for his perquisite of the hides of cattle the Chamār has to act as the general village drudge in the northern Districts and is always selected for the performance of *bigār* or forced labour. When a Government officer visits the village the Chamār must look after him, fetch what grass or fuel he requires, and accompany him as far as the next village to point out the road. He is also the bearer of official letters and messages sent to the village. The special Chamār on whom these duties are imposed usually receives a plot of land rent-free from the village proprietor. Another of the functions of the Chamār is the castration of the young bullocks, which task the cultivators will not do for themselves. His method is most primitive, the scrotum being held in a cleft bamboo or a pair of iron pincers, while the testicles are bruised and rubbed to pulp with a stone. The animal remains ill for a week or a fortnight and is not

15. The Chamār as general village drudge.

worked for two months, but the operation is rarely or never fatal. In the northern Districts the Chamārs are said to be very strong and to make the best farmservants and coolies for earthwork. It is a proverb that ' The Chamār has half a rib more than other men.' Notwithstanding his strength, however, he is a great coward, this characteristic having probably been acquired through centuries of oppression. Many Chamār women act as midwives. In Raipur the cultivators give her five annas at the birth of a boy and four annas for a girl, while well-to-do people pay a rupee. When the first child of a rich man is born, the midwife, barber and washerman go round to all his friends and relations to announce the event and obtain presents. It is a regular function of the Chamārs to remove the carcases of dead cattle, which they eat without regard to the disease from which the animal may have died. But a Chamār will not touch the corpse of a pony, camel, cat, dog, squirrel or monkey, and to remove the bodies of such animals a Mehtar (sweeper) or a Gond must be requisitioned. In Raipur it is said that the Chamārs will eat only the flesh of four-legged animals, avoiding presumably birds and fish. When acting as a porter the Chamār usually carries a load on his head, whereas the Kahār bears it on his shoulders, and this distinction is proverbial. In Raipur the Chamārs have become retail cattle-dealers and are known as Kochias. They purchase cattle at the large central markets of Baloda and Bamnidih and retail them at the small village bazārs. It is said that this trade could only flourish in Chhattīsgarh, where the cultivators are too lazy to go and buy their cattle for themselves. Many Chamārs have emigrated from Chhattīsgarh to the Assam tea-gardens, and others have gone to Calcutta and to the railway workshops at Kharagpur and Chakardharpur. Many of them work as porters on the railway. It is probable that their taste for emigration is due to the resentment felt at their despised position in Chhattīsgarh.

16. Social status.   The Chamār ranks at the very bottom of the social scale, and contact with his person is considered to be a defilement to high-caste Hindus. He cannot draw water from the common well and usually lives in a hamlet somewhat removed

from the main village.   But in several localities the rule is
not so strict, and in Saugor a Chamār may go into all parts
of the house except the cooking and eating rooms.   This is
almost necessary when he is so commonly employed as a farmservant.   Here the village barber will shave Chamārs and the
washerman will wash their clothes.   And the Chamār himself
will not touch the corpse of a horse, a dog or any animal
whose feet are uncloven ; and he will not kill a cow though
he eats its flesh.   It is stated indeed that a Chamār who once
killed a calf accidentally had to go to the Ganges to purify
himself.   The crime of cattle-poisoning is thus rare in Saugor
and the other northern Districts, but in the east of the
Provinces it is a common practice of the Chamārs.   As is
usual with the low castes, many Chamārs are in some repute
as Gunias or sorcerers, and in this capacity they are frequently
invited to enter the houses of Hindus to heal persons possessed of evil spirits.   When children fall ill one of them is
called in and he waves a branch of the *nīm*[1] tree over the
child and taking ashes in his hand blows them at it ; he is
also consulted for hysterical women.   When a Chamār has
had something stolen and wishes to detect the thief, he takes
the wooden-handled needle used for stitching leather and
sticks the spike into the sole of a shoe.   Then two persons
standing in the relation of maternal uncle and nephew hold
the needle and shoe up by placing their forefingers under
the wooden handle.   The names of all suspected persons are
pronounced, and he at whose name the shoe turns on the
needle is taken to be the thief.

The caste do not employ Brāhmans for their ceremonies,
but consult them for the selection of auspicious days, as this
business can be performed by the Brāhman at home and he
need not enter the Chamār's house.   But poor and despised
as the Chamārs are they have a pride of their own.   When
the Dohar and Marātha Chamārs sell shoes to a Mahār they
will only allow him to try on one of them and not both, and
this, too, he must do in a sitting posture, as an indication of
humility.   The Harale or Marātha Chamārs of Berār[2] do not
eat beef nor work with untanned leather, and they will not
work for the lowest castes, as Mahārs, Māngs, Basors and

---

[1] *Melia indica.*   [2] *Berār Census Report* (1881), p. 149.

Kolis. If one of these buys a pair of shoes from the Chamār the seller asks no indiscreet questions ; but he will not mend the pair as he would for a man of higher caste. The Satnāmis of Chhattīsgarh have openly revolted against the degraded position to which they are relegated by Hinduism and are at permanent feud with the Hindus ; some of them have even adopted the sacred thread. But this interesting movement is separately discussed in the article on Satnāmi.

17. Character.

In Chhattīsgarh the Chamārs are the most criminal class of the population, and have made a regular practice of poisoning cattle with arsenic in order to obtain the hides and flesh. They either mix the poison with mahua flowers strewn on the grazing-ground, or make it into a ball with butter and insert it into the anus of the animal when the herdsman is absent. They also commit cattle-theft and frequently appear at the whipping-post before the court-house. The estimation in which they are held by their neighbours is reflected in the proverb, ' Hemp, rice and a Chamār ; the more they are pounded the better they are.' " The caste," Mr. Trench writes, " are illiterate to a man, and their intellectual development is reflected in their style of living. A visit to a hamlet of tanning Chamārs induces doubt as to whence the appalling smells of the place proceed—from the hides or from the tanners. Were this squalor invariably, as it is occasionally, accompanied by a sufficiency of the necessaries of life, victuals and clothing, the Chamār would not be badly off, but the truth is that in the northern Districts at all events the Chamār, except in years of good harvest, does not get enough to eat. This fact is sufficiently indicated by a glance at the perquisites of the village Chamār, who is almost invariably the shoemaker and leather-worker for his little community. In one District the undigested grain left by the gorged bullocks on the threshing-floor is his portion, and a portion for which he will sometimes fight. Everywhere he is a carrion-eater, paying little or no regard to the disease from which the animal may have died." The custom above mentioned of washing grain from the dung of cattle is not so repugnant to the Hindus, owing to the sacred character of the cow, as it is to us. It is even sometimes considered holy food :—" The zamīndār of Idar, who is named Naron Dās, lives with such austerity that his only food is grain which has passed through oxen and has been separated from their dung ; and this kind of aliment the Brāhmans consider pure in the highest degree." [1] Old-fashioned cultivators do not muzzle the bullocks treading out the corn, and the animals eat it the whole time, so that much passes through their bodies undigested. The Chamār will make several maunds (80 lbs.) of grain in this way, and to a cultivator who does not muzzle his bullocks he will give a pair of shoes and a plough-rein and yoke-string. Another duty of the Chamār is to look after the *banda* or large underground masonry chamber in which grain is kept. After the grain has been stored, a conical roof is built and plastered over with mud to keep out water. The Chamār looks after the repairs of the mud plaster and in return receives a small quantity of grain, which usually goes bad on the floor of the store-chamber. They prepare the threshing-floors for the cultivators, making the surface of the soil level and beating it down to a smooth and hard surface. In return for this they receive the grain mixed with earth which remains on the threshing-floor after the crop is removed.

Like all other village artisans the Chamār is considered by the cultivators to be faithless and dilatory in his dealings with them ; and they vent their spleen in sayings such as the following :—" The Kori, the Chamār and the Ahīr, these are the three biggest liars that ever were known. For if you ask the Chamār whether he has mended your shoes he says, ' I am at the last stitch,' when he has not begun them ; if you ask the Ahīr whether he has brought back your cow from the jungle he says, ' It has come, it has come,' without knowing or caring whether it has come or not ; and if you ask the Kori whether he has made your cloth he says, ' It is on the loom,' when he has not so much as bought the thread." Another proverb conveying the same sense is, ' The Mochi's to-morrow never comes.' But no doubt the uncertainty and delay in payment account for much of this conduct.

[1] *Rāsmāla*, i. 395, quoting from the *Ain-i-Akbari*.

Chasa,[1] **Tasa** (also called **Alia** in the Sonpur and Patna States).—The chief cultivating caste of Orissa. In 1901 more than 21,000 Chasas were enumerated in Sambalpur and the adjoining Feudatory States, but nearly all these passed in 1905 to Bengal. The Chasas are said[2] by Sir H. Risley to be for the most part of non-Aryan descent, the loose organisation of the caste system among the Uriyas making it possible on the one hand for outsiders to be admitted into the caste, and on the other for wealthy Chasas who gave up ploughing with their own hands and assumed the respectable title of Mahanti to raise themselves to membership among the lower classes of Kāyasths. This passage indicates that the term Mahanti is or was a broader one than Karan or Uriya Kāyasth, and was applied to educated persons of other castes who apparently aspired to admission among the Karans, in the same manner as leading members of the warlike and landholding castes lay claim to rank as Rājpūts. For this reason probably the Uriya Kāyasths prefer the name of Karan to that of Mahanti, and the Uriya saying, 'He who has no caste is called a Mahanti,' supports this view. The word Chasa has the generic meaning of 'a cultivator,' and the Chasas may in Sambalpur be merely an occupational group recruited from other castes. This theory is supported by the names of their subdivisions, three of which, Kolta, Khandait and Ud or Orh are the names of distinct castes, while the fourth, Benatia, is found as a subdivision of several other castes.

Each family has a *got* or sept and a *varga* or family name. The *vargas* are much more numerous than the *gots*, and marriages are arranged according to them, unions of members of the same *varga* only being forbidden. The sept names are totemistic and the family names territorial or titular. Among the former are *bachhās* (calf), *nāgas* (cobra), *hasti* or *gaj* (elephant), *harin* (deer), *mahumāchhi* (bee), *dīpas* (lamp), and others ; while instances of the *varga* names are Pitmundia, Hulbulsingia, Giringia and Dumania,

---

[1] From papers by Mr. Parmeshwar Misra, Settlement Superintendent, Rairakhol, and Mr. Rasānand, Siresh-tedār, Bāmra.

[2] *Tribes and Castes of Bengal*, art. Chasa.

all names of villages in Angul State ; and Nāyak (headman),
Mahanti (writer), Dehri (worshipper), Behera (cook), Kandra
(bamboo-worker), and others.   The different *gots* or septs
revere their totems by drawing figures of them on their
houses, and abstaining from injuring them in any way.   If
they find the footprints of the animal which they worship,
they bow to the marks and obliterate them with the hand,
perhaps with the view of affording protection to the totem
animal from hunters or of preventing the marks from being
trampled on by others.   They believe that if they injured
the totem animal they would be attacked by leprosy and
their line would die out.   Members of the *dīpas* sept will
not eat if a lamp is put out at night, and will not touch a
lamp with unclean hands.   Those of the *mahumāchhi* or
bee sept will not take honey from a comb or eat it.   Those
of the *gaj* sept will not join an elephant kheddah.   Some of
the septs have an Ishta Devata or tutelary Hindu deity to
whom worship is paid.   Thus the elephant sept worship
Ganesh, the elephant-headed god, and also do not kill rats
because Ganesh rides on this animal.   Similarly the *harin*
or deer sept have Pāwan, the god of the wind, as their Ishta
Devata, because a deer is considered to be as swift as the
wind.   It would appear then that the septs, each having
its totem, were the original divisions for the restriction of
marriage, but as these increased in size they were felt to
debar the union of persons who had no real relationship
and hence the smaller family groups were substituted for
them ; while in the case of the old septs, the substitution
of the Hindu god representing the animal worshipped by
the sept for the animal itself as the object of veneration is
an instance of the process of abandoning totem or animal
worship and conforming to Hinduism.   In one or two cases
the *vargas* themselves have been further subdivided for the
purpose of marriage.   Thus certain families of the Padhān
(leader, chief) *varga* were entrusted with the duty of readmitting persons temporarily put out of caste to social
intercourse, for which they received the remuneration of a
rupee and a piece of cloth in each case.   These families
were called the Parichha or ' Scrutinisers ' and have now
become a separate *varga*, so that a Parichha Padhān may

marry another Padhān. This is a further instance of the process of subdivision of exogamous groups which must take place as the groups increase in size and numbers, and the original idea of the common ancestry of the group vanishes. Until finally the primitive system of exogamy disappears and is replaced by the modern and convenient method of prohibition of marriage within certain degrees of relationship.

3. Status and customs of the caste.
The Chasas do not marry within the same *varga*, but a man may usually take a wife from his mother's *varga*. A girl must always be wedded before arriving at adolescence, the penalty for breach of this rule being the driving out of the girl to seclusion in the forest for a day and a half, and a feast to the caste-fellows. If no husband is available she may be married to an arrow or a flower, or she goes through the form of marriage with any man in the caste, and when a suitable partner is subsequently found, is united with him by the form of widow-marriage. Widows may marry again and divorce is also allowed. The dead are usually buried if unmarried, and burnt when married. The Chasas worship the Hindu deities and also the village god Grāmsiri, who is represented by a stone outside the village. At festivals they offer animal sacrifices to their agricultural implements, as hoes and hatchets. They employ Brāhmans for religious ceremonies. They have an aversion to objects of a black colour, and will not use black umbrellas or clothes woven with black thread. They do not usually wear shoes or ride horses, even when they can afford these latter. Cultivation is the traditional occupation of the caste, and they are tenants, farmservants and field-labourers. They take food from Rājpūts and Brāhmans, and sometimes from Koltas and Sudhs. They eat flesh and fish, but abjure liquor, beef, pork and fowls. Their social position is a little below that of the good agricultural castes, and they are considered somewhat stupid, as shown by the proverb :

> *Chasa, ki jāne pasār katha,*
> *Padili bolai dons ;*

or 'What does the Chasa know of the dice? At every throw he calls out "twenty."'

Chauhān.[1]—A small caste of village watchmen and labourers in the Chhattīsgarh Division. They are also known as Chandel by outsiders. In 1911 the Chauhāns numbered 7000 persons in the Raipur and Bilāspur Districts, and the adjoining Feudatory States. The caste claim themselves to be of Rājpūt origin, and say that their ancestors came from Mainpuri, which is the home of the Chauhān clan of Rājpūts. A few of their section names are taken from those of Rājpūt clans, but the majority are of a totemistic nature, being called after animals and plants, as Nāg the cobra, Neora the mongoose, Kolhia the jackal, Kamal the lotus, Pat silk, Chānwar rice, Khānda a sword, and so on. Members of each sept worship the object after which it is named at the time of marriage, and if the tree or animal itself is not readily available, they make a representation of it in flour and pay their respects to that. Thus members of the Bedna or sugarcane sept make a stick of flour and worship it. They will not kill or eat their sept totem, but in some cases, as in that of the Chānwar or rice sept, this rule is impossible of observance, so the members of this sept content themselves with abstaining from a single variety of rice, the kind called Nāgkesar. Families who belong to septs named after heroic ancestors make an image in flour of the ancestral saint or hero and worship it. The caste employ Brāhmans for their marriage and other ceremonies, and will not take food from any caste except Brāhmans and their Bairāgi *gurus* or spiritual preceptors. But their social position is very low, as none except the most debased castes will take food or water from their hands, and their hereditary calling of village watchman would not be practised by any respectable caste. By outsiders they are considered little, if at all, superior to the Pankas and Gāndas, and the most probable theory of their origin is that they are the descendants of irregular alliances between immigrant Rājpūt adventurers and the women of the country. Their social customs resemble those of other low castes in Chhattīsgarh. Before the bridegroom starts for a wedding, they have a peculiar ceremony known as Naodori. Seven small earthen cups full of water are placed on the boy's head, and

[1] This article is based principally on notes taken by Mr. Hīra Lāl at Bhatgaon.

then poured over him in succession. A piece of new cloth
is laid on his head, and afterwards placed seven times in
contact with the earth. During this ritual the boy keeps his
eyes shut, and it is believed that if he should open them
before its completion, his children would be born blind.
When the bride leaves her father's house she and all her
relatives mourn and weep noisily, and the bride continues
doing so until she is well over a mile from her own
village. Similarly on the first three or four visits which she
pays to her parents after her wedding, she begins crying
loudly a mile away from their house, and continues until she
reaches it. It is the etiquette also that women should cry
whenever they meet relatives from a distance. In such cases
when two women see each other they cry together, each
placing her head on the other's shoulder and her hands at
her sides. While they cry they change the position of their
heads two or three times, and each addresses the other
according to their relationship, as mother, sister, and so on.
Or if any member of the family has recently died, they call
upon him or her, exclaiming 'O my mother! O my sister!
O my father! Why did not I, unfortunate one, die instead
of thee?' A woman when weeping with a man holds to
his sides and rests her head against his breast. The man
exclaims at intervals, 'Stop crying, do not cry.' When
two women are weeping together it is a point of etiquette
that the elder should stop first and then beg her companion
to do so, but if it is doubtful which is the elder, they sometimes go on crying for an hour at a time, exciting the younger
spectators to mirth, until at length some elder steps forward
and tells one of them to stop. The Chauhāns permit the
remarriage of widows, and a woman is bound by no restrictions
as to her choice of a second husband.

The goddess Dūrga or Devi is chiefly revered by the
caste, who observe fasts in her honour in the months of
Kunwār (September) and Chait (March). When they make
a *badna* or vow, they usually offer goats to the goddess, and
sow the *Jawaras* or Gardens of Adonis in her name, but
except on such occasions they present less costly articles, as
cocoanuts, betel-leaves, areca-nuts and flowers. On the
Dasahra festival they worship the *lāthi* or stick which is the

badge of office of the village watchman. They were formerly addicted to petty theft, and it is said that they worshipped the *khunta* or pointed rod for digging through the wall of a house. The caste usually burn the dead, but children whose ears or noses have not been pierced are buried. Children who die before they have begun to eat grain are not mourned at all, while for older children the period of mourning is three to seven days, and for adults ten days. On the tenth day they clean their houses, shave themselves and offer balls of rice to the dead under the direction of a Brāhman, to whom they present eating and drinking vessels, clothes, shoes and cattle with the belief that the articles will thus become available for the use of the dead man in the other world. The Chauhāns will not eat fowls, pork or beef, and in some places they abstain from drinking liquor.

Chhīpa, Rangāri, Bhaosar, Nirāli, Nilgar.—The Hindu caste of cotton printers and dyers. They are commonly known as Chhīpa in the northern Districts and Rangāri or Bhaosar in the Marātha country. The Chhīpas and Rangāris together number about 23,000 persons. In the south of the Central Provinces and Berār cotton is a staple crop, and the cotton-weaving industry is much stronger than in the north, and as a necessary consequence the dyers also would be more numerous. Though the Chhīpas and Rangāris do not intermarry or dine together, no essential distinction exists between them. They are both of functional origin, pursue exactly the same occupation, and relate the same story about themselves, and no good reason therefore exists for considering them as separate castes. Nīlgar or Nirāli is a purely occupational term applied to Chhīpas or Rangāris who work in indigo (*nīl*); while Bhaosar is another name for the Rangāris in the northern Districts. *1. Constitution of the caste.*

The Rangāris say that when Parasurāma, the Brāhman, was slaying the Kshatriyas, two brothers of the warrior caste took refuge in a temple of Devi. One of them, called Bhaosar, threw himself upon the image, while the other hid behind it. The goddess saved them both and told them to adopt the vocation of dyers. The Rangāris are descended *2. Its origin and position.*

from the brother who was called Bhaosar and the Chhīpas from the other brother, because he hid behind the image (*chhipna*, to hide). The word is really derived from *chhāpna*, to print, because the Chhīpas print coloured patterns on cotton cloths with wooden stamps. Rangāri comes from the common word *rang* or colour. The Chhīpas have a slightly different version of the same story, according to which the goddess gave one brother a needle and a piece of thread, and the other some red betel-leaf which she spat at him out of her mouth ; and told one to follow the vocation of a tailor, and the other that of a dyer. Hence the first was called Chhīpi or Shimpi and the second Chhīpa. This story indicates a connection between the dyeing and tailoring castes in the Marātha Districts, which no doubt exists, as one subcaste of the Rangāris is named after Nāmdeo, the patron saint of the Shimpis or tailors. Both the dyeing and tailoring industries are probably of considerably later origin than that of cotton-weaving, and both are urban rather than village industries. And this consideration perhaps accounts for the fact that the Chhīpas and Rangāris rank higher than most of the weaving castes, and no stigma or impurity attaches to them.

3. Caste subdivisions.

The caste have a number of subdivisions, such as the Malaiyas or immigrants from Mālwa, the Gujrāti who come from Gujarāt, the Golias or those who dye cloth with *goli ka rang*, the fugitive aniline dyes, the Nāmdeos who belong to the sect founded by the Darzi or tailor of that name, and the Khatris, these last being members of the Khatri caste who have adopted the profession.

4. Marriage and other customs.

Marriage is forbidden between persons so closely connected as to have a common ancestor in the third generation. In Bhandāra it is obligatory on all members of the caste, who know the bride or bridegroom, to ask him or her to dine. The marriage rite is that prevalent among the Hindustāni castes, of walking round the sacred post. Divorce and the marriage of widows are permitted. In Narsinghpur, when a bachelor marries a widow, he first goes through a mock ceremony by walking seven times round an earthen vessel filled with cakes ; this rite being known as Langra Biyāh or the lame marriage. The caste burn their dead, placing the head to the north. On the day of Dasahra the

CHHĪPA OR CALICO-PRINTER AT WORK.

Chhīpas worship their wooden stamps, first washing them and then making an offering to them of a cocoanut, flowers and an image consisting of a bottle-gourd standing on four sticks, which is considered to represent a goat. The Chhīpas rank with the lower artisan castes, from whose hands Brāhmans will not take water. Nevertheless some of them wear the sacred thread and place sect - marks on their foreheads.

The bulk of the Chhīpas dye cloths in red, blue or black, 5. Occupa-
with ornamental patterns picked out on them in black and tion.
white. Formerly their principal agent was the *al* or Indian mulberry (*Morinda citrifolia*), from which a rich red dye is obtained. But this indigenous product has been ousted by alizarin, a colouring agent made from coal-tar, which is imported from Germany, and is about thirty per cent cheaper than the native dye. Chhīpas prepare *sāris* or women's wearing-cloths, and floor and bed cloths. The dye stamps are made of teakwood by an ordinary carpenter, the flat surface of the wood being hollowed out so as to leave ridges which form either a design in curved lines or the outlines of the figures of men, elephants and tigers. There is a great variety of patterns, as many as three hundred stamps having been found in one Chhīpa's shop. The stamps are usually covered with a black ink made of sulphate of iron, and this is fixed by myrobalans ; the Nīlgars usually dye a plain blue with indigotin. No great variety or brilliancy of colours is obtained by the Hindu dyers, who are much excelled in this branch of the art by the Muhammadan Rangrez. In Gujarāt dyeing is strictly forbidden by the caste rules of the Chhīpas or Bhaosars during the four rainy months, because the slaughter of insects in the dyeing vat adds to the evil and ill-luck of that sunless time.[1]

[1] *Bombay Gazetteer, Hindus of Gujarāt,* p. 178.

CHITĀRI

1. Origin and traditions. **Chitāri, Chiter, Chitrakār, Mahārana.** — A caste of painters on wood and plaster. Chiter is the Hindustāni, and Chitāri the Marāthi name, both being corruptions of the Sanskrit Chitrakār. Mahārana is the term used in the Uriya country, where the caste are also known as Phāl-Barhai, or a carpenter who only works on one side of the wood. Chitāri is further an occupational term applied to Mochis and Jīngars, or leather-workers, who have adopted the occupation of wall-painting, and there is no reason to doubt that the Chitāris were originally derived from the Mochis, though they have now a somewhat higher position. In Mandla the Chitrakārs and Jīngars are separate castes, and do not eat or intermarry with one another. Neither branch will take water from the Mochis, who make shoes, and some Chitrakārs even refuse to touch them. They say that the founder of their caste was Biskarma,[1] the first painter, and that their ancestors were Rājpūts, whose country was taken by Akbar. As they were without occupation Akbar then assigned to them the business of making saddles and bridles for his cavalry and scabbards for their swords. It is not unlikely that the Jīngar caste did really originate or first become differentiated from the Mochis and Chamārs in Rājputāna owing to the demand for such articles, and this would account for the Mochis and Jīngars having adopted Rājpūt names for their sections, and making a claim to Rājpūt

---

[1] A corruption for Viswakarma, the divine artificer and architect.

descent. The Chitrakārs of Mandla say that their ancestors belonged to Garha, near Jubbulpore, where the tomb of a woman of their family who became *sati* is still to be seen. Garha, which was once the seat of an important Gond dynasty with a garrison, would also naturally have been a centre for their craft.

Another legend traces their origin from Chitrarekha, a nymph who was skilled in painting and magic. She was the friend of a princess Usha, whose father was king of Sohāgpur in Hoshangābād. Usha fell in love with a beautiful young prince whom she saw in a dream, and Chitrarekha drew the portraits of many gods and men for her, until finally Usha recognised the youth of her dream in the portrait of Aniruddha, the grandson of Krishna. Chitrarekha then by her magic power brought Aniruddha to Usha, but when her father found him in the palace he bound him and kept him in prison. On this Krishna appeared and rescued his grandson, and taking Usha from her father married them to each other. The Chitāris say that as a reward to Chitrarekha, Krishna promised her that her descendants should never be in want, and hence members of their caste do not lack for food even in famine time.[1] The Chitāris are declining in numbers, as their paintings are no longer in demand, the people preferring the cheap coloured prints imported from Germany and England.

The caste is a mixed occupational group, and those of Marātha, Telugu and Hindustāni extraction marry among themselves. A few wear the sacred thread, and abstain from eating flesh or drinking liquor, while the bulk of them do not observe these restrictions. 2. Social customs.

Among the Jīngars women accompany the marriage procession, but not with the Chitāris.

Widow-marriage is allowed, but among the Mahārānas a wife who has lived with her husband may not marry any one except his younger brother, and if there are none she must remain a widow. In Mandla, if a widow marries her younger brother-in-law, half her first husband's property goes to him finally, and half to the first husband's children.

---

[1] The story, however, really belongs to northern India. Usha is the goddess of dawn.

If she marries an outsider she takes her first husband's property and children with her. Formerly if a wife misbehaved the Chitāri sometimes sold her to the highest bidder, but this custom has fallen into abeyance, and now if a man divorces his wife her father usually repays to him the expenses of his marriage. These he realises in turn from any man who takes his daughter. A second wife worships the spirit of the dead first wife on the day of Akhātīj, offering some food and a breast-cloth, so that the spirit may not trouble her.

3. Birth and childhood.

A pregnant woman must stay indoors during an eclipse; if she goes out and sees it they believe that her child will be born deformed. They think that a woman in this condition must be given any food which she takes a fancy for, so far as may be practicable, as to thwart her desires would affect the health of the child. Women in this condition sometimes have a craving for eating earth; then they will eat either the scrapings or whitewash from the walls, or black clay soil, or the ashes of cowdung cakes to the extent of a small handful a day. A woman's first child should be born in her father-in-law's or husband's house if possible, but at any rate not in her father's house. And if she should be taken with the pangs of travail while on a visit to her own family, they will send her to some other house for her child to be born. The ears of boys and the ears and nostrils of girls are pierced, and until this is done they are not considered to be proper members of the caste and can take food from any one's hand. The Chitāris of Mandla permit a boy to do this until he is married. A child's hair is not shaved when it is born, but this should be done once before it is three years old, whether it be a boy or girl. After this the hair may be allowed to grow, and shaved off or simply cut as they prefer. Except in the case of illness a girl's hair is only shaved once, and that of an adult woman is never cut, unless she becomes a widow and makes a pilgrimage to a sacred place, when it is shaved off as an offering.

4. The evil eye.

In order to avert the evil eye they hang round a child's neck a nut called *bajar-battu,* the shell of which they say will crack and open if any one casts the evil eye on the child. If it is placed in milk the two parts will come together again.

They also think that the nut attracts the evil eye and absorbs
its effect, and the child is therefore not injured.   If they
think that some one has cast the evil eye on a child, they
say a charm, '*Ishwar, Gauri, Pārvati ke ān nazar dur ho
jao,*' or ' Depart, Evil Eye, in the name of Mahādeo and
Pārvati,' and as they say this they blow on the child three
times ; or they take some salt, chillies and mustard in
their hand and wave it round the child's head and say,
' *Telin kī lāgi ho, Tamolin kī lāgi ho, Marārin kī ho,
Gorania (Gondin) kī ho, oke, oke, parparāke phut jāwe,*'
' If it be a Telin, Tambolin, Marārin or Gondin who
has cast the evil eye, may her eyes crack and fall out.'
And at the same time they throw the mustard, chillies
and salt on the fire so that the eyes of her who cast the
evil eye may crack and fall out as these things crackle in
the fire.

If tiger's claws are used for an amulet, the points must
be turned outwards.   If any one intends to wish luck to a
child, he says, ' *Tori balayān leun,*' and waves his hands round
the child's head several times to signify that he takes upon
himself all the misfortunes which are to happen to the child.
Then he presses the knuckles of his hands against the sides of
his own head till they crack, which is a lucky omen, averting
calamity.   If the knuckles do not crack at the first attempt, it
is repeated two or three times.   When a man sneezes he will
say ' Chatrapati,' which is considered to be a name of Devi,
but is only used on this occasion.   But some say nothing.
After yawning they snap their fingers, the object of which,
they say, is to drive away sleep, as otherwise the desire will
become infectious and attack others present.   But if a child
yawns they sometimes hold one of their hands in front of
his mouth, and it is probable that the original meaning of
the custom was to prevent evil spirits from entering through
the widely opened mouth, or the yawner's own soul or spirit
from escaping ; and the habit of holding the hand before the
mouth from politeness when yawning inadvertently may be
a reminiscence of this.

The following are some cradle-songs taken down from a   5. Cradle-
Chitrakār, but probably used by most of the lower Hindu   songs.
castes :

1. Mother, rock the cradle of your pretty child. What is the cradle made of, and what are its tassels made of?
   The cradle is made of sandalwood, its tassels are of silk.
   Some Gaolin (milkwoman) has overlooked the child, he vomits up his milk.
   Dasoda [1] shall wave salt and mustard round his head, and he shall play in my lap.
   My baby is making little steps. O Sunār, bring him tinkling anklets!
   The Sunār shall bring anklets for him, and my child will go to the garden and there we will eat oranges and lemons.
2. My Krishna's tassel is lost, Tell me, some one, where it is. My child is angry and will not come into my arms.
   The tears are falling from his eyes like blossoms from the *bela* [2] flower.
   He has bangles on his wrists and anklets on his feet, on his head a golden crown and round his waist a silver chain.

The *jhumri* or tassel referred to above is a tassel adorned with cowries and hung from the top of the cradle so that the child may keep his eyes on it while the cradle is being rocked.

3. Sleep, sleep, my little baby; I will wave my hands round your head [3] on the banks of the Jumna. I have cooked hot cakes for you and put butter in them; all the night you lay awake, now take your fill of sleep.
   The little mangoes are hanging on the tree; the rope is in the well; sleep thou till I go and come back with water.
   I will hang your cradle on the banyan tree, and its rope to the pīpal tree; I will rock my darling gently so that the rope shall never break.

The last song may be given in the vernacular as a specimen:

4.
> *Rām kī Chireya, Rām ko khet.*
> *Khaori Chireya, bhar, bhar pet.*
> *Tan munaiyān khā lao khet,*
> *Agao, labra, gāli det;*
> *Kahe ko, labra, gāli de;*
> *Apni bhuntia gin, gin le.*

or—

The field is Rāma's, the little birds are Rāma's; O birds, eat your fill; the little birds have eaten up the corn.

---

[1] Krishna's mother.

[2] Little white flowers like jasmine. This simile would be unlikely to occur to the ordinary observer who sees a Hindu child crying.

[3] *Tori balayān leun.* For explanation see above.

The surly farmer has come to the field and scolds them ; the little birds say, ' O farmer, why do you scold us ? count your ears of maize, they are all there.'

This song commemorates a favourite incident in the life of Tulsi Dās, the author of the Rāmāyana, who when he was a little boy was once sent by his *guru* to watch the crop. But after some time the *guru* came and found the field full of birds eating the corn and Tulsi Dās watching them. When asked why he did not scare them away, he said, ' Are they not as much the creatures of Rāma as I am ? how should I deprive them of food ? '

The Chitāris pursue their old trade, principally in Nāgpur city, where the taste for wall-paintings still survives ; and they decorate the walls of houses with their crude red and blue colours. But they have now a number of other avocations. They paint pictures on paper, making their colours from the tins of imported aniline dyeing-powders which are sold in the bazār ; but there is little demand for these. They make small pictures of the deities which the people hang on their walls for a day and then throw away. They also paint the bodies of the men who pretend to be tigers at the Muharram festival, for which they charge a rupee. They make the clay paper-covered masks of monkeys and demons worn by actors who play the Rāmlīla or story of Rāma on the Rāmnaomi festival in Chait (March) ; they also make the *tāzias* or representations of the tomb of Hussain and paper figures of human beings with small clay heads, which are carried in the Muharram procession. They make marriage crowns ; the frames of these are of conical shape with a half-moon at the top, made from strips of bamboo ; they are covered with red paper picked out with yellow and green and with tinfoil, and are ornamented with borders of date-palm leaves. The crowns cost from four annas to a rupee each. They make the artificial flowers used at weddings ; these are stuck on a bamboo stick and at the arrival and departure of the bridegroom are scrambled for by the guests, who take them home as keepsakes or give them to their children for playthings. The flowers copied are the lotus, rose and chrysanthemum, and the imitations are quite good. Sometimes the bridegroom is

6. Occupation.

surrounded by trays or boxes of flowers, carried in procession and arranged so as to look as if they were planted in beds. Other articles made by the Chitrakār are paper fans, paper globes for hanging to the roofs of houses, Chinese lanterns made either of paper or of mica covered with paper, and small caps of velvet embroidered with gold lace. At the Akti festival[1] they make pairs of little clay dolls, dressing them as male and female, and sell them in red lacquered bamboo baskets, and the girls take them to the jungle and pretend that they are married. Formerly the Chitrakārs made clay idols for temples, but these have been supplanted by marble images imported from Jaipur. The Jīngars make the cloth saddles on which natives ride, and some of them bind books, the leather for which is made from goat-skin, and is not considered so impure as that made from the hides of cattle. But one class of them, who are considered inferior, make leather harness from cow-hide and buffalo-hide.

Chitrakathi, Hardas.[2]—A small caste of religious mendi-cants and picture showmen in the Marātha Districts. In 1901 they numbered 200 persons in the Central Provinces and 1500 in Berār, being principally found in the Amraoti District. The name, Mr. Enthoven writes,[3] is derived from *chitra*, a picture, and *katha*, a story, and the professional occupation of the caste is to travel about exhibiting pictures of heroes and gods, and telling stories about them. The community is probably of mixed functional origin, for in Bombay they have exogamous section-names taken from those of the Marāthas, as Jādhow, More, Powār and so on, while in the Central Provinces and Berār an entirely different set is found. Here several sections appear to be named after certain offices held or functions performed by their members at the caste feasts. Thus the Atak section are the caste headmen; the Mānkari appear to be a sort of substitute for the Atak or their grand viziers, the word

---

[1] Commencement of the agricultural year.

[2] This article is partly based on a paper by Mr. Bijai Bahadur, Naib-

Tahsīldār, Bālāghāt.

[3] *Bombay Ethnographic Survey*, draft article on Chitrakathi.

Mānkar being primarily a title applied to Marātha noblemen, who held an official position at court ; the Bhojni section serve the food at marriage and other ceremonies ; the Kākra arrange for the lighting ; the Kothārya are store-keepers ; and the Ghoderao (from *ghoda*, a horse) have the duty of looking after the horses and bullock-carts of the castemen who assemble. The Chitrakathis are really no doubt the same caste as the Chitāris or Chitrakārs (painters) of the Central Provinces, and, like them, a branch of the Mochis (tanners), and originally derived from the Chamārs. But as the Berār Chitrakathis are migratory instead of settled, and in other respects differ from the Chitāris, they are treated in a separate article. Marriage within the section is forbidden, and, besides this, members of the Atak and Mānkari sections cannot intermarry as they are considered to be related, being divisions of one original section. The social customs of the caste resemble those of the Kunbis, but they bury their dead in a sitting posture, with the face to the east, and on the eighth day erect a platform over the grave. At the festival of Akhatīj (3rd of light Baisākh) [1] they worship a vessel of water in honour of their dead ancestors, and in Kunwār (September) they offer oblations to them. Though not impure, the caste occupy a low social position, and are said to prostitute their married women and tolerate sexual licence on the part of unmarried girls. Mr. Kitts [2] describes them as " Wandering mendicants, sometimes suspected of associating with Kaikāris for purposes of crime ; but they seem nevertheless to be a comparatively harmless people. They travel about in little huts like those used by the Waddars ; the men occasionally sell buffaloes and milk ; the women beg, singing and accompanying themselves on the *thāli*. The old men also beg, carrying a flag in their hand, and shouting the name of their god, Hari Vithal (from which they derive their name of Hardās). They are fond of spirits, and, when drunk, become pot-valiant and troublesome." The *thāli* or plate on which their women play is also known as *sarthāda*, and consists of a small brass dish coated with

---

[1] May–June. The Akhatīj is the beginning of the agricultural year.
[2] *Berār Census Report* (1881), para-graph 206. The passage is slightly altered and abridged in reproduction.

wax in the centre; this is held on the thigh and a pointed stick is moved in a circle so as to produce a droning sound. The men sometimes paint their own pictures, and in Bombay they have a caste rule that every Chitrakathi must have in his house a complete set of sacred pictures ; this usually includes forty representations of Rāma's life, thirty-five of that of the sons of Arjun, forty of the Pāndavas, forty of Sīta and Rāwan, and forty of Harishchandra. The men also have sets of puppets representing the above and other deities, and enact scenes with them like a Punch and Judy show, sometimes aided by ventriloquism.

1. General notice.

Cutchi or **Meman, Kachhi, Muamin.**— A class of Muhammadan merchants who come every year from Gujarāt and Cutch to trade in the towns of the Central Provinces, where they reside for eight months, returning to their houses during the four months of the rainy season. In 1911 they numbered about 2000 persons, of whom five-sixths were men, this fact indicating the temporary nature of their settlements. Nevertheless a large proportion of the trade of the Province is in their hands. The caste is fully and excellently described by Khān Bahādur Fazalullah Lutfullah Farīdi, Assistant Collector of Customs, Bombay, in the *Bombay Gazetteer.*[1] He remarks of them : " As shopkeepers and miscellaneous dealers Cutchis are considered to be the most successful of Muhammadans. They owe their success in commerce to their freedom from display and their close and personal attention to and keen interest in business. The richest Meman merchant does not disdain to do what a Pārsi in his position would leave to his clerks. Their hope and courage are also excellent endowments. They engage without fear in any promising new branch of trade and are daring in their ventures, a trait partly inherited from their Lohāna ancestors, and partly due to their faith in the luck which the favour of their saints secures them." Another great advantage arises from their method of trading in small corporations or companies of a number of persons either relations or friends. Some of these will have shops in the great centres of trade, Bombay and Calcutta, and others in

---

[1] Vol. ix. part. ii. *Muhammadans of Gujarāt*, p. 57.

different places in the interior. Each member then acts as correspondent and agent for all the others, and puts what business he can in their way. Many are also employed as assistants and servants in the shops ; but at the end of the season, when all return to their native Gujarāt, the profits from the different shops are pooled and divided among the members in varying proportion. By this method they obtain all the advantages which are recognised as attaching to co-operative trading.

According to Mr. Farīdi, from whose description the remainder of this article is mainly taken, the Memans or more correctly Muamins or ' Believers' are converts from the Hindu caste of Lohānas of Sind. They venerate especially Maulāna Abdul Kādir Gīlāni who died at Baghdād in A.D. 1165. His sixth descendant, Syed Yūsufuddīn Kordiri, was in 1421 instructed in a dream to proceed to Sind and guide its people into the way of Islām. On his arrival he was received with honour by the local king, who was converted, and the ruler's example was followed by one Mānikji, the head of one of the *nukhs* or clans of the Lohāna community. He with his three sons and seven hundred families of the caste embraced Islām, and on their conversion the title of Muamin or ' Believer' was conferred on them by the saint. It may be noted that Colonel Tod derives the Lohānas from the Rājpūts, remarking of them : [1] " This tribe is numerous both in Dhāt and Talpūra ; formerly they were Rājpūts, but betaking themselves to commerce have fallen into the third class. They are scribes and shopkeepers, and object to no occupation that will bring a subsistence ; and as to food, to use the expressive idiom of this region where hunger spurns at law, ' Excepting their cats and their cows they will eat anything.' " In his account of Sind, Postans says of the Lohānas : " The Hindu merchants and bankers have agents in the most remote parts of Central Asia and could negotiate bills upon Candahār, Khelāt, Cābul, Khiva, Herāt, Bokhāra or any other marts of that country. These agents, in the pursuit of their calling, leave Sind for many years, quitting their families to locate themselves among the most savage and intolerant

2. Origin of the caste.

[1] *Rājasthān*, ii. p. 292.

tribes." This account could equally apply to the Khatris, who also travel over Central Asia, as shown in the article on that caste ; and if, as seems not improbable, the Lohānas and Khatris are connected, the hypothesis that the former, like the latter, are derived from Rājpūts would receive some support.

The present Pīr or head of the community is Sayyid Jāfir Shāh, who is nineteenth in descent from Yūsufuddīn and lives partly in Bombay and partly in Mundra of South Cutch. "At an uncertain date," Mr. Farīdi continues, "the Lohāna or Cutchi Memans passed from Cutch south through Kāthiāwār to Gujarāt. They are said to have been strong and wealthy in Surat during the period of its prosperity (1580—1680). As Surat sank the Cutchi Memans moved to Bombay. Outside Cutch and Kāthiāwār, which may be considered their homes, the Memans are scattered over the cities of north and south Gujarāt and other Districts of Bombay. Beyond that Presidency they have spread as traders and merchants and formed settlements in Calcutta, Madras, the Malabar Coast, South Burma, Siam, Singapore and Java ; in the ports of the Arabian Peninsula, except Muscat, where they have been ousted by the Khojas ; and in Mozambique, Zanzibar and the East African Coast."[1] They have two divisions in Bombay, known as Cutchi or Kachhi and Halai.

3. Social customs. Cutchis and Memans retain some non-Muhammadan usages. The principal of these is that they do not allow their daughters and widows to inherit according to the rule of Muhammadan law.[2] They conduct their weddings by the Nikāh form and the *mehar* or dowry is always the same sum of a hundred and twenty-five rupees, whatever may be the position of the parties and in the case of widows also.

---

[1] *Bombay Gazetteer, l.c.*

[2] In recording this point Mr. Farīdi gives the following note : " In 1847 a case occurred which shows how firmly the Memans cling to their original tribal customs. The widow of Hāji Nūr Muhammad of the Lakariya family demanded a share of her deceased husband's property according to Muhammadan law. The *jamā-at* or community decided that a widow had no claim to share her husband's estates under the Hindu law. Before the High Court, in spite of the ridicule of other Sunnis, the elders of the Cutchi Memans declared that their caste rules denied the widow's claim. The matter caused and is still (1896) causing agitation, as the doctors of the Sunni law at Mecca have decided that as the law of inheritance is laid down by the holy Korān, a wilful departure from it is little short of apostasy. The Memans are contemplating a change, but so far they have not found themselves able to depart from their tribal practices."

They say that either party may be divorced by the other for conjugal infidelity, but the *mehar* or dowry must always be paid to the wife in the case of a divorce. The caste eat flesh and fowls and abstain from liquor. Most of them also decline to eat beef as a consequence of their Hindu ancestry, and they will not take food from Hindus of low caste.

DAHĀIT[1]

1. Origin of the caste.

Dahāit, Dahāyat.—A mixed caste of village watchmen of the Jubbulpore and Mandla Districts, who are derived from the cognate caste of Khangārs and from several of the forest tribes. In 1911 the Dahāits numbered about 15,000 persons in the Central Provinces, of whom the large majority were found in the Jubbulpore District and the remainder in Bilāspur, Damoh and Seoni. Outside the Province they reside only in Bundelkhand. According to one story the Dahāits and Khangārs had a common ancestor, and in Mandla again they say that their ancestors were the door-keepers of the Rājas of Mahoba, and were known as Chhadī-dar or Darwān ; and they came to Mandla about 200 years ago, during the time of Rāja Nizām Shāh of the Rāj-Gond dynasty of that place. In Mandla the names of their subdivisions are given as Rawatia or Rautia, Kol, Mawāsi, Sonwāni and Rajwāria. Of these Kol and Rajwār are the names of separate tribes ; Mawāsi is commonly used as a synonym for Korku, another tribe; Sonwāni is the name of a sept found among several of the primitive tribes ; while Rāwat is a title borne by the Saonrs and Gonds. The names Rautia and Rajwāria are found as subdivisions of the Kol tribe in Mīrzāpur,[2] and it is not improbable that the

[1] This article is based on papers by Mr. Vithal Rao, Naib-Tahsīldār, Bilāspur, and Messrs. Kanhya Lāl and Pyāre Lāl Misra of the Gazetteer office.

[2] Crooke, *Tribes and Castes*, art. Kol.

Dahāits are principally derived from this tribe.   The actual name Dahāit is also given by Mr. Crooke as a subdivision of the Kols, and he states it to have the meaning of 'villager,' from *dehāt*, a village.   The Dahāits were a class of personal attendants on the chief or Rāja, as will be seen subsequently.   They stood behind the royal cushion and fanned him, ran in front of his chariot or litter to clear the way, and acted as door-keepers and ushers.   Service of this kind is of a menial nature and, further, demands a considerable degree of physical robustness ; and hence members of the non-Aryan forest tribes would naturally be selected for it.   And it would appear that these menial servants gradually formed themselves into a caste in Bundelkhand and became the Dahāits.   They obtained a certain rise in status, and now rank in the position of village menials above their parent tribes.   In the Central Provinces the Dahāits have commonly been employed as village watchmen, a post analogous to that of door-keeper or porter.   The caste are also known as Bhāldār or spearmen, and Kotwār or village watchmen.

The subcastes returned from the Mandla District have already been mentioned.   In Bilāspur they have quite different ones, of which two, Joharia and Pailagia, are derived from methods of greeting.   Johār is the salutation which a Rājpūt prince sends to a vassal or chief of inferior rank, and Pailagi or 'I fall at your feet' is that with which a member of a lower caste accosts a Brāhman.   How such names came to be adopted as subcastes cannot be explained. The caste have a number of exogamous groups named after plants and animals.   Members of the Bel,[1] Rusallo and Chheola[2] septs revere the trees after which these septs are named.   They will not cut or injure the tree, and at the time of marriage they go and invite it to be present at the ceremony.   They offer to the tree the *maihar* cake, which is given only to the members of the family and the husbands and children of daughters.   Those belonging to the Nagotia sept[3] will not kill a snake, and at the time of marriage they deposit the *maihar* cake at a snake-hole. Members of the Singh (lion) and Bāgh (tiger) septs will not

2. Internal structure : totemism.

---

[1] *Aegle Marmelos.*   [2] *Butea frondosa.*   [3] *Nāg*, a cobra.

kill a tiger, and at their weddings they draw his image on a wall and offer the cake to it, being well aware that if they approached the animal himself, he would probably repudiate the relationship and might not be satisfied with the cake for his meal.

3. Marriage and other customs.

Prior to a marriage a bride-price, known as *sukh* or *chāri*, and consisting of six rupees with some sugar, turmeric and sesamum oil, must be paid by the parents of the bridegroom to those of the bride ; and in the absence of this they will decline to perform the ceremony. At the wedding the couple go round the sacred post, and then the bridegroom mingles the flames of two burning lamps and pierces the nose of the image of a bullock made in flour. This rite is performed by several castes, and is said to be in commemoration of Krishna's having done so on different occasions. It is probably meant to excuse or legitimise the real operation, which should properly be considered as sinful in view of the sacred character of the animal. And it may be mentioned here that the people of the Vindhyan or Bundelkhand Districts where the Dahāits live do not perforate the nostrils of bullocks, and drive them simply by a rope tied round the mouth. In consequence they have little control over them and are quite unable to stop a cart going downhill, which simply proceeds at the will of the animals until it reaches the level or bangs up against some obstacle. In Bilāspur a widow is expected to remain single for five years after her husband's death, and if she marries within that time she is put out of caste. Divorce is permitted, but is not of frequent occurrence. The caste will excuse a married woman caught in adultery once, but on a second offence she must be expelled. If a woman leaves her husband and goes to live with another man, the latter must repay to her husband the amount expended on his marriage. But in such a case, if the woman was already a widow or *kari aurat*,[1] no penalty is incurred by a man who takes her from her second husband. A man of any good cultivating caste who has a *liaison* with a Dahāit woman will be admitted into the community. An outsider who desires to become a member of the caste must clean his house, break

---

[1] Kept woman, a term applied to a widow.

his earthen cooking-pots and buy new ones, and give a meal to the caste-fellows at his house. He sits and takes food with them, and when the meal is over he takes a grain of rice from the leaf-plate of each guest and eats it, and drinks a drop of water from his leaf-cup. This act is equivalent to eating the leavings of food, and after it he cannot re-enter his own caste. On such occasions a rupee and a piece of cloth must be given to the headman of the caste, and a piece of cloth to each member of the *panchāyat* or committee. The headman is known as Mirdhān, and a member of the committee as Diwān, the offices of both being hereditary. The caste worship the Hindu and village gods of the locality. They have a curious belief that the skull of a man of the Kāyasth (writer) caste cannot be burnt in fire, and that if it is placed in a dwelling-house the inmates will quarrel. A child's first teeth, if found, are thrown into a sacred river or on to the roof of a house with a few grains of rice, in order that the second teeth may grow white and pointed like the rice. The Jhālar or first hair of a boy or girl is cut between two and ten years of age and is wrapped in a piece of dough and thrown into a sacred river. Women are tattooed on the back of the hands, and also sometimes on the shoulder and the arms above the elbow, but not on the feet or face.

The Dahāits are now commonly employed as village watchmen and as guards or porters (*chaukidār*) of houses. In Bilāspur they also carry litters and work as navvies and stonebreakers like the Kols. Here they will eat pork, but in Jubbulpore greater regard is paid to Hindu prejudice, and they have given up pork and fowls and begun to employ Brāhmans for their ceremonies. The men of the caste will accept cooked food from any man of the higher castes or those cultivators from whom a Brāhman will take water, but the women are more strict and will only accept it from a Brāhman, Bania, Lodhi or Kurmi. *4. Social position.*

In past times the Dahāits were the personal attendants on the king. They fanned him with the *chaur* or yak-tail whisk when he sat in state on the royal cushion. This implement is held sacred and is also used by Brāhmans to fan the deities. On ordinary occasions the Rāja was fanned by a pankha made of *khaskhas* grass and wetted, but not so that *5. Former occupations: door-keeper and mace-bearer.*

the water fell on his head. They also acted as gate-keepers of the palace, and had the title of Darwān. The gate-keeper's post was a responsible one, as it lay on him to see that no one with evil intentions or carrying secret arms was admitted to the palace. Whenever a chief or noble came to visit the king he deposited his arms with the porter or door-keeper. The necessity of a faithful door-keeper is shown in the proverb : "With these five you must never quarrel : your Guru, your wife, your gate-keeper, your doctor and your cook." The reasons for the inclusion of the others are fairly clear. On the other hand the gate-porter had usually to be propitiated before access was obtained to his master, like the modern chuprāssie ; and the resentment felt at his rapacity is shown in the proverb : " The broker, the octroi moharrir, the door-keeper and the bard : these four will surely go to hell." The Darwān or door-keeper would be given the right to collect dues, equivalent to those of a village watchman, from forty or fifty villages. The Dahāits also carried the *chob* or silver mace before the king. This was about five feet long with a knob at the upper end as thick as a man's wrist. The mace-bearer was known as Chobdār, and it was his duty to carry messages and an-nounce visitors ; this latter function he performed with a degree of pomposity truly Asiatic, dwelling with open mouth very audibly on some of the most sounding and emphatic syllables in a way that appeared to strangers almost ludicrous,[1] as shown in the following instance : " On advancing, the Chobdārs or heralds proclaimed the titles of this princely cow-keeper in the usual hyperbolical style. One of the most insignificant-looking men I ever saw then became the destroyer of nations, the leveller of mountains, the exhauster of the ocean. After commanding every inferior mortal to make way for this exalted prince, the heralds called aloud to the animal creation, ' Retire, ye serpents ; fly, ye locusts ; approach not, iguanas, lizards and reptiles, while your lord and master condescends to set his foot on the earth.' "[2] The Dahāits ran before the Rāja's chariot or litter to clear the way for him and announce his coming ; and it

---

[1] Moor's *Hindu Infanticide*, p. 133.
[2] James Forbes, *Oriental Memoirs*, i. p. 313.

was also a principal business of the caste to carry the royal umbrella above the head of the king.

The umbrella was the essential symbol of sovereignty in Asia like the crown in Europe. "Among the ancient Egyptians the umbrella carried with it a mark of distinction, and persons of quality alone could use it. The Assyrians reserved it for royal personages only. The umbrella or parasol, says Layard, that emblem of royalty so universally adopted by Eastern nations, was generally carried over the king in time of peace and sometimes even in war. In shape it resembled very closely those now in common use ; but it is always seen open in the sculptures. It was edged with tassels and usually decorated at the top by a flower or some other ornament. The Greeks used it as a mystic symbol in some of their sacred festivals, and the Romans introduced the custom of hanging an umbrella in the basilican churches as a part of the insignia of office of the judge sitting in the basilica. It is said that on the judgment hall being turned into a church the umbrella remained, and in fact occupied the place of the canopy over thrones and the like ; and Beatian, an Italian herald, says that a vermilion umbrella in a field argent symbolises dominion. It is also believed that the cardinal's hat is a modification of the umbrella in the basilican churches. The king of Burma is proud to call himself The Lord of Twenty-four Umbrellas, and the Emperor of China carries that number even to the hunting-field." [1] In Buddhist architecture the 'Wheel of Light' symbolising Buddha is over-shadowed by an umbrella, itself adorned with garlands. At Sānchi we find sculptured representations of two and even three umbrellas placed one above the other over the temples, the double and triple canopies of which appear to be fixed to the same handle or staff as in the modern state umbrellas of China and Burma. Thus we have the primary idea of the accumulated honour of stone or metal discs which sub-sequently became such a prominent feature of Buddhist architecture, culminating in the many-storied pagodas of China and Japan. [2] Similarly in Hindu temples the pinnacle

6. The umbrella.

---

[1] Rajendra Lāl Mitra, *Indo-Aryans*, i. p. 263.

[2] *Journal of Indian Art and Industry*, xvi., April 1912, p. 3.

often stands on a circular stone base, probably representing an umbrella.

The umbrella of state was apparently not black like its successor of commerce, but of white or another colour, though the colour is seldom recorded. Sometimes it was of peacock's feathers, the symbol of the Indian war-god, and as seen above, in Italy it was of red, the royal colour. It has been suggested that the halo originally represented an umbrella, and there is no reason to doubt that the umbrella was the parent of the state canopy.

7. Significance of the umbrella.

It has been supposed that the reason for carrying the umbrella above the king's head was to veil his eyes from his subjects, and prevent them from being injured by the magical power of his glance.[1] But its appearance on temples perhaps rather militates against this view. Possibly it may have merely served as a protection or covering to the king's head, the head being considered especially sacred as the seat of life. The same idea is perhaps at the root of the objection felt by Hindus to being seen abroad without a covering on the head. It seems likely that the umbrella may have been held to be a representation of the sky or firmament. The Muhammadans conjoined with it an *aftāda* or sun-symbol; this was an imitation of the sun, embroidered in gold upon crimson velvet and fixed on a circular framework which was borne aloft upon a gold or silver staff.[2] Both were carried over the head of any royal personage, and the association favours the idea that the umbrella represents the sky, while the king's head might be considered analogous to the sun. When one of the early Indian monarchs made extensive conquests, the annexed territories were described as being brought under his umbrella; of the king Harsha-Vardhana (606–648 A.D.) it is recorded that he prosecuted a methodical scheme of conquest with the deliberate object of bringing all India under one umbrella, that is, of constituting it into one state. This phrase seems to support the idea that the umbrella symbolised the firmament. Similarly, when Visvāmitra sent beautiful maidens to tempt the good king Harischandra he instructed

[1] Dr. Jevons, *Introduction to the History of Religion*, p. 60.

[2] *Private Life of an Eastern King*, p. 294.

them to try and induce the king to marry them, and if he would not do this, to ask him for the Puchukra Undi or State Umbrella, which was the emblem of the king's protecting power over his kingdom, with the idea that that power would be destroyed by its loss. Chhatrapati or Lord of the Umbrella was the proudest title of an Indian king. When Sivaji was enthroned in 1674 he proclaimed himself as Pinnacle of the Kshatriya race and Lord of the Royal Umbrella. All these instances seem to indicate that some powerful significance, such as that already suggested, attached to the umbrella. Several tribes, as the Gonds and Mundas, have a legend that their earliest king was born of poor parents, and that one day his mother, having left the child under some tree while she went to her work, returned to find a cobra spreading its hood over him. The future royal destiny of the boy was thus predicted. It is commonly said that the cobra spread its hood over the child to guard it from the heat of the sun, but such protection would perhaps scarcely seem very important to such a people as the Gonds, and the mother would naturally also leave the child in the shade. It seems a possible hypothesis that the cobra's hood really symbolised the umbrella, the principal emblem of royal rank, and it was in this way that the child's great destiny was predicted. In this connection it may be noticed that one of the Jain Tirthakārs, Pārasnāth, is represented in sculpture with an umbrella over his head ; but some Jains say that the carving above the saint's head is not an umbrella but a cobra's hood. Even after it had ceased to be the exclusive appanage of the king, the umbrella was a sign of noble rank, and not permitted to the commonalty.

The old Anglo-Indian term for an umbrella was 'roundel,' an early English word, applied to a variety of circular objects, as a mat under a dish, or a target, and in its form of 'arundel' to the conical handguard on a lance.[1] An old Indian writer says : " Roundels are in these warm climates very necessary to keep the sun from scorching a man, they may also be serviceable to keep the rain off ; most men of account maintain one, two or three roundeliers, whose office is only to attend their master's motion ; they are very

---

[1] *Hobson-Jobson, s.v.* ' Roundel.'

light but of exceeding stiffness, being for the most part made
of rhinoceros hide, very decently painted and guilded with
what flowers they best admire. Exactly in the midst thereof
is fixed a smooth handle made of wood, by which the
Roundelier doth carry it, holding it a foot or more above his
master's head, directing the centre thereof as opposite to
the sun as possibly he may. Any man whatever that will
go to the charge of it, which is no great matter, may have
one or more Katysols to attend him but not a Roundel ;
unless he be a Governor or one of the Council. The same
custom the English hold good amongst their own people,
whereby they may be distinguished by the natives." [1] The
Katysol was a Chinese paper and bamboo sunshade, and the
use of them was not prohibited. It was derived from the
Portuguese *quito-sol,* or that which keeps off the sun. [2] An
extract from the *Madras Standing Orders,* 1677-78, prescribed : " That except by the members of this Council,
those that have formerly been in that quality, Chiefs of
Factories, Commanders of Ships out of England, and the
Chaplains, Rundells shall not be worn by any men in this
town, and by no woman below the degree of Factors' Wives
and Ensigns' Wives, except by such as the Governor shall
permit." [3] Another writer in 1754 states : " Some years
before our arrival in the country, they (the E. I. Co.) found
such sumptuary laws so absolutely necessary, that they gave
the strictest orders that none of these young gentlemen
should be allowed even to hire a Roundel boy, whose business it is to walk by his master and defend him with his
Roundel or umbrella from the heat of the sun. A young
fellow of humour, upon this last order coming over, altered
the form of his Umbrella from a round to a square, called it
a Squaredel instead of a Roundel, and insisted that no order
yet in force forbade him the use of it." [4] The fact that the
Anglo-Indians called the umbrella a roundel and regarded
it as a symbol of sovereignty or nobility indicates that it was
not yet used in England ; and this Mr. Skeat shows to be
correct. " The first umbrella used in England by a man in

---

[1] Old English manuscript quoted by
Sir R. Temple in *Ind. Ant.* (December
1904), p. 316.

[2] *Hobson-Jobson, s.v.* ' Kittysol.'
[3] *Hobson-Jobson, s.v.* ' Roundel.'
[4] *Hobson-Jobson, ibidem.*

the open street for protection against rain is usually said
to have been that carried by Jonas Hanway, a great traveller,
who introduced it on his return from Paris about 1750,
some thirty years before it was generally adopted.

"Some kind of umbrella was, however, occasionally used
by ladies at least so far back as 1709 ; and a fact not generally known is that from about the year 1717 onwards, a
'parish' umbrella, resembling the more recent 'family'
umbrella of the nineteenth century, was employed by the priest
at open-air funerals, as the church accounts of many places
testify."[1] This ecclesiastical use of the umbrella may have
been derived from its employment as a symbol in Italian
churches, as seen above. The word umbrella is derived
through the Italian from the Latin *umbra*, shade, and in
mediaeval times a state umbrella was carried over the
Doge or Duke at Venice on the occasion of any great
ceremony.[2]

Even recently it is said that in Saugor no Bania
dare go past a Bundela Rājpūt's house without getting
down from his pony and folding up his umbrella. In
Hindu slang a 'Chhatawāli' or carrier of an umbrella was
a term for a smart young man ; as in the line, 'An umbrella
has two kinds of ribs ; two women are quarrelling for the
love of him who carries it.' Now that the umbrella is free
to all, and may be bought for a rupee or less in the bazār,
the prestige which once attached to it has practically disappeared. But some flavour of its old associations may still
cling to it in the minds of the sais and ayah who proudly
parade to a festival carrying umbrellas spread over them to
shade their dusky features from the sun ; though the Rāja,
in obedience to the dictates of fashion, has discarded the
umbrella for a *sola-topi*.

Daharia.[3]—A caste of degraded Rājpūts found in Bilās- 1. Origin
pur and Raipur, and numbering about 2000 persons. The and
                                                           traditions.

---

[1] W. W. Skeat, *The Past at our
Doors*.

[2] Skeat, *ibidem*, p. 95.

[3] This article is compiled from
papers by Mr. Bahmanji Muncherji,

Extra Assistant Commissioner ; Mr.
Jeorākhan Lāl, Deputy Inspector of
Schools, and Pandit Pyāre Lāl Misra,
ethnographic clerk. The historical
notice is mainly supplied by Mr. Hīra
Lāl.

Daharias were originally a clan of Rājpūts but, like several others in the Central Provinces, they have now developed into a caste and marry among themselves, thus transgressing the first rule of Rājpūt exogamy. Colonel Tod included the Daharias among the thirty-six royal races of Rājasthān.[1] Their name is derived from Dāhar or Dāhal, the classical term for the Jubbulpore country at the period when it formed the dominion of the Haihaya or Kālachuri Rājpūt kings of Tripura or Tewar near Jubbulpore. This dynasty had an era of their own, commencing in A.D. 248, and their line continued until the tenth or eleventh century. The Arabian geographer Alberuni (born A.D. 973) mentions the country of Dāhal and its king Gāngeya Deva. His son Karna Daharia is still remembered as the builder of temples in Karanbel and Bilahri in Jubbulpore, and it is from him that the Daharia Rājpūts take their name. The Haihaya dynasty of Ratanpur were related to the Kālachuri kings of Tewar, and under them the ancestors of the Daharia Rājpūts probably migrated from Jubbulpore into Chhattīsgarh. But they themselves have forgotten their illustrious origin, and tell a different story to account for their name. They say that they came from Baghelkhand or Rewah, which may well be correct, as Rewah lies between Chhattīsgarh and Jubbulpore, and a large colony of Kālachuri Rājpūts may still be found about ten miles north-east of Rewah town. The Daharias relate that when Parasu-rāma, the great Brāhman warrior, was slaying the Kshatriyas, a few of them escaped towards Ratanpur and were camping in the forest by the wayside. Parasurāma came up and asked them who they were, and they said they were *Daharias* or wayfarers, from *dāhar* the Chhattīsgarhi term for a road or path; and thus they successfully escaped the vengeance of Parasurāma. This futile fiction only demonstrates the real ignorance of their Brāhman priests, who, if they had known a little history, need not have had recourse to their invention to furnish the Daharias with a distinguished pedigree. A third derivation is from a word *dahri* or gate, and they say that the name of Dahria or Daharia was conferred on them by Bimbaji Bhonsla, because of the bravery with which they held the gates of Ratanpur against his attack. But history

[1] Tod's *Rājasthān*, i. p. 128.

is against them here, as it records that Ratanpur capitulated
to the Marāthas without striking a blow.

As already stated, the Daharias were originally a clan   2. Sept
of Rājpūts, whose members must take wives or husbands   and
from other clans.   They have now become a caste and   subsept.
marry among themselves, but within the caste they still
have exogamous groups or septs, several of which are named
after Rājpūt clans as Bais, Chandel, Baghel, Bundela, Mainpuri Chauhān, Parihār, Rāthor and several others.   Certain
names are not of Rājpūt origin, and probably record the
admission of outsiders into the caste.   Like the Rājpūts,
within the sept they have also subsepts, some of which are
taken from the Brāhmans, as Parāsar, Bhāradwāj, Sāndilya,
while others are nicknames, as Kachariha (one who does not
care about a beating), Atariha, Hiyās and others.   The
divisions of the septs and subsepts are very confused, and
seem to indicate that at different times various foreign
elements have been received into the community, including
Rājpūts of many different clans.   According to rule, a man
should not take a wife whose sept or subsept are the same
as his own, but this is not adhered to ; and in some cases
the Daharias, on account of the paucity of their numbers
and the difficulty of arranging matches, have been driven to
permit the marriage of first cousins, which among proper
Rājpūts is forbidden.   They also practise hypergamy, as
members of the Mainpuri Chauhān, Hiyās, Bisen, Surkhi
and Bais septs or subsepts will take girls in marriage from
families of other septs, but will not give their daughters to
them.   This practice leads to polygamy among the five
higher septs, whose daughters are all married in their own
circle, while in addition they receive girls from the other
groups.   Members of these latter also consider it an honour
to marry a daughter into one of the higher septs, and are
willing to pay a considerable price for such a distinction.
It seems probable that the small Daraiha caste of Bilāspur
are an inferior branch of the Daharias.

The Daharias, in theory at any rate, observe the same   3. Social
rules in regard to their women as Brāhmans and Rājpūts.   customs.
Neither divorce nor the marriage of widows is permitted,
and a woman who goes wrong is finally expelled from the

caste. Their social customs resemble those of the higher Hindustāni castes. When the bridegroom starts for the wedding he is dressed in a long white gown reaching to the ankles, with new shoes, and he takes with him a dagger ; this serves the double purpose of warding off evil spirits, always prone to attack the bridal party, and also of being a substitute for the bridegroom himself, as in case he should for some unforeseen reason be rendered unable to appear at the ceremony, the bride could be married to the dagger as his representative. It may also be mentioned that, before the bridegroom starts for the wedding, after he has been rubbed with oil and turmeric for five days he is seated on a wooden plank over a hole dug in the courtyard and bathed. He then changes his clothes, and the women bring twenty-one small *chukias* or cups full of water and empty them over him. His head is then covered with a piece of new cloth, and a thread wound round it seven times by a Brāhman. The thread is afterwards removed, and tied round an iron ring with some mango leaves, and this ring forms the *kankan* which is tied to the bridegroom's wrist, a similar one being worn by the bride. Before the wedding the bride goes round to the houses of her friends, accompanied by the women of her party singing songs, and by musicians. At each house the mistress appears with her forehead and the parting of her hair profusely smeared with vermilion. She rubs her forehead against the bride's so as to colour it also with vermilion, which is now considered the symbol of a long and happy married life. The barber's wife applies red paint to the bride's feet, the gardener's wife presents her with a garland of flowers, and the carpenter's wife gives her a new wooden doll. She must also visit the potter's and washerman's wives, whose benisons are essential ; they give her a new pot and a little rice respectively. When the bridegroom comes to touch the marriage - shed with his dagger he is resisted by the bride's sister, to whom he must give a rupee as a present. The binding portion of the marriage consists in the couple walking seven times round the marriage-post. At each turn the bridegroom seizes the bride's right toe and with it upsets one of seven little cups of rice placed near the marriage-post. This is probably a symbol of fertility. After it they worship seven pairs of little wooden boxes smeared with vermilion and called *singhora* and *singhori* as if they were male and female. The bridegroom's father brings two little dough images of Mahādeo and Pārvati as the ideal married pair, and gives them to the couple. The new husband applies vermilion to his wife's forehead, and covers and uncovers her head seven times, to signify to her that, having become a wife, she should henceforth be veiled when she goes abroad. The bride's maid now washes her face, which probably requires it, and the wedding is complete. The Daharias usually have a *guru* or spiritual preceptor, but husband and wife must not have the same one, as in that case they would be in the anomalous position of brother and sister, a *guru's* disciples being looked upon as his children. The Daharias were formerly warriors in the service of the Ratanpur kings, and many families still possess an old sword which they worship on the day of Dasahra. Their names usually end in Singh or Lāl. They are now engaged in cultivation, and many of them are proprietors of villages, and tenants. Some of them are employed as constables and chuprāssies, but few are labourers, as they may not touch the plough with their own hands. They eat the flesh of clean animals, but do not drink liquor, and avoid onions and tomatoes. They have good features and fair complexions, the traces of their Rājpūt blood being quite evident. Brāhmans will take water from them, but they now rank below Rājpūts, on a level with the good cultivating castes.

Dāngi.—A cultivating caste found almost exclusively in the Saugor District, which contained 23,000 persons out of a total of 24,000 of the caste in the Central Provinces in 1911. There are also considerable numbers of them in Rājputāna and Central India, from which localities they probably immigrated into the Saugor District during the eleventh century. The Dāngis were formerly dominant in Saugor, a part of which was called Dāngiwāra after them. The kings of Garhpahra or old Saugor were Dāngis, and their family still remains at the village of Bilehra, which with a few other villages they hold as a revenue-free grant.

1. Origin and traditions.

The name of the caste is variously derived. The traditional story is that the Rājpūt king of Garhpahra detained the palanquins of twenty-two married women of different castes and kept them as his wives. The issue of the illicit intercourse were named Dāngis, and there are thus twenty-two subdivisions of the caste, besides three other subdivisions who are held to be descended from pure Rājpūts. The name is said to be derived from *dāng*, fraud, on account of the above deception. A more plausible derivation is from the Persian *dāng*, a hill, the Dāngis being thus hillmen ; and they may not improbably have been a set of robbers and freebooters in the Vindhyan Hills, like the Gūjars and Mewātis in northern India, naturally recruiting their band from all classes of the population, as is shown by ingenious implication in this story itself. '*Khet men bāmi, gaon men Dāngi*,' or 'A Dāngi in the village is like the hole of a snake in one's field ' is a proverb which shows the estimation in which they were formerly held. The three higher septs may have been their leaders and may well have been Rājpūts. Since they have settled down as respectable cultivators and enjoy a good repute among their neighbours, the Dāngis have disowned the above story, and now say that they are descended from Rāja Dāng, a Kachhwāha Rājpūt king of Narwar in Central India. Nothing is known of Rāja Dāng except a rude couplet which records how he was cheated by a horse-dealer :

> *Jitki ghori tit gayi*
> *Dāng hāth karyāri rahi,*

'The mare bolted to the seller again, leaving in Dāng's hand nothing except the reins.'

The Dāngis have a more heroic version of this story to the effect that the mare was a fairy of Indra's court, who for some reason had been transformed into this shape and was captured by Rāja Dāng. He refused to give her up to Indra and a battle was about to ensue, when the mare besought them to place her on a pyre and sacrifice her instead of fighting. They agreed to do this, and out of the flames of the pyre the fairy emerged and floated up to heaven, leaving only the reins and bridle of the mare in Rāja Dāng's hand.

Yet a third story is that their original ancestor was Rāja
Nipāl Singh of Narwar, and when he was fighting with Indra
over the fairy, Krishna came to Indra's assistance. But
Nipāl Singh refused to bow down to Krishna, and being
annoyed at this and wishing to teach him a lesson the god
summoned him to his court. At the gate through which
Nipāl Singh had to pass, Krishna fixed a sword at the height
of a man's neck, so that he must bend or have his head cut
off. But Nipāl Singh saw the trick, and, sitting down,
propelled himself through the doorway with his head erect.
The outwitted god remarked, ' *Tum bare dāndi ho*,' or ' You
are very cunning,' and the name Dāndi stuck to Nipāl
Singh and was afterwards corrupted to Dāngi. There can
be little doubt that the caste are an offshoot of Rājpūts of
impure blood, and with a large admixture of other classes of
the population. Some of their sept names indicate their
mixed descent, as Rakhya, born of a potter woman, Dhoniya,
born of a washerwoman, and Pavniya, born of a weaver
woman. In past times the Dāngis served in the Rājpūt
and Marātha armies, and a small isolated colony of them is
found in one village of Indora in the Nāgpur District, the
descendants of Dāngis who engaged in military service under
the Bhonsla kings.

The Dāngis have no subcastes distinguished by separate
names, but they are divided into three classes, among whom
the principle of hypergamy prevails. As already seen, there
were formerly twenty-five clans, of whom the three highest, the
Nahonias, Bhadonias and Nadias, claimed to be pure Rājpūts.
The other twenty-two clans are known as Baīsa (22) or
Prithwipat Dāngis, after the king who is supposed to have been
the ancestor of all the clans. Each of his twenty-two wives
is said to have been given a village for her maintenance, and
the clans are named after these villages. But there are now
only thirteen of these local clans left, and below them is a
miscellaneous group of clans, representing apparently later
accretions to the caste. Some of them are named from the
places from which they came, as Mahobia, from Mahoba,
Narwaria, from Narwar, and so on. The Solakhia sept is
named after the Solanki Rājpūts, of whom they may be the
partly illegitimate descendants. The Parnāmi sept are

2. Caste sub-divisions.

apparently those who have the creed of the Dhāmis, the followers of Prānnāth of Panna. And as already seen, some are named from women of low caste, from whom by Dāngi fathers they are supposed to be descended. The whole number of septs is thus divided into three groups, the highest containing the three quasi-Rājpūt septs already mentioned, the next highest the thirteen septs of Prithwipat Dāngis, and the lowest all the other septs. Pure Rājpūts will take daughters in marriage from the highest group, and this in turn takes girls of the Prithwipat Dāngis of the thirteen clans, though neither will give daughters in return ; and the Prithwipat Dāngis will similarly accept the daughters of the miscellaneous septs below them in marriage with their sons. Matches are, however, not generally arranged according to the above system of hypergamy, but each group marries among its own members. Girls who are married into a higher group have to be given a larger dowry, the fathers often being willing to pay Rs. 500 or Rs. 1000 for the social distinction which such an alliance confers on the family. Among the highest septs there is a further difference between those whose ancestors accepted food from Rāja Jai Singh, the founder of Jaisinghnagar, and those who refused it. The former are called Sakrodia or those who ate the leavings of others, and the latter *Deotaon ki sansār*, or the divine Dāngis. Pure Rājpūts will take daughters only from the members of the latter group in each sept. Marriage within the sept or *baink* is prohibited, and as a rule a man does not marry a wife belonging to the same sept as his mother or grandmother. Marriage by exchange also is not allowed, that is, a girl cannot be married into the same family as that in which her brother has married.

3. Marriage.　　Girls are generally married between seven and twelve and boys between ten and twenty, but no stigma attaches to a family allowing an unmarried girl to exceed the age of puberty. The bridegroom should always be older than the bride. Matches are arranged by the parents, the horoscopes of the children being compared among the well-to-do. The zodiacal sign of the boy's horoscope should be stronger than that of the girl's, so that she may be submissive to

him in after-life. Thus a girl whose zodiac sign is the lion
should not be married to a boy whose sign is the ram,
because in that case the wife would dominate the husband.
There is no special rule as to the time of the betrothal, and
the ceremony is very simple, consisting in the presentation
of a cocoanut by the bride's father to the bridegroom's
father, and the distribution of sweets to the caste-fellows.
The betrothal is not considered to have any particularly
binding force and either party may break through it.
Among the Dāngis a bridegroom-price is usually paid,
which varies according to the social respectability of the
boy's sept, as much as Rs. 2000 having been given for
a bridegroom of higher class according to the rule of
hypergamy already described. But no value is placed on
educational qualifications, as is the case among Brāhmans
and Kāyasths. The marriage ceremony is conducted according to the ritual prevalent in the northern Districts, and
presents no special features. Two feasts are given by the
bride's father to the caste-fellows, one consisting of *katchi*
food or that which is cooked with water, and another of
pakki food cooked with *ghī* (butter). If the bride is of
marriageable age the *gauna* or sending away ceremony is
performed at once, otherwise it takes place in the third or
fifth year after marriage. At the *gauna* ceremony the
bride's cloth is tied to that of the bridegroom, and they
change seats. Widow-marriage is not fashionable, and the
caste say that it is not permitted, but several instances are
known of its having occurred. Divorce is not allowed, and
a woman who goes wrong is finally expelled from the caste.
Polygamy is allowed, and many well-to-do persons have
more than one wife.

The Dāngis pay special reverence to the goddess Durga
or Devi as the presiding deity of war. They worship her
during the months of Kunwār (September) and Chait (March),
and at the same time pay reverence to their weapons of war,
their swords and guns, or if they have not got these, to
knives and spears. They burn their dead, but children are
usually buried. They observe mourning for three days for
a child and for ten days for an adult, and on the 13th day
the caste-fellows are feasted. Their family priests, who are

4. Religious and social customs.

Jijhotia Brāhmans, used formerly to shave the head and beard when a death occurred among their clients as if they belonged to the family, but this practice was considered derogatory by other Brāhmans, and they have now stopped it. The Dāngis perform the *shrādhh* ceremony in the month of Kunwār. The caste wear the sacred thread, but it is said that they were formerly not allowed to do so in Bundelkhand. They eat fish and flesh, including that of wild boars, but not fowls or beef, and they do not drink liquor. They take *pakki* food or that cooked without water from Kāyasths and Gahoi Banias, and *katchi* food, cooked with water, from Jijhotia and Sanādhya Brāhmans. Jijhotia Brāhmans formerly took *pakki* food from Dāngis, but have now ceased to do so. The Dāngis require the services of Brāhmans at all ceremonies. They have a caste *panchāyat* or committee. A person who changes his religion or eats with a low caste is permanently expelled, while temporary exclusion is awarded for the usual delinquencies. In the case of the more serious offences, as murder or killing of a cow, the culprit must purify himself by a pilgrimage to a sacred river.

5. Occupation and character.

The Dāngis were formerly, as already stated, of a quarrelsome temperament, but they have now settled down and, though spirited, are of a good disposition, and hardworking cultivators. They rank slightly above the representative cultivating castes owing to their former dominant position, and are still considered to have a good conceit of themselves, according to the saying :

> *Tin men neh terah men,*
> *Mirdang bajāwe dere men,*

or 'Though he belong neither to the three septs nor the thirteen septs, yet the Dāngi blows his own trumpet in his own house.' They are still, too, of a fiery disposition, and it is said that the favourite dish of gram-flour cooked with curds, which is known as *karhi*, is never served at their weddings. Because the word *karhi* also signifies the coming out of a sword from its sheath, and when addressed to another man has the equivalent of the English word 'Draw' in the duelling days. So if one Dāngi said it to another, meaning to ask him for the dish, it might result in

a fight.   They are very backward in respect of education and
set no store by it.   They consider their traditional occupation to be military service, but nearly all of them are now
engaged in agriculture.   At the census of 1901 over 2000
were returned as supported by the ownership of land and
3000 as labourers and farmservants.   Practically all the
remainder are tenants.   They are industrious, and their
women work in the fields.   The only crops which they
object to grow are *kusum* or safflower and *san*-hemp.   The
Nahonia Dāngis, being the highest subcaste, refuse to sell
milk or *ghī*.   The men usually have Singh as a termination
to their names, like Rājpūts.   Their dress and ornaments
are of the type common in the northern Districts.   The
women tattoo their bodies.

Dāngri.[1]—A small caste of melon and vegetable
growers, whose name is derived from *dāngar* or *dāngra*, a
water-melon.   They reside in the Wardha and Bhandāra
Districts, and numbered about 1800 persons in 1911.   The
caste is a mixed one of functional origin, and appears to be
an offshoot from the Kunbis with additions from other
sources.   In Wardha they say that their ancestor was one
of two brothers to whom Mahādeo gave the seeds of a juāri
plant and a water-melon respectively for sowing.   The
former became the ancestor of the Kunbis and the latter of
the Dāngris.   On one occasion when Mahādeo, assuming
the guise of a beggar, asked the Dāngri brother for a water-
melon, he refused to give it, and on this account his descendants were condemned to perpetual poverty.   In fact, the
Dāngris, like the other market-gardening castes, are badly off,
possibly on account of their common habit of marrying a
number of wives, whom they utilise as labourers in their
vegetable gardens ; for though a wife is better than a hired
labourer for their particular method of cultivation, where
supervision is difficult and the master may be put to serious
loss from bad work and petty pilfering, while there is also
much scope for women workers ; yet on the other hand
polygamy tends to the breeding of family quarrels and to

---

[1] This article is based on notes taken by Pandit Pyāre Lāl Misra in Wardha,
and Mr. Hirā Lāl in Bhandāra.

excessive subdivision of property. The close personal supervision which is requisite perhaps also renders it especially
difficult to carry on the business of market-gardening on a
large scale. In any case the agricultural holdings of the
Mālis and Dāngris are as a rule very small. The conclusion
indicated by the above story that the Dāngris are an offshoot
from the Kunbi caste of cultivators appears to be correct ;
and it is supported by the fact that they will accept food
cooked with water from the Baone Kunbis. But their subcastes show that even this small body is of very heterogeneous composition ; for they are divided into the Teli, the
Kalār, the Kunbi and the Gādiwān Dāngris, thus showing
that the caste has received recruits from the Telis or oilmen
and the Kalārs or liquor-sellers. The Gādiwān, as their
name denotes, are a separate section who have adopted the
comparatively novel occupation of cart-driving for a livelihood. In Wardha there is also a small class of Pānibhar
or waterman Dāngris who are employed as water-bearers,
this occupation arising not unnaturally from that of growing
melons and other crops in river-beds. And a few members
of the caste have taken to working in iron. The bulk of
the Dāngris, however, grow melons, chillies and brinjals on
the banks or in the beds of rivers ; but as the melon crop is
raised in a period of six weeks during the hot season, they
can also undertake some ordinary cultivation. When the
melons ripen the first fruits are offered to Mahādeo and
given to a Brāhman to ensure the success of the crop.
When the melon plants are in flower, a woman must not
enter the field during the period of her monthly impurity, as
it is believed that she would cause the crop to wither.
While it may safely be assumed that the Dāngris originated
from the great Kunbi caste, it may be noted that some of
them tell a story to the effect that their original home was
Benāres, and that they came from there into the Central
Provinces ; hence they call themselves Kāshi Dāngri, Kāshi
being the classical name for Benāres. This legend appears
to be entirely without foundation, as their family names,
speech and customs are alike of purely Marāthi origin. But
it is found among other castes also that they like to pretend
that they came from Benāres, the most sacred centre of Hin-

duism. The social customs of the Dāngris resemble those of
the Kunbis, and it is unnecessary to describe them in detail.
Before their weddings they have a curious ceremony known
as Dewat Pūja. The father of the bridegroom, with an axe
over his shoulder and accompanied by his wife, goes to a
well or a stream. Here they clean a small space with cowdung and make an offering of rice, flowers, turmeric and
incense, after which the man, breaking his bangle from
off his wrist, throws it into the water, apparently as a pro-
pitiatory offering for the success of the marriage. It is not
stated what the bangle is made of, but it may be assumed
that a valuable one would not thus be thrown away. As
among some of the other Marātha castes, the bridegroom
must be wrapped in a blanket on his journey to the bride's
village. If a bachelor desires to espouse a widow he must
first go through the ceremony of marriage with a swallow-
wort plant. Polygamy is freely permitted, and some Dāngris
are known to have as many as five wives. As already
stated, wives are of great assistance in gardening work, which
demands much hand-labour. Divorce and the remarriage
of widows are allowed. The Dāngris commonly bury the
dead, and they place cotton leaves over the eyes and ears of
the corpse. In Bhandāra they say that this is done when
it is believed the dead person was possessed by an evil spirit,
and there is possibly some idea of preventing the escape of
the spirit from the body. In Wardha the Dāngris have
rather a bad reputation, and a saying current about them is
' *Dāngri beta puha chor,*' or ' A Dāngri will steal even a
shred of cotton ' ; but this may be a libel.

DARZI

LIST OF PARAGRAPHS

1. General
notice.

Darzi, Shimpi, Chhīpi, Sūji.—The occupational caste of tailors.   In 1911 a total of 51,000 persons were returned as belonging to the caste in the Central Provinces and Berār. The Darzis are an urban caste and are most numerous in Districts with large towns.   Mr. Crooke derives the word Darzi from the Persian *darz*, meaning a seam.   The name Sūji from *sui*, a needle, was formerly more common.   Shimpi is the Marātha name, and Chhīpi, from Chhīpa a calico-printer or dyer, is another name used for the caste, probably because it is largely recruited from the Chhīpas.   In Bombay they say that when Parasurāma was destroying the Kshatriyas, two Rājpūt brothers hid themselves in a temple and were protected by the priest, who set one of them to sew dresses for the idol and the other to dye and stamp them.   The first brother was called Chhīpi and from him the Darzis are descended, the name being corrupted to Shimpi, and the second was called Chhīpa and was the ancestor of the dyers. The common title of the Darzis is Khalīfa, an Arabic word meaning 'The Successor of the Prophet.'   Colonel Temple says that it is not confined to them but is also used by barbers, cooks and monitors in schools.[1]   The caste is of comparatively recent formation.   In fact Sir D. Ibbetson wrote [2] that "Darzi, or its Hindi equivalent Sūji, is purely

---

[1] *Proper Names of the Punjābis*, p. 74.
[2] *Punjab Census Report* (1881), para. 645.

466

an occupational term, and though there is a Darzi guild in every town, there is no Darzi caste in the proper acceptation of the word.   The greater number of Darzis belong perhaps to the Dhobi and Chhīmba castes, more especially to the latter."

The Darzis, however, are now recognised as a distinct caste, but their mixed origin is shown by the names of their subcastes and exogamous sections.   Thus they have a Bāman subdivision named after the Brāhman caste.   These will not take food from any other caste except Brāhmans and are probably an offshoot from them.   They are considered to be the highest subdivision, and next to them come the Rai or Rāj Darzis.   Another subcaste is named Kaithia, after the Kāyasths, and a third Srivāstab, which is the name of a well-known subcaste of Kāyasths derived from the town of Srāvasti, now Sahet Mahet in the Gonda District.[1]   In Betūl the Srivāstab Darzis are reported to forbid the remarriage of widows, thus showing that they desire to live up to their distinguished ancestry.   A third subcaste is known as Chamarua and appears to be derived from the Chamārs. Other subcastes are of the territorial type as Mālwi, Khāndeshi, Chhattīsgarhi, Mathuria and so on, and the section or family names are usually taken from villages.   Among them, however, we find Jugia from Jogi, Thākur or Rājpūt, Gūjar, Khawās or barber, and Baroni, the title of a female Dhīmar. Mr. Crooke gives several other names.

It may thus reasonably be concluded that the Darzis are a caste of comparatively recent origin, and the explanation is probably that the use of the needle and thread in making clothes is a new fashion.   Buchanan remarks : " The needle indeed seems to have been totally unknown to the Hindus, and I have not been able to learn any Hindi word for sewing except that used to express passing the shuttle in the act of weaving. . . ."   " Cloth composed of several pieces sewn together is an abomination to the Hindus, so that every woman of rank when she eats, cooks or prays, must lay aside her petticoat and retain only the wrapper made without the use of scissors or needle " ; and again, " The dress of the Hindu men of rank has become nearly the same with

2. Subdivisions.

3. Sewn clothes not formerly worn.

---

[1] Crooke's *Tribes and Castes*, art. Darzi.

that of the Muhammadans [1] who did not allow any officer employed by them to appear at their *levées* (Durbars) except in proper dress.   At home, however, the Hindu men, and on all occasions their women, retain almost entirely their native dress, which consists of various pieces of cloth wrapped round them without having been sewn together in any form, and only kept in their place by having their ends thrust under the folds."   And elsewhere he states : " The flowering of cotton cloth with the needle has given a good deal of employment to the Muhammadan women of Maldeh as the needle has never been used by the Hindus." [2]   Darzi, as has been seen, is a Persian word, and in northern India many tailors are Muhammadans.   And it seems, therefore, a possible hypothesis that the needle and the art of sewing were brought into general use by the Moslem invaders.   It is true that in his *Indo-Aryans* [3] Mr. Rājendra Lāl Mitra combats this hypothesis and demonstrates that made-up clothes were known to the Aryans of the Rig-Veda and are found in early statuary.   But he admits that the instances are not numerous, and it seems likely that the use of such clothes may have been confined to royal and aristocratic families. It is possible also that the Scythian invasions of the fifth century brought about a partial relapse from civilisation, during which certain arts and industries, and among them that of cutting and sewing cloth, were partially or completely lost.   The tailor is not the familiar figure in Hindu social life that he is, for example, in England.   Here he is traditionally an object or butt for ridicule as in the saying, ' Nine tailors make a man,' and so on ; and his weakness is no doubt supposed to be due to the fact that he pursues a sedentary indoor occupation and one more adapted to women than men, the needle being essentially a feminine implement.   A similar ridicule, based no doubt on exactly the same grounds, attaches in India to the village weaver, as is evidenced by the proverbs given in the articles on Bhulia, Kori, and Jolāha. No reason exists probably for the contempt in which the weaver class is held other than that their work is considered to be more fitting for women than men.   Thus in India the

---

[1] Buchanan's *Eastern India*, Martin's edition, ii. pp. 417, 699.
[2] *Ibidem*, p. 977.   [3] Vol. i. pp. 178-184.

weaver appears to take the place of the tailor, and this leads to the conclusion that woven and not sewn clothes have always been commonly worn.

In the Central Provinces, at least, the Darzi caste is practically confined to the towns, and though cotton jackets are worn even by labourers and shirts by the better-to-do, these are usually bought ready-made at the more important markets. Women, more conservative in their dress than men, have only one garment prepared with the needle, the small bodice known as *choli* or *angia*. And in Chhattīsgarh, a landlocked tract very backward in civilisation, the *choli* has hitherto not been worn and is only now being introduced. Though he first copied the Muhammadan and now shows a partiality for the English style of dress for outdoor use, the Hindu when indoors still reverts to the one cloth round the waist and a second over the shoulders, which was probably once the regular garb of his countrymen. For meals the latter is discarded, and this costume, so strange to English ideas, while partly based on considerations of ceremonial purity, may also be due to a conservative adherence to the ancient fashion, when sewn clothes were not worn. It is noticeable also that high-caste Hindus, though they may wear a coat of cloth or tasar silk and cotton trousers, copying the English, still often carry the *dupatta* or shoulder-cloth hanging round the neck. This now appears a useless encumbrance, but may be the relic of the old body-cloth and therefore interesting as a survival in dress, like the buttons on the back of our tail-coats to which the flaps were once hooked up for riding, or the seams on the backs of gloves, a relic of the time when the glove consisted simply of finger-lengths sewn together.[1] More recently the *dupatta* has been made to fulfil the function of a pocket-handkerchief, while the educated are now discarding the *dupatta* and carry their handkerchiefs in their pockets. The old dress of ceremony for landowners is the *angarkha*, a long coat reaching to the knees and with flaps folding over the breast and tied with strings. This is worn with pyjamas and is probably the Muhammadan ceremonial costume as remarked by Buchanan. In its correct form, at, least it has no buttons,

[1] Webb's *Heritage of Dress*, p. 33.

and recalls the time when a similar state of things prevailed
in English dress and the 'trussing of his points' was a
laborious daily task for every English gentleman.   The
ghundis or small pieces of cloth made up into a ball, which
were the precursors of the button, may still be seen on the
cotton coats of rustics in the rural area.

The substitution of clothes cut and sewn to fit the body
for draped clothes is a matter of regret from an artistic
or picturesque point of view, as the latter have usually a
more graceful appearance.   This is shown by the difficulty
of reproducing modern clothes in statuary, trousers being
usually the despair of the sculptor.   But sewn clothes, when
once introduced, must always prevail from considerations
of comfort.   When a Hindu pulls his *dhoti* or loin-cloth
up his legs and tucks it in round his hips in order to run
or play a game he presumably performs the act described
in the Bible as 'girding up his loins.'

4. Occupa-
tion.
The social customs of the Darzis present no features
of special interest and resemble those of the lower castes
in their locality.   They rank below the cultivating castes,
and Brāhmans will not take water from their hands.
Though not often employed by the Hindu villager the
Darzi is to Europeans one of the best known of all castes.
He is on the whole a capable workman and especially good
at copying from a pattern.   His proficiency in this respect
attracted notice so long ago as 1689, as shown in an
interesting quotation in the *Bombay Gazetteer* referring to
the tailors of Surat : [1] " The tailors here fashion clothes
for the Europeans, either men or women, according to every
mode that prevails, and fit up the commodes and towering
head-dresses for the women with as much skill as if they
had been an Indian fashion, or themselves had been
apprenticed at the Royal Exchange.   (The commode was
a wire structure to raise the cap and hair.) "   Since then the
Darzi has no doubt copied in turn all the changes of
English fashions.   He is a familiar figure in the veranda
of the houses of Europeans, and his idiosyncrasies have
been delightfully described by Eha in *Behind the Bungalow.*

[1] *Bombay Gazetteer*, *Hindus of Gujarāt*, p. 180, quoting from Ovington,
Voyage to Surat, p. 280.

His needles and pins are stuck into the folds of his turban, and Eha says that he is bandy-legged because of the position in which he squats on his feet while sewing. In Gujarāt the tailor is often employed in native households. " Though even in well-to-do families," Mr. Bhimbhai Kirpāram writes,[1] "women sew their bodices and young children's clothes for everyday wear, every family has its own tailor. As a rule tailors sew in their own houses, and in the tailor's shop may be seen workmen squatting in rows on a palm-leaf mat or on cotton-stuffed quilts. The wives and sons' wives of the head of the establishment sit and work in the shop along with the men. Their busy time is during the marriage season from November to June. A village tailor is paid either in cash or grain and is not infrequently a member of the village establishment. During the rains, the tailor's slack season, he supplements his earnings by tillage, holding land which Government has continued to him on payment of one-half the ordinary rental. In south Gujarāt, in the absence of Brāhmans, a Darzi officiates at Bhāwad marriages, and in some Brāhman marriages a Darzi is called with some ceremony to sew a bodice for the bride. On the other hand, in the Pānch Mahals and Rewa Kantha, besides tailoring Darzis blow trumpets at marriage and other processions and hold so low a position that even Dhedas object to eat their food." It seems clear that in Gujarāt the Darzi caste is of older standing than in northern India, and it is possible that the art of sewing may have been acquired through the sea trade which was carried on between the western coast and Arabia and the Persian Gulf. Here the Darzi has become a village menial, which he is not recorded as being in any other part of India.

Like the weaver, the Darzi is of a somewhat religious turn of mind, probably on account of his sedentary calling which gives him plenty of time for reflection. Many of them belong to the Nāmdeo sect, originated by a Chhīpa or dyer, Nāmdeo Sādhu. Nāmdeo is said to have been a contemporary of Kabīr and to have flourished in the twelfth or thirteenth century. He was a great worshipper of the

5. Religion.

---

[1] *Bombay Gazetteer, Hindus of Gujarāt*, p. 180.

god Vithoba of Pandharpur and is considered by the Marāthas to be their oldest writer, being the author of many Abhangs, or sacred hymns.[1] He preached the unity of God, recognising apparently Vithoba or Vishnu as the one deity, and the uselessness of ceremonial. His followers are mainly Dhobis and Chhīpas, the two principal castes from whom the Darzis have originated.[2] Nāmdeo's sect was thus apparently a protest on the part of the Chhīpas and Dhobis against their inferior position in the caste system and the tyranny of the Brāhmans, and resembled the spiritual revolt of the weavers under Kabīr and of the Chamārs under Ghāsi Dās and Jagjīwan Dās.

In Berār it is stated [3] that "the Simpi caste has twelve and a half divisions; of these the chief are known as the Jain, Marāthi and Telugu Simpis. The Jain Simpis claim the hero Rimināth as a caste-fellow, while the Marāthas are often Lingāyats and the Telugu division generally Vaishnavas." Before beginning work in the morning the Darzi bows to his scissors or needle and prays to them for his livelihood for that day.

The Darzi's occupation, Mr. Crooke remarks, is a poor one and held rather in contempt. The village proverb runs, ' *Darzi ka pūt jab tak jīta tab tak sīta*,' ' The tailor's boy will do nothing but sew all his life long.' Another somewhat more complimentary saying is, ' *Tanak si suiya tak tak kare aur lākh taka ko banj kare*,' or ' The tiny needle goes *tuk tuk*, and makes merchandise worth a lakh of rupees.' The Hindustani version of both proverbs is obviously intended to give the sound of a needle passing through cloth, and it is possible that our word ' tuck ' has the same origin.

1. General notice.

Dewār.[4] — (Derived from Devi, whom they worship, or from Diābār, ' One who lights a lamp,' because they always practise magic with a lighted lamp.) A Dravidian caste of beggars and musicians. They numbered about 2500 persons

[1] *Bombay Gazetteer, Nasik*, p. 50.

[2] According to another account Nāmdeo belonged to Mārwār. Mr. Maclagan's *Punjab Census Report* (1891), p. 144.

[3] *Berār Census Report* (1881), para. 231.

[4] This article is partly based on a note by Mr. Gokul Prasād, Tahsīldār, Dhamtari.

in 1911 and are residents of the Chhattīsgarh plain. The Dewārs themselves trace their origin from a Binjhia named Gopāl Rai, who accompanied Rāja Kalyān Sai of Ratanpur on a visit to the Court of Delhi in Akbār's time. Gopāl Rai was a great wrestler, and while at Delhi he seized and held a *mast* elephant belonging to the Emperor. When the latter heard of it he ordered a wrestling match to be arranged between Gopāl Rai and his own champion wrestler. Gopāl Rai defeated and killed his opponent, and Kalyān Sai ordered him to compose a triumphal song and sing it in honour of the occasion. He composed his song in favour of Devi Maha Mai, or Devi the Great Mother, and the composition and recitation of similar songs has ever since been the profession of his descendants the Dewārs. The caste is, as is shown by the names of its sections, of mixed origin, and its members are the descendants of Gonds and Kawars reinforced probably by persons who have been expelled from their own caste and have become Dewārs. They will still admit persons of any caste except the very lowest.

The caste has two principal divisions according to locality, named Raipūria and Ratanpūria, Raipur and Ratanpur having been formerly the two principal towns of Chhattīsgarh. Within these are several other local subdivisions, *e.g.* Navāgarhia or those belonging to Nawāgarh in Bilāspur, Sonākhania from Sonākhān south of the Mahānadi, Chātarrājiha from Chāter Rāj, in Raipur, and Sārangarhia from Sārangarh State. Some other divisions are either occupational or social ; thus the Baghurra Dewārs are those who tame tigers and usually live in the direction of Bastar, the Baipāri Dewārs are petty traders in brass or pewter ornaments which they sell to Banjāra women, and the Lohār and Jogi Dewārs may be so called either because their ancestors belonged to these castes, or because they have adopted the profession of blacksmiths and beggars respectively. Probably both reasons are partly applicable. These subdivisions are not strictly endogamous, but show a tendency to become so. The two main subcastes, Raipūria and Ratanpūria, are distinguished by the musical instruments which they play on while begging. That of the Raipūrias is a sort of rude

2. Subdivisions.

fiddle called *sārangi*, which has a cocoanut shell as a resonator with horsehair strings, and is played with a bow. The Ratanpūrias have an instrument called *dhungru*, which consists of a piece of bamboo about three feet long with a hollow gourd as a resonator and catgut strings. In the latter the resonator is held uppermost and rests against the shoulder of the player, while in the former it is at the lower end and is placed against his waist. The section names of the Dewārs are almost all of Dravidian origin. Sonwānia, Markām, Marai, Dhurwa, Ojha, Netām, Salām, Katlām and Jagat are the names of well-known Gond septs which are also possessed by the Dewārs, and Telāsi, Karsayal, Son-Mungir and others are Kawar septs which they have adopted. They admit that their ancestors were members of these septs among the Gonds and Kawars. Where the name of the ancestor has a meaning which they understand, some totemistic observances survive. Thus the members of the Karsayal sept will not kill or eat a deer. The septs are exogamous, but there is no other restriction on marriage and the union of first cousins is permissible.

3. Marriage customs. Adult marriage is usual, and if a husband cannot be found for a girl who has reached maturity she is given to her sister's husband as a second wife, or to any other married person who will take her and give a feast to the caste. In some localities the boy who is to be married is sent with a few relatives to the girl's house. On arrival he places a pot of wine and a nut before the girl's father, who, if he is willing to carry out the marriage, orders the nut to be pounded up. This is always done by a member of the Sonwāni sept, a similar respect being paid to this sept among some of the Dravidian tribes. The foreheads of the betrothed couple are smeared with the nut and with some yellow-coloured rice and they bow low to the elders of the caste. Usually a bride-price of Rs. 5 or 10 is then paid to the parents of the girl together with two pieces of cloth intended for their use. A feast follows, which consists merely of the distribution of uncooked food, as the Dewārs, like some other low castes, will not take cooked food from each other. Pork and wine are essential ingredients in the feast or the ceremony cannot be completed. If liquor is not available, water from the house of a Kalār (distiller) will do instead, but there is no substitute for pork. This, however, is as a rule easily supplied as nearly all the Dewārs keep pigs, which are retailed to the Gonds for their sacrifices. The marriage ceremony is performed within three or four months at most after the betrothal. Before entering the Mandwa or marriage-shed the bridegroom must place a jar of liquor in front of his prospective father-in-law. The bridegroom must also place a ring on the little finger of the bride's right hand, while she resists him as much as she can, her hand having previously been smeared with castor oil in order to make the task more difficult. Before taking the bride away the new husband must pay her father Rs. 20, and if he cannot do this, and in default of arrangements for remission which are sometimes made, must remain domiciled in his house for a certain period. As the bride is usually adult there is no necessity for a *gauna* ceremony, and she leaves for her husband's house once for all. Thereafter when she visits the house of her parents she does so as a stranger, and they will not accept cooked food at her hands nor she at theirs. Neither will her husband's parents accept food from her, and each couple with their unmarried children form an exclusive group in this respect. Such a practice is found only among the low castes of mixed origin where nobody is certain of his neighbour's standing. If a woman has gone wrong before marriage, most of the ceremonies are omitted. In such a case the bridegroom catches hold of the bride by the hair and gives her a blow by way of punishment for her sin, and they then walk seven times round the sacred pole, the whole ceremony taking less than an hour. The bride-price is under these circumstances reduced to Rs. 15. Widow-marriage is permitted, and while in some localities the new husband need give nothing, in others he must pay as much as Rs. 50 to the relatives of the deceased husband. If a woman runs away from her husband to another man, the latter must pay to the husband double the ordinary amount payable for a widow. If he cannot afford this, he must return the woman with Rs. 10 as compensation for the wrong he has done. The Dewārs are also reported to have the practice of mortgaging their wives or making them over temporarily to a creditor in return for a loan. Divorce is allowed for the usual causes and by mutual consent. The husband must give a feast to the caste, which is looked on as the funeral ceremony of the woman so far as he is concerned ; thereafter she is dead to him and he cannot marry her again on pain of the permanent exclusion of both from the caste. But a divorced woman can marry any other Dewār. Polygamy is freely allowed.

4. Religion and social practices. The Dewārs especially worship Devi Maha Mai and Dūlha Deo. To the former they offer a she-goat and to the latter a he-goat which must be of a dark colour. They worship their *dhungru* or musical instrument on the day of Dasahra. They consider the sun and the moon to be brother and sister, and both to be manifestations of the deity. They bury their dead, but those who are in good circumstances dig up the bones after a year or two and burn them, taking the ashes to a sacred river. Mourning lasts for seven or ten days according as the deceased is unmarried or married, and during this time they abjure flesh and oil. Their social rules are peculiar. Though considered impure by the higher castes, they will not take cooked food from a Brāhman, whom they call a Kumhāti Kīda, or an insect which effects the metamorphosis of others into his own form, and who will therefore change them into his own caste. Nor will they take cooked food from members of their own caste, but they accept it from several of the lower castes including Gonds, whose leavings they will eat. This is probably because they beg from Gonds and attend their weddings. They keep pigs and pork is their favourite food, but they do not eat beef. They have a tribal council with a headman called Gaontia or Jemādar, who always belongs either to the Sonwāni or Telāsi section. Among offences for which a man is temporarily put out of caste is that of naming his younger brother's wife. He must also abstain from going into her room or touching her clothes. This rule does not apply to an elder brother's wife.

5. Occupation. The Dewārs are professional beggars, and play on the musical instruments called *dhungru* and *sārangi* which have already been described. The Ratanpūrias usually celebrate in an exaggerated style the praises of Gopāl Rai, their mythical ancestor. One of his exploits was to sever with a single sword-stroke the stalk of a plantain inside which the Emperor of Delhi had caused a solid bar of iron to be placed. The Raipūrias prefer a song, called Gujrīgīt, about curds and milk. They also sing various songs relating how a woman is beloved by a Rāja who tries to seduce her, but her chastity is miraculously saved by some curious combination of circumstances. They exorcise ghosts, train monkeys, bears and tigers for exhibition, and sell ornaments of base metal. In Raipur the men take about performing monkeys and the women do tattooing, for which they usually receive payment in the shape of an old or new cloth. A few have settled down to cultivation, but as a rule they are wanderers, carrying from place to place their scanty outfit of a small tent and mattress, both made of old rags, and a few vessels. They meet at central villages during the Holi festival. The family is restricted to the parents and unmarried children, separation usually taking place on marriage.

Dhākar.[1]—A small caste belonging solely to the Bastar State. In 1911 they numbered 5500 persons in Bastar, and it is noticeable that there were nearly twice as many women as men. The term Dhākar connotes a man of illegitimate descent and is applied to the Kirārs of the Central Provinces and perhaps to other castes of mixed Rājpūt origin. But in Bastar it is the special designation of a considerable class of persons who are the descendants of alliances between Brāhman and Rājpūt immigrants and women of the indigenous tribes. They are divided, like the Halbas, into two groups—Purāit or pure, and Surāit or mixed. The son of a Brāhman or Rājpūt father by a Rāwat (herdsman) or Halba mother is a Purāit, but one born from a woman of the Muria, Marār, Nai or Kalar castes is a Surāit. But these latter can become Purāits after two or three generations, and the same rule applies to the son of a Dhākar father by a Halba or Rāwat woman, who also ranks in the first place as a Surāit. Descendants of a Dhākar father by a Muria or other low-caste woman, however, always remain Surāits.

1. Origin and subdivisions.

---

[1] This article is based entirely on a paper by Rai Bahādur Panda Baijnāth, Superintendent, Bastar State.

The Purāits and Surāits form endogamous groups, and the latter will accept cooked food from the former. The more respectable Dhākars round Jagdalpur are now tending, however, to call themselves Rājpūts and refuse to admit any one of mixed birth into their community.

One legend of their origin is that the first Dhākar was the offspring of a Brāhman cook of the Rāja of Bastar with a Kosaria Rāwat woman ; and though this is discredited by the Dhākars it is probably a fairly correct version of the facts. An inferior branch of the caste exists which is known as Chikrasār ; it is related of them that their ancestors once went out hunting and set the forest on fire as a method of driving the game, as they occasionally do still. They came across the roasted body of a dog in the forest and ate it without knowing what animal it was. In the stomach, however, some cooked rice was found, and hence it was known as a dog and they were branded as dog-eaters. As a penalty the Rāja imposed on them the duty of thatching a hut for him at the Dasahra festival, which their descendants still perform. The other Dhākars refuse to marry or eat with them, and it is clear from the custom of thatching the Rāja's hut that they are a primitive and jungly branch of the caste.

2. Marriage.

If a girl becomes with child by a member of the caste she is made over to him without a marriage, or to the man to whom she was previously betrothed if he is still willing to take her. Neither is she expelled if the same event occurs with a man of any higher caste, but if he be of lower caste she is thrown out. Marriages are usually arranged by the parents but an adult girl may choose her own husband, and she is then wedded to him with abbreviated rites so that her family may avoid the disgrace of her entering his house like a widow or kept woman. Formerly a Dhākar might marry his granddaughter, but this is no longer done. When the signs of puberty first appear in a girl she is secluded and must not see or be seen by any man. They think that the souls of dead ancestors are reborn in children, and if a child refuses to suck they ask which of their ancestors he is and what he wants, or they offer it some present such as a silver bangle, and if the child then takes to the breast they give away the bangle to a Brāhman. The sixth day after a child is born the paternal aunt prepares lamp-black from a lamp fed with melted butter and rubs it on the child's eyes and receives a small present.

The period of mourning or impurity after a death must terminate with a feast to the caste-men, and it continues until this is given. Consequently the other caste-men subscribe for a poor member, so that he may give the feast and resume his ordinary avocations. On this occasion one of the guests puts a small fish in a leaf-cup full of water, which no doubt represents the spirit of the deceased, and all the mourners touch this cup and are freed from their impurity. A Brāhman is also invited, who lights a lamp fed with melted butter and then asks for a cow or some other valuable present as a recompense for his service of blowing out the lamp. Until this is done the Dhākars think that the soul of the departed is tortured by the flame of the lamp. If the Brāhman is pleased, he pours some curds over the lamp and this acts as a cooling balm to the soul. When a member of the family dies the mourners shave the whole head with beard and moustache.

3. Funeral rites.

The Dhākars are mainly engaged in cultivation as farm-servants and labourers. Like the Halbas, they consider it a sin to heat or forge iron, looking upon the metal as sacred. They eat the flesh of clean animals, but abstain from both pigs and chickens, and some also do not eat the peacock. A man as well as a woman is permanently expelled for adultery with a person of lower caste, the idea of this rule being no doubt to prevent degradation in the status of the caste from the admission of the offspring of such unions. If one Dhākar beats another with a shoe, both are temporarily put out of caste. But if a man seduces a caste-man's wife and is beaten with a shoe by the husband, he is permanently expelled, while the husband is readmitted after a feast. On being received back into caste intercourse an offender is purified by drinking water in which the image of a local god has been dipped or the Rāja of Bastar has placed his toe. Like other low castes of mixed origin, they are very particular about each other's status and will only accept cooked food from families who are well known to them. At caste feasts each family or group of families cooks for

4. Occupation and social status.

itself, and in some cases parents refuse to eat with the family into which their daughter has married and hence cannot do so with the girl herself.

1. Traditions and structure of the caste.

Dhangar.[1]—The Marātha caste of shepherds and blanket-weavers, numbering 96,000 persons in the Central Provinces and Berār. They reside principally in the Nāgpur, Wardha, Chānda and Nimār Districts of the Central Provinces and in all Districts of Berār. The Dhangars are a very numerous caste in Bombay and Hyderābād. The name is derived either from the Sanskrit *dhenu*, a cow, or more probably from *dhan*,[2] wealth, a term which is commonly applied to flocks of sheep and goats. It is said that the first sheep and goats came out of an ant-hill and scattering over the fields began to damage the crops of the cultivators. They, being helpless, prayed to Mahādeo to rescue them from this pest and he thereupon created the first Dhangar to tend the flocks. The Dhangars consequently revere an ant-hill, and never remove one from their fields, while they worship it on the Diwāli day with offerings of rice, flowers and part of the ear of a goat. When tending and driving sheep and goats they ejaculate 'Har, Har,' which is a name of Mahādeo used by devotees in worshipping him. The Dhangars furnished a valuable contingent to Sivaji's guerilla soldiery, and the ruling family of Indore State belong to this caste. It is divided into the following subcastes : Varādi or Barāde, belonging to Berār ; Kānore or Kānade, of Kanara ; Jhāde, or those belonging to the Bhandāra, Bālāghāt and Chhindwāra Districts, called the Jhādi or hill country ; Lādse, found in Hyderābād ; Gādri, from *gādar*, a sheep, a division probably consisting of northerners, as the name for the cognate caste of shepherds in Hindustān is Gadaria ; Telange, belonging to the Telugu country ; Marāthe, of the Marātha country ; Māhurai from Māhur in Hyderābād, and one or two others. Eleven subcastes in all are reported. For the purposes of marriage a number of exogamous groups or septs exist which may be classified according to their nomenclature as titular and totemistic, many having also the

---

[1] Compiled mainly from a paper by Kanhya Lāl, clerk in the Gazetteer office.
[2] Cf. the two meanings of the word 'stock' in English.

names of other castes.   Examples of sept names are : Powār,
a Rājpūt sept ; Dokra, an old man ; Mārte, a murderer or
slayer ; Sarodi, the name of a caste of mendicants ; Mhāli, a
barber ; Kaode, a crow ; Chambhāde, a Chamār ; Gūjde, a
Gūjar ; Juāde, a gambler ; Lamchote, long-haired ; Bodke,
bald-headed ; Khatīk, a butcher ; Chāndekar, from Chānda ;
Dambhāde, one having pimples on the body ; Halle, a he-
buffalo ; Moya, a grass, and others.   The sept names show
that the caste is a functional one of very mixed composition,
partly recruited from members of other castes who have
taken to sheep-tending and generally from the non-Aryan
tribes.

A man must not marry within his own sept or that of   2. Mar-
his mother, nor may he marry a first cousin.   He may wed   riage.
a younger sister of his wife during her lifetime, and the
practice of marrying a girl and boy into the same family,
called Anta Sānta or exchange, is permitted.   Occasionally
the husband does service for his wife in his father-in-law's
house.   In Wardha the Dhangars measure the heights of a
prospective bride and bridegroom with a piece of string and
consider it a suitable match if the husband is taller than the
wife, whether he be older or not.   Marriages may be infant
or adult, and polygamy is permitted, no stigma attaching to
the taking of a second wife.   Weddings may be celebrated
in the rains up to the month of Kunwār (September), this
provision probably arising from the fact that many Dhangars
wander about the country during the open season, and are
only at home during the rainy months.   Perhaps for the
same reason the wedding may, if the officiating priest so
directs, be held at the house of a Brāhman.   This happens
only when the Brāhman has sown an offering of rice, called
Gāg, in the name of the goddess Rāna Devi, the favourite
deity of the Dhangars.   On his way to the bride's house
the bridegroom must be covered with a black blanket.
Nowadays the wedding is sometimes held at the bridegroom's
house and the bride comes for it.   The caste say that this
is done because there are not infrequently among the
members of the bridegroom's family widows who have
remarried or women who have been kept by men of higher
castes or been guilty of adultery.   The bride's female

relatives refuse to wash the feet of these women and this provokes quarrels. To meet such cases the new rule has been introduced. At the wedding the priest sits on the roof of the house facing the west, and the bride and bridegroom stand below with a curtain between them. As the sun is half set he claps his hands and the bridegroom takes the clasped hands of the bride within his own, the curtain being withdrawn. The bridegroom ties round the bride's neck a yellow thread of seven strands, and when this is done she is married. Next morning a black bead necklace is substituted for the thread. The expenses of the bridegroom's party are about Rs. 50, and of the bride's about Rs. 30. The remaining procedure follows the customary usage of the Marātha Districts. Widows are permitted to marry again, but must not take a second husband from the sept to which the first belonged. A considerable price is paid for a widow, and it is often more expensive to marry one than a girl. A Brāhman and the mālguzār (village proprietor) should be present at the ceremony. If a bachelor marries a widow he must first go through the ceremony with a silver ring, and if the ring is subsequently lost or broken, its funeral rites must be performed. Divorce is allowed in the presence of the caste *panchāyat* at the instance of either party for sufficient reason, as the misconduct or bad temper of the wife or the impotency of the husband.

3. Religion.   Mahādeo is the special deity of the Dhangars, and they also observe the ordinary Hindu festivals. At Diwāli they worship their goats by dyeing their horns and touching their feet. One Bahrām of Nāchangaon near Pulgaon is the tutelary deity of the Wardha Dhangars and the protector of their flocks. On the last day of the month of Māgh they perform a special ceremony called the Deo Pūja. A Dhīmar acts as priest to the caste on this occasion and fashions some figures of idols out of rice to which vermilion and flowers are offered. He then distributes the grains of rice to the Dhangars who are present, pronouncing a benediction. The Dhīmar receives his food and a present, and it is essential that the act of worship should be performed by one of this caste. In their houses they have Kul-Devi

and Khandoba the Marātha hero, who are the family deities. But in large families they are kept only in the house of the eldest brother. Kul-Devi or the goddess of the family is worshipped at weddings, and a goat is offered to her in the month of Chait (March). The head is buried beneath her shrine inside the house and the body is consumed by members of the family only. Khandoba is worshipped on Sundays and they identify him with the sun. Vithoba, a form of Vishnu, is revered on Wednesdays, and Bālāji, the younger brother of Rāma, on Fridays. Many families also make a representation of some deceased bachelor relative, which they call Munjia, and of some married woman who is known as Mairni or Sāsin, and worship them daily.

The Dhangars burn their dead unless they are too poor to purchase wood for fuel, in which case burial is resorted to. Unmarried children and persons dying from smallpox, leprosy, cholera and snake-bite are also buried. At the pyre the widow breaks her bangles and throws her glass beads on to her husband's body. On returning from the burning *ghāt* the funeral party drink liquor. Some gānja, tobacco and anything else which the deceased may have been fond of during his life are left near the grave on the first day. Mourning is observed during ten days on the death of an adult and for three days for a child. Children are usually named on the twelfth day after birth, the well-to-do employing a Brāhman for the purpose. On this day the child must not see a lamp, as it is feared that if he should do so he will afterwards have a squint. Only one name is given as a rule, but subsequently when the child comes to be married, if the Brāhman finds that its name does not make the marriage auspicious, he substitutes another and the child is afterwards known by this new name. The caste employ Brāhmans for ceremonies at birth and marriage. They eat flesh including fowls and wild pig, and drink liquor, but abstain from other unclean food. They will take food from a Kunbi, Phūlmāli or a Sunār, and water from any of the good cultivating castes. A Kunbi will take water from them. The women of the caste wear bracelets of lead or brass on the right wrist and glass bangles on the left. Permanent or temporary excommunication from caste

4. Birth, death and social status.

is imposed for the usual offences, and among those visited with the minor penalty are selling shoes, touching the carcase of a dog or cat, and killing a cow or buffalo, or allowing one to die with a rope round its neck. No food is cooked for five weeks in a house in which a cat has died. The social standing of the caste is low.

5. Occupation.

The traditional occupation of the Dhangars is to tend sheep and goats, and they also sell goats' milk, make blankets from the wool of sheep, and sometimes breed and sell stock for slaughter. They generally live near tracts of waste land where grazing is available. Sheep are kept in open and goats in roofed folds. Like English shepherds they carry sticks or staffs and have dogs to assist in driving the flocks, and they sometimes hunt hares with their dogs. Their dress consists frequently only of a loin-cloth and a blanket, and having to bear exposure to all weathers, they are naturally strong and hardy. In appearance they are dark and of medium size. They eat three times a day and bathe in the evening on returning from work, though their ablutions are sometimes omitted in the cold weather.

1. Original and classical records.

Dhānuk.—A low caste of agriculturists found principally in the Narsinghpur District, which contained three-fourths of the total of nearly 7000 persons returned in 1911. The headquarters of the caste are in the United Provinces, which contains more than a lakh of Dhānuks. The name is derived from the Sanskrit *dhanuska*, an archer, and the caste is an ancient one, its origin as given in the Padma Purāna, quoted by Sir Henry Elliot, being from a Chamār father and a Chandāl or sweeper mother. Another pedigree makes the mother a Chamār and the father an outcaste Ahīr. Such statements, Sir H. Risley remarks in commenting on this genealogy,[1] serve to indicate in a general way the social rank held by the Dhānuks at the time when it was first thought necessary to enrol them among the mixed castes. Dr. Buchanan[2] says that the Dhānuks were in former times the militia of the country. He states that all the Dhānuks

---

[1] *Tribes and Castes of Bengal*, art. Dhānuk.

[2] *Eastern India*, i. 166, as quoted in Crooke's *Tribes and Castes*.

were at one time probably slaves and many were recruited
to fill up the military ranks—a method of security which
had long been prevalent in Asia, the armies of the Parthians
having been composed entirely of slaves. A great many
Dhānuks, at the time when Buchanan wrote, were still slaves,
but some annually procured their liberty by the inability of
their masters to maintain them and their unwillingness to
sell their fellow-creatures. It may be concluded, therefore,
that the Dhānuks were a body of servile soldiery, recruited
as was often the case from the subject Dravidian tribes ;
following the all-powerful tendency of Hindu society they
became a caste, and owing to the comparatively respectable
nature of their occupation obtained a rise in social position
from the outcaste status of the subject Dravidians to the
somewhat higher group of castes who were not unclean but
from whom a Brāhman would not accept water. They did
not advance so far as the Khandaits, another caste formed
from military service, who were also, Sir H. Risley shows,
originally recruited from a subject tribe, probably because
the position of the Dhānuks was always more subordinate and
no appreciable number of them came to be officers or leaders.
The very debased origin of the caste already mentioned as
given in the Padma Purāna may be supposed as in other
cases to be an attempt on the part of the priestly chronicler
to repress what he considered to be unfounded claims to a
rise in rank. But the Dhānuks, not less than the other
soldier castes, have advanced a pretension to be Kshatriyas,
those of Narsinghpur sometimes calling themselves Dhānkarai
Rājpūts, though this claim is of course in their case a pure
absurdity. It is not necessary to suppose that the Dhānuks
of the Central Provinces are the lineal descendants of the
caste whose genealogy is given in the Purānas ; they may be
a much more recent offshoot from a main caste, formed in a
precisely similar manner from military service.[1] Mr. Crooke[2]
surmises that they belonged to the large impure caste of
Basors or basket-makers, who took to bow-making and thence
to archery ; and some connection is traceable between the

---

[1] Cf. the two perfectly distinct groups
of Paīks or foot-soldiers found in
Jubbulpore and the Uriya country.

[2] *Tribes and Castes of the N.W.P.
and Oudh*, art. Basor.

Dhānuks and Basors in Narsinghpur. Such a separation must
probably have occurred in comparatively recent times, inasmuch as some recollection of it still remains. The fact that
Lodhis are the only caste besides Brāhmans from whom the
Dhānuks of Narsinghpur will take food cooked without water
may indicate that they formed the militia of Lodhi chieftains
in the Nerbudda valley, a hypothesis which is highly probable
on general grounds.

2. Mar-
riage.

In the Central Provinces the Dhānuks have no subcastes.[1]
The names of their *gotras* or family groups, though they
themselves cannot explain them, are apparently territorial :
as Māragaiyān from Māragaon, Benaikawār from Benaika
village, Pangarya from Panāgar, Binjharia from Bindhya or
Vindhya, Barodhaya from Barodha village, and so on.
Marriages within the same *gotra* and between first cousins
are prohibited, and child-marriage is usual. The father of
the boy always takes the initiative in arranging a match,
and if a man wants to find a husband for his daughter he
must ask the assistance of his relatives to obtain a proposal,
as it would be derogatory to move in the matter himself.
The contract for marriages is made at the boy's house and is
not inviolable. Before the departure of the bridegroom for
the bride's village, he stands at the entrance of the marriage-
shed, and his mother comes up and places her breast to his
mouth and throws rice balls and ashes over him. The former
action signifies the termination of his boyhood, while the
latter is meant to protect him on his important journey.
The bridegroom in walking away treads on a saucer in which
a little rice is placed. Widow - marriage and divorce are
permitted.

3. Social
rank and
customs.

A few members of the caste are tenants and the bulk of
them farmservants and field - labourers. They also act as
village watchmen. The Dhānuks eat flesh and fish, but not
fowls, beef or pork, and they abstain from liquor. They will
take food cooked without water from a Brāhman and a
Lodhi, but not from a Rājpūt ; but in Nimār the status of
the caste is distinctly lower, and they eat pig's flesh and the
leavings of Brāhmans and Rājpūts. The mixed nature of

---

[1] The following particulars are from
a paper by Kanhyā Lāl, a clerk in the
Gazetteer office belonging to the Educational Department.

the caste is shown by the fact that they will receive into the community illegitimate children born of a Dhānuk father and a woman of a higher caste such as Lodhi or Kurmi. They rank as already indicated just above the impure castes.

DHANWĀR

1. Origin and traditions.

Dhanwār, Dhanuhār.[1]—A primitive tribe living in the wild hilly country of the Bilāspur zamīndāri estates, adjoining Chota Nāgpur. They numbered only 19,000 persons in 1911. The name Dhanuhār means a bowman, and the bulk of the tribe have until recently been accustomed to obtain their livelihood by hunting with bow and arrows. The name is thus merely a functional term and is analogous to those of Dhāngar, or labourer, and Kisān, or cultivator, which are applied to the Oraons, and perhaps Halba or farmservant, by which another tribe is known. The Dhanwārs are almost certainly not connected with the Dhānuks of northern India, though the names have the same meaning. They are probably an offshoot of either the Gond or the Kawar tribe or a mixture of both. Their own legend of their origin is nearly the same as that of the Gonds, while the bulk of their sept or family names are identical with those of the Kawars. Like the Kawars, the Dhanwārs have no language of their own and speak a corrupt form of Chhattīsgarhi Hindi. Mr. Jeorākhan Lāl writes of them :—
" The word Dhanuhār is a corrupt form of Dhanusdhār or a holder of a bow. The bow consists of a cleft piece of bamboo

---

[1] This article is based almost entirely on a monograph by Mr. Jeorākhan Lāl, Deputy Inspector of Schools, Bilāspur.

488

and the arrow is made of wood of the *dhāman* tree.[1] The
pointed end is furnished with a piece or a nail of iron called
phani, while to the other end are attached feathers of the
vulture or peacock with a string of tasar silk. Dhanuhār
boys learn the use of the bow at five years of age, and kill
birds with it when they are seven or eight years old. At
their marriage ceremony the bridegroom carries an arrow
with him in place of a dagger as among the Hindus, and
each household has a bow which is worshipped at every
festival." According to their own legend the ancestors of
the Dhanuhārs were two babies whom a tigress unearthed
from the ground when scratching a hole in her den, and
brought up with her own young. They were named Nāga
Lodha and Nāgi Lodhi, *Nāga* meaning naked and *Lodha*
being the Chhattīsgarhi word for a wild dog. Growing up
they lived for some time as brother and sister, until the deity
enjoined them to marry. But they had no children until
Nāga Lodha, in obedience to the god's instructions, gave his
wife the fruit of eleven trees to eat. From these she had
eleven sons at a birth, and as she observed a fortnight's
impurity for each of them the total period was five and a
half months. In memory of this, Dhanuhār women still
remain impure for five months after delivery, and do not
worship the gods for that period. Afterwards the couple
had a twelfth son, who was born with a bow and arrows in
his hand, and is now the ancestral hero of the tribe, being
named Karankot. One day in the forest when Karankot
was not with them, the eleven brothers came upon a wooden
palisade, inside which were many deer and antelope tended
by twelve Gaoli (herdsmen) brothers with their twelve sisters.
The Lodha brothers attacked the place, but were taken
prisoners by the Gaolis and forced to remove dung and other
refuse from the enclosure. After a time Karankot went in
search of his brothers and, coming to the place, defeated the
Gaolis and rescued them and carried off the twelve sisters.
The twelve brothers subsequently married the twelve Gaoli
girls, Karankot himself being wedded to the youngest and
most beautiful, whose name was Maswāsi. From each couple
is supposed to be descended one of the tribes who live in

---

[1] *Grewia vestita.*

this country, as the Binjhwār, Bhumia, Korwa, Mājhi, Kol, Kawar and others, the Dhanuhārs themselves being the progeny of Karankot and Maswāsi. The bones of the animals killed by Karankot were thrown into ditches dug round the village and form the pits of *chhui mithi* or white clay now existing in this tract.

The Dhanuhārs, being a small tribe, have no endogamous divisions, but are divided into a number of totemistic exogamous septs. Many of the septs are called after plants or animals, and members of the sept refrain from killing or destroying the animal or plant after which it is named. The names of the septs are generally Chhattīsgarhi words, though a few are Gondi. Out of fifty names returned twenty are also found in the Kawar tribe and four among the Gonds. This makes it probable that the Dhanuhārs are mainly an offshoot from the Kawars with an admixture of Gonds and other tribes. A peculiarity worth noticing is that one or two of the septs have been split up into a number of others. The best instance of this is the Sonwāni sept, which is found among several castes and tribes in Chhattīsgarh ; its name is perhaps derived from *Sona pāni* (Gold water), and its members have the function of readmitting those temporarily expelled from social intercourse by pouring on them a little water into which a piece of gold has been dipped. Among the Dhanuhārs the Sonwāni sept has become divided into the Son-Sonwāni, who pour the gold water over the penitent ; the Rakat Sonwāni, who give him to drink a little of the blood of the sacrificial fowl ; the Hardi Sonwāni, who give turmeric water to the mourners when they come back from a funeral ; the Kāri Sonwāni, who assist at this ceremony ; and one or two others. The totem of the Kāri Sonwāni sept is a black cow, and when such an animal dies in the village members of the sept throw away their earthen pots. All these are now separate exogamous septs. The Deswārs are another sept which has been divided in the same manner. They are, perhaps, a more recent accession to the tribe, and are looked down on by the others because they will eat the flesh of bison. The other Dhanwārs refuse to do this because they say that when Sīta, Rāma's wife, was exiled in the jungles, she could not find a cow to worship and so revered a bison in its stead. And they say that the animal's feet are grey because of the turmeric water which Sīta poured on them, and that the depression on its forehead is the mark of her hand when she placed a *tīka* or sign there with coloured rice. The Deswārs are also called Dui Duāria or 'Those having two doors,' because they have a back door to their huts which is used only by women during their monthly period of impurity and kept shut at all other times. One of the septs is named Manakhia, which means 'man-eater,' and it is possible that its members formerly offered human sacrifices. Similarly, the Rakat-bund or 'Drop of blood Deswārs' may be so called because they shed human blood. A member of the Telāsi or 'Oil' sept, when he has killed a deer, will cut off the head and bring it home ; placing it in his courtyard, he suspends a burning lamp over the head and places grains of rice on the forehead of the deer ; and he then considers that he is revering the oil in the lamp. Members of the Sūrajgoti or sun sept are said to have stood as representatives of the sun in the rite of the purification of an offender.

Marriage within the sept is prohibited, and usually also between first cousins. Girls are commonly married a year or two after they arrive at maturity. The father of the boy looks out for a suitable girl for his son and sends a friend to make the proposal. If this is accepted a feast is given, and is known as Phūl Phulwāri or 'The bursting of the flower.' The betrothal itself is called Phaldān or 'The gift of the fruit'; on this occasion the contract is ratified and the usual presents are exchanged. Yet a third ceremony, prior to the marriage, is that of the Barokhi or inspection, when the bride and bridegroom are taken to see each other. On this occasion they exchange copper rings, placing them on each other's finger, and the boy offers vermilion to the earth, and then rubs it on the bride's forehead. When the girl is mature the date of the wedding is fixed, a small brideprice of six rupees and a piece of cloth being usually paid. If the first signs of puberty appear in the girl during the bright fortnight of the month, the marriage is held during the dark fortnight and vice versa. The marriage-shed is built in the form of a rectangle and must consist of either seven or nine posts in three lines. The bridegroom's party

3. Marriage.

comprises from twenty to forty persons of both sexes. When they arrive at the bride's village her father comes out to meet them and gives them leaf-pipes to smoke. He escorts them inside the village where a lodging has been prepared for them. The ceremony is based on that of the local Hindus with numerous petty variations in points of detail. In the actual ceremony the bride and bridegroom are first supported on the knees of two relatives. A sheet is held between them and each throws seven handfuls of parched rice over the other. They are then made to stand side by side ; a knot is made of their cloths containing a piece of turmeric, and the bride's left hand is laid over the bridegroom's right one, and on it a *sendhaura* or wooden box for vermilion is placed. The bride's mother moves seven times round the pair holding a lighted lamp, at which she warms her hand and then touches the marriage-crowns of the bride and bridegroom seven times in succession. And finally the couple walk seven times round the marriage-post, the bridegroom following the bride. The marriage is held during the day, and not, as is usual, at night or in the early morning. Afterwards, the pair are seated in the marriage-shed, the bridegroom's leg being placed over that of the bride, with their feet in a brass dish. The bride's mother then washes their great toes with milk and the rest of their feet with water. The bridegroom applies vermilion seven times to the marriage-post and to his wife's forehead at the parting of her hair. The couple are fed with rice and pulses one after the other out of the same leaf-plates, and the parties have a feast. Next morning, before their departure, the father of the bride asks the bridegroom to do his best to put up with his daughter, who is thievish, gluttonous and so slovenly that she lets her food drop on to the floor ; but if he finds he cannot endure her, to send her home. In the same manner the father of the boy apologises for his son, saying that he cares only for mischief and pleasure. The party then returns to the bridegroom's house.

4. Festivities of the women of the bridegroom's party. During the absence of the wedding party the women of the bridegroom's house with others in the village sing songs at night in the marriage-shed constructed at his house. These are known as Dindwa, a term applied to a

man who has no wife, whether widower or bachelor.   As
they sing, the women dance in two lines with their arms
interlaced, clapping their hands as they move backwards
and forwards.   The songs are of a lewd character, treating
of intrigues in love mingled with abuse of their relatives and
of other men who may be watching the proceedings by
stealth.   No offence is taken on such occasions, whatever
may be said.   In Upper India, Mr. Jeorākhān Lāl states
such songs are sung at the time of the marriage and are
called *Naktoureki louk* or the ceremony of the useless or
shameless ones, because women, however shy and modest,
become at this time as bold and shameless as men are at the
Holi festival.   The following are a few lines from one of
these songs :

The wheat-cake is below and the urad-cake is above.   Do you see
    my brother's brother-in-law watching the dance in the narrow
    lane.[1]
A sweetmeat is placed on the wheat-cake ; a handsome young black-
    guard has climbed on to the top of the wall to see the dance.
When a woman sees a man from afar he looks beautiful and attractive :
    but when he comes near she sees that he is not worth the trouble.
I went to the market and came back with my salt.   Oh, I looked
    more at you than at my husband who is wedded to me.

Several of the ceremonies are repeated at the bride- 5. Conclu-
groom's house after the return of the wedding party.   On sion of the
                                                            marriage.
the day following them the couple are taken to a tank
walking under a canopy held up by their friends.   Here they
throw away their marriage-crowns, and play at hiding a
vessel under the water.   When they return to the house a
goat is sacrificed to Dulha Deo and the bride cooks food in
her new house for the first time, her husband helping her,
and their relatives and friends in the village are invited to
partake of it.   After this the conjugal chamber is prepared
by the women of the household, and the bride is taken
to it and told to consider her husband's house as her
own.   The couple are then left together and the marriage
is consummated.

The remarriage of widows is permitted but it is 6. Widow-
                                                    marriage
not considered as a real marriage, according to the and
                                                     divorce.

[1] The term brother's brother-in-law is abusive in the same sense as brother-in-
law (*sāla*) said by a man.

saying: " A woman cannot be anointed twice with the marriage oil, as a wooden cooking - vessel cannot be put twice on the fire." A widow married again is called a *Churiyāhi Dauki* or ' Wife made by bangles,' as the ceremony may be completed by putting bangles on her wrists. When a woman is going to marry again she leaves her late husband's house and goes and lives with her own people or in a house by herself. The second husband makes his proposal to her through some other women. If accepted he comes with a party of his male friends, taking with him a new cloth and some bangles. They are received by the widow's guardian, and they sit in her house smoking and chewing tobacco while some woman friend retires with her and invests her with the new cloth and bangles. She comes out and the new husband and wife bow to all the Dhanwārs, who are subsequently regaled with liquor and goats' flesh, and the marriage is completed. Polygamy is permitted but is not common. A husband may divorce his wife for failing to bear him issue, for being ugly, thievish, shrewish or a witch, or for an intrigue with another man. If a married woman commits adultery with another man of the tribe they are pardoned with the exaction of one feast. If her paramour is a Gond, Rāwat, Binjhwār or Kawar, he is allowed to become a Dhanwār and marry her on giving several feasts, the exact number being fixed by the village Baiga or priest in a *panchāyat* or committee. With these exceptions a married woman having an intrigue with a man of another caste is finally expelled. A wife who desires to divorce her husband without his agreement is also turned out of the caste like a common woman.

7. Childbirth.   After the birth of a child the mother receives no food for the first and second, and fourth and fifth days, while on the third she is given only a warm decoction to drink. On the sixth day the men of the house are shaved and their impurity ceases. But the mother cooks no food for two months after bearing a female child and for three months if it is a male. The period has thus been somewhat reduced from the traditional one of five and a half months,[1] but it must still be highly inconvenient. At the expiration of the time of impurity the

[1] See commencement of this article.

earthen pots are changed and the mother prepares a meal for the whole household.   During her monthly period of impurity a woman cooks no food for six days.   On the seventh day she bathes and cleans her hair with clay, and is then again permitted to touch the drinking water and cook food.

The tribe bury the dead.   The corpse is wrapped in an old cloth and carried to the grave on a cot turned upside down.   On arrival there it is washed with turmeric and water and wrapped in a new cloth.   The bearers carry the corpse seven times round the open grave, saying, ' This is your last marriage,' that is, with the earth.   The male relatives and friends fill in the grave with earth, working with their hands only and keep their backs turned to the grave so as to avoid seeing the corpse.   It is said that each person should throw only five handfuls.   Other people then come up and fill in the grave, trampling down the surface as much as possible.   For three days after a death the bereaved family do not cook for themselves but are supplied with food by their friends.   These, however, do not give them any salt as it is thought that the craving for salt will divert their minds from dwelling on their loss.   The tribe do not perform the *shrāddh* ceremony, but in the month of Kunwār, on the day corresponding to that on which his father died, a man feeds the caste-fellows in memory of him.   And at this period he offers libations to his ancestors, pouring a double handful of water on the ground for each one that he can remember and then one for all the others.   While doing this he stands facing the east and does not turn to three different directions as the Hindu custom is.   The spirit of a man who has been killed by a tiger becomes Baghia Masān or the tiger imp, and that of a woman who dies in childbirth becomes a Churel.   Both are very troublesome to the living.

The principal deities of the Dhanwārs are Thākur Deo, the god of agriculture, and Dūlha Deo, the deity of the family and hearth.   Twice a year the village Baiga or medicine-man, who is usually a Gond, offers a cocoanut to Thākur Deo.   He first consecrates it to the god by placing it in contact with water and the small heap of rice which

8. Disposal of the dead.

9. Religion.

lies in front of his shrine, and then splits it asunder on a
stone, saying, '*Jai Thākur Deo*,' or 'Victory to Thākur
Deo.' When any serious calamity befalls the tribe a goat
is offered to the deity. It must also be first consecrated to
him by eating his rice ; its body is then washed in water
and some of the sacred *dūb*[1] grass is placed on it, and the
Baiga severs the head from the body with an axe. Dūlha
Deo is the god of the family and the marriage-bed, and
when a Dhanwār is married or his first son is born, a goat
is offered to the deity. Another interesting deity is Maiya
Andhiyāri, or the goddess of the dark fortnight of the
month. She is worshipped in the house conjointly by
husband and wife on any Tuesday in the dark fortnight of
Māgh (January-February), all the relatives of the family
being invited. On the day of worship the husband and
wife observe a fast, and all the water which is required for
use in the house during the day and night must be brought
into it in the early morning. A circular pit is dug inside
the house, about three feet deep and as many wide. A
she-goat which has borne no young is sacrificed to the
goddess in the house in the same manner as in the sacrifice
to Thākur Deo. The goat is skinned and cut up, the skin,
bones and other refuse being thrown into the hole. The
flesh is cooked and eaten with rice and pulse in the evening,
all the family and relatives, men and women, eating together
at the same time. After the meal, all the remaining food
and the water including that used for cooking, and the new
earthen pots used to carry water on that day are thrown
into the pit. The mouth of the pit is then covered with
wooden boards and plastered over with mud with great
care to prevent a child falling into it ; as it is held that
nothing which has once gone into the pit may be taken out,
even if it were a human being. It is said that once in the
old days a man who happened to fall into the pit was
buried alive, its mouth being covered over with planks of
wood ; and he was found alive when the pit was reopened
next year. This is an instance of the sacrificial meal,
common to many primitive peoples, at which the sacred
animal was consumed by the worshippers, skin, bones and

[1] *Cynodon dactylon.*

all. But now that such a course has become repugnant to
their more civilised digestions, the refuse is considered sacred
and disposed of in some such manner as that described.   The
goddess is also known as Rāt Devi or the goddess of the
night ; or Rāt Mai, the night mother.   The goddess Maswāsi
was the mythical ancestress of the Dhanwārs, the wife of
Karankot, and also the daughter of Maiya Andhiyāri or
Rāt Mai.   She too is worshipped every third year in the
dark fortnight of the month of Māgh on any Tuesday.
Her sacrifice is offered in the morning hours in the forest
by men only, and consists also of a black she-goat.   A site
is chosen under a tree and cleaned with cowdung, the bones
of animals being placed upon it in a heap to represent the
goddess.   The village Baiga kills the goat with an axe
and the body is eaten by the worshippers. Maswāsi is
invoked by the Dhanwārs before they go hunting, and
whenever they kill a wild boar or a deer they offer it to her.
She is thus clearly the goddess of hunting.   The tribe also
worship the spirits of hills and woods and the ghosts of the
illustrious dead.   The ghosts of dead Baigas or medicine-
men are believed to become spirits attending on Thākur
Deo, and when he is displeased with the Dhanwārs they
intervene to allay his anger.   The brothers of Maswāsi, the
twelve Gaolis, are believed to be divine hunters and to
haunt the forests, where they kill beasts and occasionally
men.   Six of them take post and the other six drive the
beasts or men towards these through the forest, when they
are pierced as with an arrow.   The victim dies after a few
days, but if human he may go to a sorcerer, who can extract
the arrow, smaller than a grain of rice, from his body.   In
the month of Aghan (November), when the grass of the
forests is to be cut, the members of the village collectively
offer a goat to the grass deity, in order that none of the
grass-cutters may be killed by a tiger or bitten by a snake
or other wild animal.

The Dhanwārs are fervent believers in all kinds of 10. Magic
magic and witchcraft.   Magic is practised both by the and witch-
Baiga, the village priest or medicine-man, who is always a craft.
man and who conducts the worship of the deities mentioned
above, and by the *tonhi*, the regular witch, who may be a

man or woman. Little difference appears to exist in the methods of the two classes of magicians, but the Baiga's magic is usually exercised for the good of his fellow-creatures, which indeed might be expected as he gets his livelihood from them, and he is also less powerful than the *tonhi*. The Baiga cures ordinary maladies and the bites of snakes and scorpions by mesmeric passes fortified by the utterance of charms. He raises the dead in much the same manner as a witch does, but employs the spirit of the dead person in casting out other evil spirits by which his clients may be possessed. One of the miracles performed by the Baiga is to make his wet cloth stand in the air stiff and straight, holding only the two lower ends. He can cross a river walking on leaves, and change men into beasts. Witches are not very common among the Dhanwārs. A witch, male or female, may be detected by a sunken and gloomy appearance of the eyes, a passionate temperament, or by being found naked in a graveyard at night, as only a witch would go there to raise a corpse from the dead. The Dhanwārs eat nearly all kinds of food except beef and the leavings of others. They will take cooked food from the hands of Kawars, and the men also from Gonds, but not the women. In some places they will accept food from Brāhmans, but not everywhere. They are not an impure caste, but usually live in a separate hamlet of their own, and are lower than the Gonds and Kawars, who will take water from them but not food. They are a very primitive people, and it is stated that at the census several of them left their huts and fled into the jungle, and were with difficulty induced to return. When an elder man dies his family usually abandon their hut, as it is believed that his spirit haunts it and causes death to any one who lives there.

11. Social rules.

A Kawar is always permitted to become a Dhanwār, and a woman of the Gond, Binjhwār and Rāwat tribes, if such a one is living with a Dhanwār, may be married to him with the approval of the tribe. She does not enjoy the full status of membership herself, but it is accorded to her children. When an outsider is to be admitted a *panchāyat* of five Dhanwārs is assembled, one of whom must be of the Mājhi sept. The members of the *panchāyat* hold out their right hands, palm upwards, one below the other, and beneath them the candidate and his wife place their hands. The Mājhi pours water from a brass vessel on to the topmost hand, and it trickles down from one to the other on to those of the candidate and his wife. The blood of a slaughtered goat is mixed with the water in their palms and they sip it, and after giving a feast to the caste are considered as Dhanwārs. Permanent exclusion from caste is imposed only for living with a man or woman of another caste other than those who may become Dhanwārs, or for taking food from a member of an impure caste, the only ones which are lower than the Dhanwārs. Temporary exclusion for an indefinite period is awarded for an irregular connection between a Dhanwār man and woman, or of a Dhanwār with a Kawar, Binjhwār, Rāwat or Gond ; on a family which harbours any one of its members who has been permanently expelled ; and on a woman who cuts the navel-cord of a newly-born child, whether of her own caste or not. Irregular sexual intimacies are usually kept secret and condoned by marriage whenever possible. A person expelled for any of the above offences cannot claim readmission as a right. He must first please the members of the caste, and to do this he attends every caste feast without being invited, removes their leaf-plates with the leavings of food, and waits on them generally, and continually proffers his prayer for readmission. When the other Dhanwārs are satisfied with his long and faithful service they take him back into the community. Temporary exclusion from caste, with the penalty of one or more feasts for readmission, is imposed for killing a cow or a cat accidentally, or in the course of giving it a beating ; for having a cow or bullock in one's possession whose nostrils or ears get split ; for getting maggots in a wound ; for being beaten except by a Government official ; for taking food from any higher caste other than those from whom food is accepted ; and in the case of a woman for saying her husband's name aloud. This list of offences shows that the Dhanwārs have almost completely adopted the Hindu code in social matters, while retaining their tribal religion. A person guilty of one of the above offences must have his or her head shaved by a barber, and make a pilgrimage to the shrine of Narsingh Nāth in Bodāsāmar zamīndāri ; after having accomplished this he is purified by one of the Sonwāni sept, being given water in which gold has been dipped to drink through a bamboo tube, and he provides usually three feasts for the caste-fellows.

12. Dress and tattooing.
The tribe dress in the somewhat primitive fashion prevalent in Chhattīsgarh, and there is nothing distinctive about their clothing. Women are tattooed at their parents' house before or just after marriage. It is said that the tattoo marks remain on the soul after death, and that she shows them to God, probably for purposes of identification. There is a saying, ' All other pleasures are transient, but the tattoo marks are my companions through life.' A Dhanwār will not take water from a woman who is not tattooed.

13. Names of children.
Children are named on the *chathi* or sixth day after birth, and the parents always ascertain from a wise man whether the soul of any dead relative has been born again in the child so that they may name it after him. It is also thought that the sex may change in transmigration, for male children are sometimes named after women relatives and female after men. Mr. Hīra Lāl notes the following instance of the names of four children in a family. The eldest was named after his grandfather ; the second was called Bhālu or bear, as his maternal uncle who had been eaten by a bear was reborn in him ; the third was called Ghāsi, the name of a low caste of grass-cutters, because the two children born before him had died ; and the fourth was called Kausi, because the sorcerer could not identify the spirit of any relative as having been born again in him. The name Kausi is given to any one who cannot remember his sept, as in the saying, ' *Bhūle bisāre kausi got*,' or ' A man who has got no *got* belongs to the Kausi *got*.' Kausi is said to mean a stranger. Bad names are commonly given to avert ill-luck or premature death, as Boya, a liar ; Labdu, one smeared with ashes ; Marha, a corpse ; or after some physical defect as Lati, one with clotted hair ; Petwa, a stammerer ; Lendra, shy ; Ghundu, one who cannot walk ; Ghunari, stunted ; or from the place of birth, as Dongariha or Pahāru, born on a hill ; Banjariha, born in brushwood, and so on. A man will not mention the names of his wife, his son's wife or his

sister's son's wife, and a woman will not name her husband
or his elder brother or parents.   As already stated, a woman
saying her husband's name aloud is temporarily put out of
caste, the Hindu custom being thus carried to extremes, as is
often the case among the lower castes.

The tribe consider hunting to have been their proper
calling, but many of them are now cultivators and labourers.
They also make bamboo matting and large baskets for storing
grain, but they will not make small bamboo baskets or fans,
because this is the calling of the Turis, on whom the Dhanwār
looks down.   The women collect the leaves of *sāl*[1] trees and
sell them at the rate of about ten bundles for a pice (farthing)
for use as *chongis* or leaf-pipes.   As already stated, the tribe
have no language of their own, but speak a corrupt form
of Chhattīsgarhi.

14. Occu-
pation.

[1] *Shorea robusta.*

DHĪMAR[1]

LIST OF PARAGRAPHS

1. General notice.

Dhīmar, Kahār, Bhoi, Pālewār, Baraua, Machhandar.— The caste of fishermen and palanquin-bearers. In 1911 the Dhīmars numbered 284,000 persons in the Central Provinces and Berār, being most numerous in the Marātha Districts. In the north of the Province we find in place of the Dhīmars the Kahārs and Mullāhs, and in the east or Chhattīsgarh country the Kewats. But the distinction between these castes is no more than nominal, for in some localities both Kahār and Kewat are returned as subcastes of Dhīmar. In some parts of India the Bhois and Dhīmars are considered as separate castes, but in the Central Provinces they are not to be distinguished, both names being applied indiscriminately to the same persons. The name of Bhoi perhaps belongs more particularly to those who carry litters or palanquins, and that of Dhīmar to the fishermen. The word Dhīmar is a corruption of the Sanskrit Dhīvara, a fisherman. Bhoi is a South Indian word (Telugu and Malayalam *boyi*, Tamil *bovi*), and in the Konkan people of this class are known as Kahār Bhui. Among the Gonds Bhoi is con-

---

[1] This article is based partly on papers by Mr. Govind Moreshwar, Head Clerk, Mandla, and Mr. Pancham Lāl, Naib-Tahsīldār, Sihora. Much of the interesting information about the occupations of the caste was given to the writer by Bābu Kāli Prasanna Mukerji, Pleader, Saugor.

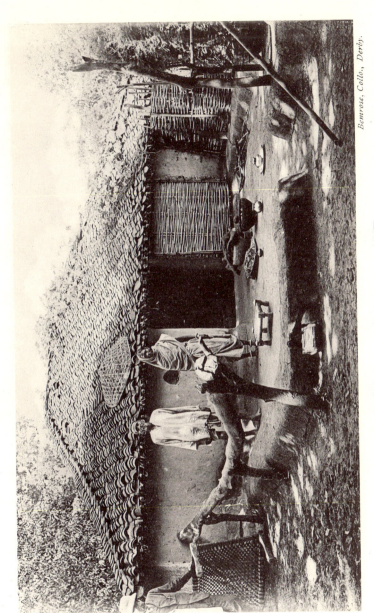

DHĪMAR OR FISHERMAN'S HUT.

Bemrose, Collo., Derby.

sidered as an honorific name or title ; and this indicates that a large number of Gonds have become enrolled in the Dhīmar or Kahār caste, and consider it a rise in status. Pālewār is the name of the Telugu fishermen of Chānda. Machhandar signifies one who catches fish.

The caste has a large number of subdivisions of a local or occupational nature ; among occupational names may be mentioned the Singaria or those who cultivate the *singāra* nut, the Nadha or those who live on the banks of streams, the Tānkiwālas or sharpeners of grindstones, the Jhīngas or prawn-catchers, the Bansias and Saraias or anglers (from *bansi* or *sarai*, a bamboo fishing-rod), the Bandhaiyas or those who make ropes and sacking of hemp and fibre, and the Dhurias who sell parched rice.   These last say that their original ancestors were created by Mahādeo out of a handful of dust (*dhūr*) for carrying the palanquin of Pārvati when she was tired.   They are probably the same people as the Dhuris who also parch grain, and in Chhattīsgarh are considered as a separate caste.   Similarly the Sonjhara Dhīmars wash for gold, the calling of the separate Sonjhara caste. The Kasdhonia Dhīmars wash the sands of the sacred rivers to find the coins which pious pilgrims frequently drop or throw into the river as an offering when they bathe in it. The Gondia subcaste is clearly an offshoot from the Gond tribe, but a large proportion of the whole caste in the Central Provinces is probably derived from the Gonds or Kols, members of this latter tribe being especially proficient as palanquin-bearers.   The Suvarha subcaste is named after the *suar* or pig, because members of this subcaste breed and eat the unclean animal ; they are looked down on by the others.   Similarly the Gadhewāle Dhīmars keep donkeys, and are despised by the other subcastes who will not take food from them.   They use donkeys for carrying loads of wood, and the bridegroom rides to his wedding on this animal ; and among them a donkey is the only animal the corpse of which can be touched without conveying pollution. The Bhanāre Dhīmars appear to be named after the town of Bhandāra.

2. Subcastes.

A large number of exogamous groups are also returned, either of a titular or totemistic nature : such are Bāghmār, a

3. Exogamous groups.

tiger-slayer ; Ojhwa, from Ojha, or sorcerer ; Guru pahchān, one who knows his teacher ; Midoia, a guardian of boundaries, from *med*, a boundary or border ; Gidhwe, a vulture ; Kolhe, or jackal ; Gadhekhāya, a donkey-eater ; and Kastūre, musk ; a few names are from towns or villages, as Tumsare from Tumsar, Nāgpurkar from Nāgpur ; and a few from other castes as Mādgi, Bhoyar, Pindāria from Pindāri, a freebooter ; Gondia (Gond) and Gondhali ; and Kachhwāha, a sept of Rājpūts.

4. Marriage.

Marriage is prohibited between members of the same sept and also between first cousins. In many localities families do not intermarry so long as they remember any relationship to have existed between them. In Mandla, Mr. Govind Moreshwar states, the Nadha and Kehera sub-castes do not intermarry ; but if a man desires a girl of the other subcaste he can be admitted into it on giving a feast to the caste-fellows according to his means, and thus marry her. Two families may exchange daughters in marriage. A maiden who goes wrong with a man of the caste or of any higher caste may be readmitted to the community under penalty of a feast to the caste and of having a lock of her hair cut off. In the Hindustāni Districts women do not accompany the marriage procession, but in the Marātha Districts they do. Among the Bhanāra Dhīmars of Chānda the wedding may be held either at the bride's or the bride-groom's house. In the former case a bride-price of Rs. 16 is paid, and in the latter one of Rs. 20, because the expenses of the bride's family are increased if the wedding is held at her house. A custom exists among the poorer Dhīmars in Chānda of postponing the marriage ceremony to avoid expense ; a man will thus simply take a girl for his wife, making a payment of Rs. 1-4 or twenty pence to her father and giving a feast to the community. She will then live in his house as his wife, and at some subsequent date, perhaps in old age, the religious ceremony will be held so that the couple may have been properly married before they die. In this fashion the weddings of grandparents, parents and children have all been celebrated simultaneously. The Singaria Dhīmars of Chhindwāra grow *singāra* or water-nut in tanks, and at their weddings a crocodile must be killed and eaten.   The Sonjharas or gold-washers must also have a crocodile, but they keep it alive and worship it, and when the ceremony is concluded let it go back again to the river. It is natural that castes whose avocations are connected with rivers and tanks should in a manner deify the most prominent or most ferocious animal contained in their waters.   And the ceremonial eating of a sacred animal has been recorded among divers peoples all over the world.   At a Dhīmar marriage in Bhandāra a net is given to the bridegroom, and *sidori* or cooked food, tied in a piece of cloth, to the bride, and they walk out together as if going to a river to fish, but the bride's brother comes up and stops them.   After a wedding in Mandla they kill a pig and bury it before the door of the bridegroom's house, covering it with earth, and the bride and bridegroom step over its body into the house. Widow-marriage is freely permitted ; in Mandla the marriage of a widow may be held on the night of any day except Sunday, Tuesday and Saturday.   Divorce is allowed, but is of rare occurrence.   Adultery on the part of a wife will be frequently overlooked, and the extreme step of divorcing her is only taken if she creates a public scandal.   In such a case the parties appear before a meeting of the caste, and the headman asks them whether they have determined to separate.   He then breaks a straw in token of the disruption of the union, and the husband and wife must pronounce each other's names in an audible voice.[1]   A fee of Rs. 1-4 is paid to the headman, and the divorce is completed.[2]   In some localities the woman's bangles are also broken.   In Jhānsi the fine for keeping a widow is ten rupees and for living with the wife of another man sixty rupees.

Children are named either on the day of birth or the twelfth day afterwards.   The women place the child in a cradle, spreading boiled wheat and gram over its body, and after swinging it to and fro the name is given.   Sweets or boiled wheat and gram are distributed to those present.   In Berār on the third day after a birth cakes of juāri flour and buttermilk are distributed to other children ; on the fifth

5. Child-birth.

---

[1] As a rule a husband and wife never address each other by name.

[2] Among Hindus it is customary to give a little more than the proper sum on ceremonial occasions in order to show that there is no stint.   Thus Rs. 1-4 is paid instead of a rupee.

day the slab and roller used for grinding the household corn
are washed, anointed and worshipped ; on the twelfth day
the child is named and shortly after this its head is shaved.[1]

6. Disposal of the dead.

The bodies of the dead are usually buried, cremation
being beyond the means of Dhīmars.　Children whose ears
have not been pierced are mourned only for one day, and
others for ten days.　When a body has been burnt the
ashes are consigned to a tank or river on the third day, or
if the third day be a Sunday or a Wednesday, then on
the fifth day.　In Berār, Mr. Kitts remarks,[2] the funeral
ceremony of the Dhīmars resembles that of the Gonds.
After a burial the mourners repair to the deceased's house
to drink ; and subsequently each fetches his own dinner and
dines with the chief mourner.　At this time he and his
family are impure and the others cannot take food prepared
by him ; but ten days afterwards when the mourning is
over and the chief mourner has bathed and shaved they
again dine with him, and on the next day the caste is
feasted.　During the period of mourning a lighted lamp is
daily placed outside the house.　When the period of mourning expires all the clothes of the family are washed and their
house is newly whitewashed.　There is no subsequent
annual performance of funeral rites as among the higher
Hindus ; but at the Akshayatritiya or commencement of
the agricultural year the head of the household throws at
each meal a little food into the fire, in honour of his dead
ancestors.

7. Religion.

One of the principal deities of the Dhīmars[3] as of other
low castes is Dulha Deo, the deified bridegroom.　They
fashion his image of *kadamb*[4] wood and besmear it with
red lead.　In Berār they also pray to Anna Pūrna, the
Corn-giving goddess of Madras corresponding to Durga or
Devi, whose form with that of her horse is engraved on
a brass plate and anointed with yellow and red turmeric.
When about to enter a river or tank for fishing or other
purposes they pray to the water-god to save them from
being drowned or molested by its denizens.　They address
a river as Ganga Mai or 'Mother Ganges' in order to

---

[1] *Berār Census Report* (1881), p. 133.
[2] *Ibidem, l.c.*　　　[3] *Ibidem, l.c.*　　　[4] *Anthocephalus kadamba.*

FISHERMEN IN DUG-OUTS OR HOLLOWED TREE TRUNKS.

Bemrose, Collo., Derby.

propitiate it by this flattery. Those who are employed on
ferry-boats especially venerate Ghatoia[1] Deo, the god of
ferries and river-crossings. His shrine is near the place
where the boats are tied up, and ferry contractors keep a
live chicken in their boat to be offered to Ghatoia on the
first occasion when the river is sufficiently in flood to be
crossed by ferry after the breaking of the rains. Other
local godlings are the Bare Purakh or Great men, a collective
term for their deceased ancestors, of whom they make silver
images ; Parihār, the soul of the village priest ; Baram Deo,
the spirit of the banyan tree ; and Gosain Deo, a deified
ascetic. To the goddess Devi they offer a black she-goat
which is eaten ceremonially, and when they have finished,
the bones, skin and all the other remains of the animal are
placed in a pit inside the house. If anything should fall
into this pit it must be buried with the remains of the
offering and not taken out. And they relate that on one
occasion a child fell into the pit, and the parents, setting
obedience to the law of the goddess above the life of their
child, buried it alive. But next year when the sacrifice
was again made and the pit was opened, the child was
found in it alive and playing. So they say that the goddess
will save the life of any one who is buried in the pit with
her offering. When a widower marries a second time his
wife sometimes wears a *tāwīz* or amulet in the shape of a
silver box containing charms round her neck in order to
ward off the evil machinations of her predecessor's spirit.

The occupations of the Dhīmar are many and various. **8. Occupa-**
He is primarily a fisherman and boatman, and has various **tion :**
kinds of nets for taking fish. One of these is of triangular **fisherman.**
shape about 150 feet wide at the base and 80 feet in
height to the apex. The meshes vary from an inch wide
at the top to three inches at the bottom. The ends of the
base are weighted with stones and the net is then sunk into
a river so that the base rests on its bed and the top is held
by men in boats at the surface. Then other Dhīmars beat
the surface of the water for some distance with long bamboos
on both sides of the net, driving the fish towards it. They

---

[1] From *ghāt*, a steep hillside or slope; hence a river-crossing because of the
banks sloping down to it.

call this a *kheda*, the term used for a beat of the forest for game.

Another method is to stretch a long rope or cord across the river, secured on either bank, with baited hooks attached to it at short intervals. It is left for some hours and then drawn in. When the river is shallow one wide-bottomed boat will be paddled up the stream and a line of men will wade on each side beating the water with bamboos so as to make the small fish jump into the boat. Or they put a little cotton-seed on a stone in shallow water, and when the fish collect to eat the seed a long circular net weighted with pieces of iron is let down over the stone. Then the upper end is drawn tight and the fishermen put their hands inside and seize the little fish. The Dhīmar is also regularly employed as a worker on ferries. His primitive boat made from the hollowed trunk of a tree and sometimes lashed in couples for greater stability may still be seen on all rivers. He makes his own fishing-nets, knitting them on a stick at his leisure while he is walking along or sitting down to smoke and talk. He worships his fishing-nets at the Diwāli festival, and his reverence for the knitted thread is such that he will not touch or wear a shoe made of thread, because he thinks that the sacred article is debased by being sewn into leather. When engaged in road-work the Dhīmars have unsewn sandals secured to the feet with strips of leather. It is a special degradation to a Dhīmar to be struck with a shoe. He has a monopoly of growing *singāra* [1] or water-nuts in tanks. The fruit of this plant has a taste somewhat between a cocoanut and a potato, with a flavour of soap. It can be taken raw and is therefore a favourite comestible for fast days when cooked food is forbidden. It is also sold at railway stations and the fresh fruit is prescribed by village doctors as easy of digestion. The Dhīmar grows melons, cucumbers and other vegetables on the sandy stretches along the banks of streams, but at agriculture proper he does not excel.

9. Water-carrier.

The Dhīmar's connection with water has led to his becoming the water-carrier for Hindus, or that section of the community which can afford to employ one. This is

[1] *Trapa bispinosa.*

more especially the case in the Hindustāni Districts where
women are frequently secluded and therefore cannot draw
water for the household, while in the Marātha Districts
where the women go to the well no water-bearer is required.
In this capacity the Dhīmar is usually the personal servant
of the village proprietor, but in large villages every house
has a *ghinochi*, either an earthen platform or wooden stand
just outside the house, on which four or five earthen water-
pots are kept.   These the Dhīmar fills up morning and
evening and receives two or three annas or pence a month
for doing so.   He also brings water for Government servants
when they come to the village, and cleans their cooking-
vessels and prepares the hearth with fresh cowdung and
water in order to cleanse it.

If he cleans the mālguzār's vessels he gets his food for
doing so.   When the tenants have marriages he performs
the same duties for the whole wedding party and receives a
present of one or two rupees and some clothes if the families
are well off, and also his food every day while the marriage
is in progress.   In his capacity of waterman the title Baraua
is used to him as an honorific method of address ; and to his
wife Baroni.   In a hot country like India water is revered
as the source of relief, comfort and life itself, like fire in cold
countries, and the waterman participates in the regard paid
to his element.

Another business of the Dhīmar's is to take sweet potatoes
and boiled plums to the fields at harvest-time and sell them.
He supplies water for drinking to the reapers and receives
three sheaves a day in payment.   On the fifteenth of Jesth
(May) the Dhīmar goes round to the cultivators, throwing his
fishing-net over their heads and receives a small present.

At the period prior to the introduction of wheeled transport when palanquins or litters were largely used for travelling, the carriers belonged to the Kahār caste in northern
India and to the Dhīmars or Bhois in the south.   Though
litters are now practically not used for travelling except
occasionally by high-caste women, a survival of the old
custom is retained in the marriage ceremony, the bride and
bridegroom being always carried back from the marriage-
shed to the temporary lodging of the bridegroom in a *pālki*,

10. Palan-
quin-
bearer and
personal
servant.

though for the longer journey to the bridegroom's village some less cumbrous conveyance is utilised. Four Dhīmars carry the *pālki* and receive Rs. 1-4. Well-to-do people will be carried in procession round the town. When employed by the village proprietor the Dhīmar accompanies him on his journey, carrying his cooking-vessels and other necessaries in a *banhgi* or wooden cross-bar slung across the shoulders, from which two baskets are suspended by loops of rope. Water he will always carry in a *banhgi* and never on his head or shoulders. From waterman and litter-carrier the Dhīmar has become a personal servant; it is he to whom the term 'bearer' as designating a body-servant was first applied because he bears or carries his master in a *pālki* and his clothes in a *banhgi*. He is commonly so employed in native houses, but rarely by Europeans, whether because he is too stupid or on account of caste objections of his own. When employed as a cook the Dhīmar or his wife is permitted to knead flour with water and make it into a cake which the Brāhman will then take and put on to the girdle with his own hands. He can also boil water and pour pulse into the cooking-pot from above so long as he does not touch the vessel after the food has been placed in it. He or she will also take any remains of food which is left in the cooking-pot as this is not considered to be polluted, food only becoming polluted when the hand touches it on the dish after having touched the mouth. When this has happened all the food on the dish becomes *jūtha* or leavings of food, and as a general rule no caste except the sweepers will eat the leavings of food of another caste or of another person of their own. Only the wife, whose meal follows her husband's, will eat his leavings. As a servant the Dhīmar is very familiar with his master; he may enter any part of the house, including the cooking-place and the women's rooms, and he addresses his mistress as 'Mother.' In northern India Mr. Crooke states that the Kahārs are sometimes known as Mahra, from the Sanskrit Mahila, a woman, because they have the entry of the female apartments. When he lights his master's pipe he takes the first pull himself to show that it has not been tampered with, and then presents it to him with his left hand placed under his

right elbow in token of respect.   Maid-servants also frequently belong to the Dhīmar caste, and it often happens that
the master of the household has illicit intercourse with them.
Hence there is a proverb, ' The king's son draws water and
the water-bearer's son sits on the throne,' similar intrigues
on the part of high-born women with their servants being
not unknown.   The Dhīmar often acts as a pimp, this being
an incident of his profession of indoor servant.

Another occupation of the Dhīmar's is to sell parched
grain and rice to travellers in markets and railway stations
like the Bharbhūnja and Dhuri.   This he can do because of
his comparative social purity, as all castes will take water
and cakes and sweetmeats from his hands.   Some Dhīmars
and Kewats also weave hemp-matting and gunny-bags, but
such members of the caste rank lower than the others and
Brāhmans will not take water from them.   Another calling
by which a few Dhīmars find support is that of breeding
pigs.   One would think it a difficult matter to make a living
out of the village pig, an animal abhorred by both Hindus
and Muhammadans as the most unclean of the brute creation,
and equally abjured by Europeans as unfit for food.   But
the pig is in considerable demand by the forest tribes for
sacrifice to their deities.   The Dhīmar participates in the
sacrifice to Nārāyan Deo described in the article on Mahār,
when a pig is eaten in concert by several of the lower castes.
Lastly, the business of rearing the cocoons of the tasar silk-
worm is usually in the hands of Dhīmars and Kewats.
While the caterpillars are feeding on leaves and spinning
their cocoons these men live in the forests for two months
together and watch the *kosa-bāris* or silk-gardens, that is the
blocks of trees which are set apart for the purpose of rearing
the caterpillars.   During this period they eat only once a
day, abstain from meat and lentils, do not get shaved and
do not visit their wives.   When the eggs of the caterpillars
are to be placed on the trees they tie a silk thread round
the first tree to be used and worship it as Pāt Deo or the
god of silk thread.   On this subject Mr. Ball writes : [1] " The
trees which it is intended to stock are carefully pollarded
before the rains, and in early spring the leaves are stocked

11. Other
occupa-
tions.

[1] *Jungle Life in India*, p. 137.

with young caterpillars which have been hatched in the
houses. The men in charge erect wigwams and remain on
the spot, isolated from their families, who regard them for
the time being as unclean. During the daytime they have
full occupation in guarding the large green caterpillars from
the attacks of kites and other birds. The cocoons are
collected soon after they are spun and boiled in a lye of
wood-ash, and the extracted chrysalids must then be eaten
by the caretakers, who have to undergo certain ceremonial
rites before they are readmitted into the society of their
fellows. The effect of the boiling in the lye is the removal
of the glutinous matter, which renders it possible to wind off
the silk." The eating of the caterpillars is no doubt a
ceremonial observance like that of the crocodile at weddings.
They are killed by the boiling of the cocoons and on this
account members of good castes will not engage in the
business of rearing them. The abstention from conjugal
intimacy while engaged in some important business is a
very common phenomenon.

12. Social
status.

The social status of the Dhīmar is somewhat peculiar.
Owing to his employment as palanquin-bearer, cook and
household servant he has been promoted to the group of
castes who are ceremonially clean, so that Brāhmans in
northern India will take water and food cooked in butter
from his hands. But by origin he no doubt belongs to the
primitive or non-Aryan tribes, a fact which he shows by his
appearance and also by his customs. In diet he is the reverse
of fastidious, eating crocodiles, tortoises and crabs, and also
pork in the Marātha Districts, though in the north where he
is employed by Brāhmans as a personal servant he abstains
from this food. With all this, however, the Dhīmars practise
in some social matters a pharasaical strictness. In Jubbulpore
Mr. Pancham Lāl records that among the four subcastes of
Rekwār, Bant, Barmaian and Pabeha a woman of one subcaste will not partake of any food cooked by one of another
division. A man will take any kind of food cooked by a
man of another subcaste, but from a woman only such as is
not mixed with water. A woman will drink the water held
in the metal vessel of a woman of another division, but not
in an earthen vessel ; and in a metal vessel only provided

that it is brought straight from the well and not taken from the *ghinochi* or water-stand of such woman's house.   A man will take water to drink from the metal or earthen vessel of any other Dhīmar, male or female.   In Berār again Mr. Kitts states[1] that a Bhoi considers it pollution to eat or drink at the house of a Lohār (blacksmith), a Sutār (carpenter), a Bhāt (bard), a washerman or a barber ; he will not even carry their palanquins at a marriage.

Once a year at the Muharram festival the Dhīmars will eat at the hands of Muhammadans.   They go round and beg for offerings of food and take them to the Fakīr, who places a little before the *tāzia* or tomb of Husain and distributes the remainder to the Dhīmars and other Hindus and Muhammadans who have been begging.   Except on this occasion they will eat nothing touched by a Muhammadan.   The Dhīmar, the Nai or barber, and the Bāri or indoor servant are the three household menials of the northern Districts, and are known as Pauni Parja.   Sometimes the Ahīr or grazier is an indoor servant and takes the place of the Dhīmar or the Bāri.   These menials are admitted to the wedding and other family feasts and allowed to eat at them.   They sit in a line apart from the members of the caste and one member of the family is deputed to wait on them.   Their food is brought to them in separate dishes and no food from these dishes is served to guests of the caste.

Permanent expulsion[2] from caste is inflicted only for marrying, or eating regularly, with a man or woman of some other low caste ; but in the case of unmarried persons the latter offence may also be expiated.   Temporary exclusion is imposed for killing a cat, dog or squirrel, getting maggots in a wound, being sentenced to imprisonment[3] or committing adultery with a person of any low caste.   One who has

---

[1] *Berār Census Report* (1881), p. 132.

[2] The following notice of caste offences is from Mr. Govind Moreshwar's paper.

[3] Not probably on account of the commission of a crime, but because being sentenced to imprisonment involves the eating of ceremonially impure food.   These rules are common to most Hindu castes, and the Dhīmars are taken only as a typical example.   They seem to have little or no connection with ordinary morality.   But in Jhānsi Mr. Crooke remarks that a Kahār is put out of caste for theft in his master's house.   This again, however, might be considered as an offence against the community, tending to lower their corporate character in their business, and as such deserving of social punishment.

committed any of the above offences must be purified by
the Batta of the caste, that is a person who takes the sins
of others upon himself.　The Batta conducts the culprit to
a river and then causes him to bathe, cuts off a lock of his
hair, breaks a cocoanut as a sacrifice, and gives him a little
cowdung and milk to eat.　Then they proceed to eat
together ; the Batta eats five mouthfuls first and declares
that he has taken the sin of the offender on himself ; the
latter gives the Batta Rs. 1-4 as his fee, and is once more
a proper member of the community.　In Berār a Bhoi who
has been put out of caste is received back by his fellows
when he has drunk the water touched by a Brāhman's toe,
and has feasted them with a bout of liquor.　In towns the
caste are generally addicted to drink, and no marriage or
other social function is held without a sufficient supply of
liquor.　They also smoke *gānja* (Indian hemp).

13. Legend
of the
caste.
　　　　The Dhīmars are proverbially of a cheerful disposition,
though simple and easily cheated.　When carrying *pālkis* or
litters at night they talk continually or sing monotonous
songs to lighten the tedium of the way.　In illustration of
these qualities the following story is told : One day when
Mahādeo and Pārvati were travelling the goddess became
very tired, so Mahādeo created four men from the dust, who
bore her in a litter.　On the way they talked and laughed,
and Pārvati was very pleased with them, so when she got
home she told them to wait while she sent them out a reward.
The Bhois found that they could get plenty of liquor, so
they went on drinking it and forgot all about going for the
reward.　In the meantime a Mārwāri Bania who had heard
what the goddess said, waited at the door of the palace,
and when the servants brought out a bag of money he
pretended that he was one of the Bhois and got them to
give him the money, with which he made off.　After a time
the Bhois remembered about the reward and went to the
door of the palace to get it, when the goddess came out and
found out what had happened.　The Bhois then wept and
asked for another reward, but the goddess refused and said
that as they had been so stupid their caste would always
be poor, but at the same time they would be cheerful and
happy.

DHOBA

Dhoba.[1]—A small caste belonging to the Mandla District 1. General and apparently an offshoot from one of the primitive tribes. notice. They have never been separately classified at the census but always amalgamated with the Dhobi or washerman caste. But the Mandla Dhobas acknowledge no connection with Dhobis, nor has any been detected. One Dhoba has indeed furnished a story to the Rev. E. Price that the first ancestor of the caste was a foundling boy, by appearance of good lineage, who was brought up by some Dhobis, and, marrying a Dhobi girl, made a new caste. But this is not sufficient to demonstrate the common origin of the Dhobas and Dhobis. The Dhobas reside principally in a few villages in the upper valley of the Burhner River, and members of the caste own two or three villages. They are dark in complexion and have, though in a less degree, the flat features, coarse nose and receding forehead of the Gond ; but they are taller in stature and not so strongly built, and are much less capable of exertion.

The caste has twelve exogamous septs, though the list 2. Exogamous is probably not complete. These appear to be derived divisions. from the names of villages. Marriage is forbidden between the Bāghmār and Bāghcharia septs, the Marātha and Khatnāgar and Marālwati septs and the Sonwāni and

---

[1] This article is partly based on an account of the caste furnished by Mr. H. F. E. Bell and drawn up by Mr. F. R. R. Rudman in the *Mandla District Gazetteer.*

Sonsonwāni septs. These septs are said to have been subdivided and to be still related. The names Bāghmār and
Bāghcharia are both derived from the tiger; Sonwāni is
from Sona-pāni or gold-water, and the Sonsonwāni sept
seems therefore to be the aristocratic branch or *crême de la
crême* of the Sonwānis. The children of brothers and sisters
may marry but not those of two sisters, because a man's
maternal aunt or *mausi* is considered as equivalent to his
mother. A man may also marry his step-sister on the
mother's side, that is the daughter of his own mother by
another husband either prior to or subsequent to his father,
the step-sister being of a different sept. This relaxation
may have been permitted on account of the small numbers
of the caste and the consequent difficulty of arranging
marriages.

3. Mar-
riage
customs.
The bridegroom goes to the bride's house for the wedding,
which is conducted according to the Hindu ritual of walking
round the sacred post. The cost of a marriage in a fairly
well-to-do family, including the betrothal, may be about
Rs. 140, of which a quarter falls on the bride's people.
Divorce and the remarriage of widows are permitted. A
pregnant woman stops working after six months and goes
into retirement. After a birth the woman is impure for five
or six days. She does not appear in public for a month,
and takes no part in outdoor occupations or field-work until
the child is weaned, that is six months after its birth.

4. Funeral
rites.
The dead are usually buried, and all members of the
dead man's sept are considered to be impure. After the
funeral they bathe and come home and have their food
cooked for them by other Dhobas, partaking of it in the
dead man's house. On the ninth, eleventh or thirteenth
day, when the impurity ends, the male members of the sept
are shaved on the bank of a river and the hair is left lying
there. When they start home they spread some thorns and
two stones across the path. Then, as the first man steps
over the thorns, he takes up one of the stones in his hand
and passes it behind him to the second, and each man
successively passes it back as he steps over the thorns, the
last man throwing the stone behind the thorns. Thus the
dead man's spirit in the shape of the stone is separated from

the living and prevented from accompanying them home. Then a feast is held, all the men of the dead man's sept sitting opposite to the *panchāyat* at a distance of three feet. Next day water in which gold has been dipped is thrown over the dead man's house and each member of the sept drinks a little and is pure.

The head of the caste is always a member of the Sonwāni sept and is known as Rāja.   It is his business to administer water in which gold has been dipped (*sona-pāni*) to offenders as a means of purification, and from this the name of the sept is derived.   The Rāja has no deputy, and officiates in all ceremonies of the caste ; he receives no contribution from the caste, but a double share of food and sweetmeats when they are distributed.   The other members of the Panch he is at liberty to choose from any *got* or sept he likes.   When a man has been put out of caste for a serious offence he has to give three feasts for readmission. The first meal consists of a goat with rice and pulse, and is eaten on the bank of a stream ; on this occasion the head of the offender is shaved clean and all the hair thrown into the stream.   The second meal is eaten in the yard of his house, and consists of cakes fried in butter with rice and pulse. The offender is not allowed to partake of either the first or second meal.   On the third day the Rāja gives the offender gold-water, and he is then considered to be purified and cooks food himself, which the caste-people eat with him in his house.   A man is not put out of caste when he is sent to jail, as this is considered to be an order of the Government.   A man keeping a woman of another caste is expelled and not reinstated until he has put her away, and even then it is said that they will consider his character before taking him back.   A man who gets maggots in a wound may be readmitted to caste only during the months of Chait and Pūs.

5. Caste *panchāyat* and social penalties.

The Dhobas act as priests of the Gonds and are also cultivators.   Their social position is distinctly higher than that of the Gonds and some of them have begun to employ Brāhmans for their ceremonies.   They will eat the flesh of most animals, except those of the cow-tribe, and also field-mice, and most of them drink liquor, though the more prominent

6. Occupation and social customs.

members have begun to abstain. The origin of the caste is very obscure, but it would appear that they must be an offshoot of one of the Dravidian tribes. In this connection it is interesting to note that Chhattīsgarh contains a large number of Dhobis, though the people of this tract have until recently worn little in the way of clothing, and usually wash it themselves when this operation is judged necessary. Many of the Dhobis of Chhattīsgarh are cultivators, and it seems possible that a proportion of them may also really belong to this Dhoba caste.

DHOBI

LIST OF PARAGRAPHS

Dhobi, Wārthi, Baretha, Chakla, Rajak, Parit.— The professional caste of washermen. The name is derived from the Hindi *dhona*, and the Sanskrit *dhav*, to wash. Wārthi is the Marātha name for the caste, and Bareth or Baretha is an honorific or complimentary term of address. Rajak and Parit are synonyms, the latter being used in the Marātha Districts. The Chakla caste of Madras are leather-workers, but in Chānda a community of persons is found who are known as Chakla and are professional washermen. In 1911 the Dhobis numbered 165,000 persons in the Central Provinces and Berār, or one to every hundred inhabitants. They are numerous in the Districts with large towns and also in Chhattīsgarh, where, like the Dhobas of Bengal, they have to a considerable extent abandoned their hereditary profession and taken to cultivation and other callings. No account worth reproduction has been obtained of the origin of the caste. In the Central Provinces it is purely functional, as is shown by its subdivisions ; these are generally of a territorial nature, and indicate that the Dhobis like the other professional castes have come here from all parts of the country. Instances of the subcastes are : Baonia and Berāria from Berār ; Mālwi, Bundelkhandi, Nimāria, Kanaujia, Udaipuria from Udaipur ; Madrasi, Dharampuria from Dharampur, and so on. A separate subcaste is formed of

1. Character and structure of the caste.

519

Muhammadan Dhobis. The exogamous groups known as *khero* are of the usual low-caste type, taking their names from villages or titular or professional terms.

Marriage within the *khero* is prohibited and also the union of first cousins. It is considered disgraceful to accept a price for a bride, and it is said that this is not done even by the parents of poor girls, but the caste will in such cases raise a subscription to defray the expenses of her marriage. In the northern Districts the marriages of Dhobis are characterised by continuous singing and dancing at the houses of the bridegroom and bride, these performances being known as *sajnai* and *birha*. Some man also puts on a long coat, tight down to the waist and loose round the hips, to have the appearance of a dancing-girl, and dances before the party, while two or three other men play. Mr. Crooke considers that this ritual, which is found also among other low castes, resembles the European custom of the False Bride and is intended to divert the evil eye from the real bride. He writes :[1] " Now there are numerous customs which have been grouped in Europe under the name of the False Bride. Thus among the Esthonians the false bride is enacted by the bride's brother dressed in woman's clothes ; in Polonia by a bearded man called the Wilde Braut ; in Poland by an old woman veiled in white and lame ; again among the Esthonians by an old woman with a brickwork crown ; in Brittany, where the substitutes are first a little girl, then the mistress of the house, and lastly the grandmother.

" The supposition may then be hazarded in the light of the Indian examples that some one assumes on this occasion the part of the bride in order to divert on himself from her the envious glance of the evil eye." Any further information on this interesting custom would be welcome.

The remarriage of widows is allowed, and in Betūl the bridegroom goes to the widow's house on a dark night wrapped up in a black blanket, and presents the widow with new clothes and bangles, and spangles and red lead for the forehead. Divorce is permitted with the approval of the caste headman by the execution of a deed on stamped paper.

---

[1] *Folklore of Northern India,* vol. ii. p. 8.

After a birth the mother is allowed no food for some days except country sugar and dates.   The child is given some honey and castor-oil for the first two days and is then allowed to suckle the mother.   A pit is dug inside the lying-in room, and in this are deposited water and the first cuttings of the nails and hair of the child.   It is filled up and on her recovery the mother bows before it, praying for similar safe deliveries in future and for the immunity of the child from physical ailments.   After the birth of a male child the mother is impure for seven days and for five days after that of a female.

The principal deity of the Dhobis is Ghatoia, the god of the *ghāt* or landing-place on the river to which they go to wash their clothes.   Libations of liquor are made to him in the month of Asārh (June), when the rains break and the rivers begin to be flooded.   Before entering the water to wash the clothes they bow to the stone on which these are beaten out, asking that their work may be quickly finished ; and they also pray to the river deity to protect them from snakes and crocodiles.   They worship the stone on the Dasahra festival, making an offering to it of flowers, turmeric and cooked food.   The Dhobi's washing-stone is believed to be haunted by the ghosts of departed Dhobis when revisiting the glimpses of the moon, and is held to have magical powers.   If a man requires a love-charm he should steal a *supāri* or areca-nut from the bazār at night or on the occasion of an eclipse.   The same night he goes to the Dhobi's stone and sets the nut upon it.   He breaks an egg and a cocoanut over the stone and burns incense before it.   Then he takes the nut away and gives it to the woman of his fancy, wrapped up in betel-leaf, and she will love him. Their chief festivals are the Holi and Diwāli, at which they drink a great deal.   The dead are buried or burnt as may be convenient, and mourning is observed for three days only, the family being purified on the Sunday or Wednesday following the death.   They have a caste committee whose president is known as Mehtar, while other officials are the Chaudhri or vice-president, and the Badkur, who appoints dates for the penal feasts and issues the summons to the caste-fellows.   These posts are hereditary and their holders receive presents of a rupee and a cloth when members of the caste have to give expiatory feasts.

5. Occupation: washing clothes.   Before washing his clothes the Dhobi steams them,[1] hanging them in a bundle for a time over a cauldron of boiling water.   After this he takes them to a stream or pond and washes them roughly with fuller's earth.   The washerman steps nearly knee-deep into the water, and taking a quantity of clothes by one end in his two hands he raises them aloft in the air and brings them down heavily upon a huge stone slab, grooved, at his feet.   This threshing operation he repeats until his clothes are perfectly clean.   In Saugor the clothes are rubbed with wood-ashes at night and beaten out in water with a stick in the morning.   Silk clothes are washed with the nut of the *rītha* tree (*Sapindus emarginatus*) which gives a lather like soap.   Sir H. Risley writes of the Dacca washermen :[2] " For washing muslins and other coloured garments well or spring water is alone used ; but if the articles are the property of a poor man or are commonplace, the water of the nearest tank or river is accounted sufficiently good.   Indigo is in as general use as in England for removing the yellowish tinge and whitening the material.   The water of the wells and springs bordering on the red laterite formation on the north of the city has been for centuries celebrated, and the old bleaching fields of the European factories were all situated in this neighbourhood.   Various plants are used by the Dhobis to clarify water such as the *nirmali* (*Strychnos potatorum*), the *piu* (*Basella*), the *nāgphani* (*Cactus indicus*) and several plants of the mallow family.   Alum, though not much valued, is sometimes used."   In most Districts of the Central Provinces the Dhobi is employed as a village servant and is paid by annual contributions of grain from the cultivators.   For ordinary washing he gets half as much as the blacksmith or carpenter, or 13 to 20 lbs. of grain annually from each householder, with about another 10 lbs. at seedtime or harvest.   When he brings the clothes home he also receives a meal or a *chapāti*, and well-to-do persons give him their old clothes as a present.   In return for this he washes all the clothes of the family two or three times a month, except the loin-cloths

---

[1] Sherring's *Hindu Castes*, i. 342-3.   [2] *Tribes and Castes*, art. Dhobi.

and women's bodices which they themselves wash daily. The Dhobi is also employed on the occasion of a birth or a death. These events cause impurity and hence all the clothes of all the members of the family must be washed when the impurity ceases. In Saugor when a man dies the Dhobi receives eight annas and for a woman four annas, and similar rates in the case of the birth of a male or female child. When the first son is born in a family the Dhobi and barber place a brass vessel on the top of a pole and tie a flag to it as a cloth and take it round to all the friends and relations of the family, announcing the event. They receive presents of grain and money which they expend on a drinking-bout.

The Dhobi is considered to be impure, and he is not allowed to come into the houses of the better castes nor to touch their water-vessels. In Saugor he may come as far as the veranda but not into the house. His status would in any case be low as a village menial, but he is specially degraded, Mr. Crooke states, by his task of washing the clothes of women after child-birth and his consequent association with puerperal blood, which is particularly abhorred. Formerly a Brāhman did not let the Dhobi wash his clothes, or, if he did, they were again steeped in water in the house as a means of purification. Now he contents himself with sprinkling the clean clothes with water in which a piece of gold has been dipped. The Dhobi is not so impure as the Chamār and Basor, and if a member of the higher castes touches him inadvertently it is considered sufficient to wash the face and hands only and not the clothes. 6. Social position.

Colonel Tod writes[1] that in Rājputāna the washermen's wells dug at the sides of streams are deemed the most impure of all receptacles. And one of the most binding oaths is that a man as he swears should drop a pebble into one of these wells, saying, " If I break this oath may all the good deeds of my forefathers fall into the washerman's well like this pebble." Nevertheless the Dhobi refuses to wash the clothes of some of the lowest castes as the Māng, Mahār and Chamār. Like the Teli the Dhobi is unlucky, and it is a bad omen to see him when starting on a journey or going out in the morning. But among some of the

[1] *Annals and Antiquities of Rājasthān.*

higher castes on the occasion of a marriage the elder members of the bridegroom's family go with the bride to the Dhobi's house. His wife presents the bride with betel-leaf and in return is given clothes with a rupee. This ceremony is called *sohāg* or good fortune, and the present from the Dhobin is supposed to be lucky. In Berār the Dhobi is also a Balūtedār or village servant. Mr. Kitts writes of him :[1] "At a wedding he is called upon to spread the clothes on which the bridegroom and his party alight on coming to the bride's house ; he also provides the cloth on which the bride and bridegroom are to sit and fastens the *kankan* (bracelet) on the girl's hand. In the Yeotmāl District the barber and the washerman sometimes take the place of the maternal uncle in the *jhenda* dance ; and when the bridegroom, assisted by five married women, has thrown the necklace of black beads round the bride's neck and has tied it with five knots, the barber and the washerman advance, and lifting the young couple on their thighs dance to the music of the *wājantri*, while the bystanders besprinkle them with red powder."

In Chhattīsgarh the Dhobis appear to have partly abandoned their hereditary profession and taken to agriculture and other callings. Sir Benjamin Robertson writes of them :[2] "The caste largely preponderates in Chhattīsgarh, a part of the country where, at least to the superficial observer, it would hardly seem as if its services were much availed of ; the number of Dhobis in Raipur and Bilāspur is nearly 40,000. In both Districts the washerman is one of the recognised village servants, but as a rule he gets no fixed payment, and the great body of cultivators dispense with his services altogether. According to the *Raipur Settlement Report* (Mr. Hewett), he is employed by the ryots only to wash the clothes of the dead, and he is never found among a population of Satnāmis. It may therefore be assumed that in Chhattīsgarh the Bareth caste has largely taken to cultivation." In Bengal Sir H. Risley states[3] that "the Dhobi often gives up his caste trade and follows the profession of a writer, messenger or collector of rent (*tahsīldār*), and it is

---

[1] *Berār Census Report* (1881), p. 155.
[2] *Central Provinces Census Report* (1891), p. 202.   [3] *Loc. cit.*

an old native tradition that a Bengali Dhobi was the first interpreter the English factory at Calcutta had, while it is further stated that our early commercial transactions were carried on solely through the agency of low-caste natives. The Dhobi, however, will never engage himself as an indoor servant in the house of a European."

Like the other castes who supply the primary needs of the people, the Dhobi is not regarded with much favour by his customers, and they revenge themselves in various sarcasms at his expense for the injury caused to their clothes by his drastic measures. The following are mentioned by Sir G. Grierson : [1] '*Dhobi par Dhobi base, tab kapre par sābun pare*,' or 'When many Dhobis compete, then some soap gets to the clothes,' and 'It is only the clothes of the Dhobi's father that never get torn.' The Dhobi's donkey is a familiar sight as one meets him on the road still toiling as in the time of Issachar between two bundles of clothes each larger than himself, and he has also become proverbial, '*Dhobi ka gadha neh ghar ka neh ghāt ka*,' 'The Dhobi's donkey is always on the move'; and 'The ass has only one master (a washerman), and the washerman has only one steed (an ass).' The resentment felt for the Dhobi by his customers is not confined to his Indian clients, as may be seen from Eha's excellent description of the Dhobi in *Behind the Bungalow*; and it may perhaps be permissible to introduce here the following short excerpt, though it necessarily loses in force by being detached from the context: "Day after day he has stood before that great black stone and wreaked his rage upon shirt and trouser and coat, and coat and trouser and shirt. Then he has wrung them as if he were wringing the necks of poultry, and fixed them on his drying line with thorns and spikes, and finally he has taken the battered garments to his torture chamber and ploughed them with his iron, longwise and crosswise and slantwise, and dropped glowing cinders on their tenderest places. Son has followed father through countless generations in cultivating this passion for destruction, until it has become the monstrous growth which we see and shudder at in the Dhobi."

7. Proverbs about the Dhobi.

---

[1] *Bihār Peasant Life*, *s.v.* Dhobi.

It is also currently believed that the Dhobi wears the clothes of his customers himself.   Thus, 'The Dhobi looks smart in other people's clothes'; and '*Rājāche shiri, Paritāche tiri*,' or 'The king's headscarf is the washerman's loin-cloth.'   On this point Mr. Thurston writes of the Madras washerman : " It is an unpleasant reflection that the Vannāns or washermen add to their income by hiring out the clothes of their customers for funeral parties, who lay them on the path before the pall-bearers, so that they may not step upon the ground.   On one occasion a party of Europeans, when out shooting near the village of a hill tribe, met a funeral procession on its way to the burial-ground.   The bier was draped in many folds of clean cloth, which one of the party recognised by the initials as one of his bed-sheets.   Another identified as his sheet the cloth on which the corpse was lying.   He cut off the corner with the initial, and a few days later the sheet was returned by the Dhobi, who pretended ignorance of the mutilation, and gave as an explanation that it must have been done in his absence by one of his assistants." [1]   And Eha describes the same custom in the following amusing manner : " Did you ever open your handkerchief with the suspicion that you had got a duster into your pocket by mistake, till the name of De Souza blazoned on the corner showed you that you were wearing some one else's property ?   An accident of this kind reveals a beneficent branch of the Dhobi's business, one in which he comes to the relief of needy respectability.   Suppose yourself (if you can) to be Mr. Lobo, enjoying the position of first violinist in a string band which performs at Parsi weddings and on other festive occasions. *Noblesse oblige* ; you cannot evade the necessity for clean shirt-fronts, ill able as your precarious income may be to meet it.   In these circumstances a Dhobi with good connections is what you require.   He finds you in shirts of the best quality at so much an evening, and you are saved all risk and outlay of capital ; you need keep no clothes except a greenish-black surtout and pants and an effective necktie. In this way the wealth of the rich helps the want of the poor without their feeling it or knowing it—an excellent arrange-

[1] *Ethnographic Notes in Southern India*, p. 226.

ment.   Sometimes, unfortunately, Mr. Lobo has a few clothes of his own, and then, as I have hinted, the Dhobi may exchange them by mistake, for he is uneducated and has much to remember ; but if you occasionally suffer in this way you gain in another, for Mr. Lobo's family are skilful with the needle, and I have sent a torn garment to the wash which returned carefully repaired." [1]

Dhuri.[2]—A caste belonging exclusively to Chhattīsgarh, which numbered 3000 persons in 1911. Dhuri is an honorific abbreviation from Dhuriya as Bāni from Bania. The special occupation of the caste is rice-parching, and they are an offshoot from Kahārs, though in Chhattīsgarh the Dhuris now consider the Kahārs as a subcaste of their own. In Bengal the Dhuriyas are a subcaste of the Kāndus or Bharbhūnjas. Sir H. Risley states that "the Dhurias rank lowest of all the subcastes of Kāndus, owing either to their having taken up the comparatively menial profession of palanquin-bearing, or to their being a branch of the Kahār caste who went in for grain-parching and thus came to be associated with the Kāndus." [3]   The caste have immigrated to Chhattīsgarh from the United Provinces.   In Kawardha they believe that the Rāja of that State brought them back with him on his return from a pilgrimage.   In Bilāspur and Raipur they say they came from Badhār, a pargana in the Mīrzāpur District, adjoining Rewah.   Badhār is mentioned in one of the Rājim inscriptions, and is a place remembered by other castes of Chhattīsgarh as their ancestral home.   The Dhuris of Chhattīsgarh relate their origin as follows : Mahādeo went once to the jungle and the damp earth stuck to his feet. He scraped it off and made it into a man, and asked him what caste he would like to belong to.   The man said he would leave it to Mahādeo, who decided that he should be called Dhuri from *dhūr*, dust.   The man then asked Mahādeo to assign him an occupation, and Mahādeo said that as he was made from dust, which is pounded earth, his work should

1. Origin and sub-divisions.

1 *Behind the Bungalow.*
2 This article is mainly compiled from papers by Mr. Gokul Prasād, Naib-Tahsīldār, Dhamtari, and Pyāre   Lāl Misra, a clerk in the Gazetteer office.
3 *Tribes and Castes of Bengal*, art. Kāndu.

be to prepare *cheora* or pounded rice, and added as a special distinction that all castes including Brāhmans should eat the pounded rice prepared by him. All castes do eat *cheora* because it is not boiled with water. The Dhuris have two subcastes, a higher and a lower, but they are known by different names in different tracts. In Kawardha they are called Rāj Dhuri and Cheorākūta, the Rāj Dhuris being the descendants of personal servants in the Rāja's family and ranking above the Cheorākūtas or rice-pounders. In Bilāspur they are called Badhāria and Khawās, and in Raipur Badhāria and Desha. The Khawās and Desha subcastes do menial household service and rank below the Badhārias, who are perhaps later immigrants and refuse to engage in this occupation. The names of their exogamous sections are nearly all territorial, as Naugahia from Naogaon in Bilāspur District, Agoria from Agori, a pargana in Mīrzāpur District, Kāshi or Benāres, and a number of other names derived from villages in Bilāspur. But the caste do not strictly enforce the rule forbidding marriage within the *gotra* or section, and are content with avoiding three generations both on the father's and mother's side. They have probably been driven to modify the rule on account of the paucity of their numbers and the difficulty of arranging marriages. For the same reason perhaps they look with indulgence on the practice, as a rule strictly prohibited, of marriage with a woman of another caste of lower social rank, and will admit the children of such a marriage into the caste, though not the woman herself.

2. Marriage. Infant-marriage is in vogue, and polygamy is permitted only if the first wife be barren. The betrothal is cemented by an exchange of betel-leaves and areca-nuts between the fathers of the engaged couple. A bride-price of from ten to twenty rupees is usually paid. Some rice, a pice coin, 21 cowries and 21 pieces of turmeric are placed in the hole in which the marriage post is erected. When the wedding procession arrives at the girl's house the bridegroom goes to the marriage-shed and pulls out the festoons of mango leaves, the bride's family trying to prevent him by offering him a winnowing-fan. He then approaches the door of the house, behind which his future mother-in-law is standing,

and slips a piece of cloth through the door for her. She takes this and retires without being seen. The wedding consists of the *bhānwar* ceremony or walking round the sacred pole. During the proceedings the women tie a new thread round the bridegroom's neck to avert the evil eye. After the wedding the bride and bridegroom, in opposition to the usual custom, must return to the latter's house on foot. In explanation of this they tell a story to the effect that the married couple were formerly carried in a palanquin. But on one occasion when a wedding procession came to a river, everybody began to catch fish, leaving the bride deserted, and the palanquin-bearers, seeing this, carried her off. To prevent the recurrence of such a mischance the couple now have to walk. Widow-marriage is permitted, and the widow usually marries her late husband's younger brother. Divorce is only permitted for misconduct on the part of the wife.

The Dhuris principally worship the goddess Devi. Nearly all members of the caste belong to the Kabīrpanthi sect. They believe that the sun on setting goes through the earth, and that the milky way is the path by which the elephant of the heavens passes from south to north to feed on the young bamboo shoots, of which he is very fond. They think that the constellation of the Great Bear is a cot with three thieves tied to it. The thieves came to steal the cot, which belonged to an old woman, but God caught them and tied them down there for ever. Orion is the plough left by one of the Pāndava brothers after he had finished tilling the heavens. The dead are burnt. They observe mourning during nine or ten days for an adult and make libations to the dead at the usual period in the month of Kunwār (September-October). *3. Religious beliefs.*

The proper occupation of the caste is to parch rice. The rice is husked and then parched in an earthen pan, and subsequently bruised with a mallet in a wooden mortar. When prepared in this manner it is called *cheora*. The Dhuris also act as *khidmatgārs* or household servants, but the members of the Badharia subcaste refuse to do this work. Some members of the caste are fishermen, and others grow melons and sweet potatoes. Considering that they *4. Occupation and social status.*

live in Chhattīsgarh, the caste are somewhat scrupulous in the matter of food, neither eating fowls nor drinking liquor. The Kawardha Dhuris, however, who are later immigrants than the others, do not observe these restrictions, the reason for which may be that the Dhuris think it necessary to be strict in the matter of food, so that no one may object to take parched rice from them. Rāwats and Gonds take food from their hands in some places, and their social status in Chhattīsgarh is about equivalent to that of the Rāwats or Ahīrs. A man of the caste who kills a cow or gets vermin in a wound must go to Amārkantak to bathe in the Nerbudda.

1. Origin and traditions.

Dumāl.[1] — An agricultural caste found in the Uriya country and principally in the Sonpur State, recently transferred to Bihār and Orissa. In 1901, 41,000 Dumāls were enumerated in the Central Provinces, but only a few persons now remain. The caste originally came from Orissa. They themselves say that they were formerly a branch of the Gaurs, with whom they now have no special connection. They derive their name from a village called Dumba Hadap in the Athmālik State, where they say that they lived. Another story is that Dumāl is derived from Duma, the name of a gateway in Baud town, near which they dwelt. Sir H. Risley says : " The Dumāls or Jādupuria Gaura seem to be a group of local formation. They cherish the tradition that their ancestors came to Orissa from Jādupur, but this appears to be nothing more than the name of the Jādavas or Yādavas, the mythical progenitors of the Goala caste transformed into the name of an imaginary town."

2. Subdivisions.

The Dumāls have no subcastes, but they have a complicated system of exogamy. This includes three kinds of divisions or sections, the *got* or sept, the *barga* or family title and the *mitti* or earth from which they sprang, that is, the name of the original village of the clan. Marriage is prohibited only between persons who have the same *got*, *barga* and *mitti* ; if any one of these is different it is allowed. Thus a man of the Nāg *got*, Padhān *barga* and Hindolsai *mitti* may marry a girl of the Nāg *got*, Padhān *barga* and

---

[1] This article is taken almost entirely from a paper drawn up by Mr. Hīra Lāl, Extra Assistant Commissioner.

Kandhpadā *mitti* ; or one of the Nāg *got*, Karmi *barga* and Hindolsai *mitti* ; or one of the Bud *got*, Padhān *barga* and Hindolsai *mitti*. The *bargas* are very numerous, but the *gots* and *mittis* are few and common to many *bargas* ; and many people have forgotten the name of their *mitti* altogether. Marriage therefore usually depends on the *bargas* being different. The following table shows the *got*, *barga* and *mitti* of a few families :

Got.	Barga.	Mitti.
Nāg (cobra)	Padhān (chief)	Hindolsai
Nāg	Karmi (manager)	Unda (a village in Athmalik)
Nāg	Behra (Palki-bearer)	Kandhpada (a village in Athmalik)
Nāg	Mahākul (great family)	Do. do.
Nāg	Mesua (shepherd)	Dalpur (a village in Baud)
Nāg	Karan (writer)	Kandhpada (a village in Athmalik)
Nāg or Nāgesh	Mahākul (great family)	Bāmanda (a village in Baud)
Bud (a fish)	Kolta (caste)	Kandhpada (a village in Athmalik)
Bud (a fish)	Baghār (buffalo)	Do do.
Bichhū (scorpion)	Mahākul (great family)	Bāmada (a village in Baud)

The only other *gots* besides those given above are Kachhap (tortoise), Ulūk (owl) and Limb (*nim*-tree). The *gots* are thus totemistic, and the animal or plant giving its name to the *got* is venerated and worshipped. The names of *bargas* are diverse. Some are titles indicating the position of the founder of the family in life, as Nāik (leader), Padhān (chief), Karmi (manager), Mahākul (great family) and so on. Others are derived from functions performed in sacrifices, as Amāyat (one who kills the animal in the sacrifice), Gurandi (one who makes a preparation of sugar for it), Dehri (priest), Bārik (one who carries the god's umbrella), Kamp (one who is in charge of the baskets containing the sacred articles of the temple). Another set of *bargas* are names signifying the performance of menial functions in household service, as Gejo (kitchen-cleaner), Chaulia (rice-cleaner), Gadua (*lotā*-bearer), Dāng (spoon-bearer), Ghusri (cleaner of the dining-place with cowdung). Other names of *bargas* are derived from the caste's traditional occupation of grazing cattle, as Mesua or Mendli (shepherd), Gaigariya (milkman), Chhānd (one who ties a rope to the legs of a cow when milking her). These names are interesting as showing that the Dumāls before taking to their present occupation of agriculture were temple servants, household menials and cattle-herds, thus fulfilling the functions now performed by the Rāwat or Gaur caste of graziers in Sambalpur. The names of the *mittis* or villages show that their original home was in the Orissa Tributary Mahāls, while the totemistic names of *gots* indicate their Dravidian origin. The marriage of first cousins is prohibited.

3. Marriage.   Girls must be married before adolescence, and in the event of the parents failing to accomplish this, the following heavy penalty is imposed on the girl herself. She is taken to the forest and tied to a tree with thread, this proceeding signifying her permanent exclusion from the caste. Any one belonging to another caste can then take her away and marry her if he chooses to do so. In practice, however, this penalty is very rarely imposed, as the parents can get out of it by marrying her to an old man, whether he is already married or not, the parents bearing all the expenses, while the husband gives two to four annas as a nominal contribution. After the marriage the old man can either keep the girl as his wife or divorce her for a further nominal payment of eight annas to a rupee. She then becomes a widow and can marry again, while her parents will get ten or twenty rupees for her.

The boy's father makes the proposal for the marriage according to the following curious formula. Taking some fried grain he goes to the house of the father of the bride and addresses him as follows in the presence of the neighbours and the relatives of both parties : " I hear that the tree has budded and a blossom has come out ; I intend to pluck it." To which the girl's father replies : " The flower is delicate ; it is in the midst of an ocean and very difficult to approach : how will you pluck it ? " To which the reply is : ' I shall bring ships and *dongas* (boats) and ply them in the ocean and fetch the flower.' And again : " If you do pluck it, can you support it ? Many difficulties may stand in the way, and the flower may wither or get lost ; will it be possible for you to steer the flower's boat in the ocean of time, as long as it is destined to be in this world ? " To which the answer is : ' Yes, I shall, and it is with that

intention that I have come to you.' On which the girl's
father finally says : 'Very well then, I have given you the
flower.' The question of the bride's price is then discussed.
There are three recognised scales—Rs. 7 and 7 pieces of
cloth, Rs. 9 and 9 pieces of cloth, and Rs. 18 and 18 pieces
of cloth. The rupees in question are those of Orissa, and
each of them is worth only two-thirds of a Government
rupee. In cases of extreme poverty Rs. 2 and 2 pieces of
cloth are accepted. The price being fixed, the boy's father
goes to pay it after an interval ; and on this occasion he
holds out his cloth, and a cocoanut is placed on it and
broken by the girl's father, which confirms the betrothal.
Before the marriage seven married girls go out and dig
earth after worshipping the ground, and on their return
let it all fall on to the head of the bridegroom's mother,
which is protected only by a cloth. On the next day
offerings are made to the ancestors, who are invited to
attend the ceremony as village gods. The bridegroom is
shaved clean and bathed, and the Brāhman then ties an iron
ring to his wrist, and the barber puts the turban and marriage-
crown on his head. The procession then starts, but any
barber who meets it on the way may put a fresh marriage-
crown on the bridegroom's head and receive eight annas or
a rupee for it, so that he sometimes arrives at his destination
wearing four or five of them. The usual ceremonies attend
the arrival. At the marriage the couple are blindfolded and
seated in the shed, while the Brāhman priest repeats _mantras_
or verses, and during this time the parents and the parties
must continue placing nuts and pice all over the shed. These
are the perquisites of the Brāhman. The hands of the couple
are then tied together with _kusha_ grass (_Eragrostis cynosu-
roides_), and water is poured over them. After the ceremony
the couple gamble with seven cowries and seven pieces of
turmeric. The boy then presses a cowrie on the ground
with his little finger, and the girl has to take it away, which
she easily does. The girl in her turn holds a cowrie inside
her clenched hand, and the boy has to remove it with his
little finger, which he finds it impossible to do. Thus the boy
always loses and has to promise the girl something, either to
give her an ornament or to take her on a pilgrimage, or to

make her the mistress of his house. On the fifth or last day of the ceremony some curds are placed in a small pot, and the couple are made to churn them ; this is probably symbolical of the caste's original occupation of tending cattle. The bride goes to her husband's house for three days, and then returns home. When she is to be finally brought to her husband's house, his father with some relatives goes to the parents of the girl and asks for her. It is now strict etiquette for her father to refuse to send her on the first occasion, and they usually have to call on him three or four times at intervals of some days, and selecting the days given by the astrologer as auspicious. Occasionally they have to go as many as ten times ; but finally, if the girl's father proves very troublesome, they send an old woman who drags away the girl by force. If the father sends her away willingly he gives her presents of several basket-loads of grain, oil, turmeric, cooking-pots, cloth, and if he is well off a cow and bullocks, the value of the presents amounting to about Rs. 50. The girl's brother takes her to her husband's house, where a repetition of the marriage ceremony on a small scale is performed. Twice again after the consummation of the marriage she visits her parents for periods of one and six months, but after this she never again goes to their house unaccompanied by her husband. Widow-marriage is allowed, and the widow may marry the younger brother of her late husband or not as she pleases. But if she marries another man he must pay a sum of Rs. 10 to Rs. 20 for her, of which Rs. 5 go to the Panua or headman of the caste, and Rs. 2 to their tutelary goddess Parmeshwari. The children by the first husband are kept either by his relatives or the widow's parents, and do not go to the new husband. When a bachelor marries a widow, he is first married to a flower or *sahara* tree. A widow who has remarried cannot take part in any worship or marriage ceremony in her house, not even in the marriage of her own sons. Divorce is allowed, and is effected in the presence of the caste *panchāyat* or committee. A divorced woman may marry again.

4. Religious and social customs.
The caste worship the goddess Parmeshwari, the wife of Vishnu, and Jagannāth, the Uriya incarnation of Vishnu. Parmeshwari is worshipped by Brāhmans, who offer bread

and *khīr* or rice and milk to her; goats are also offered
by the Dehri or Mahākul, the caste priest, who receives the
heads of the goats as his remuneration.   They believe in
witches, who they think drink the blood of children, and
employ sorcerers to exorcise them.   They worship a stick
on Dasahra day in remembrance of their old profession of
herding cattle, and they worship cows and buffaloes at the
full moon of Shrāwan (July-August).   During Kunwār, on
the eighth day of each fortnight, two festivals are held.   At
the first each girl in the family wears a thread containing
eighteen knots twisted three times round her neck.   All the
girls fast and receive presents of cloths and grain from their
brothers.   This is called Bhaijiuntia, or the ceremony for
the welfare of the brothers.   On the second day the mother
of the family does the same, and receives presents from her
sons, this being Puājiuntia, or the ceremony for the welfare
of sons.   The Dumāls believe that in the beginning water
covered the earth.   They think that the sun and moon are
the eyes of God, and that the stars are the souls of virtuous
men, who enjoy felicity in heaven for the period measured
by the sum of their virtuous actions, and when this has
expired have to descend again to earth to suffer the agonies
of human life.   When a shooting star is seen they think it
is the soul of one of these descending to be born again on
earth.   They both burn and bury their dead according to
their means.   After a body is buried they make a fire over
the grave and place an empty pot on it.   Mourning is
observed for twelve days in the case of a married and for
seven in the case of an unmarried person.   Children dying
when less than six days old are not mourned at all.   During
mourning the persons of the household do not cook for
themselves.   On the third day after the death three leaf-
plates, each containing a little rice, sugar and butter, are
offered to the spirit of the deceased.   On the fourth day
four such plates are offered, and on the fifth day five, and
so on up to the ninth day when the Pindas or sacrificial
cakes are offered, and nine persons belonging to the caste
are invited, food and a new piece of cloth being given to
each.   Should only one attend, nine plates of food would
be served to him, and he would be given nine pieces of

cloth. If two or more persons in a family are killed by a
tiger, a Sulia or magician is called in, and he pretends to
be the tiger and to bite some one in the family, who is then
carried as a corpse to the burial-place, buried for a short
time and taken out again. All the ceremonies of mourning
are observed for him for one day. This proceeding is believed to secure immunity for the family from further attacks.
In return for his services the Sulia gets a share of everything in the house corresponding to what he would receive,
supposing he were a member of the family, on a partition.
Thus if the family consisted of only two persons he would
get a third part of the whole property.

The Dumāls eat meat, including wild boar's flesh, but
not beef, fowls or tame pigs. They do not drink liquor.
They will take food cooked with water from Brāhmans and
Sudhs, and even the leavings of food from Brāhmans.
This is probably because they were formerly the household
servants of Brāhmans, though they have now risen somewhat in position and rank, together with the Koltas and
Sudhs, as a good cultivating caste. Their women and girls
can easily be distinguished, the girls because the hair is
shaved until they are married, and the women because they
wear bangles of glass on one arm and of lac on the other.
They never wear nose-rings or the ornament called *pairi* on
the feet, and no ornaments are worn on the arm above the
elbow. They do not wear black clothing. The women
are tattooed on the hands, feet and breast. Morality within
the caste is lax. A woman going wrong with a man of
her own caste is not punished, because the Dumāls live
generally in Native States, where it is the business of the
Rāja to find the seducer. But she is permanently excommunicated for a *liaison* with a man of another caste. Eating
with a very low caste is almost the only offence which
entails permanent exclusion for both sexes. The Dumāls
have a bad reputation for fidelity, according to a saying :
'You cannot call the jungle a plain, and you should not call
the Dumāl a brother,' that is, do not trust a Dumāl. Like
the Ahīrs they are somewhat stupid, and when enquiry was
being made from them as to what crops they did not grow,
one of them replied that they did not sow salt. They are

good cultivators, and will grow anything except hemp and turmeric. In some places they still follow their traditional occupation of grazing cattle.

Fakīr.[1]—The class of Muhammadan beggars. In the 1. General Central Provinces the name is practically confined to notice. Muhammadans, but in Upper India Hindus also use it. Nearly 9000 Fakīrs were returned in 1911, being residents mainly of Districts with large towns, as Jubbulpore, Nāgpur and Amraoti. Nearly two-fifths of the Muhammadans of the Central Provinces live in towns, and Muhammadan beggars would naturally congregate there also. The name is derived from the Arabic *fakr*, poverty. The Fakīrs are often known as Shāh, Lord, or Sain, a corruption of the Sanskrit Swāmi, master. Muhammad did not recognise religious asceticism, and expressly discouraged it. But even during his lifetime his companions Abu Bakr and Ali established religious orders with Zikrs or special exercises, and all Muhammadan Fakīrs trace their origin to Abu Bakr or Ali subsequently the first and fourth Caliphs.[2] The Fakīrs are divided into two classes, the Ba Shara or those who live according to the rules of Islam and marry ; and the Be Shara or those without the law. These latter have no wives or homes ; they drink intoxicating liquor, and neither fast, pray nor rule their passions. But several of the orders contain both married and celibate groups.

The principal classes of Fakīrs in the Central Provinces 2. Principal are the Madari, Gurujwāle or Rafai, Jalāli, Mewāti, Sada orders. Sohāgal and Nakshbandia. All of these except the Nakshbandia are nominally at least Be Shara, or without the law, and celibate.

The Madari are the followers of one Madar Shāh, a converted Jew of Aleppo, whose tomb is supposed to be at Makhanpur in the United Provinces. Their characteristic badge is a pair of pincers. Some, in order to force people to give them alms, go about dragging a chain or lashing their legs with a whip. Others are monkey- and bear-

---

[1] This article is mainly compiled from Sir E. D. Maclagan's *Punjab Census Report* (1891), pp. 192-196, the article on Fakīr in the Rev. T. P. Hughes' *Dictionary of Islām,* and the volume on *Muhammadans of Gujarāt* in the *Bombay Gazetteer,* pp. 20-24.
[2] Hughes, p. 116.

trainers and rope-dancers. The Madaris are said to be proof against snakes and scorpions, and to have power to cure their bites. They will leap into a fire and trample it down, crying out, ' *Aam Madar, Aam Madar.*'[1]

The Gurujwāle or Rafai have as their badge a spiked iron club with small chains attached to the end. The Fakīr rattles the chains of his club to announce his presence, and if the people will not give him alms strikes at his own cheek or eye with the sharp point of his club, making the blood flow. They make prayers to their club once a year, so that it may not cause them serious injury when they strike themselves with it.

The Jalālias are named after their founder, Jalāl-ud-dīn of Bokhāra, and have a horse-whip as their badge, with which they sometimes strike themselves on the hands and feet. They are said to consume large quantities of *bhāng*, and to eat snakes and scorpions ; they shave all the hair on the head and face, including the eyebrows, except a small scalp-lock on the right side.

The Mewāti appear to be a thieving order. They are also known as Kulchor or thieves of the family, and appear to have been originally a branch of the Madari, who were perhaps expelled on account of their thieving habits. Their distinguishing mark is a double bag like a pack-saddle, which they hang over their shoulders. The Sada or Mūsa Sohāg are an order who dress like women, put on glass bangles, have their ears and noses pierced for ornaments, and wear long hair, but retain their beards and moustaches. They regard themselves as brides of God or of Hussan, and beg in this guise.

The Nakshbandia are the disciples of Khwaja Mīr Muhammad, who was called Nakshband or brocade-maker. They beg at night-time, carrying an open brass lamp with a short wick. Children are fond of the Nakshband, and go out in numbers to give him money. In return he marks them on the brow with oil from his lamp. They are quiet and well behaved, belonging to the Ba Shara class of Fakīrs, and having homes and families.

The Kalandaria or wandering dervishes, who are

[1] *Punjab Census Report* (1891), p. 196.

GROUP OF GURUJWĀLE FAKĪRS.

Benrose, Collo., Derby.

occasionally met with, were founded by Kalandar Yusuf-ul-Andalusi, a native of Spain. Having been dismissed from another order, he founded this as a new one, with the obligation of perpetual travelling. The Kalandar is a well-known figure in Eastern stories.[1]

The Maulawiyah are the well-known dancing dervishes of Constantinople and Cairo, but do not belong to India.

The different orders of Fakīrs are not strictly endogamous, and marriages can take place between their members, though the Madaris prefer to confine marriage to their own order. Fakīrs as a body are believed to marry among themselves, and hence to form something in the nature of a caste, but they freely admit outsiders, whether Muhammadans or proselytised Hindus.

Every Fakīr must have a Murshid or preceptor, and be initiated by him. This applies also to boys born in the order, and a father cannot initiate his son. The rite is usually simple, the novice having to drink sherbet from the same cup as his preceptor and make him a present of Rs. 1-4 ; but some orders insist that the whole body of a novice should be shaved clean of hair before he is initiated. The principal religious exercise of Fakīrs is known as Zikr, and consists in the continual repetition of the names of God by various methods, it being supposed that they can draw the name from different parts of the body. The exercise is so exhausting that they frequently faint under it, and is varied by repetition of certain chapters of the Korān. The Fakīr has a *tasbīh* or rosary, often consisting of ninety-nine beads, on which he repeats the ninety-nine names of God. The Fakīrs beg both from Hindus and Muhammadans, and are sometimes troublesome and importunate, inflicting wounds on themselves as a means of extorting alms. One beggar in Saugor said that he would give every one who gave him alms five strokes with his whip, and attracted considerable custom by this novel expedient. Some of them are in charge of Muhammadan cemeteries and receive fees for a burial, while others live at the tombs of saints. They keep the tomb in good repair, cover it with a green cloth and keep a lighted lamp on it, and appropriate the

3. Rules and customs.

----

[1] Hughes' *Dictionary of Islam*, art. Fakīr.

offerings made by visitors. Owing to their solitude and continuous repetition of prayers many Fakīrs fall into a distraught condition, when they are known as *mast*, and are believed to be possessed of a spirit. At such a time the people attach the greatest importance to any utterances which fall from the Fakīr's lips, believing that he has the gift of prophecy, and follow him about with presents to induce him to make some utterance.

END OF VOL. II

Printed by R. & R. CLARK, LIMITED, *Edinburgh*.